Paradigms and Processes

Paradigms and Processes

Selected Papers of Arnold Wilson

IPBOOKS.net
International Psychoanalytic Books
International Psychoanalytic Books (IPBooks)
New York • www.IPBooks.net

IPBooks Inc
International Psychoanalytic Books (IPBooks)
Queens, NY
Online at: www.IPBooks.net

Interior book design by Maureen Cutajar, gopublished.com

ISBN: 978-1-949093-68-1

ACKNOWLEDGMENTS AND APPRECIATION

The selected papers that are gathered here reflect many years of writing. Several of them were published in journals that are not easily accessible to the psychoanalytic reader. No book chapters previously published are in this volume. The intention of gathering these journal chapters is to depict an interdisciplinary-infused psychoanalysis, as seen through the eyes of a clinical psychoanalyst. At times, my excursions can take me to unusual places, but what is constant is that if I felt that any topic did not bear on the clinical situation, it was not included in this collection. Nor were papers I felt were redundant with one another.

Various chapters have been presented at one time or another at many places, including but not limited to the New Jersey Psychoanalytic Society, the American Psychoanalytic Association, Chicago Institute for Psychoanalysis, Institute for Psychoanalytic Training and Research, University College in London, International Psychoanalytic Association, Columbia Center for Psychoanalytic Training and Research, and the New York Psychoanalytic Institute. Selections from several chapters as well have been presented as the Heinz Hartman II Award Lecture, Ernst and Gertrude Ticho Award Lecture, and the Sigmund Freud Award Lecture. The Ticho Lectureship Prize is awarded yearly to an analyst at mid-career by the Gertrude and Ernst Ticho Foundation, to whom I am grateful.

The papers are categorized into five sections, each with a characteristic line of investigation into psychoanalysis. The first is titled Paradigms and Processes. In this section: Chapter 1 was published in 2003, as "Ghosts of Paradigms Past: The Once and Future Evolution of Psychoanalysis," *Journal of the American Psychoanalytic*

Association 51:825–56. Chapter 2 was published in 1989, as "Affect and the Compulsion to Repeat: Freud's Repetition Compulsion Revisited," *Psychoanalysis and Contemporary Thought* 12:243–290. My co-author was Carol Malatesta, a lifespan developmental psychologist. Chapter 3 was published in 1985, as "Dynamic Interpersonal Processes and the Inpatient Holding Environment," *Psychiatry* 48(4):341–357. My co-author was Ira Levine, who at the time was the Medical Director of the Yale Psychiatric Institute, where I was on the staff. The Yale Psychiatric Institute was then one of the last long-term care psychoanalytic hospitals left in the United States. Chapter 4 was published in 2009, as "Theorizing About Theorizing: An Examination of the Contributions of William I. Grossman to Psychoanalysis," *Journal of the American Psychoanalytic Association* 57:9–36. Chapter 5 was published in 1995, as "Mapping the Minds of Relational Psychoanalysis: Some Critiques, Questions, and Conjectures," *Psychoanalytic Psychology* 12:9–29. This chapter was originally given at a panel of Division 39 (Psychoanalysis) of the American Psychological Association about structural analysts critiquing relational analysts, which was organized with Alan Sugarman. Publication of this chapter was facilitated by the urging of Bertram Cohler, then editor of this journal. Chapter 6 was published in 2015, as "Science Studies, Context, and Psychoanalysis," *American Imago* (Special Issue on Psychoanalysis as a Critical Methodology: Interdisciplinary Applications) 72:211–228.

The second section is titled Observations on Analyzability. In this section: Chapter 7 was published in 1999, as "Analyzability Redux: From 'Analyzable' to Preparable for Analysis." *Annual of Psychanalysis* 37:127–141. This paper was initially prepared for and presented at the symposium entitled The Fusion of Science, Art, and Humanism" honoring John E. Gedo on his 70th Birthday, sponsored by the Chicago Psychoanalytic Institute and Society, October 18, 1997. Chapter 8 was published in 2004, as "Analytic Preparation: The Creation of an Analytic Climate with Patients Not Yet in Psychoanalysis," *Journal of the American Psychoanalytic Association* 52:1041–1073. Chapter 9 was published in 1989, as "Levels of Adaptation and Narcissistic Psychopathology," *Psychiatry* 52:218–236. Chapter 10 was published in 1999, as "A Conjoint Phase of Treatment Involving a Severely Disturbed Adolescent Boy and His Father," *Psychoanalytic Quarterly* 68:21–51.

The third section is titled Vygotsky and Psychoanalysis. In this section: Chapter 11 was published in 1992, as "An Investigation into Some Implications of a Vygotskian Perspective on the Origins of Mind: Psychoanalysis and Vygotskian Psychology, Part I," *Journal of the American Psychoanalytic Association* 40:357–387. My co-author was Lissa Weinstein. Chapter 12 was published in 1992, as "Language and the Psychoanalytic Process: Psychoanalysis and Vygotskian Psychology, Part II," *Journal of the American Psychoanalytic Association* 40:725–759. My co-author was Lissa Weinstein. Chapter 13 was published in 1996, as "The Transference and the Zone of Proximal Development," *Journal of the American Psychoanalytic Association* 44:167–200. These papers were sparked by many conversations on the topic with Jerome Bruner, who conveniently had an office down the hall from mine. My co-author was again Lissa Weinstein. I hasten to add that Lissa Weinstein's contributions to these three papers were at least as significant as mine, and our incredible collaboration was a high point in my career.

The fourth section is titled The Epigenetic Rating System (EARS). During my decade on the faculty of the clinical psychology program at the New School for Social Research in New York

City, I embarked on an empirical research program aimed at measuring and operationalizing certain psychoanalytic constructs. In this section: Chapter 14 is an unpublished scoring manual for the EARS. Chapter 15 was published in 1994, as "Affectivity in Opiate and Cocaine Abusers," *Psychiatry* 57:333–347. My co-author was Daniel Keller. Chapter 16 was published in 1998, as "Affective Experiences and Levels of Self-Organization in Maternal Postpartum Depression," *Psychoanalytic Psychology* 15:396–419. My co-author was Micka Menos. Chapter 17 was published in 1997, as "Adolescent Suicidality in Urban Minorities and Its Relationship to Conduct Disorders, Depression, and Separation Anxiety," *Journal of the American Academy of Child and Adolescent Psychiatry* 36:75–84. My co-author was Marilyn Feldman. Over the years, many colleagues worked with me on various EARS projects. In addition to the above-mentioned co-authors; my thanks go to Julia Prillaman, Steven Passik, Jeffrey Faude, Ann Turner, Gloria Miele, Mark Kuras, Janet Boller, Rebecca Scarpellino, Julie Abrams, Eve Gordon, Alicia Camlibel, and Andrew Morrall,

The fifth section is titled Surviving the Holocaust. In this section: Chapter 18 was published in 1982, as "Aftermath of the Concentration Camp: The Second Generation," *Journal of the American Academy of Psychoanalysis* 10:289–335. My co-author was Erika Fromm. Having herself found sanctuary at the University of Chicago, she was a refugee from prewar Europe and survived against steep odds. She derived more than an academic satisfaction at seeing the paper reach the light of publication. Chapter 19 was published in 1985, as "On Silence and the Holocaust: A Contribution to Clinical Theory," *Psychoanalytic Inquiry* 5:63–84. This manuscript was solicited for the volume by Dori Laub and Nanette Auerhahn, to whom I am grateful.

Publication of this book was expedited through the gentle persistence of Arnold Richards, editor of this psychoanalytic book series. Several of the papers were read and critiqued prior to publication by William Grossman. Production of this book was overseen by Sonny and Lillian Viltzen. My enormous appreciation to all of my compatriots cannot be overstated.

DEDICATION

I dedicate this book to my three children. Each are remarkable in their own way. Raising them has never failed to fill me with awe and has profoundly rounded out my sense of the significance of life in its totality.

Jared Henry Wilson,
whose name means one who descends to rule.

Samuel Benjamin Wilson,
"Nunc scio quid sit amor."

Julia Claire Wilson,
fiercely loving defender of the moral order, and all that is beautiful and good.

CONTENTS

III. Lev Vygotsky and Psychoanalysis

IV. The Epigenetic Assessment Rating System (EARS)

Contents

I was very pleased when my good friend and colleague, Arnold Wilson, asked me to write an introduction to his book of collected papers. We have been friends for over twenty years and have spent many an evening, along with our wives, talking about our lives, our children's lives, and our dedication to helping our patients deal with their own struggles. I have always been impressed with his devotion to his patients and particularly with his intellectual efforts to make sense of those struggles. There have been a number of instances when he asked me to evaluate his patients for the use of medication and to monitor those cases with him. We shared many cases. I was impressed with not only his willingness to use medications when he thought they could be of help but also his knowledge about psychotropic medications themselves.

It is rare indeed to read a book of collected papers, all of which are of consistently high quality, such as this one. Arnold is a psychoanalyst equally at home discussing psychoanalytic theory, psychoanalytic practice, the contributions of academic psychologists, as well as empirical studies of such contemporary issues as cocaine addiction, postpartum depression, and survivors of the Holocaust and their children. This collection, covering such a wide range of topics, demonstrates Arnold's intellectual gifts and his ability to integrate ideas from a number of disciplines and viewpoints. This book is also a testimony to the breadth of his interest in everything related to the workings of the mind. The book is divided into five sections, the first three dealing with various psychoanalytic topics demonstrating Wilson's extraordinary grasp of psychoanalytic theory and psychoanalytic practice.

The first paper in Section I. Paradigms and Processes, is "Ghosts of Paradigms Past: The Once and Future Evolution of Psychoanalytic Thought." Wilson writes, "I hope to show how prevailing psychoanalytic theories represent transformations of the past, and how these theories allow us to reconstruct a theoretical past as well as particular processes of development and change that determine the evolution of psychoanalytic theory...also how conflict, defense, and compromise characterize the relationship between the core commitments of different theories that have existed within an interactive context of one sort or another." Here he introduces the ideas of Imre Lakatos to psychoanalysis. The second paper "Affect and the Compulsion to Repeat" revisits Freuds' concept of the repetition compulsion, emphasizing that "it is more exact to reserve the term 'repetition compulsion' for the motivation underlying primal repetition, and 'transference' for the motivation and sequelae of symbolic repetition."

In "Dynamic Interpersonal Processes and the Inpatient Holding Environment," Wilson states that "the primary function of a psychiatric holding environment is the delivery to the patient of the normative services which the nuclear family customarily provides. In order to provide this, the hospital, like the optimal family, holds both by restraining and by facilitating."

The next paper in this section serves as a tribute to his close friend, colleague, and mentor, Dr. William Grossman. It is entitled "Theorizing about Theorizing: An Examination of the Contributions of William Grossman to Psychoanalysis" He stresses that "Grossman sought to detail the many subtle factors infusing Freudian theory, from its initial sources to its consolidation as a system, to its embrace in the mind of an analyst who will use it, and on to the many iterations of its progress on the way to being applied in the clinical situation. This progression assumes a recognition of the analyst's need to be at once experiencer and observer." In "Mapping the Mind in Relational Psychoanalysis: Some Critiques, Questions and Conjectures," Wilson argues that the maps of the mind proposed by relational psychoanalysts pull clinical theory too far toward environmental factors and goes on to identify potential clinical dilemmas that follow from that view.

The second section entitled "Observations on Analyzability," deals primarily with the clinical practice of psychoanalysis and the theories that inform it. In "Analyzability Redux: From Analyzable to Preparable for Analysis," Wilson posits that "analyzability is not an entity that can exist outside of context. In psychoanalysis, context always changes, as the prevailing emotional climate of the hour varies. Psychoanalysts who locate analyzability inside an analysand rather than as wedded to the shifting tides of multiple contexts have made an egregious error, one that is damaging in many ways—to the patient, not to mention to the field of psychoanalysis itself." He continues to discuss issues of analyzability in the paper entitled "Analytic Preparation: The Creation of an Analytic Climate with Patients not yet in Analysis." In this paper he examines some relations between analytic preparation, analytic interaction, and the interpretation of transference.

The paper on "Levels of Adaptation and Narcissistic Psychopathology" examines how an "understanding of the dimensions of empathic abilities, paranoia, levels of depression, grandiosity , and defensive uses of denial and disavowal can lend a broad explanatory range to the understanding" of two levels of narcissistic psychopathology, and how we can assess both successful and unsuccessful adaptation to the outer world and the inner world in narcissistic disorders. This section concludes with a paper describing an unusual conjoint treatment of an adolescent boy and his father. The conjoint therapy "complemented the son's individual therapy and led to a stable, hence analyzable transference."

The third section, "Vygotsky and Psychoanalysis," consists of three papers published in the 1990s in the *Journal of the American Psychoanalytic Association* and co-authored with his friend and colleague Dr. Lissa Weinstein. These papers introduce the psychoanalytic community to the work and theories of the Russian psychologist Lev Vygotsky who proposed an analysis of language, thought, and internalization that has direct relevance to the concerns of psychoanalysis. The authors write that "our adaptation of Vygotsky's views expands upon Freud's assigned role to language in the topographic model," emphasizing particularly Vygotsky's views on the genesis and utilization of word meanings. They elaborate on Vygotsky's theory of thinking and speaking and the structure and interplay of language and thought. Wilson and Weinstein also suggest that Vygotsky's methodology of understanding the mind is comparable to the analyst who derives his clinical data from the analytic situation. In "Psychoanalysis and the ZPD," they introduce Vygotsky's concept of the zone of proximal development, which was adduced in order to make sense of how and why two people, in conjunction, can mobilize the intrapsychic and inter-psychological resources that make cognitive and psychological growth possible for the less developed member of the dyad. There is an extensive discussion of the distinction and similarities between the transference and the therapeutic alliance.

Section IV, "The Epigenetic Assessment Rating System" (EARS), contains four papers detailing the use of that measurement system. In one study, Wilson demonstrates that "opiate and cocaine abusers' affect tolerance and affect expression were significantly impaired as compared to normals." Using the EARS and other tests in urban minority adolescents, he found that relying on depressive symptomatology to identify suicidality overlooks the importance of the presence of a diagnosis of conduct disorder and separation anxiety. Once again, using the EARS and other tests, he studies maternal postpartum depression and finds a global regression to earlier levels of personality organization

The final section, "Surviving the Holocaust," contains two papers. The first, "On Silence and the Holocaust: A Contribution to Clinical Theory," is a study of the children of holocaust survivors. Wilson suggests here that "tolerance for certain affects which are holocaust sequelae is enhanced by the commitment to historical explanation and that such a narrative commitment, when supported by a therapeutic holding environment, constitutes a facilitative element of the treatment process." In the final paper, "Aftermath of the Concentration Camp: The Second Generation," he concludes that "the Holocaust seems to exert an influence on either health or illness in the children, depending upon how the parents adapted to postwar life and to their parenting functions."

Arnold Wilson's collected papers offer the reader insight into a gifted psychoanalytic theorist's mind at work, whether in the clinician's chair, engaging in empirical studies, or integrating the work of other psychoanalytic thinkers. It has been a privilege and a pleasure to write this introduction to his book.

Martin S. Willick, M.D.
Teaneck, NJ, 2019

I. Paradigms and Processes

GHOSTS OF PARADIGMS PAST: THE ONCE AND FUTURE EVOLUTION OF PSYCHOANALYTIC THOUGHT

An example of the psychoanalytic mode of thought is put forward concerning how psychoanalytic theories have historically been constituted and transformed. The model of world hypotheses, characterized by multiple irresolvable truth claims, captures the nature of most psychoanalytic theorizing until about 1970. Each of two world hypotheses—one grounded in intrapsychic conflict (seen when the analyst observes from outside the transference) and the other in interpersonal internalization (seen when the analyst observes from inside the bidirectional interactive processes)—is an autonomous and self-sufficient aggregate. The stance taken by the analyst-observer with respect to the analytic interaction is key to seeing how the two world hypotheses are made manifest in clinical work and in theory. By contrast, the model of competing programs captures the essential nature of most psychoanalytic theorizing since about 1970 and is characterized by the necessity of each progressively evolving through a particular kind of commerce with its neighbors. Such commerce is necessary when a program is in danger of degenerating. In this way of thinking, there is a fundamental tension between classical psychoanalysis adapting to the demands and exigencies of its particular and ever-evolving historical niche, and simultaneously retaining the core commitments that guarantee continuity. Honoring the forces of progression displaces the quest for truth as a paramount goal of psychoanalysis. A developmental lag in recognizing this transformation has hindered progress toward a comparative, process-centered psychoanalysis.

A particular "psychoanalytic mode of thought" has been conceptualized that to Freud was a research instrument. This mode of thought has been examined by Grossman (1993, 1998), who delineates the constituent parts of this form of investigation that Freud applied in a variety of contexts: the understanding of clinical material and other clinical concerns, the nature of mental organization, and various sociocultural processes. Freud's model of psychoanalytic investigation was based on his analytic method and was characterized by the application of a psychological model to thinking about theories. This approach incorporated the means by which past mental life is discovered in the present. It examines processes of development and change that are the basis of the reconstruction of the past. The same model organizes every hierarchical level of investigation, ranging from the intrapsychic conflict observed in clinical analysis to the development of the highest forms of human thought. It recognizes the duality of conscious and unconscious factors in all ideas and cultural products. In an attempt to address these issues in a multiplicity of contexts, the investigatory framework was constructed using hierarchical and interactional principles, with hierarchies arrayed in a complemental series, featuring defense, conflict, and compromise at every level, and operations that transform the levels in turn into levels of ever higher complexity, which act recursively to reorder past experiences.

This psychoanalytic mode of thought will be used here to understand aspects of the history of psychoanalytic theorizing. We can understand that history much as an analyst understands the history of a patient. I hope to show how prevailing psychoanalytic theories represent transformations of the past, and how these theories allow us to reconstruct a theoretical past as well as particular processes of development and change that determine the evolution of psychoanalytic theory. I hope to show also how conflict, defense, and compromise characterize the relationship between the core commitments of different theories that have existed within an interactive context of one sort or another. Finally, I will present an analogue of Freud's complemental series by examining the inherent tension of a theory between progression and degeneration, which also involves a relationship between preserving a theory's hard core and the need to adapt to creative input from the outside, and results from the use of the theory clinically, or at times in other applications. Freud's concept of the complemental series is that all disposition to neurosis is the result of the variable interplay and mutual interdependence of constitution and experience at every point in development; although they are conceptual alternatives, constitution and environment both require the other for their very expression.

Two World Hypotheses in Psychoanalysis

Whereas David Rapaport was fond of describing what he did as "thinking about thinking," what I am attempting here is to consider "how we think we are thinking" about psychoanalysis. The line of reflection I propose does not address particular clinical issues, though it does bear profoundly, if indirectly, on such issues. My point of departure is the observation that if there is any single factor that sets the current intellectual world off from, say, the world of fifty years ago, it is that there are as many forms of potentially valid knowledge as there are agreed on criteria for the establishment of that knowledge. We can only ruefully shake our heads at the memory of the days when it was believed that a good scientific theory was one that corresponded with observable facts, possessed minimal excess meaning, could be supported or falsified by observable facts, and allowed new observed facts to be predicted. In our more rough-and-tumble times, the knowledge context of any explanatory theory must be established immediately and clearly so as to avoid confusion later on. No longer can any serious discipline act as if value systems and metatheory need not be assessed. This is the only way now to adjudicate between different points of view with an eye to identifying a good theory.

Such an examination of psychoanalysis, one that blends elements of its epistemology with its clinical theory, is what I have in mind here. I hold that the evolution of psychoanalytic thought is characterized by a key transition, from a duality of divergent and irreconcilable world hypotheses to a plurality of competing programs capable of dialogue and mutual influence. Before that transition, psychoanalytic views emphasized the primacy of either endogenous or exogenous motivational factors, and so set up camp in a world hypothesis whose constructs were irreconcilable and indeed incommensurable with those of the other world hypothesis. For the last few decades, however, any novel psychoanalytic thinking has had to move beyond these world hypotheses. The cycle of pitting interpersonal (exogenous) and intrapsychic (endogenous) theories against each other has simply grown too wearisome and destructive for the field to tolerate, and its seemingly endless permutations fail to offer any further prospect for deeper or more discerning theorizing.

Since the dawn of epistemology over two millennia ago, a primary concern has been this: Faced with rival claims about the world that rely on a body of evidence, how can we use that evidence to rationally adjudicate those claims? In a way reminiscent of how Aristotle responded to Plato's mystical theory of forms, modern science has created taxonomies for almost everything in sight, in the comforting hope that comparative empirical tests might allow such adjudication. Over thirty years ago, however, this effort, like the Aristotelian categories, foundered, as a period of postpositivism was ushered in. This was a profound reaction against the narrow-mindedness of positivism, yet the reaction proved equally limited. It promoted a subtly disguised relativism, featuring such assertions as that there simply are different and incompatible worlds, and that different views are not translatable into one another, construct reality differently, and simply must coexist without any exchange that might push matters forward. In my view, there is no single greater danger to the perpetuation of the classical psychoanalytic tradition than the possibility that psychoanalytic theory will degenerate into the freewheeling relativism that says anything goes and that one point of view cannot validly be compared to another. In my reading of current literature across the sciences, this view is facing rigorous opposition, in part because ironically it shares many of the assumptions of the positivist view it crowded out (for a virtual manifesto of this position, see Laudan 1996).

Although a circumspect and respectful pluralism has received excellent press in recent years, in a kind of natural sympathy for the notion that there are no essential properties in the things we study and no best method with which to study them, pluralism is best viewed of as a temporary state of affairs in psychoanalysis. Our diverse body of theory will grapple with new and unforeseen demands in the face of evolutionary and synthetic tendencies. Pluralism has a certain contemporary appeal. because historically it has taken the place of an ideological intolerance in which adherents of a regnant theory label other positions misguided, wrong, or just plain crazy. In this sense, pluralism stands politically for a healthier state of affairs. Nonetheless, it suffers from problems of clarity that can be teased out from its political appeal. If contradictory views can each make truth claims and the evolution of ideas is no longer a desideratum, a pluralistic world is at best fragmented, at worst paralyzed. Certainly, the pursuit of truth as an overarching value in psychoanalysis is a mixed blessing, a dogged and rather concrete construal of psychoanalysis as science. It is difficult, of course, to think of anyone baldly opposed to the search for truth; the rub is its inordinately high ranking in the hierarchy of values embraced by many analysts. By contrast, contemporary pragmatists certainly appreciate truth, embrace it as something they would rather have than be without, but see its preeminence in doing science as constraining and obstructing a more important task, the solving of real-world problems. In the recent psychoanalytic literature there has been a spate of disturbing attacks on the idea that there is any truth or reality at all that an analyst can rely on as an anchor (for a critique of this view, see Eagle, Wolitsky, and Wakefield 2001); these pronouncements can be viewed as symptoms of pluralism at its worst. The more practical position is that rival theories can indeed be adjudicated, but through methods intrinsic to the work psychoanalysts do, rather than through extrinsic methods that fail to take into account the nature of psychoanalytic activity.

The procedures of comparative investigation must include translation rules that allow the comparison of entities in adjacent disciplines, as Kitcher (1992) has proposed. This is an old problem and no simple task, for in psychoanalysis, as in other inquiries into the mind, the areas divided have been studied in an isolation that breeds self-referential circularities and native languages quite difficult to translate into other tongues. However, certain types of conversation between disciplines, it has been found, promote these creative translations that make for a helpful conversation between bodies of knowledge nested in different disciplines. Freud (1912–1913), in the preface and in the introduction to the third essay in *Totem and Taboo,* offers a clear and thought-provoking discussion of the methodological problems of interdisciplinary work for the psychoanalyst. Freud might well have been pleased that today there is a thriving field called psychoneuroimmunology. To be sure, managing such border negotiations is a daunting challenge, and a considerable literature has developed around the notion of incommensurability (see Kuhn 1962).The challenge to incommensurability has been, although is not necessarily, characterized by a resurgence of the values of what used to be called pragmatism, in the patchwork tradition stretching from William James to Richard Rorty.

Before we can test our way into the future, we must first think our way into it. This is to be done initially not from the bottom-up tradition of empirical comparison, but through model building from the top down—theory construction followed by the gathering of data that is probative. A robust comparative psychoanalysis has been lacking over the last half-century because, for the most part, analysts have been unable to get beyond what can best be described as the acceptance of two predominant world hypotheses—the intrapsychic and the interpersonal. Pitting one against the other creates a caricature of testing the validity of psychoanalytic propositions. These world hypotheses have been implicit from the start, and are largely responsible for the tedious repetitiveness of some of the great debates of psychoanalysis. One can leapfrog from the famous Marienbad conference of 1937, where the issue was whether interpretation or introjection of the analyst's benign presence is the primary mutative factor in treatment, to the self psychology / conflict psychology controversies thirty years later over the interpretation of aggression vs. the empathic resolution of the experience of selfobject transferences, and then to the relational challenge to contemporary structural analysis another thirty years later. In this latest episode, relationalists propose that nuances of the relationship are the primary fulcrum for intervention and that insight into intrapsychic activity is of secondary significance. Alter the vocabulary a tad to account for terminological fashion, and the arguments on both sides over the years are remarkably, and numbingly, alike. In each instance, a by now uninteresting set of contrasts is presented: the interpersonal or intrapsychic, relationship or insight, interpretation or empathy. How can we account for this repetitiveness, that fuels so much passion yet advances the field so little? Sociopolitically, it is certainly true that many of these debates were characterized by polarization into competing schools and camps, and by a failure to develop more discriminating theory in response to potentially useful critiques. Methodologically, instances of either/or thinking have abounded, as have the personality shortfalls of various men and women.

Most important of all, however, psychoanalysis, having created within itself these two world hypotheses, was fated to irresolvable debates. The overarching thematic similarities of controversies over the course of psychoanalytic history suggests that there are repetitive forms lurking, an underlying architecture capable of producing endless theoretical content in infinite permutations and transformations.

World hypotheses were first studied by the philosopher Stephen Pepper (1942), and the notions of scientific revolution, separate worlds, and incommensurable realities find their origins in Pepper, whose work preceded that of the better-known Thomas Kuhn. Pepper finds in world hypotheses the fundamental reason for the lack of cross-theoretical progress across much of science. A world hypothesis is a symbolic scheme for the arrangement of data. He depicts incommensurable clusters of data and theory lying side by side, self-contained hypotheses generated by underlying root metaphors, each autonomous of the other, each of which possesses profound explanatory powers when any new datum is brought within the purview of a theory. Truth becomes remarkably promiscuous; a world hypothesis confers objectivity on all data it can encompass within its explanatory web, which it imparts through the powers of condensation and ideational motility inherent in metaphor.

A root metaphor is a guiding assumption that is imperceptibly converted into theory (for example, man-as-machine, or man-as-organism; for a current take on how prevalent and mischievous the expansion of core metaphors indeed is, in general and particularly with respect to the cognitive unconscious, see Lakoff and Johnston 1999). A world hypothesis is derived from these underlying root metaphors that must be inferred rather than directly observed, and metaphor works to pull facts inside and confer objectivity upon them through metaphor's inevitable participation in the construction of theory. World hypotheses are the elaborated root metaphors, self-contained collections of lower-level models (for a discussion of levels of models, see Black 1962), and data that can explain virtually any phenomenon. It is the nature of a world hypothesis to be metatheoretical, invisible to the naked eye; all one can see are the derivatives, so to speak, made visible by a programmatic amplification of the prevailing root metaphor.

Of essential importance to Pepper is that data cannot be presented in such a way as to adjudicate between competing world hypotheses, because each can explain anything plausibly and each has virtually universal scope. Since each can in principle integrate and explain virtually any datum it addresses, the actual tension between different world hypotheses is between different epistemologies (characterized by how each purports to know, rather than what each claims to know), rather than between data-testing theories in which one or the other proves superior. Since the testing of data cannot adjudicate between theories located within different world hypotheses, most empirical tests aimed at doing so become fundamentally irrelevant. Successful empirical testing can be accomplished only within, rather than between, world hypotheses.

Pepper speaks of six world hypotheses, but none are rooted in any field he more broadly classified as science. The identification of world hypotheses as structures determining core methods and phenomena can usefully be conducted by any and all investigatory fields, not just psychoanalysis. For the purposes of psychoanalysis, there is no reason to assume the commonality or universality of Pepper's original six. In much the same way that I identify two world hypotheses as native to psychoanalysis, Overton (1994, 1998) has identified two—mechanismic and organismic—as native to life-span developmental psychology. Overton argues that in life-span developmental psychology the organismic and mechanistic world hypotheses provide the most basic concepts and categories for any understanding of data, are unlimited in scope, incompatible and irreconcilable, and at bottom have remarkably different implications for the study of the course of life. I suggest that the same conditions were the case for the intrapsychic and interpersonal world hypotheses in psychoanalysis. However, whereas Overton borrows his world hypotheses explicitly from Pepper (that is, they are two of the six Pepper depicted), I identify the two world hypotheses of psychoanalysis from my imagination—my own take on the history of psychoanalytic ideas. I do not use the word imagination lightly; all science begins in imagination, which is a necessary forerunner to even the most intensive empirical scrutiny.

Although the topic has not been formally investigated at great length, it is intriguing to consider how and why psychoanalysis produced its own unique world hypotheses. Clinical sciences have ground rules different from those of the academic sciences. One can speculate that these world hypotheses follow from how psychoanalysis gathers its data, and from the unique characteristics of the clinical situation, in conjunction with the distinctive interpretive demands the clinical situation makes on theorists and clinicians alike.

Certainly, others have explored this general area within psychoanalysis. For example, it has been proposed that psychoanalytic data must be understood within the context of tragic and ironic visions of reality (Schafer 1970), and that these different visions of reality produce incommensurable data from the romantic and comic visions (see also Messer and Winoker 1980; Strenger 1991). This seems to me a way of saying what I am proposing; like me, these theorists believe that the data yielded by the psychoanalytic situation are metatheoretically saturated, and that world hypotheses (quite like what Schafer calls visions of reality) are their guarantor.

I have suggested that world hypotheses are not universal; neither are they immutable. To hold that they are is to invite the frustrations of a conceptual straitjacket. Pepper himself does not really speak to the issue of how world hypotheses can be bypassed. The power of thought always stands ready to create ideas that can alter the forces of history, and thereby its course. World hypotheses are human constructs, not immutable facts of nature. We create them rather than find them, and so we can supersede them once they are identified. In support of my views, and arrayed against the continuation of the world hypotheses model, witness the following: (a) in contemporary science, many of the philosophical arguments for multiple worlds have not held up under scrutiny; and (b) incommensurability, the idea that rival ontologies are unable to understand each other because of native languages that defy translation, has not held up, as such translations have been successfully undertaken in many sciences. Laudan

(1996) argues against incommensurability by showing that the supposed fact that scientists who subscribe to radically different theories about the natural world cannot understand one another does not preclude the possibility that, if they share certain meta-goals, they may be able to agree on the relative successes and failures of their respective theories. They need merely count the number of problems each theory has solved. The point is that the incommensurability of theories at the object-level does not entail incommensurability at the meta-level. Non-translatability does not inevitably lead to relativism. In fact, establishing relations of mutual translatability between two world views is a precondition for determining that they are different. In addition, (c) the underdetermination of theory by data problem, the idea that any theory can be reconciled with any evidence, has been weakened, as it has been shown that evidence is not impotent in choosing between rival conceptions of the world; and (d) the thesis of methodological subjectivity—that a paradigm's standards for determining the adequacy of proposed solutions to problems, make its own solutions appear strong and others weak, has not held up. It has been repeatedly been shown that there are standards that crisscross paradigms, and these can be used to choose between paradigms. In psychoanalysis, the thesis of methodological subjectivity has likewise not held up as the conceptual bell ringer of the thesis of separate worlds. The reason for this, simply put, is that psychoanalysis does not progress by paradigm shifts, nor does it thrive in isolation. The thesis of methodological subjectivity, as exemplified by Kohut and Brenner, to assert the uniqueness of the standards and methods used to assess their particular theories, will be discussed later.

Rorty (1998) and Laudan (1984, 1990, 1996) have dedicated volumes to sketching such objections. Although Rorty has long been identified with the postmodern turn and Laudan has been a staunch advocate of natural-scientific methods, both identify themselves as neopragmatists. Also to be noted are the contributions of Gholson and Parker (1985) and O'Donohue (1993), who have examined metascientific theories in psychology in a manner other than Kuhnian.

Contemporary psychoanalysis appears in many ways to be a zeitgeist. If, in fact, it is, then separate worlds within it are not as conceptually distinct as meets the eye. Spence (1982) has noted that the underdetermination of theory by data in psychoanalysis, and hence the necessity of a kind of hermeneutic reading not truly driven by evidence, occurs only when data are presented so loosely that the underlying empirical soil is not visible. Others have made the point even more strongly. At a microscopic level of clinical inquiry, when a sufficient amount of clinical data is exposed, I have always found that while there may be many ways to help a patient, some ways are better than others. Theory may inevitably color data, but it need not do so to the point of saturation.

In contemporary psychoanalysis, there is no reason to hold onto the notion of separate and incommensurable worlds; today, we are challenged by difficulties of translation and criteria for comparison that are not well thought out or easily implemented (for a first step toward such translation, see Kitcher 1992). I will take this up more explicitly later, when I discuss how the contributions of Laudan and Lakatos allow us to recognize, name, and move toward an evolutionary view, in contrast to the ideas of Kuhn, whose endorsement of discontinuities over time makes it difficult to determine whether evolution or devolution is at play. Laudan and Lakatos, I argue, allow us to move past Pepper's world hypotheses, and their ideas best describe the current state of psychoanalysis.

The Intrapsychic (Conflict) and the Interpersonal (Internalization)

The root metaphor (or operational referent) of the intrapsychic world hypothesis is ideational conflict; that of the interpersonal world hypothesis is internalization. Contemporary structural analysts and relational analysts alike certainly struggle to make systematic sense of the relation of conflict to internalization. The former trace their lineage back to Freud, yet strive to evolve along with the times. Contemporary structural analysts speak of both conflict and internalization as fulcrums for clinical intervention, yet the psychoanalytic situation (the couch, sessions at least four times a week, free association) has not historically been adequately studied as lending itself to the treatment of processes of internalization. Indeed, Gray (1987) states explicitly that his close monitoring theory is therapeutic to the extent that it maximizes the role of conflict and minimizes the role of internalization in psychoanalysis, and that his approach is applicable to patients who have a "greater capacity for non-internalizing solutions" (p. 149).

Internalization is defined by the body of propositions that follow from the view that taking in the analyst's attributes, or any experiential equivalents, is the primary means by which analytic change takes place. Although from the intrapsychic perspective internalization is certainly handled in a detailed and far-reaching manner (see Schafer 1968; Meissner 1981). I will take a different tack, in that I will speak of internalization as it has been employed by those who have intellectually campaigned within its distinct world hypothesis, who regard it as a superordinate theory that can explain everything and that implicates particular interventions. Those adhering to this definition of internalization generally advocate a position of discontinuity from classical analysis and believe that a new start is called for. By contrast, internalization, as viewed from within the intrapsychic world hypothesis, is smoothly integrated into the history of psychoa-nalysis and does not lead to a new school of thought.

As for conflict, I adhere to the following definition. Conflict is the particular form of mental functioning producing ideation characterized by compromise formation, and therefore more or less accessible to interpretation in terms of one or both bipolar coordinates of the ideas or wishes involved. I note and will avoid the circularity of one way of handling a particular feature of this definition—that the mind's total composite output is, a priori, ideational conflict between existing psychic macro- and/or mi-crostructures or representations. That approach makes conflict an assumption, in no way testable or falsifiable in the clinical sit-uation, and hence theory rather than data-driven. It is not at all elegant to create such a tautology and then believe that the ob-servations that follow flow from objective facts. However, the definition escapes tautology if taken simply as a characterization of what is seen from an angle of observation from which prob-lems are to be considered. Here it is a question not of testing the fact of conflict, but of determining the concept's goodness of fit.

Once this is recognized, another important point arises con-cerning how to understand intrapsychic conflict. If an analyst cannot discern compromise between competing wishes that can be reached through interpretation, or whose derivatives are po-tentially revealed through transformations of thought (e.g., primary to secondary process through dream work), then one is justified in speaking of ideational intrapsychic life not seemingly characterized by intrapsychic conflict.

To do so does not invalidate the intrapsychic world hypothe-sis, because various permutations of conflict color all other mental elements. In this way, ideational qualities other than con-flict can certainly be conceived within the intrapsychic world hypothesis, and the role of conflict will thereby be more readily understood. For example, Hartmann's conflict-free sphere of the ego, or deficits defined as the absence of conflict, at bottom refer to one or another fate of conflict. In this sense, the assumption of conflict (or of internalization, for that matter) may be seen as an instance of what Searle (1992) refers to as constitutive principles, each of which evokes and requires an entire conceptual system and must be assessed in relation to the entire system. Constitutive principles create the possibility of the activities they regulate and an area of investigation around them.

The intrapsychic world hypothesis incorporates intrapsychic conflict, as well as other elements, and these other elements are understood in relation to conflict. However, in traversing world hypotheses, crucial boundaries may blur because of loose or sliding definitions and other vagaries of language. An example may be seen in the notion of conflict between self and others, Mitchell's notion of conflict between relational configurations (1988). This is in no way equivalent or even comparable to intrapsychic conflict; the two share only a surface linguistic concurrence, a common language that obscures rather than clarifies.

I will now introduce an idea somewhat akin to what in psychoanalysis has been called points of view—angles of observation. Just as Freud (1915) spoke of an adequate metapsychological explanation as consisting of multiple points of view, one can begin to think of the advantages and liabilities of multiple angles of observation in psychoanalytic explanation. An angle of observation places the observer in a particular location and thus determines what is seen. Angles of observation refer to the where of the origins of an observation. In most theorizing, they are implicit rather than explicit. Viewing analytic data from one angle or another brings into necessary focus the unwavering, unrelenting influence of the observer on what is observed. Much of what is often assumed to exist in an analytic context is, in fact, observer-dependent and profoundly changes as the observational field is altered. Observer categories are often confused for objective categories, and, as Nagel (1986) reminds us, objective truth is usually not to be found by traveling as far away from one's personal perspective as possible, in search of a world that "simply exists and has no perspectival center" (p. 27).

I will use the phrase "outside the transference" to refer to the angle of observation that allows the observer to bring the intrapsychic domain most clearly into view. The angle of observation that affords the observer a good view of the interpersonal domain will be denoted as inside the bidirectional processes (Wilson 1999). Many factors will influence where a particular observation originates, but most will migrate to one or the other of these angles of observation. The world hypotheses organized around conflict and internalization have lent themselves, respectively, to these two different angles of observation.

When systematically elaborated, these angles of observation in psychoanalysis lead to two visions of how analytic dyads work together. Elsewhere, I have discussed these two visions, and how the particulars of the intrapsychic world hypothesis (conflict) are metaphorized into the "differentiated dyad," and the particulars of the interpersonal world hypothesis (internalization) are metaphorized into the "attached dyad" (Wilson and Prillaman 1997). What is seen and described from the angle of the attached dyad is analogous to the view of the analyst positioned inside the flux of bidirectional processes of the analytic dyad. This is in contrast to what is seen and described by the analyst positioned outside the transference and observing its externalized fantasy content. This view assumes a fundamental differentiation between individuals that is not present in the other view. In the attached dyad, the analysand is seen to be struggling to integrate and cope with the analyst's actual personage, and this appearance follows from the assumption of the hegemony of dissociation prevalent in the current relational literature (Bromberg 1994), an issue that long ago preoccupied Ferenczi. Viewed from this angle, derivatives from the dynamic unconscious are far more difficult to see, and are clouded by the give-and-take of interaction; the interpersonal scene, rather than unconscious derivatives, readily comes to occupy one's attention. Theory crafted from this angle, inside the bidirectional interpersonal processes, can make the bid to remain outside the transference appear misguided, sadistic, or foolish, serving only to punish the patient from the analyst's position of untempered authority.

When the analyst is positioned outside the transference and perceives clinical matters through the lens of the assumption of a differentiated dyad, the analysand is more readily perceived to be struggling with unconscious forces that overwhelm him or her from within. The classical vision of transference follows from the assumption of the hegemony of repression, and what crystallizes into view as the analysand freely associates are the thematic derivatives that are traced and attributed to a dynamic unconscious. Theory crafted from this angle of observation promotes the impression that the analyst's bid to remain inside the bidirectional processes is simplistic, shortsighted, and superficial, serving only to obscure the gold provided by transference analysis. What is seen from each set of assumptions makes the other's assumptions appear degraded.

To restate: A great deal of psychoanalytic theory over its history has been crafted from the angle of regarding the mind of the analysand as if two differentiated sentient beings are interacting in a particular way. This is how intrapsychic conflict is most clearly witnessed and tends to privilege processes we have heretofore called intrapsychic. By contrast, processes of internalization are more readily seen by looking at an analysand's mind from the perspective of two attached beings, and, although both are sentient, neither mind is boundaried by the skin (Wertsch 1990). Mental processes are thus distributed into a kind of homegrown collectivity. In this way of regarding the mind, the minds of analyst and analysand hook together, largely through the auspices of the communicational medium of affects and language (Cavell 1993; Wilson and Weinstein 1992).

Another important point inevitably follows. Synthesis at a lower level of abstraction (i.e., at the level of observation and data) cannot be a compromise; rather, psychoanalysts must hold out for new ideas that are free of the mischief of world hypotheses. Since these ideas of how analysis works stem from incompatible world hypotheses, simple syntheses are not possible. Efforts to create a synthesis at that lower level will be defeated unless some resolution occurs at higher levels of abstraction, in the sense invoked by Waelder (1962). This is why, if synthesis is to be a goal, it is necessary that we leave behind in our wake world hypotheses viewed as superordinate principles dictating incommensurability. The difference between synthetic and what I will call pseudosynthetic forces is crucial: synthetic forces transcend world hypotheses, whereas pseudosynthetic forces bolster them.

I now turn to some features of transference and interaction to further illustrate my argument. I will compare two views on analytic interaction and the role of the transference, those of Stern (1998) and Boesky (1991). Theorists from within the internalization perspective, such as Stern, have tended to emphasize the here-and-now transference and experience-near phenomena in their writing. Contemporary Freudian analysts, like Boesky, make some use of these concepts but maintain that a certain amount of distance from patients is necessary if they are to abstract from the immediacy of their experience and understand what they are going through and how their mind works. For

Stern and other relational thinkers, the more feeling-laden and authentic the analytic connection, the more viable the treatment.

But pseudosynthetic forces naturally come into play that obscure clarity of vision. A relational analyst does not go on to abjure insight, although he or she will hold that the more the analysis is situated in the here and now, the immediacy of experience, the more productive is the analysis. This emphasis on mutative factors associated with experiencing within the hour is counterbalanced by some acknowledgment of the role of self-awareness, self-reflection, and the detached ability to understand what one is going through—the very hallmark of the intrapsychic perspective. This reaching toward common ground, however, serves only to obscure the fundamental difference between the two perspectives.

Such an approach to interaction can be contrasted with a similar line of demarcation, noticed by Boesky (1991), but from an intrapsychic perspective. With respect to the role of the object in transference, Boesky notes that any emphasis on authenticity is deceptive and unreal, because the analysand is experiencing an authentic relationship with a transference imago, rather than with another person. To pursue authenticity in this manner is therefore impossible, ultimately manipulative, and can only shunt a patient away from adequate reality testing. Clarity comes with freedom from the cloudiness of interaction, for this is the path to increased objectivity. However, the interpersonal context is liberally acknowledged as providing a background that enables the dyad to elevate the transference to its preeminent position. Again reaching for common ground, but remaining ensconced within a world hypothesis, the appearance of overlap is misleading, pseudosynthetic.

In the terms of this discussion, one has to settle one's position with respect to the transference, which means with respect to world hypotheses. Inside the bidirectional processes, one can, and should be, authentic, because authenticity helps in promoting internalization. If one is positioned outside the transference, though, authenticity makes little or no sense as a goal, because it interferes with the task of creating and then analyzing the externalizations that are the basis of the transference. One can see clearly that the positions judiciously acknowledge one another but are fundamentally set apart; any lower-level synthesis concerning the role of transference interaction will very likely vex both positions.

A more theoretical example will make my point even more clear. Take the construct of projective identification. Its assumptions are nested within the people-are-attached view metaphorized from the internalization world hypothesis, from which it derives its clinical scope and explanatory range. From the people-are-separate view metaphorized from the conflict world hypothesis, the notion of projective identification can be reformulated to appear silly, if not downright magical, and therefore absurd. When minds exist in some kind of ontological conjunction (Beebe and Lachmann (2002) have vividly demonstrated, experimentally and conceptually, that this is a plausible view of the mind's origins) and paraverbal communication is privileged, the mechanism of projective identification makes perfect sense. When minds are separated by a sharp demarcation between selves, and each is seen as processing information fully apart from the other, the mechanism is much harder to justify, and in fact can be explained by constructs more native to the intrapsychic view.

Research Programs vs Paradigms and World Hypotheses

When Freud introduced the structural model in 1923, it was intended to complement the topographic model sketched out in chapter 7 of *The Interpretation of Dreams*. Yet, according to Gray (1982), it took some six or seven decades, because of a "developmental lag" to properly integrate the wide-ranging significance of the shift. I think we are seeing a similar developmental lag with respect to the need to transcend these world hypotheses, and it is important to see whether we can hurry things along. There was a striking confluence of global events, concerning how things are to be thought about, that rocked the world of ideas in the 1970s and 1980s. Generally speaking, categories characterized by certainty broke down virtually everywhere one looked. The student rebellions in France and United States had challenged and overturned prevailing assumptions of authority, and the approach to how people can legitimately come to know what they set out to study took a sharp turn toward greater complexity. The linguistic turn and the arrival of critical theory created an intellectual arena in which method and critique take precedence over preformed categories. Balsam (2002) identifies 1970 as the year in which a new definition of female psychology began to work its way into public and psychoanalytic ways of thinking, although she points an accusing finger at a developmental lag, similar to the one identified by Gray, in properly integrating this vision some thirty years later. It was as if a new Foucauldian episteme had arisen in psychoanalysis, a shift in the form an explanation should take. Coincidentally, the year 1970 marked the first English-language publication of the Hungarian philosopher Imre Lakatos.

Within psychoanalysis, there was a veritable explosion of new ways of thinking, not all of it welcome by those who considered themselves the guardians of professional standards. It is well documented how phenomena like demedicalization, the expulsion of analysts from medical schools and universities, and the decrease in the number of analytic patients have changed the landscape of traditional psychoanalysis. What I would add to these significant sociological events is the growing inadequacy of world hypotheses as a way to make sense of psychoanalytic propositions and explain psychoanalytic data. I date the transition from world hypotheses to multiple competing research programs (of which more shortly) to the period beginning around 1970.

As Gray has noted with respect to the structural model and Balsam with respect to female psychology, there is a developmental lag, also one that continues to this very day, in apprehending the significance of this transition. However, it is not hard to see how these developmental lags came about. In psychoanalysis, a claim of truth or of special significance becomes clearer and is usually recognized only in retrospect. Some kind of developmental lag is thus inevitable, though not necessarily one as tenacious as the stalled transition from the intrapsychic and interpersonal world hypotheses.

Some analysts who have studied the history of how psychoanalytic knowledge accrues cite Kuhn and his work on revolutions as if he were the definitive authority. Certainly, Kuhn's *The Structure of Scientific Revolutions* (1962) is the most widely cited book in the history of philosophy; yet there is abundant evidence of its lack of applicability to anything psychoanalytic. It is conceptually geared to the hard sciences, and even there its precision and explanatory range are open to severe doubt; Kuhn does not even mention the soft or social sciences. Nonetheless, for whatever reasons, when the recent evolution of psychoanalysis is discussed, the specter of Kuhn seems to dominate the field, and his theory of paradigms is discussed as if it were the only choice open to us. This is puzzling since, outside of psychoanalysis, Kuhn's ideas attract nowhere near this degree of exclusive attention (Leahey 1992).

I suggest that Kuhn's idea of paradigm shifts and scientific revolution fails to accurately explain the organization of knowledge (or the lack thereof) in psychoanalytic history. Applying the concept of Kuhnian paradigms to psychoanalysis presents grave problems. Whereas Spezzano (1998), arguing in favor of a revised version of the paradigm concept, stretches to identify three plausible definitions of paradigm, Weinberg's article in the *New York Review of Books* (1998) states that twenty different interpretations of the word are to be found in Kuhn's classic. In his otherwise thoughtful paper, Spezzano goes on to identify telling problems in the notion of paradigms, but rather than leave the Kuhnian empire, he returns to Kuhn's writings and identifies a weaker Kuhnian construct, a disciplinary matrix, as the central concept defining differences between groups. Spezzano clearly sees the fatal flaws in the Kuhnian paradigm argument, but does not take the fateful step of looking elsewhere; instead, he opts for a weaker argument that is not fundamentally different from the stronger one. If one draws on Lakatos's version of the advancement of knowledge, rather than that of Kuhn in 1962 (he did do some later revisionary work that tends to be overlooked), psychoanalysis would be seen as not monolithic with respect to the rest of the intellectual world, and as hardly characterized by a single dominant paradigm at any given time. This view has far more appeal than the version of Kuhnian paradigm obsolescence, as interpreted by Mitchell (1988) and others. The irony is that Mitchell draws on a philosophy of science that allows for but one dominant paradigm at a time, while at the same time calling for pluralism—even while an historical methodology more in keeping with his call for pluralism is within arm's reach.

To locate progress in psychoanalytic theorizing and conceptually ground it, we must look elsewhere. The concept of paradigm shifts has never provided an accurate characterization of psychoanalytic theory in evolution, and Pepper's views on world hypotheses seem better suited to explain the early organization of psychoanalytic theories and how they evolved. As psychoanalysis developed, the views of Lakatos came closer to the mark. Lakatos (1976) explicitly spoke of research programs as replacements for the concept of paradigms. Lakatos's views (1978) allow for the side-by-side simultaneous existence of multiple programs that more or less draw on one another. In fact, Lakatos assumes as the norm the simultaneous existence, over time, of several competing research programs in some degree of intimate commerce with one another. In doing so, he disagrees with Kuhn, not about the presence of conflict between paradigms, but rather about the criteria by which the new is determined to have become the predominant position in a field. Lakatos argues against Kuhn's "gestalt switch" notion of change and in favor of what he considers more rational and evolutionary criteria. In making some of Kuhn's basic assumptions more differentiated, rational, and accessible, he shows that research programs coexist and can be either degenerating or progressing. Two types of "progression," empirical and theoretical, are the result of experimentation. Empirical progressions receive experimental support, while theoretical progressions are theories that lead to new predictions. If neither type of progression is occurring, a program is deemed "degenerating." Unlike a progressive research program, a degenerating research program has ceased generating testable hypotheses.

It is important to note that a degenerating program can borrow from an adjacent program and spring back to life, capable again of generating testable hypotheses, and therefore revitalized, back on the road to growth (see Gholson and Parker 1985). Such borrowing is a sign of fitness and often defines the passage into a new era. Precisely this process is under way in contemporary Freudian psychoanalysis.

What Laudan (1996) adds to the mix are original and creative ways to think about how to evaluate the newly emergent hypotheses that define the viability of what he calls a research tradition.

Lakatos (1978; Lakatos and Musgrave 1970) tends in the main to appreciate empirical factors, whereas Laudan explicitly identifies a wider range of factors, conceptual factors in particular, as crucial in the appraisal of theories, and as independent of a theory's experimental success or failure. Certainly, to date, the conceptual factors in psychoanalysis have been largely independent of its experimental successes and failures. Research traditions are not rigid guidelines set to inhibit growth, but rather allow for growth by accumulating "theory clusters" over time in order to support a core base of knowledge. Theory clusters are characterized by what Lakatos (1978) calls "core commitments." This notion has some overlap with Kuhn's use of the same phrase. A research program has a substantial and irrefutable core that is protected by "dispensable hypotheses." Core commitments are important to identify, but rarely are they transparent. Unlike Lakatos, Laudan believes that core commitments do not have to be stated explicitly in order to play a central role in a research tradition. Rather, a research tradition is defined by implicit core commitments, generating theory clusters that often go unnoticed until quite late.

The idea that such a view better describes the recent history of psychoanalysis can now be taken up. In a psychoanalytic culture marked by commitments to incommensurable world hypotheses, individuals like Ferenczi or Jung are easily dismissed, and their ideas (if not they themselves) are seen as crazy; in a psychoanalytic culture marked by competition among research programs, these same ideas are more likely to be evaluated for their visionary potential. Lakatos's model of scientific change aptly depicts the once degenerating and now rejuvenated flavor of classical psychoanalytic theory. It is hard to deny that traditional psychoanalysis, in its glorious and irritating stubbornness, flirted with but averted its demise as a respected form of knowledge. Now it is clearer why. No research tradition in psychoanalysis is obsolete simply because a rival tradition for a time generates more interesting testable hypotheses. Its proponents can revive it if so motivated, and this is indeed the picture at present (for a celebration of precisely this state of affairs, see Friedman 1997). It can best reemerge from a degenerating state when its modes of inquiry are altered.

What binds a research program and keeps it cohesive is that its core commitments pass relatively unchanged through successive theories in the program. It can borrow methods and ideas from adjacent programs when it degenerates, but the core commitments remain the bulwark of the program. Such matters can be recognized only in retrospect. In studying the classical tradition of psychoanalysis, we must identify its core commitments, which remain constant even as it evolves. Paradoxically, only by conceptualizing clear boundaries can interdisciplinary dialogue fruitfully occur. Only by articulating what traditional analysis is at its very core can analysts come face to face with prospects for progression. The possibility for dialogue leading to conflict and compromise, between proponents of different points of view in contemporary psychoanalysis and between psychoanalysis and its intellectual neighbors, hinges on their being able to deeply understand one another. And to do so, layers of obscuring simplifications and other devices bidding to protect core commitments must be peeled away, and the core commitments of each point of view made explicit. Otherwise, traditional psychoanalysis will never arrive at an understanding of what is intrinsic to it, and it will become a protean blur of evanescent myths.

Recall that I am arguing that Pepper's world hypothesis concept explained the progress in psychoanalysis up to a certain point, but then gave way, some thirty or so years ago, to Lakatos's idea of competing research programs. One might wonder, at this juncture, how one can change horses in midstream. Why would Lakatos's version of history kick in as an explanatory device at a certain moment, when Pepper's version had until then been a better explanatory device? Lakatos himself would have no problem with this. He recognizes that all historiographic accounts are themselves born into a sea of anomalies, and that it is only rational to abandon one account if at some point a better one becomes available. The method of Lakatos is explicitly historical and temporally specific, much like Marx's historicization of political economy or Vygotsky's historical analysis of human ontogeny.

The concept of history is key here. Kuhn put forward an historicism that is decidedly elemental and nonevolutionary. Karl Popper, Lakatos's teacher and a favorite sparring partner (for a description of this most interesting relationship, see Kadvany 1999) fiercely opposed historicism (though he did not consider science ahistorical). But his criterion of falsification fails because it does not say enough about how successive theories cohere or fail to cohere over time, or why some contradictions are ignored for long periods, while others are picked up and become refutations. To Lakatos, the appropriate unit of analysis is not the theory, or even the proposition, but rather the examined sequence of historically related theories in flux over a unit of time. A research program is the sum of the changes of a set of theories over a specified historical period.

Since change rather than stasis is his general focus, Lakatos (1976), like a good pragmatist, substitutes the consideration of methodology for an objective notion of truth in determining the merits of a theory. The mark of a good scientist is not how one responds to challenges to the truth of one's favored theory (say, by jettisoning it), but rather how one navigates the passage to the next stage of a specific program. The triumph of progress trumps the purity of a truth claim. Lakatos is not debunking the notion of an objective truth, for he is quite concerned with the relation between methodology and truth. Anyone who offers a methodology for science must claim that following the given rules will more than likely lead science toward the truth. However, the preemptive significance of inductivism and falsification collapses before the tribunal of history. Lakatos (1978) speaks to this in responding to a critique by Kuhn that he sweeps aside details of history that do not suit his purposes: "I hold that all histories of science are always philosophies fabricating examples. But, equally, all physics or any kind of empirical assertion (i.e., theory) is 'philosophy fabricating examples.' Surely since Kant and Bergson, this is a commonplace. But, of course, some fabrications in history are better than others. And I offer sharp criteria using which one can compare rival fabrications both in physics and in its history, and I claim that my fabrications contained more truth then Kuhn's" (vol. 1, p. 192).

In fact, because we anchor explanation in an historical context, and history is so fluid, an argument can be made that it is to be expected that meta-explanations of changes in the structure of how ideas proliferate will themselves naturally change. Theories, after all, are not timeless if they are grounded in a critical historicism. The history of ideas is disjunctively nonlinear, and the contradictions of one stage of evolution are different from the contradictions of another. All historiographic research programs will inevitably have their anomalies. None can explain everything; all have internal inconsistencies. Philosophies of science are thus "born refuted," and anomalies are history's way of guaranteeing that any methodology will be overtaken by a competitor, or will generate its own seeds for change. A theory, like a child, is born into a ready-made world with a distinctive lineage. Freud (1927, p. 21) made the analogous point that children are born into particular ways of thinking and take on this heritage of ideas just as they do the multiplication table. But any theory over time becomes a progressively poorer description of what it strives to account for, and any philosophy of science is born out of phase with scientific practice. By the time an idea has reached the stage of being formulated within a theory, it is already late in the half-life of its usefulness. As Lakatos said (Kavadny 2001, p. 226), some of the most interesting questions involve the interaction of actual standards and putative standards.

Since any methodology will be calibrated and to some extent falsified by history, it is only in hindsight that this can be recognized; this is exactly what we can see now concerning what began in psychoanalysis three decades ago. Psychoanalysis has lived this shift without explicitly conceptualizing it. Indeed, it was probably inevitable that the streams emerging from the intrapsychic and interpersonal world hypotheses would diverge before they could converge.

With this in mind, as we survey the world of contemporary psychoanalysis, something crucial swims into focus. We can never comfortably settle for living and working in a pluralistic world of theories. Pluralism is a weak explanation; a stronger one now suggests itself. It is an historical and not a pluralistic world that contemporary psychoanalysis inhabits, a world bathed in changes imposed by time and by the remarkably demanding processes of evolution. The turn to other theories and points of view is not so much an acknowledgment of complementary pieces as an embrace of the need to borrow in order to grow. Freud's psychoanalytic point of view always relied on stratified hierarchies, in which lower levels are transformed through conflict and defense into higher levels. Partisans of particular views should take heart; one's point of view should be defended, but only by looking forward rather than backward, by deploring isolation and periodically seeking to plunder the riches of other points of view for one's own purposes. Whereas most boundaries in analytic theory were carved out in defense of a psychoanalytic school of thought, now they function as constraints. If pluralism was ever a feasible concept, it was only because psychoanalysts myopically put a static, cross-sectional sample slice under their specimen microscopes, rather than taking a dynamically unfolding longitudinal view.

Toward a More Synthetic Knowledge in Psychoanalysis

Leonard Bernstein is reputed to have said that the most powerful moment in music he ever witnessed was Maria Callas's projecting a whisper to the far reaches of an auditorium in order to reach the entire audience. He noted that it was more awesome to witness this than the incendiary operatic power of Richard Tucker breaking a crystal glass with his voice. Similarly, there is a striking forcefulness behind the quiet rejuvenation of a degenerating research program that is more compelling than the clamor of a scientific revolution. Tailoring new or imported ideas and ways of thinking to its own fit is how a degenerating program can reverse course and become progressive. The history of any science is one of wars of attrition between degenerating and progressing research programs. A discipline can remain scientific only so long as the progressive forces triumph over the degenerating ones. Change tends to come to a progressive program from carrying forward its own internal logic, predicting facts that are not only new but were once undreamed of, while change tends to come to a degenerating program in response to external criticism. Isolation is, therefore, a dangerous state of affairs, if a field is to avoid lapsing into pseudoscience.

Lakatos added something more specific here, the notion that a leading idea is the core of a research program. A leading idea is a set of commitments that cannot be abandoned without abandoning the research program in its totality. Laudan sought to modify this principle by showing that core commitments do not rigidly determine the development of a theory. The hard core of commitments is protected by a belt of auxiliary hypotheses that shields it from critique and potential falsification. A program always seeks to deflect criticism away from its hard core toward its protective belt, which is dispensable and can evolve along with changes in the empirical constitution of the program. The hard core, by contrast, is resistant to change, which would undermine the entire program.

For psychoanalysis at the present time, ensuring a progressive program involves moving beyond the intrapsychic and interpersonal world hypotheses into a more synthetic theory. It would be interesting to recast these world hypotheses as leading ideas, core commitments shielded by protective belts of auxiliary hypotheses. This exercise might conceptually link these world hypotheses with the ideas of a progressive research program. Much of the nomological net of classical metapsychology can be considered just such a protective belt of auxiliary hypotheses. Modifying or rejecting aspects of the structural, topographic, or genetic point of view acts silently to protect the core commitments of psychoanalysis. To see this, allows us to consider how psychoanalysis can continue to evolve, in a way that is at present not well understood or mapped out. It also allows psychoanalysis to put to rest the notion that its ability to provide ready answers, its sense of already possessing the necessary conceptual tools, is a mark of its maturity.

The *Standard Edition* can usefully be read in its entirety as a case study of how to avoid isolation and exclusionary, paradigm-like claims. It should now be clear that a serious problem with world hypotheses is that, in making paradigmatic claims, they breed isolation and degenerating programs, with no blueprint for a program's revival. Freud's sense of the provisional nature of all his discoveries is a constant reminder that analytic theory cannot be die-cast. Given his followers' overzealous protection of his insights, the failure of psychoanalytic ideas to thrive was perhaps inevitable. In this light, I want now to examine some of the ideas advanced in works by Brenner (1982) and Kohut (1977), virtual manifestos of paradigm-like world hypotheses. In these ideas, we can witness important progress, yet they also illustrate how the invisibility of the prevailing world hypotheses was an obstacle to forward movement. A strong statement of psychoanalytic isolation is made by Brenner. He argues that psychoanalysis, because of its unique method, produces unique data that cannot be equated with data generated with other methods. Brenner believes there is something distinctive about the analytic method that allows the observer to see things not perceptible using other clinical methods, such as psychotherapy or laboratory experimentation. He does allow for consideration of material from other fields of observation, but only so long as it comports with psychoanalytic findings. But psychoanalytic data are not in fact unique, and data that can modify earlier observations can be gathered in a variety of circumstances and settings. Psychoanalytic data stemming from analysands who free associate on the couch are undeniably distinctive, but we can ask whether the distinctiveness stems from the analytic method itself or from the prevailing world hypotheses that lead analysts to interpret data in particular ways. In other words, the question is not whether psychoanalytic data are intrinsically unique, but how they become distinctive through the method of collecting data or through the interpretation of the data once it has been collected.

Although at first glance Brenner's view is plausible and has appeal, at second glance it is revealed as another paradigmatic argument that fails to move psychoanalysis as a body of knowledge forward. This will become evident as we compare his views with those of Kohut, who advances another paradigmatic argument. When Kohut (1977) first declared that the psychology of the self "in the wider sense" was independent of the object-libidinal line of development of classical psychoanalysis, he like Brenner was making a paradigmatic claim of incommensurability. Yet he too used the couch, free association, and four or five sessions per week. Indeed, Kohut and Brenner analyzed similar patients. If Brenner's argument, then, about the uniqueness of the analytic method is correct, why, we must ask, did Kohut not generate data compatible with Brenner=s? Though their overt methods were identical, one can hardly find two less compatible bedfellows.

The culprit is the existence of competing world hypotheses, stealthily invading our notions of the psychoanalytic method. What this juxtaposition of Brenner and Kohut demonstrates, in point of fact, is that the psychoanalytic method does not yield unique data; rather, prior to reflection, it starts with historically embedded world hypotheses that exist independent of the attribution of facticity to clinical observations. Behavioral features of the psychoanalytic method were the same for Kohut and for Brenner, but interpretation and formulation of data and how these are then presented to the patient are a more important and fundamental part of the method. What they interpret is different, and generates markedly different possibilities for the further elaboration of both interpretation and theory, not to mention the behavior of analyst and patient during the analysis. In the future, discussions of the psychoanalytic method should stress its interpretive elements and downplay the behavioral ones. It was the seductions of covert world hypotheses, not the overt method used to collect the data, that determined the radically different nature of the data described, respectively, by Brenner and by Kohut.

Conclusion

Freud's psychoanalytic mode of thought was employed to understand a variety of matters about which he was curious, each according to the same principles, though they may operate in different contexts. These matters include clinical material, the structure and organization of the mind, psychoanalytic anthropology, and how technique yields analytic results. It is interpretation, in its endless permutations, but necessarily through the lens of the psychoanalytic mode of thought, that defines their commonality and is the core of contemporary Freudian thinking. Although I have drawn here on extra-analytic sources to find my way through the argument, I have throughout used the psychoanalytic mode of thought to interpret their contribution to the history of psychoanalytic theorizing. I am optimistic that traditional psychoanalysis has moved to regain its footing as a progressive program. But I believe another shift, equally significant, has taken place. We now have a more mature science, one less wedded to finding and demonstrating facts spun out of itself, and more committed to its effectiveness in problem solving. To see progress, to be able to say that now there is a better theory, we must make it axiomatic that our aim is to render psychoanalysis workable in the modern world. As Laudan (1984) reminds us, theories constrain methods, while methods justify theories; but because aims and theories must harmonize with one another, aims in turn justify methods. The importance of this shift in the aims of psychoanalysis, and therefore in its methods and theories, cannot be emphasized enough. It is indeed a jungle out there, an evolutionary struggle for survival. Small wonder that Hull (1988) devotes such careful attention to showing how the forces affecting the survival of a theory are so little different from those affecting the survival of a species.

Then again, too often the quest for truth appears coolly distant from the human concerns that psychoanalysis traffics in. Psychoanalysis has been haunted, and perhaps we are hamstrung, by the apparent nobility of that quest. Davidson (2000) suggests that the failure of psychoanalysis to come to grips with truth has occurred because analysts have not resolved the tension between an independent conception and a human creation of truth. Choosing sides, he points to the interactive properties of language and discourse as one way out of this cul-de-sac. Although aiming his remarks to psychoanalysts, he does not note the marriage of convenience between the world hypotheses of psychoanalysis and the quest for truth. A century of chasing truth at all costs under the high-flying banner of world hypotheses has led us to where we stand today; it is now time to end, once and for all, this increasingly suffocating grip.

The relentless inquisitiveness and openness that promote a flow of commerce in ideas and methods in perpetuity are the hallmarks of a progressive program. A progressive psychoanalytic program looks forward and backward, inward and outward. It looks forward to what can be newly accommodated, and backward in order to manage its core commitments. A progressive psychoanalytic program looks outward not to support what it already knows, for that is merely a rear-guard action. It appropriates in order to expand its inner vision and generate new hypotheses, to defeat rivals, to protect its core commitments, to claim new conceptual turf. Edelman and Tononi (2000) have pointed out, tongue in cheek, how philosophers are at bottom best at troublemaking. But to solve most of the problems philosophers so usefully identify, in our times we do better to turn to disciplines like psychology, psychoanalysis, and neurobiology. What we need is to plot out a progressive psychoanalytic program, organized around the task of crafting theoretical models, at all levels of abstraction, that makes clear what is required for psychoanalysis to move toward the kind of synthetic knowledge that lays to rest the legacy of world hypotheses from our first century.

REFERENCES

Balsam, R. (2002). Integrating male and female elements in a woman's gender identity. *Journal of the American Psychoanalytic Association* 49:1335–1360.

Beebe, B., & Lachmann, F. (2002). *Infant Research and Adult Treatment: Co-Constructing Interactions.* Hillsdale, NJ: Analytic Press.

Black, M. (1962). *Models and Metaphors.* Ithaca: Cornell University Press.
Boesky, D. (1991). The psychoanalytic process and its components. *Psychoanalytic Quarterly* 59:550–584.

Brenner, C. (1982). *The Mind in Conflict.* New York: International Universities Press.

Bromberg, P. (1994). Speak! That I may see you: Some reflections on dissociation, reality, and psychoanalytic listening. *Psychoanalytic Dialogues* 4:517–548.

Cavell, M. (1993). *The Psychoanalytic Mind: From Freud to Philosophy.* Cambridge, MA: Harvard University Press.

Davidson, D. (2000). On truth. In *Whose Freud? The Place of Psychoanalysis in Contemporary Culture,* Eds. P. Brooks & A. Weoloch, pp. 300–303. New Haven,CT.: Yale University Press.

Eagle, M., Wolitsky, D., & Wakefield, J. (2001). The analyst's knowledge and authority. *Journal of the American Psychoanalytic Association* 49:457-490.

Edelman, G., & Tononi, G. (2000). *A Universe of Consciousness: How Matter Becomes Imagination.* New York: Basic Books.

Freud, S. (1900). The interpretation of dreams. *Standard Edition* 4/5.

———(1912-1913). Totem and taboo. *Standard Edition* 13:1–161.

———(1915). The unconscious. *Standard Edition* 14:166–215.

———(1923). The ego and the id. *Standard Edition* 19:3–66.

———(1927). The future of an illusion. *Standard Edition* 21:5–56.

Friedman, L. (1997). Ferrum, ignis, and medicina: Return to the crucible. *Journal of the American Psychoanalytic Association* 45:1–35.

Gholson, B., & Parker, P. (1985). Kuhn, Lakatos, and Laudan: Applications in the history of physics and psychology. *American Psychologist* 40:755–769.

Gray, P. (1982). "Developmental lag" in the evolution of technique for psychoanalysis of neurotic conflict. *Journal of the American Psychoanalytic Association* 30:621–655.

———(1987). On the technique of analysis of the superego: An introduction. *Psychoanalytic Quarterly* 61:130–154.

Grossman, W. (1993). Hierarchies, boundaries, and representation in a Freudian model of mental organization. In *Hierarchical Concepts in Psychoanalysis,* Eds. A. Wilson & J. Gedo, pp. 170–202. New York: Guilford Press.

———(1998). Freud's presentation of the psychoanalytic mode of thought in *Totem and Taboo* and his technical papers. *International Journal of Psychoanalysis* 79:469–486.

Hull, D. (1988). *Science as a Process: An Evolutionary Account of the Social and Conceptual Development of Science.* Chicago: University of Chicago Press.

Kadvany, J. (1999). The extraterritoriality of Imre Lakatos: A conversation with Janos Kadvany. In *Paranoia within Reason,* ed. G. Marcus. Chicago: University of Chicago Press, pp. 39–64.

———(2001). *Imre Lakatos and the Guises of Reason.* Durham: Duke University Press.

Kitcher, P. (1992). *Freud's Dream.* Cambridge, MA: MIT Press.

Kohut, H. (1977). *The Restoration of the Self.* New York: International Universities Press.

Kuhn, T. (1962). *The Structure of Scientific Revolutions.* Chicago: University of Chicago Press.

Lakoff, G., & Johnson, M. (1999). *Philosophy in the Flesh: The Embodied Mind and Its Challenge to Western Thought.* New York: Basic Books.

Lakatos, I. (1976). *Proofs and Refutations,* Eds. J. Worrall & E. Zahar. Cambridge & New York: Cambridge University Press.

———(1978). *Philosophical Papers,* Eds. J. Worrall & G. Currie. 2 vols. Cambridge & New York: Cambridge University Press.

———& Musgrave, A., EDS. (1970). *Criticism and the Growth of Knowledge.* Cambridge & New York: Cambridge University Press.

Laudan, L. (1984). *Science and Values.* Berkeley: University of California Press.

———(1990). *Science and Relativism.* Chicago: University of Chicago Press.

———(1996). *Beyond Positivism and Relativism.* Boulder, CO: Westview Press.

Leahey, T. (1992). The mythical revolutions of American psychology. *American Psychologist* 47:308–318.

Meissner, W. (1981). *Internalization in Psychoanalysis.* Psychological Issues Monograph 50. New York: International Universities Press.

Messer, S., & Winokur, M. (1980). Psychoanalysis and behavior therapy: Limits to their integration. *American Psychologist* 35:818–827.

Mitchell, S. (1988). *Relational Concepts in Psychoanalysis: An Integration.* Cambridge, MA: Harvard University Press.

Nagel, T. (1986). *The View from Nowhere.* New York: Oxford University Press.

O'Donohue, W. (1993). The spell of Kuhn on psychology: An exegetical elixir. *Philosophical Psychology* 6:267–287.

Overton, W. (1994). The arrow of time and cycles of time: Concepts of change, cognition, and embodiment. *Psychological Inquiry* 5:215–237.

———(1998). Developmental psychology: Philosophy, concepts, and methodology. In *Theoretical Models of Human Development,* Ed. R.M. Lerner, pp. 107–188. New York: Wiley.

Pepper, S. (1942). *World Hypotheses.* Berkeley: University of California Press.

Rorty, R. (1998). *Truth and Progress.* Cambridge & New York: Cambridge University Press.

Schafer, R. (1968). *Aspects of Internalization.* New York: International Universities Press.

———(1970). The psychoanalytic vision of reality. *International Journal of Psychoanalysis* 51:279–297.

Searle, J. (1992). *The Rediscovery of the Mind.* Cambridge, MA: MIT Press.

Spence, D. (1982). *Narrative and Historical Truth.* New York: W.W. Norton & Company.

Spezzano, C. (1998). The triangle of clinical judgment. *Journal of the American Psychoanalytic Association* 46:365–388.

Stern, D. (1997). *Unformulated Experience: From Dissociation to Imagination in Psychoanalysis.* Hillsdale, NJ: Analytic Press.

Strenger, C. (1991). *Between Hermeneutics and Science.* New York: International Universities Press.

Waelder, R. (1962). Psychoanalysis, scientific method, and philosophy. In *Psychoanalysis: Observation, Theory, Application, pp. 248–272.* New York: International Universities Press.

Weinberg, S. (1998). The revolution that didn't happen. *New York Review of Books,* October 8, pp. 48–52.

Wertsch, J. (1990). *Voices of the Mind.* Cambridge, MA: Harvard University Press.

Wilson, A. (1999). Analyzability redux: From analyzable to preparable for analysis." *Annual of Psychoanalysis* 37:127–141.

———& Prillaman, J. (1997). Early development and disorders of internalization. In *The Neurobiological and Developmental Basis for Psychotherapeutic Intervention,* Eds. M. Moskowitz, M., C. Monk, C. Kaye, & S. Ellman, pp. 189–234. Northvale, NJ: Jason Aronson.

———& Weinstein (1992). Language and the psychoanalytic process: Psychoanalysis and Vygotskian psychology, part II. *Journal of the American Psychoanalytic Association* 40:725–759.

CHAPTER 2

AFFECT AND THE COMPULSION TO REPEAT: FREUD'S REPETITION COMPULSION REVISITED

Introduction

To a certain extent, it is through repetition that we are assured of some basic and fundamental continuities—of self-continuity and object relations. We seek familiarity and obtain mastery by repeating, thereby guaranteeing ourselves that not every situation will be new, that we can navigate through a variety of recognizable situations employing tried-and-true adaptive styles that work. The comfort in routines and the recognition of repetitive experiences enable us to focus our attention on a wide span of problems and situations because we are not preoccupied with the management of each moment as if it were novel. However, repetition is a double-edged sword. We can impose it in places where it does not belong, at which time it can overtake the conscious controls we exert over our lives, imposing unwelcome consequences of long-forgotten personal history on situations where novelty would be preferable. When repetition is thus out of our control, when we are not conscious of nor can we discern the nature of the repetitive patterning, and especially when the fragment of repetition is beyond symbolic mediation, we may then speak of a "repetition compulsion" that can dominate our lives in subtle but telling ways.

We intend to distinguish two types of repetition within the broad spectrum of potential repetitive human action. We then suggest that it makes sense to reserve the term "repetition compulsion" as a motivational explanation for the type to be called *primal repetition.*[1] The first type we will call *symbolic repetition.* For now, let us postpone a discussion of symbolic repetition in order to focus concerted attention on primal repetition. We will demonstrate that primal repetition originates at an earlier period in human development than does symbolic repetition. Primal repetitions tend to contain and carry the actual experiential content of the early dyadic interaction between caregiver and child, specifically the affectively laden content. What is carried in primal repetition is less influenced over time by maturational factors than is symbolic repetition. Although more fixed in the personality organization and corresponding to the texture of actual early object relations, this type of repetition is exceedingly difficult to discern in the analytic situation of the adult patient because its epigenesis is during preverbal and presymbolic development, and therefore its original causes are beyond the reach of verbal and memorial access.

The conceptualization and articulation of primal repetition will be the major task of this paper. In order to discuss and elaborate upon the distinction between primal and symbolic repetition, we will marshal and examine evidence chiefly from two sources: first, accumulated evidence gathered from within the clinical situation; second, recent discoveries in psychological research on the primacy of early emotional processes in human development and personality.

---

[1] The choice of the word "primal" to denote this form of repetition follows from Freud's tendency to use this term as an adjective to characterize basic and fundamental underlying processes of many different types. For example, Freud spoke of primal instincts (1915a, p. 124). primal repression (1915b, p. 181). and, of course, the primal scene, the primal horde, and primal words

Transference and Repetition

Historically, repetition and transference have overlapped in clinical theory construction. What is subject to repetition through the phenomena of transference is an important question for psychoanalysis. At first glance, it would seem obvious that what gets repeated are early "relationships." This follows from the well-known definition of transference by Greenson (1965): transference is the experience of feelings, drives, attitudes, fantasies, and defenses toward a person in the present that are a repetition of reactions originating in regard to significant persons of early childhood. There are, however, certain problems with this formulation; it tends to disarm us with its obviousness, but, at second glance, it is unclear what it means to repeat a relationship. Like the famed mythological Hydra, a monster who grew two new heads whenever one was severed, when we think we understand transference repetition, more and deeper facets of the concept almost automatically ensue upon close inspection, and the concept sprouts new heads.

One clear and present danger, brought into focus by recent advances in the study of the psychology of thinking, is that any pattern match between patients' contemporaneous thoughts or actions and their remembered reports of their parents can be understood reflexively by the analyst as transference, without necessarily assessing whether it constitutes a true repetition or simply more or less random overlap in the finite set of potential human actions. The human mind easily confuses correlations for contingencies, creating causal explanations when none in fact exist, a version of magical thinking found in adulthood (D'Andrade, 1975; Schweder, 1977). A related problem in the philosophy of science has been addressed by Popper (1959), who, quarreling with the appeal to similarity as a basis of scientific comparison, notes that "with a little ingenuity" we can find repetition in *some* respects between any members of any finite set of different situations. As he puts it, "Anything can be said to be a 'repetition' of anything, if only we adopt the appropriate point of view" (p. 422). As argued by the philosopher Adolf Grünbaum (1984), the *post hoc ergo propter hoc* fallacy presents us with the logic of a similar pitfall. Thus, we seek more precision. Does Greenson's definition of transference, "repeating a relation-ship," mean that we have some kind of preformed mental template of our caregivers and in adulthood seek out others whom we can fit within this primary template with a minimal degree of incongruity? Is the seeking-after-repetition one of affective contours? Cognitive or form similarities? Smell or pheromone recognition? Behavior? Critical moments? Modes of need gratification? Feelings for an-other, feelings induced by another, thoughts of or fantasies about, wishes for, or physical sensations induced by another? To clarify what is meant by the phrase "repeat a relationship," it follows that we should examine which unique or particular characteristics of an early object relationship are subject to being repeated.

In setting the stage for our depiction of primal repetition, it is also important to notice that several psychoanalysts, especially those working with severely disturbed patients and those inter-ested in studying the influence of infancy and early child-hood upon later psychological processes, have described how at times the genetic roots of transference and repetition are not subjec-tively accessible. Frank (1969), for example, spoke of that which is "unrememberable and unforgettable," elaborating on his no-tion of passive primal repression as an explanation for the continuing effects of preverbal experiences upon the psychic re-ality of adults. The introduction of early, presymbolic (psychobiological) modes of representation thus introduces a complication into understanding the nature of the earliest repe-tition. If these early modes of representation influence the content of what is subject to being repeated, we must somehow find a place for them within theoretical models that illuminates the subtle texture of the analytic process.

Repetition: A Historical Perspective

The problem of repetition has long been of fascination to philosophy, the discipline that historically was a stepparent to many contemporary social sciences. Recall Nietzsche's fascination with the theme of the Eternal Return. In *Thus Spake Zarathustra* (1892), the sheer prospect of inevitable and unavoidable repetition becomes one of the organizing hinges of Nietzsche's struggle with Zarathustra's incipient madness. Then, too, Kierkegaard (1843) wrote extensively about the relationship between repetition and memory in ways that presage the later findings of Freud. To Freud, it was only the systematic and scientific discipline of psychoanalysis that could unlock the mysteries behind the principle of repetition. Freud's fascination with repetition led him to postulate a *compulsion* to activate in action unchecked repetitions of early experiences. The key word in Freud's definition of the principle of repetition is *compulsion*. Freud's choice of terms implies that he was trying to grapple with a phenomenon that is not of a tendency to repeat, as befitting a probabilistic stimulus-response model, but of an inevitability to repeat, an inability to prevent a repetition due to a prepotent unconscious motivating factor.

In Freud's evolving intellectual struggle with the factors that produce repetition, the concepts of repetition and the repetition compulsion took on multiple meanings, designating different clinical phenomena at different times in his corpus of writings. In his early writings, Freud has what we will call *a broad* view of repetition, which is not distinguishable from the repetition compulsion. In his later writings, most noticeably after 1920, he develops a *narrow* view in which the repetition compulsion is quite circumscribed, clearly and inextricably aligned with his final dual-instinct theory. This distinction corresponds to a conceptual disentanglement of the repetition compulsion from new discoveries in the theory of transference.

In Freud's early writing on the subject of repetition, he sought to understand what it is that determines this compulsion to repeat, what it is that is swept up in the unconscious momentum toward repetition rather than novel experience, compelling a person to repeat rather than recollect. Freud (1914b) pondered this question:

> The patient reproduces instead of remembering, and he reproduces according to the conditions of the resistance; we may now ask what it is exactly that he reproduces or expresses in action. The answer is that he reproduces everything in the reservoirs of repressed material that has already permeated his general character—his inhibitions and disadvantageous attitudes of mind, his pathological traits of character. He also repeats during the treatment all his symptoms [p. 371].

Here we see Freud looking through the lens of clinical analysis, with limited interest in the archaeology of psychic origins. Freud appears to be more interested in establishing the viability of the construct of repetition for clinical psychoanalysis than in vouchsafing its coherence for metapsychological theory construction. In this broad view, repetition is seen to gather momentum from displaced action, which constitutes a resistance against recollecting. Transference is seen as a "playground" through which actions should be allowed to decompose, first into words, and then, ideally, into early memories (recollections). Through the gathering of the transference, the "impulse to remember" achieves priority over the "compulsion to repeat."

Transference, thus, is an "intermediate realm between illness and real life, through which the journey from one to the other must be made" (p. 154). In lieu of the successful handling of the transference, the compulsion to repeat asserts itself, and action triumphs over recollection as the patient becomes victimized by the recrudescence of infantile experiences that are subject to repression, and, thus, reenactment.

Earlier, we were unable to specify what is repeated through transference, and now we ask a related question: What gets repeated through the compulsion to repeat? Unless the compulsion to repeat and transference are synonymous, it is only by understanding this difference that we can appreciate how Freud's views on repetition and transference gradually diverged. The causal relationship between repressed memories and symptom formation is primary for Freud in 1914, in keeping with the utility of the topographic model with which he was working. Symptoms, "pathological traits," and "disadvantageous attitudes" are all subject to repetition. Since repressed memories underlie all repetitive activity, it is clear that to Freud that there is no hard and fast distinction between transference repetition and the compulsion to repeat. This was the case despite the fact that Freud had spoken of the "compulsion to repeat" as early as *Studies on Hysteria* (Breuer and Freud, 1895, p. 105). We must recall the context of this 1914 paper. Written at about the same time as the earliest of the series of *Papers on Metapsychology,* this was a time in the growth of psychoanalysis when Freud was trying to establish the hegemony of recollection, and when he did not have a truly sophisticated developmental view of the mental abilities that define psychological capacities and limitations (see Schimek, 1975). Freud himself was quite concerned with how the past is played out in the present and the conundrum of what to do with non-memories subject to repetition, for he was to return to the problem six years later, in order to seek a redefinition of sorts, when the solution takes an unusual and dizzying twist with the advent of Thanatos. The compulsion to repeat reappears, but now married to drive theory and biological destiny, a fate from which it was destined never to return for the remainder of Freud's life. Thanatos thus becomes an original cause of repetition, beyond repressed memories.

Freud's return to the problem of repetition in 1920 occurred in his monograph *Beyond the Pleasure Principle*, where, brooding about the death of a favored grandchild, the savagery of war, and preoccupied with the inevitability of his own death, he introduced the enigmatic conservative principle of Thanatos, the death instinct, the regressive urge of which symptoms are but a dramatic manifestation, a superordinate motive ground into our every cell to return to the primal origins from which we evolved millions of years ago. This monograph, often viewed by psychoanalysts as a strange interlude in a succession of clinically important papers because of its abstract logic and lack of empirical referents, can also be read as shedding new and important light on the principle of repetition. We can now more clearly illuminate differences between transference repetition and the repetition compulsion. The repetition compulsion is intended to account for more primitive phenomena, such as masochism and separation distress, which are neither allied with the reality principle nor regulated by the pleasure principle.

As Klein (1976) notes, from this monograph a truly dynamic ego psychology may have sprung but Freud's primary allegiance is not to the clinical process but to a new packaging of instinct theory. Perhaps if Freud's attention had been drawn more to the content of repetitive phenomena beyond the pleasure principle and how we clinically manage these instinctual derivatives, we would have had a clearer statement of his position on this question. The only empirical referents in the entire monograph are to the anecdotal "fort-da" game of a one-and-a-half-year-old infant observed by Freud (his grandson), which is used to illustrate how children can make active what is passive and pleasurable what is unpleasurable. The monograph gets increasingly abstract and speculative as it continues.

After 1939, the concept of the repetition compulsion appears to have generally vanished in American psychoanalysis. A search of titles of five of the major psychoanalytic journals (*Journal of the American Psychoanalytic Association, International Journal of Psychoanalysis* and *International Review of Psychoanalysis, Psychoanalytic Quarterly, Psychoanalytic Study of the Child*) indicates that the term "repetition compulsion" appears once between the years 1920 through 1950 (Bibring, 1943). It appears once again between 1951 and 1961 (Toman, 1955), and three times between 1962 and 1972 (Lipin, 1963; Gifford, 1964; Sigal, 1969). By contrast, the theory underlying the concept of repetition as distinct from a compulsion had been incorporated within the theory of transference and subjected to intensive scrutiny and empirical test in the clinical situation. The neglect of the repetition compulsion deserves a short discussion, for its reemergence in recent years (Loewald, 1971; Klein, 1976; Gedo, 1979, 1981) corresponds to the opening of psychoanalysis to the preoedipal years and an increased interest in the widening scope of psychoanalysis. We suspect two factors: first, that the marriage between the suppositions of the death instinct (Thanatos) and the repetition compulsion was an unhappy one in the eyes of most psychoanalysts, such that they avoided investigation of theoretical problems associated with the repetition compulsion because they wished to steer clear of the death instinct; second, the predominant emphasis on oedipal pathology and strict canons of analyzability led to a relative lack of interest in those severe pathologies seen to be afflicted mainly or predominantly by the forces attributable to the repetition compulsion, and so consequently the theory embodied in the conceptualization of transference was sufficient to explain repetitive human action observed in most patients.

We will now examine the problem of the death instinct and its exile from the mainstream of psychoanalytic theorizing. In Waelder's (1962) hierarchy of metapsychological explanation, the death instinct is placed at the highest level of abstraction, far removed from clinical observation and generalization, the levels of abstraction from which data and inferences are most often employed in psychoanalytic practice. The death instinct is aligned with many of the most problematic of Freud's philosophical assumptions, such as the Constancy Principle, whose evidential basis Freud derived from the dated guiding assumptions of nineteenth-century Newtonian physics. Although psychoanalysts may have wished to avoid the stigma of association with the death instinct, we think that, by 1924, in *The Economic Problem of Masochism*, the unhappy theoretical relationship between the death instinct and the repetition compulsion had been modified by Freud. In this paper, he divorced the death instinct from the Constancy Principle, at which time the repetition compulsion could have been brought into the mainstream of psychoanalytic theory without being tied to an eccentric cosmology. The theoretical armamentarium was in place, so that psychoanalysis could have approached the repetition of the earliest and least understood aspects of psychological life.

It is necessary to examine briefly the antecedents of one of Freud's assumptions inherent in the death instinct, the Constancy Principle, a drive to return to a state of nonorganic inertness characterized by pleasure in lack of stimulation. In Freud's evolving views on instinct theory, we may see several precursors to the conservativism of the death instinct. In *The Neuro-Psychoses of Defense*, Freud (1894) wrote:

There is something which should be differentiated (an amount of affect, a sum of excitation), something having all the attributes of a quantity—although we possess no means of measuring it—a something which is capable of increase, decrease, displacement, and discharge, and which extends itself over the memory-traces of an idea like an electric charge over the surface of the body [p. 75].

Written roughly in the same period as the decision to bar the *Project for a Scientific Psychology* (1895) from publication, Freud has set the stage for pleasure to be the diminution of sensation. Eleven years later, in *Three Essays on the Theory of Sexuality* (1905), the road is further paved by introducing the theory underlying the Constancy Principle:

The character of tension of sexual excitement is connected with a problem, the solution of which is as difficult as it would be important for the conception of the sexual process. Despite all divergence of opinion regarding it in psychology, I must firmly maintain that a feeling of tension must carry with it the character of displeasure. I consider it conclusive that such a feeling carries with it the impulse to alter the psychic situation and thus act incitingly, which is quite contrary to the nature of the perceived pleasure [p. 68].

The instincts were yet to undergo a number of incarnations, retaining their conservative cast, appearing in *On Narcissism* (1914a) as ego-libido and object-libido, in *Instincts and Their Vicissitudes* (1915a) as sexual and self-preservative instincts, and then in 1920 as Eros and Thanatos. However, even after this monograph, Freud continued to struggle with what to do with the death instinct. We think that shortly after 1920, he saw that his line of reasoning was leading him into a cul-de-sac. His radical dualism failed to provide him with intellectual leverage.

With more clinical evidence and the logical contradictions of Thanatos in hand, he could no longer support a view of the organism in which the stimulus thermostat was optimally set at zero, that is, as a seeker after no sensation, nor in which the polarities of instinct are the prime movers of psychological life. Note how in *The Economic Problem of Masochism* (1924), he retains the concept of the death instinct, but renounces its conservativism:

> Every "pain" coincides with a heightening, every pleasure with a lowering, of the stimulus-tension existing in the mind; the Nirvana Principle (and the pleasure principle which is assumed to be identical with it) would be entirely in the service of the death-instincts (the aim of which is to lead our throbbing existence into the stability of an inorganic state) and would have the function of warning us against the claims of the life-instincts, of the libido, which tries to disturb the course life endeavors to take.... Unfortunately, this view cannot be correct. It seems that we experience the ebb and flow of quantities of stimuli directly in perceptions of tensions which form a series, and it cannot be doubted that there is such a thing as both pleasurable tension and a "painful" lowering of tension. The condition of sexual excitement is the most striking example of a pleasurable increase of tension of this kind, but it is certainly not the only one (pp. 255–256).

Unpleasure and its agent, the death instinct, are no longer characteristic of the Constancy Principle (return to null state of excitation). This, however, turns the 1920 theory of the repetition compulsion on its ear, for if pleasure is no longer equated with the lack of excitation, then the pleasure principle needed recasting (in addition to what lay beyond it).

Because of such difficulties with the theoretical network uniting the repetition compulsion and the death instinct, Freud (1923) found a better vehicle for his views on the death instinct in the structural model. This allowed him to find more concrete clinical referents for the death instinct. In 1924, the Constancy Principle was superseded by the Nirvana Principle, in which pleasure became linked to qualitative characteristics of excitation itself rather than a return to a null state of excitation. Linking pleasure with the rise and fall of internal states of tension could lend itself to an understanding of repetition, though Freud did not take this step. The concept of the repetition compulsion thus became enmeshed within a network of poorly reasoned theoretical constructs. By 1926, in *Inhibitions, Symptoms, and Anxiety*, Freud sought to account for the repetition of traumatic experiences, but we must highlight that he did not introduce the repetition compulsion as an explanatory construct. Although the death instinct continued to play a pivotal role in his writings as late as 1937 in *Analysis Terminable and Interminable* (1937) and the posthumously published *An Outline of Psychoanalysis* (1940), the concept of the repetition compulsion gradually receded from sight because of its uneasy logical status in the rapidly evolving theory of psychoanalysis. Freud's drift toward a narrow definition of repetition was consequently thwarted.

While the theory of transference thrived in clinical psychoanalysis, after decades of neglect interest in the principle of repetition was revived and the concept expanded upon by Loewald (1971). Loewald demonstrates that, to some extent, psychoanalysis is predicated on the assumption that much of psychic reality is derived from repetition of early mental life—in the words of Klein (1976). "A potential for repetition is implicit in all the core (psychoanalytic) principles. That growth, and even life itself, is in critical ways a repetition is basic to psychoanalytic understanding and knowledge" (p. 34). Loewald remarked on the many difficulties facing an adequate definition of repetition, incorporating as it does biological and psychological manifestations, while at the same time noting how central it is to many key psychoanalytic conceptualizations. One of Loewald's important contributions is his distinction between active and passive repetition. Active repetition is akin to progressive (and normative) re-creation and is aimed at mastery of the repeated phenomena that become organized in new and creative forms. Repetition in this case implies a "reactivation on a higher level of organizing potential, which makes possible novel configurations and novel resolutions of the conflict" (p. 89). Passive repetition, called by Loewald "reproductive," is a tendency toward duplication of traumatic experience with no aim toward resolution or mastery. This distinction is important because it qualifies the pathognomonic significance of repetition and focuses on how the repetition is handled rather than on its presence or absence. However, Loewald does not discuss the antecedents to repetition, what is subject to repetition, or in what hierarchical forms active or passive repetitions occur.

Klein (1976), in his program to recast psychoanalytic theory into two distinct bodies of knowledge, one clinical and the other metapsychological, moved his explanation of repetition away from the domains of psychoeconomic and biological explanation and spoke of repetition as a product of the principles of "repression" and "reversal of voice." By this formulation Klein meant achieving mastery over a passively experienced sensation by repeating it until achieving mastery. Klein actually amplifies Loewald's distinction of active versus passive repetition, reconstruing the implications of active and passive modes within his system of psychoanalytic conceptualization. He goes further, though, by examining what is subject to repetition and notes that repetition is not a unitary phenomenon, but must be distinguished by its content, aims, and forms. Thus, Klein notes that some varieties of repetition include the following:

1. Repressed wishes or fantasies clamoring for expression
2. Replica induction, repeated aspects of an unconscious relationship
3. Automatism occurring in states of dissociation
4. Interrupted pleasurable tasks
5. Pleasure in functioning (Buhler's "Funktionlust")
6. The working-off of anxiety by repetitive behavior
7. Imitation of a model's behavior
8. Transference repetitions
9. Symbolic repetition through the sphere of artistic expression

Here, we have what was earlier termed a broad view of repetition, swallowing up the principles, rationale, and motivation for such diverse actions as transference, crucial forms of internalization (imitation, introjection, identification), and creativity. It is important to note that the breadth of scope of this formulation stands in contrast to Freud's post—1920 conceptualizations of the repetition compulsion, which we understand as Freud's attempt to define a narrow view. Klein actually brings us back to the earlier Freud of the *Papers on Metapsychology*, with his polarized juxtaposition of repetition with recollection, but Klein describes the pattern and structure of repetition more diligently and thoroughly, as if repetition is a pedestrian part of the mechanics of living. It is difficult, however, to understand this broad view of repetition as constituting some form of a *compulsion* rather than an orderly form of continuity of self-experience, which guides and frames people's lives. Klein aligns repetition with the inclination to repeat what has preceded it—an almost behavioral assumption of stimulus and response process. Such broad views are most susceptible to the "illusory correlation" problem mentioned earlier. It is also important to note that both Loewald and Klein did not attempt to weave the existing state of developmental phenomena into their views on repetition, despite their acquaintance with Piaget's concept of primary and secondary circular reactions, the earliest repetitions of self and self/other states upon which the capacity for novel (tertiary circular) reactions is based.

Gedo (1979) is concerned with the general place of the repetition compulsion within the motivational premises of psychoanalysis. He suggests that the concept of the repetition compulsion may be helpful in explaining aspects of the mysterious (and poorly understood) relationship between early psychobiological states and later psychological life. This nature view is to be carefully but sharply distinguished in theory from those object relational perspectives that are based on the nurture view of caregiver-child patternings of joint experience. He thus seeks to balance (but not reconcile) the old problem of the nature/nurture controversy in psychoanalysis in such a way that theory can be responsive to recent developments in the life sciences, a proper domain of investigation of psychobiological phenomena. To Gedo, unlike Klein, the concept of the repetition compulsion may be applied and is limited to the early nonsubjectively motivated psychobiological states of mind.

Gedo, however, like Klein (1976), holds little hope for getting much mileage out of the distinction between volition, affect, and cognition, the trichotomy into which Aristotle divided human motivation over 2,000 years ago. Rather, he chooses to frame motivational dynamics within the context of aims and goals (depending upon the mode of structural organization), which *ipso facto* are saturated with affect. As in *Beyond the Pleasure Principle* (1920), but now not conceived of in terms of drive theory, the repetition compulsion in Gedo's formulation becomes the concept applicable to the understanding of psychological phenomena beyond subjectivity, but which have a dramatic impact on the psychic functioning of adults. The gist is similar to Freud's in 1920, but empirical referents are more easily gathered in. It took sixty years to be able to reframe the repetition compulsion in terms that mesh with modern scientific findings in order to facilitate further empirical investigation. The repetition compulsion becomes a crucial and central motivational dynamic during Gedo's Modes 1 and 2 of developmental organization, in which motivation is dominated by diverse psychobiological aims, and in which the typical dangers are traumatic overstimulation and separation reactions (recall the "fort-da" game Freud described in 1920 as the referent for his concept of separation distress!). The concept of preverbal psychobiologically coded representations has multiple sources of corroboration from diverse analytic perspectives. For example, Horowitz's (1972) sensorimotor representations and Greenspan's (1979) Stages 1 and 2 of somatic intelligence are attempts to capture the psychobiological realities, in analytic terms, of the dawn of psychological life beyond the normal adult's subjective recall.

At this point, let us take stock of the relationship between symbolic and primal repetition. In order to begin to develop a more precise understanding of these processes, it is now necessary to understand further the motivation and dynamic content underlying and constituting these two processes. If we adopt the *spirit* (but not the version of philosophical anthropology) of Freud's (1920) suggestion that the repetition compulsion empowers persisting psychobiologically coded and nonsubjective aspects of mental life beyond the pleasure principle, we can proceed to a further specification of the impact of our earliest years upon the potential repetition of subsequent human action. What is required now is a conceptual disentanglement so that both concepts of repetition, primal and symbolic, have a distinct and clear explanatory range. In order to accomplish this, we will explore certain aspects of nonpsychoanalytic views of affectivity and try to understand their relevance for our theses.

Extra-analytic Perspectives on Affect Genesis: Some Implications of Recent Psychological Research for Transference and Repetition

In this section, we will review the contributions of several approaches to early affect formation outside of the psychoanalytic literature and evaluate their applicability to the argument in this paper for the place of early affectivity in primal repetition. We will begin by critically examining and evaluating evidence that the child's affectivity is the basis for primal repetition. We will define affect in infants as a particular early form of mentating and of apprehending the social world that is provided by caregivers. The nonanalytic approaches to be examined include aspects of discrete emotions theory, empirical infancy research, and experimental psychology.

These evidentiary bases to be presented pose clear problems (and, to be sure, challenges) to the theory of clinical psychoanalysis. Psychoanalysts should be wary of turning over the confirmatory basis of their developmental theory to purely observational behavioral manifestations, especially facial expressions, since adults, at least, are capable of exercising voluntary control over their facial muscles. Obviously, an adult's emotions that are felt can be suppressed or altered, and emotions that are not felt can be simulated. However, prior to the advent of self-awareness, the human child's affects have both an "outside-of-the-body" as well as "inside-of-the-body" character. Affects are externally manifest in facial expressions and body movements, and internally present as organic sensations. Some cognitive developmental researchers have striven to demonstrate that in early development there is congruence between these two, that is, between felt emotional state and overt expressive behavior (e.g., Malatesta, 1985). However, psychoanalysts have been more wary (Brenner, 1983). Few analysts would admit facial behavior without other convergent evidence from patients as a convergent criterion for psychoanalytic evidence. Nevertheless, the pioneering analytic and developmentalist Rene Spitz (1965) foresaw that while studying preverbal infants, behavioral expressions had to be considered crucial data for the determination of infant experiences, as did the psychoanalytic researchers at the Yale Child Study Center in the 1940s and 1950s, who moved toward the expansion of the scientific data base of psychoanalysis to elements outside of the clinical situation. In the wake of the work of these researchers and many others of like mind, a mature psychoanalytic view of affect formation that incorporates the first eighteen months of the infant's life, as well as one that seeks to understand the importance of affectivity in the clinical situation, will have to take into account, *pari passu*, both reconstructive evidence from the clinical analytic situation as well as observational evidence of infant and child behavior from the laboratory.

Most, although not all, approaches to the psychological origins of emotionality typically fall into one of two categories—the dimensional or the typological. Dimensional approaches stress levels of arousal, activation, or hedonic tone along a dimensional axis of increasing and decreasing quantities. In contrast, typological approaches, also known as discrete emotions theories, propose that there are a limited number of primary or fundamental emotions that are different from one another in qualitative ways. Different fundamental emotions have distinctive phenomenological, motivational, and signal properties. One type of discrete emotions theory—differential emotions theory, as formulated by Izard (1971, 1978, 1979)—is particularly concerned with the ontogenetic aspects and has guided a great deal of empirical research on the emotional development of infants and children. Discrete emotions theory proposes that these primary emotions are psychobiologically based, although socializing influences can and must developmentally modify the innate pattern. Earliest affects are motivational vectors, rather than operations resembling the "structures d'ensemble" (Piaget, 1970) of cognitive developmentalists. What is primary in early development is the stratum of psychobiologically based organic feeling states that are experienced within the context of the caregiving dyad. Unique dyadic environments provide infrastructures for the emergence and consolidation of affectivity and selfhood.

As mentioned, differential emotions theory proposes an innate concordance between motoric expressions of emotion and internal affective states, and operates on the assumption that the ontogenesis of emotionality can be understood through direct observation of infant behavior, especially during dyadic interactions with primary caretakers. Izard (1971) has suggested and presented evidence that a number of primary affects are available well before the advent of reflective self-consciousness. The inherently communicative nature of the signals of these primary affects promotes the establishment of infant-mother bonding and, therefore, the survival of infants.

Over the past decade, a substantial amount of data on infant affective development in this genre has been accumulating. Some researchers find signs of the primary emotions in evidence as early as the first *day* of life, most notably as indexed by facial expressions. For example, the facial expressions of interest, distress, and disgust are observed in neonates within appropriate contexts (Izard, 1978). Field, Woodson, Greenberg, and Cohen (1982) have presented evidence that neonates can imitate still other facial expressions posed by models. The remainder of the primary emotions are thought to emerge during the ensuing months, as they become adaptive for object relating. At the same time, we see the emergence of individual differences in affect expression. By two to four months of age, expressions of joy, sadness, surprise, and anger have been added to the repertoire; the facial expression of fear has not been reliably recorded in normal infants before six months of age, but there is some evidence of its earlier emergence among abused children (Gaensbauer, 1982). The emotions of guilt, shame, and contempt are thought to emerge relatively late in development because of their dependence on cognitive maturation and the development of the sense of self. We see, therefore, the presence of a sophisticated network of primary affectivity set within a communicational matrix in infants and toddlers prior to the development of the cognitive operations necessary for mental imagery and language.

In a functionalist analysis of individual differences in human ontogeny, we elsewhere expand upon a similar view of primary affectivity and draw some implications for research on the development of personality (Malatesta and Wilson, 1988). We describe the influential role of early affects in personality development and in the way certain character organizations become organized around particular affects that dominate and shape them. In other words, there are affect-specific organizations that can be viewed as emotion traits and that can be understood as nodal aspects of personality organization. Such affective organizations are set up initially in infancy and become consolidated over time. Emotions evolve to serve crucial adaptive functions and are most likely to be manifest in situations where adaptive behavioral responses are called for—even during infancy. For example, anger is a response that is helpful in eliminating obstacles that thwart goal-directed behavior, as when an infant struggles against the restraint of tight or binding clothing; the disgust response serves to eliminate distasteful substances from the mouth; the interest expression serves to open the eyes wide so that more of the visual environment is available for scanning, and so on. Over time, individual emotions assume a favored status in the infant's behavioral repertoire, as unfolding motor and cognitive capacities prompt and support the execution of affect-specific motivations. As indicated earlier, some emotions are present at birth and most of the primary emotions are manifest by six to seven months of age. Once the emotions are in the repertoire, individual differences can emerge. As early as one year of age, we can identify anger-dominant, sad-dominant, and fear-dominant emotional organizations in individual children. Thus, there is evidence that emotional traits representing stable and enduring emotional predispositions evolve and consolidate, beginning as early as the first year of life, depending on the nature, reliability, and chronicity of exposure to elicitors of the particular affects, as well as the nature and reliability of the outcome of affect expression.

There is evidence that the particularity of these organizations accrues from repetitive interactive experiences within the context of the early caregiving relationship. The research of Malatesta (1980) demonstrates that during play sessions, mothers of young infants cycle repetitively through certain "emotion routines"—patterns of emotional expression and emotional responses to their infants' affects. Given the infant's propensity to imitate, even during the earliest *days* of life (Field et al., 1982; Malatesta and Izard, 1984), and the ready contagion of emotion (Cohn and Tronick, 1983; Zahn-Wexler, Cummings, Iannotti, and Radke-Yarrow, 1984), it is likely that these experiences will leave an enormous emotional impression as well as establish incipient emotional/behavioral styles that then may be modified in development or become ever more highly consolidated over time. We have observed that other aspects of such communicative and interactive behavior are also stamped into the nexus of the unique dyad and thus highly repetitive (although this remains to be empirically demonstrated), so that the infant experiences redundancy and repetition of significant emotional experiences, packed within the earliest object relationship. It is an open empirical question whether it is chronicity of exposure, intensity of exposure, or an interaction of chronicity and intensity that contributes to the emotional imprint that initiates this emotional disposition. Plutchik (1980) proposes a psychoevolutionary theory of emotions' ontogenesis in which he suggests that emotions are produced by "persisting situations" but leaves unclear the mechanisms involved in transforming repetitive events into emotions. Plutchik tends to focus on responses rather than aspects of *mind*, and also does not explore the developmental implications of his theory.

We will return to the nature of the repetitive caregiver-infant choreography shortly, but first we will probe further into research implications for our understanding of affectivity. In attempting to link psychoanalytic developmental psychology with the methodology and data of direct infant observation, Stern (1983, 1985) examines subtle nuances of infant life and suggests that there is a preponderance of evidence suggesting a view of the infant as an actively constructing organism, in contrast to the traditional psychoanalytic view of the infant as passive recipient of the caregiver's ministrations. Psychoanalysis itself posits multiple models of mentation in human infants. A question posed by Stern is worth considering—Whose baby are we referring to when we speak of a psychoanalytic perspective on infancy? Freud's baby? Fairbairn's baby? Kohut's baby? Each "thinks" in different ways. Stern's research, as well as that of other infant observers (Emde, Gaensbaeur, and Harmon, 1976; Trevarthen, 1979; Sander, 1980; Kaye, 1982) suggests that the infant-mother dyad can be understood as a functional unit of bidirectional activity, with an early joint communicative capacity that exceeds in sophistication and mutually regulative capacity anything previously suspected. Indeed, the extent to which the infant and mother constitute a mutually regulating dyad from the onset of birth has led Trevarthen (1979) to describe the shared mental states in which the infant participates with the caregiver as "intersubjective" and Kaye (1982) to speak of the "attached individual." In the words of Stern, infant and mother engage in a "dance of attunement," replete with subtle signals, cues, and communications, that converge on ways and means for the caregiver to understand the infant so that she might properly provide for him. The caregiver-infant attunement is organized around the regulation of optimal arousal. Too high or too low a level of arousal in the infant can cause the caregiver to intervene and seek to reestablish an optimal level of arousal. Sander (1980, 1983) has described in detail how the infant's states of consciousness are dependent upon the ministrations of the caregiver, whose primary task is that of an external self-regulating other.[2] Drawing upon attachment research (e.g., Ainsworth, Blehar, Waters, and Wall, 1979; Schwartz, 1979), Kellerman (1983) argues that the development of distinct emotions "awaits object development, not emotion development; that is, that all emotions take objects, and without objects there can be no healthy or normal emotional organization" (p. 325). The importance of the affective availability over time and situation of the caregiver and her affective attunement to her child is highlighted in the research of Sorce and Emde (1981) and Campos and Sternberg (1980), described as "social referencing." These researchers demonstrate how toddlers, prior to the dawn of self-awareness and shortly thereafter, access others in their social field as a way of appraising the emotional impact of events. In this way, toddlers acquire "emotional information" from the caregiver, repetitively patterned over time in

---

[2] The similarity between this phenomenon and Freud's (1924) view on pleasure as constituting an optimal level of excitation in *The Economic Problem of Masochism* should be carefully noted.

characteristic ways, pertaining to modes of object relating yet integrated in a burgeoning selfhood, all prior to a capacity for the child's language to describe what is occurring. Demos (1984) likewise has described six repetitive types of infant-caregiver exchanges that constitute what she calls the infant's "affective resonance." These categories provide a basis for grasping how the infant structures characteristic affective communicational exchanges with the caregiver over time.

As we open up the preoedipal years to scrutiny, we have mobilized many competing and at times seemingly contradictory terms in order to explain the nature of the infant's earliest internalized structures, especially as internalized by the infant within the jointly regulating infant-caregiver dyad. There are many different conventions when using terms to capture the nonreducible building blocks of the organization of experience in infants. Piaget (1972), for example, spoke of an "affective schema" in a special address given to American psychoanalysts. In the same address, building on his discussion in *Play, Dreams, and Imitation* (1951), he discusses the functional relationship between affect and cognition, arguing for a conceptual independence between the two (although they function synergistically, *in situ*), Stern (1983) has described how infants possess what he terms schemas of "self-with-other," which are based upon "affect attunements" between infant and caregiver. They are pre-imagistic (i.e., organized and retained prior to capacities for evocative memory and object constancy). As mentioned, Stern uses the concept of the schema of "self-with-other" to characterize a certain type of organization, the storage of dynamic events, which he conceives of as "emotional event knowledge," rather than static entities or category knowledge. Describing their affective valence, Stern notes that his research suggests "infants have some sense of the extent to which affect and intensity of affect or arousal are 'inter-experienced' (i.e., shared mental states)" (p. 77). Schemas of self-with-other appear to be distinct from schemas of self or schemas of other, which presumably are forerunners of self and object representations.

Schemata of "self-with-other" are of three types: state sharing, state transforming, and state complementing, each characterizing a mutually regulating aspect of the caregiver-infant dyad that leads to the developmental propulsion of the infant. They are not learned; according to Stern, they are innate givens of the infant's *Anlage*—a constitutional communicational endowment. Further, due to their dynamic rather than static organization, the study of such schemata appear to fall in the natural province of psychoanalysis rather than cognitive psychology. This point deserves special emphasis: self-with-other knowledge is knowledge of dynamically occurring, affectively tinged, dyadically forged events. Such knowledge cannot be broken up into bits because to do so fractures the framework within which the knowledge is known. It is like one of Zeno's famous paradoxes—motion renders objects inscrutable because any time an object is studied in motion, it cannot be located and must be elsewhere since it is in motion. Psychoanalysis is, thus, the proper forum for the investigation and understanding of such affectively based knowledge-in-motion. Drawing upon the perspective of clinical psychoanalysis, a similar view is neatly captured by Modell's (1978) maxim that "affects are at the crossroads of biology and history" (p. 177).

Stern (1985) has suggested that infants, at the very beginning of life, experience the impact of reality without the buffer of defensive distortion. This suggests a repositioning of the relationship between cognitive development and the functional onset of defense mechanisms. According to Stern, infants' "subjective experiences suffer no distortion by virtue of wishes or defenses, but only those made inevitable by perceptual or cognitive immaturity or overgeneralization"

(p. 255). Since the caregiver-infant relationship is a mutually regulating one characterized by high intensity communications of affect-state-dependent conditions, direct infant observation leads us to conclude that early affective experiences are accurately registered before the onset of defensive operations, and that there is a core affective self that precedes the distorting effects of more advanced representational capacities. Emde (1983) has made a similar claim, and described how an "affective core" guarantees a continuity of experiencing across the life span that resists transformation by the many ways that people change. Stern also presents the hypothesis that the child's preverbal domains of self-experience (what he calls the "emergent" and "core" self) continue to exert influence throughout life at the same time as they become integrated into higher domains of selfhood. Stern's research thus can be seen to lend itself admirably to an epigenetic view of human development.

We can also appreciate how the arrival of the infant's capacity for self-recognition can lead to a dissociation of capacities of state from capacities of behavior. Kagan (1981) has shown how self-recognition, emerging during the last six months of the second year of life, entails several maturational advances, including the arrival of self-descriptive utterances. Personal pronouns begin at this age. In the infant, cognitive development begins in motor activity, in action-based behaviors that have a repetitive character—Piaget's primary and secondary circular reactions, for example. As the child matures and develops more advanced representational abilities, these actions become "interiorized," at which time the infant becomes capable of symbolic control and manipulation. During early development, the child gradually acquires the capacity to dissociate state from behavior, to disconnect expressive actions from feeling states, so that he can enact a feeling that may or may not actually be present, or experience a feeling but inhibit its behavioral manifestation. We have observed wide fluctuations, both in children and adults, in the facility by which expressive behaviors can be controlled. This has analogously been demonstrated in the course of experimental demands in a laboratory situation (Malatesta and Izard, 1984). A child may not be able to generate an angry facial expression when asked to, for example. Or an adult may constantly exhibit a contemptuous facial expression when interacting with others, yet be entirely unaware that this is the case. In large measure, the parental labeling and facilitation of emotions forges a meaning-imbued consciousness of expressive behavior as linked to internal state (Lewis and Michalson, 1983). Thus, there appears to be a crucial dissociation of state from behavior, corresponding to language acquisition and the arrival of a capacity for symbolic repetition, in the service of adaptation and interpersonal demands, as one "manages" one's emotional displays. Children learn such willful dissociation during the onset of the periods of self-recognition and language acquisition (also see Stern, 1985, who describes a somewhat similar situation in terms of "accountability" to the caregiver).

The concept of "preverbal domains" has appeared in this paper, counterposed against the concept of level of lexical representation. Some further clarification of the relationship between language development and repetition is necessary. As mentioned, at some point in human development we see a shift in tendency from primal to symbolic forms of repetition. Our contention is that this shift hinges on the acquisition of the communicative function of language, roughly toward the middle or end of the second year of life, corresponding to Stern's (1985) dating of the onset of the mechanisms of defense and Kagan's (1981) description of the dawn of self-awareness. Primal repetition does not disappear at this time; rather, it now shares the stage with symbolic repetition, and only gradually begins to re-cede from the forefront of repetitive activity as the infant matures and symbolic repetition assumes hegemony. With the development of the semiotic function, the child becomes capable of the objectification of selfhood and increasingly removed from the immediacy of ongoing experience. The emerging functions constitute a second stream of psychological motivation, meaning states with advanced representational status that run sometimes parallel to and sometimes divergent from the first stream of psychobiological motivation. We hypothesize that certain emotional experiences may escape the net of lexical appropriation and remain outside of conscious awareness and recall, still influential in the personality organization, unconscious yet exerting a repetitive claim on action with the archaic logic of prelexical mentation.

Let us explore this hypothesis further. The existence of feeling states, we have seen, precedes the capacity of language to describe them, and, in fact, language at first does a rather poor job of communicating such states (Bretherton, McNew, and Beeghly-Smith, 1981). Linguistic capacities expand with time, though there may be restricted access to primal repetitions that lie submerged in the stream of psychobiological motivation. This increasing hegemony of language was the basis for the research of Werner and Kaplan (1963), who paint a picture of how global and undifferentiated realms of preverbal experience become organized by language. The global experience organized by language is then transformed by the speech act, resulting in more articulated experiences that are separate and distinct from the earlier experience. A further refinement of this phenomena is that early language is far superior in communicating categorical information than gradient information; gradient information is the type of information of which early affect states are constituted. The advent of language introduces an original sense of alienation and estrangement into the patterning of early mental life, a radical discontinuity between that which is felt and that which attains lexical representation. It is this bifurcation that characterizes the schism into primal and symbolic repetition.

Further evidence for the primacy of affectivity may be gleaned from nondevelopmental experimental research programs. From the experimental psychology literature on affectivity, Zajonc (1980), a post-attribution social psychologist, has asserted on the basis of experimental studies of human cognitive processes that affects are not necessarily preceded by cognitions, that preferences do not require inferences, and that feeling and thinking may be under the control of separate information-processing systems in the human brain. Basch (1976) and others had earlier made this claim, that affect tends to reflect subcortical processing and cognition cortical processing (the so-called old and new brains). Both assertions are in sharp contradistinction to the generally prevailing experimental view put forth by Schacter and Singer (1962), who describe how thought or cognitive appraisal is a necessary factor for an emotional experience. In this theory, emotions are a product of nonspecific arousal and cognitive attribution. Zajonc suggests that this may be true for sustained emotional experiences, in which thought and feeling are virtually inextricable, but that "it is entirely possible that the very first stage of the organism's reaction to stimuli and the very first elements in retrieval are affective. It is further possible that we can like something or be afraid of it before we know precisely what it is and perhaps even without knowing what it is" (p. 154). Since affective appraisals of information have an independent life of their own, Zajonc believes they may differ from a cognitive system psychologically as well as biologically. Moreover, he speculates that the affect system may precede the cognitive system both phylogenetically as well as ontogenetically. Zajonc builds his case primarily with references from the experimental psychology literature, yet it is clear that he is wrestling with a problem similar to that encountered by psychoanalysts. In a more recent update, Zajonc (1984) has reaffirmed this stance and added more empirical evidence that emerged subsequent to the publication of his earlier paper.

Zajonc's work on how affect precedes cognition is complemented by a body of experimental research demonstrating that affectivity bears a causal relationship to permutations of cognitive processing, that differential mood states alter cognitive processes and influence interpersonal behavior, rather than vice versa. When a happy mood is induced under experimental mood-induction procedures, it results in increases in friendliness, optimism, altruism, and creative problem solving (Isen, 1984). The induction of sadness produces impaired cognitive performance, increased dogmatism, apathy, and conventionality (Messick, 1965; Isen, 1984). Inductions of anger have been found to have a facilitating effect upon the recall of negative information and to produce more violent imagery in free association and TAT narratives (Bower, 1981; Nasby and Yando, 1982). Thus, prevailing mood states can affect wide domains of behavior and performance, and the effects appear to be affect-specific.

Affects also appear to order social cognitions, as demonstrated in the literature concerned with episode cognition and event schemas (Schank and Abelson, 1977; Forgas, 1982). This literature not only documents the interplay between emotional and cognitive processes but also provides a particular framework for understanding how repetitive emotional experiences may lay down a foundation for the creation of psychic structure, which, in turn, determines the way in which people subsequently engage the world. According to this point of view, people possess implicit internal representations of social interactions that guide interpersonal behavior. These are representations defined not in psychoanalytic terms but within the purview of cognitive science (cf. Fodor, 1981), as cognitive schemata that divide the world into a limited number of schematized routines and images that define the essence of social behavior. They derive from the repetitive nature of social interaction in conjunction with the natural human tendency to categorize and structure the social environment. Episode cognitions differ from cognitions about nonsocial objects along a number of dimensions: first, they are imbued with a strong affective component (Bretherton, 1985), and this affective component is more important than objective episode features. Bretherton (1985) stresses the important developmental consequences that ensue from this condition: "Event schemas developed in interaction with specific persons are also the raw material from which young children construct internal (affective/cognitive) working models of the self and of significant others, including attachment figures" (p. 32). Second, these cognitions tend to be relationship oriented, that is, focused on the interaction between partners during social intercourse. Third, there is a strong individual difference component of episodic cognitions, reflecting the effect of individual differences in personality. Episodic cognitions are more than a parsimonious means of coding and structuring experience—they determine perception of others, cognition, and behavior, and instrumentally guide decision making and reorder erroneously categorized episodes so that they comply with prototypic episodic structures. Interestingly, although cognitive schemas are viewed as having a pervasive influence on the structuring of reality, especially in the realm of the interpersonal, it is affect (a certain quality or type of affect) that is the resin that sustains the connectivity among schematized routines. Since even very young, preschool-aged children show evidence of having schematized routines (Nelson, 1981; Nelson and Gruendal, 1981), we can deduce that many such affective-cognitive schemas are forged within the context of early repetitive dyadic experiences.

In concluding this section, we note that in the case of observational research on the preverbal infant, we are led to the conclusion that infants experience primary affects, jointly constructed between caregiver and self, before they are capable of establishing defense mechanisms that can mediate between competing wishes and effect compromise formations, and long before these experiences can be coded in a fashion that allows for conscious and verbal articulation. The powerful repetitive emotional experiences between infant and caregiver generate emotional patterns and response dispositions that can dramatically influence action yet remain outside of the domain of consciousness as the infant matures. An epigenetic perspective provides us with a theoretical model that can elucidate how early domains of affective knowing can persevere into adulthood. There is evidence from the experimental psychology literature that affective responses can occur before the emergence of symbolic representation, may not be accessible to consciousness, and yet may profoundly determine object relations. The literature concerned with early schema formation and episodic cognition suggests that it is from early repetitive social-interactive experiences that representations of the world and corresponding expectations about the nature of current interactions are built up over time. We will now return to the literature of psychoanalysis and attempt to assess some implications of this body of work, with the goal being an integrated, clinically based theory of repetition.

Psychoanalytic Implications

We have come a long way from the time when we thought that preoedipal clinical phenomenology marked a regressive flight from oedipal sexual anxieties and that affectivity is, as Freud described in Chapter 7 of *The Interpretation of Dreams* (1900), an epiphenomenon of drive discharge, by definition outside of the system *Ucs*. The contributions of contemporary researchers from these diverse nonpsychoanalytic perspectives have provided us with important evidence from which we, as psychoanalysts, can infer the following. First, affect can be studied apart from cognition and may constitute a separable neurophysiological and behavioral action system. Second, in human development, affective reactions precede the onset of imagistic representational capacities. Third, affective reactions are crucially important to a communicational system patterned within the nexus of the primary-caregiver—infant relationship before the infant has established an autonomous and individuated self. Fourth, these early affective reactions are not transitory states but are a form of early mentation, knowledge of earliest object-relational patterns that become bound up in the growing child's continuity of self-experiences and are essential life-enhancing ingredients of the caregiver-child attachment system. The discussion to follow calls upon the reader to transcend traditional Aristotelian categories of mind and appreciate how affect can be an early form of mentation, characterizing a channel for apprehending self and object, a form of information gathering and sending.

The caregiver attunes herself to her child, and, through a reciprocity of signals and cues, promotes the expansion of the affect array (cf. Pine, 1980), thereby expanding the infant's communicational ability. At birth, the infant becomes involved in a complex, mutually regulating dyadic relationship with the primary caregiver, which sets up an affective tone, disposition, or storehouse of affective knowledge that precedes the onset of imagistic and lexical representational capacities. Such affective knowledge is beyond the adult patient's recollective ability, yet we believe that its influence on personality organization is profound. This early affective knowledge is pre-imagistic representational dynamic knowledge of self-in-interaction with another. This sphere of affective life evolves through a circular reaction of affect sequences, originally acquired within the context of repetitive dyadic interplay, but eventually becoming an autonomous knowledge, organically embedded and important, bearing on self and other, and reflecting the apprehension of the object world in unique and particular ways.

Viewing affect as a form of early mentation, of interpersonal knowledge of self-with-other, has important implications for the manner by which we come to understand the infant's psychic reality. For example, it suggests that representations of interactions, although affectively coded, do not necessarily (although they may) correspond to the patterning of actual events if we could find them preserved in some archaeological expedition into personal history. In this sense, many psychoanalysts can find an intellectual ally in the genetic epistemology of Piaget—as well as in many modern theorists of cognitive science—who insists that knowledge is created and integrated in an active and not passive mode. Piaget called this *constructivism*. In his view, knowledge neither represents a copy of the object (copy theory or empiricism) nor takes the form of a consciousness predetermined in the subject (preformism)—it is a perpetual construction made by an ongoing exchange of information between the active organism and the responsive (maternal?) environment. In the true spirit of psychoanalysis, how the active infant construes an interaction will determine the fate of the resulting emotional event knowledge; this is why that which is internalized is often not readily apparent to an outside observer or reconstructor of events.

Earlier, we spoke of language and repetition, but did not expand on the clinical implications of our views. Adults orate using language skills, and language is an advanced form of representational capacity (Bruner, 1964; Horowitz, 1972), yet early affective knowledge is not easily accessed by language. Earliest affective knowledge, coded in enduring psychobiological representations, tends to be quiet, mute, requiring an unusual introspective capacity or empathic partnership for it to be accessed by language. As discussed by Wilson and Weinstein (1990) this perspective involves a particular relationship between language and thought beyond the word-thing presentations of the topographic model. Bruner (1986) has re-viewed and further contrasted the relationship between language and thought found in the theories of Freud, Piaget, and Vygotsky. There are large and perhaps unresolvable distinctions in the views of these three titans, which Bruner notes may be due to the cultural context within which each view is embedded. Given whom they study, where they came from, and what their intentions were, each generates a different "world" in which there is a different dialectic of language and thought which has a claim to "rightness." In our view, earliest affect embodies a form of communicative intent and therefore is a rudimentary element of thought organization, part of the dyadically forged ontogeny of mind, embodied within a transactional process through which knowledge is expressed, shared, and obtained. In our "world," we lean, in Bruner's terms, toward the Freudian view that thought can trick language, through mechanisms such as parapraxes, repression and its derivatives and so forth, and that ultimately language derives its therapeutic efficacy from the ability to express the archaic and the primally repressed. Thus, such early affective knowledge, one of the earliest forms of mentation, can be potentially discordant and unintegratable into the language system. In the adult analysand, this affective knowledge may be at first engageable in subtle nuances of affectivity rather than through language and, as a result, may be most readily brought into communicational relevance by the affective engagement of object relating, that is, through shared affect states of self-with-other. We may well be in the realm of the paraverbal. With the analysand as with the caregiver, such repetitive affective states may be gathered within the transference, and, in fact, constitute a crucial element of the transference, serving multiple functions between patient and analyst.

All this is not to say that primal repetition is a simple construct, or parsimonious in derivation. Parsimony is an oft-stipulated value of *Naturwissenschaften* that may have dire procedural implications for a *Geisteswissenschaften*. Loewald (1971) remarks that "repetition is a concept of such generality that one quickly gains the impression that it is, in one way or another, applicable to most if not all phenomena and processes of life, biological and psychological" (p. 87). We hope that moving from a broad to a narrow definition of repetition will help alleviate this problem. Nevertheless, even while we simplify, we encounter increasing degrees of complexity of a different sort: the concept of primal repetition provides us with an inroad toward a greater appreciation of how complex the early affective repertoire of the infant is and how truly complex the sequelae of primal repetition can be.

During the analytic hour, subtleties of action precipitated by the trigger of primal repetition are telescoped into prominence as an important aspect of the transference. These subtleties can then be analyzed and symbolized, moved into the domain of shared language. Such derivatives of primal repetition are precipitated by the often unspoken engagement of analyst and patient, which, in the analytic situation, at certain times can parallel the affective and communicative vectors of the caregiver-child communicative bond. As most analysts know, when close attention is paid to the paraverbal, especially affective, aspects of the communication between analyst and patient, clinical data is most precisely recorded by the analyst. The affective knowledge of this form of repetition is at times evoked when there is an establishment of (or lack of) attunement that can evoke archaic affective knowledge of self with other. This can then be worked with and brought into consciousness through the psychoanalytic process, which elevates into discourse that which had been unsayable. With neurotic patients, such affectively attuned experiences are often assumed and unspoken (Wilson, 1986). This unspoken affective encounter is well known, and at various times has been termed, under the technical umbrella of analytic neutrality, "the holding environment" (Winnicott, 1960b; Modell, 1976), "the diatrophic function of the analyst" (Gitelson, 1962), "the therapeutic alliance" (Zetzel, 1956; Greenson, 1965), or "the selfobject transference" (Kohut, 1977; Adler, 1980). All of these are terms that characterize an optimal foundation, a trust, a confluence of obscure but powerful feelings and fantasies that form the basis of an agreement through which complex processes, embodied in the symbolic repetition of disguised meanings, can be analyzed. With more severely disturbed patients, such affective communicational processes take a noisier form and require exquisite attention before symbolic repetition can be attended to (Wilson, 1986). With such severely disturbed patients, the residua of primal repetition can be initially out of synchrony with the interpretative task of the psychoanalyst, for it cannot be corroborated through introspection.

This discussion of the epigenesis of affectivity actually suggests a new conceptualization of the concept of the holding environment. In the view of certain analysts (e.g., Kohut, 1971, 1977), the soothing function of the analyst holds the patient. This formulation suggests interventions in the form of calming and pacification in order to create the holding environment. However, perhaps a more precise explanation might be that of affective "fitting-in" to

the patient. A concept such as soothing fixes the analytic intervention within a limited repertoire of kindly emotional
reactions, and fails to depict how many patients are in fact held
by an emotional ambience that is far more than soothing. When
Winnicott (1971) promotes the conditions for the patient's free
expression by allowing himself to be killed and then surviving,
he certainly does not do so by kindness. The holding function
may be better described as a form of complementarity, a co-construction of emotional ambience, one that the analyst intuitively
(or, if skillful, consciously) tailors for each patient. The fitting-in
is in part constituted of affective knowledge of both analyst and
patient, a residue of primal repetition, that serves to fulfill the
patient's need to experience trust, security, and the vision that
through the analyst's presence and the analytic process he can be
helped (Loewald, 1960; Friedman, 1969).

As infants mature and eventually become capable of symbolic
communication, archaic remnants of early affective knowledge of
self-with-other tend to recede to the inner core of the personality.
This is what Winnicott (1960a) implied when he described healthy
people, in some fundamental way, as isolates, possessing a precious
true self that they strive to maintain pristine, untouched by the demands and needs of others. Similarly, in his intellectual struggle
with the death instinct, one of the descriptors Freud was fond of was
"muteness." For example, in *The Ego and the Id* (1923), he stated that
"since we feel necessitated to it (namely, to hold to our fundamentally dualistic point of view), we gain the impression that the death
instincts are by their nature mute and that the noise [alternately
translated as "clamor"] of life proceeds for the most part from
Eros" (p. 46). We are in fundamental agreement with Freud when
he sought to define a narrow view of the repetition compulsion
and in doing so found value in the metaphor of "noise." When primal repetition results in affective noisiness, this can reflect not

only abrasions of discordant object relating but also the emotional pathology suggested by Loewald's (1971) description of passive repetition. When primal repetition is mute, this does not imply that its sequelae are not present and influential; only that what is repeated is not sufficiently discordant to result in noisiness. Affects are, we can see, what provide for a quiet fitting-in or a noisy lack of fitting-in to the cathected other.

The understanding of affectivity presented in this paper may have important clinical implications for pathology that some consider intractable to psychoanalysis. In *Beyond the Pleasure Principle* (1920). Freud cited masochism as one clinical referent that could be understood in more depth by the death instinct. The relationship between masochism and the death instinct was further elaborated with the introduction of the structural theory (1923) and tied in with the unconscious sense of guilt (as seen in the tenacious resistance to recovery) and fusion/diffusion of libido and the death instincts, as the "taming" of the death instincts by the libido is effected (1924, 1926). Resistance to recovery became elaborated over the years into the voluminous literature on the negative therapeutic reaction, a concept Freud introduced in 1923. For Freud, the death instinct was a crucial explanatory construct in the understanding of the negative therapeutic reaction. As late as in *Analysis Terminable and Interminable* (1937), describing the negative therapeutic reaction, he wrote that it represents "unmistakable indications of the presence of a power in mental life which we call the instinct of aggression or of destruction according to its aims, and which we trace back to the original death instinct of living matter" (p. 243). The discussion in this 1937 paper indicates that Freud's latest view on the subject was that the negative therapeutic reaction could not be accounted for by moral masochism (1924) or superego resistance (1926), as he had earlier sought to do. This view was amplified by Loewald (1972), who viewed the negative therapeutic reaction not as directed within the object relationship against the analyst, that is, as motivated resistance, but rather as a transcendental resistance against improvement in which the death instinct triumphs and maintains the upper hand over Eros in an unending internal life-death struggle.

The literature on the negative therapeutic reaction is vast, and we will not attempt to address the many controversies that are involved. We intend, rather, to focus on one particular aspect relevant to our thesis. While many analysts expanded on Freud's concept (Riviere, 1936; Olinick, 1964; Loewald, 1972) and strove to bring the negative therapeutic reaction within analyzable parameters, Valenstein (1973) described a particular view of the negative therapeutic reaction, which can be viewed as a specific instance of the more general principle of primal repetition. According to Valenstein, the negative therapeutic reaction has its origins as early as the first or second year of life, when the preoedipal child develops a primary attachment to pain and suffering, condensing and echoing an inconstant object tie. What he calls "primal affects"—earliest affects characterizing the emergence of the ego from the stage of primary narcissism—are created and then held to within a context of a caregiver's induction of pain and emotional suffering. To Valenstein, since such a formation is preverbal, an ego deficit ensues, and these primal affects cannot be reached by mutative psychoanalytic interpretation, which remains relatively impotent in effecting analytic change. It is the forging and adherence to the affects induced by the primary attachment to the anaclitic pain-inducing object representation that identifies the negative therapeutic reaction, as described by Valenstein, as an example of the noisiness of primal repetition.

There are many opinions on what constitutes the curative action of psychoanalysis. We know of the unconscious becoming conscious, creating ego where id had been, introjecting the analyst, the acquisition of insight, resolving the infantile neurosis through transference, the taming of drives, and so on. Probably all are applicable in some cases, and many, in most cases, for psychoanalysis does not possess one mutative factor that supersedes all others (Loewald, 1960). The discussion in this paper leads one to think that another conception of analytic change may be worth considering—that of examining and bringing insight and language to bear on the repetitive nature of recurring archaic affective knowledge to trigger particular actions, amidst certain current interpersonal configurations, one of which is the analytic transference. When insight occurs through the normal process of the analysis of transference, primal repetition can then be understood in its entirety and in its effects upon the personality organization. Lipton (1977) may have seen something similar when he attempted to grapple with the concept of analytic neutrality in the light of his sense of how psychoanalysis actually is practiced. The notion of neutrality emphasizes not taking one side of a patient's conflict. Lipton notes that between 1939 and 1948 there arose a preoccupation with relatively trivial aspects of analytic technique that overemphasized the analyst's behavior and underemphasized the analyst's purpose. Lack of responsiveness and dispassionate interpretation become the shibboleths of analytic decorum. Neutrality thus becomes something an analyst is rather than does. However, it is not possible to have *no* response to a patient, only the substitution of one response for another, for better or worse. When two people are in the same room and sharing the same analytic intent, the analyst's unresponsiveness will evoke as sure a reaction in the patient as any other action, such as telling a joke, a fondness of Freud's. Can an analyst be neutral with respect to affective knowledge? Only in a quite relative sense. Prescribed unremitting unresponsiveness in the service of neutrality also limits the freedom of the analyst to sculpt creatively an affective engagement with the patient that can become a central element serving to facilitate the elevation into words of unconscious meanings and disavowed actions.

In the light of our description, it is more exact to reserve the term "repetition compulsion" for the motivation underlying primal repetition, and "transference" for the motivation and sequelae of symbolic repetition. To do otherwise is to define repetition and transference so broadly that both become obscure. As one example of this confusion, Kohut's (1971) description of the selfobject transferences comes to mind. Kohut describes analytic scenarios in which isomorphisms of deficit-laden configurations within the earliest selfobject relationship are found in the analyses of adults. These are primal repetitions, so different from a transference that they deserve a distinct title and explanatory range. Sandler and Sandler (1978), alert to this dilemma, attempt to bridge these two perspectives. They collapse the distinction between what we call symbolic and primal repetition, as they consider both earliest fantasies and affects instrumental in the repetitive patterning of later action. They observe that "a great deal of our life is involved in the concealed repetition of early object relationships in one form or another" (p. 287). They suggest that these archaic repetitions can be understood as the striving toward actualization of persisting unconscious fantasies and that they also are characterized by affectivity because earliest wishes are object directed, and all object relational experiences must be linked with feelings, otherwise they would have no meaning to the person. In our opinion, this is an interesting effort, but the depth of the empirical evidence suggests that a conceptual distinction between affective knowledge and fantasy, and thus between the repetition compulsion and transference, is called for.

Our view is in many ways quite similar to, but more elaborated than, the view of Kernberg (1976, 1984). Kernberg describes earliest affects as a primary motivational system in infants and suggests that early affective structures serve to link the infant with the mother in a communicational matrix that both precedes and ushers in early object relations and drives. Thus, he notes that "affects ... building blocks, or constituents of drives; affects eventually acquire a signal function for the activation of drives" (Kernberg, 1984, p. 236). The drives, however, are made manifest by a specific wish toward an object. Thus, to Kernberg, until there is the capacity to wish (which brings with it the presumption of unconscious fantasy and conflictual potential), early affect states linking self with other are the central organizers of the emerging object relational potential and personality organization.

Without specifically invoking the repetition compulsion, in recent years, advocates of the concept of the psychoanalytic narrative have demonstrated telling problems with the bridges commonly built in analysis between the distant past and the present. Their solution is to render the past inchoate, unknowable, at best a story to be interpreted with only trace elements of an aboriginal reality. For instance, Spence (1982) has described how, in the present, that which is past is constantly recreated in new guises, because of inherent constraints within language, memory, and thought processes of re-creating that which actually occurred. With Spence's important caveat in mind, it becomes even more important to prevent contemporary actions not motivated by factors from the distant past, but that are brought into a meaningful relationship by the mind and interpretive activity of the analyst, from passing as repetitions. A broad definition of repetition, such as provided by Klein (1976), can lend itself to these false positives, because widening the range of repetition allows for the discovery of repetitions in broad domains of human action, and thus increases the chances that such findings are er-roneous perceptions of the analyst rather than true repetitions. Such errors are made largely because we do not have a well-thought-out sense of what it is that is repeatable in human men-tation and action. Although Spence warns us of inherent constraints in veridical representations across cross-modal syn-thesis and memory re-production, he does not speak to the issue of repetitive permutations of early affective experience nor of pre-representational phenomena. Affectivity may be more re-sistant to the permutations of narrativization than the sensory processes, as Spence cites. If language, imagery, and recollective memory processes are implicated in what we are calling symbolic repetition, then it naturally follows that there will be dramatic transformations across the life span in structure and content that are influenced by these abilities. However, the hermeneutic per-spective of the psychoanalytic narrative would seem poorly equipped to convincingly explain the repetition of experiences that are carriers of early preverbal affective experience, beyond subjectivity and narrativization. It becomes ever more crucial to conceptualize what it is that is swept up and contained by the forces of repetition. A narrow, rather than broad, definition of repetition becomes more compelling.

In conclusion, the repetition of post-lexical mental produc-tions characterized by the ability to wish and fantasize is characteristic of symbolic repetition, and the repetition of archaic affective experiences is characteristic of primal repetitions that are created and unfold through the mutually regulating infant-care-giver dyad. Because of recent advances in psychological research and psychoanalytic theory, we are now well positioned to concep-tualize the manner by which repetitive archaic affect states are first forged and then perpetuated into the adult's psychic reality in a manner related to Freud's insistence that humans possess a compulsion to repeat that which is beyond regulation by the pursuit of pleasure. If, though, pleasure is not defined, as in his early formulations, as the lack of excitation, but rather more in accord with his rather undeveloped later formulations, as the optimal rises-and-falls of excitation within the ego as a part of the earliest object relationship, then primal repetition can occur both within ("silent") as well as beyond ("noisy") the pleasure principle. We may thus conclude that the structures imposed by repetition may be more far-reaching and instrumental to psychological reality than Freud himself saw when, over the years, he struggled with the place in psychoanalytic theory of the compulsion to repeat.

References

Adler, G. (1980). Transference, real relationship, and alliance. *International Journal of Psycho-Analysis* 61:547–558.

Ainsworth, M.D.S., Blehar, M.C., Waters, E., & Wall, S. (1979). *Patterns of Attachment*. Hillsdale, NJ: Erlbaum.

Basch, M.F. (1976). The concept of affect—A reexamination. *Journal of the American . Psychoanalytic Association* 24:759–778.

Bibring, E. (1943). The conception of the repetition compulsion. *Psychoanalytic Quarterly* 12:486–519.

Bower, G. (1981). Mood and memory. *American Psychologist*, 36:129–148.

Brenner, C. (1983). *The Mind in Conflict*. New York: International Universities Press.

Bretherton, I. (1985). Attachment theory: Retrospect and prospect. In: *Growing Points of Attachment Theory and Research*, Eds. I. Bretherton & E. Walters, pp. 3–35. Chicago: University of Chicago Press.

Bretherton, I., McNew, S., & Beeghly-Smith, M. (1981). Early person knowledge as expressed in gestural and verbal communication: When do infants acquire a "theory of mind"? In: *Infant Social Cognition*, Eds. M. E. Lamb & L R. Sherrod, pp. 333-373. Hillsdale, NJ: Erlbaum.

Breuer, J., & Freud, S. (1895). Studies on Hysteria. *Standard Edition, 2.* London: Hogarth Press, 1955.

Bruner, J. (1964). The course of cognitive growth. *American . Psychologist* 19:1–15.

———(1986). *Actual Minds, Possible Worlds.* Cambridge, MA: Harvard University Press.

Campos, J., & Sternberg, C. (1980). Perception of appraisal and emotion: The onset of social referencing. In: *Infant Social Cognition,* Eds. M. E. Lamb & L. R. Sherrod. Hillsdale, NJ: Erlbaum.

Cohn, J.F., & Tronick, E.Z. (1983). Three month old infants' reaction to simulated maternal depression. *Child Development* 54:185–193.

D'Andrade, R. (1975). Memory and the assessment of behavior. In: *Measurement in the Social Sciences*, ed. T. Blalock, pp. 159–186. New York: Aldine-Atherton.

Demos, V. (1984). Empathy and affect. In: *Empathy II*, Eds. J. L. Lichtenberg, M. Bornstein, & D. Silver, pp. 9-34. Hillsdale, NJ: Analytic Press.

Emde, R. (1983). The prerepresentational self. *Psychoanalytic Study of the . Child*, 38:165–192. New Haven, CT: Yale University Press.

———Gaensbauer, T., & Harmon, R. (1976). Emotional Expression in Infancy: A

Biobehavioral Study. *Psychological Issues* 10, Monograph. 37. New York: International Universities Press.

Field, T. M., Woodson, R., Greenberg, R., & Cohen, D. (1982). Discrimination and imitation of facial expressions by neonates. *Science* 218:179–181.

Fodor, J.A. (1981). *Representations*. Cambridge, MA: Harvard University Press.

Forgas, J.P. (1982). Episode cognitions: Internal representations of inter-action routines. In: *Advances in Experimental Social Psychology*, Vol. 15. New York: Analytic Press.

Frank, A. (1969). The unrememberable and the unforgettable: Passive primal repression. *Psychoanalytic Study of the Child* 24:59–66. New York: International Universities Press.

Freud, S. (1894). The Neuro-psychoses of Defense. *Standard Edition*, 3:45–61.

———(1895). Project for a scientific psychology. *Standard Edition*, 1:295–397.

———(1900). The Interpretation of Dreams. *Standard Edition*, 4 & 5.

———(1905). Three essays on the theory of sexuality. *Standard Edition*, 7:130–243.

———(1914a). On narcissism. *Standard Edition*, 14:67–102.

———(1914b). Remembering, repeating and working-through. *Standard Edition*, 12:145–156.

———(1915a). Instincts and their vicissitudes. *Standard Edition*, 14:109–140.

———(1915b). The unconscious. *Standard Edition*, 14:164–204.

———(1920). Beyond the pleasure principle. *Standard Edition*, 18:7–64.

———(1923). The ego and the id. *Standard Edition*, 19:3–66.

———(1924). The economic problem of masochism. *Standard Edition*, 19:159–170.

———(1926). Inhibitions, symptoms, and anxiety. *Standard Edition*, 20:87–172.

———(1937). Analysis terminable and interminable. *Standard Edition*, 23:211–253.

———(1940). An outline of psychoanalysis. *Standard Edition*, 23:144–207.

Friedman, L. (1969). The therapeutic alliance. *International Journal of Psychoanalysis*

Gaensbauer, T. (1982). The differentiation of discrete affects: A case report. *Psychoanalytic Study of the. Child* 37:29–66.

Gedo, J. (1979). *Beyond Interpretation: Towards a Revised Theory for Psychoanalysis.* New York: International Universities Press.

———(1981). *Advances in Clinical Psychoanalysis.* New York: International Universities Press.

Gifford, S. (Rep.) (1964). Repetition compulsion. *Journal of the American Psychoanalytic. Association* 12:632–649.

Gitelson, M. (1962). The curative factors in psychoanalysis: The first phase of psychoanalysis. *International Journal of Psychoanalysis* 43:194–205.

Greenson, R. (1965). The working alliance and the transference. In: *Explorations in Psychoanalysis*, pp. 199-224. New York: International Universities Press, 1978.

Greenspan, S. I. (1979). Intelligence and Adaptation: An Integration of Psychoanalytic and Piagetian Developmental Psychology. *Psychological Issues*, Monograph, 47/48. New York: International Universities Press.

Grünbaum, A. (1984). *The Foundations of Psychoanalysis*. Berkeley: University of California Press.

Horowitz, M. (1972). Modes of representation of thought. *Journal of the American . Psychoanalytic Association* 20:793–819.

Isen, A. M. (1984). Toward understanding the role of affect in cognition. In: *Handbook of Social Cognition*, Eds. R. Wyler & T. Surr. Hillsdale, NJ: Erlbaum.

Izard, C.E. (1971). *The Face of Emotion*. New York: Appleton-Century-Crofts.

———(1978). On the ontogenesis of emotions and emotion-cognition relationships in infancy, In: *The Development of Affect*, Eds. M. Lewis & L.A. Rosenblum, pp. 389–413. New York: Plenum.

Izard, C.E. (1979). *The Maximally Discriminative Facial Movement Coding System (MAX)*. Newark: University of Delaware Instructional Resources Center.

Kagan, J. (1981). *The Second Year of Life: The Emergence of Self-Awareness*. Cambridge, MA: Harvard University Press.

Kaye, K. (1982). *The Mental and Social Life of Babies*. Chicago: University of Chicago Press.

Kellerman, H. (1983). An epigenetic theory of emotions in early development. In: Emotion: *Theory, Research, and Experience*, Vol. 2, Eds. R. Plutchik & H. Kellerman. New York: Academic Press.

Kernberg, O. (1976). *Object Relations Theory and Clinical Psychoanalysis*. New York: Jason Aronson.

———(1984). *Severe Personality Disorders.* New Haven, CT: Yale University Press.

Kierkegaard, S. (1843). *Repetition: An Essay in Experimental Psychology.* Princeton, NJ: Princeton University Press, 1946.

Klein, G. (1976). *Psychoanalytic Theory: A Study of Essentials.* New York: International Universities Press.

Kohut, H. (1971). *The Analysis of the Self: A Systematic Approach to the Psychoanalytic Treatment of Narcissistic Personality Disorders.* New York: International Universities Press.

———(1977). *The Restoration of the Self.* New York: International Universities Press.

Lewis, M., & Michalson, L. (1983). *Children's Emotions and Moods.* New York: Plenum.

Lipin,T. (1963). Repetition compulsion and "maturational" drive representatives. *International Journal of. Psychoanalysis* 44:389–416.

Lipton, S. (1977). The advantages of Freud's technique as shown in the analysis of the Rat Man. *International Journal of Psychoanalysis* 58:255–274.

Loewald, H. (1960). On the therapeutic action of psychoanalysis. *International Journal of Psychoanalysis* 41:16–33.

———(1971). Some considerations on repetition and repetition compulsion. *International Journal of Psychoanalysis,* 52:59–66.

———(1972). Freud's conception of the negative therapeutic reaction, with comments
on instinct theory. *Journal of the American Psychoanalytic Association* 20:235–245.

Malatesta, C. (1980). Determinants of Infant Affect Socialization: Age, Sex of Infant, and Maternal Emotional Traits. Doctoral dissertation, Rutgers University.

———(1985). Developmental course of emotion expression in the human infant. In: *The Development of Expressive Behavior,* Ed. G. Zivin, pp. 183–219. New York: Academic Press.

———Izard, C. E. (1984). Human social signals in ontogenesis: From biological imperative to symbol utilization. In: *Affective Development: A Psychobiological Perspective*, ed. N. Fox & R.J. Davidson, pp. 161-216. Hillsdale, NJ: Erlbaum.

———Wilson, A. (1988). Emotion/cognition interaction in personality development: A

functionalist analysis. *British Journal of Social Psychology* 27:91–112.

Messick, S. (1965). The impact of negative affect on cognition and personality. In: *Affect, Cognition, and Personality*, Eds. S. S. Tomkins & C. E. Izard. New York: Springer.

Modell, A.H. (1976). The holding environment and the therapeutic action of psychoanalysis. *Journal of the American. Psychoanalytic Association* 24:285–307.

———(1978). Affects and the complementarity of biological and historical meaning. *Annual of Psychoanalysis* 6:167–180.

Nasby, W., & Yando, R. (1982). Selective encoding and retrieval of affectively valent information. *Journal of Personality & Social Psychology* 43:1244–1255.

Nelson, K. (1981). Social cognition in a script framework. In: *Social Cognitive Development*, Eds. J.H. Flavell & L. Ross, pp. 97-118. Cambridge, UK: Cambridge University Press.

———Gruendal, J.M. (1981). Generalized event representations: Basic building blocks of cognitive development. In: *Advances in Developmental Psychology*, Eds. M. E. Lamb & A.L. Brown. Hillsdale, NJ: Erlbaum.

Nietzsche, F. (1892). *Thus Spake Zarathustra*, trans. T. Common. New York: Tudor, 1934.

Olinick, S. L. (1964). The negative therapeutic reaction. *International Journal of Psychoanalysis* 45:540–548.

Piaget, J. (1951). *Play, Dreams, and Imitation*. New York: W.W. Norton & Company, 1972.

———(1970). *Genetic Epistemology*. New York: W.W. Norton & Company.

———(1972). The affective unconscious and the cognitive unconscious. *Journal of the American Psychoanalytic Association* 20:249–261.

Pine, F. (1980). On the expansion of the affect array: A developmental description. In: *Rapprochement: The Critical Subphase of Separation-Individuation*, Eds. R. L. Lax, S. Bach, & J.A. Burland, pp. 217–333. New York: Jason Aronson.

Plutchik, R. (1980). *The Emotions: A Psychoevolutionary Synthesis.* New York: Harper & Row.

Popper, K. (1959). *The Logic of Scientific Discovery.* New York: Harper & Row.

Riviere, J. (1936). A contribution to the analysis of the negative therapeutic reaction. *International Journal of Psychoanalysis* 17:304–320.

Sander, L. (1980). New knowledge about the infant from current research: Implications for psychoanalysis. *Journal of the American Psychoanalytic Association* 28:181–198.

———(1983). To begin with—Reflections on ontogeny. In: *Reflections on Self Psychology*, Eds. J. L. Lichtenberg & S. Kaplan. Hillsdale, NJ: Analytic Press.

Sandler, J., & Sandler, A.M. (1978). On the development of object relationships and affects. *International Journal of Psychoanalysis* 59:285–296.

Schacter, S., & Singer, J. (1962). Cognitive, social, and physiological determinants of emotional state. *Psychoanalytic Review* 65:379–399.

Schank, R.C., & Abelson, R. (1977). *Scripts, Plans, Goats, and Understanding.* Hillsdale, NJ: Erlbaum.

Schimek, J. (1975). A critical re-examination of Freud's concept of mental representation. *International Review of Psychoanalysis* 2:171–187.

Schwartz, J.C. (1979). Childhood origins of psychopathology. *American Psychologist* 34:879–885.

Schweder, R. (1977). Likeness and likelihood in everyday thought: Magical thinking in judgements about personality. *Current Anthropology* 18:637–648.

Sigal, N.P. (1969). Repetition compulsion, acting-out, and identification with doer. *Journal of the American Psychoanalytic Association* 17:474–488.

Sorce, J.F., & Emde, R.N. (1981). Mother's presence is not enough: Effect of emotional availability on infant explorations. *Developmental Psychology* 17:737–745.

Spence, D. (1982). *Narrative Truth and Historical Truth: Meaning and Interpretation in Psychoanalysis.* New York: W.W. Norton & Company.

Spitz, R. (1965). *The First Year of Life.* New York: International Universities Press.

Stern, D. (1983). The early development of schemas of self, of other, and of "self with other." In: *Reflections on Self Psychology,* Ed. S. Kaplan. New York: International Universities Press.

Stern, D. (1985). *The Interpersonal World of the Infant.* New York: Basic Books.

Toman, W. (1955). Repetition and repetition compulsion. *International Journal of Psychoanalysis* 36:347–350.

Trevarthen, C. (1979). Communication and cooperation in early infancy: A description of primary intersubjectivity. In: *Before Speech: The Beginning of Interpersonal Communication,* Ed. M.M. Bullowa. Cambridge & New York: Cambridge University Press.

Valenstein, A.F. (1973). On attachment to painful feelings and negative therapeutic reactions. *Psychoanalytic Study of the Child* 28:365–392. New York: Quadrangle.

Waelder, R. (1962). Psychoanalysis, scientific method, and philosophy. In: *Psychoanalysis: Observation, Theory, Application.* New York: International Universities Press, 1976, pp. 248–274.

Werner, H., & Kaplan, B. (1963). *Symbol Formation: An Organismic-Developmental Approach to Language and Expression of Thought.* New York: Wiley.

Wilson, A. (1986). Archaic transference and anaclitic depression: Psychoanalytic perspectives on the treatment of severely disturbed patients. *Psychoanalytic. Psychology* 3:237–256.

———Weinstein, L. (1990). Language, thought, interiorization. *Contemporary. Psychoanalysis* 26:24–40.

Winnicott, D.W. (1960a). Ego distortion in terms of true and false self. In:

The Maturational Processes and the Facilitating Environment, pp. 140-152. New York: International Universities Press, 1965.

———(1960b). The theory of the parent-infant relationship. In: *The Maturational Processes and the Facilitating Environment*, pp.37–55. New York: International Universities Press, 1965.

———(1971). The use of an object and relating through identification. In: *Playing and Reality*, pp. 86-94. New York: Basic Books.

Zahn-Wexler, C., Cummings, E.M., Iannotti, R.J., & Radke-Yarrow, M. (1984). Young offspring of depressed parents: A population at risk for affective problems. In: *Childhood Depression*, Eds. D. Cicchetti & K. Schneider-Rosen. San Francisco: Jossey-Bass.

Zajonc, R. (1980). Feeling and thinking: Preferences need no inferences. *American Psychologist* 35:151–175.

Zajonc, R. (1984). On the primacy of affect. *American Psychologist* 39:117–123.

Zetzel, E. (1956). Current concepts of transference. In: *The Capacity for Emotional Growth*. New York: International Universities Press, 1970.

CHAPTER 3

DYNAMIC INTERPERSONAL PROCESSES AND THE INPATIENT HOLDING ENVIRONMENT

The long-term inpatient psychiatric hospital treating severely disabled patients is a complex, multifaceted institution in which many diverse people occupying different roles interact in order to accomplish the task of creating a holding environment for the patient. In this paper, we suggest that the primary function of a psychiatric holding environment is the delivery to the patient of the normative services which the nuclear family customarily provides. In order to provide this, the hospital, like the optimal family, holds both by restraining and by facilitating. Through an understanding of the strategic mental mechanisms which severely disturbed patients often employ in order to interact with and comprehend others, particularly empathy and projective identification, we may delineate more refined treatment strategies. Principles concerning the dynamics of small and large groups, patient-staff interactions, the treatment of so-called "hopeless" and negative therapeutic reaction patients, and supervision follow from these conceptualizations. In all of our explication, our perspective is guided by a systems framework but finds concrete expression in an object relational viewpoint.

In this paper, we will stress the theoretical and clinical usefulness of understanding the concepts of projective identification, empathy, and the holding environment in order to support the notion of the family paradigm as the core conceptual organizer for the hospital-based treatment of severely disturbed patients.

Our intent is to demonstrate how a conception of these processes can be both diagnostically and therapeutically useful. This paper is thus a further elaboration of those which have considered: (1) The vicissitudes of object relations during the hospital phase of treatment of severely disturbed patients (Kernberg 1976; Gossett and Lewis 1983); (2) the concept of the holding environment as reflected in the several modalities of treatment available in the hospital social system (Gunderson et al. 1981); (3) the dynamic interrelationship of intrapsychic, interpersonal, and especially transitional (Hong 1978) processes that contribute to the total therapeutic field of the hospitalized patient. The concept of the holding environment, as used in psychiatric treatment settings, derives from concepts initially conceptualized by Winnicott (1953, 1960). The concept was principally employed and developed in the context of both dyadic treatment of children and the observation of mothers and their children in pediatric settings. In the course of his therapeutic and research work, Winnicott developed the notions of transitional objects, transitional phenomena, and transitional experiences as a way of making sense out of the simultaneous need of the child to remain emotionally connected to the mother, through tactile sensations, vision, and auditory experiences, and to follow the thrust of his own developmental needs, which perforce separated him from the mother. The child, abetted by the good-enough mother's intuition, forges an intermediate space between social reality and fantasy, which allows him or her to be both with and without the mother.

The concept of the holding environment later began to be used in order to describe certain therapeutic strategies within the psychiatric hospital. The concept is particularly germane to those settings which employ psychoanalytic concepts of individual and group dynamics to explicate their therapeutic procedures (Stanton and Schwartz 1954; Edelson 1970). In the relevant literature, the concept of the holding environment is subtly changed from its original meaning and intent. For the most part, it was originally meant to evoke a positive and nurturant set of optimal conditions which help facilitate a patient's recovery, but the idea of restraint emerged as the concept evolved. Though some theorists (e.g., Kernberg 1976; Gunderson 1978) note that holding in the original context also connotes restraint, this version has remained relatively under elaborated. The restraining connotation is generally employed in relationship to aggressive activity, and the containment is viewed as a necessary precondition to personality growth. Both connotations of holding constitute the conceptual and operational links between the family and the psychiatric hospital in their relations with the patient.

Both connotations of holding (facilitating/nurturant and restraining/containing) find concrete expression in the interpersonal activities in a hospital between staff members and patients. In seeking to explicate the concept of the holding environment of the inpatient psychiatric service, we will principally explore mechanisms which span the interpersonal and the intrapsychic, showing how such factors as fantasy production and cognitive abilities are vital for an integrated understanding of the two functions of holding.

The concept of projective identification, of major importance in our investigation, was initially developed and elaborated upon by Melanie Klein (1946). It has a long and variable usage in psychoanalytic literature (Grinberg 1962; Kernberg 1975; Grotstein 1981; Ogden 1981), psychiatric literature, family literature (Berkowitz et al. 1979), and group dynamic literature (Bion 1959; Slater 1966). The concept employs two seemingly disparate terms (projection and identification), which themselves are more elemental mechanisms. The definition we will use in this paper is in accord with Ogden, who describes projective identification as a complex intrapsychic and interpersonal mechanism characterized by three phasic processes. Phase one involves the projection by the self into the other of some unwanted aspects of the self. These are usually negatively valenced self-other representations that are experienced in such phenomenologic forms as greed, hatred, envy, rage, or fear. The second phase involves the acceptance by the other of the subject's projection through reciprocal identification. This phase is usually accompanied by actual interpersonal pressure by the projector toward the recipient to accept and think of the content of the projection as his own; such pressure may take a subtle and sophisticated form, and may evoke dramatic interpersonal maneuvering. A third phase can occur when the recipient "metabolizes" (i.e., accepts, holds, and processes) the projected content, renders it less noxious through containing and modulating it within the context of his own personality system, and then, at the appropriate time, makes it available for reintrojection by the projector. Thus, projective identification carries with it a structuralist assumption of the simultaneity of the attribution of meaning and motive (Levenson 1972). This, of course, roughly parallels transference and countertransference dynamics. Thus, while not quite hybrid (Slap and Levine 1978), the concept encapsulates a two-way process, both in fantasy and in actual object-relating.

Whatever the particular definition employed, most theorists have noticed that this mechanism is one among many which people use to accomplish the complex tasks of self-development and conflict resolution. Projective identification as a mechanism serves a multiplicity of specific functions (Waelder 1942) for the normative development of the young child or, as we shall describe, the recovery of the older patient. Such functions as maintenance of a primitive object tie, communication, defense, and a spur to psychological development are present and intertwined. As a primitive object tie, projective identification facilitates a particular form of attachment to a mothering figure. It defines an attachment in which two figures are bound through the consequences of fantasy production as constituted through one relatively unformed and one relatively well-formed cognitive system. As a form of communication, projective identification promotes fantasies of oneness, sameness, or similarity. Familiarity is enhanced by locating one's own parts inside someone else (see Friedman 1969 and Loewald 1960 for similar views on the curative action of psychoanalysis). As a defense, projective identification serves to distance the self from unwanted elements, and thus may help to minimize an overload of annihilation anxiety or self-directed aggression. As a pathway to psychological development, projective identification expands the array of avenues available for coping with one's unconscious conflicts. As the recipient metabolizes the projected elements and eventually returns them in manageable forms, gradually disowned or unwanted parts of the self can be reclaimed and reintegrated (Tolpin 1971).

In using the term here, we are exploring the multiple avenues of social and interpersonal healing available to severely disturbed inpatients. Once a hospitalized patient has accomplished a projective identification (i.e., has fantasized the transfer of unwanted representations and has obtained behavioral confirmation of this by gauging the object's reactions to him), one of the extremely important initial conditions necessary for the two holding functions of the hospital has been established from the vantage point of the patient. This is not necessarily true for the staff person, who must to some extent be trained in order to have the psychological capacity and intent to metabolize such interpersonal configurations.

By the metaphor of "metabolizing," we mean that through the staff member's capacity to identify reciprocally with the patient, he or she takes on the patient's projected content, without necessarily sacrificing his own self-integration. This can occur because to the patient, the staff member is an undifferentiated other, whereas to the staff member, the patient is a differentiated other (see Pine 1976, 1979). Thus, the net effect of this process for the patient can be that he has an extended series of educative experiences, the healing core of which is to learn by successive approximations (using imitation, introjection, and identification) how to maintain self-cohesion in the presence of disavowed and projected hostile and aggressive aspects of the self.

A complex issue of both theoretical and practical clinical significance is the distinction between occurrences of projective identification and empathy. Both are modes of cognition, which lend themselves to varying degrees of accuracy in a person's capacity to know or understand the psychological world of another. The definition of empathy that we are using here is in accord with Basch (1983), who writes:

> Empathy in the formal or theoretical sense should refer only to a process of coming to know. Where 'reason' is commonly used to indicate that the judgment is supposedly being made on the basis of logic alone, i.e., unemotionally, 'empathy' should be used to indicate that a judgment is being made through a process that specifically does take one's pertinent affective responses into account. To continue the comparison, like reason, empathy does not require the participation of consciousness, but can, from the beginning to end, proceed unconsciously [p. 120].

Empathy refers to a higher order mental ability which subtends our conviction that we know what another person is feeling or thinking. The mental mechanisms which constitute a human's capacity for empathy have been the subject of scholarly debate for years. Some have argued that empathy is a special capacity to "merge" with another (Olden 1958; Schafer 1959, 1968; Green-son 1960). Others have argued in favor of a more developmentally advanced notion of empathy representing a kind of identification (Beres 1968; Beres and Arlow 1974), particularly a "trial" identification (Fliess 1942). The latter investigators follow Freud (1921), who wrote that "A path leads from identification by way of imitation to empathy, that is, to the comprehension of the mechanism by means of which we are enabled to take up any attitude at all towards another mental life" (p. 110 n.). Others have traced the gradual acquisition of the capacity for empathy from the perspective of separation-individuation (Bergman and Wilson 1984) and cognitive development (Hoffman 1978).

Several important links bridge projective identification and empathy, and several distinguish them. One link is that both empathy and projective identification can proceed unconsciously. Second, empathy, like projective identification, requires two people to accomplish one completed mental act. Third, both involve cognitive processes that require at least rudimentary self-other discriminatory capacities. However, one difference is that mature empathy requires a more advanced level of cognitive/emotional maturation than projective identification, and is thus characteristic of more advanced and differentiated developmental achievements. Thus, virtually all hospitalized patients employ projective identification, whereas fewer employ empathy in their ordinary interactions.

There are also several other important differences between the concepts. In the presence of frustration, empathy tends to decrease and projective identification to increase. As an example, in complex situations a person may think that he is empathizing with another when he is merely projecting an attribution of knowledge produced under stormy mental-state conditions. Further, when projective identification is employed, an individual's capacity for empathy tends to decrease. This is especially true when bad self-other representations are in need of ejection, for empathy would block the process of ejection. An additional important difference is that generally projective identification promotes attachment to another person, as previously discussed. Empathy does not necessarily enhance or further attachment! Notions of attachment via empathy tend to reflect the use of the concept as a phenomenological state. However, one person can know about another without necessarily becoming any more emotionally attached to him, reflecting the advanced and differentiated developmental capacities of the empathizer. As a final distinction, the person who empathizes does not necessarily aim to control the other in order to experience certainty concerning his mental content; the patient who employs projective identification aims to control the other in order to complete the act.

Having defined the concepts of holding environment, projective identification, and empathy, in order to provide a skeletal structure with which to explicate the broad range of personality, social, and biological systems necessary for the treatment of difficult patients, we shall go on in the following section to discuss associated key clinical concepts in hospital culture.

The Long-Term Inpatient Hospital and the Family Paradigm

Psychiatric hospitals are organized in accord with a variety of organizational, theoretical, and task orientations. Depending upon the length of stay, the type of patient, and the variety of treatment modalities available, the processes outlined in the introduction to this paper are of more or less central significance for the overall treatment. We shall here confine our discussion only to those hospitals which offer long-term residential treatment of severely disturbed patients. At such hospitals, staff organizations and treatment modalities often are guided by a variable combination of psychoanalytic, psychiatric, social systems, and managerial concepts (Kernberg 1980). By contrast, hospitals which offer primarily short-term, symptom-targeted treatment of a variety of conditions primarily focus on biological and social system approaches (Maxmen et al. 1974; Tucker 1983). Regardless of the particular configuration of treatment services, a common component to all the long-term residential treatment settings is that the patient lives perforce within the setting and culture for an extended period of time. The extended length of stay influences and organizes the realities of staff-patient interactions and also staff-patient-extended family interactions.

We believe that the central configuration of such hospitals is that they serve and function in loco familias (see Rubenstein and Lasswell 1966). Thus, a hospital should be organized in such a way as to provide for the patient the opportunity to transform or stabilize those sequelae of insults to his biopsychosocial development that have culminated in his present impairment. Whatever the specifics of pathogenesis within the family of origin, these sequelae are likely to be externalized during intensive treatment or hospitalization (Lidz et al. 1965; Zinner and Shapiro 1972; Giovacchini 1979). This is what is at the base of our view of the relationship of key staff functions to clinical concepts such as projective identification, empathy, and the holding environment, each of which possesses both a normative and a pathological implication.

The significance of the notion that the hospital functions in loco familias is rooted in the central developmental tasks of all people. We think that virtually all psychological treatments are a derivative of nuclear family functioning, whether these treatments are formally construed in dyadic, small- or large-group therapy, family therapy, or social treatment settings. The nuclear family, containing as it does the mother of attachment and separation (Mahler et al. 1975) and the dyads and triads of homosexual and heterosexual identifications, competitions, and learning, is expected to provide the conditions for normative psychosocial growth and development (Lidz 1968).

Processes of projective identification and empathy, and the construction of phase-, age-, and task-related holding environments, are all normative family functions. The long-term hospital, whether primarily using the fulcrum of the psychoanalytic dyad or prescribing multiple modalities of treatment, must ultimately provide opportunities for the patient to repair and revise those severe pathologic complexes which resulted from the multiple transactions of the patient (with whatever constitutional equipment he possesses) and the family, delivering whatever capacities for "good-enough developing" it possesses or can muster.

Upon arrival at a hospital, a patient presents a complex amalgam of strengths and weaknesses. The presenting behaviors result from defenses and adaptive styles produced by conflict resolution and pathological fixation, as well as deficits and nonpathological aspects of a personality system. Such a distinction is rarely clear for a considerable period of time. Furthermore, identical behaviors may at different times derive primarily from deficits or conflicts depending upon the psychosocial context; thus, the crucial aspect of an initial diagnostic procedure is to tease out more precisely those pathological components of the personality system which reflect deficit and those which reflect conflict. This allows us to make sense of surface behaviors, interpersonal dynamics, and particular attachments that the patient makes upon entry into the hospital system.

We wish to stress that the configuration of therapeutic processes prescribed upon the patient's admission is usually organized in accordance with the particular beliefs of the particular leadership of the particular hospital. Accordingly, some hospitals shun involvement with relatives of the identified patient, in order to promote the hospital as an asylum from family and the stresses of ordinary social living, and to formally protect the nascent therapeutic dyad. Usually, such asylum hospitals seek to create intense psychotherapeutic milieus. By contrast, other hospitals operate on the assumption that the identified patient is inextricably a member of the family, and that the cooperation and involvement of all or most family members is central both for the resolution of the identified individual pathological syndrome and for the development of a healthier psychosocial context for post-discharge living.

Regardless of which of these two broad types of hospital strategy are prescribed, the underlying paradigm still holds—what we have called the family paradigm—and constrains and determines practical clinical decision-making. Various kinds of staff configurations should reflect this conceptualization. There are many ways of acting in loco familias. Whatever the staff configuration, the clinical realities which may be extrapolated from the family paradigm remain in effect—and the therapeutic requirements must be met, for better or worse. Often the configuration takes the form of different staff members providing individual therapy, clinical administration, group therapy, family therapy, and recreation and activities therapy.

At the outset of treatment, both patients and staff have important tasks. From the patient's perspective, an important task is usually to find another person(s) to help him stabilize himself and prevent a regressive worsening of his experiential plight. At entry, that is frequently the dominant, though not necessarily conscious, aim of the patient.

The staff focuses on a different hierarchy of tasks. The first is to attempt to provide the conditions which will promote the patient's goal of self-stabilization, while developing a preliminary understanding of the patient's biosocial field. At the same time, some initial treatment techniques are brought into play; these are generic in nature and common to all admitted patients—e.g., the individual and family therapies, and social integration into a unit. From the vantage point of the patient, the people who are initially least important to his concerns are often the individual therapists. Some hospital staff, on the other hand, typically see the individual therapist as providing critical interventions through his understanding, organization of, and ministrations to the diverse elements of the patient's personality. In hospitals which allocate the tasks of individual therapy and clinical administration to separate persons, the individual therapist is usually an unknown quantity, as well as a figure who does not initially possess enormous practical significance in the everyday life of the patient. For many patients, it will take a long time before the individual therapist assumes practical significance. For these patients, whose object relations tend to be at a need-gratifying sensorimotor level, the benevolent neutrality of the therapist may be experienced as functionally irrelevant and unnecessary. Neutrality (a concept and technique borrowed from the description of the recommended procedural attitude of the psychoanalyst treating a neurotic patient) in these cases is of no helpful experiential import (Sullivan 1962). One of the functions of psychotherapy at this stage is to help the patient reach a level of relating whereby the therapist might be of more explicit experiential import (Hill 1955).

To the patient, the most important people during the initial period of hospitalization are often the nursing staff, clinical administrator, and family therapist, who spend the most time with the patient, are directly involved with day-to-day transactions, and regulate the arenas of social skills and peer contact. The family therapist also controls access to the parents or key relatives, who are often powerful loci of decision-making (which is only temporarily delegated to the hospital). For many patients, an even more important factor is their relationships with other patients who form peer groups. The most important initial ties many patients make in the hospital system are to other patients. Part of the initial diagnostic task is to observe the fashion in which the patient organizes these critical early involvements. The process of projective identification is probably never more actively employed by the patient nor more actively overlooked by the staff than during this phase of treatment.

An important aspect of the family paradigm is the delineation of similarities between the various functions which the staff members perform and those the nuclear family once performed. Few patients in extended inpatient treatment present with a prototypical pattern of family style and pathogeneses (Lidz 1973; Wynne and Singer 1963; Goldstein and Jones 1977). Of course, the personality system of the patient, patterned and evolved in the crucible of the family of origin's transactional processes (Reiss 1981), is further extended through multiple reshapings in the course of interaction with nonfamily persons. Thus, at any particular moment, a patient will present behaviors, communications, and subjective states which derive from different developmental levels and experiences, and which require different types of therapeutic action. This parallels the course of normal development, where different components of family functions are necessary in order to meet the evolving needs of the developing person. The extent to which the family paradigm is central to successful hospital treatment depends upon the extent to which the family of origin succeeded or failed in safeguarding the child's crucial age-specific developmental tasks.

Dynamic Interpersonal Processes and the Family Paradigm

Frequently unbeknownst to the staff, patients employ certain behaviors for purposes other than those ostensibly intended, making use of objects available for self-healing purposes (Lidz 1973). How does it come about that such serendipitous therapeutic activities occur? How do staff facilitate such activities? We believe an important link here is the operation of projective identification. Often, especially early in treatment, patients will select particular members of the treatment staff and target them for projections of unwanted mental contents. Neither the patient nor staff member will necessarily be conscious of this process. Over a period of time, the patient embarks on behaviors that are a requisite part of a completed projective identification (e.g., exerting interpersonal pressure, or relating to the recipient in a manner consistent with the particular meaning of the projection). This will be readily discerned when special attitudes that patients hold for certain staff members—or vice versa—are visible. These may be sufficiently out of synchronization with shared views of the patient as to provide other clinicians a tangible clue that a projective identification has been completed.

Similar observations have heretofore been described in transference–countertransference terms. Indeed, we think that focusing on these mechanisms highlights the preoedipal origin of the transferences of many severely disturbed patients (Pao, 1979) and is related to many of the recent psychoanalytic descriptions of the archaic forms of transference relatedness. In contrast to seeing the concept of regression as a defense against oedipal anxieties, we are here emphasizing the advantages of differentiating cognitive distortions arising from projective identification via a deficit condition, from those reflecting the biasing of perception by neurotic transference or psychological arrest. The former are not necessarily rooted in the repetition of early childhood traumata.

Further examples of similarities between the dynamic interpersonal processes occurring in the psychiatric hospital and the structural/functional organization of a "typical" nuclear family follow. In the family, these typical functions occur during the natural trajectory of the life cycle of the family members. In the hospital, we carefully attempt to organize the role structures and to select the specific people involved in those role structures in order to deliver the roughly analogous functions. We know, however, that a patient may use any staff member to accomplish any particular function despite the assigned role delegated and crafted by the hospital stewardship.

The intergenerational organization of the nuclear family is replicated and delivered at the level of the psychiatric unit. The parental tasks of absorbing aggression, promoting tolerance of affect, anxiety, and frustration, and understanding overwhelming pressures and intrapsychic tensions within the context of management are embodied in the ward group administrator. This person performs ordinary day-to-day negotiations of therapeutic statuses, collaborates with other members of the staff on management decision-making, and provides evaluations of the fitness, security, and salutariness of the patient's decisions and behaviors. As with parents, there is a constant clash of wills over negotiations for privileges and statuses. What we wish to stress is that the salubrious component in this relationship tends not to be the content of the negotiated privilege but rather the manner in which the negotiation is conducted. The patient is held, in the restraining sense, by the administrator's resoluteness in insisting upon proper behavior and morals; upon this foundation, the patient is then held, in the facilitating sense, by the administrator's parental advocacy of his readiness to enter into the less protected sectors granted by the wider world of privileged statuses.

The nursing staff as a cohort can have a function, for the patient, that is roughly analogous to that of a nonfamilial peer group. In many hospitals, nurses provide a series of modeling activities and instructional feedbacks by which the patient is helped to evolve more socially acceptable patterns of social behavior and interaction. There is also considerable overlap with the role that siblings play for each other in a family, but this function is more often enacted vis-à-vis other patients, who are parts of a supervised therapeutic culture in which confrontation, cooperation, and self-management are encouraged.

With regard to the patient's subjective experience, here the nursing staff, regardless of gender, may simultaneously serve as facilitators who allow for the creation of transitional space and transitional experiences for the patient. In the course of reintrojecting disowned parts of the self, the patient may, through a series of trials and errors, construct an intermediate zone that is co-participated in by patient and nurse, and no one else. Such a zone is evocative of Winnicott's (1953) fantasized space co-constructed and then occupied by the child and the mother, which is used by the child but provided by the mother, in the context of developing the object constancy and self-cohesion necessary for subsequent object relations.

Thus, the staff organization may reflect the ideology of the clinical administration, the intrapsychic necessities of the patient, and the reparative family functions that have been relinquished and left to the hospital to enact. In consequence, the hospital personnel must embody multiple functions in order to meet the challenge of self-reparation in the severely disturbed patient. Yet to be delineated are the complex ways in which different group processes within the hospital system bind these overlapping and intersecting functions so that a manageable therapeutic social system can be created.

We will now discuss some implications of our views on interpersonal processes as conceptualized at a system-wide level.

Some psychiatric units are organized so as to provide a series of differentiated activities for patients residing on that unit. Having discussed important clinical principles deriving from the impact of individuals on patient care, we shall now relate these ideas to the operation of the overall psychiatric program.

The patient on a psychiatric unit is involved in a complex treatment endeavor. The structure set up to provide for him differs enormously from the treatment structure of the individual patient in dyadic outpatient therapy, especially insofar as the hospital becomes responsible for management of entire sectors of the patient's life support. Most inpatients at extended care units, to varying degrees, cannot manage one or more of these sectors, owing to debilitating pathologies which interact at multiple levels. Such pathologies may be at the level of the biological, personality, or social family systems. Thus, the treatment staff must develop a comprehensive treatment plan that addresses these multiple levels and sectors. As a result, a large number of people intervene in different ways and at different levels, involving themselves in order to treat illness, disability, family problems, occupational liability, and so on. Given the number of people involved, the understanding and management of complex group dynamics become an important part of the hospital's activity. This function, akin to the instrumental leadership of the family, is carried out by clinical leadership at all levels.

We know, however, from studies of normal and abnormal small groups that the irrational frequently interferes with the primary tasks of the group (Bion, 1959; Slater, 1966; Kernberg 1980). Since important transactions in groups can be understood to occur through projective identification, such processes will often occur among multiple levels of staff and patient organization. At times, one person may well be simultaneously both recipient and initiator of an array of projective identifications. Given this understanding of group life and the mechanisms by which complex organizational tasks are accomplished, it is not surprising that we cannot predict for a given patient whether a self-reparative transaction will come from other patients or a staff member. This is, of course, a reflection of the family paradigm, wherein any member of the nuclear or extended family may play a crucial role in normative development. In the following section, we will attempt to apply these understandings of individual and group processes to the clinical problems that frequently appear in long-term residential psychiatric hospitals.

Clinical Implications

Conflict, Deficiency, and Dynamic Interpersonal Processes

Because many patients enter the hospital with congeries of symptoms which derive from deficits in neurophysiological and neurolinguistic abilities, they present a clinical picture of conflicts and deficits that are largely of unknown etiology. A comprehensive initial evaluation therefore must extend beyond formal testing to include longitudinal clinical observations and formulations. These can take place through close observation of patient-staff interactions on the unit. Fundamentally, the diagnostic process is ever evolving and continues until discharge. As the process proceeds, it makes possible the categorization of the patient's deployment of projective identification into instances that derive principally from conflict (or developmental arrest) and those that derive principally from deficit. Such a categorization is important because it defines a differential pattern of staff behavior in therapeutic ministrations to the patient.

There are different and potentially critical technical implications in dealing with patients whose conditions reflect both deficits and conflicts versus those whose pathology seems to derive primarily from fixation—that is, primarily from conflicts. A patient whose pathological behavior derives primarily from a deficit condition usually has developed a variety of characterological interpersonal strategies as an adaptation to and compensation for such a condition. These strategies may often be a focal departure point for projective identification.

If the initial conditions for projective identification occur, and are followed by the characteristic constellations of incorporations, identifications, and projections, the staff member will eventually experience the projected wishes and fantasies of the patient. This may occur in the form of a gradual vague recognition that something is wrong in the relationship with the patient and needs to be righted. Under favorable conditions, these split-off elements will be metabolized and returned in a therapeutic manner.

Up to this point, there is no true difference between handling a patient with a deficit and handling one with a conflict resulting from arrest or fixation. However, if it turns out that the mechanism was prompted by a deficit condition, then the advisability of returning the unwanted, though partially metabolized, content is different. Because the deficit still exists, and there is little or no likelihood that it can be ameliorated, a different therapeutic maneuver needs to be invoked; the patient must be made aware of the deficit and learn how to deal with his representational world in its presence. In agreement with Gedo (1979, 1981), we believe that when dealing with certain biological derivatives that are beyond conflict and, therefore, interpretation, an educational stance is required.

Thus, an essential working proposition for all clinical staff is that these prototypic (conflict or deficit) situations require different forms of clinical intervention. We recognize how difficult the accurate evaluation and analysis of this process can be, since the same surface behavior usually expresses multiple meanings and motives and condenses diverse origins. Experienced clinical staff, who may not be directly involved with the patient but who can interpret unusual patterns of staff reactions, can provide the necessary supervisory orientation, which increases the likelihood that the patient will neither receive inappropriate reactions to conflict-based behavior nor be neglected because of irremediable deficit.

An example of the confusion of a deficit condition with a conflict condition follows. An 18-year-old white male was admitted to the hospital subsequent to several episodes of assault on family members and police officers. During the premorbid period there had been a gradual but steady decline in his school work. In his friendships, there had been a marked increase in paranoid ideation and a withdrawal from any heterosexual involvements. He also began to consume more and more marijuana and alcohol. On his admission to a general hospital, he was diagnosed as suffering from a drug-induced psychosis and an underlying affective disorder. Short-term treatment was uneventful, and the patient was referred for long-term care. During the extensive evaluation procedure, we found that he was dyslexic, with a perceptual learning disorder superimposed on the dyslexia. The neuropsychological examination suggested deficits in the areas of perceptual integration and visual-motor coordination. His history suggested that hyperkinesis and attention-deficit difficulties were first apparent when he was a latency-aged child.

The patient was six feet two inches tall and extremely muscular, and devoted much time to performing a variety of exercises designed to increase his strength, which contributed to a threatening aura. The front-line staff immediately set about socializing him by focusing on his seeming obliviousness to his menacing posture and his insensitivity to how he frightened people. He was treated as if his behavior expressed unknown motives, especially a wish to frighten, impress, and dominate others.

Two important factors were overlooked. First, in a caricature of his father, he was enacting a family myth that some member of his family had to be both strong and deviant. This blended into a second factor, which was that self-tranquilization for him involved somatic, repetitive, ego-syntonic experiences. That this became incorporated into a representational world and a meaningful network of fantasies and images was hardly surprising, but that was not their primary psychological function. He was oblivious to any conflict-centered interpretation of his behavior, and attempts to deal with his behavior as conflictual derivatives were singularly unsuccessful. He produced a fantasy that the staff wanted him to stop exercising so that he would become weak and less of a menace to them (a notion not far from the preconscious expectations of some staff).

About six months into this hospitalization, a new female nurse developed a special relationship with him. She seemed to be unafraid of him, and on several occasions was remonstrated by other staff for her cavalier attitude. She was told that she was inviting disaster and that, by offering herself up as a victim, she was encouraging him to act out his aggressive impulses—that it was only a matter of time before he assaulted her or some other staff member as a displacement of his affection for her. She insisted that she did not feel fearful with him but rather sensed his considerable relief when she was present.

A closer analysis revealed that she tended to him primarily when he was exercising. In addition to other aspects of their relationship, she not only encouraged his exercises but taught him new ones. The nurse had empathically understood and metabolized an important aspect of the patient's disowned self-experience and had not

returned it to him in a form he could not cope with. She empathically knew the origin and source of the need for communication
through somatic self-soothing, and sensed that it was through
this avenue that the patient could develop psychologically in
ways which would facilitate his ability to relate to others more
successfully.

A further elaboration of the clinical manifestations of patients
with major psychological deficits deriving from neurobiological
dysfunction can be seen in those mistakenly perceived as hopeless by clinical staff. The reaction of hopelessness in treaters may
be indicative of a particular neurological deficit which leads a
patient to appear dumb, unresponsive, non-psychologically
minded, or prone to acting-out proclivities. The treatment staff
tends to cope with this by providing different technical interventions for such patients, which often are packaged as management
contracts or behavioral treatment. We have found that many so-
called hopeless patients have acquired a knack for utilizing others to process and metabolize incoming information. Often,
what appears to be stubborn or panic-driven dependency or anaclitic hunger in a deficit-ridden patient is characteristic of a
psychobiological adaptation that for him is an optimal way to
make sense out of "blooming and buzzing confusion"—through
recruiting a staff member to serve as a metabolizer of incoming
and outgoing information.

The deficits to which we have been referring encompass many
degrees and combinations of cognitive and learning disorders that
are molecular components of larger social and interpersonal processes. The understanding of patients with varying degrees of
these deficits exemplifies the value of our particular usage of the
terms empathy and projective identification. Deficits in any of the
more molecular elements tend to lead these patients to seek the
easiest route to adaptation via intrapsychic conflict resolution.

Since they can do this less easily on an intrapersonal basis, they tend to skew their intrapsychic processes in the direction of supportive containment by others. This presents major handicaps to these patients in the formation of empathic cognition. For this reason, they may be perceived as dumb, unresponsive, and so on—their reliance on projective identification and their dependency on others to secure pathways of empathy creates this often incorrect appearance.

Such seemingly hopeless patients are dependent upon the attachment to their treaters to provide those ego functions which facilitate their making rational sense out of the world. This may turn out to be a highly efficacious use of projective identification—i.e., to normalize experience—and should be distinguished from more pathological usages, such as those found in certain borderline and schizophrenic patients, and also in a broad class of patients who exhibit negative therapeutic reactions (to which we shall return later). However, once having developed projective identification as a partially successful mode of adaptation, the patient is loath to abandon it, since it leaves him in the position of employing defective empathic cognition (by virtue of the deficit) that is less adaptive. In this fashion, a dynamic linkage can result in which projective identification becomes a defensive process in the service of excluding reliance on the less effective empathic cognition.

The Problem of Over-Involvement

The term "over-involvement," frequently encountered in psychiatric hospitals, has both a colloquial and a technical meaning. The technical meaning derives largely from the social psychology and family systems literature, which is concerned with boundary violations and optimal patternings for social experiences. In this section, we will identify the forms of involvement which constitute clinical problems (and thus are labeled over-involvement; when there is no problem, there is only involvement).

"Over-involvement" inevitably implies a value judgment by the clinical observer. Its negative connotation denotes a failure of boundary maintenance, a neglect of a patient's psychodynamics, or an unwitting and perhaps unconscious pathological collusion between patient and staff member. To continue with our metaphor of the family paradigm, it is important to notice that in normative human development, there are multiple circumstances under which "over-involvement" is not only expectable but healthy and necessary. For example, Winnicott's (1956) notion of primary maternal preoccupation, which he says appears to be a quasi-psychotic state, does not imply over-involvement. We often talk about "normal symbiosis," in which we accept the idea that one who is more differentiated must meet the ordinary needs of one who is less so. The key point is the understanding of whether or not the involvement involves a developmental necessity, for identical processes may have facilitative consequences or may constitute over-involvement, depending on whether they are timed or mistimed in terms of the dictates of the life cycle. For these reasons it is difficult to discern whether a staff member's profound attachment to a patient represents for the patient a useful experience or a pathological tie reflecting the interference of the staff member's unmet needs. Of course, at times a patient can utilize a staff member's pathological tie for healing purposes. Examples of important, enduring, and facilitating involvements are not easy to identify during early stages of hospitalization; such distinctions require repeated observation over a lengthy period.

One type of over-involvement does occur when a staff member has become the recipient of a patient's projective

I. Paradigms and Processes

identification and then becomes the patient's advocate in the therapeutic community, in order to protect the patient from having to reintegrate the projected portion of the personality. The staff member may now be unwittingly acting in the service of the patient's defensive system. When this occurs, the staff member should be supervised accordingly.

Another type of over-involvement may parallel a vector of projective identification. We call this "systems over-involvement," and it may lead to severe harm to a patient. It occurs when a patient becomes involved almost exclusively with one particular staff member, so that other staff members are prevented from having a significant impact on the patient's life. It is not central to this process whether the tie is normative or pathological—the reason is less important than the reaction of the excluded staff. They may feel angry, jealous, and thwarted, and may be critical of the special staff member who is the recipient of the patient's favor or disfavor. The exclusive relationship is likely to evoke hostility toward the patient as well—in part, because of the prevailing idealization/devaluation process. When one person is identified as all good, others become persecutory figures from whom only the good object can protect the patient. The identified staff member is now in the middle of a complicated process in which he is inadvertently precipitating punitive staff reactions to the patient. In order to avoid this impasse and to avoid being split-off from a well-functioning unit, the over-involved dyad may temporarily have to reintroject powerfully valenced elements that have been displaced onto others. This is helpful to the extent that the therapeutic alliance embedded within the relationship can tolerate such difficult feelings and continue to exist.

An example of a systems over-involvement follows. A late adolescent, female schizophrenic patient was on a transitional unit, in preparation for discharge from the hospital into the surrounding community, where preparations had been made to accommodate her in continued psychotherapy and day treatment programs. Frightened by the impending change after five years of hospitalization, she developed a close involvement with her ward group administrator, centering around skirmishes over statuses; at times she transparently tried to provoke the administrator to protectively restrict her from activities she sought but feared. The involvement represented a tie to the familiar hospital and the protection it afforded and was also her preferred characteristic pattern for mobilizing significant others to contain and hence help her with her own antisocial and self-destructive tendencies. Thus, the pattern was adaptive, with a history of success in eliciting protection, despite the outward trappings of rebellion and obstinance imposed upon the manifest relationship. In this case, however, the staff on the transitional unit could not respond in the same way as the staff on a long-term unit. They asserted that the relationship was deleterious, in part because of the patient's insistence on having the administrator make every important decision concerning her fate. Accustomed to being heavily relied upon by outgoing patients, the staff punished the patient by inconsistently enforcing rules. At this point, the administrator recognized his responsibility in bringing about the situation and insisted upon a more limited relationship with the patient. He also insisted that the patient bring her diverse problems to a variety of staff members for clarification and resolution. At this time, the patient developed a deeper repertoire of characteristically stormy involvements with other staff, and a more benign discharge process was effected.

The Negative Therapeutic Reaction

In discussing the negative therapeutic reaction, Valenstein (1973) described persons whose attachment to pain is primary, signifying an original attachment to painful and inconstant objects. Early object experiences fail to become consolidated into love and trust; rather, early affects are aggressively tinged and through repetition define subsequent object relations, crystallizing in an adult formation of attachment to pain and chronic distrust of benevolent figures. This stance is maintained both as a defense and as an instinctually charged concomitant of object relations. On this early substratum may be built more sophisticated self and object experiences beyond the oral phase; thus, object relations proceed from this foundation of failed need gratification and later tend to be organized around age-related derivatives that echo the primary attachment to pain and suffering. The condensed amalgam of these developmental experiences becomes mobilized and played out in the pain and degradation of the transference neurosis or transference psychosis.

There are serious problems in the hospital-based treatment of these patients, calling for an approach that incorporates multiple staff members in order to prevent therapeutic impasse. Valenstein notes that the major disturbance in self and object relations is a reflection of an early preverbal ego defect, which is thus not accessible to psychoanalytic interpretation. These patients often stalemate their individual therapists. Therapy causes havoc because the patients do not allow anyone to metabolize their rage, remaining stable and untouched by nurturance. Such patients are also resistant to experiential nonverbal measures, which threaten to jeopardize their primary attachment to pain. They struggle to impress others with how unnecessary the experience of positive affect is to them, as if seeking to condition others to respond fearfully when wishing to express concern. When a therapist does express concern, the patient experiences comforting rage, which paradoxically both binds him to the therapist and simultaneously tears him away. In the psychiatric hospital, a way must be found to gain some leverage so that the patient can come to appreciate the way he habitually abuses other people while realizing a fulfilling emotional need.

The negative therapeutic reaction is a regularly occurring feature of the psychopathology of many of the patients seen in long-term residential settings. Such patients require firm management in order to contain their often dangerous acting out yet employ the firm management as a pathway to the establishment of preferred frustrating relationships. To the patient, such frustration does not represent limit setting—rather, it is a kind of homing beacon to the primary maternal object, and is masochistically sought after while fought against.

In treating such patients, we seek to provide the necessary complement of relationships that will allow for a minimization of the repetitive striving for painful reenactment. Such a likelihood is enhanced when the unit leadership understands that the patient's intrapsychic economy is organized around aggression that requires for its masochistic fulfillment a person who lends himself to being victimized by the projection or introjection of hostility. The phenomenon is minimized when several staff members alternately fulfill the function for the patient, until the patient no longer needs to create such relationships. This may be signaled to unit leadership when the patient finds someone in the milieu who, through a higher level capacity for empathy, understands the patient's needs and responds with nurturance in a fashion that does not prompt the preverbal repetition.

Supervision

One advantage of the type of clinical theoretical model presented here is its helpfulness in highlighting specific technical skills that must be acquired by hospital staff members. One issue of supervision we want to address is that of the front-line personnel (nurses, psychiatric assistants, occupational therapists, and so on). The supervisor must, of course, understand the dynamic interpersonal processes which we have described, not only in order to help the patients but also in order to set in motion brisk and timely ward operations. It is not necessary, however, for the frontline personnel to have an explicit conceptual understanding of the dynamic processes as long as the transactions with a particular patient (often erroneously called countertransference reactions) are subject to peer and supervisory scrutiny. Thus, the supervisor helps tease out interpersonal phenomena and allows himself to become an additional receptacle for projected mental content (Fleming and Benedek 1964), which can be worked through for the patient's ultimate benefit. In that way, the supervisor functions to restore a consensual reality orientation which serves to minimize the deleterious potential of ritualized interpersonal transactions.

The issue of supervision of the individual psychotherapy dyad has parallels to the process just described. An important difference is that the supervisor of the dyad should consciously assist the therapist in identifying and learning about the dynamic processes involved. For instance, a particularly important time in some treatments occurs when the therapy has stalled. While this can occur for a variety of reasons, it sometimes results because a therapist has unwittingly initiated a projective identification with a patient, who has come to bear the disowned and unwanted aspects of the therapist. The supervisory process should involve a sensitivity to the Janusian aspects of such an interpersonal event—i.e., the projective identification may be for the psychic benefit of the therapist and not the patient. There is often a re-representation of the dynamics of the therapy in the relationship with the supervisor (termed "parallelisms" in the psychoanalytic literature—Gediman and Wolkenfeld 1980), which may be discerned over a period of time by the kind of strain associated with the supervisee's insisting on a particular point of view to the exclusion of any other and insisting that the supervisor accede to such a point of view. The supervisor's task then is to untangle the entire process so that the therapist can be freed of the controlling aspect of the unconscious incorporation and identification which has occurred. Once having recognized the process, the therapist need not confront the patient; rather, the supervisor should gradually assume the responsibility for the reorganization of the projected elements so that the therapist can continue to bring them to consciousness gradually.

Conclusion

We will conclude with some comments on the importance of these concepts for understanding certain aspects of the relationship between the processes operating at the level of the patient-therapist dyad and those operating at the more molar level of the hospital community: Of major importance for the individual therapist working in an inpatient setting is an understanding of both the dynamics of the patient's personality and the interaction between the dyad and the rest of the community. Synthesizing the diverse aspects of the patient's personality system can be facilitated by paying close attention to the phasic patterning of various dyadic and group relationships that the patient forges in the hospital. This point has not been heavily stressed in the clinical literature, which tends to focus on the impact of individuals within larger group contexts. More attention should be paid to the natural history of well-functioning therapeutic dyads and the way in which they must integrate with and be integrated by the rest of the hospital context. One of the principles of supervision which derive from this point of view is that it is important for the dyadic supervisor to be aware of the broader psychosocial context of the patient's milieu. As discussed, the supervisor may become involved in recreating (in a new dyad with the therapist) some of the identical dynamics played out on the unit. We do not believe that the supervisor should didactically give the therapist a conceptual framework for such processes. This is better accomplished through formal seminars and through ongoing clinical activity led by the clinical unit chief. We wish to emphasize, rather, that when the supervisor unwittingly inculcates the notion that the psychotherapy occurs in a hermetically sealed context, this is likely to undermine the overall hospital-based treatment of the severely disturbed patient.

Finally, we wish to note that processes analogous to those occurring at the level of the dyad (patient and therapist) and small group (patient among front-line staff) can be observed at the level of the larger group (the unit and overall hospital community) (Edelson 1970). We refer here to the oft-observed phenomenon wherein a unit's processes reflect a basic assumptive position (Bion 1959) that is antithetical to sound patient care. In such instances, the clinical-executive leadership of the hospital or division must be able to diagnose the potentially serious disruption of task performance. Examples of events requiring intervention are the extrusion of patients, excessive and pathological sexual behaviors, or shifts to patterns of excessive work orientation. Supervision at this level is essential, because the pertinent dynamics can potentially ripple throughout the entire hospital system, leading to an overall shift to a fight mode or multiple enactments of the split-off content in diverse patient cohorts.

References

Basch, M. (1983). Empathic understanding: A review of the concept and some theoretical considerations. *Journal of the American Psychoanalytic Association* 31:101–26.

Beres, D. (1968). The role of empathy in psychotherapy and psychoanalysis. *Journal of the Hillside Hospital* 117:362–69.

———& Arlow, J.A. (1974). Fantasy and identification in empathy. *Psycho-analytic Quarterly* 43:26–50.

Bergman, A., & Wilson, A. (1984). Thoughts about stages on the way to em-pathy and the capacity for concern. In J. Lichtenberg, M. Bornstein, and D. Silver, Eds., *On Empathy*. Hillsdale, NJ: Analytic Press.

Berkowitz, D., Shapiro, L., Zinner, J., & Shapiro, E. (1979). Concurrent family treatment of narcissistic disorders in adolescence. In J. Howells, ed., *Advances in Family Psychiatry*, Vol. I. New York: International Universities Press.

Bion, W. (1959). *Experience in Groups.* New York: Basic Books.

Edelson, M. (1970). *Sociotherapy and Psychotherapy.* Chicago: University of Chicago Press.

Fleming, J. & Benedek, T. (1964). Supervision: A method of teaching psycho-analysis. *Psychoanalytic Quarterly* 33:71–96.

Fliess, R. (1942). Metapsychology of the analyst. *Psychoanalytic Quarterly* 11:211–227.

Freud, S. (1921). Group Psychology and the Analysis of the Ego. *Standard Edition* 18:65–144.

Friedman, L. (1969).The therapeutic alliance. *International Journal of Psycho-analysis* 50:139–53.

Gunderson, J. Defining the therapeutic processes in psychiatric milieus. *Psychiatry* (1978). 41:327–35.

Gediman, H.K., & Wolkenfeld, F. The parallelism phenomenon in psychoa-nalysis and supervision: Its reconsideration as a triadic system. *Psychoanalytic Quarterly* (1980). 49:234–55.

Gedo, J. (1979) *Beyond Interpretation.* New York: International Universities Press.

———*Advances in Clinical Psychoanalysis.* New York: International Universities Press, 1981.

Giovacchini, P. (1979) *The Treatment of Primitive Mental States.* Northvale, NJ: Jason Aronson.

Goldstein, M., & Jones, J. (1977). Adolescents and familial precursors of borderline and schizophrenic conditions. In P. Hartocollis, ed., *Borderline Personality Disorders.* New York: International Universities Press.

Gossett, J.R., and Lewis, J. M. (1983). *To Find a Way: The Outcome of Hospital Treatments of Disturbed Adolescents.* Northvale, NJ: Jason Aronson.

Greenson, R.R. (1960) Empathy and its vicissitudes. *International Journal of Psychoanalysis* 41:418–24.

Grinberg, L. (1962). On a specific aspect of countertransference due to the patient's projective identification. *International Journal of Psychoanalysis* 43:436–40.

Grotstein, J. (1981) *Splitting and Projective Identification.* Northvale,NJ; Jason Aronson.

Gunderson, J., Will, O., & Mosher, L., eds. (1983). *Principles and Practices of Milieu Therapy.* Northvale, NJ: Jason Aronson.

Hill, L.B. (1955). *Psychotherapeutic Interventions in Schizophrenia.* Chicago: University of Chicago Press,

Hoffman, M. (1978). Toward a theory of empathic arousal and development. In M. Lewis & L. Rosenblum, eds., *The Development of Affect. New York:* Plenum Publishing Corp.

Hong, M.H. (1978). The transitional phenomena: A theoretical integration. *Psychoanalytic Study of the Child* 33:47–79.

Kernberg, O. (1975). *Borderline Conditions and Pathological Narcissism.* Jason Aronson,

———(1976). *Object Relations Theory and Clinical Psychoanalysis.* New York: Jason Aronson.

——(1980). The individual in groups. In *Internal World and External Reality*. Northvale, NJ: Jason Aronson.

Klein, M. (1941). Notes on some schizoid mechanisms. In *Envy and Gratitude & Other Works 1946–1963*. New York: Delacorte Press, 1975.

Levenson, E. (1972). *The Fallacy of Understanding: An Inquiry into the Changing Structure of Psychoanalysis*. New York: Basic Books.

Lidz, T. 1968. *The Person*. New York: Basic Books.

——(1973). *The Origin and Treatment of Schizophrenic Disorders*. New York: Basic Books.

——Fleck, S., & Cornelison, A. (1965.) *Schizophrenia and the Family*. New York:

International Universities Press.

Loewald, H.W. (1960). On the therapeutic action of psychoanalysis. *International Journal of Psychoanalysis* 41:16–33.

Mahler, M., Pine, F., & Bergman, A. (1975.) *The Psychological Birth of the Human Infant*. New York: Basic Books.

Maxmen, J.S., Tucker, G.T., & Lebow, M. (1974). *Rational Hospital Psychiatry: The Reactive Environment*. New York: Brunner/Mazel.

Ogden, T. (1981). On projective identification. *International Journal of Psychoanalysis* 68:357–373.

Olden, C. (1958). Notes on the development of empathy. *Psychoanalytic Study of the Child* 13:505–318.

Pao, P. (1979). *Schizophrenic Disorders*. New York: International Universities Press.

Pine, F. (1976). On therapeutic change: Perspectives from a parent-child model. *Psychoanalysis and Contemporary Science* 5:537–569.

——(1979). On the pathology of the separation-individuation process as manifested in later clinical work: An attempt at delineation. *International Journal of -Psychoanalysis* (60:225–42)

Reiss, D. *The Family's Construction of Reality*. Cambridge, MA: Harvard University Press, 1981.

Rubenstein, R., & Lasswell, H.D. *The Sharing of Power in a Psychiatric Hospital.* New Haven, CT: Yale University Press, 1966.

Schafer, R. (1959) Generative empathy in the treatment situation. *Psychoanalytic Quarterly* 28:342–73.

Schafer, R. (1968) *Aspects of Internalization.* International Universities Press, 1968.

Slap, J.W., & Levine, F.J. (1978) On hybrid concepts in psychoanalysis. *Psychoanalytic Quarterly* 47:499–523.

Slater, P. (1966). *Microcosm: Structural, Psychological, and Religious Evolution in Groups.* New York: Wiley.

Stanton, A.H., & Schwartz, M.S. (1954). *The Mental Hospital.* New York: Basic Books.

Sullivan, H.S. (1962). *Schizophrenia as a Human Process.* W.W. Norton & Company.

Tolpin, M. (1971). On the beginnings of a cohesive self: An application of the concept of transmuting internalization to the study of the transitional object and signal anxiety. *Psychoanalytic Study of the Child* 26:316–52.

Tucker, G. Therapeutic Communities. In Gunderson et Al. (1983). *Principles and Practices of Milieu Therapy.* Northvale, NJ: Jason Aronson.

Valenstein, A. (1973). On attachment to painful feelings and the negative therapeutic reaction. *Psychoanalytic Study of the Child* 28:365–92.

Waelder, R. (1930). The principle of multiple function: Observations on over-determination In S. Guttman, ed., *Psychoanalysis: Observation, Theory, Application.* New York: International Universities Press.

Winnicott, D.W. (1953). Transitional objects and transitional phenomena Primary maternal preoccupation. In *Collected Papers: Through Pediatrics to Psychoanalysis. New York:* Basic Books.

———(1960). The theory of the parent-infant relationship. *International Journal of Psychoanalysis* 41:585–95.

Wynne, L.C., & Singer, M.T. (1963) Thought disorder and family relations of schizophrenics: A research strategy. *Archives of General Psychiatry* 9:191–98.

Zinner, J., & Shapiro, R. (1972). Projective identification as a mode of perception and behaviour in families of adolescents. *International Journal of Psychoanalysis* 53:523–30.

CHAPTER 4

THEORIZING ABOUT THEORIZING:
AN EXAMINATION OF THE CONTRIBUTIONS OF
WILLIAM I. GROSSMAN TO PSYCHOANALYSIS

William I. Grossman's contributions to psychoanalysis are studied in the light of an interest that suffuses his papers: the remarkably complex ways an analyst develops his or her mind in order to become an effective analyst. Grossman sought to detail the many subtle factors infusing Freudian theory, from its initial sources to its consolidation as a system, to its embrace in the mind of an analyst who will use it, and on to the many iterations of its progress on the way to being applied in the clinical situation. This progression assumes a recognition of the analyst's need to be at once both experiencer and observer. Implicit in the attempt to understand another is a self-reflective taking of oneself as an object of analysis. How an essential tension is worked out between the subjective and objective points of view is an issue that pervades Grossman's writings. This is but one instance of a larger tendency characterizing his ideas—thinking psychoanalytically about psychoanalysis itself. Factors he implicated in being a contemporary Freudian analyst are then taken up.

When William Grossman so unexpectedly passed away on June 22, 2006, psychoanalysis lost one of its giants, a formidable thinker and theorist. His work has to date not attracted the attention it merits, for a variety of reasons. One is his singular writing style; this will be taken up toward the end of this paper. A second is his refusal, carried through to the end, to reduce complicated psychoanalytic issues to factors easily grasped by the reader; he was determined to consider psychoanalytic ideas in their native complexity. Even as he tackled issues of inherent difficulty, in his hands, they seemed to become more difficult while they were in the throes of being clarified. A third reason is that he was reluctant to write papers on topics of the moment, for he was an avid reader and recognized how often old ideas return in new garb, making it necessary, in building a psychoanalytic formulation, to include history lest we repeat it. Still a fourth reason, and perhaps the most important, is the unfamiliarity of most readers with the consistent, well-developed program that undergirds and is interwoven throughout his papers.

In a bid to remedy this lack of attention, I will attempt to make some of his programmatic thinking available to a wider psychoanalytic audience. My challenge here is to convey the fertility and depth of his ideas in a necessarily abridged form without compromising the richness of his thinking. Since meeting this challenge fully is not possible, reading this paper is no substitute for a careful study of the original sources.

At no time did Grossman attempt to build a new psychoanalytic system or to integrate different psychoanalytic theories. He stayed firmly within the Freudian tradition. Yet he was acutely interested in novelty, in extending rather than confirming the Freudian legacy. In his pursuit of novelty, Freudian thinking is as if a backdrop to his investigations, so much so that at times it is difficult to grasp the links between the Freudian past and the new and original ideas he tackled. But it is always present, at times requiring a textual reading of underlying connections rather than of manifest assertions.

Without great fanfare, Grossman constructed original propositions set within Freudian theory. As I have intimated and hope to show, they constitute a coherent system. Each paper he wrote alludes directly or indirectly to the history of his own ever developing and accreting ideas. Thus, his papers must be understood as a whole. Any one on its own tells an incomplete story. They map onto one another, assume an understanding of what has been demonstrated in other papers, and extend proposals the reader unfamiliar with those other papers may not even realize are part of the argument being developed. Core ideas threading their way from paper to paper are, in this way, often hidden, recessed beneath the surface appearance of seemingly new issues. A retrospective reading can most accurately perceive this state of intellectual integrity. In all these pursuits, he was invariably "theorizing about theorizing" in ways analogous to how David Rapaport spent his career "thinking about thinking." However, unlike Rapaport, Grossman focused always on how minds operate in clinical analysis. The assumption he brought to his work was a particular observational context—the simultaneity of the analyst analyzing and the patient being analyzed. The two are inseparable; one cannot exist without the other, in life or in theory. One mind requires the other if either is to be launched into conceptual existence.

Theorizing about Theorizing

Grossman conveyed that it is easy to theorize about clinical matters psychoanalytically, but not so easy to consistently maintain a psychoanalytic perspective whose interpretive objects include the acts of the analyst himself theorizing while working clinically. Grossman thereby depicted a radical disjunction between theorizing that is self-reflective—that takes itself as its own object of investigation, and so itself is subject to psychoanalytic considerations—and theorizing that uses psychoanalysis to parse the world as most scientists would, by organizing inferences and amassing evidence. When rigorously pursued, as it is throughout

Grossman's oeuvre, the former is distinctively psychoanalytic and yields a view of clinical processes and psychoanalytic theory very different from what the latter offers.

In developing what he calls a "clinical view of theory," he assumes that prevailing psychoanalytic theories are begotten by theorists with minds in conflict and then picked up and interpreted by analysts likewise in conflict. Every clinician is seen as a theorist operating in a state of duress when, with an analysand, the analyst is subject to varying pressures to accept one line of thinking rather than another. The relationship he elaborates between theory and theorizer is reminiscent of Searle's critique (1992) of the idea that the mind functions like a computer—to wit, because even if it mostly does, the comparison fails because a sentient mind is required to interpret the digitized readout of the final product. Psychoanalysis studies the theorizer in the act of theorizing in order to understand how psychoanalytic theories can be learned and then usefully applied. As Grossman says, "I am not discussing the value of theory, the need for theory, the proofs of theory, the 'proper' uses or misuses of theory. Instead, I am reviewing the multiple ways in which the analyst's theories influence his/her mental function and are responsive to the clinical situation" (Grossman 1995c, p. 887).

The constancy and preeminence of the analyst's self-reflection is crucial for understanding the theorizer. Grossman (1967) introduced this theme early on, and it permeates all of his later thinking. This is a self-reflection different, say, from the skill pictured by Paul Gray; rather, it is a fundamental analytic tool, a hierarchically organized and multiply transformed composite with complex mental representations at several levels. The analyst's relentless self-reflection runs parallel to the ability to formulate meaningful interpretations: "when the self-analyzing analyst is interpreting the productions of the patient in conflict, both subjects are at least double systems whose relationships are a function of representation and translation" (Grossman 1995b, p. 8). There are many seductive opportunities to bypass such necessary self-reflection, but a high price is paid when this occurs during clinical activities. Grossman's self-reflection presumes an understanding of the processes at work within one's own unconscious conflicts, defenses, compromises, and wishes. At the same time, the analyst struggles to understand the same features in the mental life of the analysand and how these two streams meet in the construction of an analytic process: "Although Freud and analysts since Freud have included many kinds of issues and interests in psychoanalytic psychology, we might speak of the psychoanalytic method and theory as addressing a core issue. This issue is the effort to describe the analyst's use of his or her self-observation as a tool in the study of his or her patients and their self-observations. Clinical interpretation tests the picture of the mind that is created" (Grossman 1993, p. 192).

Psychoanalytic theories themselves were to Grossman (1992a,1995b) a combination of, but more than a set of, written principles that are right or wrong (rational), useful or not (pragmatic), adhered to or not (endorsed by what he termed, following Ludwik Fleck [1935], a "thought community"). They also become conscious and unconscious internal objects subject to a bewildering array of influences. It is virtually impossible to tease out where the logic of a public theory (Sandler 1992) ends, and that of a private theory begins. The clinical analyst's theories as they are used are far more personally elaborated than given. Public theories are, for the most part, systematically elaborated, but then, in a second step, they must be interpreted as patched together out of the motley array of an analyst's experiences, conflicts, allegiances, and hidden dialogues, with a dizzying array of internal objects exerting influence. The second step is the more important to grasp. The first is simple. One has only to read, listen, and allow oneself to be influenced. (It is, of course, not possible to know all the influences behind what Grossman calls "the analyst's views about mental reality.") Thus, questions of theory and technique are tangled up with the inevitability of subjective judgments that cannot be legislated by publicly elaborated theories. To be guided by public theories is to theorize psychoanalytically rather than to use psychoanalysis to analyze itself in order to grasp how minds work.

Grossman repeatedly insisted that even the most abstract theoretical concepts must be derived from and thus reflect the subjective experiences of both patients and analysts. No helpful theory can block or shunt aside a patient's subjective experience, which makes the generalizability of that theory a tricky undertaking. An example of such subjective origins, one of great interest to Grossman, is the enduring unconscious relationship the analyst, together with his theory, has to authority. Submission to authority contributes to adherence to, misapplication of, and rejection of theories, as well as to antitheoretical attitudes. Students of analysis inevitably learn theory as a form of received knowledge, some of which can be integrated, some of which is too jarring to the unconscious set of ideas already in place in the individual. The allegiance of any analyst to his theories as he applies them with his patients is always subject to the vagaries of transference to inner objects and to those around him. It is an important step for the developing analyst to recognize this and try to approach the challenge of theory in a manner more responsive to his developing clinical experience and less to the need to participate in one or another school of thought: "learning and teaching involve the transmission of knowledge concerning the application of a thought system. The system deals with theory and treatment as it is contextualized in the thought style of a group, the thought community. The therapist's ideas are subjective versions of some kinds of shared systems of ideas referring to theory and technique" (Grossman 2006, p. 87). In this sense, how the developing analyst learns theories parallels how the growing young adult learns about reality; both move from external to internal constraints and personalize their spin on what forms of inquiry and knowledge are necessary and useful in order to flourish within the constraints of adaptation. In his later papers, Grossman recognized the complex group origins of psychoanalytic theories and the role of thought communities in a theory's adoption and claim to objectivity. What *is* true and why, as contrasted with what *is held to be* true and why, are quite different things, and their implications branch off in different directions. The former, the natural province of philosophy, is peripheral to psychoanalysis, though at times it is brought to bear on psychological arguments and even held to steer clinical technique. The latter is more properly the focus of psychoanalysis and leads to the exploration of how and why a group coalesces and functions to determine standards of objectivity that hold the group and its signature theory together. Thus a thought community is created that gives the group's theory a transpersonal life of its own and an authority one level removed from any individual authority.

An individual analyst's relationship to authority is subtle and finds powerful expression in conflicts about how he can justify interventions to himself. As the analyst reaches into his memories in order to find such justifications, there is a regretful tendency to lose self-reflection and instead repeat something already known or done, thereby reducing open principles of technique to fixed rules for behavior. Justifying interventions in this way is both the cause and the effect of the kind of intrapsychic conflict that hinders an analysis. Doing so stands in sharp contrast to an authentic self-reflective psychoanalytic understanding. Once again, in such circumstances, the only possible antidote is continuous self-reflection, which allows the analyst to explore his own mind, his conflicts, and the uses of theory that ensue. The young analyst can thereby clear away obstacles to his development toward enhanced clinical effectiveness. It is an illusion to think that a new theory or technique can bypass this necessity. Since all observations and interventions are necessarily theory-laden, and the analyst's relationship to internalized authorities is largely unconscious, such self-reflection bears a heavy burden. Young analysts learn to understand, rely on, and nurture what can be thought of as a Freudian self, which, as I will show, is a complex web of fantasy.

Hierarchical Models of Freudian Psychoanalysis for Our Times

In "Hierarchies, Boundaries, and Representation in a Freudian Model of Organization," Grossman (1992b, 1993) explicated hierarchical thinking as central to the psychoanalytic way of making sense of a broad range of phenomena. He was convinced that this was how Freud represented psychoanalytic thought across the breadth of his many interests. This is one of the most telling and incisive investigations ever conducted into Freudian theory.

In this paper, Grossman boldly stated that Freud consistently used a hierarchical model of everything he sought to understand in making sense of nature's diversity. Although it appears that Freud's views are being revealed here, the possibility cannot be overlooked that they are as much Grossman's, or perhaps his even more. As so often happens when one interlocutor is deeply immersed in the ideas of another, their thoughts merge, and it is difficult to be precise about where the ideas of one begin and those of the other end. At any rate, Grossman held that this model served Freud as the touchstone of the traditional psychoanalytic method, the foundation of his theory, the core commitment from which all else followed. The model Grossman constructed, and attributed to Freud, allowed psychoanalysts for the first time to draw a conceptual boundary around traditional analysis. Thus, an abstract method of traditional analysis was defined and could be taught. No longer did analysts have to lean on affiliation to a school, the immediate surround of colleagues, or authorities cited in their papers in order to draw that boundary.

Freud's hierarchical method is architectural, not explicitly stated, and must be discerned. It does not leap out at the interpreter. Grossman puts it this way: "My purpose is to show that Freud presented a model by the use of rhetoric, analogies, metaphors, and his reflections on theory formation. Moreover, this model unifies the more abstract aspects of the theory and its clinical applications ... and ... when this model is recognized in Freud's work, the theory and the various stages of its development show a greater coherence" (Grossman 1993, p. 172).

The prototypical mind pictured here is a hierarchical structure of agencies, functions, and fantasy organizations. In the model Freud elaborated, each hierarchical level is recursively organized according to the same fundamental principles, yet the content is remarkably different as represented at the different levels. These fundamental principles include conflict, compromise, defense, representation, and reconstruction. Different content represented in dramatically different guises at different levels disguise these core principles. Across the boundaries of the mental system characterizing each level, translation of the contents of one system leads to their being represented in another. Grossman termed such varied content the "mind's products."

Repeated editing and translation account for many properties of the different systems represented at the various levels. Complexity results from the combination of relatively simple relations and the repetition of the same operations, reconstructed through interpretation. Grossman believed this way of modeling unites Freud's investigations into culture, religion, art, history, and clinical psychoanalysis.

Grossman's examination of theorizing as a psychoanalytic activity, and of the significance of hierarchical levels, went even deeper in a paper in which he introduced the stunning notion of "the psychoanalytic mode of thought" (Grossman 1998). This effort stands as a companion piece to the paper on hierarchies (Grossman 1992b, 1993), in that the psychoanalytic mode of thought is conceptualized as inherently hierarchical. In the 1998 paper, Grossman hypothesized that Freud's anthropological excursion in *Totem and Taboo* (1912–1913) is based on the same clinical psychoanalytic method expressed in the contemporaneous technical papers (most specifically, Freud 1912a,b). In doing so, Grossman suggested that there is a particular psychoanalytic mode of thought, characterizing the form of investigation Freud applied in a variety of contexts—the understanding of clinical material and other clinical concerns, the nature of mental organization, and various sociocultural processes.

The psychoanalytic mode of thought organizes every hierarchical level of investigation, ranging from the intrapsychic conflict observed in clinical analysis to the development of the highest intellectual forms of human thought. As in the earlier paper, hierarchies are arrayed in a series and feature defense, conflict, and compromise at every level, operations that transform the content of one level into the content of levels of ever higher complexity, which then act recursively to reorder past experiences. Processes of transformation alter the coding of content but maintain a dynamic relationship between levels. Reconstruction, as a way of understanding these transformations, becomes a central feature of the psychoanalytic mode of thought.

It cannot be emphasized enough that the psychoanalytic mode of thought is not specific to individuals self-identified as psychoanalysts. Grossman holds that the psychoanalytic mode of thought is central to Freud's thinking, but many analysts do not employ it, and many nonanalysts do. For example, Grossman was excited by top-notch historians of science and certain neuroscientists, admired how they could reconstruct the stages of the history of a particular idea or theme, with iterations of the idea segmented at different eras and in different ways, and found in their grasp of the evolution of their scientific knowledge the exact features of the psychoanalytic mode of thought he described as originating with Freud. The idea that some scholars in other disciplines think psychoanalytically like Freud, while some analysts do not, is at first glance counterintuitive, but, on second thought, it grabs the imagination. It opens doors into how higher-level bodies of thought can be approached in a way that gets behind what each purport to be and say. Historians of science use hierarchical arrangements, much as Freud did, and develop models that are remarkably proximate to the psychoanalytic mode of thought. They share the same hierarchical boundary concept. As Grossman (1993) puts it, "The idea of boundaries between levels in a hierarchy is an important concept. . . . translation is one of the relationships defining the boundary. That is, the boundary is a conceptual boundary characterized by the different organizations of the systems so that one must be translated into the other . . . " (p. 179).

Grossman believed that the biological side of Freud's complemental series was such a boundary concept and provided a basis that supported the psychoanalytic mode of thought. Thus, biology is first and foremost to a psychoanalyst an object of thought in theory (not to be mistaken for a material reality), one that promotes his ability to make important clinical and conceptual distinctions. It is not necessary for the clinical analyst to grasp specific biological processes. It is important, though, that the analyst know how these processes work, because this provides an analogical set of ideas that can stimulate the analyst to think in new, possibly unforeseen ways. This is what is meant by biology as an object of thought.

Once outlined and clarified, the psychoanalytic mode of thought can be transported to a wide variety of situations and stands on its own as a way of thinking. It can be taught and learned. It spans the clinical and nonclinical arenas, and in this sense can serve as a very real bridge between psychoanalysis and related forms of thought. Thus, the psychoanalytic mode of thought is located on the border of progress and preservation. Through its gates, psychoanalysis can trace other key boundaries—for example, between traditional and nontraditional psychoanalysis, psychoanalysis and neuroscience, theory and practice. This allows for lucid exchanges, both within Freudian psychoanalysis and between it and its neighbors. Good conceptual boundaries help sharpen the positions on either side. The essentials of each can then be clearly defined and put forward for consideration. Grossman's articulation of the psychoanalytic mode of thought highlights how the past of psychoanalysis can be preserved in a way that underlines core continuities for its future

The Freudian Self

How an analyst conceives of an individual's self-description, including his own, is crucial to clinical psychoanalysis. The term *self* as an explanation of this has a long and contentious history, in and out of psychoanalysis. Grossman opposed conceiving the self as an entity and then trying to locate it with respect to other mental constructs. Instead, he chose to explain the significance and the very experience of the self by way of intrapsychic fantasy (Grossman 1982, 1984). The fantasies of the self constitute its significance and experience. Fantasy itself is unusual because it is both an aspect of mental organization and can transform it, inasmuch as fantasy underlies all conscious experience. The concept of the self is a special kind of fantasy: "the self-state . . . is everyday language about an everyday fantasy about a fantasized entity, the 'self'. . . It seems to be a concrete entity, and is treated like an experiential 'fact'. . . The self, then, is a special fantasy with its own language and referents" (Grossman 1982, pp. 925–926).

The complex fantasy of the self and its experience derives from both subjectively oriented clinical data and objectively oriented theory. As usual for Grossman, subjectivity and objectivity are fused into an overall explanation for a phenomenon, yet each maintains its own universe of explanation (Grossman 1991a). What makes the fantasy of the self special—it is different from any other fantasy—is that it is created and stretches along two conceptual axes. Both axes have two coordinates, one of subjectivity, the other of objectivity. The first axis joins the everyday personal experience of the self with the relation between the self and the world of things. For example, an individual's ideas about himself, to Grossman a theory of sorts, are everyday personal experiences. So are the delusions of a schizophrenic.

But for the analyst to construct this first axis properly, another type of theory must also be put into play, one that is different from a person's ideas about himself. This requires a second axis, one that is distinctively psychoanalytic. The concrete events of the clinical situation and the subjective experience of the patient are at one end of this axis, and a mosaic of systematic, theoretical concepts are at the other end. Both axes (the "everyday-personal-philosophical" and "the psychoanalytic-clinical-theoretical") contribute the type of experience that infuses the fantasies of the self and allows the analyst to tease apart multiple constructions in making sense of the clinical data.

During an analysis, Grossman proposes, three sorts of analytic construction stretch along both axes: "Freud constructed a psychoanalytic theory of mind, the analyst constructs the mind of the patient, and the patient constructs his own experience in speaking about himself. That these three activities have a similar form . . . is built into the psychoanalytic model of mental activity . . ." (Grossman 1982, p. 922). The analyst must first grasp how different each of these constructions is, and then make clinical sense of them to establish an interpretive line. Fantasies of the self, joining the two axes with these multiple constructions, now stand revealed as remarkably complex, condensing multiple theories, constructions, and viewpoints.

Grossman believes that important technical issues—tact, timing, dosage of interpretations—are at stake when the analyst conceives of the self either as a fantasy organization or as a structure. The understanding of fantasies of the self includes the analyst's participation in the unending equilibration between objectivity and subjectivity. In terms of clinical application, the analyst trying to understand what the patient means when he refers to himself in his associations must take the point of view of the patient, thereby affirming a unity between the subjectivity of the spoken present and the reconstructed past. At the same time, he must maintain a position of objectivity with respect to these subjective elements, striving for an objective view of his own subjective reactions to the patient, as well as of the patient's subjective communications.

The technical handling and interpretation of self-description are delicate matters. Self-description analyzed as fantasy brings many potential complications, such as stirring up narcissistic investments, the patient's need to protect his way of seeing things, or the emergence of anxiety, all of which may be missed when the analyst is guided by the theory of the self as an entity or endopsychically perceived state. These reactions are more accessible than when the self is conceived as a stable entity, because then they are seen as fixed attributes that limit the scope and effectiveness of interpretation.

For Grossman, then, the idea of self as structure is itself an analytic fantasy. The fantasy of an "actual structure" reflects quite complex meanings of observable organizations of the patient, but now condensed. The notion of an actual structure simplifies what is in the observable mix. This is why Grossman can say that the idea that psychoanalysis needs a self as structure is itself a fantasy, even while it reflects a misunderstanding. It is not that Freudian theory is inadequate. It is, rather, that it is misunderstood. Grossman aimed to show that the proposals offered by analysts who argue that a self as structure is needed do not update or refute Freud as much as they expose a misapplication of Freudian principles.

Perhaps Grossman's perspective on the self was a subtle response to the self psychology of Heinz Kohut, whose name receives only brief mention in the first self-as-fantasy paper (a favorable comment with respect to self-state dreams). It was published in 1982, when Kohut's influence on American psychoanalysis was at its apex. Despite its astuteness, however, the paper has to my knowledge not been mentioned alongside Loewald's well-known book review essay (1973) or other comparisons of traditional psychoanalysis and self psychology. Grossman was always generous to colleagues in print; it was not his style to directly criticize another analyst or theory. When in disagreement, he preferred to stipulate his position in great depth, and then allow readers to draw their own conclusions on the merits.

Such a model, of self as fantasy and as illuminated by the theory of fantasy, is an example of Grossman elaborating his own ideas within the bounds of Freudian theory. But while consistent with Freud, it also extends Freud's views into new areas. Grossman always made it clear that if Freud's views were to be extended, they must first be properly clarified. This was his method also in his investigation of female sexuality.

Female Sexuality

Freud's understanding of female sexuality was of great interest to Grossman. Objecting early on to the concept of penis envy, he showed that it collapsed central conflicts involving a sense of identity, narcissistic sensitivity, and problems with aggression, expressed in terms of general envy and a sense of worthlessness, inadequacy, damage, and deprivation (Grossman and Stewart 1976). Penis envy was a metaphor, Grossman noted, not a concrete guide for clinical interpretation. It was as if the metaphor had been reified and made into the blueprint of a stable universal fantasy. He was quite concerned (see Grossman and Simon 1969) about how analysts use and abuse metaphors and analogies in order to communicate their ideas in the language of theory. Given advancements in the psychoanalytic understanding of female sexuality over the last twenty-five years, it is now hard to imagine how a paper explaining this concreteness could once have been viewed as a strikingly innovative contribution.

His investigation of female sexuality deepened over time and became more subtle. He recognized that most controversies over Freud's ideas about female sexuality were not at bottom about sexuality; rather, they were echoes of other matters requiring clarification and more precise definition. Employing a textual reading of Freud's writings on the topic (Grossman 1976a), he showed why this was so. These controversies, which tended to interpret Freud as antagonistic to women, isolated specific problems and then assessed them out of context, apart from the conceptual matrix in which they were embedded.

It was this overliteral, concrete approach that Grossman worked to correct: "It is not the merit of particular ideas that interests us so much as their function in the process of creating a systematic theory. We have no arguments about whether any particular idea is sufficient in its own right, as no idea is. We take it for granted that Freud, read literally, is wrong in many respects with regard to his generalizations, assumptions, and conclusions about women, men, and human nature. However, his analyses of these matters are important for their function in the development of our current understanding of concepts . . ." (Grossman and Kaplan 1988, p. 344).

His sense of the prevailing incompleteness of understanding of this complex topic prompted him to show how Freud's controversial hypotheses on female psychology are optimally understood as deriving from three different methodological sources: (1) Freud's nontechnical and empirical, but not necessarily psychoanalytic, observations presented as clinical findings; (2) a normative reconstructed narrative of female development, the case for everyone and therefore no one; and (3) a technical view informed by clinical psychoanalytic observations that address particular dynamic processes in treatment and development, and that has no bearing on fixed outcomes (Grossman and Kaplan 1988). These technical views are not tied to the traits of (1) or the narratives of (2), but rather owe their allegiance to clinical processes. This analysis offers a much more accurate and sympathetic portrayal of the evolution of Freud's struggle to grasp these issues, his ever evolving attempt to understand female sexuality. Freud is presented at his scholarly best, questioning himself, assessing new lines of investigation—a more perspicacious view than blanket dismissals of Freud as blithely lost in this thicket.

The relationship between these three methodological trends is complicated, and it is useful to keep in mind that each yields a different vision concerning female sexuality. Each comes primarily from a different stage of Freud's thought, although in several of his papers they overlap as descriptions. It is easy to blur the three. Grossman and Kaplan note that Freud did not have a consistent voice concerning such matters.

Taken together, the three strands have historically been the basis for a general psychoanalytic grasp of female sexuality, but each expresses a particular view that from the perspective of another may be considered "wrong." When unraveled, however, the strands can be seen to reflect different stages of Freud's thought, allowing a clearer reading of Freud's multifaceted and evolving view of female sexuality. Formulations of female sexuality put forward by Freud can hence be seen as provisional, and his hypotheses can be argued pro and con much more readily. An excellent demonstration of how separating the three strands clarifies the psychoanalytic understanding of female homosexuality is presented in Auchincloss and Vaughan (2001).

How Psychoanalytic Controversies Illuminate Ideas in Conflict

In the anatomy of psychoanalytic controversies, Grossman found an opportunity to more deeply grasp the texture of theory. Psychoanalytic controversies, he noted, are complex and opaque events. Some lead to profound change beyond the contested ideas, while others simply disappear. The reasons for the survival of some lie beneath the manifest content of the ideas contested. On one level, Grossman was investigating two figures prominent in the history of psychoanalytic controversy—Wilhelm Reich (Grossman 1976b) and Karen Horney (Grossman 1986a). However, he used the controversies each kindled in order to address his primary focus, the forces determining how psychoanalytic ideas change over time. Comparing the controversies raised by Horney and Reich opens up the question of how psychoanalysis is to handle those who deviate from the mainstream. After all, most of Jung's "heretical" ideas would today seem tame, and the contemporary scientific world takes acupuncture, ESP, and meditation quite seriously.

Grossman believed that psychoanalytic controversies are waged over fundamental models disguised as specific problems. His working idea was that beneath the overt quarrels of any controversy, more fundamental ideas are in conflict, obscured behind the pyrotechnics of personal animosities, diversionary theoretical struggles, and group-centered debates that disguise rather than clarify what is really at issue. When these ideas are viewed from the distance provided by history, what was hidden by the manifest debates and then worked out can be seen more clearly. In this regard, Grossman drew a useful distinction between manifest and latent theoretical issues, paralleling the concept of manifest and latent clinical content. When controversies flare, underlying models that are on the cusp of revision can best be viewed.

Such was the case in the well-known controversy between Horney and Freud in the 1930s, which ostensibly was about the nature of female sexuality. Female sexuality became the manifest theoretical issue through which more fundamental but latent differences were argued and worked out. Grossman documents how the real struggle was over the role of biological models and their implementation in a clinical theory. Freud's model of biology was adaptational, with roots in the thought of Charles Darwin, Herbert

Spencer, and Hughlings Jackson. Horney's view of the relationship between biology and psyche was quite different. She rejected the concept of constitutional bisexuality and replaced it with "primary heterosexuality," thereby allowing conceptual space for "primary femininity." Her rejection of Freud's genetic point of view is actually an allegiance to a new view of the role of biology in development, a view that led to her revised understanding of the Oedipus complex and male and female development; it also laid the groundwork for the arrival on the psychoanalytic scene of a focus on preoedipal phenomena. After her, these ideas became largely commonplace and were accepted within the psychoanalytic mainstream.

Horney's fate was not to be shared by Wilhelm Reich. Grossman examines the latter's career, as he does Horney's, to arrive at a larger point about psychoanalysis. To evaluate a psychoanalytic oeuvre, the author's intentions, rooted in conflict, must be noted. Reich declared himself the true successor to Freud, the next Freud-like figure in psychoanalysis, since he alone drove the libido theory to its logical conclusions. Grossman views this as reflecting a flagrant, starkly narcissistic need. In telltale narcissistic fashion, Reich insisted that his contributions had to be accepted, and only on his terms. This created a controversy, but it was one of mixed value. Reich's reputation, Grossman believes, owes as much to his ability to ignite outrage as to the originality of his ideas. In *Character Analysis,* Reich (1933) advocated replacing the analysis of symptoms with the analysis of character. As we saw with Horney, Reich put forward ideas that today are uncontroversial. However, Grossman reads the book as a confused, overpersonalized work that repetitively and incorrectly insists how before its author, analysts analyzed symptoms, and, after him, character traits. Reich always put himself in front of the throngs he wanted to convert to his views, but instead he converted them into a firing squad. His theoretical ideas were invariably enmeshed within whatever personality nuances led to his need to promote controversy. It was, Grossman suspects, the failure of these ideas to create a controversy large enough to satisfy him that led to the later work on orgone boxes and the renunciation of his earlier Marxism. Contemporary psychoanalysis does not take Reich's ideas seriously, not because they do not merit investigation, but because he politicized his ideas by way of his insistent alienation.

Sadomasochism

The potentially destructive impact of reductionism of any type concerned Grossman. He contested any tendency to find simple answers to complex questions. Thus, when he turned to the important subject of sadomasochism, Grossman (1986b) brought out the futility of seeking a single source, cause, origin, or essence that would unite the many psychoanalytic ideas on the subject: "The term masochism is used to allude to a variety of developmental end-points for which we have no reason to assume a common developmental pathway. What is necessary is a better understanding of the developments of pleasures and sufferings and their relationship to cognitive development . . ." (p. 405).

The concept of sadomasochism is a product of the intersection of many threads (Grossman 1991b), including data from adult psychoanalysis, infant observation, and the study of abused children and traumatized adults. These streams of data then had to be studied from three perspectives: the functions of fantasy, the expression and regulation of aggression, and the role of pain in evoking specific behaviors. These are the specific psychological factors that infuse sadomasochism. Such an integrative formulation, so much more detailed than a reconstruction of early fantasies (reduction to linear explanation) or an embellished model of trauma (reduction to social explanation), bridges the conceptual divide between the mental life of early childhood and the complex mental structures of neurotics and adults with perversions and severe character disorders. Here Grossman spells out a version of Freud's complementary series, a conceptualization of how actual experience and psychological experience are simultaneous, in equilibrium with each other, and blend into any explanation, with particular emphasis on neurosis or trauma.

I would point out a subtle feature of the work on sadomasochism. On the surface, Grossman departs from his affinity for theorizing about theories and theoreticians and enters the more heavily trafficked world of describing a clinical syndrome. However, sadomasochism itself is secondary here to a variant of theorizing. The contribution in this case is the model, not what is said about sadomasochism, which is quite derivative, more so than any of Grossman's other contributions. It is as if he is fashioning a blueprint for how psychopathology in a broad sense ought to be studied, thereby showing how his ideas about theorizing and science can be pragmatically actualized. More than in any of his other work, Grossman mutes his own voice in the act of interpreting. This foray into sadomasochism relies heavily on the manifest content of what Freud said, his patois, rather than Grossman's interpretation of how Freud thought.

This is a highly original model that can usefully be applied not only to sadomasochism, but to other clinical pictures where aggression, fantasy, and trauma are deeply implicated, such as perversion or fetishism. Indeed, it can be applied as a more general model to psychopathology not focused so readily on aggression. This model resists reduction, integrates the biological with the psychological, suggests how pathological development can unfold, unites trauma with the role of fantasy, postulates an interplay between inner motivation and the external factors that determine its course, and provides conceptual space for contemporary psychological research findings, all without sacrificing the richness of Freudian thinking.

There are particulars in Grossman's model of sadomasochism, but these are less important than how these particulars operate within the model. Grossman posits three central assumptions: (1) pain and painful affects are sources of aggression; (2) the need to express and regulate aggression plays an important role in the development of psychic structure; (3) child abuse and trauma impair the ability to use fantasy for the mastery of impulses.

1. Traumatized children are known to provoke attacks on themselves and to attack others. Traumatized people, adults or children, respond to traumatic treatment with destructive and self-destructive behavior. Thus, what appears painful to an observer may be pleasurable to the traumatized individual. These painful (to the individual) activities can then become sources of pleasure and shape the development of sexuality. Painful experiences in children are often mediated by the reactions of caregivers to the children's aggression, making the relationship between early trauma and later development a complex issue. There are motives for self-injury that serve to control aggression, one of which is to obtain control over the object. The fate of the aggression becomes the model for superego formation.

2. The stereotyped, automatic, and repetitive behaviors characterizing the need to seek or inflict pain tend to not readily respond to analytic interpretation. Pain becomes a goal due to its relationship to aggression. Somatic pain is the source of aggression, just as stimulation of an erotogenic zone is a source of sexual pleasure. Pain and painful affect evoke aggression toward others, who are perceived as more powerful, dangerous, or threatening, and potentially

pleasurable experience (such as sexual activity) is recruited to the cause of preserving such crucial relationships, leading to the rise of sadomasochistic fantasy and related ways of managing aggression.

3. Fantasy is instrumental in a child's mastery of traumatic experience. When a child is abused, the workings of fantasy are impaired, and a ripple effect then implicates central ego functions in the sequelae of the abuse. A reversal of trauma in the adult incorporates a synthesis of object relations and bodily sensations into fantasy that serves as a corrective.

For Grossman, clearly, there is no simple, streamlined formula for understanding sadomasochism. Opposition to reductionism is seen as well in Grossman's investigation into the role and place of hierarchical thinking in Freud and, by extension, in psychoanalysis as a science.

Psychoanalysis and Scientific Inquiry

Inquiry into clinical methodology in all its incarnations fascinated Grossman. Using as a platform for his own views a discussion of a target paper by Howard Shevrin, he sought to specify the relationship between science and psychoanalysis (Grossman 1995a). Most discussions on experimentation and the testing of methodologies, he considered narrow and insufficiently thought out. Too often, he thought, advocates put forward their methodological preferences as unarguably superior to rival notions. But to Grossman, no method had a peremptory claim to universal superiority. He believed that identifying psychoanalysis as an exclusively interpretive discipline or as a subset of natural science is a retreat from many of its key aspects. As concepts, psychoanalysis and science share the feature of covering too many activities, interests, and points of view to be characterized by a single arm of epistemology. Thus, it is important to analyze the component features of each in order to understand their interrelationships, which when viewed in this way defy simple explanation.

The various methods available for use, necessary because of the limitations of any single one, do not necessarily fit well together. Too often, methodological synergy is invoked—to placate others in a pluralistic world or to salve one's scientific conscience—when the approach actually taken is thoughtlessly additive. The problem is to determine how methods and interests can be fitted to the domains they seek to investigate. When they are, psychoanalytic science is being done well, and it does not matter whether laboratory experiments or case descriptions generate the data. Neurobiology and narration are a priori on equal footing. The primary difference between them is how they are used and the level at which they are deployed in investigating psychoanalysis. To find the proper fit, though, psychoanalysis must be clearly defined, so that what is researched is in fact psychoanalysis and not something else. Grossman was insistent that psychoanalysis not turn itself into something that can be researched using methods appropriate only to other treatments. What is recognizable to the analytic clinician must be recognizable to the analytic researcher, and vice versa.

Ensuring that it is psychoanalysis (or one of its discrete features) being studied and not something else requires the articulation and sharing of an "observational context" for those who wish to engage in probative discussions and tests. Grossman's idea of an observational context allows two people in scientific dialogue to glimpse what the other is actually referring to, so that they minimize talking past each other; a shared conservational context is a prerequisite for dialogue free of category errors. This is a daunting challenge, but I believe the psychoanalytic mode of thought I have described above provides just such a context. To be sure, some comparative studies (some of them experimental) involve methods and interests that are not in themselves psychoanalytic. Yet psychoanalysis itself is not homogeneous in its activities and overall structure, and in fact some activities and structures attributed to it are not exclusively psychoanalytic. To be outside of psychoanalysis is therefore not an insoluble problem, as long as the observational context can be shared.

The challenge is then to coordinate—not integrate—diverse approaches to the acquisition of psychoanalytic knowledge. A scientific approach to the question of what psychoanalysis is and is not is possible only if methods, interests, goals, and domains are specified before an investigation proceeds. The sum total of investigations reflects the disunity of psychoanalysis; their subsequent coordination is the ongoing process of science in the best sense of the word. This way of thinking about science must be carefully distinguished (Grossman 2000b) from an alternative model in which the organization of mental function called metapsychology is derived from the basic aphasia / nervous system model introduced in Freud's *On Aphasia* (1891) to explain how sensory information is organized in the brain.

Once again Grossman theorizes about theorizing, noting that the onus is on the depth of the psychoanalytic investigator's thinking, which implicates his or her conflicts. Grossman joins philosophers like Feyerabend, Kuhn, and Lakatos in regarding science (in which he includes psychoanalysis) as primarily an endless human enterprise, not fundamentally a rational one.

Only the myopia induced by assuming the narrowest definition of science—a series of decisive experimental proofs—can lead analysts to overlook the degree to which many other factors (social prestige, epistemological preference) play a role in the development and acceptance of a theory. Grossman was very concerned about how advocates of one method simplify and caricature its rivals to score rhetorical points. The science of psychoanalysis is very much under the sway of the interplay between objectivity and subjectivity.

Subjectivity and Objectivity

There is an essential tension in psychoanalytic theory between the subjective and the objective points of view. Both must be taken into account in considering all of a patient's experiences. Any psychology that takes the patient's communication of subjective experience as a starting point will inevitably be immersed in this tension between subjectivity and objectivity. The analyst must strive to maintain a position of objectivity even as he plunges into the patient's subjectivity and his own. One of Grossman's favorite passages from Freud bears on this: "we shall have to investigate [the] system's psychological characteristics, and we shall do so once again by reference to the similar systems which we find constructed by neurotics. . . . the 'secondary revision' of the content of dreams. And we must not forget that, at and after the stage at which systems are constructed, two sets of reasons can be assigned for every psychical event that is consciously judged—one set belonging to the system and the other set real but unconscious" (Freud 1912–1913, p. 65). Here Grossman found in Freud his own bedrock view, that every event in a life, every judgment an analyst makes, must be assigned two facets—its own public bid for objectivity and the inevitable subjectivity that is built into the nature of psychoanalysis itself, married to the inescapable objectivity necessary to make sense of that subjectivity. Objectivity and subjectivity implicate and are suffused with one another.

Theories based on direct infant observation may attempt to evade this tension between subjective and objective points of view by assuming that observed behavior can be treated as equivalent to the infant's mental activities. This blurs the distinction between subjective and objective by converting subjective meaning into explicitly behavioral observations. By contrast, theories assuming the priority of irreducible subjectivity shirk the responsibility of looking for objectivity where it can be found.

What is necessary is not to balance the two perspectives, so as to integrate objectively obtained knowledge with the inevitably subjective nature of clinical psychoanalysis. This is a Solomon-like solution, cutting both into half for the sake of appeasing the demands of the principals. More to the point is to grasp the intricacies of their embedded and intertwined relationships.

In embarking on this, Grossman finds it useful to distinguish between conscious and unconscious theorizing. In doing so, he coins the useful term *inescapable objectivity* (Grossman, 2006) as a counterweight to the overreach of the currently popular notion of irreducible subjectivity. He feels that the meteoric rise of subjectivity minimizes the role of conscious and rational points of view. Subjectivity necessarily implicates a kind of objectivity that is established by the analytic pair, and that can be thought of as a kind of conjoint objectivity about subjectivity:

> ...psychoanalysis needs a counterpoint to the closed-in subjectivity of psychic reality... a kind of objectivity with regard to subjectivity of the therapeutic couple is established on the basis of shared conscious judgment and emotional response... we cannot do without some idea of objectivity and the idea that in some way our shared points of view point to some kind of objective reality" (Grossman 2006, p. 93).

Without the stabilizing effect of objectivity, subjectivity would become for the analyst a menace rather than what it is, a necessary asset invaluable in grasping the nature of his data.

166

Subjectivity covers a wide terrain, since the analyst at work dwells amid a welter of his own constructions. To Grossman, the analyst at work is always caught in the intersection of these constructions, each stemming from a different source, which are necessary input if what is happening in an analysis is to be understood. Constructions are an inevitable consequence of the analyst's mental activity, his only access to psychoanalytic data, and so should not be thought of as secondary to a perception of some un-reality. Each construction is composed of complex compromise formations. The past, the mind of the patient, and the analyst's theories (public and private) are all sources of the analyst's constructions, and these converge to have an effect on clinical decision making. At times, the cascade of constructions threatens to overwhelm the analyst's ability to make rational sense of what he does and understands while analyzing. This is why there must be a tropism toward objectivity. Rationality, according to Grossman, is possible only because there is a stable backdrop, a world of objectivity, largely beyond the reach of these constructions, but there—as a buttress to ensure that they can be drawn into the psychoanalytic mode of thought.

When this trade-off is replaced by the illusions of a factual objectivity free of subjectivity, psychoanalysis becomes a caricature of itself, a way of thinking with a veneer but no inside, a way of conceiving behaviors that are formulaic and lack any justification other than the tyranny of rules and prescriptions. Objectivity, when it stands apart from its origins in subjectivity, is usually a signal that oversimplification is at work and crucial data are being overlooked. Mere belief can thus parade destructively as an objectivity resistant to deeper scrutiny.

And what if this sense of the role of construction is accepted at face value? One can then say that my interpretation of Grossman's ideas is itself a construction, and that my own compromise formations and set of unconscious loyalties, different from those of Grossman, invade the ideas of this paper, making it as much about me as about him. It is not a problem that this paper is really about me, caught by the reader in the act of interpreting Grossman. The problem appears only when this consideration is overlooked, and my paper is read as an objective explanation of Grossman's views. But Wilson interpreting Grossman does not realize any finality, and things do not stop there. As this paper is read, the reader is constructing a version of my construction of Grossman. Yet there is still an original Grossman beyond my construction. (It is not hard to see why reading original sources is so crucial.) Grossman's understanding of how psychoanalytic knowledge is constructed infuses my paper. Envisioning how I construct Grossman, and how the reader constructs me, is consistent with how clinical psychoanalysis parses the psychological processes it strives to account for.

How Grossman Wrote About Psychoanalysis

I alluded at the outset of this paper to Grossman's singular writing style. His writings demand of the reader a certain kind of interpretation now to be described. If the reader of his papers looks for knowledge or technical tips to be taken away, as a gourmet chef might consult a cookbook for instructions and measured ingredients to get a dish just right, he is doomed to frustration, amid a pervasive sense that there is more here than can be readily grasped. There are few proclamations. A reader's hunger for answers is not gratified; rather, the reader is pushed toward another kind of appetite—for the inherent value of eloquent inquiry into ever deeper questions.

Grossman's writings have a remarkably high ratio of new ideas to canonical text, if such a formula can be imagined. At times, they resemble telegraphic speech in which the speaker assumes, often mistakenly, that the listener can follow his reasoning, when to follow his words is an enormous effort, because of the wealth of meaning compressed into minimal speech. These writings, tautly composed, require an interpretive approach like that needed to understand a well-crafted poem. There is a tightness in the relationship between ideas and text that requires focused attention, in conjunction with a relaxation of the urge to know too soon. Grossman's ideas must be seen through to, actively discovered rather than passively received, and this often requires several readings.

A psychoanalytic orientation means to Grossman that a clinical inference is not complete unless it relentlessly takes itself as an object. Any drift away from this reflectiveness is likely to interrupt a concatenating chain that is in perpetual motion, a kind of reductio ad infinitum whose only end is the limits of the intellect. This vision of psychoanalytic thought accounts for why each of his papers presents a mounting crescendo of ideas. Each sentence contains a new idea that reorganizes the idea of the preceding sentence and prepares for another new idea in the next. This recursive chain proceeds until the paper ends, the reader bumping into a virtual "to be continued" sign. No idea stands still in Grossman's writing for very long. Each new idea adds a layer of additional significance to the preceding ideas, as if understanding naturally exists in a slow upward spiral. Ideas the reader locks into as he reads along morph slowly into something else. Ideas are developed, not frozen once stipulated. The reader must learn to suspend the hope that once something is clearly understood, that understanding will remain stable going forward. This is a style that requires getting used to.

In Grossman's writings, different conceptual levels require translation into one another, exemplifying the same processes that characterize the psychoanalytic mode of thought. Grossman, in relation with his reader, is akin to the analyst at work interpreting levels of analytic material, who is likewise akin to the Freudian theorist with his multiple hierarchical axes. The psychoanalytic mode of thought cannot be turned off. It organizes everything Grossman reads, writes, says, and does in the professional arena.

Coda: On Identifying Oneself

Although what is entailed in being a Freudian analyst was never addressed at length by Grossman, the question nevertheless preoccupied him, and his views on the subject are to be found throughout his papers. Some principles grafted together from various snippets may help me focus my inquiry here. In Freudian thought, Grossman discovered a great deal of curiosity and openness, not requiring an acceptance on faith of data, propositions, or systems. Being Freudian, Grossman felt, includes openly and curiously approaching many things crafted by humans, in the clinical sphere and elsewhere. He was deeply appreciative of Freud's vigilance regarding how the small details characterizing the relationship between complex systems of premises and the personal alter the very nature of psychoanalysis itself. A favorite thinker Grossman repeatedly quoted was Albert Einstein, invariably to the effect that here too was a champion of fresh and nondogmatic ways of locating the personal embedded within otherwise rule-driven complex systems.

William Grossman never saw a contradiction between being a serious and dedicated Freud scholar and seeking new psychoanalytic ideas. To say he was a Freud scholar does not imply that he was an unabashed apologist for Freud. He considered Freud a visionary, a thinker whose ideas were essential for past and future alike, yet he always pointed out instances where Freud was inconsistent or mistaken. He always sought to place the problems he tackled in the context of Freud's evolving ideas and stressed the importance of understanding that evolution as he joined others in assessing, revising, and creating psychoanalytic theories. For him, Freud's ideas were timeless, always parked at the back of his mind even as he chased down and appreciatively wrestled with all the novel ideas psychoanalysis was examining.

There is a fundamental and necessary tension, Grossman believed, between certain aspects of self-identification as a Freudian analyst. One of them is this: a true psychoanalytic description is rendered only when the observer is simultaneously the experiencer. Both aspects must be accounted for, everywhere and at all times, but it is the diachronic nature of description to make it appear that they blink on and off when actually they coexist in real time. From the outside, Freudian psychoanalysis appears to be a set of interconnected premises, but from the inside, because the analyst must of necessity experience the clinical process, it is transformed into something intensely personal that often resists those premises. This being at once both inside and outside, observer and experiencer simultaneously, is a tension that cannot be bypassed.

An opponent of psychoanalytic pluralism in the contemporary sense, Grossman did not look toward integration as the solution for problems. He did, however, insist upon the necessity of multiple ways of thinking about clinical phenomena (Grossman 2000a, 2002). He believed that no single thought style or perspective could adequately explain all analytic data. He felt that this feature captured and organized the critical approach of analysts who mapped out original territory; he repeatedly cited as examples Freud, Hartmann, and Schafer. Everything, in order to be properly understood psychoanalytically, must be examined from multiple angles or seen in the light of multiple hierarchical codes. Grossman called this "the multiple viewpoints method" (1993, p. 187). Nothing can be completely seen as it appears from a single perspective. Typically, a perspective is characterized by a particular locus (e.g., things are viewed from the angle of the ego, the superego, or adaptation) or kind of thinking (e.g., they are viewed in the light of unconscious, preconscious, or conscious components). Each locus or kind of thinking is native to psychoanalysts. What is important is that all psychoanalytic concepts are moving targets, as perceptions from multiple perspectives accrete. Seeing from multiple perspectives makes psychoanalytic observations come alive. Freudian theory is synthetic rather than integrative.

What might be termed "theory-centrism" characterizes Grossman's view of the approach of a Freudian analyst. What I mean by this term is that analysts are much more suffused by private theory than they publicly declare or believe themselves to be. An analyst's theories are infused by every far-reaching aspect of his psyche, and this expanded sense of theory then determines more than is often attributed to a theory. Theory centrism affects how the analyst understands himself and how he understands others. Every analyst's theory is distinctive, personal, and unique; all the while, it takes its place in the various conformist demands of the organizational side of psychoanalysis. The former tends to be quiet and the latter noisy, but Grossman would have this reversed, the priority resting on the privateness of the inner storms, of which the outer compromises are largely a reflection. Every analyst dwells in both private and public domains and must reconcile the demands of both. He or she has powerful public allegiances to a defining group, yet is at the same time a silent theorist of one embedded within the viselike grip of the thought community he or she is aligned with.

The only way to understand how this can be so, according to Grossman, is through the tradition begun by Freud and handed down to us by generations of interpreters. Grossman read most things psychoanalytic and then some, but, unless it could explain this foundational theory centrism, it could not contribute to the world he envisioned. No brilliant twists of theory could move him unless this foundation was made clear.

To be Freudian is not necessarily to accept drives, infantile sexuality, the structural model, or the reality principle, to cite Freud or Hartmann or anyone in particular in one's papers, to wear suits or tweed jackets, or to enshrine what Freud or anyone else said. Nor is it particularly important what school an analyst explicitly identifies himself with, because whichever one it is, it is but one thought community among the many in which all analysts participate. Rather, it is all about specific premises and how they are handled. Freudians do not necessarily follow the premises they consciously hold allegiance to—that is the trap of illusory objectivity and uncritical participation in a thought community. Instead, Freudians strive to look beyond those premises, continuously reflecting on their implications as they find expression in new thought. In the surround of changing clinical contexts, each analyst participates in a theory of his or her own conscious and unconscious construction, caught amid multiple streams of input, and needing to think a way through this flood to a clinical realization that must be regarded as uncertain, that can change at a moment's notice. The necessity of subjective judgments in myriad conditions means that an analyst is wise to be wary of the chimera of rote theory, to distrust feelings of certainty or the conviction that one clinical intervention is incontrovertibly right and another wrong. Each Freudian analyst attends to streams of private experience, public data, and clinical theory, all of which are constructions of a particular analyst at a particular moment. A

Freudian analyst does not lose sight of being guided in this reflection by the very premises whose implications are being examined. Mastering these conflicting forces so that they yield clinical insight is not an easy task, but, to Grossman, it is what the personal development of an analyst is all about. These nested principles characterize what it meant to Grossman to be a Freudian in the current world of psychoanalysis.

References

Auchincloss, E.L., & Vaughan, S.C. (2001). Psychoanalysis and homosexuality. *Journal of the American Psychoanalytic Association* 49:1157–1186.

Fleck, L. (1935). *Genesis and Development of a Scientific Fact.* Chicago: University of Chicago Press, 1979.

Freud, S. (1891). *On Aphasia.* New York: International Universities Press, 1953.

———(1912a). The dynamics of transference. *Standard Edition* 12:99–108.

———(1912b). Recommendations to physicians practising psycho-analysis. *Standard Edition* 12:111–120.

———(1912–1913). Totem and taboo. *Standard Edition* 13:1–161. Grossman, W.I. (1967).

Reflections on the relationships of introspection and psychoanalysis. *International Journal of Psychoanalysis* 48:16–31.

———(1976a). Discussion of 'Freud and Female Sexuality'. *International Journal of Psychoanalysis* 57:301–305.

———(1976b). Knightmare in armor: Reflections on Wilhelm Reich's contributions to psychoanalysis. *Psychiatry* 39:376–385.

———(1982). The self as fantasy: Fantasy as theory. *Journal of the American Psychoanalytic Association* 30:919–937.

———(1984). The self as fantasy: Fantasy as theory, II. In *Psychoanalysis: The Vital Issues,* ed. J.E. Gedo & G.H. Pollock, pp. 395–412. New York: International Universities Press.

———(1986a). Freud and Horney: A study of psychoanalytic models via the analysis of a controversy. In *Psychoanalysis: The Science of Mental Conflict: Essays in Honor of Charles Brenner,* ed. A.D. Richards & M.S. Willick, pp. 65–87. Hillsdale, NJ: Analytic Press.

———(1986b). Notes on masochism: A discussion of the history and development of a psychoanalytic concept. *Psychoanalytic. Quarterly* 55:379–413.

———(1991a). Contemporary perspectives on self: Toward an integration. *Psychoanalytic Dialogues* 1:149–160.

———(1991b). Pain, aggression, fantasy, and concepts of sadomasochism. *Psychoanalytic Quarterly* 60:22–52.

———(1992a). Comments on the concept of the analyzing instrument. *Journal of Clinical Psychoanalysis* 1: 261–271.

———(1992b). Hierarchies, boundaries, and representation in a Freudian model of mental organization. *Journal of the American Psychoanalytic Association* 40:27–62.

———(1993). Hierarchies, boundaries, and representation in a Freudian model of mental organization [expanded version]. In *Hierarchical Concepts in Psychoanalysis,* ed. A.Wilson & J. Gedo, pp. 170-202. New York: Guilford Press.

———(1995a). Commentary on "Psychoanalysis as science" by H. Shevrin. *Journal of the American Psychoanalytic Association* 43:1004–1015.

———(1995b). Freud and Einstein. Unpublished paper.

———(1995c). Psychological vicissitudes of theory in clinical work. *International Journal of Psychoanalysis* 76:885–899.

———(1998). Freud's presentation of the psychoanalytic mode of thought in *Totem and Taboo* and his technical papers. *International Journal of Psychoanalysis* 79:469–486.

———(2000a). The "Hartmann Era": On the interplay of different ways of thinking. In *The Hartmann Era,* ed. M.S. Bergmann, pp 117–142. New York: Other Press.

———(2000b). Review of *Freud and His Aphasia Book*, by Valerie Greenberg. *International Journal of Psychoanalysis* 81:603–606.

———(2002). Hartmann and the integration of different ways of thinking. *Journal of Clinical Psychoanalysis* 11:271–293.

———(2006). Some perspectives on relationships of theory and technique. In *Psychoanalysis: From Practice to Theory*, ed. P. Fonagy & J. Canestri, pp. 87–102. London: Whurr.

———& Kaplan, D.M. (1988). Three commentaries on gender in Freud's thought: A prologue on the psychoanalytic theory of sexuality. In *Fantasy, Myth, Reality: Essays in Honor of Jacob A. Arlow*, Eds. H.P. Blum, Y. Kramer, A.K. Richards, & A.D. Richards, pp. 339–369. New York: International Universities Press.

———& Simon, B. (1969). Anthropomorphism: Motive, meaning and causality in psychoanalytic theory. *Psychoanalytic Study of the Child* 4:78–114.

———& Stewart, W.A. (1976). Penis envy: From childhood wish to developmental metaphor. *Journal of the American Psychoanalytic Association* 24(Suppl.):193–212.

Loewald, H. (1973). Review of *The Analysis of the Self: A Systematic Approach to the Treatment of Narcissistic Personality Disorders*, by Heinz Kohut. *Psychoanalytic Quarterly* 42:441–451.

Reich, W. (1933). *Character Analysis*, transl. V.R. Carfagno. New York: Farrar, Straus & Giroux, 1980.

Sandler, J. (1992). Reflections on developments in the theory of psychoanalytic technique. *International Journal of Psychoanalysis* 73:189–198.

Searle, J.R. (1992). *The Rediscovery of the Mind*. Cambridge, MA: MIT Press.

CHAPTER 5

MAPPING THE MIND IN RELATIONAL PSYCHOANALYSIS: SOME CRITIQUES, QUESTIONS, AND CONJECTURES

Mind maps in psychoanalysis consist of hypothetical constructs, first posited and then interwoven, for generating conceptual leverage so that the analyst may make useful clinical interventions. An infinite number are conceivable; they must be tested in the clinical situation for efficacy. Maps of the mind proposed by relational analysts are examined and critiqued as pulling clinical theory too far toward environmental factors. Potential clinical dilemmas that then follow are identified. A dichotomous view that parses relational from other psychoanalytic views is discussed as a strategy that limits necessary clinical theory-building and evolution. A view of mind maps that attempt to coordinate a balanced view between endogenous and exogenous pressure is recommended and linked to some available evidence from human development. Questions concerning the role of representations and the developmental course of the structures in the mind are taken up.

One of the daunting tasks of any model of psychoanalytic psychology is to map the mind with constructs that will help to make sense of human nature within a particular context. How one sets about this task will largely determine the model's theoretical extrapolations that follow (although seemingly independent of the choice of mind maps). The units chosen to map the mind thus constitute decisive decisions about one's view of human nature, if one builds a clinical theory consistent with such units.

The choice of hypothetical constructs is a necessary and fateful step in one's approach in all of psychology, not just psychoanalysis. It is virtually an obligation of theorists with new propositions to commit to one or another mind map. For example, cognitive scientists map the mind with such entities as images or propositional and linguistic representations. Then, adherents of different views test comparative models and try to make as much sense out of the mind as they can. Psychoanalysts likewise use a variety of entities to map the mind, ranging from Freud's tripartite macrostructures to an impressive array of more recent recastings. These mind maps, too, can be tested, but not in the same way as the mind of cognitive science.

The mind, then, can be mapped in many ways, depending on one's intentions. Different psychological theorists have markedly different intentions, leading to the oft-observed yet still controversial call to use multiple maps of the mind to account for the complex data of psychoanalysis. Calling for such an ecumenical approach to psychoanalytic theory does not imply that a unitary theory is not on the horizon. Psychoanalysis, among all the human and social sciences, has a markedly different intention than other scholarly disciplines. The controversies in most other disciplines bear only indirectly on the most preemptive intention of psychoanalysis—to treat patients—of using constructs for the purpose of promoting a clinical process that effects structural change. Mind mapping in psychoanalysis thus must be responsive to data gathered from within its native data base, the clinical situation. Other psychological areas have their own native databases and are not likewise accountable for data from the clinical situation. For all its epistemological flaws, Freud's structural model was based on just such data—the clinical situation—and for some psychoanalysts it represents the touchstone against which another mind map should be measured (Shevrin, 1989).

It follows from this healthy and, for now, necessary pluralism that the constructs used to map the mind cannot be evaluated as true or false. Because the constructs are chosen with the intention of providing explanation within a particular context, evaluation can only be in terms of how they adapt to the overriding aims inherent in stipulating them. Comparisons between different mind maps thus must be studied in the light of the contexts within which they are postulated.

Because truth and falsity propositions possess such a complicated role in this arena, and absolute empirical truth claims are not at issue, other avenues can be introduced to evaluate a mind map. In mapping the mind, psychologists are forced to rely on hypothetical constructs because the mind is not like a naturally occurring landscape that when mapped has actual space–time coordinates to locate points against. To provide for some evaluative test of an internal map, there must be some accountability, some referents against which to determine the usefulness of a hypothetical construct. One gate of entry for psychologists must be some unit of behavior, broadly defined; otherwise, the construct might function as untestable dogma (e.g., Freud's death instinct). The unit of behavior could range from lowly reflex reactions to the highest of cortical processes, making meaning through language use. Once anchored in this way, inferential leaps into higher levels of abstraction and generalization become necessary. Such a hypothetical construct must both be internally coherent with respect to other constructs and provide for correspondence with some publicly available events. There is a bidirectional flow, from theory to data and from data to theory and from behavior to inference and from inference to behavior— an unending dialectic that constantly alters all.

The broader and sweeping the constructs of the mind map, the less precise the units mapped and the increasingly expansive the domain of action to be encompassed by a particular unit. These large units are often characteristic of the cognitive behavioral attempt to map the mind. In general, the more precise and intricate the constructs selected to map the mind, the more imperceptible they are, and so they can blend readily into the actual processes of psychoanalytic interventions. Its dazzling intricacy and the way in which the form of the constructs lent themselves to clinical interactions is part of the genius and attraction of chapter 7 of Freud's (1900) *The Interpretations of Dreams*. Hence, when clinical work is going well, psychoanalytic theory is invisible to a conjectural onlooker, who can see only conversation phrased in the everyday language of emotion and action. Good clinical theory can most readily be found in small bursts, at the interstices of moments of decision making by the analyst, and is characterized by offering subtle direction to conversation. These invisible small bursts are empowered by, among other factors, the mind maps the analyst ascribes to the analysand. Good clinical theory follows from good mind mapping.

Among the social and human sciences, psychoanalysis historically has been the approach to the mind that emphasized the most complex units of a mind map. Psychoanalysis has of necessity been opposed to the classical principle of parsimony of explanation, one of the stalwart values of Baconian scientific method. Such bedrock clinical concepts as the principle of multiple function or overdetermination bring this point home. Yet, the more complicated the mapping is, the more difficult it is to coordinate the units so that they exist in some harmonious and nonredundant (coherent) relation with each other. At times, this has produced in the psychoanalytic literature what can almost read like mind maps passing as metapsychological fictions, especially older forays into the energic turmoil of the inner world using the language of cathexis and homeostasis. Such a fate was also characteristic of some

overly ambitious efforts in ego psychology to push Freud's structural model forward by positing new microstructures to fit in with
the macrostructures to account for perplexing clinical data from
within the clinical situation. A good mind map in psychoanalysis
seeks to balance simplicity and complexity, coherence and correspondence, but always seeks to make better sense of clinical data
than do other such maps.

Freud's structural model ably served as the gold standard for
cohorts of psychoanalysts in mapping the mind. It now appears
to be in its twilight as the final arbiter for organizing clinical data
and making sense of clinical processes. One of its most venerable
defenders, Brenner (1982) took a position in support of the
structural model,[1] arguing that it best explains the data gathered
within the analytic situation. He asserted that data generated by
the psychoanalytic method is qualitatively different than other
kinds of psychological data gathered employing other methods.
In my estimation, his argument does not distinguish between origins and outcomes. Freud's structural model was generated
(origins) in the clinical situation but is not married to it (outcome). The outcome of any set of constructs comprising a mind
map can be tested in the analytic situation. The origins of constructs are irrelevant. It is the outcome—the test of how well
perplexing clinical data are explained—that must be evaluated.

Further, ever-evolving mind maps must be tested if psychoanalysis is to honor its future and not its past. However, one can

---

[1] Brenner (1993) renounced Freud's structural model, arguing that all of the macrostructures are in essence compromise formations. He therefore recommended that it
makes more exact clinical sense to conceive of their constituent microprocesses as
particular compromise formations. This seems to me to hold true even if one does not
regard these microprocesses as compromise formations. Any view of them as com-
prised of virtually any sort of microprocesses fulfills the same requirements of
exactness cited by Brenner and leads to the same recommendation, the jettisoning of
the structural model.

retain the idea of the clinical situation as generating a unique form of data (the psychoanalytic method) without necessarily advocating the structural model, as Brenner (1982) seemed to suggest organically follows. Whereas some psychoanalysts probing such matters will proceed independent of the clinical situation and so will certainly go on scoring rhetorical points with and against each other in often endlessly sterile theoretical debates, ultimately any new contribution inevitably will be assessed and survive or perish according to its applicability to the native data base of psychoanalysis, analyst, and analysand in what Greenacre (1954/1971) termed the uniquely *emotionally tilted* conversation known as analytic process. Who will provide the next generation of mind maps? The heirs apparent to Freud's structural model compose a large part of the contemporary excitement in psychoanalysis. Contenders will have to cope with tests of virtually unprecedented complexity, accountability, and therefore scrutiny and critique.

Paradigm Shifts and Psychoanalysis Without the Structural Model

Psychoanalysis is currently in a state of vibrant ferment, with multiple mind maps striving for prominence. Over one decade ago, a similar ferment was referred to by Wallerstein (1982) as the great metapsychological debate. In more recent times, the arguments have become increasingly bound up with clinical ideas, and the more metatheoretical issues seem to have receded from sight somewhat. It is to the credit of theorists such as Mitchell (1988) and Greenberg (1991) for reviving some of these crucial metatheoretical issues. The more refined advances in clinical theory of the last decade are thereby joined, pari passu, with more refined advances in metatheory.

One assumption running through Western thought is that the mind is *intra-mental*. That is, the mind is a secluded entity, individualized by whatever boundaries separate individuals from one another. Recently, this assumption has been challenged, with a newly arisen, acute interest in the social determination of the mind. Some have gone so far as to challenge the notion of a mind as bounded by or contained within a single person. Wertsch (1991), for example, eloquently described from a Vygotskian and Bakhtinian perspective what he terms "the mind that extends beyond the skin" (p. 14). Some psychoanalysts have followed suit as the trickle has become a torrent. From all the subfields within psychoanalysis, there has been movement in this direction. The relational approach in psychoanalysis has contributed such candidates as the *embodied mind* (Fast, 1992) and the *relational mind* (Mitchell, 1988) to this dialogue.

Mitchell's (1988) clarion call for a relational mind echoes his argument (Greenberg & Mitchell, 1983) concerning dichotomous paradigms between relational and drive psychologies, which merits careful attention. He put forward his view as exemplifying a paradigm change and cited many integrative theorists as exemplars of contemporary "model mixing" (e.g., Kernberg, Gedo, Sandler, Kohut, and Pine). However, the finality with which he invoked the concept of a Kuhnian scientific revolution to buttress his argument for a dichotomized world of relational in opposition to drive theories, that leaves the old (drive) world behind, may give one pause. Let us return to Kuhn (1962) and examine what he intended.

According to Kuhn (1962), a paradigm shift involves a shift of professional commitments in a scientific community from one paradigm to another. This includes redefining the problem field, the methods, and the acceptable standards of solution. Normal science generates anomalies, which despite adjustment, require a paradigm change of categories and procedure. Kuhn specified as well the conditions for the abandonment of a paradigm. He noted that (a) new hypotheses emerge so that the old paradigm no longer has a special status, (b) the new hypotheses are more aesthetic and promise to solve more problems more economically, and (c) the proponents of a new paradigm formulate new techniques and arguments that win general acceptance in the scientific community. Greenberg and Mitchell first issued their call for such a paradigm shift within psychoanalysis in 1983. By Kuhnian criteria, Mitchell's (1988) version of relational psychoanalysis failed these criteria. New procedures are not required by existing crises after adjustment, and there is not a professional consensus in the scientific community; the existing paradigm has not been discredited, and the new paradigm has not demonstrated that it solves more problems more economically. I suggest that contemporary psychology and psychoanalysis do not evolve by paradigm shifts the way other sciences do, as specified by Kuhn. Greenberg (1991) himself appeared to have similar misgivings about a paradigm shift when he noted that he attempts "the unfinished business not of combining the models but of trying to extract from each of them what best fits with my understanding of people generally and of my patients in particular" (p. viii). Greenberg's efforts, thus, militate against one of the prime characteristics of a paradigm shift: the redefinition of the very concept of objectivity itself in a science. Mitchell's pronouncement of a scientific revolution seems to be premature.

Yet, it has been persuasively argued that the present era in psychoanalytic theorizing is privy to a reevaluation of the relation between the intrapsychic and the interpersonal, the inner and the outer, and the individual and the social.[2] Of this, there is little

---

[2] These pairings, suggestively simple, are actually not dichotomies. Decades ago, in speaking to the importance of the social, Loewald (1951) made the telling point that to the infant, the concept of the social makes no sense, because what is inside and outside do not constitute cognitive categories that are present. Likewise, he reasoned in the psychic reality of adults, the same point holds.

doubt across all of psychology as well. I use as an example the current status of cognitive science. The study of cognitive processes, which has been dominant in psychology over the last two decades, has been enriched by what has been termed *social* or *situated cognition*. In situated cognition, the effort is to conceive of cognitive processes as nested within particular fluid social subcultures that must be included in any meaningful analysis. However, situated cognition does not discard the working notion that cognition has internal referents, or that situated cognition emerges from a different paradigm or "root metaphor" than cognition in general. By expanding the field of inquiry to include situated cognition, the study of cognition in general is amplified.

Other disciplines have tended to integrate the social or situational aspects of their corpus with the preexisting base from whence they emerged, not sought to dichotomize and therefore divorce them. Mitchell's (1988) claim that psychoanalysis should join into these cross-disciplinary currents and likewise retool into an unmixed, pure relational perspective is not an accurate rendition of the current state of scientific affairs. The current psychoanalytic climate is more properly viewed as (a) epistemic evolution and not revolution, (b) postmodern in its orientation, (c)focusing attention on how something is known rather than what is known, (d) invoking a principled pluralism, (e) emphasizing the constructivist role of language and semiotics (which Mitchell seems to agree with), and (f) one that expands on rather than forecloses the multiple directions from which to appreciate the mind.

To be true to the times, postmodern psychoanalysis should be dialogic, abide by accepted scholarly standards for the evolution of its theory, and be open to change through critique and testing. The most important work and the most trenchant theorizing on the current scene hinges on questions raised by these standards.

Such crucial work, within a field in rapid flux, characterizes the turmoil on the current scene, not bifurcating into drive versus relational camps. When psychoanalysis is dichotomized, and relational analysts identify as "orthodoxy" anything that is not explicitly relational in nature, strains can be recognized, not as a Kuhnian paradigm shift but rather as a regression away from progress by principled critique among a plurality of voices and positions. To be sure, anomaly generation may be forthcoming, but as yet an integrated, complementary perspective fulfills the task of pushing along analytic progress with modern social and philosophical thought, which is an admirable intent of most contemporary relational theorists.

In contemporary structural psychoanalysis (loosely defined here as one which traces its lineage to Freud), threads of these aforementioned controversies about the individual embedded within a sociocultural milieu have appeared, for example, in the questions raised over what Balint (1968) termed *one-person* versus *two-person psychologies*. The question of one-person versus two-person psychologies itself reflects an artificial distinction. One-person and two-person psychologies can and have been encompassed within the set of proposals of one such classical theorist. I cite two rather different examples in Otto Kernberg and John Gedo.

From the perspective of internalized object relations, Kernberg (1976) suggested that all early internalizations and the units of the mind are inherently social. The basic building block of psychic structure is the self–other–affect unit, which is an internal amalgam of that which had been external—a unit of self and other in affective interaction, subject to the subsequent effects of the primarily internal mental climate. Gedo (1979) described how early life is inherently social and, as the person matures, there is a progressive interiorization of functional capacities, so that ultimately what was public becomes private. The early social domain is part of an expectable maturational blueprint proceeding according to the rules of human epigenesis, and both early structures and a lack of expectable structures live on as a potential endpoint for regression in all people. Both of these theorists move away from stark environmentalism by building in a hierarchical explanation for how psychic conflict and the maturational effects of human development remake these early internalizations. Both Kernberg and Gedo rely on a developmental perspective to overcome the intrapsychic versus interpersonal dichotomy. The earlier the phenomena constituting the mind, the more likely it is to be saturated by explicitly object relational considerations, whereas later phenomena are more likely to be drawn into ideational conflict. Further, both do not fail to map their respective versions of the mind systematically while retaining a significant, albeit balanced, place for the relational nature of the human's ontogeny of mind and selfhood.

The metapsychology of Freud and his followers, as condensed and summarized by Rapaport and Gill (1959). was a top-down approach to clinical data; now, psychoanalysts are able to deploy a bottom-up approach that makes the top-down approach obsolete. In other words, Freud's metapsychology could steer and organize data when it served as a substitute for systematically observed and formulated principles for understanding thought and action in clinical and theoretical psychoanalysis. This availability of clinical data at the level of the compromise formation is what informed Brenner's aforementioned discarding of the structural model. Now, the level of inquiry at a lower level (Waelder, 1962/1976) than metapsychology is what is at issue. The accumulation of clinical lore for over a century has released a burden on metapsychology and can usefully guide the clinical analyst. In other words, clinical theory resides closer to metapsychology than ever before.

In recent years, profound challenges to both the metapsychological and the clinical aspects of psychoanalysis have been hurled by infancy research, neurobiological findings, longitudinal (prospective) studies of personality development and outcome, the amplification of the concept of narration into psychoanalysis, and the cognitive revolution in psychology that began in the 1960s. Freud might well have welcomed such challenges, as he indicated when discussing the value of an earlier abandoned model. In discussing the value of the topographic model in *An Autobiographical Study*, Freud (1925) wrote, "Such ideas as these are part of a speculative superstructure of psychoanalysis, any portion of which can be abandoned or changed without loss or regret the moment its inadequacy has been proved" (p. 33).

We live in an exciting time, and the tension between the competing new views will hopefully force their advocates to push their points of view as far as is possible to unveil implicit assumptions, integrative possibilities, and clinical implications. A test of the usefulness of a particular view is how far it can be pushed without either collapsing into logical contradiction or leading to untenable treatment recommendations. Such theory driving is a welcome development—a laudable example is Schafer's (1970) assessment of the contribution of Heinz Hartmann to psychoanalysis, in which Schafer expresses his appreciation of the genius of Hartmann, not because Hartmann ultimately was correct in much of what he undertook, but rather because he bravely lent his career to progress in psychoanalysis through the boldness of his assertions and his willingness to subject his formulations to various forms of testing. One of the recent contenders that has generated a good deal of excitement within psychoanalysis is the relational approach, put forward in the admirable spirit of dialogue and furthering psychoanalytic thought. It is their approach to mapping the mind to which I now turn my attention.

Relational Maps of The Mind

Recent perspectives on relational theory in psychoanalysis (e.g., Greenberg, 1991; Greenberg & Mitchell, 1983; Mitchell, 1988) attempted to tackle some of the problems outlined earlier. Reading these works, an immediate concern is that the solutions offered run the risk of shackling the analyst to an environmentalist position. In addition, the solutions offered fail to integrate vast amounts of evidence from other perspectives. These concerns follow from the decisions by these theorists as to how they map their respective versions of the mind. At times, it is hard to see clearly a mind that is being mapped at all.

Mitchell (1988) presented the explicitly relational view, in which, as noted, the mind is primarily viewed as a relational mind. He set the stage for his proposals by asserting that the distinction between a monadic theory of mind and a relational theory of mind is sometimes characterized as a one-person versus two-person psychology (p. 5). As I understand him, a monadic theory of mind is one responsive to endogenous pressures rather than external pressures. The implication is that one cannot have a theory of endogenous origin, or internal motivation, and yet partake in a two-person psychology. This view consistently follows from Mitchell's assertion that "mind seeks contact, engagement with other people" (p. 3). and as well in postulating two different, isolated, non-interwoven paradigms. However, this definition conflates the structure of the mind with an action of the person. The mind is not awarded a status in which it merits constructs independent of social relations. This solution of going beyond the structural model is to dispense with psychic structure itself. The clinician who maps the mind this way is limited to interventions that are pulled to the external, with little or no anchoring in the internal. The give-and-take of relationship factors is the priority, and the mind disappears from view.

In theory, too, whole sections of psychoanalytic history that are based on one or another notion of a dynamic unconscious (e,g., the theory of thought, the type of work David Rapaport took upon himself to examine) are minimized in one fell swoop. Ironically, it was Rapaport, the foremost architect of mind maps of his time, who was profoundly concerned with the same general arena of theorizing but had different assumptions; he always sought ways to conceptualize a mind that was not enslaved by either drives or the environment. Throughout his writings, he sought a balance between drive and environment, while always preserving the fundamental role of the dynamic (not descriptive) unconscious. He maintained, with reference to activity and passivity (1953) and the role of cognitive structures (1957a) and of ego autonomy (1957b), that drives are what protect people from a stimulus response like enslavement to the environment, and the environment is what protects the mind from prioritizing endogenous pressures. Rapaport suggested that autonomy of the ego from the id and the environment were reciprocal, and that excessive autonomy from either one meant enslavement to the other.

One reason why internal constructs help the clinical psychoanalyst is that they carve out units of psychic activity that exist in some counterpoint to each other—an example of which is being in conflict. That is, one element dynamically wards another off, thereby producing anxiety and intrapsychic defense that appear in the form of interpersonal resistance. When the mind is by definition seen to be seeking contact with other people, ideational conflict between mental elements in the mind becomes readily replaced by interpersonal actions as the target of interpretation. Mitchell (1988) argued that his is a conflict theory because it stipulates conflict between a person and his or her environment. This is quite different from what most contemporary analysts define as intrapsychic conflict—namely, ideational conflict between mental elements warding each other off, not a theory of rough-and-tumble human life. Of course, it is an empirical question whether Mitchell's definition of conflict leads to interventions that produce more efficacious results than interpretation of ideational conflict.

When internal mind mapping is relinquished as a guide to channeling inferences and interventions, one concern is that clinical theory will move toward environmental determination of the most distressing aspects of mental life. This is by now an old story in the history of psychoanalytic dissent, yet one that, it appears, must periodically be resurrected. Given the volatility of transference and the prevalence of projection in virtually every analytic case (Cooper, 1993). one runs the danger of blaming external figures for their pathogenic impact rather than carefully seeking to understand how even such people are psychologically utilized for various purposes, many of which are not consciously accessible. From the perspective of internalized object relations, this follows the cleavages of splits and projective maneuvers rather than analyzes the use of good and bad inner objects. Virtually all analysands, at one time or another, make the case with complete conviction that they are innocent victims of a marauding world. One does not want to minimize the pathogenicity of external trauma, but one also does not want to place such trauma on a pedestal, from where it can crowd out the internal amplifications that are likewise pathogenic.

A possibility is that with nonabused analysands, this can usefully be worked with; for example, it may be due to an unconscious beating fantasy that points toward masochistic gratifications. Or, it can be established that the memory or account of an external attack is veridical, and the dyad can then usefully examine how the conditions came to pass and whether the analysand might have unconsciously brought them about. Of course, holding to this line of intrapsychic illumination grimly and at all costs is technically incorrect, potentially overlooks expectable stresses of living, can be felt by an analysand as tactless, and is therefore at times contraindicated. However, to restate the point, a theory is in danger of supporting and following rather than explaining and analyzing an analysand's defensive activity when it moves toward prioritizing social determination. If the defense is externalization of one sort or another, locating a culprit rather than helping the analysand understand the defensive maneuver disavowing personal agency might lead to a short-term alliance but a failure of adaptation over the long course.

Psychoanalytic history further suggests that when a theory skews toward social determination, there arises the possibility of the analyst moving toward a stance of standing in for the benevolent nurturance, which the analyst thinks is necessary to undo what went wrong. Concomitantly, there is a tendency to move away from the value of acquiring insight and toward the nonspecific therapeutic factors of the relationship. Kohut's (1977) midcourse views come to mind in this respect. *The Clinical Diary of Sandor Ferenczi* (Ferenczi, 1988) vividly documents some courageous early technical experiments in this genre that, with the benefit of accumulated experience, many modern analysts now find somewhat hair-raising. Interpretation and the specification of conflicts that are out of awareness becomes superseded by the mutual search for authentic contact, as insight is superseded by relationship factors as primary mutative factors in analysis. However, this lens can and has been refocused, and these two families of processes are seen as not necessarily involved in a zero-sum game; Pine (1993) depicted how relationship factors come into play in his view, and he set the stage for structural change at the moment of interpretation. The two are inextricably packaged together. Whereas some analysts agree with the technical approach that emphasizes the relationship rather than insight, other analysts rue that there is then limited leverage for insight into how an analysand comes to understand (a) how he or she is pitted against himself or herself, (b) how memory and unconscious fantasy can wreak havoc, (c)how unstable one's motivation is to live well and have pleasure, and (d) an appreciation of the myriad number of ways by which internal resources are mobilized during the course of analysis (i.e., structural change).

When the analytic focus is on adaptively overcoming malevolent external forces, several technical changes inevitably follow. The concept of optimal frustration becomes obsolete because it induces an analytic regression that suddenly has no place within the overall goals of the treatment. Free association is of limited value and seems to be superseded by the concept of dialogue— two people speaking according to conventional rules of discourse rather than one person associating and then two people examining thematic derivatives within and around which key conflicts coalesce. The role of the unconscious seems to play a far lesser role when this transpires. Transference shifts to being something the analyst strives to be within rather than out of, and so the technical principle of using the transference as best one can to help the analysand to see the contribution of externalized fantasy or conflict may be replaced by the dyad's jointly participating co-constructions. Then, the concept of a transference neurosis dissipates, and the potential deepening of the transference becomes more of a threat than an opportunity. The rationale for deepening the intensity of transference, heating up what negativity is on the analytic surface, becomes unclear. In his "good hour" article, Kris (1956) described how a considerable and significant amount of analytic work can be accomplished only under the aegis of the negative phase of transference. This good hour is distinguished from the "deceptively good hour" by the presence of compliance in the latter, in which compliance serves the aim of winning the analyst's love, which overshadows the therapeutic value of the truly integrative acquisition of insight. Here, Kris argued for the value of more, not less, emphasis on negativity, in which the only alternative is compliance.

Unfortunately, there is very little actual clinical process data reported by Mitchell (1988), so it is difficult to evaluate how his views address these key clinical concerns. What is reported tends to be anecdotal, so the reader's grasp on the material tends to be more theory-driven than data-driven. This, of course, is a ubiquitous and far-ranging problem with virtually all psychoanalytic writing. I am not interested in critiquing the problem endemic to psychoanalysis of a lack of primary data; for the purposes of this article, I am more interested in pointing out that the technical recommendations of psychoanalysis are logical outgrowths of the mind maps adopted.

Greenberg (1991, p. 145) has clearly seen the concerns raised and mobilizes against them. In fact, it seems as if his revamped theory of drives implies a rejection of his own earlier call (Greenberg & Mitchell, 1983) for a separate dichotomized relational paradigm. He moves toward populating the interiority of the mind with hypothetical constructs and an appreciation of both exogenous and endogenous pressures in motivation. His solution to the problem of how to map the mind is to highlight the significance of representations and to assert that "we cannot grasp meaning without some idea of motive" (p. 86) and thereby posit drives of safety and effectance. However, it is not clear that this choice solves the vexing problems he is tackling. The nature of the pathway between intentionality and motivation, and that of a mind mapped by representations, are ones that remain unclear. For example, once having discarded the "somatic strategy" (chap. 4). where do the drives to safety and effectance originate? How are they psychologically structured? Does one expect to see derivatives, and, if so, how do they come about? Such connections must be specified for a view to be tested and have scientific credibility. Further, though a representational theory of mind is one that allows for interiorized mental elements, it continues to postulate a particular relationship to external reality that remains potentially troublesome, and that is now examined.

To wit, the question that emerges is, is a theory of representations enough to map the mind with to free it from the enslavement of the environment? In 1923, Freud faced a related question concerning the etiologic role of intrapsychic conflict and the environment. Moving from the topographic to the structural concepts, and seeking to understand such phenomena as negative therapeutic reaction, masochism, and sequelae of war-related trauma, the superego concept was introduced. Whether one agrees with the use of the superego concept, it is virtually axiomatic that interpreting and working with unconscious and self-lacerating guilt plays a huge role in the therapeutic benefit provided to many analysands. It is difficult to imagine a theory of psychoanalytic treatment that attributes little or no role to guilt. This period of Freud's theorizing can be thought of as his struggle to explain why the savagery of internalized condemnation that could be directed against the self or against others as aggression was so often far more violent than the actual conditions that gave rise to it. So, although the superego, and the ego ideal for that matter, was thought of as a representational structure, it was actually that and more. A consideration that therefore emerges is if mapping the mind with representations alone is sufficient to account for such clinical phenomena.

The role of representations within a mind mapped to explain such clinically crucial pathogenic phenomena arises as a key factor.

Friedman's (1978) decry of "the barren prospect of a representational world" warns of the contradictions and theoretical fuzziness of many recent psychoanalytic contributions to a theory of representations. There are two related problems that I now address concerning how Greenberg maps the mind with representations.

First, as Friedman (1978) noted, the idea of representation has increasingly become concretized in theory as one form or another of a visual image. The representation as image, though, does not have the mind-mapping power that theorists of representations originally meant to convey (e.g., Jacobson, 1964; Sandler & Rosenblatt, 1962) because the concept of image is too broad and not a sufficient abstraction to provide leverage to understand the mind in a way necessary for the conduct of psychoanalysis. This is not mere nitpicking; Friedman demonstrated that when the image representation is narrowly defined, it becomes too concrete to explain ways in which people are more than simply involved in commerce with others. When a representation is broadly defined, it becomes virtually synonymous with the person and then loses a capacity to distinguish among such mental elements as symbols, memory traces, and fantasy structures. Then, representations still require some additional theoretical entity to abstract their implications into clinical meaningfulness. To quote Friedman,

> In short, if representation as image is too trivial to be theoretically useful, representation as the world-for-the-person—the experienceable world—is too encompassing. We must abstract certain features from the "everything" in order to have items to talk about [p. 219].

Thus, because both narrow and broad definitions of a representation present such problems, Friedman concluded that representations alone cannot map the mind.

Second, when image representations (images of the external that are remade internally) become supraordinate, theories of the mind portray, to use Rorty's (1979) wry phrase, a "mirror of nature." Rorty's entire book is a broad assessment of the intellectual mischief wrought when the mind is viewed as representing external things and events. Goodman (1968) attacked the idea of a unitary world known by the image representation in the following way.

> To make a faithful picture (representation) comes as close as possible to copying the object as it is. This simple-minded injunction baffles me: for the object before me is a man, a swarm of atoms, a complex of cells, a fiddler, a fool, and much more. If none of these constitute the object just as it is, then none is *the* way the object is. I cannot copy all these at once: and the more nearly I succeeded, the less would the result be a realistic picture [p. 6].

Within psychoanalysis, Schafer (1968b) saw the problem of atomistic units that can compose mind which additively summate to meaningfulness, and, in his metapsychological examination of processes of internalization, he opted for a narrowed definition of the concept of the representation. For him, a representation is an ideational content of subjective experience, and one that generally conveys the environment's regulations. He did this to distinguish representations from other metapsychologically defined components of the mind, such as the structured ego system, to make them non-redundant in terms of their explanatory range. As a result, representations can interact with other psychic structures—the concept of mental elements with both internal and external origins and loci pitted against each other is thereby preserved. Representations exist within the ego system. To Greenberg (1991), in contrast, the representation is not part of a larger mapping; rather, representations themselves constitute the mind. His task was then to stipulate how the mind is not environmentally regulated, which Greenberg attempted to avoid by postulating drives of safety and effectance.

When a representation, as Greenberg (1991) defined it, is used to funnel what is outside inside, the resultant referent is of an image; the origins of the representation inevitably are social, and marks a representation as an internal reflection of the external. Thus, although he spoke at length of mind as an active agency, Greenberg cleaved the mind to the environment by positing representations as the units of mind mapping on one hand, and he liberated it by positing endogenous drives on the other. This sets up an enormous tension that makes theoretical coordination between drives and representations a very difficult task.

If the origins of representations are social, it becomes a feat of great facility to successfully develop how there is a deep and abiding link with aspects of drive, such as intentionality and motivation, which have no obvious relationship to a reflected or imaged external world. Schematizing the structure of the mind so as to account for drives and external reality preoccupied Freud ever since his *On Aphasia* monograph in 1891, as Grossman (1992) recently showed. It remains a challenge for Greenberg to develop such a schematic overview that can generate original hypotheses, withstand testing, provide for interplay with other maps of the mind, explain complex psychoanalytic data, and provide his version of the mind with scientific credibility overall.

Greenberg will certainly further develop his views on representational units so that they will be theoretically better coordinated with such factors and accountabilities. Parenthetically, it has been suggested elsewhere (Wilson & Weinstein, 1992a, 1992b) that this might be accomplished by mapping the mind in ways that follow from some recent developments in linguistics. To briefly mention this line of thinking, contemporary psychoanalysis can move beyond the image representation concept and opt for the notion of language as a representational tool that engages the world, rather than serving to set the stage for a mirror of the real. One can view the supraordinate task of the representation as grappling with the world rather than copying it (cf. Cavell, 1989). Thus, representations developed along linguistic lines become what Goodman (1984) termed a natural referential unit of the representational world—one that would more naturally follow from Greenberg's other theoretical views and which readily brings along some of the accompanying attributes that Greenberg specified that a representation possesses.

The attributes that Greenberg cited include the idea that representations are not passively achieved, but are actively constructed and therefore in some ways have built-in adaptive and coping characteristics. Another attribute cited by Greenberg of active representations is that they can be gauged not only by their stability but also by how well they achieve communicability. Representations are also not determined originally by input, but by their bidirectional engagement with other inner and outer objects.

Because the issue of activity and passivity of the representation arises, the conundrum of the active–passive dimension merits careful attention. Greenberg (1991) spotted the problem, but it remains a thorny issue, and this is again due to how he mapped his version of the relational mind. The point is made by several psychoanalysts, most directly by Schafer (1968a), updating some of Rapaport's (1953) concerns—that a sophisticated psychoanalytic explanation of the active–passive dimension, one of Freud's (1915) three polarities of an instinct, was complicated and certainly beyond any simple solution, because the active–passive polarity was played out on so many levels of theory, behavior, and intrapsychic activity. One must always ask, active or passive with respect to what—one structure with respect to another? The person with respect to the environment? Is the person with the unconscious guilt of a fate neurosis, who repeatedly sees to it that he or she emerges as the victim of malevolent forces, active or passive? A satisfactory accounting of activity and passivity in psychoanalysis is remarkably complicated. When there is intrapsychic conflict, the dimension of active–passive becomes difficult to pin down. It is only when there is no mind mapped by structures that the more streamlined version emerges, whereby the person and the environment are tied into a kind of balanced reciprocity in which only one or the other is active specifically at the expense of the other's passivity.

Yet, it is interesting that so often when making new proposals, psychoanalytic theorists suggest as if new a view of the person as an active construer of mental life—as if activity can be reduced to the notion of the person acting on rather than reacting to the environment, and as if any classical analysts advocate a view of person-as-passive. Both Greenberg and Mitchell in their respective volumes tend to rely on constructivist and postmodern arguments concerning human nature to make this critique. When Greenberg (1991) said, "the representation is thus an active construction—in truth a creation—that embodies the event's meaning to the subject" (p. 173), he seemed to want to make the representation active with respect to everything. There is, between the lines, a streamlining of this unrelenting tension between activity and passivity in all its bedeviling complexity that stubbornly refuses to evaporate, and one that follows from how Greenberg's choice of units that map the mind (representations) tax his theoretical proposals.

When dichotomizing between environment and drive, between individual and social, Greenberg and Mitchell (1983) failed to provide the tools for superseding these polarities. Rather, they

came down on one side of them. A dialectical option, as stipulated by Ogden (1992), is not present in Greenberg and Mitchell,
which Greenberg (1991) attempted to rectify in his critique of
earlier relational views, observing that "relational theorists differ
from Freud in the sorts of drives they have substituted for libido
and aggression, and in their failure to specify the nature of these
drives" (p. 89). The Greenberg and Mitchell analysis is one of a
solipsistic individual in a relational universe. Consequently, their
views led them to reject the social components of endogenous
motivations and the internal components of exogenous pressures. This tension ultimately is why they were led to mind maps
that accept the limits of such dichotomies as endogenous–exogenous, rather than superseding each of them.

A Proposition of Compatibility

Relational thinking is not new, as the recent rediscovery of Ferenczi
makes clear. What is new is the insistence that such a view is inherently incompatible with other psychoanalytic models. However,
there are many currently prevailing psychoanalytic views bidding
for attention that are likewise not drive models, and it remains puzzling why nonrelational analysts are categorized in this way. In
dichotomizing the field of psychoanalysis into drive and relational
models, and then repeatedly using prestructural (topographic) concepts from early Freud (examples are cited by Bachant & Richards,
1993) as if such concepts are characteristic of modern psychoanalysis, and by grouping all nonrelational analysts under the rubric of
drive—including those who explicitly disavow classical drive theory—Greenberg and Mitchell (1983) and Mitchell (1988) have
painted a picture of modern psychoanalysis that makes it difficult
to tell where and how their critique applies to drive and non-drive
concepts as they are used in the current psychoanalytic world.

It is my point of view that relational concepts are not incompatible in any meaningful way with modern classical analysis, which has such a diverse group of theorists within its subscription net. Accordingly, I now take up the proposal, which Mitchell (1988) considered and rejected, that relational considerations can be hierarchically ordered and form part and parcel of an undergirding that is the edifice on which intrapsychic structuralization and conflict rest. This has also been described elsewhere (Wilson & Gedo, 1993).

The concept of conflict is an assumption brought to some aspects of mental life at particular moments during an analysis by most modern classical analysts. It is embedded in various theories of hypothetical constructs that map the mind, ranging from American ego psychology to British theorists of internalized object relations to the so-called neo-Kleinians of London. It is hard to imagine how there can be a direct test of the role of conflict in the clinical situation. Rather, one might bootstrap their way to tests of the role of conflict (Glymour, 1980). One way to attempt that is to evaluate the propositions that the mutative interpretation of mental elements in conflict depends on a foundation or structural base that is essentially relational in origin and nature, an undergirding that allows for the necessary organization so that internal mental elements can appear on the scene in psychological development and with stability in the transference in clinical work. Such a foundation is usually described as a consequence of parent–child interaction and as a naturally occurring aspect of postnatal life. Sandler and Sandler (1978) took up how one consistent view can accommodate the sequelae of actual interactions and the effects of wishes and fantasies. Several theorists use the term *self* to describe such a base, and their views tend to be developmental in nature. This is Gedo's (1979) Modes I and II, Mahler's (1975) subphase of separation–individuation, and Lichtenberg's (1983) description of the role of infancy research in abetting a reformulation of traditional psychoanalytic theories. All are attempts to describe an interactive base on which successful self-regulation is built and on which rests maturationally advanced skills. Tyson (1991). in fact, suggested that one task of interpretation is to bring heretofore unconflicted mental elements that have origins in such interactions into ideational conflict.

What therefore follows is that relationally derived mental elements are present and utilized in the treatment of all analysands. However, these relationally derived elements, which are then internalized and constituted as enduring psychic structure, tend to become most conspicuous in clinical work with severely disturbed patients. The more regressed at any one moment a patient is, the more likely he or she is to demonstrate these relational structures in the transference. Note that this does not relegate relational factors to regressed or psychopathological people; rather, it is an expectable phenomenon of transference life for all analysands in the inevitable regression induced by the transference. It follows that one might characterize clinical technique that emerges from this set of developmental hypotheses as a one-person psychology used to analyze two-person interactions, or of seeking to create the conditions through analysis that allow for externalized two-person interactions, which can then be reinternalized in a one-person frame.

Mitchell (1988) might well object to this line of thinking, as he rejected the notion of relational needs as characteristic of earlier experience, a variant of what he critiqued as "infantilism" (pp. 134-150). Through Mitchell's argument about what he termed the "developmental tilt," he consolidated for relational factors the forms of mentation that other analysts have assigned to the sphere of ideational conflict. Thus, he objected that psychoanalytic theorists have "slid in" the "modern baby" beneath "Freud's baby." His view that the relational baby (and, by extension, relational factors) does not underlie other ideational structures (and, by extension, Freud's baby) seems a logical extension of his basic premises, which as noted entails the repudiation of interiorized mind mapping constructs.

A problem is that it is not just the classical psychoanalytic baby with which he now must intellectually contend. It is a huge domain of developmental psychology, and these findings cannot be overlooked. Although Mitchell (1988) cited several examples from observational research and mobilized other arguments in support of his view on the developmental tilt and of the inherently relational child—whose mind does not develop along a dimension of social to private—what is required to find support for this proposal is a different perspective on development than is known to much of developmental psychology, whose findings suggest that mind does unfold along this axis and that once self-regulation is more or less achieved, mental life splits off from the immediacy of environmental factors (see Stern, 1985; Werner & Kaplan, 1963). The solely relational baby contradicts crucial known developmental findings. In this sense, Mitchell commits the same fallacy that classical analysts have often been called to task for—constructing a baby from a priori theoretical premises or from (re)constructed data from the clinical situation that is tendentiously theory-saturated, a baby that does not jibe with observational findings. Most analysts make recourse to what is known about the child in pointing to clinical concepts and technical recommendations (i.e., using childhood and human development as far-reaching metaphors for constructing theory about what goes on in the clinical situation). The concept of the inherently relational child requires a mind that does not develop towards what Vygotsky called *privatized*, and so one persuasive version of human development must be remodeled.

Thus, there is an enormous array of clinical data and clinical theory, as well as developmental theory and research, which Mitchell must account for, that lends support to children's progression along the dimension of public to private, with internal structures that progress from more global to more differentiated. By contrast, in the view of development that seems to logically follow from Mitchell's views, the growing person's mind moves neither from more social to more private, as Stern[3] and many others have suggested, nor from more global to more differentiated. The nature of skills changes, but earlier is not necessarily less competent. This overall approach, which seems intellectually defensible and has some evidential support in developmental psychology, has been termed by Wertsch (1991) "heterogeneity despite genetic hierarchy" (p. 97). Wertsch examined some evidence that different forms of mental functioning emerge at different periods in development, but that later ones are not inherently more powerful or efficacious than earlier ones. In this view, pointing to *earlier* or *later* as axes of assigning qualities to developmental attributes is incorrect. This is the developmental argument that Mitchell's views seem to imply; otherwise childhood experience appears irrelevant to ongoing experience. Once stated, these propositions can be scrutinized and tested. Evaluating these propositions is again a question of marshalling evidence from within and without the clinical situation.

In conclusion, contemporary structural analysis is more beholden to solving clinical problems and evaluating clinical data than to any of the theoretical models of mind of Freud. It does have some tendencies to torpor when not subject to critique, when

---

[3] Stern (1985) is cited because Mitchell enlisted his views in support of Mitchell's version of the relational mind; in fact, Stern's views seem by contrast to lend evidence against rather than in support of Mitchell's views. Stern located the beginning split in experience, leading to a private mind at the period of and dovetailing with speech acquisition, around 12 months of age, wherein he dated the onset of intrapsychic conflict.

it hides in the unchallenged certainties of the Institute, or in ad hominem assertions of privilege with respect to scholarly disputation. Many modern structural psychoanalysts recognize the value of interactive processes and focus the spotlight of scrutiny on it (e.g., Jacobs, 1991; Renik, 1993). To this, a debt is owed Greenberg, Mitchell, and others who have brought this perspective out vividly and argued for it with enthusiasm. It can be and is being joined with a century of hard-won knowledge from clinical observation about what constitutes useful therapeutic process. Young and energetic analysts are now emerging who have whetted their teeth on this newer perspective, and it is now making its mark in the clinical literature, as the inevitable intellectual struggle for its place in technique and theory becomes energized. The contemporary psychoanalytic understanding of the mind has likewise been broadened by its encounter not only with modern views of cultural and social influences, but also with vastly more knowledge bases than used to infuse psychoanalysis. The opportunity to push forward has never knocked quite so loud.

References

Bachant, J., & Richards, A. (1993). Review essay: Relational concepts in psychoanalysis. *Psychoanalytic Dialogues* 3, 431–460.

Balint, M. (1968). *The Basic Fault: Therapeutic Aspects of Regression*. London: Tavistock.

Brenner, C. (1982). *The Mind in Conflict*. New York: International Universities Press.

Cavell, M. (1989). Solipsism and community: Two concepts of mind in philosophy and psychoanalysis. *Psychoanalytic Contemporary Thought* 12, 587–613.

Cooper, A.M. (1993). Paranoia: A Part of Most Analyses. *Journal of the American Psychoanalytic Association* 41:423–442.

Fast, I. (1992). The embodied mind: Toward a relational perspective. *Psychoanalytic Dialogues* 2, 389–410.

Ferenczi, S. (1988). *The Clinical Diary of Sandor Ferenczi* (J. Dupont, Ed.). Cambridge, MA: Harvard University Press.

Freud, S. (1900). The interpretation of dreams. *S.E.*, 4 & 5.

———(1915). Instinct and their vicissitudes. *S.E.*, 14, 109–140.

———(1923). The ego and the id. *S.E.*, 19, 3–66.

———(1925). An autobiographical study. *S.E.*, 20, 3–74.

Friedman, L. (1980). The Barren Prospect of a Representational World. *Psychoanalytic Quarterly* 49:215–233.

Gedo, J. (1979). *Beyond Interpretation: Towards a Revised Theory of Psychoanalysis*. New York: International Universities Press.

Glymour, C. (1980). *Theory and Evidence*. Princeton, NJ: Princeton University Press.

Goodman, N. (1968). *Languages of Art*. New York: Bobbs-Merrill.

———(1984). *Of Mind and Other Matters*. Cambridge, MA: Harvard University Press.

Greenacre, P. (1971). The role of transference: Practical considerations in relation to psychoanalytic therapy. In *Emotional growth* (Vol. 2, pp. 627–640). New York: International Universities Press. (Original work published 1954).

Greenberg, J. (1991). *Oedipus and Beyond: A Clinical Theory*. Cambridge, MA: Harvard University Press.

———& Mitchell, S. (1983). *Object Relations in Psychoanalytic Theory*. Cambridge, MA: Harvard University Press.

Grossman, W. I. (1992). Hierarchies, Boundaries, and Representation in a Freudian Model of Mental Organization. *Journal of the American Psychoanalytic. Association.* 40:27–62.

Jacobs, T. (1991). *The Use of the Self*. Madison, CT: International Universities Press.

Jacobson, E. (1964). *The Self and the Object World*. New York: International Universities Press.

Kernberg, O. (1976). *Object Relations Theory and Clinical Psychoanalysis.* New York: Jason Aronson.

Kohut, H. (1977). *The Restoration of the Self.* New York: International Universities Press.

Kris, E. (1956). On Some Vicissitudes of Insight in Psycho-Analysis. *International Journal of Psychoanalysis* 37:445–455.

Kuhn, T. (1962). *The Structure of Scientific Revolution.* Chicago: University of Chicago Press.

Lichtenberg, J. (1983). *Psychoanalysis and infant research.* Hillsdale, NJ: The Analytic Press.

Loewald, H. (1951). Ego and reality. In *Papers on Psychoanalysis* (pp. 3–20). New Haven, CT: Yale University Press.

Mahler, M., Pine, F., & Bergman, A. (1975). *The Psychological Birth of the Human Infant.* New York: Basic Books.

Mitchell, S. (1988). *Relational Concepts in Psychoanalysis: An Integration.* Cambridge, MA: Harvard University Press.

Ogden, T. H. (1992). The Dialectically Constituted/Decentred Subject of Psychoanalysis. I. the Freudian Subject. *International Journal of Psychoanalysis.* 73:517–526.

Pine, F. (1993). A Contribution to the Analysis of the Psychoanalytic Process. *Psychoanalytic* Quarterly 62:185–205.

Rapaport, D. (1953). Some metapsychological considerations concerning activity and passivity. In M. Gill (Ed.). *Collected Papers* (pp. 530–568). New York: Basic Books.

———(1957a). Cognitive structures. In M. Gill (Ed.). *Collected Papers* (pp. 631–664). New York: Basic Books.

———(1957b). The theory of ego autonomy: A generalization. In M. Gill (Ed.). *Collected Papers* (pp. 722–744). New York: Basic Books.

———& Gill, M. M. (1959). The Points of View and Assumptions of Metapsychology. *International Journal of Psychoanalysis* 40:153–162.

Renik, O. (1993). Analytic Interaction: Conceptualizing Technique in Light of the Analyst's Irreducible Subjectivity. *Psychoanalytic* Quarterly 62:553–571.

Rorty, R. (1979). *Philosophy and the Mirror of Nature.* Princeton, NJ: Princeton University Press.

Sandler, J., & Rosenblatt, B. (1962). The concept of the representational world. *Psychoanalytic Study of the Child* 23, 128–148.

———J. & Sandler, A. (1978). On the Development of Object Relationships and Affects. *International Journal of Psychoanalysis* 59:285–296.

Schafer, R. (1968). On the Theoretical and Technical Conceptualization of Activity and Passivity. *Psychoanalytic Quarterly* 37:173–198.

———(1968b). *Aspects of Internalization.* New York: International Universities Press.

———(1970). An Overview of Heinz Hartmann's Contributions to Psychoanalysis. *International Journal of Psychoanalysis* 51:425–446.

Shevrin, H. (1984). The Fate of the Five Metapsychological Principles. *Psychoanalytic Inquiry.* 4:33–58.

Stern, D. (1985). *The Interpersonal World of the Infant.* New York: Basic Books.

Tyson, R. (1991). Psychological Conflict in Childhood. In S. Dowling (Ed.). *Conflict and Compromise* (pp. 31–48). Madison, CT: International Universities Press.

Waelder, R. (1976). Psychoanalysis, scientific method, and philosophy. In *Psychoanalysis: Observation, Theory, Application* (pp. 248–274). New York: International Universities Press. (Original work published 1962).

Wallerstein, R. (1982). Foreword. In D. Spence, Ed. *Narrative truth and Historical Truth: Meaning and Interpretation in Psychoanalysis* (pp. 9–14). New York: W.W. Norton & Company.

Werner, H., & Kaplan, B. (1963). *Symbol Formation: An Organismic–Developmental approach to Language and Expression of Thought.* New York: Wiley.

Wertsch, J. (1991). *Voices of the Mind.* Cambridge, MA: Harvard University Press.

Wilson, A. & Gedo, J. (Eds.). (1993). *Hierarchical Concepts in Psychoanalysis.* New York: Guilford Press.

———& Weinstein, L. (1992a). An investigation into some implications for psychoanalysis of Vygotsky's views on the origins of mind: Psychoanalysis and Vygotskian Psychology, Part I. *Journal of the American Psychoanalytic. Association* 40, 357–387.

———& Weinstein, L. (1992). Language and the Psychoanalytic Process: Psychoanalysis and Vygotskian Psychology, Part II. *Journal of the American Psychoanalytic Association* 40:725–759.

CHAPTER 6

ANALYZABILITY REDUX: FROM "ANALYZABLE" TO "PREPARABLE FOR ANALYSIS"

When considering analysis with a prospective patient, the analyst's mindset can usefully be focused on determining if and how the patient can be prepared for analysis, rather than if he or she is analyzable. Preparation for analysis is a deceptively complex and challenging task. Concepts such as the "zone of proximal development" (ZPD) and "apraxia," both borrowed from adjacent disciplines (Russian linguistics and neuropsychology, respectively), have been introduced into the psychoanalytic lexicon precisely because they are useful in making sense of what can and must be done in order to prepare a patient for analysis. The vocabulary and technical recommendations all classical analysts are schooled in are actually more native to the midphase and beyond than to the opening phase of treatment, which can no longer be conceived of as a kind of trial of analyzability.

The concept of analyzability is at the heart of the clinical enterprise, yet it is sorely in need of clarification, for few central concepts in psychoanalysis have been treated so cavalierly and carelessly as this one. In the aftermath of the sea changes sweeping over contemporary psychoanalysis, never again can analyzability be treated as a simple empirical manner, with clinical failures thought to result from personality deformations in the patient that are made apparent when faced by an analyst who strives to limit him or herself to interpretive interventions. Analyzability is not a given and timeless fact of nature embedded within a person's character and history; it is a fluid concept pointing to a lived activity that every moment redefines itself. In a particular sense, the concept is also profoundly wedded to theory and hence cannot be regarded as theory-free. The tie-in with theory becomes clearer when one recognizes that analyzability is so broad and encompassing a concept that it frames any theoretical difference between competing approaches to psychoanalysis, since superior results with more patients are the clarion calls of virtually any push toward revision

Analyzability is not an entity that can exist outside of context. In psychoanalysis, context always changes, as the prevailing emotional climate of the hour varies. Psychoanalysts who locate analyzability inside an analysand rather than as wedded to the shifting tides of multiple contexts have made an egregious error, one that is damaging in many ways—to the patient, not to mention to the field of psychoanalysis itself. Empirically studying the analytic process by seeking to predict successful analyzability employing preexisting static factors as variables—outside of context—is a notoriously haphazard affair[1], and few analysts trust the results enough to allow them to influence their practices.

A domain is a unit of time and place wherein prediction has the potential to hold up, be meaningful, and be successful. One of the classic difficulties with prediction in any and all social science studies conducted over time has been the failure to specify appropriate domains, and a temptation to seek prediction out of domain, a seductive but invariably fruitless undertaking. The tendency to craft theory on the basis of reconstructive data that is not influenced by prospective data is a tipoff that out of

---

[1] See the Wallerstein (1987) report on the Menninger Research Project, the Weber et al. Series of 4 reports from the Columbia University Center for Psychoanalytic Training and Research, and the series of papers by Kantrowitz and her colleagues in Boston for ample documentation of this state of affairs.

domain inquiries might be in play. An example might be the idea that rapprochement-level trauma results in later borderline personality organization. Out of domain predictions often fail because they do not take into account the multiplicity of intervening factors and transformations that can veer the predicted phenomena into another direction. Time is assumed to be a neutral variable, which it never is. Often, linear out of domain predictions end up as "fishing expeditions", only comprehensible from the awesomely deceptive power of *post hoc, ergo propter hoc*, thereby conflating prediction with post-diction. Classic examples of out of domain predictions in social science include predicting adult intelligence from the IQ of an infant, or behavior from a single event with no clear conceptual linkage—such as suicidality from a Rorschach response. Even when, in such research, there is a significant statistical correlation between process and outcome variables, it rarely exceeds the so-called "magical" soft social science correlation of .30. This is hardly a satisfactory state of affairs when the high stakes of clinical work are at issue, when the query has such immediate gravity as potentially harmful consequences to another person.

We seek to predict out of domain, though, because this allows us to make more daring, and therefore more interesting, predictions. If only we could predict outcome from the beginning of an analysis to the end! There is usually a trade-off between the degree of interest a question has and its domain status. For example, it is safe to predict rain if one looks out the window and sees gray threatening clouds, more daring to say that it will rain on the first Sunday two months hence. The explanation for the latter prediction, if it comes to pass, will almost certainly be more interesting than that for the former, yet it is out of domain unless there is a clarity to the theoretical explanation that adds to what we already know about predicting rain. Hypothetico-deductive science values the latter more than the former, due to its desirable features of vulnerability and falsifiability. So social scientists tiptoe between the Scylla of uninteresting safe predictions that are in domain and the Charybdis of potentially valuable daring predictions that can easily be out of domain.

The ongoing shifting dynamic context bounded by the analytic process observed in the clinical situation is the domain of psychoanalysis. When it comes to analysis, static factors must be nested in this dynamic context for prediction to be meaningful. This is a variation of Luborsky et al.'s (1988) point that the mutual interaction of personality disposition factors and process variables will need to be more clearly assessed if more valid prediction of psychotherapeutic outcome is to be achieved.

Diagnosing the contexts that determine analyzability is not as easy as it initially appears. As noted, analyzability connotes an ongoing process between two people, not a timeless attribute abstractly residing in the psychic structure of an analysand. As a process in dynamic flux, it is poorly defined statically or metapsychologically; this is an example of what Ryle (1943) would term a category error. Since it is a process, it must be studied over time and in different units than the necessary generalizations that psychoanalytic theory might otherwise provide for. The units of study must be both smaller and more interactive; every empirical study of analyzability to date has not fully apprehended this. Since theory tends to be timeless, and analytic process inextricably intertwined with flux over time, it is probably true that all psychoanalytic theory speaks to larger units of generalization that are insufficiently interactive than is clinically called for, but that is one hazard of the nested relationship between theory that is written and data that is lived and must be tested.

Depending upon one's theoretical predilections, and defined in terms of process, it is important to recognize that all analysands will go in and out of moments of analyzability. The interactive moment is thus the unit at issue. Seen this way, one can usefully see that I am replacing a categorical with a continuous or dimensional definition of analyzability. Perhaps the differences in analyzability between different individuals has to do with how an analysand interacts with the personal attributes and theoretical preferences of the analyst, as made manifest through technique, and pulls oneself into what I have elsewhere called the zone of proximal development (ZPD), but which is in essence a dynamic process characterized by the ability to learn from the setting i.e., "analyzability." At this point, I wish to introduce 2 terms that will help further the discussion—ZPD and apraxia. I (Wilson and Weinstein, 1996) introduced the concept of the ZPD into psychoanalysis, borrowed from the Russian polyglot Lev Vygotsky. The ZPD provides the transference with its mutative potential. Just as the transference provides the motivation for the recruitment of objects to accomplish its purposes (repetition), the ZPD leads to the recruitment of objects in order to accomplish its purposes (to learn by ushering individuals into a speech and internalization community). Under the sway of the transference, objects are sought so that early dysregulating experiences can be repeated and provided the opportunity of a better resolution. The ZPD works in tandem with the transference, capitalizing on the impetus provided, allowing for the possibility of internalization, a beneficial outcome to transference repetition which otherwise would have no agent of conflict resolution. In analysis, when the transference and the ZPD enjoin smoothly, the potential outcome is "insight" in a broad sense. The processes of the ZPD define the optimal interpersonal context of psychoanalysis, one that allows the intrapsychic to be best reached by analytic interventions.

The notion of apraxia was introduced into psychoanalysis by John Gedo (see Gedo, 1988) and borrowed from clinical neuropsychology. While explicating a certain type of incapacity or inability, it has, in my judgement, mistakenly been equated with the concept of "deficit." Actually, in this case the term deficit is ambiguous—psychological inabilities that often prove to be clinically transient tend to be called deficits and should be distinguished from neurophysiological deficits, which have actual cortical referents. Perhaps an alternatively useful way to conceive of apraxia is related to how Bion depicts the transformation of a beta element into an alpha element. According to Bion, the child possesses prerepresentational knowledge, which requires certain ministrations of the caregiver in order to be elevated into representational knowledge. If these subtle ministrations are lacking, representational knowledge is not realized, and the child will suffer symptoms (e.g., psychophysiological reactions) as a consequence of the failed necessary transformation. If you substitute functions for knowledge and analysands for children, this model is quite similar to what I believe Gedo is pointing to. The analysand lacks overt functions (such as emotional self-regulation) or skills (such as processing information), whose mature unfolding is potentiated by the ministrations of the analyst. By thinking of these skills and functions as existing in nascent forms (rather than lacking), and being brought to fruition through the analytic interaction, Gedo's concept of apraxia lines up with my construal of the ZPD. The seeds for a model of "preparation for analyzability" are conceptually planted and technical concerns that follow can now swim into focus. The concept of a ZPD process implies that, more often than not, to be analyzable is to be in a particular receptive relationship to oneself and/or the analyst and the analytic situation. So-called analyzable people are those who spend more time learning within this same particular receptive relationship from a particular analyst than those who are termed unanalyzable, with some critical threshold serving as a cut-off that probably varies from analyst to analyst. We know all too painfully well that, in general, entry into this process has little to do with intelligence, sophistication, or any identifiable ego function. Both Greenacre (1971) and Stone (1961) once provocatively hypothesized it had to do primarily with the dynamics of the early stage of language acquisition and the implications thereof for separation from objects, but let us not fall prey to the genetic fallacy and bury our understanding in the inchoate past. As Rothstein's (1994) claim reminds us—that analyzability can only be determined after rather than before an analysis begins—these key factors remain a mystery today. For now, I suggest the issue of analyzability becomes synonymous with the issue of how to co-produce a particular climate—of being able to learn from the unique processes forged by the analytic situation. Whatever the case, this process-centered definition of analyzability makes clear that a challenge facing any dyad undertaking an analysis in the beginning is how to maximize moments of analyzability so that they accrete, in order that the process can beneficially unfold.

Before proceeding, let us now take a sidestep. One question emerging with more and more salience in contemporary psychoanalytic thought is: Who is to bear the burden of failure when treatment does not succeed, and what goes wrong when an analysis goes wrong? Classical analysts tend to favor faulting the patient, whereas more recently some, such as those who in describing themselves often use the term intersubjectivist, have implicated the analyst for his or her failures of empathy. Others have addressed poor analyst-patient matches, still others the role of poor technique, or unwieldy countertransference, or obsolete theoretical views—all variations on a theme. But now there is a new contender in this horse-race—having some overlap with all of these but also orthogonal to most. Here is where the theoretical contributions of John Gedo loom large. In Gedo's view, we now have a new context within which to situate analyzability. Failure will result from the analyst's allegiance to a nonpsychobiological psychoanalysis, to a theory of semiotics that excludes phenomena beyond interpretation, and one which overlooks the hierarchical stratification of the mind. In some hands, this can masquerade in drag as allegiance to a conflict psychology or to a solely dynamic unconscious, in others to the insistence upon the hegemony of empathy or a fixed sequence of transference unfoldings, and so on. The unit of analysis he proposes is the analyst in interaction with apraxic skills of the analysand. The shift to a psychobiological psychoanalysis brings along with it a quiet revolution in theory and, hence, in the concept of analyzability. Off we go now in some quite original directions.

What can possibly be meant by this phrase "psychobiological" (a term introduced by Adolph Meyer) psychoanalysis? A simple definition implies those endowed mental attributes that operate automatically, but which, although potentiated and shaped by interactive experiences, are not by and large created *de novo*. This simple definition spawns, though, an entirely widened and original framework for conceiving of and evaluating the range of possible therapeutic interventions. The complex relationship between mind and brain is further dimensionalized when one looks towards the views of such individuals as Gerald Edelman, whose book *Bright Air, Brilliant Fire* is dedicated to Sigmund Freud.

A brief glimpse at the theory of Gerald Edelman (1987), which he terms Neural Darwinism, shows how the false dichotomy between biological and psychological creates mischief. This is particularly so when applied to the developmental history of the human organism. To Edelman, earliest social experiences are inevitably "biologized" as under the influence of what he terms "value" cortical neurons literally migrate into neural networks that are forged by the demands of adaptation. In other words, the actual physical substrate of the brain's hardwiring provides a record of the adaptive demands of early experiences. Spanning the realms of biochemical processes, to neuroanatomy, to consciousness itself, Neural Darwinism takes place on a multitude of levels. Together they form a biological base, upon which higher order consciousness is built through the intersection of perception, memory, and the development of categorization; this foundation is entirely outside of awareness, although consciousness rests on such a scaffold. The core of Edelman's self and of consciousness, like Gedo's self-organization, is thus intrinsically psychobiological. Modell's breathtaking appropriation of Edelman's views for the benefit of psychoanalysis, integrating the implications of "nachträglichkeit" with clinical technique, stands forth as one of the most interesting efforts to remodel psychoanalytic theory in recent years. The implications of all this intriguing work is that literally boundaries between biological and psychological, mental and physical, collapse when one views early mental life from Edelman's and Modell's perspective. Along with multiple other findings from cognitive neuroscience, we have come to recognize how the psychological activation of certain neural pathways literally shapes the final cortical hardware that originates in the endowed rudimentary genetic blueprint. In this way, the biology of cortical architecture is a final product of the psychological states that lent it form.

Returning to our central concern about analyzability, it will become increasingly obvious that significant if not decisive aspects of the debate have been left out more or less routinely, especially in the light of the previous discussion of psychobiology. It was not long ago that analytic purity dictated referral to another analyst if one wished to convert from psychotherapy to psychoanalysis. When I was a candidate, I was taught that I should refer any therapy patient seen for any considerable length of time on to someone else for analysis, because the analytic transference was *ipso facto* contaminated by the therapy. Nowadays, of course, conversion has become virtually a cottage industry of its own, and analysts are experimenting widely and in interesting ways with the parameters of conversion. However, there remains a hidden assumption—despite this minimized expectation of the purity of transference, what is still implied in most approaches to conversion is that there is a qualitative shift in procedures between therapy and analysis, with the gold of psychoanalysis still the endpoint and the copper of therapy still the means to an end. Technique remains essentially unchanged by the evolution we observe in the experimentation with conversion, although individuals such as Gill (1982) have certainly tinkered with the mix by locating its essence in variables other than the frequency of sessions. There is therapy and there is analysis, and often a patient requires a trial period of the former in order to be able to tolerate the latter. Let us consider the implications that follow when a psychobiological set of assumptions are on the conceptual table. An intriguing set of possibilities now present themselves. To wit, can we seamlessly closet the principles aimed at furthering the patient's analyzability in therapy within analysis proper? Can what has been called "ego-building" as a necessary forerunner to implementation of the standard analytic procedure be included under the umbrella of a normatively expectable classical analysis? Can there be the necessary degree of flexibility early on in the analytic procedure so as to foster the necessary stability of the personality organization, that might allow for a midphase that more closely approximates what we have often assumed is analysis? Does such an approach to technique have implications for whom we can analyze?

A key question faced in the beginning of any analysis is this: How can we maximize moments of analyzability so that they accrete in a way that helps the process unfold beneficially? The answers to such questions as these depend upon more than any single set of implications: clearly involved is the critical need that they be answered in light of the complex view of analyzability mentioned above, that is, addressing psychobiological concerns and implicating process in its moment-by-moment fluidity.

In many cases, early on in the treatment, seemingly no amount of insight will help settle the issues of how an analysis is to progress. The analyst comes to recognize the relative intractability of these issues to interpretation early in the analysis. Such issues must be lived, at times in an agonized way, in order to be seen, named, and grappled with. When interpreted early on in the analysis, the analysand might only hear criticism, the threat of abandonment, or an accusation, superseding the semantic content of the words comprising the interpretation. Persistent early interpretation will more than likely drum the analysand out of treatment, a fate Ellman (1991) also cautions against. For many analysands, it is imperative that the psychic reality of the patient expand and take over the room, enveloping the analyst, so that the analyst's comments are phrased inside this version of psychic reality. Brute facts are at best immaterial, at worst destructively invasive. Early on, anything suggesting a separate reality apart from the one generated by the patient is too jarring, and jams up the analysis. One particularly articulate analysand who grasped this put it this way—"It is like this is an artificial world that is realer than real, and out there is a real world that is fundamentally artificial." Winnicott captures something of the basis for this line of thinking when he wryly notes that the analyst interprets so as not to show how much he knows, but rather to show how much he does not know. An ongoing and key tension throughout the opening phase is between prioritizing the psychic reality of the analysand with the assumption that forward movement inevitably leads to the loss of the preeminence of one's psychic reality and the embrace of another's. Living out an issue implies the analyst's accepting and positioning oneself inside the analysand's psychic reality. In this sense, no matter how peculiar or jolting the patient's views of the analyst in the transference are, in a certain sense the patient is always right in what he or she says, in the sense that accepting their version of events prioritizes their psychic reality, and marks the psychoanalytic situation as the distinctive site where the expansion of their psychic reality occurs. It is by accepting this state of affairs that processes of internalization come to be known, and therefore it is through promoting this climate that such processes are best approached

Now, here is an important corollary, one that has dominated analytic technique since the concepts of transference and countertransference were contemplated by Freud as he puzzled over how he failed young Dora in her treatment. It is this: Transference must be assiduously protected against contamination. Excessive concerns about reality, knowledge about and perception of the analyst, the improvident activity of the analyst, and so on, have all been thought to work against the opportunity to stand outside of the transference and analyze it. Without denying that this is a procedural approach that in general is useful, we may still ask: Is this truly the case at all times?

I am presently in the later phases of an analysis with a patient I saw in twice weekly therapy for seven years before he moved onto the couch and upped the frequency to four times weekly. The transference is an analyzable one, seemingly unblemished by the seven years of therapy. Every analyst I know tells similar stories. Yet, the assumption it exposes as fallacious is rarely taken to task, that there is a one-way street between the multiple forms intimate personal contact can take and the ability to conduct an analysis. One can go from analysis to such contact, but not vice versa. A more reasonable view is that transforming psychotherapy into analysis entirely depends upon how the therapy—and the reality contact—are handled.

Paying careful attention to some of the themes Gedo has been sounding for the past two decades means that the obverse of the assumption noted above seems more nearly correct for certain analysands: early supportive interventions involving a high degree of personal contact can actually deepen and enrich the unfolding of the transference and the opportunity to conduct analysis with a certain scope of patients. I hasten to add that by supportive techniques, I mean those interventions that are experienced by the patient as supportive, not those the analyst has preconfigured to equate with propping-up, such as the offer of an unequivocal benign or warm relationship or hollow, empty encouragement. Early on, few interventions can be experienced as genuinely supportive by a patient as offering concrete assistance with an apraxic skill. It is an understanding of clinical technique emanating from certain psychobiological postulates that makes this clear.

In sizing up this situation, some writers have criticized Gedo for failing to analyze the transference, and see him instead operating within it to produce spurious nonspecific therapeutic results. Such a criticism implicitly endorses the abovementioned assumption, and fails to grapple with the possibility that first operating within the transference (by alleviating apraxia) can actually enhance the later analytic possibilities for interpreting transference. Even more importantly, however, such criticism fails to decenter from its own world view, and accept the validity of Gedo's: Addressing apraxia as a psychobiological phenomenon frees the capacity for analyzing transference rather than impeding it.

In endorsing this view, in a recent paper, I proposed the following hypothesis: An analyst strives to be inside the ZPD but outside of the transference. I was trying to describe a necessary tension that exists in the mind of the analyst. When neutrality, anonymity, and abstinence are recognized as relative rather than absolute aims of the analyst by which to steer an analysis, the inevitable tradeoffs between being inside the ZPD and outside the transference that occur in the tempestuous currents of an hour become part of the necessary and usual aspects of guarding the analytic process. This definition of analytic process emphasizes complex goals that require constant and ongoing vigilance by the analyst, and do not readily translate into procedural attitudes such as neutrality, abstinence, and anonymity. Of course, in using words like inside and outside, I am speaking metaphorically, but this distinction is key. Being inside the transference is defined as playing a kind of symbiotic role, that of abetting the self-regulation of the analysand, whereas being outside the transference is defined as a kind of emotional separateness, an approach that assumes two separate sentient persons, in which the analyst is not making him or herself available for that kind of recruitment serving the regulatory stability of the analysand. Since the analyst is separate, projection of unconscious fantasy via the transference will be clearer and interpretable to the analyst, who is now optimally positioned to comment on such processes. Being inside and outside the transference are constructs often conflated in much current analytic theorizing. Those analysts on the contemporary scene who speak of the co-construction of the transference cannot be really analyzing the transference because they are not striving as best as possible, once some necessary spadework is done, to move towards situating themselves outside of it.

It is my contention that, in his writing, Gedo provides psychoanalysis with recommendations that bears on each of these important points. He provides a remarkably new and fresh spin on conversion, such that what once was a rough-hewn shift now becomes an invisible transition, organically proceeding, with no scars in its wake. There is no discontinuity between therapy and analysis, because there is only analysis, which now incorporates the aims that traditionally had been assigned to therapy and which contraindicated analysis. It has to do with apraxia-as-biological- phenomena that proceeds side-by-side with resistance-as-psychological-phenomena. The hardware that is the brain must be fully operative for the software that is the semiotics of mind to effectively perform its task of "meaning production." This has been of late opened up to specifically analytic exploration through the contributions of Levin (1992) and Schore (1994), both of whom have spelled out how much analytically related behavior is brain-regulated.

In the aftermath of his approach, the concept of analytic conversion can be thought of as largely replaced by the concept of "*analytic preparation*." Analysis does not begin with therapy and then evolve through conversion because, in Gedo's way of thinking, they are seamless, and all cases more or less proceed through organically occurring phases. Since Ferenczi there have been analysts who have argued that analysis be defined in terms of goals rather than by any particular technical procedure, and Gedo has championed this view for many years (Gedo and Gehrie, 1993). It is certainly the case that not all preparations are finished, and thus formal analysis is not embarked upon in a large number of cases, but here one can argue that the problem in most cases is that time ran out, not that there is intractable pathology preventing the transition from one set of ordered procedures to another. Thus, preparation/conversion becomes a process applicable in most or all cases, not an abrupt shift impacting upon only a few cases. The conversion is an automatic adjustment to those processes that indicate a patient is prepared to embark upon self-exploration and learn from the experiences in front of them. The new view of conversion follows axiomatically from Gedo's theory of apraxia. According to Gedo, we all have apraxias, which are made manifest in our inability to learn from each another. There is no point in the analyst waiting for a neurotic transference to unfold when psychological circumstances prevent an analysand from learning from the processes inherent in analysis. This conclusion follows from the idea that preparedness for analysis via overcoming apraxia is not limited to severely disturbed patients, but exists for any and all analysands. When Gedo (1996) tells us that only one analysand he began with over the last two decades prematurely terminated, and all others were brought to a relatively satisfactory conclusion, and the only difference between these treatments and the ones he conducted earlier in his career was that he paid preemptive attention early on to apraxias, then we must sit up and pay attention, for these are results that count. Accordingly, Gedo (1993) notes that the major change in the evolution of his technique came when he began handling apraxias as soon as they appeared, without waiting for them to wreak havoc. And, as we hear, in an informal study of his success rate, the rate of analysands successfully helped dramatically jumped. All told, in his career, Gedo (1997, personal communication) reports he undertook 62 analyses. 50 terminated in a mutually agreed-upon way with satisfactory results. Six had to be changed to psychotherapy, with variable outcomes, and six were interrupted with poor outcome; all those with poor outcome were individuals with a hidden psychotic core, usually covered over by a false self.

Now, I do not want to get caught up in the research methods of the data-gathering involved, only to say that any time a senior analyst makes a claim of such remarkable success, it is certainly worth a second or third look. Allow me to repeat myself to highlight the key point: instead of waiting for the transference to coalesce around symbolically-coded themata, as one would expect would be the case were the issues dynamically unconscious, Gedo recommends actively handling as early as is possible the analysand's inability to learn (i.e., to take in, to make use of the analytic situation). This goes far beyond the analysis of resistance, as I will soon specify.

Now, when I use the word "handling" I actually mean much more than meets the eye. The closer one looks here, the more mysterious the sight. In one book, Gedo refers to handling apraxias as a "technology of instruction." This instruction is not lecturing as if from a podium to students, it is a specifically psychoanalytic version of instruction, one that lends itself to maximizing the "know-how" of procedural cortical processing. In this way, a subtle remediation of sorts must take place for the analysand to repair such a learning function. If this is as efficacious as it is billed, then psychoanalysis is on the brink of some quite important steps. It profoundly alters our understanding of analyzability. So, a handling of apraxia takes us on a related journey, this time into the realm of the presymbolic.[2] In other words, analyzability is linked to a particular view of early development, one which stresses that which is psychobiological and "beyond interpretation." Here, as far as I can see, Gedo's view of psychoanalysis profoundly departs from that of many others. His assumption is that, if a personality organization is akin to a house, the 3rd floor can only be sturdy if the 1st floor is rock solid. To renovate the 3rd floor while the 1st floor is collapsing is foolish. The 1st or foundation floor must be built of different

---

[2] Presymbolic may be the wrong word here. Many semioticians deny there is such a thing as nonsymbolic in any act of intentionality. Charles Sanders Pierce, for example, long ago trifurcated all communication into the symbol, the icon, and the index, which in a sense can be thought of as a statement that symbolic-nonsymbolic is erroneously nominal (one or the other). Nonsymbolic also implies that communication can be unintentional, a topic hotly contested among contemporary philosophers of mind.

materials than other levels because it has to bear the burden of more weight. In other words, the epigenetic hierarchical model implies a different slant on the nature of analytic activity and receptivity, since waiting for iconic themes to coalesce when in the presence of apraxia can only lead to the apraxic skill becoming more acute and debilitating.

Now, a crucial question can be asked: What is the relationship between apraxia and resistance? I propose the following analogy: resistance is to intrapsychic conflict as apraxia is to internalization. Put another way, resistance is to psychological processes as apraxia is to psychobiological processes. My current explication, then, aims at articulating a distinction between the mind's impediments to moving forward and the brain's impediments to moving forward. Clinically, how can the analyst make the call that allows him or her to adjudicate between phenomena that accomplish the same task (impeding progress), in which the mental content may well-nigh be virtually identical, yet stem from different places of origin and require markedly different interventions? Here, once again, the all-important notion of *process* as an accretion of many interactive moments as the key unit of psychoanalysis becomes superordinate. Everything that takes place of lasting importance in psychoanalysis takes a long time, and requires patience. Few things that happen the first time are definitively settled. We are not purveyors of a rapid, overly efficient treatment. We rely on repeated instances to lend enumerative weight to our inferences, all the while remaining sensitive to eliminative disconfirmatory evidence. That two sets of data can appear on the surface virtually identical yet in one instance suggest resistance and in another apraxia is sobering. It speaks to the limitations we can have in our technical certainty. More importantly, it speaks to the necessity of the analyst taking chances, not being afraid to be wrong, and thinking dialectically (in the classic Hegelian sense, in which any idea automatically assumes and creates its antithesis). In a thera-peutically ambitious analysis, things must go wrong in order for them to eventually go right. The analyst must welcome things go-ing wrong, be flexible enough to backtrack with a deeper understanding of the etiological picture, and resume moving for-ward on one or the other of a highly interwoven and mutually regulating set of tracks.

So, repetition is the problem for the analysand, but the ally of the analyst, because it guarantees that we do not have to act decisively after one occurrence of any event. Repetition is a complicated piece of business; it may also be that repetition is the personality organi-zation putting forward a healing potential, in order to provide an opportunity for some kind of change (Wilson and Malatesta, 1989). What went wrong, in essence, repeats in order to provide an oppor-tunity to be made right. Process in analysis has to do with testing hypotheses against the data we encounter, not fitting the data we encounter into the Procrustean bed of our pet theories. One should in general not worry about missing an opportunity for an interven-tion with an analysand, instead one should prepare for the next inevitable occurrence of that same opportunity. In other words, rep-etition embedded within the ongoing flux of analytic process provides the venue for an analyst to test to see whether apraxia or resistance is present when looking at any one iteration of the kalei-doscopic vision produced through analysis. Resistance implicates volition, apraxia does not. Resistance—the mind at work—suggests that intervention must allow for the analysand's solution to a con-flict that prevents him or her from moving forward. Apraxia—the brain at work—suggests that intervention must aid the analysand in overcoming a difficulty towards which insight tends not to be keyed, which lends itself to a pattern of symbiotic recruitment of objects, and which requires cognitive/affective bolstering to enable the analysand to resume a forward movement.

In his papers, Gedo has gone beyond the repair of apraxias in delineating how such tests might proceed. An entire recent book (Gedo, 1995) is dedicated to the "languages of psychoanalysis," that is, how an analyst can and must establish multiple forms—characterized by the concept of "levels"—of communication with an analysand, or else the clock will simply tick and nothing useful will happen. That this can take such paraverbal shapes as humming a tune, scolding an analysand in righteous indignation, blocking the exit door during a storm of rage, or utilizing the affectivity in the countertransference (all of which Gedo reports in one or another case) to advantage sharpens our focus and captures our interest, because now the lines are more tautly drawn. We can see how he creates the conditions for the necessary channels of connection so that the analytic transactions can then unfold. These will probably vary from analyst to analyst, so a "how-to-repair-apraxias" paper is of less interest than a clearly laid out conceptual explanation of the whys and wherefores. It is clear, however, that this question—how do analysands learn from the analysis?—is one of the most pressing questions on the current landscape.

The history of the concept of analyzability can now be updated. First, there was "analyzable" as a patient variable. This was superseded by questions like—analyzable by whom? and—what is the analyzable dyad?—and so on, in other words, patient-therapist interactive variables. With the widening scope in the last few decades and the findings from such empirical studies as Wallerstein's (1987) integrated into contemporary clinical theory, we saw a mélange of supportive techniques inserted side-by-side with the older gold of interpretation from classical analytic theory. Now, in the aftermath of the so-called "decade of the brain," we are well positioned not so much to shore up the question of who is analyzable, but to note that it is now the wrong question.

To get the answers we need, we must ask the right questions. In this instance, the proper questions are these: How can this patient, assuming that he or she is not psychotic or sociopathic, be prepared for analysis? What actions on the part of the analyst are necessary for the analysand to be able to eventually free associate and externalize intrapsychic conflict?

Although I am not aware that he has consistently voiced this view, Gedo (1981) asserts that anyone who is not psychotic nor sociopathic can be usefully treated by analysis, if certain of his technical precepts are observed. Why is this? Obviously if many individuals not fitting this description lie down on a couch and start free associating to a relatively silent analyst, all hell will break loose. There is an enormous appeal to wrestling with this question, because it opens doors we all yearn to walk through but cannot because we are afraid of what we might find out. But John Gedo, through his *oeuvre*, says he has been there, and it looks safe. And it is so because they can be prepared for the ardors of the analytic situation, if the analyst lets him or herself break free from traditional restraints and do what is necessary to realize this state of affairs. Analyzability can only be assessed after a patient has undergone the preparation for analysis that is in and of itself the early phase of the procedure.

There will certainly be those who do not agree with the views adduced here. It cannot be doubted, however, that the stakes are high indeed. It is sobering to notice that the contemporary world of American culture is now questioning the very relevance of psychoanalysis. We cannot go on ignoring the world that prevails around us. This is not to say that we should adapt to it. That is to say, in a world where the brain matters more than the mind, a psychobiological psychoanalysis opens up a venue for an interesting conversation. In a world where symptom alleviation counts more than character or structural change, the rapid attention to the amelioration of apraxias has great appeal, particularly to the suffering patient. In a medical milieu that renders empirical demonstration of efficacious outcomes the literal basis for the existence of any clinical procedure, the claims of demonstrable success can even be intoxicating. For all of these reasons, these ideas now urgently require testing in the clinical situation by a goodly number of analysts committed to a fair trial.

But, in a crucial way, analysis has always stood outside of the mainstream and has always served as a prod for culture to evolve, so there is no fundamental reason to lose heart. As we approach the end of the millennium, it may bode well to recall how Freud committed the well-known 4th blow against mankind, and shook the world. Although the revolutionary insights psychoanalysis once offered by and large seem to have been digested, and it is unlikely that in its current incarnation it can regain its former luster, this should not be taken to mean that progress is not being made, or that current innovations might not once again emerge so that psychoanalysis might yet shake the foundation of our world. Erikson once remarked that in Freud's *fin de siècle* it was sexuality that was repressed, while in modern American culture it is parenthood. That which was once revolutionary is now regarded as commonplace, that which was once commonplace is now all too often burdensome, and in these transformations psychoanalysis must refind its soul. Too many people scream that we must defeat managed health care, whereas too few people scream that psychoanalysis must traffic preemptively in the evolution of ideas, and therefore develop new and more useful ways of modeling the mind and the treatment situation, in particular embracing what we know about method and representation from cognitive science and neurobiology. The problem, dear Horatio, lies not in the stars but in ourselves, so let us now say it is time to move forward, holding out the hope that we can rally and find a shape, a form, a message that can once again grab the cultural and intellectual world that prevails around us, shake it up, and give it something fresh and invigorating to contend with under the imprimatur of contemporary structural psychoanalysis.

References

Edelman, G. (1987). *Neural Darwinism*. New York: Basic Books.

Ellman, S. (1991). *Freud's Technique Papers*. Northvale, N.J.: Jason Aronson.

Gedo, J. (1981). *Advances in Clinical Psychoanalysis*. New York: International Universities Press.

——(1988). *The Mind in Disorder*. Hillsdale, N.J.: Analytic Press.

——(1993). *Beyond Interpretation*. Hillsdale, N.J.: Analytic Press.

——(1996). *The Languages of Psychoanalysis*. Hillsdale, N.J.: Analytic Press.

——& Gehrie, M. (1993). *Impasse and Innovation in Psychoanalysis*. Hillsdale, NJ: Analytic Press.

Gill, M. (1982) *Analysis of Transference*, Vol. I. New York: International Universities Press.

Greenacre, P. (1968/1971). The psychoanalytic process, transference, and acting out. In: *The Capacity for Emotional Growth, Vol. II, pp. 762–776*. New York: International Universities Press.

Levin, F. (1992). *Mapping the Mind*. Hillsdale, N.J.: Analytic Press.

Luborsky, L.; McLellan, A.T.; Woody, G.E.; O'Brien, C.P.; & Auerbach, A. (1985). Therapeutic success and its determinants. *Archives of General Psychiatry* 42:602–611.

Rothstein, A. (1994). A perspective on doing a consultation and making the recommendation of analysis to a prospective analysand. *Psychoanalytic Quarterly* 63:680–695.

Ryle, G. (1943). *The Concept of Mind*. Chicago: University of Chicago Press.

Schore, A. (1994). *Affect Regulation and the Origin of the Self*. Hillsdale, NJ: Erlbaum.

Stone, L. (1961). *The Psychoanalytic Situation*. New York: International Universities Press.

Wallerstein, R. (1986). *Forty-Two Lives in Treatment*. New York: Guilford.

Wilson, A. and Malatesta, C. (1989). Affect and the compulsion to repeat: Freud's repetition compulsion revisited. *Psychoanalysis and Contemporary Thought* 12: 243–290.

Wilson, A. & Weinstein, L. (1996). The transference and the zone of proximal development. *Journal of the American Psychoanalytic Association* 44:167–200.

II. Observations on Analyzability

CHAPTER 7
_____

SCIENCE STUDIES, CONTEXT, AND PSYCHOANALYSIS

Introduction

Psychoanalysis has recently made great strides in investigating its borders with friendly neighboring fields, such as neuroscience, developmental psychology, and cultural studies, among others. The yield from these investigations has been impressive. One contemporary area, however, has escaped psychoanalytic investigation, perhaps because its composition is hybrid, its subject matter somewhat parochial, and its own borders somewhat unclear. This area goes by several titles, often science studies or at times Science and Technology studies, which for the purposes of this essay I will abbreviate as STS. As a field of inquiry, STS came of age in the last few years.[1] It focuses on how knowledge is produced in and through modern science, set against the background of the history of science. Uncovering the secret life of objectivity across history and within historical contexts provides a unifying thread for this field, whose better known figures include Peter Galison, Bruno Latour, Arnold Davidson, Lorraine Daston, Karin Knorr Cetina, Ian Hacking, Donna Haraway, Mario Biagioli, Barbara Herrnstein Smith, and Andrew Pickering. STS is internationally based and discipline-nonspecific. Its practitioners include, from among other disciplines, philosophers, sociologists,

_____
[1] A virtual manifesto of STS is laid out in Latour's (1999) discussion.

psychologists, historians, and physicists. Overlooking this area has come at a cost for psychoanalysis, for STS directly and persuasively speaks to one side of a long and destructive debate within psychoanalysis about truth and objectivity. The reverse, however, is also the case: the productivity of psychoanalytic understanding over the years strengthens, as a natural experiment, many STS assertions.

Psychoanalysis can address ideas originating in other fields—in this case, STS—in two ways. Each has its advantages and disadvantages, and it is important to be clear about the risks. The first way imports ideas from outside the field into psychoanalysis. Primarily analysts exercise this input option, and they must guard against the risk of naturalizing imported ideas. A second way exports psychoanalytic ideas to other fields. Here primarily nonanalysts, or analysts who are conversant in other fields, take the lead and they must keep in mind the risk of sterilizing psychoanalytic ideas. Exploring the implications of STS for psychoanalysis, this essay examines both how psychoanalysis can incorporate ideas from STS and how STS can draw upon psychoanalytic thought. It utilizes both approaches in its comparative and integrative *modus operandi.*

Efforts to compare or integrate different fields of science, it should be noted, often risk too much trafficking in nouns, by which I mean a tendency to set up entities that require agreement about definitions. For example, witness the concreteness of the question: What is a transference? Years ago, Darius G. Ornston (1985) noted that Strachey's translation of Freud created entities, whereas the terms were originally intended to represent dynamic processes. Once set up as entities, terms must be invented and reinvented anew. Debates about them become cast as definitional and conceptual, when actually they are better differentiated as linguistic and process-related. STS terms such as "trading zones"

(Galison, 1999) or "trade languages" (Fuller, 1995), for example, describe a dynamic system whereby representatives of different discourses (languages) usefully negotiate how to speak with (translate) one another. Thus, when both STS and psychoanalysis approach the problem of objectivity and subjectivity, we must carefully undo this problem by never losing sight of the systems within which they participate. Many STS scholars affirm that all objectivities and subjectivities are nested, encased, and self-perpetuating within a larger frame that contains other nested objectivities as well as subjectivities. Such understanding, important for this essay, helps us to avoid setting up entities that minimize process factors. Finally, in the interface of STS and psychoanalysis, it is important to distinguish between clinical methods and scientific methods. Psychoanalysis and STS employ discipline-specific techniques of study utilizing both sets of methods. In psychoanalysis, clinical method is how what patient and analyst do with one another is formalized and thus known; in STS, a quasi-clinical methodology proceeds by focusing on the secret lives of scientists and their medium. Scientific method, on the other hand, is the technology of understanding applied to any system, be it psychoanalytic or not.

Scientific and Historical Praxis

A significant trend in contemporary STS emphasizes the relationship between theory and practice as a central concern across all sciences. We see this trend in Galison's (1997a, 1997b) investigations of the disunities of the physical sciences, Hacking's (1992) studies of the surprising complexities of the culture of experimentation, Davidson's (1996) investigation into styles of reasoning in psychiatry, and finally Latour's (2005) effort to provide a framework to rid science of impractical, endlessly circular abstract models. These and other individuals are heavy lifters in the so-called "Science Wars" that have embroiled the study of method. Deploying various concepts and scrutinizing practice as it unfolds, they expose the inadequacy of many putatively explanatory theories and demonstrate the complexities of practice. A clearer picture of actual practice emerges, yielding a different kind of emphasis on the subject at hand.[2] Their contributions emphatically reject old debates—words like relativism or realism simply do not appear in their writings except as conceptual foils—or recast those debates into new ones, successfully sharpening our conceptual tools.

STS scholars examine science as an unfolding, historical practice, specifying heretofore hidden factors within a key finding. A significant scientific advance is understood in its own unique context and in terms of the reverberations of crucial past events—often secret, invisible, or out of the awareness of the germane individuals, like a niched unconscious. Tracking what unfolds over time, the reader of STS scholarship becomes a witness to how events produce ripples that were not heretofore causally linked to the original event. The unique context of a scientific discovery is brought into a relationship with the greater overall world—and not necessarily with the actions called at that particular time "science." By employing such a method, for example, Galison (2012) illustrates how the idea of "censorship" reverberates in multiple guises throughout Freud's life and career. His reading of Freud—as one whose multiple intellectual contributions are joined by a commitment to honor the hegemony or, perhaps, trauma of censorship—is new and original.

The historical approach of STS illuminates complexity and paradoxes in various aspects of science. As with the analysis of

---

[2] Sidney Morgenbesser's oft-told joke is applicable here, to the effect that pragmatism is wonderful in theory but lousy in practice.

transference, a red thread from the present to the past is necessary to imbue the analysis with significance. Similarly, history with no tie to the dynamic present is enervated, without vitality. We have several examples of imaginative STS undertakings, in which secrets of the past are unveiled and history reassembled. Ludwik Fleck's (1979) investigation of the then prevailing understanding of syphilis and the Wasserman reaction, when contrasted with contemporary understandings, led to his ideas about the social nature of hard facts. Latour's (1999) investigation of Pasteur's work led to Latour's theory of human and nonhuman actants (microbes are ascribed agency!) and how events in the material world undergo transactions that allow them to be transformed into scientific knowledge. Knorr Cetina's (1999) inquiry discovered how the historical culture of laboratories created a disunity of current knowledge societies. Finally, Galison (2004) explored how the coordination of clocks for Einstein and the creation of maps for Poincaré quietly sparked a still reverberating revolution. Galison uncovered how these seemingly mundane tasks were products of a culture that was then ready—once the coordinating clock and creating map problems were solved—to move on to the novel notions of simultaneity in time and space, making possible the explanations leading to Einstein's principle of relativity. Who would have conceived that quantum physics and relativity would have their roots in earlier puttering with maps and clocks?

Interpreting the Present and the Past

Various principles bridge the world of psychoanalytic ideas and the world painted by historians of science. I begin with general, compatible principles of interpretation.

1. Both the analyst with a patient and the historian of science—aiming to uncover the as yet inchoate past to grasp a deeper

understanding of the present—rely on reconstruction of the past for insight into the present. Both reconstruct the past with all the available evidence at their disposal.

2. Both emphasize transference dynamics—in the analysis, the transference to the analyst, and in STS, the historical figure to his milieu, especially the important people in his or her life.

3. Both emphasize the tracking of intrapsychic conflict over time. Individuals over time will participate in conflict, defense, and compromise, and these will be seen in both the intrapsychic life of an individual and in interpersonal relationships.

4. Both identify successive registrations of ideas reorganized at different hierarchical levels on the way to a present incarnation, which Freud (1913, pp. 182–183) first defined as the essence of psychoanalysis and which was to evolve into the genetic point of view of metapsychology. Grossman (1992) has argued that hierarchical modeling defines the central organizing method underlying all the categories of Freud's thought, what Grossman termed "the psychoanalytic mode of thought." The same can be said for the differing approaches of STS.

5. Both reconceptualize the present in light of the past so that the present is available for understanding. The freshly excavated past brings out the contexts of the present that otherwise would not be seen.

6. Both assume a past draped in mystery. The historian of science does not address a past that has been repressed or forgotten, but rather one that was never assembled. The analyst, too, has access to a past that can be known through careful scrutiny of seemingly unimportant details and subsequent imaginative assembly. The history of a particular interpretive line will then have some reciprocal relationship with the history of the context within which it appeared.

7. Both view interpretation of the data gathered by their methods as necessary. Interpretation formalizes the shared history of a

context. When a context is identified and knowable, a necessary foundation is created for interpretation to be followed up on.

8. Both rely upon the scrutiny of multiple variables and employ, in the complexity of their subject matter, a method explained by Robert Waelder (1936) as the principle of multiple function.

9. Both assume that no person is a solitary thinker and emphasize the role of unconscious factors (see for example Davidson's 1987 paper on how to read the history of psychoanalysis as exemplified by Freud's 1905 *Three Essays on the Theory of Sexuality*).

10. Both reject linear explanations of causality. Both emphasize how, when properly done, what swims into focus are the equipotentiality (all roads lead to Rome) and multipotentiality (one road leads everywhere) of cause-effect explanations (Cicchetti & Rogosch, 1996). In other words, many causes can lead to one effect, and one cause can lead to many possible effects.

11. Both regard every event as unique. The uniqueness of every momentary event puts to the test a quiet yet powerful assumption that what is expressed or enacted has application and meaning beyond the particular moment or situation—Fonagy's (2003) *bête noir* of endless inductions. Weak theories and not-worked-out methodologies dwell in universals; strong theories and mature methodologies deal in specifics and instances. The human mind seems to have a lust to generalize, to break down distinctions, a by-product perhaps of the innate psychological necessity of classification. Empirically based science and hermeneutics are, at bottom, two traditions for legitimizing different types of generalization. These two traditions come into conflict most violently over what is considered a legitimate form of generalization, and generalizations have a way of creating contexts in which these violent conflicts fester.

12. For both psychoanalysis and STS, context is the necessary backdrop for even the most minimal comparisons between ideas in conflict. Boesky (2008) demonstrates how context allows different ideas to be compared with one another in psychoanalysis, in turn preventing the chaos of having no empirical mooring, the nightmare that almost everybody fears.

Personal Epistemology and Contextual Understanding

Keeping these general principles of interpretation in mind, we turn to particular implications for psychoanalysis. As mentioned above, a central organizing focus of STS is that it (and perhaps most of modern science itself) best concerns itself with context-specific methods, a point first made and defended by Thomas Nickles (1987).[3] Such a notion has become the centerpiece of a contemporary broad-based reform of how humans can best understand nature. Applied to psychoanalysis, it emphasizes that each context in analysis is a mini-epistemic culture embedded within larger epistemic cultures (Knorr Cetina, 1999). Each context generates standards of reason, which someone within that context assumes to be true or false. In psychoanalysis, context has as one of its sources the repetition of developmental levels that are brought out and worked through in an analysis. But context also operates internally, infuses itself into the very ideas, word meanings, atmosphere, and non-semantic (syntactical and pragmatic) communications that bracket how people understand one another. The same words and ideas can have a different significance when spoken in different contexts. Context distills

---

[3] Grice's (1989) conversational implicatures (pragmatics). Searle's (1979) problem of zero context (speech act theory), and Kagan's (2006) embededness (developmental psychology) are examples of context-dependent methods from various fields outside of psychoanalysis.

and frames all understanding of a phenomenon during analytic dialogue, its crucial significance becoming especially apparent when something is on the way to being brought out or understood. Understanding this in analysis requires theoretical approaches, but such theoretical inquiries evolve into clinical questions within the overarching context, the psychoanalytic situation.

Once a context is established, a self-reproducing cycle is set in place. The cycle is recursive in nature: a context reappears in a somewhat similar guise time after time, even becoming self-perpetuating. In analysis, the term refers to a process that occurs when one of the steps of a procedure involves rerunning the entire procedure but not necessarily successfully reproducing it. Each reiteration of the procedure has a patina of oldness and newness. One patient began an analytic hour by saying: "I would like to pick up where we left off, but I do not feel able." The procedure, in other words, can be rerun but not reproduced. What has been once analyzed is never done and over. Memories are always significant even when recalled over and over, providing information about that context in that hour. Nothing old in analysis is ever obsolete. Such self-perpetuation in clinical work is analogous to the cycle that "habitus" undergoes as described by the social theorist Pierre Bourdieu (1991). As Bourdieu explains, social entities constituted by way of language, first conceived in demands stemming from a particular practice and then inevitably abstracted outside of that particular context, remain capable of revitalization when linked anew to that practice.

STS scholars have sought to show that no context has or lacks objectivity. Rather, context arbitrates objectivity. This recognition, in which the STS literature remains ahead of the psychoanalytic literature, yields remarkably novel ways of thinking about historical and current events—and courses of action with patients. For psychoanalysts to conduct their work, the question whether something is true or false outside of a context can usefully be placed to one side in favor of investigating how the complicated attributions of true and false are employed within a given context. In clinical practice, what is held to be "true" in one moment and one context is not necessarily held to be true in another, although the same analyst and patient are at work.[4] What is important is not what is or is not "really" true or false—for analysts the Cassandra call of ontology—but rather the important boundary between ontology and what can be called "personal epistemology." As a psychoanalyst, I am interested in personal epistemology, how analyst and patient work together to develop what could be put forward as objectively true. such an understanding of objectivity has a quite human face in both STS (Fleck, 1979) and psychoanalysis (Grossman, 1995), and personal epistemology can serve as a bridge between the two fields. As Simon Blackburn (2005) writes:

> I believe that ignoring the context and purpose of explanations is responsible for much of the confusion and the heat in debates in the philosophy of science. in my view, it is right both to say that we believe Jupiter has four moons because it has, and right to avoid the issue of how many it has if we are explaining why Galileo did and others did not take the telescope to be a reliable device for registering that number of moons. (p. 183)

In both STS and psychoanalysis, personal epistemology is constituted by two factors, as determined by lived practice: first,

---

[4] Commenting on the search for a common ground that could further all psychoanalytic inquiry, Roy Schafer (1990) wrote that in the "making, breaking, and remaking of contexts—there is common ground" (p. 50)—a common ground that would not imply a conservative value system or disavow progress. Context sets the upper limit on what is the only common ground that can be found among different groups of analysts.

the thought-communities at play, and, second, what the interpreter and the interpreted at work come to believe to be true and false. An understanding of personal epistemology is far more important to the clinical analyst than detailing programmatically how psychoanalysis can proceed through testing by an evolutionary falsification doctrine.[5]

What some call objectivity and correlate with positivism Galison (1998) calls "mechanical objectivity" a leftover, as he suggests, from the nineteenth century, with its idealization of and conviction in context-less certainty. Galison prefers a critical definition of objectivity, one with roots also in the nineteenth century, but one that emphasizes the concept as a pragmatically employed instrument to accomplish the many and often contradictory tasks of science. Documenting the emergence of scientific objectivity as revealed in images from scientific atlases, he and Daston (2007) recount how lofty epistemic ideals fused with workaday practices. Such an understanding of objectivity bears upon Owen Renik's (1993) concept of irreducible subjectivity. In psychoanalysis, irreducible subjectivity inescapably assumes objectivity somewhere— so that it can be recognized as subjectivity. Attention to context thus leads to the recognition that there can be no subjectivity without a necessarily implicated objectivity and lends substance to John R. Searle's argument that states, "We can have an epistemically objective science of a domain that is ontologically subjective" (1993, p. 9). Jonathan Lear (2003) presents a remarkably similar idea in psychoanalysis, as do Galison and Daston (2007, see chapter five) with their concept of "structural objectivity," a model that they derive from the late nineteenth century. Objectivity in clinical psychoanalysis, which can have several different aspects and meanings,I defend as an ideal that analysts in their work hope to approximate so as to develop and sustain confidence in their

---

[5] See the many related arguments in STS of Galison and Stump (1996).

contextualized procedures. In psychoanalysis, following Daston and Galison's argument regarding scientific objectivity, questions of how one or more contexts "lack" or "possess" objectivity can be pushed aside in favor of critical objectivity and an understanding of the multiple perceived realities involved in psychoanalytic work.

Psychoanalysis and STS share the presumption that real events anchor fluctuations of perception, including those induced by multiple contexts. The notion of real events, however, can take different forms. Hacking (1983) has described how events (or effects) are relative in the sense that they are bound to the ability to recreate them: effects depend on a person's skill but they still cross theories and styles of reasoning. Although not involved with STS, Hilary Putnam (1987) refers to "ontological realism," the idea of having a base or foundation from which everything else emerges. "Common-sense realism," which is the native habitat of psychoanalysis, is the view that so far as human knowledge is concerned, what a thing really is in itself and our ideas of what that thing is can never be separated in a dichotomous way. Each of these, in different ways, emphasizes an aboriginal reality that is unchanging despite the changing face of how it is perceived. Both STS and psychoanalysis rely on a variant of the same argument—that there are theory resilient effects in the world, which cross and are therefore independent of or prior to theories seeking to depict them, and that are known insofar as they keep being used. since these effects are the main objects studied by modern scientists and analysts, such resilient effects are enough to argue for a firm notion of realism.[6] Many core notions of psychoanalysis (e.g., effects of transference, derivatives of intrapsychic conflict) make common sense, cross theories in this way, and thereby qualify to possess such realism.

---

[6] See a similar argument with respect to STS but regarding different matters in Stump (1992).

Context does not remake reality but influences the perception of it. Thus, the central tenets of psychoanalysis when understood in context still are bound to a real world of objects. This fundamental recognition allows analysts to do their clinical work: there are no different worlds, only the inevitability of different ways of parsing the world. Fluctuations induced by context can remake a person's sense of reality, but those fluctuations can be precisely known analytically because of our reliance on the stability of the world. Stated another way, psychoanalytic technique creates the stabilities that allow for a focus on the instabilities, and both clinicians and practitioners of STS recognize that a backdrop of stability is necessary to address the inevitability of such instabilities.

Aware of its multiple contexts, psychoanalysis proceeds by way of provisional understandings of actual events. External realities are cast provisionally during an analysis (Schafer, 2003) in accord with what the patient is trying to get to.[7] Since it is evolution within the context of external realities that concerns psychoanalysis, what a patient says about events—including their history—is seen in constant motion. The perception of external realities in psychoanalysis thus qualifies as what Biagioli (1993), among many others, calls situated knowledge, that is, partial understandings that are produced and located specifically in a particular place at a particular time and are neither arbitrary nor fixed. At issue here is what Thomas Nagel (1985) refers to as "the view from nowhere," according to which alternative lines of sight on the same raw phenomena must remain provisional, forever engaging in commerce with other lines of sight that construe matters differently. Neither psychoanalysis nor STS play what Haraway (1991) calls

---

[7] Schafer (1992) in another place suggests that external reality is not even a psychoanalytic concept. Likewise, recall Loewald's proposal that the concept of the social makes no sense to the child.

"the God trick"—the act of appearing to see everything from no-where in particular. instead, analysts free themselves in their clinical work from notions of inner and outer as fixed points of reference, so that inner and outer can be seen for how they func-tion contextually, i.e., as permeable. All perceptions, even in their narrowness, draw from a broader sense of the world than any one perception allows (Galison, 1997b). Similarly, every observation a patient makes of external reality reflects the transference, and every transference perception offers a commentary on the pa-tient's relationship to external reality.

The Demise of Dichotomous Thinking

The view from STS can influence not only the analyst's clinical vi-sion but also his or her understanding of the link between theory and practice. In a word, STS opposes the imperialism of theory, or the inclination to take theory as primary, and sees theory as misap-plied when it ignores context. Multiple models and theories constantly operate behind the scenes (Fuller, 2007). Contextual thinking offers insight into our use of them, allowing us to take our bearings and to determine what form of intervention is appropriate at what time: context—not model, not theory, not technique—is primary. Theory thus derives its value from context.

Psychoanalysis requires an open mind toward the inherent theoretical disunity that becomes visible when context is empha-sized. As Galison and Stump (1996) have illustrated, disunity is not a foible to be overcome but the natural resting state of all contemporary sciences, and psychoanalysis is no exception. The claim that one theory or method necessarily supersedes another, without assessing contextual relevance, remakes psychoanalysis into the image of the now invading theory or method. Instead, context promotes a specifically psychoanalytic understanding of dichotomy, offering insight into how seemingly fixed binaries—art and science, hermeneutics and experiment, mind and nature, soft (social) and hard (natural) approaches to data assessment—are actually permeable. Each apparent opposite must draw on context in order to make its own case successfully. Thus Freud (1923[1922]), although determined to present psychoanalysis as a science, still discussed it also as "an interpretative art" (p. 238). It is context that makes the case for interpretation as midway between and connected to both science and art. Context forces the realization that any dichotomy is not merely what it purports to be: there is a third engendered by the prevailing context.

STS has documented how the vicissitudes of context cannot be escaped, even by turning to the dry laboratory or the experiment as a pure culture of context-less inquiry. Galison (1987) has depicted how experimentation has a "life of its own," and how this life can be independent of the constraints of the actual theory being tested. Hacking (1992) calls experimentation "a style of reasoning" that displays the same self-stabilizing tendencies as in any other style of reasoning, outlining what can be thought of as a philosophy of contextual experimentation, Galison and Hacking underscore how context determines the very essence of experimentation itself, and how what is found can be understood realistically. They explain how there is no such thing as a pure experiment, only an experimental context no different from any other context. An investigator might offer a context clothed in the garb of methodological certainty for study and, with no attention to context, perhaps the consumer as well as the investigator can be blinded by a double-blind study. Galison (1997a) puts the point simply and clearly: "We can speak of conditions of experimentality, focusing on the constraints that allow (or disallow) forms of laboratory argumentation" (p. 671).

For quite a long time, analysts have fretfully envisioned "Rosetta Stones" to guide translation—between mind and body, between different methods of inquiry. Yet, the demise of dichotomy allows context to promote what STS authors have termed border skirmishes, trading zones, and trade languages. A "border skirmish" between adjacent and rival perspectives and methods stands in support of a democracy of perspectives and methods. Each scientific context is determined by a particular method, but method must acclimate to context, not vice versa. Latour (2004) has likewise argued that what is fatal to the democracy of methods becomes fatal to the healthy development of various practices within the same branch of science.

STS has investigated how an important historical context—think also of psychoanalytic theory and practice—can propagate its own language and how those languages conflict with one another. One significant byproduct of such border skirmishes will be the development of a "trade language" (Fuller, 1995) that spans contexts. A trade language is a hybrid tongue, one that serves to break down cultural barriers associated with two or more original languages. different languages intermingle, leading to the creation of a new language—a trade language consisting of exchanges between two or more systems that compete for explanatory space. Such trade languages arise from contexts skirmishing with one another over their respective borders. Thus when a trade language emerges, it remains open whether the language will signify the creation of a new context or will remain an artifact of inadequate communication, leaving intact borders and a situation of stasis—but also a reminder of the potential to produce new contexts.

As STS and different psychoanalytic theories demonstrate, context is not intrinsic to one or another epistemology, but is, instead, virtually limitlessly plastic. it is also vulnerable to being reduced to a particular epistemology, and such reduction from a stand-alone concept to a specific and limited definition of context inflicts a further obfuscating fate on other reductions with which it comes into contact (Smith, 2006). Context in that way can become formalized in the ideas of a single theorist and made vulnerable to being pulled into an interpretive context within one or another favored epistemology to the exclusion of others. When it is drawn into a single epistemology, it becomes an entity—one whose definition is brought into a network of concepts that determine its meaning within the network's own tolerance for plasticity. Context, in this sense, can and has been imported and used to buttress contemporary epistemologies.[8]

Conclusion

Psychoanalytic theory today is characterized by the silent onset of trade languages that tend to be pursued by those interested in comparative therapeutics and integrative formulations. Concepts, terms, and other diction from different theories become mingled as part of this effort. The origin of much of contemporary psychoanalytic parlance, therefore, represents the outcome of a collision of systems of different contexts and their respective cultures. Still, because a new trade language can be a harbinger of more far-reaching changes to come, it merits paying careful attention to the use of such terminologies. In the history of science, Galison (1999) has explored the significance of the "trading zone," an arena in which quite different activities or theories from divergent and competing sources can be locally coordinated, without having to reconcile the global differences on which they are based. Trading zones are characterized by trade languages—the new words and ways of speaking brought into existence by such zones. In psychoanalysis, two or

---

[8] See Latour's (1999, pp. 116–133) depiction of how necessary it was to move readily from one epistemology to another without creating paradox that allowed for the discovery of yeast peculiar to lactic acid.

more contexts can come to form a trading zone with a corresponding trade language. such a process can be witnessed in both the
clinical situation and the development of theory. Indeed, a case can
be made that the recent evolution of psychoanalytic principles,
loosely packaged as "pluralistic," is the function less of the successful
integration of different theories than of the development of new
trade languages. Practitioners employing different languages speak
to and influence one another, and the collision of each new trade
language forges different theoretical viewpoints. Still, trading zones
and trade languages characterize progress at a potential price: the
myriad advantages and disadvantages of what is termed "interpenetration," integration of viewpoints that ends in interpenetration,
risks becoming static and uncritical. To be useful, such integration
must retain the dynamic and critical form of two programs jostling
one another. Through such integration, we can give concrete expression to Nagel's (1985) claim that the clash of viewpoints over
particular phenomena—rather than the quest for the discovery of
new phenomena—opens up the most compellingly important vis-
tas of human understanding.

References

Biagioli, M. (1993). *The Practice of Science in the Culture of Absolutism*. Chi-
    cago: University of Chicago Press.
Blackburn, S. (2005). *Truth: A Guide*. Oxford: Oxford University Press.
Boesky, D. (2008). *Psychoanalytic Disagreements in Context*. New York: Jason
    Aronson.
Bourdieu, P. (1991). *Language and Symbolic Power*. Cambridge, MA: Har-
    vard University Press.
Cicchetti, D., & Rogosch, F. (1996). Equifinality and multifinality in develop-
    mental psychopathology. *Development and Psychopathology* 8 (4):597–
    600.

Daston, l., & Galison, P. (2007). *Objectivity*. Cambridge, MA: Zone Books.

Davidson, A. (1987). How to do the history of psychoanalysis: A reading of Freud's three essays on the theory of sexuality. *Critical Inquiry 13* (2):252–277.

———(1996). Styles of reasoning, conceptual history, and the emergence of psychiatry. in P. Galison & D. Stump (Eds.). *The Disunity of Science: Boundaries, Contexts, and Power*, pp. 75–100. Stanford: Stanford University Press.

Fleck, L. (1979). *Genesis and Development of a Scientific Fact*. Chicago: University of Chicago Press.

Fonagy, P. (2003). Some complexities in the relationship of psychoanalytic theory to technique. *Psychoanalytic Quarterly 72* (1):13–47.

Freud, S. (1905) Three essays on the theory of sexuality. *Standard Edition* 7:125–243.

———(1913). The claims of psychoanalysis to scientific interest. *Standard Edition* 13:163–190.

———(1923 [1922]). Two encyclopedia articles. *Standard Edition* 18:235–259.

Fuller, S. (1995). Talking metaphysical turkey. in P. Galison & D. Stump (Eds.). *The Disunity of Science: Boundaries, Contexts, And Power* (pp. 170–188). Stanford: Stanford University Press.

———(2007). *New Frontiers in Science and Technology Studies*. Malden, MA: Polity Press.

Galison, P. (1987). *How Experiments End*. Chicago: University of Chicago Press.

———(1997a). Material culture, theoretical culture, and delocalization. in D. Pestre & J. Krige (Eds.). *Science in The Twentieth Century* (pp. 669–682). Amsterdam: Harwood Publishers.

———(1997b). *Image and Logic: A Material Culture of Microphysics*. Chicago: University of Chicago Press.

———(1998). Judgment against objectivity. in C. Jones & P. Galison, Eds. *Picturing Science, Producing Art*, pp. 327–359. New York: Routledge.

———(1999). Trading zone: Coordinating action and belief. in M. Biagioli (Ed.). *The Science Studies Reader* (pp. 137–160). New York: Routledge.

———(2004). *Einstein's Clocks, Poincaré's Maps: Empires of Time*. New York: W.W. Norton & Company.

———(2012). Blacked-out spaces: Freud, censorship and the re-territorialization of mind. *British Journal for the History of Science* 45:235–266.

———& Stump, D. (1996). *The Disunity of Science: Boundaries, Contexts, and Power*. Stanford: Stanford University Press.

Grice, P. (1989). *Studies in the Way of Words*. Cambridge, MA: Harvard University Press.

Grossman, W. (1992). Hierarchies, boundaries, and representation in a Freudian model of mental organization. *Journal of the American Psychoanalytic Association 40* (1):27–62.

Grossman, W. (1995). Psychological vicissitudes of theory in clinical work. *International Journal of Psychoanalysis* 76:885–899.

Hacking, J. (1983). *Representing and Intervening*. New York: Cambridge University Press.

———(1992). 'Style' for historians and philosophers. *Studies in History and the Philosophy of Science 23* (1):1–20.

Haraway, d. (1991). *Simians, Cyborgs, And Women: The Reinvention of Nature*. London: Routledge.

Kagan J. (2006). *An Argument for Mind*. New Haven: Yale University Press.

Knorr Cetina, K. (1999). *Epistemic cultures: How the Sciences Make Knowledge*. Cambridge, MA: Harvard University Press.

Latour, B. (1999). *Pandora's Hope: Essays on the Reality of Science Studies*. Cambridge, MA: Harvard University Press.

———(2004). *Politics of Nature: How to Bring the Sciences into Democracy*. Cambridge, MA: Harvard University Press. Latour, B. (2005). *Reassembling the Social: An Introduction to Actor–Network Theory*. Oxford: Oxford University Press.

Lear, J. (2003). *Therapeutic Action: An Earnest Plea for Irony*. New York: Other Press.

Nagel, T. (1985). *The View from Nowhere.* New York: Oxford University Press.

Nickles, T. (1987). From natural philosophy to metaphilosophy of science. in P. Achinstein & R. Kargon (Eds.). *Kelvin's Baltimore Lectures and Modern Theoretical Physics: Historical and Philosophical Perspectives,* pp. 507–541. Cambridge, MA: MIT Press.

Ornston, D. (1985). Freud's conception is different from Strachey's. *Journal of the American Psychoanalytic Association 33*:379–412.

Putnam, H. (1987). *The Many Faces of Realism.* Lasalle, IL: Open Court.

Renik, O. (1993). Analytic interaction: Conceptualizing technique in light of the analyst's irreducible subjectivity. *Psychoanalytic Quarterly 62*:553–571.

Schafer, R. (1990). The search for common ground. *International Journal of Psychoanalysis 71*:49–52.

———(1992). *Retelling a life: Narration and dialogue in psychoanalysis.* New York: Basic Books.

———(2003). Knowing another person psychoanalytically. in R Shafer, *Insight and Interpretation: The Essential Tools of Psychoanalysis,* pp. 133–152. New York: Other Press.

Searle, J.R. (1979). *Expression and meaning: Studies in the theory of speech acts.* Cambridge & New York: Cambridge University Press.

———(1993). The problem of consciousness. *Social Research 60* (1):3–16.

Smith, B.H. (2006). *Scandalous Knowledge: Science, Truth, and the Human.* Durham, NC: Duke University Press. Stump, D. (1992). Naturalized philosophy with a plurality of methods. *Philosophy of Science 59*:456–460.

Waelder, R. (1936). The principle of multiple function. *Psychoanalytic Quarterly 5*:45–62.

CHAPTER 8

ANALYTIC PREPARATION: THE CREATION OF AN ANALYTIC CLIMATE WITH PATIENTS NOT YET IN ANALYSIS

The art and science of beginning an analysis has a life of its own and can be considered in many ways quite apart from its later stages. An incremental path forward is smoothed for patients who are not yet prepared to analyze, and builds eventually into something readily recognizable as an analysis. The term *analytic preparation* refers to this set of processes. Early on, the analyst is concerned less with facilitating an early replica of an idealized analysis than with facilitating the mutual adaptation of patient and analyst as they begin to negotiate a "thought community." Since analytic preparation is not an entity, it does not neatly overlap in real time with the opening phase as usually described, does not have a discrete beginning or end, and does not abruptly shift midstream into analysis proper. Some relations between analytic preparation, analytic interaction, and the interpretation of transference are examined.

This paper takes up issues that are not in my judgment elsewhere adequately addressed, or generally regarded as topics meriting special consideration. I am concerned with how to understand what goes on in the period between a patient's initial contact with an analyst and the point, if it ever occurs, that this new arrivee fits the profile of the capable, introspective analytic patient some clinical principles implicitly presume he or she must be. The tasks the analyst is faced with during this period are complex, at times seemingly contradictory to one another, and at times quite unlike those characterizing the analytic setting as it is often depicted. For convenience' sake, I will introduce a heuristic and term the bundle of processes characterizing these tasks *analytic preparation.* The principles to be developed are applicable to patients who begin in a psychotherapy and eventually convert to analysis, as well as to those who arrive wishing to embark on an analysis. It is a big bite taking on these issues, and although I believe the central issues of concern can be clearly defined and witnessed, I suspect, given the current sprawl of views within psychoanalysis, that they cannot at present be resolved to everyone's satisfaction.

Throughout this paper, I will elaborate a particular view of the beginning of analysis—that analyst and patient must first learn how to adapt to each other. This process of mutual adaptation is unending, and analytic preparation is its earliest history. Once this mutual adaptation is established as a viable goal by both individuals (establishing it as such is itself part of the process). it is constantly transformed and refined by the stepwise developments that occur in an ever-deepening analysis.

Analyst and patient, when they begin together, construct a distinctive partnership, with striking parallels to what has been termed a "thought community" (Fleck 1979). This particular thought community of two negotiates, develops, and then proceeds within its very own constantly changing criteria of objectivity, in a broad sense. Such a thought community is possessed by, even as it possesses, its members. Over time, it becomes more stable and consistent than its component members, who tend to be driven by quite fluctuating and contradictory motives. A thought community works to bring into existence new objects, or so modifies old objects that they appear in a new way, with new properties, and with new relations and distinctions vis-à-vis other objects. Since it takes on a stability that is beyond the reach of either member's ability, acting alone, to influence it, an analysis is constituted by more than the individual inputs of analyst and patient.

Both patient and analyst are independently and simultaneously embedded within multiple thought communities. Beginning an analysis to a patient amounts to creating new criteria for objectivity that are nested within other such criteria, reflecting both outer allegiances (e.g., to family, ethnicity, nationality, the facts of science) and inner allegiances (e.g., to objects of merger fantasy or objects of idealization). The beginning patient will have to figure out, given the nature of his or her anxieties, how to cope with the unfolding dangers and opportunities for gratification involved with creating and then living within this one increasingly influential thought community. Although it is taxing for a patient to participate in several such thought communities at the same time, it is necessary if the insights of analysis are to take root in a life.

Seen in this way, analyst and beginning patient pass in and out of an equilibrium characterized by a developing degree of shared understandings. This equilibrium—based on an ever-precarious balance between these shared understandings and various factors working against them—can never be taken for granted, even from one moment to the next, even though the base of shared understanding itself expands. If the analyst or the patient comes to assume that this equilibrium can be presumed without analyzing, their dialogue will lag behind what is fundamental to analysis—the necessary examination of the dynamics of the transference. For the patient to arrive at a recognition that this tension characterizes analytic work, and is a desirable state of affairs, is the outcome of a long and complicated set of processes. It cannot be assumed, treated as if it should already be in a patient's repertoire, nor should its absence be viewed as an insurmountable obstacle when beginning with a patient. Analytic preparation is also about how the dyad can best come to realize this all-important principle, of coming to monitor and usefully analyze these endless momentary perturbations.

The particular views of the analyst on how analysis works are of importance to the analyst and of interest to the patient during analytic preparation because their earliest negotiations must be conducted with some plan in the analyst's mind, a plan the patient must sooner or later reckon with (for more on negotiations in psychoanalysis, (see A. Goldberg 1987). Analytic preparation is saturated with the impact of giving birth to both participants' fantasies and ideas of how to let implicit and explicit theories guide the unfolding of events, including specifying each participant's particular responsibilities. Usually the analyst leads the way, but the patient need not so readily follow. It is not necessary for the patient to endorse the analyst's interpretation of how theory will affect them, as long as the analyst is careful to subject the issue to continuing analysis.

In a volume dedicated to the opening phase of analysis, Jacobs (1990) remarks how precious little has been written on the subject, a complaint echoed by Brenner (1990) in the same book. With both the opening phase and analytic preparation, there is certainly a need to conceptually demarcate analytic preparation from what follows, the opening phase from the middle and end phases. With both, the underlying assumptions have been that what characterizes analysis proper—how it is understood, described, and put into effect—likewise characterizes the earliest contact. The challenges of analytic preparation, though, are not synonymous with those of the traditional opening phase. To address the distinctiveness of analytic preparation, I propose that certain elements of the clinical theory central to contemporary American psychoanalysis be tailored for a slightly different fit.

What Analysis Can Realistically Ask of
Its Theories on Beginning

I am trying here to lay out a mindset for the clinical analyst. Although I will be touching on some abstractions concerning the role of theory, my primary concern is with how analysts can usefully think about what they do with what they know about a patient, and how analysis can then proceed. My aims here resemble those of Galison (2003), whose project is to show how scientists can bring together more directly the abstract and concrete levels of their thought, thereby allowing the levels to better illuminate each other.

Virtually every psychoanalytic author who has examined the opening phase agrees in principle that in the early going the clinician, to allow the new patient to settle in, should be "flexible" in applying the typical analytic procedures. However, the idea of flexibility is more complicated than might at first be evident. Understanding the intricacies of the relations between theory and technique requires a distinctively psychoanalytic grasp of what theory does to technique during analytic preparation. This topic is currently of widespread general interest; thus, Almond (2003) perceives the importance of this relation of analyst to theory, and refers to it as the holding function of theory. But he focuses on the comfort and downplays the subtle yet profound tensions around adherence to theory, often involving an internal clash of directives. Friedman (1989) has noted how the hidden role of theory is to set comfortable limits on the analyst's behavior, a narrowing of options that makes the clinical situation, with all its inherent anxieties, more bearable. The key point with respect to analytic preparation is that the analyst is internally pressured to adhere and yet not to adhere, both at once, and is forced into a set of compromises called flexibility.

Even so, flexibility is the wrong term to apply to technique during analytic preparation. It erroneously implies that a lack of flexibility characterizes later analytic work. Subtly implied also is that analytic preparation is a poorer but necessary version of what takes place later, when technique will be cleaner and disturbing departures will snap into place. Then, too, idealizing adherence to a set of standardized behaviors betrays a misunderstanding of the relation between theory and technique in psychoanalysis. I will have more to say about this.

The pressing issue is how analyst and patient adapt not only to one another but also to the analytic principles that they believe govern, at least in part, what they are there to do. This has bred two conceptual problems—how the analyst is to behave and how the analyst's initiatives should be limited. The first is a problem of prescription; the second, of proscription.

Let us begin with the first. How analyst and patient adapt to theory has been widely interpreted as revolving around how the analyst behaves with the patient. Thus, one theory has the analyst doing one thing, while another prescribes an entirely different course of action, and each claims to be correct. Yet it is not at all clear that an invariantly correct technical way to behave with patients, or even different classes of patients, can at present (or ever) be identified.

This problem has been glimpsed by Boesky (2004), who makes the point that most clinical disputes between theorists have more to do with how evidence is handled than with the nature of true disagreement, the resolution of which tends to remain unknown. The evidence that is required to make a proper determination—depending on the context of an analysand's associations or an in-depth clinical report—is too often selectively reported, or not adequately weighed, or not properly fitted to a particular explanation. Inadequate reporting of empirical evidence foments theoretical disputes. Different kinds of evidence are suitable for the different levels of abstraction that characterize psychoanalytic theories, and most disagreements take place at very high levels of abstraction. Yet it is clinical evidence at a low level of abstraction that influences clinical decisions, which are only indirectly affected by broader generalizations. Since an adjudicative turn to clinical evidence trumps theory in this way, what to do becomes localized at a remove from theoretical prescription. But Boesky does not squarely confront the implications. Can it be that, even when evidence is fairly mobilized and considered, we cannot do what he in fact assumes we can—that is, decisively adjudicate between two approaches? Does not evidence conform to conceptions just as profoundly as conceptions do to evidence?

The two solutions most often proposed to this problem of prescription implicate (1) underdetermination and (2) induction. Both vex, and neither truly solves the problem. It does not illuminate the problem to state that any technical prescription will be underdetermined by clinical data during the opening phase (see Edelson 1984), though certainly this is so. Nor is it adequate to hold, with Fonagy (2002), that there is a decisive way to harness the limitless engine of induction. Fonagy himself identifies a danger lurking in induction, a malicious tendency toward the overspecification of theory. To specify how to behave under different conditions, at different times, and with different patients is to suggest that prescribing an analyst's behavior entails first an act of generalization whereby patients are taken to instantiate a category. However, this necessary step commits analysis to the sort of nomothetic generalizations that are fundamentally at odds with analytic methodology. The more abstract way of thinking characteristic of psychoanalytic theory does not so readily issue into "rules" and can translate into a multitude of credible ways to behave with even a single patient. To say this is not to endorse technical anarchy or a pluralism devoid of critical dialogue; it is to say only that thinking about analytic matters trumps the prescription of rules. Thus, both of these solutions to the problem of how theory prescribes are helpful, but stop short of the mark. Both are solutions displaced onto psychoanalysis from other methodological domains.

Turn now to the problem of how theory proscribes. Many analytic authors line up in support of one theoretical perspective or another in order to limit the clinical initiatives of the analyst in a way they have come to prefer. One line becomes correct and the other incorrect, but both lines work stealthily to impose their version of limits on what is deemed technically acceptable. This is a mischievous problem, and currently there is a movement afoot to loosen the hold of theory's proscriptive grip in the service of eclecticism, openness, and pluralism. But the problem goes deep and cannot be solved simply by our being receptive to other views. A bid to solve this problem can easily become cast in caricature—the topsy-turvy trumpeting of advances in technique that consists of reporting interventions once considered shocking (countertransference disclosures, dramatic departures from neutrality, and so on) whose purported success is held to debunk the proscriptions of rival points of view, all too often set up as straw men. Although any prod to thinking anew about clinical matters is to be welcomed, it is the assumption underlying theory's proscriptive authority, rather than the context of what is proscribed, that bedevils analytic progress.

All of these ways of adapting to the impact—prescriptive or proscriptive—of our theories follow from a common conception of the relation between theory and technique. According to this view, theory is the master of technique, and the analyst is the purveyor of techniques based on the theories he or she has accepted. I regard this assumption as external to psychoanalysis. Our clinical theory is different from the theories of other forms of psychological intervention in at least one fundamental way.

Nonanalytic theories, typically considered more "evidence-based," are held to the scientific obligation of mirroring what actually takes place between patient and therapist. For example, in manualized treatments, the therapist complies with what the manual instructs him or her to do, and departures are by definition errors.

In stark contrast, how an analyst finds guidance to act, moving from the realm of precepts to the realm of understanding, and then to the realm of acting, is among the most interesting clinical questions. There are many intervening steps between what an analyst understands and what an analyst does. The field that understanding carves out can afford to be—and indeed should be—broad and multifactorial, whereas the field carved out by action is narrow, as any action excludes other actions, often equally plausible, that might have been taken. Thus, everything an analyst does may be seen as the affirmation of one view and the renunciation of another that may approximate it in plausibility. It follows that analytic theory of technique is at bottom about understanding how to understand, from which follows the understanding of how to act, which can so readily be mired in an anxious ambiguity.

Recall that from the beginning of analytic history there was an understanding that the opening phase requires specific departures from standard operating procedure. Freud, (1912, 1913), in his papers on technique, sought to persuade by using the rhetorical strategy of prescribing fixed rules, and then describing instances in which departures from them were necessary: "I think I am well advised . . . to call these rules 'recommendations' and not to claim any unconditional acceptance for them" (1913, p. 123). There is good reason for this. On the surface, Freud might seem to be arguing with himself, but this appearance is misleading. Freud always worked out matters from the assumption of a dynamic process; he used the analogy of rules in various contexts only to convey his ideas, not to develop them. His discussion of the opening phase, like much of his writing on other topics, first emphasizes the conceptual side of a problem, which is invariably complex and hard to understand. Once the conceptual side is worked out, then and only then does Freud present rules and precepts, which he uses to communicate and exemplify his thinking but never forthwith to represent it. Rules caricature the analytic method, Freud said sternly in an admonishing letter to his restless disciple Ferenczi (see Grubrich-Simitis 1986). When reading Freud, we must always take note of his method of exposition. It was his followers, not Freud, who embraced a taxing exactitude of codified rules.

But is there, then, a standard operating procedure in the opening phase? If, from the outset, all we can find is the advice to depart from any such procedure, rules become a stalking-horse for an unworldly technical purity. Freud (1913) metaphorized the notion of rules in the opening phase by comparing them with principles in the opening game in chess. Authors seeking systematization over the years have sought to modify Freud's rules by laying out new ones, or the groundwork for departures from the rules, old and new, appropriate to the opening phase. However, rules are no less rules for being new. In quiet allegiance to the hegemony of rules, Glover (1955) and Fenichel (1941) in emphasizing elasticity, and Gitelson (1962) in conceptualizing the diatrophic function of the analyst, each focused on what an analyst should do and be, rather than on what and how an analyst should think. It is not a huge leap from the rules of the opening game in chess to the rules of a manualized treatment. That is the price paid for embracing the rule-bound rather than the conceptually driven side of Freud's forays into psychoanalytic technique.

From the clinical mindset I am advancing, there follows a need to develop a way of approaching the tasks and dilemmas of the clinician during analytic preparation, with the assumption that the clinician's technical skill need not be restrained by explicit prohibitions or guided by prescription.

Diagnosing a Person is Diagnosing a Process

Psychoanalytic theory is not scripture meant to be followed by rote, or, failing that, put out of mind. Rather, when put into practice, analytic theory constantly renews and refreshes itself because it is filtered through the joint experience of two individuals; theorizing in most natural sciences assumes that the world is subject to examination and classification, but that the theorizer is a constant. However, when the theorizer has an unconscious, employs defenses, and struggles with intrapsychic conflict, and when this is built into the theory itself, the essential nature of that theory dramatically shifts. This view of psychoanalytic theory has been examined by Grossman (1995), who has explored the roles, each of which has quite different effects, that theories play in the analyst's mind, both preconsciously and unconsciously. Even though psychoanalytic theories operate to some extent the way any general scientific theory does, (i.e., by bringing provisional ideas into conjunction with observations to order our understanding of things), they also do much more, because of the manner in which they are arrayed within the analytic setting. The conflicted mental functioning of the analyst cannot be factored out of any equation having to do with theory. The hold of theories on an analyst comes to resemble that of unconscious fantasies, as they intermittently come and go in consciousness, and their influence waxes and wanes in piecemeal fashion. Theories become internal objects, imbued with the transferences to authority that characterize the professional context of our field. In this sense, theories sustain intensely personal internal conversations with a medley of influential friends and foes. Theories are inevitably understood through the lens of the analyst's compromise formations, and thereby are rendered idiosyncratic. For these reasons, psychoanalysts do not obey or disobey theories; rather, they obey or disobey their own internal injunctions in consultation with ever evolving internal objects swayed by many factors. In this sense, it is impossible for an analyst to be merely guided by theories.

Further, during analytic preparation analysts are drawn to theories and then must step clear of them, depart from them, as children playing tag must leave home base, where they are safe, if the game is to continue. They may return to home base in order to avoid being tagged, but the game itself is played out away from this base. Searl (1936) long ago implied that a helpful function of theory is to buttress the analyst's weaknesses during moments when things are not going well or according to plan. Psychoanalytic theories function like touchstones in the bidirectional stream of processes we take as our data. Analysts rely on theories in observing, formulating, and intervening, all according to how they unconsciously interpret their own mental life, that of the patient, and their theory of choice; processes then unfold that must eventually be brought back to the theories to be assessed again; this recursive set of arrangements is unending.

This situation shows why it is not so important whether a particular psychoanalytic theory is right or wrong. Our theories cannot be held accountable for what analysts do with patients. Nor can they be adequately tested the way theories are tested in other sciences. The test can only be pragmatic: to grasp what an analyst does with them by understanding what they first do to him or her.

Since psychoanalytic theories function in this manner, so different from the theories of natural science, which have a fixed, constant theorizer, it follows that any diagnosis of what clinically occurs is as much the diagnosis of a process as of a person, since it inevitably implicates the interaction of two minds in dialogue, each in conflict.

I am taking a slant quite different from Hoffman's "throwing away the book" (1994); out of ambivalence regarding technique in general, he views the book as too easily upsetting the fragile balance between authoritarian and spontaneous ways of being with patients. We interpret different books. I agree that no analysis can be satisfactorily mapped by technical formulations, but only if these are understood prescriptively and proscriptively, and as exhaustive of the possibilities. Wittgenstein (1953) clearly sees this issue as widespread and laughs at the absurdity and uselessness of a map as large as the region it represents—which a "complete" map would have to be. I am saying that analysts have no need to throw away the book, because the book is so remarkably accommodating. Every analyst has a different version of the book, and this is inevitable. To throw away the book is to throw away the subjectivity of the analyst, which is yoked during the back-and-forth flow between what is understood and what is done. Hoffman interprets the unforgiving book of ink and paper, whereas mine is the book of psychoanalysis as anyone interprets its application in practice, and which cannot possibly be discarded. This unit—this "book"—is thus irreducible with respect to the inevitability of clinical judgments.

In what follows, I will examine analytic preparation with this understanding of theory and technique in mind. There are many streams that feed the way analysts understand the earliest contacts during a treatment that may—and only may—lead to an analysis. I will not address them all, but rather will focus on a few specific issues that are in general overlooked or given short shrift in the literature, more so than in the oral tradition of clinical psychoanalysis. But first, I will further illustrate the major problem.

The Problem of Beginning

Some of the controversially heightened distinctions between different analytic theories would not be as pressured, and greater clarity would be had, if we better distinguished the aims of the different phases of an analysis. The processes at play when beginning, deepening, and ending an analysis are more varied and phase-specific than meets the eye. Drawing such key clinical distinctions can make or break an analysis. To illustrate, I will compare two fundamental papers addressing self- destructiveness and the outer limits of analyzability—one by Betty Joseph on patients addicted to near-death, the other by Hans Loewald on the nature of repetition. Both papers are still widely read and can be found on many institutes' syllabi. Written ten years apart, both appear to be concerned with a remarkably similar set of clinical problems, as each addresses masochism, guilt, and malignant narcissism in similar patients, and each invokes Freud's concept of the death instinct for explanatory purposes. Both depict similar clinical difficulties and impasses, and both advocate an analysis at a frequency of four or five sessions weekly. Both analysts are often thought of as seminal contributors to object relations theory. The differences between these two papers are thus quite striking.

Practicing in America, Loewald (1972) described a personality constellation in the analysand that to him configured an outer limit to analyzability. He spoke of a predisposition to negative therapeutic reaction that marked certain nonpsychotic and nonsociopathic individuals as treatment refractory. His emphasis with them was on analyzing the transference. The inability of the analytic dyad to successfully do so was taken to confirm their status as unanalyzable. Practicing in London, Joseph (1982) described a feature she termed *addiction to near-death*. Like Loewald, she described a kind of masochism that leads to analytic intransigence. In contrast to Loewald, however, she made no reference whatever to a role for sexuality. Her emphasis was more on the countertransference—transference being viewed as the total situation—and, in sharp contrast to Loewald, she regarded these individuals as analyzable, though she does speak to the arduousness and remarkably long duration of such analyses. Since both seem to have described similar analysands—guilty, profoundly masochistic, nonpsychotic individuals who need to defeat the analyst and embrace death—the fact that Loewald admitted defeat and Joseph claimed success should give one pause.

Interpreting these papers with respect to one another, anyone can construct a story, and many are plausible. My bid to make sense of the comparison is to demonstrate that Joseph prioritizes the bidirectional emotional currents, with countertransference accorded equal status with transference, whereas Loewald privileges the analysis of the transference, particularly in the early going. As their discussions unfold, these emphases emerge as unquestioned assumptions of their analytic viewpoints. But there is more to my story. I suggest that aspects of Joseph's approach might be more useful with such difficult patients early on, and aspects of Loewald's later in treatment. Loewald describes more difficulty engaging his patients early on, whereas it is unclear what Joseph means by saying that her patients were successfully analyzed by the end. It is unclear, that is, whether she regarded the adequate working through of conflicts, for Loewald the sine qua non of a successful analysis, as a metric of success. Thus, Loewald stressed the technical precept that the analyst remains outside of the transference in order to analyze it, whereas Joseph stressed the analyst's necessary entry into the processes inside the interaction in order to create the conditions for a viable analysis. Joseph expects less of the patient, at least at the outset, then does Loewald, and focuses her attention on helping the patient realize many of the attributes Loewald expects to be already present in an analyzable patient. Where Loewald looks for greater objectivity, more likely to piece together evidence from the data of the patient's comments and actions, Joseph seems content to regard as adequate navigational tools the subjectivities available to her, especially how Kleinian concepts and countertransference inform one another. One can imagine that an optimal balance between these factors naturally occurred in these analyses, but it is not reflected in these authors' reports.

Open-Ended Processes, Not Entities

Understanding beginnings is complicated by how, over time, the processes of clinical psychoanalysis, described so that they may be communicated and understood, relentlessly become recast as entities. Complexities are typically simplified, collapsed into concrete things, when this is done. Entities are easier to wrap one's mind around, play with through theory, and generalize from, than are processes. However, processes are closer to the marrow of clinical realities. The insidious transformation of processes into entities subtly degrades clear description and promotes pseudo-understanding. Processes lend themselves to careful and deep description, whereas entities tend to the creation of new terms and categories that do not always advance our understanding of an issue.[1] We do best to be vigilant about this ubiquitous tendency to attribute "thingness" to protean processes, and to avert such a drift whenever possible. Thus, one often hears of "interpretation" or "the resistance," with no

---

[1] New terms and categories are welcome but require a clear argument with respect to their status for general acceptance, showing how they are superior to an older term or category. It is not sufficient to justify them by their "newness." Otherwise we are in danger of erecting a Tower of Babel, in which the cure by nomenclature is more harmful than the ailment.

accompanying description, as if these bare terms automatically convey a shared understanding.

The term a*nalyzability* well instances this conceptual drift into reification. While the term may usefully serve as a short-hand designation for a combination of attributes characterizing an individual, to think of analyzability as an entity or trait within a person is to concretize an abstracted bundle of processes that can be manifest and therefore known only in the analytic situation. Rudolf Loewenstein would often comment about a prospective patient that he or she was not "analyzable now" (William Grossman, personal communication). Green (1975) said that the key question is not whether a patient is analyzable, but rather whether the patient is "analyzable by me." Both are pointing in the same direction, to the preemptive significance of analytic processes over static entities.

In sound clinical descriptions, processes exist in a flow of time, whereas entities tend to be frozen by being placed outside of that flow. In weaker descriptions, clinical hypotheses are then stipulated as if analysis were timeless, not anchored in the different coloration of the aims and evolving processes that characterize the different phases of an analysis. But the flow of time imposes markedly different presses on different phases of analytic work, to which theory must be responsive. The result is that some clinical ideas can, from the angle of time passing, take on a frozen appearance, too brittle to evolve the way processes do. These ideas can usefully be stated more conditionally, better fitted to particular moments than to broad sweeps of time. When expansively stated, they easily overgeneralize about time and process, and therefore colonize and attempt to govern too much conceptual turf. The more timelessly an idea is conceived, the more it ends up accommodating and explaining too much. The tendency of theory to be located with respect to too little time and therefore too many entities has particularly hindered thinking about analytic preparation.

Compared to the written tradition of psychoanalysis, the oral tradition exemplified by supervision is far more responsive to the circumstances of time and process. Something similar may be true of scholarly traditions more generally. Derrida (1978) has alerted us to many of the remarkable differences between written and oral practices, the prototype of each of which he calls a text. He depicts written texts as independent of the oral circuit of communication, and thus as less immediately present, knowable, and personally accountable than spoken texts. Because written texts lack certain elements of dialogicity—the immediate feedback and self-correcting loop of oral texts—they are more resistant to change. However, they are also more permanent and so persevere as evanescent oral texts cannot; because the latter are not cumulative as written texts are, they seem predestined to constantly rediscover the same things. This is why the raw phenomena of clinical work, one type of practice, cannot be cast as timelessly as the theories used to explain them, a different type of practice, in Derrida's sense.[2]

In the consultation with a prospective patient, analytic preparation initiates a particular kind of evolving diagnostic intention in which the diagnostic target is the process rather than the patient. It then makes clinical sense to think about beginning a process sufficiently open-ended that the analyst can envision a number of viable treatment paths, some of which might well result in an analysis, but do not necessarily.

To do this would be a giant step toward eliminating the

---

[2] In most clinical sciences, the publication of research results trails far behind the hot necessities and novel opportunities to be found in hands-on patient care. Implementing research findings so that they become part of a clinical tradition is a serious problem; the lag can be many years in duration, and at times the translation simply fails.

embarrassing phrase "analytic failure" in describing patients who prefer, or are better qualified for, psychotherapeutic or psycho-pharmacological treatments. Any treatment should be seen as a success if it leads to the patient's receiving a lasting benefit. This is only common sense. After all, the attribution of failure in an analysis is too often made from the perspective of the analyst. Seen through the eyes of the patient, what the analyst views as a failure may well be a success. All too often, privileging analysis over other treatments reflects the needs of the analyst as much as those of the patient. Only when analyst and patient, working to-gether, can get beyond the idea that analysis is in all cases to be preferred, can they really talk to one another. Indeed, the ideali-zation of analysis in so many ways hinders, rather than facilitates, the emergence of a specifically analytic process.

Patients seen today have many treatment options and often enter a psychological treatment of any sort with a heightened concern for therapeutics; far less often than was once the case they envision the benefits of an introspective journey. Many pro-spective patients are concerned, rightly or wrongly, that there is a disconnect between the cultivation of analytic processes and treatment outcome. Renik (2001), in a paean to pragmatism, has described how the patient's experience of therapeutic benefit is his superordinate goal, influencing virtually every decision he makes and what is arrived at with patients. Renik's remarks sharpen the more general point made by Bader (1994)that ther-apeutic goals have tended to be underemphasized in favor of what he calls "process goals," and that this has led to failure in a recursively organized feedback loop that could have served as a useful corrective. This feedback loop has the potential to advance analytic theorizing by harnessing the all-important factor of ap-prehending benefit from the perspective of the patient. But this requires building a conceptual bridge with a patient, between the priority of processes and the likelihood of benefit, and this is an important aspect of analytic preparation.

The very terminology we use to grasp what analysts do influences theory through the power of language to organize the categories that order perceptions. Exploring this requires an investigation of some of the ways language itself can subtly influence the understanding of analytic preparation.

A Borrowed Language Leading to Problems of Conceptualization

The issue I am examining here, that of a dedicated language that has emigrated outside its original domain, is a special instance of a widely recognized and more general problem. Languages are in large part defined by domains of usage. The more general problem was stated by Whitehead (1947) who, musing over an argument proposed by a rival, noted that "most of the muddles of philosophy are . . . due to using a language which is developed from [another] point of view to express a doctrine based upon entirely alien concepts" (p. 117). In the instance of analytic preparation, which shares its language with analysis proper, we are not examining domains quite so disjunct. The solution is not to fashion a separate language, but merely to recognize the problem and its consequences.

From the very beginning, there has been a certain tension between wide and narrow definitions of key terms in psychoanalysis. In general, the more timeless the theory, the more likely it is that wider definitions come into play, and this has clear implications for how clinical phenomena are understood. Conversely, the more a theory accounts for the factor of time passing, as I have argued is necessary for analytic preparation, the more likely a narrow and therefore more precise definition will be put forward. This tension between narrow and broad definitions can be found in Freud's writings.

Take the example of resistance. In 1925, shortly after Freud's remarkable engagement with the core issues that can derail an analysis—traumatic neurosis (1920), negative therapeutic reaction (1923), and masochism (1924)—he added the following curious footnote to *The Interpretation of Dreams*:

> The proposition laid down in these peremptory terms—'whatever interrupts the progress of analytic work is a resistance'—is easily open to misunderstanding. It is of course only to be taken as a technical rule, as a warning to analysts. It cannot be disputed that in the course of an analysis various events may occur the responsibility for which cannot be laid upon the patient's intentions. His father may die without his having murdered him; or a war may break out which brings the analysis to an end. But behind its obvious exaggeration the proposition is asserting something both true and new. Even if the interrupting event is a real one and independent of the patient, it often depends on him how great an interruption it causes; and resistance shows itself unmistakably in the readiness with which he accepts an occurrence of this kind or the exaggerated use which he makes of it (1900, p. 517).

In the face of his array of startling discoveries, each of which exemplified the precise understanding of complex mental phenomena that prevent an analysis from moving forward, Freud widens the concept, saying that there are many ways to understand resistance, and that the only unifying thread is that it is whatever interrupts the progress of an analysis. He sought to make resistance a broad concept, spanning and transcending multiple angles of observation. This dramatically alters the presentation of his idea.

In broadening his definition of resistance, Freud is making a general methodological statement, that analysts should always look for unconscious motives in resistance. This is not a specific technical statement, and thus freezes time. It serves to eradicate differences between early and later forms of resistance to analyzing.

It is not unusual to hear of early "intractable resistances" and the like, that in essence suggest processes that grind the analysis to a halt. However, it is customarily held that to resist is to put forward a counterforce to a currently pressing force. Therefore, the whole concept of resistance by definition implies a forward movement that is being fought against. It is all about conflicts, but the conflicts stemming from getting an analysis going are different from the conflicts preventing an analysis from duly proceeding once under way. The complex affects accompanying the two (e.g., guilt, anxieties, the dynamics of repetition, and so on) are often of different sorts. It invites imprecision to say that the analysand who sizes up the analytic situation for its safety, whom Sandler (1960) so aptly described, is resisting. It seems more reasonable to reserve the term *resistance* for times in the analysis when the possibility of a surge forward—structural change—must be stopped by the ego's or the superego's unconscious prohibitions.

A second difference observed when an early failure to progress is distinguished from later resistance implicates the ever-evolving demands for involvement that the patient makes on the analyst. At times, early impediments to progress may usefully be thought of as drawing on interactive dynamics, whereas later on resistances may draw more on the dynamic unconscious of the patient. Schafer (1992) has described how resistance is all too often assumed when unanalyzed countertransference is more to the point. Schafer's observations must be considered as more general than absolute, since one would not want to say that if the countertransference were properly analyzed, there would not be a resistance left in the patient. A related notion is suggested by Boesky (1990)who notes that resistances can be understood as the byproduct of the joint input of analyst and patient working together. Again, Boesky's point is a general one, leaving room for alternatives. The factors in opposition noted by Boesky and Schafer represent forms of analytic understanding that are only at great peril pitted against each other in a zero-sum game.

To say that resistances are produced either intrapsychically or interpersonally overlooks two cardinal features of analytic observations. First, because phenomena are observed and described from various perspectives, one or another of which will be favored, the same phenomena tend to be treated as if the phenomena themselves and not simply the descriptions are different. Second, over time, the analyst's participation is not a constant; thus, the meaning of resistance can evolve over the course of an analysis. Schafer's and Boesky's proposals can usefully be thought of as time-bound and context-clad, when qualified in this manner.

A similar situation holds with unfreezing time with respect to interpretation. As with resistance, the functions of interpretation may evolve over the course of an analysis. Early on, analysts do not necessarily interpret in order to convey various nuances of their understanding of how the patient's mind is working.

An analyst may interpret early on for many other reasons, quite different from the reasons for interpreting during later stages of the analysis. One such reason is to move a process along. To prepare the dyad to get to the next interpretation, so that the response to interpretation is itself interpretable, the analyst crafts a concatenated series of interpretations that build on one another. Loewald once informally commented that early interpretations are useful because they set the table for what is to come by creating flux, and without flux there can be no analysis. This introduction of flux highlights for the patient the significance of sequence, and promotes the availability of causal inference between elements that might otherwise appear unrelated. Early on, inexact or incorrect interpretations can always summon the awesome power of placebo and suggestion, but even an accurate interpretation, if it does not catalyze and then prod a sequence that moves things forward, is of little use. A second reason analysts may interpret early on is to establish an original position against which subsequent shifts in space between analyst and patient may be measured. Early interpretation sets up a process by which analysts position and reposition themselves in relation to their patients; interpretations of this sort convey aspects of the analyst's subjectivity that are thereby made available for use by the patient (for a related discussion, see Aron 1992). Still a third reason can be gleaned from observations of the linguist Jackendoff (1984) who observes that words when spoken allow the speaker to select and then hold a problem in view long enough that the problem can be worked on in multiple contexts. This has analytic significance: by interpreting, an analyst identifies and crystallizes the inchoate form of a conflict and gives it narrative life. Once so named, it can be approached from many different angles.

Outside the Transference, Inside the Interaction

I have been discussing certain characteristics of the analytic situation meant to highlight the distinctive properties of analytic preparation. I will now propose and defend the following idea: analytic preparation at its best has to do with the analyst's striking an optimal balance between being "outside the transference" and "inside the interaction." What I have elsewhere called, after Vygotsky (who originated the concept), the zone of proximal development, or ZPD, is a particular take on analytic interaction and its significance (Wilson and Weinstein 1996). Here I will focus on the facilitative role of analytic interaction in creating an affect-laden context that promotes learning and smooths the path for the analysis of transference.

The concept of interaction allows for a clear focus on how analytic patients are ushered into a thought community, and thereby allows the unique kind of learning that characterizes the analytic situation to be identified and implemented. Analytic work proceeds through interaction initially so as to create the pre-stages for viable transference interpretation later on. Thus, through interaction, what develops is an analytic space within which the analyst is able to formulate mutative interpretations that can be assimilated by the patient. The end goal of interaction is not for the analyst to serve as a new object, or to repair conflicts, but to create the conditions for the patient to evoke conflicts in a way that does not interfere with their being analyzed and worked through.

Analyzing the transference assumes that the analyst is a separate object on whom, through projection, the patient's neurosis is externalized. But with regard to analytic preparation, the familiar picture is more complicated. The processes at play within the dyad early on are Janus-like. They lead the analyst to want to go in opposite directions, at times virtually at once. When inside the interaction, conditions will arise that lead the analyst to strive to be outside the transference. At other moments, the analyst is outside the transference, and conditions arise that make it advantageous to push toward being inside the interaction. Paradoxically, being first competently inside the interaction allows the analyst later on to be successfully positioned outside the transference. Situating oneself outside the transference at inopportune moments, instead of being inside the interaction, invites problems of trust. Overlooking the opportunity to enter the interaction is not how an analyst can best move toward the goal of the analysis of intrapsychic life.

Considering interaction this way allows a rethinking of how to begin analysis. It now becomes clearer why the early unfolding of the transference does not have to be protected as assiduously as traditionally recommended, especially when its protection pushes the dynamics of interaction into the background. The inevitable compromises between being inside the interaction and outside the transference, which must occur in the rapid currents of an hour, become part of the necessary and usual means whereby the continuity of the analytic process is safeguarded. In other words, sound analytic process is a sequenced series of tradeoffs, determined by the flux of clinical data, between these two ways of thinking about how the analyst proceeds with patients.

I am describing a necessary tension that exists in the mind of the analyst during the early period of patient contact. Perfectly balancing this tension is obviously an ideal, impossible to fully achieve but nonetheless a marker to steer by. Since clinical material does not cleanly migrate into one or the other, an analyst must find a balance between being inside the interaction and outside the transference. Balancing between them, and recognizing the inevitability of tradeoffs, requires constant vigilance by the analyst.

With respect to analytic preparation, when neutrality is understood as a process rather than as an entity defined by a rigid set of rules, it becomes clear that every analysis requires a goodness-of-fit approximation of the concept. Analytic neutrality is not the necessary backdrop for psychoanalytic treatment, but rather is the outcome of a long and arduous collaboration, as Stone (1961) was only the first to argue. Before the analyst can ask the question "Neutral with response to what?" he or she first must ask "Neutral with respect to when?" Early on, the analyst strives not so much to be doggedly neutral, with any departure seen as an error, as to communicate ideas in a neutral fashion when that is useful for the patient. It is the failure to appreciate the difference between neutrality as a fluctuating goal and as prescriptive, normative behavior that has led many—including Greenberg (2002) in an otherwise quite thoughtful contribution—to inveigh against the idea of neutrality as fundamental. As many analyses proceed, more and more it is the patient and not the analyst who strives to protect the goal of neutrality. When eventually the analyst's position on neutrality is understood and endorsed by the analysand as a useful part of the analysis, this is the end rather than the beginning of a sequenced process—the outcome, not the precondition, of a viable analysis. The negotiation of neutrality, like everything else crucial in analysis, must be conceptualized as a process—in this case, a long series of negotiations, tests, and bumps-and-bruises, at times lasting several years, that precedes the stage in which the analyst's neutrality truly comes to serve the forward thrust of the analytic dyad. To put a fine point on it, analytic neutrality is the desired optimal state when the analyst is positioned outside the transference, but not when the analyst is inside the interaction.

When Analysis is Done on the Move

The metaphors of inside and outside positions of the analyst have to do with how analysts are invariably *on the move*, sensitive to how they position themselves (Wilson, 2005). Without such movement, a constant repositioning in order to adapt to fluctuations in the affective envelope enclosing the pair, patients will be called on to hyperadapt, and will have to constrain their wishes and actions. Analysts can usefully be attentive to the problem of patients' hyperadaptation during analytic preparation, which usually stems from their analyst's desire to implement a midphase analytic frame before the dyad is prepared to make full use of it.

Movement as I speak of here refers to how analysts locate themselves with respect to the patient's perceptions. Even during a session, the analyst's distance from the analysand's externalizations will fluctuate. Analysts move outside the transference through the judicious promotion of analytic neutrality and optimal frustration, thereby inviting the entry of transference fantasies into the analytic space. At other times, they move inside the interaction and by participating in bidirectional emotional processes create an analytic space in which two personalities engage each other within an affective envelope. The analyst positioned outside the transference, in order to gather it, has moved toward relative anonymity and neutrality in an effort to maximize the benefit for the patient of analyzing the transference. The analyst who is positioned inside the flow of bidirectional processes has moved in the opposite direction, toward interactive involvement.

Analysts once tended to move in the former direction whenever they could, while today many tend to prefer the latter direction. Few prefer to feel free to move in either direction. Different lines of analytic theory tend to be tilted toward one or the other, even if taking the other somewhat into account. In the clinical situation, analysts can acquire sensitivity to the need to move in either direction at a moment's notice. The clinical elasticity appropriate to the opening phase alluded to earlier is a sense of freedom to move in either direction or both, as the clinical data dictate, a fluidity of response that takes a nonobligatory stance with respect to one theoretical approach or another. This is somewhat unnatural, because one's clinical mindset is not oriented toward two such seemingly contradictory stances. But, in fact, they are not contradictory; inside and outside are artifactual categories not found in nature and are relative to a point of view.

There is no compelling reason, other than allegiances extraneous to the analytic dyad—to schools, theories, former analysts, supervisors (see Spezzano 1997)—for analysts to seek to position themselves exclusively either outside the transference or inside the bidirectional processes. Either position, it should be noted, may lend itself to a heated or a detached emotional climate. The two stances are in practice mutually enhancing, and it is a central theoretical task of contemporary psychoanalysis to weave a coherent technical tapestry that privileges movement in both directions, at the analyst's discretion.

Several cohorts of analytic candidates and clinical psychology doctoral students I have taught were initially puzzled at what such a synthesis entails in its clinical application, but soon caught on. It was hard for them at first to fully grasp the implications of an analyst's stance as either inside or outside the flow of processes. Over time the issues involved became clearer to me: my students were struggling to conceptually span two psychoanalytic world hypotheses, the intrapsychic and the interpersonal, each of which generates tremendous centripetal forces of loyalty (see Wilson 2003). I was asking them to be globally inclusive of what seemed to be two incommensurable sets of assumptions. It swam into focus for the students when they jettisoned the limits imposed by their loyalties and recognized that being inside the bidirectional processes and being outside the transference are not unambiguous absolutes or concrete recommendations; they are merely heuristic aids to clinical judgment, to decisions that analysts make on the basis of psychological states observed in the patient and in themselves.

Analytic Preparation and Beyond

Analytic preparation can be characterized as having the following features.

1. Analytic preparation is a generic term denoting an attitude taken toward patients in their initial contact with an analyst. It does not have a discrete beginning or end anchored to other clinical concepts, though it does begin and end. It is not coterminous with the opening phase as conventionally described, but itself goes through phases as the treatment progressively deepens.

2. Analytic preparation prizes the clinical initiatives of the analyst, and as a mode of thought cannot be reduced to hard-and-fast technical precepts.

3. Analytic preparation can begin before and continue long after a patient has accepted the formal trappings of an analysis (e.g., sessions four or five times weekly and use of the couch).

4. Analytic preparation assumes that an analyst is always anticipating the myriad paths a treatment can follow, some but not all of which result in a formal psychoanalysis.

5. Analytic preparation implies that the analyst is as comfortable steering an ongoing treatment away from as toward a formal analysis, and that the analyst does not view the choice of other treatments as "analytic failure."

6. Analytic preparation is easily and safely modified, unlike a trial of analysis, if it appears that a patient, for whatever reason, either does not want to move forward toward analysis or demonstrates warning signs that suggest the dyad are not suited to one another.

7. Analytic preparation respects the process of trial-and-error diagnosis, and regards diagnosis of the process, rather than of the patient, as crucial and continuing as long as the patient is in treatment.

8. Analytic preparation honors and considers as indivisible both transference analysis and analytic interaction; the latter is more salient in the early phase of treatment, the former more salient as the analysis progresses.

To properly do their work, analysts need to think at various levels of abstraction, with any number of possible actions issuing from their thought. Waelder (1962) warned long ago that it is necessary to locate analytic concepts along hierarchical gradients of access to interpretation, generalizability, and distance from clinical data. Yet concepts that are more abstract and therefore further removed from clinical data must nonetheless be translated into concrete plans for action, and thus are inevitably filtered through the prism of clinical judgment. Analytic preparation as a principle applies to all levels of abstraction, but at lower levels actual clinical decisions must be arrived at.[3] Locating analytic preparation solely at the level of clinical decision making, however, would strip higher-level concepts of their abstract reach and in the process oversimplify them. The path from one level to another is indirect, with many streams of input, each of which will in part determine a clinical decision. In this section, I will try to further describe how abstract thinking about analytic preparation gives rise to clinical decisions, but I intend the business of translation to be the figure, and specific technical considerations the ground, of the picture painted.

Coordinating mutual intentions is central to analytic preparation. This is touched on in a number of interesting contributions to the analytic literature. S. Goldberg (1994) has discussed the significance of a patient's "theory of pathogenesis." His concern is how patients construct a life narrative that explains their pathology, as well as what is required to overcome it. Goldberg notes that a patient's theory of pathogenesis is jointly determined by the attitudes of both patient and analyst toward history, process, and interpretation. Ticho (1972) has discussed the need to coordinate what he calls the treatment goals and the life goals of the patient.

---

[3] In this regard, Rubenstein's discussion (1975) of hierarchical levels of clinical and general hypotheses dealt with the same problem.

He speaks of the significance of this coordination with respect to termination, whereas I am invoking its significance with respect to the opening phase. In other words, the patient comes into analysis with certain life goals, such as getting married or making more money. The analyst, by contrast, wants treatment goals to come to the fore, such as for the patient to develop better affect tolerance or to learn to be self-analytic. One of the aims of analysis is to coordinate the two sets of goals, and many analyses fail because such issues are never properly addressed. Like the patient's theory of pathogenesis, the coordination of treatment goals and life goals is a joint product of the analytic pair; it is not the responsibility of the patient alone.

Both of these contributions address the potential for divergence between analyst and patient with respect to their fundamental but often unstated intentions toward each other and to the way each understands what as a dyad they do and what they can usefully accomplish. It is important not to assume that analyst and analysand are clear about just what each wants from the other. Goldberg and Ticho show how difficult it is for the two to be on the same page even when it is the conscious sense of both that they are in agreement. Bion (1963) has described an incorrigible, treatment-threatening form of this difficulty in his discussion of "reversible perspective," which he sees as the lethal product of a patient's psychotic parts. With respect to analytic preparation, it is useful to focus on something akin to what Ticho and Goldberg have described. Analyst and patient collaborate in identifying and working toward a jointly forged and mutually acceptable theory of pathogenesis and theory of cure. The patient enters analysis and shortly thereafter develops a set of views about what went wrong, what is needed to make it right, and how the benefits and liabilities of the analytic situation can lend themselves to accomplishing the latter. What went wrong will dynamically be linked to a sense of what is needed to make it right. At times there is a temptation for the analyst to simply abide by the patient's theory, but there is a danger here, for usually to do so is to capitulate to a defense rather than analyze it. Clashes between analyst and patient over their evolving shared theories are inevitable. Patients can develop a view of what is necessary to make things right as a way to avoid change rather than embrace it. Yet there is danger also if one member of the dyad takes the lead without effecting a true analytic dialogue involving both. Sometimes developing this dialogue is difficult because defenses serving to minimize anxiety prevent direct discussion of the issues. A major task of analytic preparation, then, is to develop and coordinate jointly authored "theories" of cure and pathogenesis that analyst and patient can comfortably embrace.

There are as many varieties of analytic preparation as there are analyses. No technical formulation fits all cases. To wit: early on in some analyses, when salient conflicts are interpreted the analysand might hear only criticism, the threat of abandonment, or an accusation. Persistent early interpretation can be overwhelming and will more than likely drum this analysand out of treatment. In such cases, early on in the treatment, seemingly no amount of insight will allow an analysis to progress. Often such issues must be lived, at times in an agonized way, in order to be seen, named, and grappled with. In other instances, the psychic reality of the patient expands and takes over the room, enveloping the analyst, whose comments must be phrased within the analysand's psychic reality, and looking outward rather than inward toward the resolution of paired wishes in conflict, for some of the reasons Kris (1985) provides in his discussion of divergent conflicts of ambivalence. What Searle (1995) terms "brute facts" are at best immaterial here, at worst destructively invasive. In either case, the analyst must take the side of the patient with respect to whatever he or she is experiencing in the transference. At such times, the analyst must also appreciatively adopt the frame of reference of the patient with respect to his or her capacity to understand the sheer fact that the transference is operative. It was Kohut's sensitivity to such matters that has led many classical analysts who do not identify themselves as self psychologists to find some of his ideas of particular value during the opening phase of the treatment of quite vulnerable individuals.

A central tension in analytic preparation is between honoring the analysand's psychic reality and recognizing that forward movement diminishes the hold that psychic reality has over the patient. Living out an issue implies the analyst's accepting and entering the analysand's psychic reality, without a quarrel. Often the patient's view of the analyst in the transference is jolting. Accepting this version of events privileges the analysand's psychic reality; by not clashing with it, the analyst facilitates the expansion of that psychic reality in the psychoanalytic situation. Greenacre (1954) once described the analytic setting as characterized by an "emotional tilt"; I would add that there is often also present a "psychic reality tilt." Analysts in their interpreting must address this as a necessary initial imbalance, but it is one they can progressively interpret their way out of, until eventually the patient can tolerate their take on things. This is in some ways similar to the empathic mode depicted by Schwaber (1998).

On some occasions, however, the analyst will contest confusion, bolster external and internal reality testing, and clarify communication so that analyst and patient do not talk past each other. A related tactic is to educate the analysand to effectively communicate with the analyst, for the time being assigning psychic reality more or less to the background. Gedo (1996) has described many clever and practical ways this can be done. His ideas follow from his conviction that all too often mental contents (e.g., the themes of unconscious fantasies) are less important than the way the mind processes and makes use of information, factors he considers psychobiological, hardwired, and hence beyond sub-jectivity. For Gedo, mental contents have no more significance than the manifest content of a dream; they pop up in endless per-mutations, seemingly but not really meaningful, in this way akin to the delusions of a schizophrenic. Exploring them offers analytic mileage only after a shared language is forged, one that promotes sorting out how the workings of both minds can contribute to each accurately understanding the other. Such specifically tar-geted interventions might be useful for certain analysands; for some, they are perhaps the only way they can pass through ana-lytic preparation. One might recall that Freud (1919), sympathetic at the time to some of Ferenczi's efforts, explicitly endorsed an "ac-tive technique" at particular moments and with particular patients, on the condition that "the principle of abstinence" be maintained. Freud specified that drive satisfaction was off limits, and that the technique should consist of "energetic oppositions to premature substituted satisfactions" (p. 164).

Still another viable preparation for analysis can be understood using the concept of analyst-as-passion-amplifier. An affective en-velope encases the analytic dyad, and slavish attention to proper technique can, if all clinical interventions are made through this most narrow of lenses, drain off the passion for analyzing or pre-vent its ever being kindled. With some analysands (e.g., those with impaired affect tolerance or affect blunting, or those with per-verse, as-if, or impostor tendencies). whatever genuine passions are mustered within the affective envelope can be amplified to provide a motivational basis for the work to follow. I identify this amplification as a task for the analyst under certain circumstances; I am offering a variation on a theme put forward by Boesky (1990). His point was that unless the analytic dyad is dragged through the mud of impassioned enactment, which he notes is often triggered by resistances introduced by the analyst, the analysis is likely to become a sterile, intellectualized failure. I suggest that with some analysands, unless nascent passions are amplified by the analyst, derivatives of intrapsychic conflict will not be made available for interpretation and the analysis will not progress. I think Ogden (1989) was driving at a similar dynamic in his recommendation that with patients who experience the paranoid-schizoid phenomena characteristic of an overreliance on projective identification (e.g., emptiness, persecutory anxiety) sessions early on should include efforts by the analyst to facilitate the creation of *analytic* significance that stokes their passion.

Concluding Remarks

How, then, can psychoanalysts best understand situations in which, early in a treatment, both parties are willing to go forward, the patient has no debilitating psychopathology, and yet an analysis does not thrive? I am proposing an alternative to three standard views of the matter: that it is due (1) to the patient, who is considered "unanalyzable"; (2) to the analyst, who is regarded as insensitive, or as a poor theorist or technician; or (3) to the analyst-patient pair, regarded as a bad match. I view these situations rather as a natural outcome when the type of thought community I have described has for whatever reasons not developed. Aspects of all three of these factors come into play, but only within a multifactorial structure that does not privilege one of them in a reductive or simplistic manner.

Ever since the concepts of transference and countertransference were first contemplated by Freud (1905), puzzling in print over how he had failed his feisty adolescent neighbor Dora in her brief treatment, the assumption that transference must be assiduously protected against contamination has dominated analytic technique. Excessive concerns about reality, knowledge of the analyst, the improvident breach of a neutral stance, and so on have been thought to work against the analyst's ability to stand outside the transference and analyze it. This assumption can now be recast in a more realistic, process-oriented, and time-bound way: early on, the contamination of transference in certain ways is inevitable, desirable, and necessary to prepare analysands for the later emergence of the analytic transference, and indeed for whatever else is to come. The word *contamination* is of course used here tongue in cheek, for in this way of looking at analysis its connotation is inverted; no longer a pejorative, contamination now refers to a laying of foundations for the later prospect of in-creased objectivity in transference analysis. Today, the several rationales for the exceptions to protecting transference from contamination are more interesting to think about than the rationale for the invariant protection of this fundamental feature of psychoanalysis.

I have sketched some of the ways in which the beginning of an analysis has a life of its own. Analytic preparation bears the same relation to a complete analysis as a human embryo does to an adult person. Neither analytic preparation nor an embryo is a true homunculus of its later incarnation. Both require many emergent transformations in order to realize their predestined morphology, and each stage prior to transformation has its own maturational structure that must be clearly understood and successfully passed through. An idealized, timelessly conceived analysis is a group fantasy that has distorted, if not always our actual practice, then at least its inscription in the literature.

Accordingly, I suggest that except in cases of profound false-self pathology, sociopathy, or psychosis, the judgement of "analyzability" can be made with any degree of confidence only after a patient has undergone a preparation for analysis. This is not a "trial of analysis" of the sort Freud (1913) recommended, in which a patient is given the opportunity to undergo the procedures he or she will be expected to master. If it is a trial, the analyst is seeing if the analysand will sink or swim; if it is a preparation for analysis, the analyst is struggling to do everything possible to help him or her to first float. Analytic preparation is inextricably bound up with the myriad questions bearing on whether and in what ways analyst and patient can grasp the fundamental need for a mutual coordination of intentions, itself a process subject to analysis, that each must promote. When this works out well, the analyst can freely and with appreciation move from a comfort with relative subjectivity to a comfort with relative objectivity, even as the analysand progresses from an emphasis on the trials of interaction to the concerns of analyzing the transference.

Throughout this paper, I have sought to present ideas provisionally, while not being shy about pitting them against other ideas. I have done so not just because any analytic hypothesis about clinical work can readily be countered by clinical data, rendered in some fashion or another, but also because it is so remarkably difficult, yet essential, not to confuse observer-created categories with naturally occurring categories, and to thereby install in our collective understanding a picture unreflective of the analytic setting in which our actual clinical efforts bear fruit. The fault lines identified can be cleaved apart for purposes of theoretical exposition, and I have indeed done just that, but they also tend to disappear when brought face to face with the unyielding demands of helping patients. We must reexamine the assumption that there is a clear and inevitable path from one analytic theory or another to any specific technical principle, and that therefore any specific technical principle belongs to any one theory. It follows, then, that theories can be asked to do different things—such as orient analysts to the fantastically ambiguous landscapes within which we must somehow find our way, rather than provide technical guidance (as if, I hope to have shown, analysts could ever truly be guided by one explicit theory as opposed to another).

The decisions faced by analyst and patient around beginning an analysis are where these issues usually have their sharpest impact on the clinical situation. Over and over I am impressed by how the world categorized by theory is so easily finessed into yielding greater clarity than the world categorized by practice, which with dispatch humbles us when we regard matters as definitive, and I have tried to honor this discrepancy in my discussion of analytic preparation. No one has made the point more clearly than Bruno Latour (1999) that throughout much of science what to the discerning observer at the level of theory looks unconnected stands revealed at the level of daily practice as tightly intertwined. *Technical* is a good adjective, he goes on to say, *technique* a lousy noun. From such observations, all else I am trying to get at in this paper about beginning an analysis follows. We are now realizing that we face a problem of conflicting sets of categories, none of which is to be regarded as superordinate, that must be untangled and clarified. Theories tend to afford us categories that are preformed and that lurk, waiting to be refound in our field of observation, whereas practice affords us the opportunity to create new categories (indeed, it requires that we do so), though these must be based on principles that link up with the tasks of clinical work. The evolution of clinical theories about beginning can move psychoanalysis more and more in the direction of addressing the gap between these two terrains: what we do, and how we explain what we do and are all about.

References

Almond, R. (2003). The holding function of theory. *Journal of the American Psychoanalytic Association* 51:131–154.

Aron, L. (1992). Interpretation as expression of the analyst's subjectivity. *Psychoanalytic Dialogues* 2:475–507.

Bader, M. (1994). The tendency to neglect therapeutic aims in psychoanalysis. *Psychoanalytic Quarterly* 63:246–270.

Bion, W. (1963). *Elements of Psycho-Analysis.* London: Heinemann.

Boesky, D. (1990). The psychoanalytic process and its components. *Psychoanalytic Quarterly* 59:550–584.

———(2004). Psychoanalytic controversies and clinical evidence: A model of clinical disputes. Paper presented to the International Psychoanalytical Association, New Orleans, March 12.

Brenner, C. (1990). On beginning an analysis. In *On Beginning an Analysis,* ed. T.J. Jacobs & A. Rothstein,pp. 47-56.Madison, CT: International Universities Press, pp. 47–56.

Derrida, J. (1978). *Writing and Difference.* Chicago: University of Chicago Press.

Edelson, M. (1984). *Hypothesis and Evidence in Psychoanalysis.* Chicago: University of Chicago Press.

Fenichel, O. (1941). An outline of psychoanalysis. *Psychoanalytic Quarterly* 10:169–173.

Fleck, L. (1979). *Genesis and Development of a Scientific Fact.* Chicago: University of Chicago Press.

Fonagy, P. (2002). Some complexities in the relationship of psychoanalytic theory to technique. *Psychoanalytic Quarterly* 72:13–48.

Freud, S. (1900). The interpretation of dreams. *Standard Edition* 4/5.

———(1905). Fragment of an analysis of a case of hysteria. *Standard Edition* 7:7–122.

———(1912). The dynamics of transference. *Standard Edition* 12:99–108.

———(1913). On beginning the treatment. *Standard Edition* 12:123–144.

———(1919). Lines of advance in psycho-analytic therapy. *Standard Edition* 17:159–168.

———(1920). Beyond the pleasure principle. *Standard Edition* 18:7–64.

———(1923). The ego and the id. *Standard Edition* 19:12–66.

———(1924). The economic problem of masochism. *Standard Edition* 19: 159–170.

Friedman, L. (1989). *The Anatomy of Psychotherapy*. Hillsdale, NJ: Analytic Press.

Galison, P. (2003). *Einstein's Clocks, Poincaré's Maps: Empires of Time*. New York: W.W. Norton & Company.

Gedo, J. (1996). *The Languages of Psychoanalysis*. Hillsdale, NJ: Analytic Press.

Gitelson, M. (1962). The curative factors in psychoanalysis: The first phase of psychoanalysis. *International Journal of Psychoanalysis* 43:194–205.

Glover, E. (1955). *The Technique of Psycho-Analysis*. New York: International Universities Press.

Goldberg, A. (1987). Psychoanalysis and negotiation. *Psychoanalytic Quarterly* 56:109–129.

Goldberg, S. (1994). The evolution of patients' theories of pathogenesis. *Psychoanalytic Quarterly* 63:54–83.

Green, A. (1975). The analyst, symbolization and absence in the analytic setting: On changes in analytic practice and analytic experience (in memory of D.W. Winnicott). *International Journal of Psychoanalysis* 56:1–22.

Greenacre, P. (1954). The role of transference: Practical considerations in relation to psychoanalytic therapy. *Journal of the American Psychoanalytic Association* 2:671–684.

Greenberg, J. (2002). Psychoanalytic goals, therapeutic action, and the analyst's tension. *Psychoanalytic Quarterly* 71:651–678.

Grossman, W. (1995). Psychological vicissitudes of theory in clinical work. *International Journal of Psychoanalysis* 76:885–899.

Grubrich-Simitis, I. (1986). Six letters of Sigmund Freud and Sándor Ferenczi on the interrelationship of psychoanalytic theory and technique. *International Review of Psychoanalysis* 13:259–277.

Hoffman, I. (1994). Dialectical thinking and therapeutic action in the psycho-analytic process. *Psychoanalytic Quarterly* 63:187–218.

Schwaber, E. (1998). From whose point of view? The neglected question in analytic listening. *Psychoanalytic Quarterly* 67:645–661.

Searl, M. (1936). Some queries on principles of technique. *International Journal of Psychoanalysis* 17:471–493.

Searle, J. (1995). *The Construction of Social Reality*. New York: Free Press.

Spezzano, C. (1998). The triangle of clinical judgment. *Journal of the American Psychoanalytic Association* 46:365–388.

Stone, L. (1961). *The Psychoanalytic Situation*. New York: International Universities Press.

Ticho, E. (1972). Termination of psychoanalysis: Treatment goals, life goals. *Psychoanalytic Quarterly* 41:315–333.

Waelder, R. (1962). Psychoanalysis, scientific method, and philosophy. *Journal of the American Psychoanalytic Association* 10:617–637.

Whitehead, A. (1947). *Essays in Science and Philosophy*. New York: Philosophical Library.

Wilson, A. (2003). Ghosts of paradigms past: The past and future evolution of psychoanalysis. *Journal of the American Psychoanalytic Association* 51:825–855.

———(2005). Analytic positions, repetition, and the organization of emotional memory. *Psychoanalytic Inquiry* 25:440–454.

———& Weinstein, L. (1996). The transference and the zone of proximal development. *Journal of the American Psychoanalytic Association* 44:167–200.

Wittgenstein, L. (1953). *Philosophical Investigations*. Oxford: Blackwell.

CHAPTER 9
_____

LEVELS OF ADAPTATION AND
NARCISSISTIC PSYCHOPATHOLOGY

Why, one might reasonably query, do some narcissistic characters serve time as seemingly successful presidents of corporations while others serve time as seemingly impaired inpatients on psychiatric units? I will offer some observations on this unusual clinical phenomenon and suggest that it is useful to distinguish between two clinical presentations of narcissistic character psychopathology, which I will call, for the sake of expedience, Level 1 and Level 2.1 I will then examine (1) how an understanding of the dimensions of empathic abilities, paranoia, levels of depression, grandiosity, and defensive uses of denial and disavowal can lend a broad explanatory range to the understanding of these levels, and (2) how we can assess both successful and unsuccessful adaptation to the outer world and the inner world in narcissistic disorders. Moreover, it is important to distinguish between being well adapted and being emotionally healthy, which are quite different in meaning and intent. I use the term Level 1 to refer to the more poorly adapted presentation, and the term Level 2 to refer to the more successfully adapted narcissistic presentation. Characteristics of Level 1 narcissistic pathology dispose a patient to an adaptation that is similar to the description of the narcissistic patient who is often described as borderline; characteristics of Level 2 narcissistic pathology dispose a patient to a high-flying and superficially successful adaptation in which the patient can competently navigate the occupational and social demands of an external world despite the presence of severe object relational impairments. While a difference in adaptation is highlighted, emotional well-being is not within the exclusive province of either's characteristic adaptive skills.

In this paper, I examine the dimensions of empathic ability, paranoia, depression, grandiosity, and defense processes because they are of distinguishing importance to the understanding of narcissistic pathology and its relationship to levels of adaptation. These dimensions are embedded in a multileveled conception that is developmental in nature, and I suggest that a continuum is a better way than a typology to grasp the similarities and differences between levels. Thus, I have found it clinically helpful to think of levels along particular dimensions (Wilson et al. 1990a), with relative proximity to one extreme at any given time along a particular dimension as the key diagnostic issue. In most cases of narcissistic disorder, there is a subtle blending of the dimensions discussed in this paper. As I will describe, in narcissistic states a paranoid style may blend into paranoid symptoms, or true grandiosity may blend into pseudograndiosity, or disavowal into denial. During the course of treatment of a narcissistic patient, a clinician will recognize individual shades of gradations of these dimensions. What causes a narcissistic patient to shift from one extreme to another, under what conditions and for how long, and the relationship of the different dimensions to each other in different narcissistic characters are intriguing topics for further inquiry.

I will be discussing and elaborating upon the following fundamental and interrelated points, as schematically represented in Table 1.

1. *Empathy:* I will show that Level 2 narcissistic pathology promotes a capacity for selective empathy, which allows the narcissist to appear at times as if he/she possesses true insight

into others. Specifically, he appears adept at detecting others' baser motives, yet he is motivated to keep many aspects of the other unknown. Level 1 narcissistic pathology promotes a more marked lack of empathic skill, in which the other's psychological state is not known because of a more *generalized difficulty in making any empathic connection at all.*

2. *Narcissistic grandiosity:* I will distinguish between Level 2 "true grandiosity,' which is subjectively experienced self-centeredness that serves as a defense against multiple unconscious fantasies of inferiority, rage, and envy, and Level 1 "pseudograndiosity,' a nonsubjective and relatively inaccessible self-referentiality that places an oceanically expansive self at the center of the doings of the object world.

3. *Narcissist's proclivity toward paranoia:* I will describe how Level 2 promotes a scanning and hypervigilant paranoid cognitive style, leading to adaptive buoyancy, while Level 1 lays a foundation for the appearance of paranoid symptoms, resulting in the debilitating effects of overt paranoid symptomatology.

4. *Prototypical depressive affect:* I will describe how Level 2 leads to the narcissist's contending with guilt-ridden depression. In so doing, an "immunity system" against depression comes into play, through which others, whom I term "proxies," become the carriers of projected motives and feelings that contribute to guiltiness and depression. The result is controlling and sadistic object relations that shield the narcissist from awareness of and exposure to his underlying aggression, depression, rage, and envy. Level 1 narcissists contend in the main with empty or anaclitic depression. The Level 1 narcissist develops a style of recruiting important others to

be metabolizers of incoming information, leading to severe dependency and separation conflicts and masochistically tinged object relations driven by fears of object loss. Thus, conscious depressive experiences in the narcissist can be minimized when at Level 2, whereas such depressive experiences are amplified when at Level 1.

Table 1
KEY DIMENSIONS OF THE TWO LEVELS
OF NARCISSISTIC PATHOLOGY

Dimension	*Level 2 Form*	*Level 1 Form*
Adaptation	Hypertrophied	Compromised
Empathy	Selective Empathy	Failed Empathy
Grandiosity	True Grandiosity	Pseudograndiosity
Paranoia	"Buoyant" Paranoia	"Debilitating" Paranoia
Depression	Guilty Depression	Empty Depression
Primary Defense	Disavowal	Denial

5. *Defensive blocking of information from perception and attention, leading to gradations of self-awareness:* I suggest that Level 2 narcissistic pathology has as a base the defense of disavowal, the second censorship, in which the relationship between the signifier and the signified is primarily at issue. The emotional meaningfulness of language is altered so that the meanings of certain words are stripped of the significance that allows for integration into the self (and thus the capacity for therapeutic change). Level 1 narcissistic pathology has as a base the defense of denial rather than disavowal. In my definition, denial results in attempts to shut out threatening elements of external reality because knowledge itself is dangerous and threatens a fragile adaptive status in the object world. Thus,

denial in Level 1 is defensively mobilized against actual knowledge; disavowal in Level 2 is mobilized against meanings that the person cannot tolerate.

Narcissism and Psychodiagnosis

William James once remarked that if one wants to truly understand religiosity, one should study the most religious person at his most religious moment. In this vein, as I highlight differences between Level 1 and Level 2 forms of narcissistic pathology, my discussion may initially generate a somewhat skewed picture, a purer picture than one generally sees in a clinic or therapy practice. Kernberg, too, has remarked on the relative rarity of a "pure culture" of narcissism. It is important to note that when I speak of two pure types of narcissistic pathology, fundamentally I am adopting the sociologist Max Weber's point that even though purified types exist only as heuristics, as heuristics they have pedagogic utility (Weber 1947). Clinical depictions of this sort often tend to be more messy than clean; it is my impression from the clinical situation that Level 1 characteristics tend to bundle together apart from Level 2 characteristics in narcissistic pathology, and vice versa, but this remains to be tested in formal empirical research. Aspects of multiple character styles invariably interdigitate across time and situational factors within one personality organization.

For purposes of bridge-building and translation to other diagnostic systems, it may be helpful first to locate the discussion within the bailiwick of manifest symptomatology. If one looks for parallel coordinates with Axis Il of DSM- IV, Level 2 narcissistic pathology involves traits seen in some narcissistic personalities either with paranoid or obsessional traits or accompanying personality disorders. Level 1 narcissistic pathology involves traits seen in some narcissistic personalities either with borderline, dependent, impulsive or histrionic traits or accompanying personality disorders. When making such comparisons, we must keep in mind that many character-disordered patients present with dual diagnoses, with Axis I diagnoses, and/or a multiple diagnosis on Axis Il, thus rendering isomorphic equivalences simplistic and misleading.

While much at present remains to be learned about narcissistic pathology, it has emerged as a central concern of clinicians and researchers. Clarity in the purposes of psychodiagnosis may help with efforts to understand some ambiguities currently extant concerning diagnostic practice with such patients. Recall Holt's (1968) observation concerning psychoanalytic diagnostic psychological testing, that "diagnoses are not addresses of buildings into which people may be put, but landmarks with respect to which people may be located" (p. 14). In other words, to clinical diagnosticians, the logic of between-group differences is handled differently than when employed by a scientist seeking to unveil a fact hidden amidst a welter of data. Psychodynamic clinicians have a different set of responsibilities.

They sketch the psychic terrain of individuals who display similar modes of psychic functioning without losing an ipsative focus, rather than reduce the personality organization to the least common denominators that discriminate preselected groups. What is extraneous error variance or, as it is sometimes aptly termed, "noise" to the descriptive diagnostician is a central focus of the concern for individual differences of the psychodynamic diagnostician, because within the noise is contained the dynamics of particular therapeutic importance.

The logic of psychoanalytic diagnosis, which reached its apex in the pyrotechnic brilliance of David Rapaport, was finetuned at the Menninger Foundation by the urgent need to understand patients as soon and thoroughly as possible so that therapeutic interventions could be informed by a keen knowledge of the patient's personality structure and psychodynamics. Prediction of transference, treatability, and patient-therapist matching emerge as the fulcrums of this diagnostic style. Thus, a psychoanalytic diagnosis emphasizes that which is therapeutically of pragmatic use—i.e., the structure of personality, with emphases upon thought organization, drive-defense configurations, styles of defense, and characteristic modes of object relating. It also belabors the point of view of adaptation. This purpose leads clinicians to eschew values irrelevant to the task of linking diagnosis with therapy (such as speculatively loose inferences concerning genetic reconstructions, or far-reaching guesses about possible infantile origins of psychopathology or facile correlations with psychosexual stage theory, the so-called genetic fallacy). At the same time, how many papers does one find in current journals that fail to heed Holt's warning that "a great deal of time has been wasted in the effort to set up dynamic diagnostic categories, which would be characterized by common etiological sequences, or 'impulse-defense configurations.' Such an approach lends itself to discrete rubrics even less well than the nomenclature of descriptive psychiatry" (p. 13). To the extent that a dynamically informed psychotherapy is valued, we are then led to ask—is there not a necessity for a diagnostic approach that emphasizes factors central to therapy side by side with one that emphasizes classification? Psychodynamically informed diagnostic practice is not opposed to descriptive diagnostics but should not, as Holt implies, adopt its methods lest it lose its purpose.

In the years since Rapaport and his students delved so deeply into the art and science of psychodiagnostics, two well-known scientific "revolutions" have occurred—in psychology a cognitive one and in psychiatry a biological one. Some predict that these twin revolutions will ultimately lead to the most important and lasting contributions to clinical methods coming out of our times, and I see no reason to have grave doubt that this will be the case. While many psychodynamic clinicians recently have worked to incorporate object-relational concepts to complement and update the ego psychological analysis of Rapaport and his colleagues, a further step to expand the frontiers of psychodynamic psychodiagnosis can be the encompassing of certain of these cognitive and biological factors (many are not germane in any foreseeable way). I intend this not in the neuropsychological sense of finding functional and structural deficits (which constitutes a different diagnostic purpose) but as an integrative move within the realm of psychodynamic theory construction per se.

There is a natural relationship between brain-behavior analysis and psychoanalysis (Reiser 1984) that is sparked by recent advances in the science of neurobiology (e.g., Kandel 1983) but is actually an exploration that rekindles Freud's earliest hopes for psychoanalysis, as discussed in his *Project for A Scientific Psychology,* written in 1895. The lens of this relationship, though, also brings into focus a host of critical questions, some of them as old as the study of philosophy itself. For example, many investigators have longed for the Rosetta Stone that would allow the mapping of brain events onto psychology. The philosopher Steven Toulmin (1978) emphasizes how this mapping is not just a matter of simply uncovering brain-behavior isomorphisms but also is itself subject to prevailing trends in the theory of natural science. In the last 100 years, these have revolved around the vicissitudes of transformation of first energy and then information (the first and second laws of thermodynamics, respectively). This mapping remains an ideal not yet, and perhaps never, fully attainable. Some theorists believe that such mapping can never be attained because brain events and psychological events occupy separate domains of knowledge, and descriptions are not interchangeable between the two domains (Brenner 1983; Edelson 1984).

For the purpose of the present paper, we might think of the brain and the mind as constituting different "phases" of cortical activity. However, because we acknowledge the influence of brain activity does not mean that psychological phenomena can be found anywhere else other than "in meanings" (Basch 1983), a view that respects different semantic and conceptual discontinuities between these domains. Hadley (1983) suggests that in the representational system we can find the bridging concept between mind and brain. Using the representational system as a "middle-level" construct pointing to aspects of subjectivity may give us additional leverage to understand narcissistic pathology; it also brings us into a realm in which biological and cognitive factors can play a role.

Another classic philosophical question, that of "will," also finds current expression in the controversy concerning conflict versus deficit—in narcissistic states in particular and psychoanalysis in general. This question disappears as a problem when one conceptualizes conflict as possible at a psychobiological level (Wilson et al., in press, b), similar to what Klein (1976) conceived of as the principle of resolution of developmental incompatibilities. Therefore, it is not possible to endorse, as do Stolorow and Lachman (1980), the notion that there are two kinds of narcissists—with those grounded in developmental arrest having different genetic roots than those contending with conflictual drive derivatives. Such a distinction immediately strikes me as forced, antidevelopmental, and propitiating, prematurely foreclosing upon the important yield to be mined in the ongoing controversy concerning the clinical merits of conceptions of developmental arrest and psychic conflict. I have never seen clinically—nor can I imagine—a patient who suffers from developmental arrest and does not also have later conflictual derivatives, or someone with conflictual derivatives who is not also contending with preverbal influence on his or her personality structure.

Perhaps a more useful distinction than that of conflict or deficit is one of subjective or nonsubjective representational capacity (Wilson and Malatesta, 1989). Experiences represented beyond (or, put another way, prior to) subjective accessibility can appear to be deficit-laden because of the patient's relative imperviousness to interpretation of discernible ideational conflict. In the variant of narcissistic pathology I call Level 1, much early and influential mentation may be beyond awareness and memorial retrieval and not subject to the kind of repression that lifts in response to interpretation. Rather, we may be dealing with representational capacities that are "conflicted" but do not lend themselves to lexical forms of communication because they are internalized at a developmental level prior to the acquisition of mental abilities that underlie the capacity for subjectivity—e.g., evocative memory and the codification of language. I will return to this issue in the discussion on denial and disavowal.

Empirical evidence (Wilson et al., (1990) suggests that multimodal regression resulting in the crossing of a boundary between subjective and presubjective states is an important precipitant of psychiatric hospitalization. Presubjective is defined as the manifestations of interactively forged mental structures that were internalized prior to the ontogenetic dawn of reflective self-awareness and have not been successfully integrated into higher forms of symbolic representation. Evidence on the critical issues concerning presubjective representational capacity has been converging, as addressed from the varying perspectives of clinical psychoanalysis (Frank 1969; Gedo 1988); developmental psychoanalysis (Greenspan 1979; Emde 1983); infancy research (Stern 1983, 1985; Lichtenberg 1983); from cognitively oriented psychoanalysis (Horowitz 1972; Basch 1981); and neurophysiology (Brown 1976). Wilson, Passik, and Faude (1990) assess this research and the potential for a new look in theory construction from the perspective of psychoanalysis, which they define as incorporating evidence from the clinical situation as well as from infancy research and developmental psycholinguistics.

What are some implications of the discussion on subjectivity for the understanding of narcissistic disorders? At lower levels of adaptation, much of the psychological life of Level 1 persons is beyond subjectivity; this in small part accounts for their intractability to the expressive expectations of psychotherapeutic treatment. Much psychological life can be sensed subjectively by the Level 2 narcissist but is not necessarily in the realm of introspection because of conflicts in meaning derivation. Some aspects of psychic life can be accessed in consciousness and represented in images and language but cannot be meaningfully integrated into the self because they are blocked by disavowal, the second censorship. This distinction is exemplified in the everyday language of these Level 2 narcissistic patients, where they are more able to symbolize their distinctive personality structures. For example, in their everyday language, such a narcissist is likely to use words reflecting the symbolization of conflicts over imperiousness and haughtiness. Likewise, when given psychological tests, he or she may be likely to have imperious content on the Rorschach, such as "crowns" or a "coat of arms," or on the TAT, where one such patient saw a "man swinging above pedestrian functionaries, unconcerned with the problems of little people." It is not unusual for these patients to depict events by using militaristic metaphors or language laced with highly aggressive, overtly paranoid, or combative content, barely disguising sadistic or exploitive intent. Narcissists with Level 1 trends are less likely to symbolize their narcissistic orientation. They are more likely to be self-referential and to produce frankly symbiotic imagery in their images and language and on psychological tests—important symbols, to be sure, but not distinctively narcissistic and more often conceptually associated with borderline phenomena.

With this background in mind, I will now proceed to explore the particular dimensions of narcissism in order to vivify the discussion of subjectivity and presubjectivity that I believe can clarify the clinical and theoretical implications of varying levels of narcissistic pathology.

Narcissism and Empathy

The concept of empathy has a long and variable usage in psychoanalytic theory. It has been used to suggest a capacity for trial identification, (Fliess 1942), a type of merger experience (Olden 1958), a generative mix of identification and merger (Schafer 1959), a phenomonological state with healing attributes (Kohut 1959), and an advanced cognitive ability with which a person acquires subtle knowledge of the other (Shapiro 1974). I prefer that the term denote a fine-tuned and sophisticated psychological ability to interpret correctly and thus know another's pertinent cognitive and affective states and communications (Levine and Wilson 1985). This definition circumvents the potential for reification that exists when one employs the concept with reference to an intersubjective state possessing healing attributes (Kohut) or ties the term into abstract metapsychological principles of internalization (see Buie 1981).

Because the capacity for empathy underlies all aspects of object relating, it is important to study in the narcissistic characters the structure and content of empathy, incorporating both how the other is known and what in the other is known. Knowing, anticipating, and smoothly meshing with others emerges as an important faculty for the narcissistic character who will successfully adapt to life. Likewise, the inability to adapt to life brings with it a primary failure in key empathic skills.

The Level 2 narcissist displays, simultaneously, sophisticated empathy juxtaposed with blithe insensitivity, both functioning with respect to particular aspects of the other's mental life. This selective empathy operates in such a way that even when he/she understands complex ideoaffective life in others, his empathy is not necessarily accurate even though it is rich and complex or results in a subjective belief in the certainty of his empathy. Aspects of the other are known but are divorced from their natural psychological context. The mechanisms involved are similar to but also somewhat different from those observed in projective identification. A feeling state that had previously not been present is not induced in the other through the interpersonal disowning and identifying characteristic of projective identification. Rather, selective empathy leads to a narrowed range of vision, the perception of certain mental states divorced from the richness of an overall organic psychological context. The isolated mental state is often—although not always—one of baseness. The other is then treated in such a way so as to create the conditions for the elevation into felt experience of these isolated states. The other will often experience these as novel, unexpected, or ego-alien. Others are induced to experience undesirable wishes, affects, and thoughts. Selective empathy in narcissism promotes a selective attunement with and capability of isolating and raising to felt experience others' more base motives. Such a narcissist is especially adept at empathically perceiving through projection his own base aspects of self-experience in others. Thus, through his capacity for selective empathy, he is best at recognizing emotional replicas or caricatures of himself. This, of course, is most apparent during treatment as phases of idealizing or narcissistic mirroring transference.

The narcissist who empathizes in this manner will pursue the comfort of familiarity through the creation of a proxy to be empathized with, although the proxy is known as an exaggerated caricature of his own negative self-image. The narcissist at these times will attempt to create replicas or facsimiles of himself in others by attempting to recognize and highlight narcissistically tinged motives in others that are similar to those he himself possesses. The need to be rid of affects such as guilt and envy impels him to create a proxy and thereby free himself of these debilitating states. Thus, guilt and envy are central to the distorted empathy; they are motives that he is exquisitely attuned to in others but tends to be blind to in himself. The Level 2 narcissist who uses empathy in this way often prides himself upon his perspicacity regarding others' motives. He knows others' surreptitious motives in a way that no one else can. He can trumpet his or her superior morality because he is clear about how base others are. Because the other's motives are empathically perceived as predatory or malevolent, the other must be guarded against, outwitted, and exploited. The other is perceived as a source of danger whom the narcissist must disarm for fear of aggressive actions he might take against the narcissist himself. The other is guilty of psychological crimes; he emerges as a natural target of aggression because he or she deserves to be punished for his wrongdoings and attacked for his dangerous potential threat. When an attack is not possible, the narcissist may attempt to disarm the other's potential danger (seen because of the projection of his own guilt, envy, and aggression) by a well-developed ability to understand the other's weak points, vulnerabilities, and frailties.[1] This constitutes a paranoid resolution to the problem of knowing the other through empathy. At the same time, such others must be dominated and controlled in order to forestall their potentially threatening competitiveness and dangerousness. Others are disarmed and undermined because the narcissist knows how dangerous they are and can be.

This selective empathy should be carefully distinguished from

---

[1] This is similar to Krohn's (1974) notion of "borderline empathy."

true insight into others, which is characterized by greater accuracy and realism. Aside from the sheer structural flaws in his empathy, the Level 2 narcissist has a restricted empathic field. He does not empathize with many people around him because he deems them not worthy of the empathic effort, which involves a tremendous expenditure of energy and attention. The decision to try to empathize with someone is made in a consciously calculating fashion. An empathic connection is most readily made with those (proxies or idealized objects) who can provide a mirroring effect for his grandiosity, those who may constitute a threat requiring paranoid vigilance, or those who, because of exploitiveness and ambitiousness, are perceived as of pragmatic use.

These views on empathy in certain narcissistic patients are largely in agreement with Easser (1974), who has discussed the empathic inhibitions in narcissistic patients similar to those I depict as at Level 2. Her description is of a group of narcissistic patients who "appear highly engaged with their environment and in most instances are successful in terms of real attainments, scholastic or vocational, but obtain little satisfaction or pleasure from their accomplishments, remaining bitter and dissatisfied" (p. 559). Easser emphasizes the motivated defensive nature of failures in empathy, a defensive avoidance of a painful tension state—hence her term "inhibition." At a more abstract level of conceptualization, such patients also suppress their capacity for empathic response to others as a defense protecting an illusion of grandiose oedipal triumph, an illusion necessary for the maintenance of a primary unmodulated core of childhood omnipotence. She reports success with a treatment strategy of challenging the blockage in empathy. When the core of omnipotence is treated and modulated, empathic inhibitions are no longer defensively required; others, including the therapist, can be more accurately empathized with, true intimacy can result, and a flood of oedipal material appears in the analysis. This clinical recommendation emphasizing the conflicted nature of narcissistic empathizing is in line with those emerging from my conceptualizations regarding narcissism.

By contrast, the Level 1 narcissist has difficulty using an empathic view that can facilitate adaptation in the object world. His/her empathic knowledge of others tends to be derived from quite basic ways of knowing the other—such as affect contagion, affect sharing, mutual cuing, and sheer guesswork, some of the early forerunners of mature empathy (Buie 1981; Bergman & Wilson 1984; Demos 1984). When treating these patients, one comes to see a lifelong pattern characterized by a failure of empathic knowing. Information about the object world is shut out in order that grandiosity can be maintained and conflicts about self-referentiality kept to a minimum. It is an expensive price, for when the Level 1 narcissist does need to empathize with another, his resolution of failed empathy causes him to pay the price of profound isolation and neediness. Usually his isolation allows him to be alone and triumphantly untroubled by conflictual others who threaten to deflate him with their demands. He is isolated yet dependent; he must empathize at times. Whereas Level 2 empathizing results in knowing other's baser motives, Level 1 empathizing results in the cultivation of another who can compensate for his failed empathy. The Level 1 narcissist establishes an acute dependency orientation to a poorly differentiated other; he often seems preoccupied with his own motives and needs in his quest to recruit others who might help him make sense out of the world or who might serve as auxiliary empathizers or metabolizers (see Kernberg 1975, following Melanie Klein) of information. This is not a deficit condition; the obtaining of knowledge is a dangerous avocation indeed, which is why denial is such a crucial defense. It is a task best left to the other, who can then be held accountable for such information. Through such empathizing, the self maintains passivity, free to suffer from masochistic surrender and to be a victim of the troubling information, whose origins lie in the agency of the other. To truly know the other, to empathize, is to truly understand one's own plight. Meaningful knowledge strips him of his primary self-referential orientation, jeopardizes anaclitic object ties, and exposes him to painful conflicts concerning the coordination of multiple goals and aims. Thus, I agree with Robbins' (1982) comment that "some instances of narcissistic personality . . . may best be understood in terms of pathology of symbiotic bonding' (p. 457).

How can one distinguish between the lack of empathy of the narcissistic characters and the more autistic empathic mode of those with deeply regressed psychotic mental organizations? To summarize, the Level 2 narcissist selectively empathizes, tending to recognize baseness and similarity of self-experience largely for the purpose of projectively averting the felt experience of guilty and otherwise intolerable mental content. Through projection, these negatively valenced mental states are perceived and experienced in the agency of the other, and therefore prompt and justify sadism and opportunism. The Level 1 narcissist tends to be dynamically motivated not to apprehend—i.e., not to have a theory of the mind of the other—because of the interpersonal dangers that ensue when such knowledge is recognized and must be acted upon. The more regressed, psychotic patient, on the other hand, is beyond theorizing that others possess minds to be empathized with. This discussion of empathic abilities will find multiple resonances throughout the paper, inasmuch as empathy serves as a foundation for many of the clinical issues that follow.

Narcissism and Grandiosity

The next distinction I wish to draw in narcissistic pathology is be-tween the "true grandiosity" of Level 2 and the pseudograndiosity" of Level 1- me grandiosity leads to self-centeredness; pseudogran-diosity leads to self-referentiality. True grandiosity is a phenomenon that requires verification in the social sphere; pseudograndiosity is an assumption brought to every aspect of life. Here, too, we can observe a multilevel phenomenon. Kernberg (1976) notes that many narcissistic personalities fall within the level of low (borderline) character pathology, while others are organized at intermediate or high levels of character pathology. His descrip-tion of "pseudosublimatory" potential in narcissists (Kernberg 1975), which he defines as "the capacity for active, consistent work in some areas which permits them partially to fulfill their ambitions of greatness and of obtaining admiration from others" (p. 229), sets the backdrop for the study of how the grandiose character structure of some narcissists promoted abilities that allow them to realize their vaulting aspirations, while others are not so socially and inter-personally adroit.

The narcissistic patient with pseudograndiosity does not really ascribe to this own greatness—i.e., to belief that he is superior to others, with accompanying need to make others seem inferior in order to constantly document such superiority. Rather, pseudograndiosity results in a sense of preeminence and belief that he/ she is at the center of the machinations of the world around him. Pseudograndiosity promotes a Ptolemic view of the self in the object world; he or she inadvertently ascribes special aspects to the self because of an empathic failure to recognize what occurs between and within other people. The Level 1 narcissistic character may be understood to possess pseudograndiosity, remi-niscent of the cognitively prelogical child whose expansiveness and egocentrism are grounded in the bending of all or most information in relationship to the hegemony of the self. A narcissistic patient evidencing pseudograndiosity truly believes in his own preeminence and is generally impervious to contrary evidence. He tends to suffer from but not be dominated by the motivational impetus of unconscious rage or envy, except insofar as these affective experiences are secondary to his oceanic expansiveness. Latent aggression is mobilized by the thwarting of dependency needs rather than by jealousy, envy, or competitiveness. A cognitive perceptual style focusing on sensory impressions and global feeling states predominates, which prevents him from obtaining a realistic factual picture of the object world. One such patient, B., when not depressed had new grandiose ambitions during many of her early treatment hours. One hour she was going to be a world famous opera singer; the next hour she described herself as wishing to become a great doctor who would discover the cure for cancer. Exploration of these fantasies showed that B. was not so much driven by a need for compensatory acclaim in order to counteract unconscious fantasies of inferiority; rather, a hidden grandiosity led her to believe in her preeminence, and she naively conceived of the world as a place where she naturally was going to shine in whatever tasks she set for herself. Her grandiose aims were not always resistances against awareness of fragility and inferiority. They were also uncoordinated expressions of expansiveness relatively unchecked by a sense of realistic limitations in the object world. This brief vignette also illustrates how, from the perspective of observing ego capacity, pseudograndiosity is often evident when constantly fluid aims and goals can exist simultaneously without awareness of contradiction.

By contrast, the Level 2 narcissist is likely to evidence what I call true grandiosity. True grandiosity is employed largely in the service of a defensive mobilization against the threatening awareness of fantasies of myriad forms of inferiority. Unconscious rage and envy are more in evidence, and projective mechanisms enable the narcissistic patient to externalize troubling qualms of guilt that arise from impulses of conscious, preconscious, and unconscious aggressivity. True grandiosity is used to diminish others in relation to the self and, in conjunction with projection, to make others the carriers for disowned projected mental content. Me grandiosity goes hand in hand with paranoia; through projections of paranoid mental content, undesirable or bad selfexperience is located in others, freeing the self to be perceived in a grandiose way, almost as a caricature of goodness and virtue. Projection aids the identification in others of the particular fears, anxieties, and wishes springing from the self that the narcissist believes are to be used to humiliate and degrade him. This presupposes a basic capacity to adequately discriminate self from other.

Also prominent among the disowned projected mental contents is guilt over rageful and envious wishes. However, such guilt is often relatively untroubling in the daily functioning of true grandiosity. This manner of unburdening oneself from guilt has an important relationship to the actual origins of guiltiness, for we could expect such patients to be more troubled by such clearly unpleasant affect. It is important to understand how the guilt is handled. True grandiosity, in order to be sustained in narcissism, requires an interpersonal "funneling." The actions and wishes of the other are seen as a cry for guilt and punishment. Guilt is easily projected onto certain objects, empathically (mis)perceived in others. These others then come to be seen as malevolent opportunists, a description that more accurately characterizes the narcissist himself. This Dorian Gray-like phenomenon is central to the narcissist's degree of adaptive competence. It can cause the narcissist to appear sociopathic. Perhaps for a similar reason Kernberg (1975, 1984) considers the antisocial personality a subgroup of the narcissistic personality. Kernberg notes that narcissists "characteristically adapt themselves to the moral demands of the environment because they are afraid of the attacks to which they would be subjected if they do not conform, and because this submission seems to be the price they have to pay for glory and admiration" (1975, p. 232). The narcissist tending toward Level 2 is not sociopathic, which requires the lack of development or absence of guilt feelings; rather, he generates guilt feelings but is expert at ridding himself of them so that guilt does not often appear to be a central focus of his life or his psychopathology. The funneling of guilt is the basis for an immunity system with respect to depression (which will be discussed in the section on depression). In treatment a key juncture occurs, usually after the "cocoon" holding environment (Modell 1976) is in place, at which time through the effects of interpretation the therapeutic process blocks the ejection of guilt. The therapist must then prevent the patient from suffering the same fate as Dorian Gray, who died when his döppelganger—a portrait of himself—could no longer represent and absorb his split-off tarnished self-experience, which was too destructive to reintroject after projection to the portrait.

True grandiosity, since it is a defense against fantasies of multiple inadequacies, must constantly be confirmed and reconfirmed. The grandiose aims become insatiable and lead to a parasitic dependence, to becoming a predator of others who can provide the narcissist with an unending stream of evidence for illusion of status, power, money, fame, beauty, or brilliance. By contrast, pseudograndiosity results in perplexity and confusion. Pseudograndiosity leads a narcissist to live in a "different world" (Bach 1985) than others. It is a world misperceived, slanted toward and crafted around the hegemony of the self. Thus, both grandiosity and pseudograndiosity lead to dependent object relations, but of different sorts. Pseudograndiosity leads to a dependency upon others to serve a basic orienting or regulating function, if the world is to be accurately empathized with, while true grandiosity leads to a dependency upon selected others (proxies) to provide the evidence so that the unconscious fantasies of multiple inferiorities can be counteracted by a steady stream of evidence of brilliance, wealth, power, fame, or beauty. This is not the dependency of intimacy, which when it occurs can lead the narcissist to feel that he is leaving himself open to being exploited and results in hostility and envy. Rather, this is a parasitic dependency entered into for the purpose of furthering narcissistic aims of self aggrandizement.

Narcissism and Paranoia

Paranoia is often considered to be the most pathological of all the thinking or cognitive styles (Shapiro 1965). This is in part because of the paranoid's lack of accessibility to therapeutic alliance—or to any intimate relationship. Paranoia leads to chronic suspiciousness, a searching mode of perception that causes such individuals to overlook the obvious because they are seeking nuances that confirm their already existing suspicions of conspiracy and persecution. The search is for underlying truths of the world, which invariably turn out to be just what the paranoid person imagined these truths to be. Such individuals think they see through objective givens and focus on details that confirm their worst fears, unable to distinguish situations in which their paranoid fears are justified from situations where they are imagined. The paranoid, because of his chronic distancing patterns and his extensive use of projection and projective identification to superimpose distrust and hostility onto even benign situations, often guarantees that the plots and conspiracies he imagines actually evolve (Millon 1981). Paranoid trends are usually detectable in most instances of severe psychopathology. In this section I wish to draw an important distinction between paranoid symptoms and a paranoid cognitive style, which will help to further distinguish between Level 2 and Level 1 forms of narcissistic pathology.

I would like to pay particular attention to the consequences when a paranoid cognitive style is a significant element of Level 2 pathology. Paranoia can at times facilitate adaptation, because it leads to hyperalertness in which all aspects of the real have to be examined, even if not believed. To many patients who use paranoia for this purpose, nurturance and attunement to others is the problem and not the solution. Bursten (1973) notes that many paranoid narcissists "lead active and productive lives—especially in vocations where skepticism, suspiciousness, and criticism are important components" (p. 290). For these patients, paranoid hypervigilance serves a stabilizing function that defensively averts the emergence of core conflicts that are not paranoid in origin. Paranoia enhances self-other differentiation because the object is constantly kept at a distance and treated as an adversary, thus leading to the illusion that the Level 2 narcissist is more differentiated than he in fact is. This function of paranoia can also facilitate the illusion of a capacity for true empathy (as mentioned, Level 2 empathy is actually a rudimentary form, bereft of the understanding of tenderness, love, or affection, and reflecting selective insights into others' baser motives). Thus, one patient, T., had built his life around elaborate countermeasures designed to protect him from inevitable attacks launched by those who surrounded him at his job, attacks that never materialized. In therapy, his introspection revolved around such questions as: if others could not be known as persecutors, then how could such people be known? And who was he if not someone who fought against these bad people? The realization that he did not require such richly elaborated and staunchly held protection, that he could relax his guard and branch out into areas of life that were more potentially gratifying, precipitated a major depression and the emergence of regressed material ultimately necessary for the successful resolution of the treatment.

Although paranoia is usually a maladaptive thinking style, for some schizophrenics and for narcissists in particular it can engender an adaptive buoyancy. The aggressive use of paranoia can push away others so that one's core psyche remains hidden. An interesting double-edged aspect of paranoia in some ways links certain narcissists and schizophrenics in their usage of paranoia. The schizophrenic, threatened by the dread of annihilation and the apprehension of the collapse of selfhood, can utilize paranoia as a way of maintaining a safer distance from other people; in this way he attempts to avert fantasized threats and to overarticulate self-other differentiation as a defense against the fusion that constitutes the wish and threat. Thus, in narcissistic and schizophrenic disturbances, paranoia helps a patient conceal from others the depth of disturbance by highlighting adaptive capabilities and minimizing the perception of intrapsychic structural factors.

In Level 1 narcissistic character, paranoid symptoms are interwined with pseudograndiosity. Such a narcissist, who skews all information toward the self, displays paranoid-like ideas of reference that readily evolve into symptoms, without the hypervigilance and perceptual scanning capacity that provides the constant flow of information that can be used for adaptive ends by the classic paranoid patient. By contrast, the Level 2 narcissist presents with a paranoid *cognitive style* without flagrant paranoid symptoms. Thus, he can utilize the adaptive advantages of paranoia—a well-developed cognitive style that results in (1) high levels of selective empathy regarding others' motives, (2) manipulative abilities, and (3) a shrewdness in making his way through life.

The tacit assumption of the Level 1 narcissist is that all is directed toward him. This results in a severe vulnerability to paranoid-like psychopathology, because the Level 1 narcissist produces in others persecutory actions in response to his interpersonal oblivious-ness, unremitting self-referentiality, exquisite sensitivity to and dread of aloneness, and tendency to offend. This has been amply documented by Millon (1981), who describes how such patients seek to create an atmosphere that provokes others to act as antic-ipated, which "serves to provoke almost everyone into exasperation and anger" (p. 381). Thus, the lack of a successful paranoid cognitive style can contribute to the onset of the more debilitating paranoid symptoms. Paranoid Symptoms do not re-quire a paranoid cognitive style. The Level 1 narcissist tends to develop paranoid-like symptoms because of the ineptness related to conflicts in navigating in the object world, while possessing a core grandiose self that simultaneously makes him believe that he is at the center of his psychological universe. This promotes a severance from the demands of the object world. Suspiciousness and persecutory delusion-like beliefs result when such a patient examines how he has become severed from these demands. He believes himself the key to why events occur and yet stumbles his way through the most basic social situations. Others do indeed persecute him, in subtle but telling ways. A continuum of para-noid functioning in narcissists suggests that at lower levels of adaptive organization, paranoid symptoms appear, whereas at higher levels of adaptive organization, a paranoid style prevails, generally without the visible presence of disrupting paranoid symptoms. This may be why Millon has noted that more poorly functioning narcissists readily slip into paranoid-like conditions. Psychotic-like signs are the extreme effects when the Level 1 nar-cissist is frustrated in his object-seeking, dependent, yet pseudograndiose aims. This helps to explain my clinical impres-sion that most Level 1 narcissistic characters, when they regress under stress, more often appear schizophrenic than borderline.

Levels of Depression and Narcissism

Clinical observation leads me to suggest that the more poorly adapted the narcissist, the more likely it is that he will suffer from an anaclitic form of depression. The developmentally earlier expression of depressive affect (the anaclitic or empty form) is tied to fantasies of the inevitable loss of the loved object and may thus be of relevance to the dependency and subsequent rage that can threaten the narcissist's ability to adapt to interpersonal situations. Guilt-ridden depression, in contrast, is characterized by ego ideal conflicts, self-condemnation, fear of loss of the object's love or approval, and envy of the object's affections (Blatt 1974). The narcissist struggling with guilt-ridden depression, when he feels needy and when there is a failure of the depressive immunity system (to be described), may tend to avoid other people because his failure to rid himself of these intolerable feelings engenders fantasies that he has done something wrong and deserves punishment or reprimand. Conversely, the narcissist with anaclitic depressive affect may desperately seek out others and establish clinging and manipulative relationships, because of his sense of himself as empty and in need of external support, regulation, and attunement. Anaclitic object-seeking is an overriding aim of the Level 1 narcissist and an overriding fear of the Level 2 narcissist. The defensive postures employed by narcissistic patients to manage or contain such depressive experiences are central to their level of adaptation.

The experience of emptiness in narcissistic characters is an affective experience central to depression. Narcissists at Level 2 and Level 1 have quite different sensations of emptiness. The narcissist of Level 1 experiences the emptiness of depletion, a suffering induced by the inescapable need of others for external regulatory activities when no one is available for such a purpose. By himself, such a narcissistic patient feels unable to allay his overwhelming inner tensions, yet he is incapable of negotiating the travails of a successful object relationship through which such regulation could be accomplished.

Feeling states of emptiness in the narcissist of Level 2 are also well-documented clinical phenomena. Kernberg (1975) connected certain narcissists' subjective experiences of emptiness and boredom with their inability to experience depression as well as with their constant devaluation of others. To Kernberg, the narcissist's imperiousness, arrogance, and derision do not prevent intense feelings of loneliness, depression, and isolation. These patients are vulnerable to the emptiness of thwarted dreams, of failed aspirations, of guilty rage and fear, of envy without the possibility of resolution, of involuntary submission to others secretly considered inferior, of castration fears and their equivalents. This state of emptiness is more a consequence of ego-ideal conflicts than of failed dependency longings, as in Level 1 states of empty depression. Such a narcissist's need to avoid the experience of guilt serves as a spur to action, unlike the experience of guilt in many other kinds of patients, to whom guilt acts as a preventative to action that will cause further experiences of distress. These patients are especially skilled at ridding themselves of guilt. Guilty depression is the worst medicine for a Level 2 narcissist because it is like a homing beacon attracting amplified feelings of inferiority, vulnerability, and critical self-appraisal. Guilt threatens the very nature of the narcissist's defensive organization. This is why, for these patients, a critical facet of their object relations functions like an immunity system that averts (defends against) experiences of depression. One of the interpersonal dilemmas of the narcissist is that others, who can be perceived as possessing the disowned guilt and baseness and who provide adoration and tribute, are needed badly. However, the same people who serve such an important function can and do inflict the most hurtful emotional wounds upon the narcissist, by repudiating the passive-receptive roles designated to them.

My term for the other upon whom the narcissist depends in this way is the narcissist's proxy.[2] Usually narcissists tending toward Level 2 require a proxy if they are to effectively manage their rage, envy, guilt, and depression. A proxy can be a love partner, an underling at work, a friend, a fantasized object relationship, or at any one time a combination of these. The proxy is an example of an object choice that fulfills distinctively narcissistic needs, a true self-object. The proxy is made to feel derivatives of the badness that the narcissist is unable to allow himself to experience. The disturbed object tie to the proxy in part accounts for why most narcissistic patients tend to live emotionally constricted and isolated lives. They move from exploitive involvements with one object after another in rapid fashion, first becoming pathologically entangled and later finding it necessary to discredit the proxy. Without a proxy, many narcissistic patients will have no one to carry disowned and projected selfexperience, which is the undergirding of his or her paranoid style. Narcissists without a proxy become vulnerable to severe states of depression, because of the possibility that their guiltiness, exploitiveness, enviousness, and ragefulness will become conscious and be attributed to the self.

In a fundamental way, the attachment to the proxy represents the flip side of the well-known phenomenon of the narcissist's

---

[2] Wangh (1962) has likewise conceptualized a particular Interpersonal ego defense as "evocation of a proxy." Wangh ties this defensive maneuver to unresolved symbiotic needs and a fundamental failure in the formation of an identity. Wangh defines a proxy as someone who is used to experience feelings, exercise functions, and execute actions in one's stead. Wangh also notes that patients with "highly narcissistic object relations" are particularly inclined to incite others to function as their proxies. Anna Freud (1936) also remarked upon a similar mechanism of defense, which she called altruistic surrender.

attraction to the idealized object. The proxy and the idealized object are both sought in order to bolster the self, and both are external objects with whom the narcissistic character seeks an attachment in order to avoid the pitfalls of autonomous psychological life. Both reflect the narcissist's successful separation but unsuccessful individuation, in that the psychological needs for external sources of regulation prevail but without the accompanying needs for physical proximity that often reflect impaired libidinal object constancy. The primary difference, suggestive of the unsuccessful individuation from others, is that the idealized object is imbued with the narcissist's good representations, while the proxy receives the narcissist's bad representations. More specifically, this contributes to the apparent continuity of selfhood particular to Level 2 narcissists, because the idealized object bolsters the good representations by mirroring action while the proxy aids in the elimination of the bad representations through a quid pro quo—the enactment of the immunity system against depression. What is good is kept and magnified, and what is bad is expelled and attacked, setting the stage for the emergence and interdependence of true grandiosity and sadism.

The guilt-ridden narcissist, driven by the belief that he has done something wrong and should right what is wrong (this is often a castration reaction or oedipal-like fantasy characterized by envy, competitiveness, or sexual sadism), can counteract his guilt by projection, disavowal of meaning, or the substitution of symbolic aims that quell or undo the fantasy of guilty wrong-doing. Thus, guilt feelings can also be a spur to accomplishment; the narcissist's ambitions, successes, and drive for recognition serve not only to further his grandiose aims but also to undo the unconscious guilt and facilitate its projection. The dialectic between unconscious guilt and the organization of Level 2 leads narcissistic characters to a constantly spiraling helix of action that becomes increasingly difficult to interrupt through therapy when it is efficiently furthering grandiose goals.

Denial and Disavowal in Narcissism

An important aspect of the narcissist's quality of self- and object-awareness involves the characteristic ways in which insight and knowledge are tolerated. Analyzability or treatability in an expressive psychotherapeutic modality is dependent upon the narcissist's ability to use insights generated in the clinical context. Ways of warding off insight (or knowledge in general) thus emerge as of paramount importance. This is especially true of narcissists, whose treatments are often difficult or unsuccessful despite the apparent periodic appearance of willingness and ability to grapple with conflict and develop insight into the self.

Disavowal is a particular defense against interpersonal relations and their meanings. It was first described by Freud (1927) as a defense exclusively used by fetishists who had witnessed frightening aspects of genitality but was later described (1938) within a more normative developmental sequence. In 1938, Freud spoke of disavowal as a critical defense against traumatic perceptions of external reality but not against internal demands arising from the demands of instinct, which were defended against by repression. This definition has been questioned and modified by Basch (1981), whose reformulation I will employ. Disavowal should be carefully differentiated from denial and repression. In doing so, I will rely heavily on Basch's conception of a "second censorship"[3] (the first being the repression barrier,

---

[3] Basch's concept of the second censorship is different from the concept of the second censorship as described by Sandler and Sandler (1983). Sandler and Sandler, attempting to bridge topographic and structural concepts, view the second censorship as mobilized against the content of current unconscious fantasies and thoughts, oriented not to the past but to the present and primarily functioning to avoid shame,

which defines the boundary between primary and secondary thought processes) that stands between lexical representations and the felt experience of meaningfulness of the lexical representations.

Denial refers to a process whereby incoming information registers in a sensory modality and then is bypassed, ignored, or distorted. In denial, there is a defensive distortion of actual perceptions. By contrast, disavowal may be understood as the defensive refusal to allow cognizance of a fearful or anxiety-producing state to attain meaningful emotional significance, although it can and does attain representation in language. Awareness of threatening incoming information remains accessible to introspection and thus to recollection and discourse, but the emotional meaningfulness is altered. In this way, events or fantasies of meaningful emotional significance are not responded to, attended to, or integrated into the self, despite the apparent (but misleading) potential for reflective self-awareness and self-integration. Disavowal may be understood as characteristic of a second censorship because it is mobilized against mentation that has passed through repression. Thus such thought is accessible to awareness but is stripped of emotional significance by disavowal as a further defensive operation once the "afterpressure" (Freud 1915) of repression is overcome. Repression, on the other hand, analogized by Freud (1900) as a "barrier," refers to the failure to represent in preconsciousness important aspects of lived and memorial self-experience; thus crucial elements of experience cannot become subject to the therapeutic process because the experience fails to be represented.

If this description is difficult to grasp, perhaps one example from outside of the clinical situation may help to illuminate the workings of disavowal. When Klaus Barbie, villain of the concentration

---

embarrassment, and humiliation. Basch's view is more concerned with cognitive structures and modes of representation of thought (primarily language).

camps, was recently brought to trial in Lyon, France, he repeatedly smiled with seeming contempt as victim after victim whom he had tortured was brought to testify against him and document the atrocities he had directed. It was as if the emotional significance of what he had done were magically nullified. He did not utilize denial; certainly he could recall and speak about the barbarism he had endorsed, but it seemed peripheral to him, uncannily censored as if irrelevant to his present existence, disavowed in terms of its emotional significance and potential for self-integration. Barbie, who had tortured the Frenchman Jean Moulin to death, confided in an interview (Ascherson 1983, p. 13) that "as I interrogated Jean Moulin, I felt he was myself." Here we see with stark clarity the intersecting paths of disavowal and the interpersonal funneling necessary for the immunity system against depression in a malignant narcissistic character.

An understanding of the characteristic usages of denial and disavowal may have important implications for an understanding of levels of adaptation in the narcissistic character. Disavowal is a fundamental defense of particular significance to the Level 2 narcissist, who defends by blocking the intrusion of unwanted meanings. The Level 1 narcissist, by contrast, defends by relying more upon denial than disavowal.

As indicated, the Level 1 narcissist displays visible evidence of anaclitic depression. Archaic needs predispose him or her to a hyperdependent reliance on others for internal state regulation. Yet, because of pseudograndiosity and lack of empathy with others, objects tend to be experienced as frustrating and as bad unless they continuously function as highly attuned need gratifiers. When this occurs, two processes become operative, both in the service of preserving the needed object for self-regulatory purposes. First, the badness of the object is perceived but introjected and then turned against the self. The bad object must in some ways be preserved as good. Second, denial prevents the narcissist from learning the actual facts of his object relations. Knowledge of what is actually occurring, both of the self-object tie and of the psychological life of the other, becomes dangerous and must be avoided. The resulting obliviousness is perceived by others as gandiosity because the self then becomes the reference point for social exchange. (It is in this sense related to Piaget's concept of egocentrism.) Denial fixes the pseudograndiosity and lack of empathy into others, as a way of maintaining the anaclitic attachment to the object. Such a characteristic use of denial becomes a powerful impediment to natural developmental processes, since this aspect of denial is an early defense organized in concordance with cognitive egocentrism. It results in one of the most taxing dilemmas of narcissistic patients—their most basic and pressing needs can only be met by desired people whom they are terrified of losing, and whom they can ineffectively hold onto through masochistically tinged object relations and debilitating forms of introjective identification (the taking-in of others' disowned self-experience). Unable to feel truly nurtured because of the inevitable failures of the adult in an infantile anaclitic object relationship, conflicted and unwilling either to empathize with the other or to project their badness onto the other, these narcissists remain trapped in a miasma of masochism and rudimentary affective/cognitive development, giving the mistaken appearance of being deficit-ridden rather than conflicted. Cooper (1984) has described a similar group of patients who he suggests are characterized by narcissistic/masochistic psychodynamics of this kind.

By contrast, Level 2 narcissists are prone to the use of disavowal as well as denial but tend to rely upon disavowal in conjunction with paranoid projection as a way of offsetting aspects of unwanted psychological meanings. They cannot rely heavily upon denial because paranoid hypervigilance leads them to take in their entire perceptual field. However, they do tend to dismiss features of their field of attention that they may, often mistakenly, find unimportant or unrelated to their grandiose concerns. This is not denial; phenomena are represented but are disavowed because the narcissist perceives no possibility for self-enhancement.

That disavowal and denial are both defenses at the heart of the adaptation of certain narcissists may help account for the mixed therapeutic results with such patients and the seemingly contradictory technical recommendations conceptualizing treatment strategies with them. Disavowal fuels haughtiness, while providing the external appearance of intactness because the patient's language facility and observing ego are relatively unimpaired. In contrast, for the Level 1 narcissist, denial blocks the acquisition of knowledge, and the patient is left conflicted at an archaic level, with impaired language facility to describe psychic and external realities. In treatment, it is quite clear that narcissistic patients utilizing disavowal possess a capacity for quasi-meanings but not true meanings that can be mobilized in the therapeutic task of self-change. This clinical situation is what I believe Modell (1976, 1980) sees when he invokes Winnicott's concept of the false self to describe how narcissists relate to therapists with forged or inauthentic affect states. We will benefit from further insights into technical considerations arising from the usage of disavowal—that is, the assault on meaningfulness at the juncture of the topographic systems Cs. and Pcs. This perspective lends itself to a more precise way of understanding core conflicts of the narcissist than does the distinction of conflict and deficit.

To the narcissist of Level 2, unwanted and guilty aspects of self-experience must be continuously assigned to objects (proxies). Level 2 narcissists need proxies as willing participants in this drama yet must treat them sadistically. The continued reliance on disavowal promotes a sadistic use of objects, while denial promotes a masochistic use of objects. Paranoid hypervigilance serves to preserve and maintain the sadistic resolution. Others are found to be worthy of renunciation, mistreatment, and punishment. More and more importance comes to be assigned to the self and its virtues (true grandiosity). In addition to needing grandiose confirmations and self-esteem supplies from weak others, these narcissists believe that only they themselves (or idealized others who are experienced as mirroring objects) possess what it takes to provide gratification. Thus, while denial promotes and perpetuates the Level 1 narcissistic masochistic style of directing blame and responsibility against the self and of haplessly depending on others, disavowal in conjunction with projection promotes the Level 2 narcissist's imperious style of sadistically using proxies to feel the burden of guilt. In that way the Level 2 narcissist can salve his fantasies of multiple inadequacies and continue to maintain grandiose self experience.

Modell (1975) has described what he believes is the telltale narcissistic ego defense—a massive block against affective experience. This block against affect is empowered or motivated by a fear of closeness to the object and helps create and perpetuate an illusion of self-sufficiency. Disavowal may be understood as a defense that encompasses the blocking of affect, because it is the emotional significance of closeness that must be avoided in order to preempt fantasized humiliations and sustain grandiose illusions. Modell defines affects as manifestations of "hungry" object seeking, so that affect blocking bolsters the narcissist's illusion that he needs nothing from any other person. I would view such a defense as Level 2 in nature, as a particular instance of disavowal, designed to ward off the intrusions of meaning that might contribute to the unveiling of unconscious fantasies of multiple inferiorities and underlying rage and envy.

References

Ascherson, N. (1983). The 'Bildung' of Barbie. *New York Review of Books,* November 24.

Bach, S. (1985). *Narcissistic States and the Therapeutic Process.* Northvale,NJ; Jason Aronson.

Basch, M. (1981). Psychoanalytic interpretation and cognitive transformation. *International Journal of Psychoanalysis* 62:151–75.

———(1983). Empathic understanding: A review of the concept and some theoretical considerations. *Journal of the American Psychoanalytic Association* 31:101–27.

Bergman, A., & Wilson, A. (1984). Thoughts about stages on the way to empathy and the capacity for concern. In J. Lichtenberg, M. Bornstein and D. Silver, Eds., *On Empathy.*Hillsdale, NJ: Analytic Press,

Blatt, S. (1974). Levels of object representation in anaclitic and introjective depression. *Psychoanalytic Study of the Child* 29:107–57.

Brenner, C. (1983). *The Mind in Conflict.* New York: International Universities Press.

Brown, J. (1976). Consciousness and pathology of language. In R.W. Rieber, Ed., *The Neuropsychology of Language.* New York: Plenum.

Buie, D. (1981). Empathy: Its nature and limitations. *Journal of the American Psychoanalytic Association* 29:281–307.

Bursten, B. (1973). Some narcissistic personality types. *International Journal of Psychoanalysis* 54:287–300.

Cooper, A. (1984). The unusually painful analysis:A group of narcissistic-masochistic characters. In G.H. Pollock & J. Gedo, Eds., *Psychoanalysis: The Vital Issues., Vol. 2: Clinical Psychoanalysis and Its Applications.* New York: International Universities Press.

Demos, V. (1984). Empathy and affect: Reflections on infant experience. In J. Lichtenberg, M. Bornstein & D. Silver, eds., *On Empathy.* Hillsdale, NJ: Analytic Press.

Easser, B.R. (1974). Empathic inhibition and psychoanalytic technique. *Psychoanalytic Quarterly* 43:557–80.

Edelson, M. (1984). *Hypothesis and Evidence in Psychoanalysis.* Chicago: University of Chicago Press.

Emde, R. (1983). The prerepresentational self and its affective core. *Psychoanalytic Study of the Child* 38:165–92.

Fliess, R. (1942) . The metapsychology of the analyst, Ps*ychoanalytic Quarterly* 11:211–27.

Frank, A. (1969).The unrememberable and the unforgetta· ble: Passive primal repression. *Psychoanalytic Study of the Child* 24:59–66.

Freud, A. (1936.) *The Ego and the Mechanisms of Defense.* New York: International Universities Press.

Freud, S. (1895).Project for a Scientific Psychology. *Standard Edition* 1:281–391.

———(1900–01). The Interpretation of Dreams. *Standard Edition* 4:IX–627, 5:629–686.

———(1915). Repression. *Standard Edition* 14:141–158.

———(1927). Fetishism. *Standard Edition* 21:147–158.

———(1940 [1938]). An Outline of Psycho-Analysis. *Standard Edition* 23:139–208.

Gedo, J. (1988). *The Mind in Disorder: Psychoanalytic Models of Pathology.* Hillsdale, NJ: Analytic Press.

Greenspan, S.I. (1979). Intelligence and Adaptation: An Integration of Psychoanalytic and Piagetian Developmental Psychology. In *Psychological Issues* 47–48. New York: International Universities Press.

Hadley, J. (1938). The representational system: A bridging concept for psychoanalysis and neurophysiology. *International Review of Psychoanalysis* 10:13–30.

Holt, R.)1968). Editor's Foreword. In D. Rapaport, M. Gill & R. Schafer, *Diagnostic Psychological Testing.* Rev. ed. edited by R. Holt. International Universities Press.

Horowitz, M. (1972). Modes of representation of thought. *Journal of the American Psychoanalytic Association* 20:793–819.

James, W. (1902). *Varieties of Religious Experience.* New York: Collier, 1962.

Kandel, E. From metapsychology to molecular biology: Explorations into the nature of anxiety. *American Journal of Psychiatry* (1983) 140:1277–1293.

Kernberg, O. (1975.) *Borderline Conditions and Pathological Narcissism.* Northvale, NJ: Jason Aronson.

———(1976). *Object Relations Theory and Clinical Psychoanalysis.* Northvale, NJ: Jason Aronson.

———(1984). *Seuere Personality Disorders.*New Haven,CT: Yale University Press.

Klein, G. (1976). *Psychoanalytic Theory: An Exploration of Essentials.* International Universities Press.

Kohut, H. (1959). Introspection, empathy, and psychoanalysis. *Journal of the American Psychoanalytic Association* 7:459–83.

Krohn, A. (1974). Borderline empathy and differentiation of object relations: A contribution to the psychology of object relations. *International Journal of Psychoanalytic Psychotherapy* 3:142–65.

Levine, I.,& Wilson, A. (1985). Dynamic interpersonal processes and the inpatient holding environment. *Psychiatry* 48:341–57.

Lichtenberg, J. (1983). *Psychoanalysis and Infant Research.* Hillsdale, NJ: Analytic Press.

Millon, T.(1981). *Disorders of Personality: DSM–III, Axis II.* New York: Wiley.

Modell, A. (1975). A narcissistic defence against affects. *International Journal of Psychoanalysis* 56:275–82.

———(1976). "The holding environment" and the therapeutic action of psychoanalysis. *Journal of the American Psychoanalytic Association* 24:285–307.

———(1980). Affects and their non-communication. *International Journal of Psychoanalysis* 61:259–67.

Olden, C. (1958). Notes on the development of empathy. *Psychoanalytic Study of the Child* 13:505–18.

Reiser, M. (1984). *Mind, Brain, Body.* New York: Basic Books.

Robbins, M. (1982). Narcissistic personality as symbiotic character disorder. *International Journal of Psychoanalysis* 63:457–74.

Sandler, J., & Sandler, A.M. (1983) .The 'Second Censorship', the 'Three Box Model' and some technical implications. *International Journal of Psychoanalysis* 64:413–25.

Schafer, R. (1959). Generative empathy in the treatment situation. *Psychoanalytic Quarterly* 28:342–73.

Shapiro, D. (1965). *Neurotic Styles.* New York: Basic Books.

Shapiro, T. (1974). The development and distortions of empathy. *Psychoanalytic Quarterly* 3:4–25.

Stern, D. (1983). The early development of schemas of self, of other, and of "self with other." In S. Kaplan, Ed., *Reflections on Self Psychology.* New York: International Universities Press.

———(1985). *The Interpersonal World of the Infant.* New York: Basic Books.

Stolorow, R., & Lachman, R. (1980). *Psychoanalysis of Developmental Arrest.* New York: International Universities Press.

Toulmin, S. (1978). Psychoanalysis, physics, and the mind-body problem. *Annual of Psychoanalysis,* Vol. 6. New York: International Universities Press.

Wangh, M. (1962). The "evocation of a proxy": A psychological maneuver, its use as a defense, its purpose and genesis. *Psychoanalytic Study of the Child* 17:451–69.

Weber, M. (1947). *The Theory of Social and Economic Organization.* New York: Free Press.

Wilson, A. Archaic transference and anaclitic depression: Psychoanalytic perspectives on the treatment of severely disturbed patients. *Psychoanalytic Psychology* (1986) 3:237–56.

———& Malatesta, C. (1989) Affect and the compulsion to repeat: Freud's repetition compulsion revisited. *Psychoanalysis and Contemporary Thought.*

———Passik, S., & Kuras, M. (1990). An epigenetic approach to the assessment of personality. In *Advances in Personality Assessment* : J. Butcher,

Advances in Personality Assessment, Volume 8. edited by J.N. Butcher & C.D. Spielberger, eds., Hillsdale, NJ: Lawrence Erlbaum.

————————& Faude, J. (1990). Self-regulation and its failures. In J. Masling, ed., *Empirical Studies of Psychoanalytic Theory, Vol. 3*. Hillsdale, NJ: Lawrence Erlbaum.

CHAPTER 10

A CONJOINT PHASE OF TREATMENT INVOLVING A SEVERELY DISTURBED ADOLESCENT BOY AND HIS FATHER

Was it a sin to cry when I wanted to feed at the breast?
I am too old now to feed on mother's milk, but if I were to cry for the
kind of food suited to my age, others would rightly laugh me to scorn
and remonstrate with me.

—Saint Augustine[1]

Psychoanalysis, remarkably thorough when studying most clinical matters, has not systematically investigated conditions under which conjoint treatments might be useful. Instead, such therapy has been viewed as a substitute for, rather than a complement to, individual treatments. Individuals unable to sustain the intensity of dyadic involvement are typically thought unanalyzable, but there are more ways than preparatory psychotherapy to bring along a prospective patient. The case I will describe raises the prospect that conjoint work in the treatment of severely disturbed adolescents can complement an individual treatment and can lead to lasting intrapsychic gains not accessible in an exclusively dyadic format. This follows from many of the features unique to the psychoanalytically informed treatment of adolescents, particularly the more disturbed adolescent, which calls for parameters and quite different approaches than are customary in adult analysis (Feldman & Wilson, 1997; Laufer & Laufer, 1989; Panel, 1981; Settlage, 1974).

---

[1] Error! Main Document Only.Confessions (c. 400). Translated by R.S. Pine-Coffin. New York/London: Penguin, 1961, p. 27.

In the history of psychoanalysis, one sees different lines of evolution with respect to psychoanalysis as a theory of personality as opposed to a theory of therapy (Freud, 1914). Certainly, Freud, in developing his views on personality factors, visited areas beyond the clinical situation and borrowed heavily from mythology, culture, religion, group behavior, literature, the then prevailing life sciences, and so on. The psychoanalytic theory of therapy tends to be less open to crossing the Rubicon of the bounded dyadic clinical situation. Historically, the dyad has been considered the laboratory that psychoanalysis must look to, since this is where clinical efficacy gets tested. It is hard to quarrel with this eminently reasonable view, yet perhaps nondyadic interventions can still be evaluated according to the outcome effects upon the patient within the dyadic system. In this paper, such a case is reported, formulated, and *conducted as much as possible* along the lines of psychoanalytic theory and practice. Since this case terminated, I have conducted several others in like fashion, all but one with promising results.

As far as I am aware, there is no published report in the literature describing this particular treatment configuration with an adolescent and his or her father, although such descriptions can be found in the literature on the treatment of symbiotic psychotic children (e.g., Bergman, et al., 1983) with their mothers, sometimes called tripartite treatments. In a tripartite model, both mother and child are seen as requiring help, but for the mother it is according to the vicissitudes of her contributions to the child's maturational requirements. Exclusively conjoint treatments with adolescents reported from outside of psychoanalysis, though, are frequent, although not designed to tap the intensity characterizing analysis. Many (perhaps most) clinicians, working within seat-of-the-pants necessities, fall into conjoint treatments with many adolescents, particularly those severely disturbed, dangerous to themselves or others, or those who are locked into rigid and ossified object relations with domineering others, usually family members. Thus, many eating disordered young women, excessively rebellious young men, and others whose families cannot contain their aggression find their way into such therapies. Hence, it follows that some descriptions of conjoint treatments can be found in the generic psychotherapy and family therapy literatures. But one is hard pressed to find family therapy reports that are either admixed with psychoanalytic approaches (cf., Stierlin, 1977) or do more than share a common but loose vocabulary, so interdomain translations are necessary. For example, Doane, Hill, and Diamond (1991) have described how, in what they call the "disconnected family," uninvolved behaviors (object relations) between parents and symptomatic adolescents can masquerade as intense emotional overinvolvement and connectedness. In order to treat what they term such a "disorder of communication," they warn against a premature separation process and advocate conjoint sessions promoting attachment between parents and the adolescent, followed by subsequent individual meetings with the parents and the adolescent. While they clearly describe dynamics similar to those encountered in the present case, the thoughtful interventions they recommend do not result in an intensive psychoanalytic therapy with the adolescent, which could produce enduring intrapsychic gains rather than strategic ones.

Background of the Case

The case about to be described is most atypical and was characterized by a grim symbiotic[2] struggle. The treatment was initially individual; the patient was the son, eighteen years old at the time

---

[2] Note that I use the term "symbiotic" descriptively; it does not imply an endorsement of the hypothesis that there is such an entity as a symbiotic phase during development.

of referral. In the middle of individual psychotherapy with the son, circumstances suggested an unusual direction, a once weekly conjoint therapy meeting between father and son which complemented the son's ongoing thrice weekly therapy.

The father—Mr. S—originally came for an appointment a few days before the son—Ken—was due to arrive in New York City. He provided the context for the referral, one that clinicians who work with severely impaired adolescents and young adults will find familiar. He said he was desperate. He was now, for the first time in his life, prepared to dig in his heels and face this dreadful problem, which he had hoped would disappear of its own accord. His son had terrorized everyone in the family with aggressive outbursts and erratic, frightening behavior and had been poised on the threshold of a hospitalizable disturbance for several years. The last time Ken had been home for a visit, he had gotten so angry at his father that he had punched him in the face and given him a black eye. Mr. S said he and his wife also feared for the physical safety of their daughter, Ken's half sister,for Ken recklessly initiated brutal rough-and-tumble games with her that endangered her. These were bald attempts at intimidation and dominance. Mr. S's current wife called me the day after my first appointment with Mr. S. to tell me that the return of Ken frankly endangered the marriage as well, for Ken was a source of unresolvable conflict between her and her husband.

Mr. S described how, by junior high school, things had gotten quite bad between him and his son. The year of ninth grade was a disaster for Ken. He battled his father at every turn. With the emotionally damaging birth of his younger sister, Ken had angrily left Mr. S's household to live with his biological mother. After two months he sought to return, but Mr. S would not take him back, offering as an excuse that it would be good for Ken to have continuity in school and finish the year where he was. Actually, Mr. S could not tolerate having Ken return. Ken never forgave his father for this first forced separation, and it became a central organizing dispute between the two. Ever since Ken was in the ninth grade, Mr. S and Ken had been engaged in a run-and-chase game that forced the father to frequently travel around the country to rescue his peripatetic son, who inevitably provoked some new catastrophe wherever he was. After the father's intercession, the enraged son would blame the father for his problems and soon be off again on some new escapade, always expecting to find some Nirvana-like place where he could settle down, but always setting the stage for a new, increasingly dangerous catastrophe. The two were in constant and intimate contact by telephone, negotiating Ken's next fateful step. Most recently, in desperation, Mr. S had, by telephone, placed his son in a peculiar college that was a refuge for disturbed adolescents who had no place else to go. Not surprisingly, Ken avoided classes, was socially isolated, fought with his peers when he came into contact with them, and was forthwith expelled. At the time of referral for treatment, Mr. S was panic stricken at the prospect of his son's return home after expulsion from college, for whenever Ken visited home, he attempted to destroy his father's fragile family life with his reconstituted family, a second wife, and five-year-old daughter.

In our initial meetings, Mr. S also described his and his son's childhoods and the backdrop of the father-son relationship. The case then became less stereotypic. The parents divorced when Ken was six months old, and Mr. S assumed sole custody when twenty-three years of age. Mr. S remarried when Ken was seven years old. As the primary caretaker, Mr. S insisted upon doing and being everything for Ken. He would dress him, comb his hair in the morning, take him everywhere; the two of them were inseparable during Ken's preoedipal, oedipal, and early latency years. It was a nonstop joint preoccupation with one another that admitted no outsiders. As a child, Ken regularly observed Mr. S injecting himself with amphetamines, and was brought along with him on his many escapades involving severe drug abuse, wild parties, and multiple sexual liaisons with individuals of both sexes.

Even after remarriage, Mr. S had great difficulty allowing the stepmother to break into the father-son symbiosis. Mr. S insisted upon a virtual twenty-four-hour-per-day involvement with Ken, and no one else was allowed to have any sway over Ken's upbringing. Ken signaled for help with a display of symptoms, as adolescents frequently do, but no one spotted it. For example, as an early adolescent, Ken became socially isolated and deeply involved with drugs. He once took one hundred "tabs" of LSD at one time. Although they knew there was profound trouble, both father and son collaborated around a denial of illness and refused to consult professional help.

Mr. S also told me that he felt enormous guilt over what had happened to Ken. He knew something uncanny was going on between them, and he gamely said that it had to do in some way with how his own history affected his role as a father, but he was not at all clear about what specifically was at issue. He then described how his son's psychotic-like disturbance was almost a carbon copy of a similar episode in his own adolescence that began during his first year of college. He had, in fact, been through an eleven-month psychiatric hospitalization and had been diagnosed as schizophrenic (catatonic type). During and after his hospitalization, he refused all psychotherapeutic treatment. He stressed that throughout this hospitalization he could not believe there was anything wrong with him; he believed he was being held illegally by the hospital psychiatrists, who wanted to punish him for his Bohemian counterculture lifestyle. He had the delusion that he was a notorious beatnik poet. Upon discharge from the hospital, his unorthodox lifestyle continued. He preferred to live "on the edge," as he put it. For five years, he was an amphetamine addict, injecting himself three times a day. He consumed an enormous amount of other drugs as well. He was in a profound struggle at the time with his own tyrannical father, who was soon to die.

By his late twenties, however, he was indefatigable in pursuing his professional interests, and he became quite successful occupationally. Eventually, he worked sixteen hours a day, and neglected the rest of his life and his family for many years in order to get ahead in his career. His second marriage became secondary and almost ended when he admitted to his wife that he was having an affair. Decades after his bout with psychosis, Mr. S was quite occupationally successful, despite continuing drug and alcohol abuse. His relationship with Ken became strained as the symbiotic ties overtly disappeared but without proper resolution, and Ken became a loner, an introverted and brooding late latency child.

Mr. S told me a few things about Ken's biological mother. While out on pass during his hospitalization, Mr. S met the woman he was to marry and who was to bear Ken. He married her when he was twenty-one, and they had Ken a year later. He described her as both anorectic and schizophrenic, demanding care from anyone in her orbit. An early memory Ken had was of his coming home to his father at age five after a visit to his biological mother, crying, pleading to be allowed to go live with his mother so he could take care of her, saying that someday he would be big enough to make sure that she would be well. Presently, during the time of treatment, she lived with her daughter from another marriage in a small Midwestern town and was functionally incapacitated.

Over the years, Ken had periodic but regular telephone contact with his mother. Much of this contact focused on the mother's monitoring what Ken ate, and urging him into a spiritual/religious way of life, preferably Buddhist. During Ken's early adolescence, she competed with him over who had more emotional, financial, and psychiatric difficulties, and intrusively pried into aspects of his burgeoning masculine life that Ken would understandably have wanted to keep private. She was sexually provocative with Ken, and would write him poems in which fantasized sexual contact between them was overtly described. Mr. S said that Ken's mother was and always had been fiercely competitive over who was the sickest one. A sign of any problem from an intimate would unleash this terrible competitiveness. She would call Ken on the phone, ostensibly to inquire about his life but actually to inflict her problems on him. He would console her but would become immediately physically sick with nausea and diarrhea. This, of course, carried over, and any sense he had that others wanted him to care for them precipitated a chaotic unraveling and murderous rage, although he constantly sought relationships organized in this way.

It was clear from our preliminary meetings that this case was complicated. I had immediately thought of the description of symbiotic psychosis (Mahler and Gosliner, 1955) between mother and young child, except in front of me was a father and his adolescent son. My sense was that Mr. S had tried to be a parent to the best of his abilities. Blos (1984) noted that gender polarity (father-daughter, mother-son) dominates our conception of the oedipus, yet in current psychoanalytic thinking isogendered early object relations are increasingly seen as important for the development of the self. Mr. S's inability to let anyone else into the closeness of the pair, the establishment of what looked like a symbiotic dyad with its attendant vicissitudes, and his subsequent abandonment of Ken in the ninth grade struck me as a unique departure from the classic isogendered father-son relationship, which presumes a mother. Further, symbiosis as an aspect of early object relations is usually conceived as primarily between mother and child. Although in modern times fathering is increasingly studied, rarely are the clinical phenomena related to early object relations and symbiosis viewed as primarily involving the father. Clinically, of course, gradients of father-child symbiotic-like phenomena are seen on a regular basis, but usually in the context of triadic object relations. Father-son symbiotic relationships are much less frequent than such mother-son relationships because of the boy's primal disidentification from mother and subsequent identification with father under various conflicted internal prohibitions. Stoller's (1974) major point was that boys suffer from a natural "symbiosis anxiety" with their mothers, which they must free themselves from in order to reach the father and masculine identifications—or pay a psychic price.

Beginning of the Individual Treatment

When Ken came to see me, he looked fourteen rather than eighteen. Not surprisingly, when he walked through the door, I found myself speaking to the very image of his father in manner and appearance, albeit a younger version. We arranged for individual psychotherapy, at first four times a week. Shortly thereafter, it became three times a week when he refused the fourth hour because he felt engulfed by the intensity of the therapeutic contact. The early part of the therapy consisted of his determining what possible use I could be to him, since he was less interested in treatment than he was in continuing the life-and-death struggle with his father. He said that he would give therapy a try to propitiate his father so that his father would financially support him. His most immediate problem was New York City. He insisted he needed to be immersed in nature in order to feel peaceful, and he could only do that by moving to the woods of Oregon. I felt futile and useless, and entertained periodic doubts about whether I could be of any help.

It was immediately clear that Ken appeared in or close to the schizophrenic spectrum. He had poor rapport, was extremely circumlocutional, tangential, suspicious, grandiose in his mangled speech, and was struggling to conceal a pervasive thought disorder. It was virtually impossible to understand him when he spoke; long-winded hyperbolic sentences filled with polysyllabic words and neologisms punctuated his dialogue. His object relations were devastatingly primitive. Paranoid projection and its allied defenses were rampant. He had a limited sense of time and place. He had long depersonalized periods, after which he would suddenly snap into a state of alertness with no memory of what had taken place during the last hour or two. His only interests were in Eastern religion, his route to a return to the innocence of nature. He was visibly disturbed—underweight by thirty pounds, gaunt and disheveled, vigilantly scanning the world about him in an agitated, paranoid fashion.

Nevertheless, I was not convinced he was schizophrenic, even though he met DSM-IIIR criteria. The validity of the diagnosis of schizophrenia in adolescence persevering into adulthood is always open to some question because of the fluidity of the still evolving personality organization. Maturation yet offers the opportunity for a way out of the potentially premorbid straits in which an adolescent may find himself (A. Freud, 1958; Holzman and Grinker, 1977). When I came to understand his history, it became clear that, as is often seen with youngsters struggling with incipient psychotic decompensation, moving from place to place had become a way of averting imminent decompensation. But Ken, like many adolescents, mistook physical distancing for intrapsychic individuation, and so always lived under the threat of cataclysmic object loss. Whenever the inner havoc projected outward threatened him, Ken organized around the task of moving to a new Promised Land (which, we would later come to see, represented his wish to return to a pleasurable father-son symbiosis from which he had felt so violently ejected as a child).

At the beginning of the individual treatment, Ken said that he had to take care of two things—get revenge on his father, and extract his father's fortune so that it all belonged to Ken. Several times a week, Ken would initiate a fierce battle with his father, with the intention of causing him as much distress as he could. After one such episode, Mr. S lost control and screamed at Ken that the only solution was to die himself, that he had felt such relief when his own father had died, and that perhaps he could afford his son similar relief by dying as well. Ken was determined to destroy his father's second marriage, ostensibly for revenge, but also from rageful envy, so that he could have his father all to himself. Over and over again, he raged against his father's present wife, calling her a gold digger, imagining that she had sexual wishes for him and would act on them if he would allow her, and claiming that she now had what was rightly his, Mr. S's fortune and resources. Because of the tensions between them, it was arranged for Ken to move out of the family domicile into an apartment of his own.

The Father-Son Symbiosis

The similarities between Ken's present life and his father's early one were striking. Indeed, Mr. S had impressed upon me how much Ken's psychiatric disturbance was similar to his when he was at a comparable age. Thus, one early danger for Ken was the threat of a regression to primary identification, with all the attending aggression (which, not surprisingly at the time, was a danger of psychotic proportions). There was an uncanny network of communication between them that could easily remain invisible to an outside observer. Neither of them could live with or without the other. The manner in which they treated one another was characteristic of what can usefully be described as bidirectional projective identification (Zinner and Shapiro, 1972); to wit, they produced in each other states of mind that they evacuated from within, and then fought to maintain in the other so as to feel attached. Although both bitterly complained about the other, each felt compelled to repeatedly produce in the other the very states he consciously detested, yet knew so intimately and felt so familiar with. Ken was terrified that he was like his father and was constantly struggling to disidentify from father's intrapsychic representation, much the way Greenson (1968) described disidentification from mother as a necessary step in male development.

At the same time, Ken became caught in the grip of his father's projections. Mr. S unconsciously encouraged his son to undergo a similar developmental trajectory as he had. In fact, his father told me that the only way he could understand what Ken was experiencing at any one time was by remembering what he himself had gone through under similar circumstances when he was Ken's age; he had no other way of empathically grasping his son's inner life. At other times, he had no confidence that he could understand his son. Of course, one of the reasons he so poorly understood Ken was that this empathic mode is so ineffective (see Basch, 1983) because it is grounded in a fusion of self and object. Therefore, the object cannot be seen as different from the self but must be forced to be like the self in order for some limited empathic connection to take place. It is no accident, we now see, that Mr. S brought Ken to me when Ken was the same age that Mr. S himself was when hospitalized—for he had then received treatment, and now so too could he endorse Ken's receiving treatment.

In order to develop any workable process with Ken, it was imperative that I not treat his destructive wishes for reparations as a fantasy system, no matter how uncomfortable it became for Mr.

S. I earnestly investigated their function and meaning for the conduct of the case. In this way, I earned Ken's trust. He had to know that I did not view him as the only sick one, and that I was his advocate rather than his father's agent. Only by letting him know that I thought his imagination had pockets of sanity could he gradually come to let me know how insane he believed himself to be.

The Phase of Conjoint Therapy

While Mr. S had impressed upon me how disturbed Ken was and had depicted in detail Ken's alarming history, Ken, during therapy hours, kept impressing upon me how disturbed his father was and depicting in detail his father's equally horrifying history. After stormy individual sessions in which Ken would rage against his father and refuse any understanding that might influence his rage, I would repeatedly ask myself how Ken was going to cope with the regressive pull of the protective father of symbiosis: father and son now could openly communicate only hate and fear to one another. How could he understand his feeling of being cast out of Eden into a world of near-psychosis? How could Mr. S ever reach the point where he could fulfill the parental role he longed to have but could not attain?

The individual meetings with Ken continued, but my sense was that I was missing the mark by treating only half of this remarkably intertwined dyad. Mr. S began calling me to ask me about virtually every aspect of his involvement with Ken, such as helping him to recognize and think out the implications of his feelings, providing him with some sense of parental direction, calming his overwhelming anxieties about having any contact with his son, and aiding him in planning how to proceed with Ken. I worked out with him my requirement to maintain the confidentiality of the therapy with his son. However, after consulting with Ken, I did not discourage Mr. S's calls, because I now clearly saw that the only way the case could successfully proceed was if he were treated as well. I did feel overwhelmed by the sheer amount of psychopathology over which I was assuming charge. Mr. S refused any "therapy" with another treater; he preferred my "coaching" him on what to do and say with Ken. By himself, he felt incapable of making proper fatherly decisions; however, a brilliant man, he was a very quick and astute learner. Once he grasped the fatherly function, it entered his future repertoire, although many such functions initially had a stilted and eerily affectless quality, as if they were there for the first time and required polishing before they could be smoothly integrated.

I always told Ken of the calls from his father, described their content, and indicated that I would strive as best I could to keep confidential what was raised in the individual hours. Ken not only eagerly agreed to this (he had no interest in confidentiality at this stage in the treatment; this was later to change) but urged me to convince his father that he too should seek help. It is also true that I was occasionally burdened with pressing secrets from both parties that I had to contain, which at times influenced countertransference reactions I noticed in myself in various ways. I had to work hard not to impress upon this oscillating system any solutions favored by either myself, the father, or Ken, but rather to let the course of events run as they might without the safety of anticipating an outcome. I now regard these countertransference reactions as the most potentially grave problem in the conduct of such cases. My accepting phone calls from the father, though, was soon to evolve into the conjoint phase of treatment.

I had also initiated a referral for medication, and Ken was prescribed 25 mgs. of Mellaril and 1 mg. Cogentin daily. He responded positively. Mr. S had a more profound reaction than

Ken to the question of medication. He developed the fantasy that Ken was being poisoned or would get cancer from the phenothiazine. My concern, of course, was that the taking of the medication would identify Ken as the sick partner of the father-son pair and exculpate the father. Fortunately, this was never an issue.

Actually, it was Ken who suggested to me at about this time that we begin conjoint sessions. He felt that he could only speak to his father with me present, and he thought that I would be able to help him accomplish what he wanted (which at the time was to torture his father and acquire his wealth). I thought the idea of conjoint sessions a good one, although my agenda did not overlap with Ken's, and so Ken proposed to Mr. S a weekly meeting among the three of us. Individual therapy with Ken was not enough—insights Ken acquired dissipated in the emotional volcano that erupted when he and his father were together, apart from me.

The Induction Phase

We began the conjoint sessions one hour a week, while I continued to see Ken three times weekly, and I saw again and again what the nature of their relationship was like. They were obsessed with each other. No conversation could be civil for thirty seconds without escalating into a bitter fight. Aside from their preoccupation with one another, the rest of Mr. S's and Ken's lives were characterized by isolation, avoidance of people, fearfulness, and depression. Despite the paucity of actual contact between the two of them, each was the most significant person in the world to the other. This was reflected in Ken's concurrent fantasy life. For example, later in his sessions with me, Ken's continuous fantasy was that he was so "devastated" because when he was young, his father would inject him with drugs so that he would only feel the same things that his father felt.

When Mr. S spoke to his son in a parental way, I winced at the silent violence of his comments, their intrusiveness, their imperiousness, their insensitivity, their controlling quality. For example, he would echo comments I had made to him privately but use them in a piercing and condescending way—such as that Ken's requests for money at times symbolized his wish for nurturance and at other times revenge. Ken could make no use of what was ostensibly insight but which he experienced as accusations. He would boil over with rage, unable to clearly identify the toxicity of the comments or the source of his rage. He would explode and berate his father, but for entirely displaced reasons, and it was unclear to me who was more violent, father or son, although the son was the one labeled as "violent." One of my clinical tasks was to point out how harmful such comments were, to make plain that their lack of emotional sensitivity was hurtful and worthy of attention. Specifically, I pointed out how Mr. S talked down to his son, and I sought to "lend" Ken enough ego strength to feel he could speak and be heard without fear and without finding it necessary to retreat to a near-psychotic confusion.

It soon came out that behind his rage, Ken was terrified of object loss. He would test this fear by initiating a violent quarrel, then immediately make his form of reparations by phoning his father and pretending that nothing had happened, thereby ensuring that his father was still available. I sought to put into words in our sessions, to the degree that both people could tolerate it, this and other such maneuvers that constituted their communicative system. In individual sessions with Ken, I gently interpreted to him over and over again and in many different ways the masochism implicit in his revenge—that he wanted to hurt himself on so many occasions in order to hurt his father, and that hurting himself was a high price to pay for the satisfaction of getting back at his father.

One question that was settled early on was my relative neutrality in the conjoint sessions. At first, Ken wanted me to join him in attacking his father. I refused, and told him that I could best help by lending him what it took to be able to take advantage of certain opportunities—for safe discussion he could have nowhere else or for the strength to raise anxious and fearful issues and try to overcome his rage and settle them. However, I added that if he wanted to attack his father, he was, of course, entitled to do so; I simply would not join him. The early stages were indeed characterized by multiple attacks of this sort, but soon these waned as the more important uses of the conjoint sessions emerged with clarity.

Moving the Symbiosis Forward

After both had accomplished a great deal during the conjoint sessions, I came to see that the time had come for a structural reorganization. Ken had a powerful reaction to ending each of the conjoint sessions, because he had to physically leave my office with his father to walk to the street, and he could not stand the transformation in their relationship that took place—from the "honesty" of the therapy to the "hypocrisy" of walking down the halls with him and chatting about nothing in particular. He wanted a more satisfying relationship, and he complained that he never saw his father, stepmother, and sister at their apartment because they seemed afraid of him. In this and in other ways Ken signaled me that he was ready for a new beginning with his father. Just as the individuating child requires a "gentle push" (Mahler, Pine, and Bergman, 1975), so, too, did Ken require an external push toward structural reorganization at a critical moment when he and his father were structurally prepared but unable to initiate the move on their own.

So, I called a meeting with just Mr. and Mrs. S. I reiterated to Mr. S that it was time for him to get into his own individual treatment, now more so than ever. I told him that for everybody's sake the next step in Ken's treatment was for Mr. S to overcome his avoidance of and anxiety about Ken away from my office. I suggested to both Mr. and Mrs. S that by avoiding Ken, they were trying to make me into Ken's father, and that providing money for Ken may seem virtuous by way of guilt atonement but was a pale excuse for fatherliness. Mr. S readily agreed that he had passed Ken on to me ("passing the buck," he called it) and said that, though this made him feel guilty, he simply had no time to see Ken. I suggested that he was hiding behind his schedule and that he might try to understand his fear of his son, which he could best realize in his own treatment. Further, I told them that the problem was no longer best thought of as Ken's but rather had evolved on its way to resolution into one between Ken and his father. Mr. S's immediate reaction was to panic; at first, he said he would think about it, but rather than go into therapy, he stopped drinking instead and started going to a gym four mornings a week. He also began seeing his son for dinner once a week, and tried to reintegrate Ken into the family.

This was not so much new as a new edition; they had refound each other, rekindling their early symbiotic ties, but now with the possibility of letting factors on the side of progressive maturation be internalized. What was in impasse was thus bathed in the stream of development, thereby modulating what had been unresolvable, fanatical mutual preoccupation. The more contact they had now, the more the old wounds receded and were healed. Concomitantly, Mr. S began providing Ken with more money, supporting the idea that money symbolized much more than financial currency. This casts new light on Freud's depiction of the finding of a love object, as he notes, "There are thus good reasons why a child sucking at his mother's breast has become the proto-type of every relation of love. The finding of an object is in fact a refinding of it" (1905, p. 222). In this case, even amidst the ha-tred, there was a prototype of love. There had been no breast, no suckling, only a perplexed but devoted father, himself little more than a child, barely discharged from a psychiatric hospitaliza-tion, yet within whom a prototype of love could still be refound.

Through the interventions of this period, tensions were re-duced, and gradually father and son were able to take steps toward being able to talk with each other, share their perceptions of their past, quarrel on more equal terms, and dread each other less. As this developed, Ken began less and less to dwell on leaving New York City. He alluded to not wanting to be that far from his father in the years to come. It ought not to come as a surprise that he began to appear more conventional. He seemed much clearer in his thinking, judgment, and planning. He began paying attention to how he looked and no longer appeared patently schizophrenic; he cut his hair and took pride in his grooming, stopped wearing bizarre purple clothing that was many sizes too big, and gained some much needed weight. He spoke of studying subjects in school such as anthropology and computer science. He signed up for an abnormal psychology course at the university where I was a professor. He also began exploring his numerous sexual anxieties in his individual sessions. He spoke of his wish to have a girlfriend, although his anxiety made this beyond his means at that time.

Ken began more reasonable planning for his future. He said he wanted to go to a college where there was "a lot of structure" and where other kids did not "party on drugs" all the time. He was much better related to me as well as to his father, and he be-gan to see some peers as friends. He got his first job, as a clerk in a candy store, although he lost it after a short period because of a fight with his female boss. With my assent, he decided to stop the psychotropic medication. We worked out a plan whereby he would have access to medication when he wished, and any resumption was entirely under his control, if and when he chose. He has never resumed them. He boldly told me that he trusted me and spoke of his need to see me when he left New York to go to college. He planned to visit me at least monthly for psychotherapy no matter where he lived. He began showing up at my office once or twice a week without an appointment when overtaken by some anxiety in order to work out the problem. I accommodated him whenever I could, even if only during the five-minute break I take between patients.

Ken sought to understand his relationship with his biological mother, the hidden figure in all this tumult. During the hours spent struggling to understand his relationship with his mother, he would almost burst with overwhelming rage and anxiety, yet he grasped the importance of insight into this terribly difficult and painful relationship and valiantly stayed with it despite the pain. In pursuing insight into this relationship, he realized that his preoccupation with taking care of her daughter was a new edition of how he had felt when he was a child visiting his mother on weekends and she would rush upstairs to bed, cry, and threaten him with her suicide unless he took care of her. The feelings this evoked were now displaced onto his sister. Together, we worked on how he might build an emotional "wall" so that he would not be so devastated by her phone calls, and how he would not enter into her competition with him over who was sicker.

Perhaps as important, Mr. S had tasted and embraced fatherliness. He, as much as Ken, was changed by the conjoint therapy. He developed confidence and understood how to step outside the characteristic struggles that initially defined their relationship and to turn them into dialogue rather than escalating rage situations. He invited Ken to accompany him on a four-day vacation alone, thereby offering to recapitulate the early blissful symbiotic state when each had only the other. (Ken delayed accepting this invitation, with the idea of puzzling out with me why it meant so much to him. Finally, he agreed to go, but only on condition that they not mention his biological mother while on the trip.) Shortly thereafter, Mr. S and Ken spent one week together overseas, and Ken returned as integrated as I had yet seen him. Mr. S had made great strides in dealing with the conflicted nature of his wishes toward his son. He was able to acknowledge to Ken openly that he did in fact abuse and abandon him; that in Ken's ninth-grade year he sent him away with the hope that he would disappear—but he did this when his own life was a mess, and now he would do anything to rectify what a mess he had made of Ken's life. As his fear abated, he was able to express affection in a way that did not make Ken recoil and was not suffused with what Ken experienced as hypocrisy. He bought Ken some gear for camping, and it was my impression that they were given as true gifts, were gratefully received, and neither experienced them as blackmail, reparation, or a bribe. Mr. S was much calmer, and I stopped receiving so many panicky phone calls about emergencies with Ken that another parent would see as pedestrian occurrences.

Termination Phase of the Conjoint Treatment

After about one year of weekly conjoint meetings, Ken announced to me one day in an individual session that he no longer felt the need for the father-son sessions. As he had initiated these sessions, so, too, did he conclude them. The changes in him during the interim were remarkable. The only echo of his desire for the conjoint treatments occurred during Ken's first hour after my summer vacation. He strode into my office, and without even saying hello, immediately demanded a conjoint session. Sensing an extraordinary amount of anxiety and fear, I gave him the phone, and he called his father and scheduled a meeting for a forthcoming free hour. From the start of this conjoint hour, it was clear that Ken called the meeting because he wanted the confidence of knowing that these meetings might still be available to him. He was also panicked about my going away and his father's accessibility, and he sought reassurance that both of us were still available. There were no further joint sessions after this one. Their purposes had been served, and Ken, Mr. S, and I knew the time had come to shift to the concerns of an individual therapy.

At this time, Ken was a moody, confused, but accessible young man. As the father-son symbiosis was worked through, much of the psychotic symptomatology receded. He could no longer be confused for a schizophrenic adolescent. He was preoccupied with getting a job, finding friends, meeting girls, and overcoming his inhibitions, not with getting revenge on his father, destroying himself and his father's family, and extracting his father's fortune. He did indeed find his first girlfriend that fall. He was thrilled that she was a person who kept running off to San Francisco whenever she had a conflict with her father, and he could counsel her to stay in New York City and squarely face her conflicts. He looked back on the previous five years as a grim nightmare that he had fought his way out of.

Transference and Subsequent Psychoanalytic Therapy

The conjoint weekly meeting had facilitated Ken's individual psychotherapy. To illustrate, some of the individual hours would take up a key question first raised in the conjoint sessions, and we would pursue them in more depth. At other times, Ken wanted to use the individual therapy to plan for the conjoint meetings. What might be raised, how he might respond, and how to reasonably pursue an inquiry with his father were all issues in the individual therapy but actually at the interface of the individual and conjoint meetings. In some important ways, Ken learned how individual therapy functioned through the conjoint sessions. He came to appreciate the importance of psychological causes and explanations in a way he could not prior to embarking on the conjoint sessions.

The individual psychotherapy continued for a number of years after the conjoint sessions ended. During this period, I no longer had regular contact with the father and continued to treat Ken thrice weekly. After the conjoint treatment phase closed down, the dynamic issues clustered around the 'invasion" of others into his burgeoning autonomy, his anxieties over letting down his guard, which were made manifest in pseudograndiosity and avoidance, entering a world where he might indeed fail at tasks he set himself, his wish to be passive and controlled, and idealization and perfectionism as a defense against aggression. These conflicts quickly made their way into the transference, and were usefully handled once accompanied by the analytic leverage necessary for the systematic observations required for transference resolution.

During the course of psychoanalysis, there is rarely material so consistently alive and heated up as that which stems from the transference. Nevertheless, with adolescents, there are times during which transference concerns are put to the side, since other dynamics heat up and come to occupy the patient's attention. Anna Freud particularly disagreed with the view championed by Strachey (1934) that only the interpretation of the transference is mutative (see Couch, 1995). Arlow consistently (e.g., 1987) puts forward the view that the psychoanalyst is pre-emptively concerned with interpreting unconscious fantasies, and to the extent that the analyst is enveloped in them by way of the transference, so much the better. Thus, in the pluralistic community of contemporary psychoanalysis, there is some recognition that the transference interpretation is key, but is not all.

This case demonstrates that with severely disturbed adolescents interpretation of the transference must await its proper arrival on the analytic stage. Transference is, of course, ubiquitous, as Brenner (1982) has properly noted, and Ken's transference certainly played a significant role early on. How, then, does this period of conjoint therapy intertwine with the all-important role of transference in an analytic treatment? It did not interfere with the unfolding of the transference, nor was the transference "contaminated" by the actual realities that intruded into the therapy. The dynamics of the transference constantly served as a guide to where the crucial dynamics lay, but interpretation of the transference proceeded in a zig-zag fashion.

At first, transference material was meaningless to Ken; this disinterest is not an unusual start in adolescent treatment or with narcissistic or borderline patients of any age. Thus, it was not systematically gathered as in the analysis of an adult in order to be interpreted, because its intensity was not ripe for amplification. It would have endangered rather than furthered the treatment. It was at first interpreted when its volatility frankly endangered the continuity of the treatment. Then, the conjoint phase breathed life into the transference material, while in the individual sessions we investigated Ken's sense of the processes in front of our eyes and tied this together with how he dealt with a multitude of other people and places, both real and imaginary.

This served to capture his unfolding interest in learning more about himself and his mind, rather than simply having his way with others. Much of the conjoint work was on a kind of in vivo transference constellation; after all, it involved one who had been a primary infantile object, and this later made interpretation of the transference more meaningful to Ken. This work thus deeply sharpened his sense of transference mindedness. The intrapsychic gains of the conjoint phase (insight and maturation) allowed for the liberation of the therapeutic value of examining and even intensifying the transference, which was to serve as a focus during the individual treatment that followed the termination of the conjoint work. Setting the stage for the analysis of the transference *so that it is a useful undertaking* is a tricky yet necessary prestage with many adolescents (Wilson and Weinstein, 1996).

By no means was Ken fully recovered at the time of the termination of the conjoint phase. Rather, the critical therapy marker was that the changes undergone qualified him to embark upon an intensive psychoanalytic psychotherapy, which became of greater importance than the conjoint meetings. The essential point is that the transference could be dealt with analytically, whereas when the case began, it could not. The conjoint phase had allowed for the creation of an analyzable transference, which in turn accelerated the motion of the mutative power of the psychoanalytic procedure.

Some Implications for the Theory of Therapeutic Change in Adolescents

There are many competing views on the contemporary psychoanalytic scene concerning what constitute mutative analytic factors. These range from the acquisition of insight, to remediating deficits, to promoting authenticity as one of several relationship factors, and to freeing up developmental processes that were not in synchrony with age-specific maturational expectations. Whereas discussions concerning these respective positions used to be framed in either/or terms (e.g., relationship factors versus insight), recently there is movement toward more ecumenical, nondichotomized sets of arguments. Supportive factors are now found in places where analysts had previously not looked for them (Werman, 1984), including the act of interpretation itself (Pine, 1993), and are found especially mutative with more disturbed patients (Wallerstein, 1986). Apart from the supportive factors in analysis proper, there is even the proposition that supportive psychoanalytic therapy, as a distinct technical set of interventions, aims for the same structural changes as psychoanalysis (De Jonghe, Rijnierse, & Janssen, 1992). Old embattled positions are being transcended as interactions between mutative factors embedded in the organic processes of treatment are being unpacked (Renik, 1993).

In considering the clinical evidence presented in this paper, it is scientifically presumptuous to generalize with confidence from this case to all other analytic cases in the abstract. Perhaps the data are germane to the treatment of a small subset of seriously disturbed adolescents. Perhaps the data speak more to some quite limited constellation of clinical factors common to all—or some—adolescents and/or adults. There are other possibilities as well. Whatever the nature of the generalizability may indeed be, the evidence from this case does lend support to putting forward for further general consideration a particular aspect of—or perhaps prerequisite for—therapeutic change: therapeutic benefit is in some way related to the facilitation of structural growth where there had been some form of fixation or developmental impediment. Clinical interventions, i.e., taking such a structural organization into account within one's goals for treatment, can be analogically guided by renditions of mental models pictured in psychoanalytic developmental psychology. These structural factors have, as some of their features, an indivisibly blended intrapsychic/interpersonal cast, in which objects are recruited so an individual can accomplish intrapsychic tasks unaccomplishable by oneself. These tasks, though, are not isomorphic with the typical tasks of childhood; they are better understood analogically, each requiring careful and individualized diagnostic appraisal. Mr. S and Ken accomplished something crucial through the conjoint treatment, related to what one might reasonably expect ought to have been successfully navigated many years earlier. What Ken acquired, largely through the conjoint meetings, is characterized by astonishing complexity (Wilson, Passik, and Faude, 1990). Inevitably intertwined with the compromise formations observed in intrapsychic conflict, the successful consolidation of these structural factors in most clinical work can be taken for granted. Their firm presence becomes an assumption in interpretive clinical work. If these issues flare up with such adolescents or others, it will tax the creative powers of the analyst to work effectively, because they must be carefully parsed out from the compromise formations of intrapsychic conflict and their technical implications.

What is also highlighted is how the ability to use insight is different from merely having insight. For Ken, it was necessary to first potentiate a capacity for using insight before he could assay the burden of bringing self-understanding to bear on his life. Having insight is a stilted substitute; it means little unless it can be internalized, integrated, and, hence, used. In this case, the ability to use insight rested on a preverbal structural organization that I found could be facilitated in the unusual manner of these conjoint meetings. If this structural organization was not present, insight and its brethren, conflict resolution, would not have emerged as a salient mutative factor. Speaking more generally, the translation from these shadowy processes to the verbal and paraverbal interventions of the analytic office is an important inductive undertaking in contemporary psychoanalytic theory construction.

What evidence from this case leads to these proposals? Certainly, at the point when the conjoint work was concluded, there had not been sufficient interpretation of intrapsychic conflict provided to make insight a clinical priority, as in the analysis of a neurotic patient or as would later become available for Ken. Nor did relationship factors in the transference particularly spur Ken's recovery during this time, since I was by no means a "new" object whose newness was the subject of identification (his father, in fact, was far more important to Ken than I was at the time)—nor was I one who ushered him into novel experience that provided him with a working model from which to learn about himself (that occurred later). Rather, something took place first in a series of processes between Ken and his father and only later within Ken, and it provided a foundation upon which higher-level treatment factors, such as insight, could rest. What took place was at first simultaneously intrapsychic and interpersonal, but the intrapsychic was far less accessible than the interpersonal. This is true in human development, when the intrapsychic splits off from the interpersonal and then takes on a course of its own. It was only through father and son working out their suffocating interaction that the intrapsychic world of the son could become accessible to me as a treatment factor. The intrapsychic required a set of interpersonal experiences for its accessibility, suggesting a hierarchically organized and mutually potentiating continuum between interpersonal and intrapsychic that collapses any effort at dichotomization (Wilson, 1995).

It is no accident that many of the theorists who champion the view of liberating a heretofore thwarted growth potential in analysis with adults (e.g., Loewald, 1960) cite evidence from infant research to bolster their clinical proposals. The analogue is of *developing* as distinct from *learning* about oneself; this sets up a set of linkages with child analysis and brings what is known from child analysis (especially the contributions of Anna Freud [1965], to whom being optimally positioned in the ongoing stream of expectable developmental/maturational processes was the criterion for determining mental health) into a useful conjunction with what can occur with adults. Others (e.g., Pine, 1990) who see maturation as an analytic goal, and generalize from the analogue of the developing child, note that such growth is far more visible—and more dramatic—in the treatments of severely disturbed patients. Further specification of commonalities among adaptive psychic structures and how through treatment they can be potentiated—among children, neurotic adults, and severely disturbed adults—thus emerges as a useful topic for deeper scrutiny.

Whereas Laufer and Laufer (1989) suggest that, using their approach, an analytic process is possible with severely disturbed adolescents, my finding (in other cases similarly conducted as well) is that the conjoint therapy enabled Ken to become a candidate for making use of intensive psychoanalytically informed therapy, but not for psychoanalysis proper. This may be a semantic rather than an actual difference.

In conducting a conjoint phase, a certain kind of competence is called for, one different from the typical interpretive competence of individual treatment. The clinical demands of the conjoint phase did not require me to be especially nice, or soothing, only clinically competent in a particular manner; my role was often akin to that of a diagnostician/facilitator. I had to keep alive an optimal level of tension between them, thereby enabling Ken and his father a) to avoid slipping into near-delusional and hence unresolvable issues; b) not to precipitously lose empathic sight of one another because of the rage and unpleasantness involved; and c) to move toward a new equilibrium between engagement and disengagement needs.

Once the conjoint work took place, there was a dramatically increased accessibility to many other intrapsychic issues which the engagement-disengagement issues had held in check. Such psychological processes are what Loewald was referring to when he first described a "sliding balance" (Loewald, 1952). This involves co-existing multiple levels of integration and differentiation in the child and the parent, and the way the distinction between inner and outer, social and intrapsychic, collapses when the pair navigate the task of constructing such levels—at first between them, and then, close behind, in the structural organization of the child's enduring intrapsychic life. Related issues will undoubtedly swim more into focus in the near future of psychoanalytic research. There is a sore need for more published case studies that report technical innovations and experiments in this and related genres. The fact that the conjoint phase did not take place upon a couch (which is always a judgment call with adolescents) and through the medium of free association ought not to obscure an important proposition which can be empirically tested: that perhaps many more seriously disturbed adolescents can be treated with such a psychoanalytically informed approach than has heretofore been recognized.

Postscript

At the time of the writing of this paper, it is ten years since the individual work was terminated. Ken at that time had left New York City in order to attend college in a distant city. Mr. S recently called to request an appointment in which he asked me to consult with Ken, to help Ken sort out some ambivalence about attending art school. He told me that Ken had dropped out of school, but had held a job and maintained most of the gains obtained through treatment. While meeting with Mr. S, it became clear that something else was troubling him. It soon emerged that Mr. S's wife was pregnant, and he was frightened that there would be a repeat of Ken's ninth-grade year when his sister was born and he fled his father's home to move in with his biological mother, which hastened his precipitous downhill slide. The raw materials for another symbiotic crisis were present. I agreed to do an extended consultation with Ken, who flew into New York City for a week to meet.

Only one session was necessary. Ken maintains close and blustery relations with his father, whom he now sees twice a year, but only on the condition that Mr. S journey out to his city to visit him. The consultation was successful. We cut to the chase, explored some of Ken's ambivalence about the birth of his new sibling, identified how it was reactivating some of the old symbiotic yearnings, including his wish to extract supplies and obtain revenge, and we planned how to handle these difficult feelings of abandonment and sibling displacement. It was clear that there would be no damaging repetition, nor was the situation nearly as dire as Mr. S feared.

I took the opportunity to ask Ken his memories and sense of the value of the conjoint phase. His response was telling. He paused, struggled to find the correct words, and emphatically told me that he had no memory of any of the particulars that were said during any of those hours, just something that he felt and which had never changed since. The words he found, and which he kept repeating, were that "there was a change of polarities inside of me and between me and my father." He was communicating something quite important and the words he had available did not map well onto what he was remembering (Wilson and Weinstein, 1992). The spatial metaphor of "change of polarities" (here I am condensing) expressed his sense that the structural changes taking place, simultaneously inside of him and between him and his father, strengthened him and, in doing so, loosened his need to be so preoccupied with his father. This development set the table for the dramatic and more visible changes to come—including the insights obtained in the psychodynamic therapy proper, which themselves became worth remembering, but which required for their mutative impact the girding of the structural changes that evolved out of the conjoint phase of the overall treatment.

References

Arlow, J. A. (1987). The dynamics of interpretation. *Psychoanalytic Quarterly* 61:68–87.

Basch, M. F. (1983). Empathic Understanding: A Review of the Concept and Some Theoretical Considerations. *Journal of the American Psychoanalytic Association.* 31:101–126.

Bergman, A., Schwartzman, M., Sloate, P. and Wilson, A. (1983). The Oral Deadlock: Treatment of a Psychotic Child. *Journal of the American Psychoanalytic Association.* 31:443–465.

Blos, P. (1984). Son and Father. *Journal of the American Psychoanalytic Association.* 32:301–324.

Blos, P., Sr. & Shane, M. (1981). Psychoanalytic Perspectives on the "More Disturbed" Adolescent. *Journal of the American Psychoanalytic Association* 29:161–175.

Brenner, C. (1982). *The Mind in Conflict.* New York: International Universities Press.

Couch, A.S. (1995). Anna Freud's Adult Psychoanalytic Technique: A Defence Of Classical Analysis. *International Journal of Psychoanalysis* 76:153–171.

De Jonghe, F., Rijnierse, P. & Janssen, R. (1992). The Role of Support in Psychoanalysis. *Journal of the American Psychoanalytic Association* 40:475–499.

Doane, J., Hill, W.L. & Diamond, D. (1991). A developmental view of therapeutic bonding in the family: treatment of the disconnected family. *Family Process* 30:155–176.

Feldman, M. & Wilson, A. (1997). Adolescent suicidality in urban minorities and its relationship to conduct disorders, depression, and separation anxiety. *Journal of the American Academy of Child & Adolescent Psychiatry* 36:75–84.

Freud, A. (1958). Adolescence. *Psychoanalytic Study of the Child* 13:255–278.

———(1965). *Normality and Pathology in Childhood: Assessments of Development.* New York: International Universities Press.

Freud, S. (1905). Three essays on the theory of sexuality. *Standard.Edition*, 7.

———(1914). On the history of the psycho-analytic movement. *Standard.Edition*, 14.

Greenson, R.R. (1968). Dis-Identifying from Mother: Its Special Importance for the Boy. *International Journal of Psychoanalysis*. 49:370–374.

Holzman, P.S. & Grinker, R.R., Sr. (1977). Schizophrenia in adolescence. *Adolescent Psychiatry* 5:276–292.

Laufer, M. & Laufer, M.E. (1989). *Developmental Breakdown and Psychoanalytic Treatment in Adolescence: Clinical Studies.* New Haven/London: Yale University Press.

Loewald, H.W. (1952). The Problem of Defence and the Neurotic Interpretation of Reality. *International Journal of Psychoanalysis* 33:444–449.

———(1960). On the Therapeutic Action of Psycho-Analysis. *International Journal of* Psychoanalysis 41:16–33.

Mahler, M.S. & Gosliner, B.J. (1955). On Symbiotic Child Psychosis—Genetic, Dynamic and Restitutive Aspects. *Psychoanalytic Study of the Child* 10:195–212.

Mahler, M.S., Gosliner, B.J., Pine, F. & Bergman, A. (1975). *The Psychological Birth of the Human Infant: Symbiosis and Individuation.* New York: Basic Books.

Pine, F. (1990). The concept of ego defect. In *Drive, Ego, Object, and Self: A Synthesis for Clinical Work*, pp. 198–231. New York: Basic Books.

———(1993). A Contribution to the Analysis of the Psychoanalytic Process. *Psychoanalytic Quarterly* 62:185–205.

Renik, O. (1993). Analytic Interaction: Conceptualizing Technique in Light of the Analyst's Irreducible Subjectivity. *Psychoanalytic Quarterly* 62:553–571.

Settlage, C.F. (1974). The technique of defense analysis in the psychoanalysis of an early adolescent. In *The Analyst and the Adolescent at Work*, Ed. M. Harley, pp. 3–39. New York: Quadrangle/The New York Times Book Company.

Stierlin, H. (1977). *Psychoanalysis and Family Therapy.* New York: Jason Aronson.

Stoller, R.J. (1974). Symbiosis anxiety and the development of masculinity. *Archives of. General Psychiatry,* 30:164–172.

Strachey, J. (1934). The Nature of the Therapeutic Action of Psycho-Analysis. *International Journal of Psychoanalysis* 15:127–159.

Wallerstein, R.S. (1986). *Forty-Two Lives in Treatment: A Study of Psychoanalysis and Psychotherapy.* New York: Guilford Press.

Werman, D.S. (1984). *The Practice of Supportive Psychotherapy.* New York: Brunner/Mazel.

Wilson, A. (1995). Mapping the Mind in Relational Psychoanalysis. *Psychoanalytic Psychology* 12:9–29.

Wilson, A., Passik, S.D. & Faude, J.P. (1990). Self-regulation and its failures. In *Empirical Studies in Psychoanalytic Theory,* Vol. 3, Ed. J. Masling, pp. 149-211. Hillsdale, NJ: Analytic Press.

———Weinstein, L. (1992). Language and the Psychoanalytic Process: Psychoanalysis and Vygotskian Psychology, Part II. *Journal of the American Psychoanalytic Association* 40:725–759.

———&———(1996). The Transference and The Zone Of Proximal Development. *Journal of the American Psychoanalytic Association* 44:167–200.

Zinner, J. & Shapiro, R. (1972). Projective Identification as a Mode of Perception and Behaviour in Families of Adolescents. *International Journal of Psychoanalysis* 53:523–530.

III. Lev Vygotsky and Psychoanalysis

AN INVESTIGATION INTO SOME IMPLICATIONS OF A VYGOTSKIAN PERSPECTIVE ON THE ORIGINS OF MIND: PSYCHOANALYSIS AND VYGOTSKIAN PSYCHOLOGY, PART 1

Introduction

The Russian psychologist Lev Vygotsky proposed an analysis of language, thought, and internalization that has direct relevance to the current concerns of psychoanalysts. Striking methodological and conceptual similarities and useful complementarities with psychoanalysis are discovered when one peers beneath the surface of Vygotskian psychology. Our adaptation of Vygotsky's views expands upon Freud's assigned role to language in the topographic model. We suggest that the analysand's speech offers several windows into the history of the individual, through prosody, tropes, word meaning, and word sense. We particularly emphasize Vygotsky's views on the genesis and utilization of word meanings. The acquisition of word meanings will contain key elements of the internal climate present when the word meaning was forged. Bearing this in mind, crucial theoretical questions follow, such as how psychoanalysis is to understand the unconscious fantasies, identifications, anxieties, and defenses associated with the psychodynamics of language acquisition and later language usage. We propose that the clinical situation is an ideal place to test these hypotheses.

Psychoanalysis and Language: The Context

Once the role of interactive-dyadic phenomena in the complex process of language acquisition is acknowledged, language development and usage will inevitably be seen as subject to the core psychic conflicts that characterize early childhood. However, there has been limited detailed exploration in the psychoanalytic literature of this position. Virtually every paper written on the relation between psychoanalytic theory and linguistics in the last two decades notes points of similarity between these two disciplines without focusing on their developmental interface. Their joint reconstructionist outlook is emphasized (the centrality of inferring past behavior or development from the present), as is their mutual concern with underlying structures rather than overt behavior or manifest content. Several of these papers focus on the inability of traditional psychoanalytic metatheory to explain language acquisition and usage, apart from its role in psychopathology. Others note a dearth of substantive progress in integrating the insights of modern linguistics with those of psychoanalysis. The desirability, yet difficulties, of finding a place for language within the system ego, for example, is noted repeatedly. At a panel (1968) on the relation between language and the development of the ego, the question was asked: "To what extent is the organization of the ego reflected in the language system, and to what extent does the internalized language system constitute a supraordinate regulating system of the ego?" The response was: "The process by which the normal child acquires the complex patterns of speech suggests a linguistic model for the development of psychic structure" (pp. 114–115). Yet, in this panel, the first provocative question is not satisfactorily answered, and the second bold suggestion lacks a theoretical approach that would permit further explication. Since the appearance of these predominantly ego-psychological works (e.g., Panel, 1968); (Atkin, 1969); (Panel,

1969); (Edelson, 1975); (Panel, 1977); (Shapiro, 1979), little of the called-for interdisciplinary effort has successfully taken place, although the cry has been renewed periodically (e.g., Call, 1980); (Litowitz and Litowitz, 1983); (Shapiro, 1986). Theorists had often proceeded with the hope that psychoanalysis might be joined to linguistics in order to provide the basis for a more general psychology. More recently, in the place of psychoanalysis conceptualized as a general psychology and the elaboration of its metapsychological points of view, many investigations have preferred a narrower focus on clinical theory. This trend has led away from explorations of the interstices of linguistics and psychoanalysis.

Another effort to define the relation between psychoanalysis and linguistics has led to seeking linkages to the structural linguists in the Chomskian tradition. These linguists stress a multilevel "hard-wired" perspective on language acquisition in children. Their view proposes invariant or universal aspects of language development as an essential aspect of brain maturation, independent of and/or prior to the input of earliest social phenomena. This stance led to a relative deemphasis of individual differences and the more microscopic elements of object-relating in language acquisition. Instead, correspondences such as those between characteristics of primary-process thought and those of "deep structure" were the focus of inquiry. For example, Edelheit (1969) hypothesized that phonemic acquisition acts analogously to a stimulus barrier, and serves as an *anlage* to the later mechanisms of defense by protecting the psychic apparatus from stimulus overload by ever-accruing perceptual images. An alternative effort would examine the psychodynamic context of language acquisition. This perspective might emphasize the child's motivation for, and conflicts about, acquiring and using language, broadly placed within the vicissitudes of identification. Similarly, one could examine the caregiver's array of conscious and unconscious actions and reactions toward a child that promotes or subverts language development, and how these experiences become internalized. An example of this would be Peller's (1966) concept of the mother's "regaling function" in her child's ontogenesis of speech. A parallel distinction exists in contemporary psycholinguistics, characterized by a division into the "nativist" and "social-interactionist" perspectives, and many linguists are attempting to forge some degree of amalgam of these in their research.

While the focus of the earlier papers on the psychological apparatus parallels Freud's wariness about emphasizing environmental factors after his enunciation of the central and determining role of fantasy in the 69th letter to Fliess (Freud, 1887–1902), it is nonetheless a view that requires reevaluation in the light of contemporary developments in psychoanalytic theory. Some analysts have noted that we are in the midst of a paradigm shift between other disciplines and psychoanalysis (e.g., Emde, 1988), and within the multiple schools of psychoanalysis, emphasizing points of common ground (Wallerstein, 1988). Observational research has begun to vie with reconstructive data, and has provided an impetus for some reformulation of crucial aspects of the ontogeny of mind. The newer perspectives promote the expansion of psychoanalysis to include the lifelong centrality of the psychologies of self and self-with-other, the extension of the psychoanalytic theory of motivation beyond drive psychology and cathectic investments, inquiries into models of the mind other than the structural and topographic, and the examination of the subprocesses patterned into the functions of the object for the self in object relations. The theorists who ask these questions are not necessarily retreating to a position as environmentalists or interpersonalists. As Cavell (1989a), (1989b) notes, the term "interpersonal" in recent writings need not refer to the interpersonal schools of thought in psychoanalysis, but rather to a fundamental world view that encompasses language and affect as vehicles through which the primary communicativeness of human nature is expressed, the mediums through which minds are indissolubly and nonsolipsistically linked. She argues that there is a trend in recent philosophical models to refer to how the phenomenon of meaning is dependent on an interaction between minds that is built into human nature. There is no communicational chasm between people that must be overcome in the interpersonal view, as is the case in what she terms the Cartesian view. Thus, such contributions do not necessarily deemphasize or supersede the role of the unconscious, of infantile sexuality, or of the centrality of intrapsychic reality in theory—or of the centrality of transference, defense, and resistance in technique. Areas being critically examined and challenged are classical metatheory, a narrowed definition of what constitutes psychoanalytic inquiry, the philosophical underpinnings of psychoanalysis, and the classical model of infancy and childhood (with its corresponding implications for the formation and structuralization of the mind).

As mentioned, the role of the object, theorized by Freud (1915a) as the most malleable and changeable aspect of instinctual function, and hence the least important for study, has come to receive increased attention from contemporary theorists and researchers. In developmental psycholinguistics, there is a similar shift; an unpacking of the dynamics of the social context of language acquisition is now underway. These studies depict the subtle yet complex nuances of object relations necessary for language acquisition to occur (see, for example, Olson, 1980). These researchers have proceeded with the assumption that there must be a deep interaction between the hard-wired and the social for optimal language acquisition to occur. A virtual manifesto of this line of reasoning is presented by Bruner (1983), who discusses the interreliance of Chomsky's LAD and Bruner's own concept of the LASS, the "language acquisition device" and the "language acquisition support system," which potentiates the brain's hard wiring. The LASS is the complement to the LAD; it consists of the background communicative structures that exist between caregiver and child. The LASS is constituted of interpsychological pattern structures made up of playful, gamelike, and scriptlike "formats," containing both deep and surface structure, and imbued with canonical cultural implications. Formats can be incorporated into larger interactive routines and may therefore develop a hierarchical structure. Over time, and as the child can increasingly abstract from his experience, routines can be more readily transposed or detached from their original contexts. The characteristics of the LASS are in the service of more complex regulated and imaginative cognitive, social, and emotional activities. Both the LAD and LASS serve to promote the child's entrance into the linguistic community and into the culture in general. Thus, the dynamics of the early primary relationships, the LASS, must potentiate the innate LAD described by Chomsky for language acquisition to occur, and the dynamics underlying the context will largely determine the particular registration of linguistic developments. The significance of such psycholinguistic research is *prima facie* similar to many of the newer directions in psychoanalysis. However, while developmental psycholinguistics has come to appreciate more fully the role of the object in, and the biosocial origins of, the acquisition of language, these insights have not yet found their way into a psychoanalytic theory of language acquisition, nor have they significantly influenced clinical theory.

For many years, when psychoanalysts ventured into the world of observational psychology, they seemed most comfortable with the genetic epistemology of Jean Piaget. However, recent work on mother-child interaction suggests a more tightly knit interactive structure than Piaget envisaged. As discussed by Meltzoff (1985),

Piaget's findings often do not hold up to empirical scrutiny, and the developmental timetable is flawed. For example, data suggest that infants arrive in the postuterine world with a sophisticated and operational representational system, one that channels a wide variety of adaptive behaviors. This reverses the Piagetian assumption that experience results in the formation of a representational system. Second, the root assumptions that knit together Piaget's broad stage-sequencing organizational model do not hold up well when examined in the light of contemporary theory building (see Caray, 1985). Our understanding of childhood has evolved so that infants are now seen as attached, attuned, capable, and communicative. A primarily cognitive psychology (e.g., Piaget) seems destined to be supplanted by a more broadly constructed psychology that recognizes the inherent unity of the earliest social and intrapsychic spheres (e.g., Vygotsky). This trend at present seems to cut across many of the subfields in psychology. As Dore (1989p. 256) puts it:

> We all readily believe that children acquire language in some sense. We are less ready to believe that 'language acquires children' . . . We need a theory of what happens between speakers, and especially, a theory of the interaction between how the child acquires language cognitively and how a society acquires a child functionally.

As psychoanalysts move toward recognizing wider expanses of the origins of mind, they will inevitably outgrow the model Piaget presents of a solitary cognizing child whose developmental tasks are defined as *acquiring knowledge*, and move toward a conceptualization of childhood where these tasks are defined more in terms of *action and adaptation in a communicative context*.

In this paper, we examine the relevance of the work of the polymath Lev Vygotsky for the theory and practice of psychoanalysis.

Vygotsky developed his theory of language, thought, and internalization during approximately the same chronological period as Freud, although the two were separated by a radically different cultural surround. We suggest that Vygotsky's formulations of the social and systemic elements of language acquisition can be integrated with views emphasizing innate cortical functioning (e.g., Edelson, 1972, but the first was Freud in his 1988 monograph *On Aphasia*) in order to begin to articulate a model prototype for the psychoanalytic understanding of language. Central to Vygotsky's formulation is how two people come to co-construct a "mind extending beyond the skin" (Wertsch, 1991) that leads to one person's (the child) interiorization and acquisition of language, symbolic functioning, and the further evolution of thought.

Since it is so well described elsewhere (Balkanyi, 1964); (Peller, 1966); (Panel, 1968); (Edelson, 1972); (Panel, 1977), we shall not review the entire evolution of the role played by language in Freud's thinking. Freud, in his early writings, in *On Aphasia* and in the "Project for a Scientific Psychology" (1895), gave language a central role in his initial efforts to postulate a general theory of mind. In *On Aphasia*, Freud held that word meanings develop by an accrual of linkages between an increasing number of objects and a single sound. In the "Project" (1895p. 365), Freud stipulated that language allows thoughts to become conscious. It is only through language that one is enabled to have any memory of a thought process. Language had a role in organizing one's perception of and summoning the image of the object. This was later to become formalized in the topographic model, where the attachment of a word to the visual presentation of an object formed the demarcation between the systems unconscious (ucs) and preconscious (pcs). Later, after the structural model was available to systematize his thinking, language played a diminished role in his theorizing about the origins and evolution of processes of mind.

He continued, however, to focus on language when he wrote his papers on technique and psychopathology. Psychoanalysis after Freud came to scrutinize speech and word meanings primarily as they were clearly visible in psychopathology (as exemplified in the 1911 case of Judge Schreber) and within the practical lore of clinical technique.

In sum, when Freud relinquished the seduction theory, he turned his attentions away from the role of the environment, and in doing so was unable to explain further the phenomenon of word meaning he had earlier sought to grasp in *On Aphasia*. It is in his insistence on the social context in which words take on their ongoing significance, the role they assume in the maintenance of self-regulatory processes once internalized, and the centrality of the functional value of language that Vygotsky most clearly departs from Freud's early associationist perspective. In fact, Freud and Vygotsky both initially strove to understand the categorical nature of word meanings. Vygotsky's emphasis on the sociocultural aspects of word acquisition and word meanings can be viewed as a complement to Freud's early emphasis on brain functions and his later elucidation of the emotional and pathological vicissitudes whereby word presentations and object presentations are paired or unpaired.

Vygotsky—An Introduction

Vygotsky produced his contributions to the study of the origins of mind in a world dominated by the specter of the Russian Revolution of 1917. He was debatably the single most influential Soviet psychologist of the 20th century. More recently, we have witnessed his discovery by Western thinkers as well. Because of its emphasis on *subjectivity*, which ran counter to the "vulgar materialism" now bitterly attributed to the psychology produced under Stalinist ideology, Vygotsky's writings were censored and banned in the Soviet Union in 1936 for almost two decades. They were republished and made available in 1956. His reputation and teachings during these years of official state repudiation lived on in underground publications and through the work of his students and colleagues. His writings have not been available in English except for his classic *Thought and Language*, translated in 1962 (retranslated as *Thinking and Speaking* [1987d], the version to which we will make our references), and other smatterings of writings on such diverse topics as play, processes of human development, and the relation of tools to culture, gathered in a volume titled *Mind in Society* (1978). Many of his heretofore untranslated papers are now scheduled to be translated into English in a five-part series called *The Collected Papers of L. V. Vygotsky*; the first volume was published in 1987. A more complete picture of his work will thus soon be available to the English-speaking public.

Vygotsky's writings have not yet gained wide acceptance in the West, perhaps because of the difficulty in mapping his assumptions, models, and methods onto those currently prominent here. This slow acceptance may be because his work spans and cannot be reduced to such current popular dichotomies as empiricism versus hermeneutic methodologies, biological versus sociocultural determinism, or cognition versus affect. By no means should Vygotsky be construed as a cognitive theorist! Vygotsky always saw his system as subordinating and encompassing affect, cognition, and volition (Wertsch, 1991) and as not reducible to such crudely abstracted categories. Those clinical psychoanalysts who have studied and reported on Vygotsky (e.g., Atkin, 1969); (Panel, 1969); (Shapiro, 1979); (Basch, 1981) tend to focus only briefly on his views on the relation between language and thought, without attempting an explication of their relevance for the clinical situation or how they might contribute to a psychoanalytically informed theory of language acquisition, development, and usage (speech). To date, most nonpsychoanalytic explorations of Vygotsky's works in America have emphasized a narrowly defined experimentalism that taps only fragments of the concepts he developed; we would argue that these experimental applications splinter his concepts into unrecognizable shards.

Vygotsky himself was not enthusiastic about early Freudian concepts—for example, he critiqued the pleasure principle (1987dp. 77), arguing that this concept underlies views of the infant as autistic and that inherent in the satisfaction of a need state is an adaptation to external reality. However, in a paper on issues of emotion written shortly before his death in 1932, Vygotsky (1987a) praises Freud as the first theorist of importance to correctly challenge the then prevailing notion of the biological utility of the emotions. Obviously, we can only surmise that the study of the motivational and affective aspects underlying mentation was the direction in which Vygotsky's intellectual interests would have taken him (as witnessed by his late papers [1987a], [1987b], [1987c] on problems of emotion, imagination, and play in childhood) had his career not been tragically shortened by his death at thirty-eight from tuberculosis.

Several features of Vygotskian theory deserve a careful reading by analysts. The crux of any psychoanalytic perspective on intrapsychic life must provide an explication of conflict and detail the role of the unconscious—an endorsement of Kris's (1947) well-known definition of psychoanalysis as the study of human nature viewed from the perspective of conflict. With a psychoanalytic spin, Vygotsky's theory can be seen as one concerned with the interplay of intrapsychic conflict and psychodynamics. For example, to Vygotsky a mental element cannot exist in isolation, nor can it be studied or known without an analysis of all elements—the essence of any mental element is to be interrelated with all other elements. To assign an exclusive objective to one element or structure is a conceptual error that defies the inter-functionality central to Vygotsky's method, which serves as the indissoluble link to the models of the mind of psychoanalysis that rely on the principle of multiple function put forward by Waelder (1930).

On the other hand, it would initially appear that Vygotsky's approach is devoid of formal mechanisms of unconscious structuralization. It is true that Vygotsky did not explicitly in-corporate a continuum of consciousness, nor did he label any one gradation "unconsciousness" in his theory of internalization and development. He certainly had no formal role for a dynamic unconscious, because he did not attempt to study the conflicts that lead to the peculiar and individual linkages between words and their referents. However, Vygotskian theory can help elucidate one aspect of a descriptive unconscious (Freud, 1915c). When joined with a psychoanalytic view of defense and conflict, Vygotsky's writings can provide a clinically useful explanation of how some early experiences can be represented unconsciously, not because of defensive afterpressure (Freud, 1915b), but because these expe-riences occur at a point where language cannot yet express the complexity of thought or order one's self-experience. Hence, some early forms of language and thought cannot be fully assimilated into later forms of awareness, constituting a bedrock of psychic organization that exists prior to the acquisition of self-reflection. In Vygotsky's system, self-reflection is among one of the latest cen-tral mental functions to be acquired by the child. Thus, the earliest phases of language acquisition and usage and the beginnings of the development of the self-regulating functions are not readily subject to memorial access or introspective recollection, although they are structured and exert an influence over psychic life.

We suggest that Vygotsky's methodology for understanding the mind is comparable to that of the analyst who derives his data from within the clinical situation: (1) they both focus on the in-terrelation between inner and outer stimuli and their eventual transformation into guiding psychic structure, rather than on overt behavior; (2) conflict and the assumption of active psychic processes are the bulwarks of both systems; (3) both postulate an organism in constant flux, and examine change over time as their native data base, while stressing the necessity for constantly deepening self-reflection as at the crux of development; (4) de-spite the focus of both on the centrality of meaning, neither takes methodological recourse in hermeneutic antiscientism. Both methods assume that interiorized regularities (structure from which meaning emanates) are the primary constituents of action and experience. The actual contents of consciousness can in many ways be considered epiphenomenal to the underlying or-ganizations whence they emanate; (5) Vygotsky, like most analysts, focused on the process of internalization and transfor-mation of objects into internal presences.

This last point, Vygotsky's emphasis on how regulations, rules, and structures which are originally imposed from outside come to be internalized as mental processes, is crucial. Unlike strict envi-ronmentalists who assume the internal to be a mere isomorphic reconstruction of external interpsychological processes, psycho-analysts from Freud onward as well as Vygotsky have continually iterated how internalization transforms all the structures and functions of mental process on the way from outside to inside. Within psychoanalysis, object relations theories arose to explicate the role of internalization. Yet, Vygotsky's view of the caregiver-child dyad is a more encompassing one than that of most object-relational theories, which focus on the study of the caregiver pri-marily as an object who facilitates intrapsychic structuralization. Vygotsky goes further, describing how the caregiver serves as the lo-cus through whom psychological, historical, and social phenomena are funnelled. These phenomena are naturally brought to bear on the nascent mind of the child, who is inevitably bathed in these streams of events as development unfolds. Through the caregiver, the child is united with history and culture at birth. Emde (1988) notes a related trend in contemporary psychoanalysis when he comments on the epistemic shift from "I-it" to an "I-we dialectic" in the understanding of the infant. For Vygotsky, it is almost as if the child's "we" is assumed, and the "I" develops out of it. The development of the self, while important, is not accorded the same privileged status of an idealized endpoint of development as in other approaches. We note parenthetically that many influential clinical psychoanalytic papers have promulgated Vygotskian perspectives apparently without awareness of this predecessor. Such a trend can be seen most vividly in all of the seminal clinical papers of D.W. Winnicott and some of Loewald (1960), (1973), both of whom emphasize similar elements in the analytic situation—the priority of internalization in mental life and how one person makes use of his immediate field in ineffable yet describable ways in order to refine, articulate, and develop his self.

Freud (1910p. 73), quoting the artist Leonardo, suggested: *"Nessuna cosa si può amare nè odiare, se prima non si ha cognition di quella"* . . . "One has no right to love or hate anything if one has not acquired a thorough knowledge of its nature." Since the reader may not be familiar with Vygotsky's writings, we shall offer an ongoing summary of his views throughout this paper, highlighting aspects relevant to psychoanalysis and our argument. In assessing the significance of some of Vygotsky's work for psychoanalysis, we shall suggest several possibilities, but expect to raise more questions than provide answers.

Vygotsky's Theory of Thinking and Speaking: The Structure and Interplay of Language and Thought

Object relations theorists have described how the progressive internalization of representations of significant others serve as templates around which actions are organized. The classical tradition emphasizes the massive and rapid internalization of the superego, a precipitate constituted of an amalgam of representations, the influence of the child's prevailing fantasies and physiological states, as well as the codifications and transformations of infantile value systems which become continually less personified. This new structure aids the child's efforts at self-regulation and direction through the activation of signal affects such as guilt and anxiety.

Vygotsky's work likewise represents an attempt to conceptualize how what is outside is brought inside and converted into structure. His focus on language provides an additional vantage point from which internalization can be studied, complementing those already known through analytic inquiry. To Vygotsky, all higher mental functions first appear as social ("interpsychological") processes (Vygotsky, 1981), which are interiorized ("privatized"), and transformed under the aegis of language. Vygotsky studied language in order to understand and formulate many psychological processes not explicitly related to language. He was interested in how the child's internalizations lead him to progress from being regulated by an object, to regulating the object, and eventually to being self-regulating. Language processes originate with the caregiver and are then taken over by the child, ultimately providing the child with the necessary instrumentality to challenge and overcome nature. It is through language that the child is able to monitor the actions of others, and later grows to use language to exert control over all internal processes. Not to be able to use language in this way can result in a disorder of self-regulation

(Wilson et al., 1990). Language is of necessity first spoken aloud, then it can become progressively more silent as it becomes increasingly intertwined with thought. In this evolution it comes to obey different rules, which we shall spell out. These shifts are both qualitative and quantitative—his is an epigenetic theory of new "emergence" at a particular stage along pathways of increasing intensity when critical thresholds are reached.

Why is language a supraordinate factor, superseding yet encompassing affect, cognition, and volition? Vygotsky placed language at the center of his theory of internalization for two reasons. One, he held that the child's thought can only transcend the data of immediate sensory experience with the aid of language. Thought must link with language if either are to properly unfold. As the earliest forms of thought come to be articulated through speaking, they must inevitably be placed within a linguistically defined category. The arrival of the word for a child thus allows for the combination of elements that are the beginning of complex, symbolic, categorical thought. To illustrate this point, a visual percept can only refer to a single phenomenon. A word, by contrast, categorizes as it points to and contains a class of referents. These categories can then be combined without the necessity of being bombarded by all the sensory elements to which they refer. Two, Vygotsky emphasized the instrumentality of language. Language is the premier psychological "tool" by which human actions of all sorts, those of both inner and external realities, are regulated. Language subordinates all other forms of "symbolic mediation"; it is a necessary foundation for and promotes the development of such critical mental functions as memory and planning.

To Vygotsky all language processes originate as social speech, speech to another. This process then diverges along two distinct developmental paths. One path leads to the successful acquisition of social communication; the other involves the internalization of language through a progressive movement from social speech through egocentric speech to inner speech, which is speech for self, not spoken aloud. Vygotsky thus distinguishes among these three forms of progressively interiorized speech, which develop sequentially along a gradient of public private, although they come to coexist in the repertoire of the adult. Social speech is primarily other-directed, communicative speech. In distinction, egocentric speech is an incipient form of inner speech. In contrast to formulations prior to Vygotsky of inner speech as verbal memory, "speech without sound," or as any activity prior to the act of speaking, Vygotsky defined inner speech by its function, namely being speech for oneself. If social speech is defined as the turning of thought into words, inner speech involved an opposite process, specifically the distillation of verbal speech into thought. Thus, "absence of vocalization" is a consequence of the process of inner speech, rather than its defining feature.

In line with his different assumptions, Vygotsky defined egocentric speech in contradistinction to Piaget, whose theory would predict a decreased rate of egocentric speech over the course of development, and that egocentric speech would drop out as the child became more cognitively facile and more socially oriented. Vygotsky hypothesized that egocentric speech represented a midpoint in the development of self-regulation, between external and inner speech. Vygotsky's argument was based on the developmental course of egocentric speech, namely that its incidence increases, not decreases, as the child gets older, until it reaches a plateau and then goes underground. Some related experiments in linguistics have demonstrated the manner by which words are the child's first allies in asserting self-regulation and control over his own actions (Lennenberg, 1967). Eventually this use of language becomes ingrained, and as the vast array of psychological processes that constitute self-regulation develops, egocentric speech can go underground and become silent and unarticulated, that is, it is remade into inner speech.

Before we attempt to apply his ideas about internalization to the realms of affect and action, it is important that we further clarify Vygotsky's theory of the relation of language and thought. Vygotsky was the first theorist to propose an alternative to the predominant view of his time that thought was simply silent speech (one well-known example of the time was the Watsonian view that speech was the "external concomitant of thought") or that thought and language are disjunctive phenomena. Vygotsky demonstrated that thinking and speaking are indeed separate, but are profoundly intertwined and mutually regulating. They spiral together over the course of development, and any analysis of one is incomplete without taking full stock of the other. Vygotsky (1987d, p. 250) notes:

> Thought is not expressed but completed in the word. We can, therefore, speak of the establishment (i.e., the unity of being and nonbeing) of thought in the word. Any thought strives to unify, to establish a relationship between one thing and another. Any thought has movement. It unfolds. It fulfills some function or resolves some task. This flow of thought is realized as an internal movement through several planes, as a transition from thought to word and word to thought.

As it wends its way toward expression, thought is constrained by language, while speaking is guided by the motive forces within the underlying thought processes.

Experimental-empirical tests of his ideas appeared to constitute a chronic frustration to Vygotsky, although he subscribed to the notion that these ideas must be scientifically tested. To enlist support for his theories he usually made reference to a line of evidence which he termed a *genetic analysis*, where one must study the origins of any process and all the transitions that lead up to their later forms. His genetic analysis led him to view change over time as the *only* context in which one can legitimately study the mind. He believed that without a genetic analysis only certain limited aspects of any phenomena can be described, but not the essential aspects, the inner workings, or the causal dynamics.

Thus, Vygotsky makes a distinction between the semantic and phonetic aspects of speech, which he justifies genetically by depicting how they follow different developmental paths along different genetic "domains." At first, a small phonetic unit represents for the child a large and global chunk of meaning. To illustrate, the single utterance of a child is meant to convey an idea for which an older child will later use an entire sentence. As language acquisition proceeds, phonetic production expands, but each unit comes to stand for a progressively smaller sphere of meaning. Words become less global and more precise. As a consequence, early words rarely succeed in conveying to the listener all of the sophisticated meaning with which they are driven. Nor does the word yet have the power to move the thought into a more differentiated expression. As Vygotsky (1987d, p. 251) states:

> The child's thought emerges first in a fused, unpartitioned whole. It is precisely for this reason that it must be expressed in speech as a single word. It is as though the child selects a verbal garment to fit his thought. To the extent that the child's thought is partitioned and comes to be constructed of separate parts, his speech moves from parts to a partitioned whole. Correspondingly, to the extent that the child moves in his speech from parts to the unpartitioned whole of the sentence, he can move in his thought from an unpartitioned whole to

parts . . . .The structure of speech is not a simple mirror image of the structure of thought. It cannot, therefore, be placed on thought like clothes off a rack. Speech does not merely serve as an expression of developed thought. Thought is restructured as it is transformed in speech. It is not expressed but completed in the word.

A clinical example of this initial poor fit between language and thought follows. A four-and-a-half-year-old girl with a severe language disturbance and a generalized developmental arrest was in intensive psychotherapy. Upon arriving at the therapist's office, she began her usual frozen, largely asymbolic play, which she employed in order to convey to her therapist what was going on at home. She rarely deviated from the sheer repetition of domestic events by injecting interiorized and personalized conflicts into the play. She began one session by rushing into the office, breathlessly exclaiming "breakfast, Mr. Roberts, school. Go!" She looked expectantly at the therapist, with her usual hope that he would magically understand what she was thinking. These words conveyed what to another might have taken a paragraph. A child with greater language facility might have said that when she woke up, she had breakfast that day. Then, a new bus driver had driven her to school that morning and she was frightened, because the more familiar Mr. Roberts had been missing. After that, something happened in school that had upset her, and which she now wished to play out with the therapist, and which the therapist had to ease her into, because of how overwhelmed she was by anxiety. She could not find words global enough to capture the expansiveness of her thinking—she was constantly frustrated with the precision of words and how poorly they served to communicate her thoughts. The poverty of her thought, the failure of her thinking to find expression and enrichment through language, was paralleled in her play. In both, she was unable to generate an internal dialogue that could inter-twine with thought to produce the developmental momentum that might enable her to transcend her immediate state. She could not enter into the more normalizing pathways along crucial devel-opmental lines (A. Freud, 1965), nor could she use her linguistic competence to enhance such structural capacities as self-solace and transitional object relatedness (Horton and Sharp, 1984).

At the juncture of language and thought is the concept of word meaning. Word meaning is a key concept to Vygotsky, his central unit of analysis in studying the mind. It is through the concurrence of language and thought that word meaning is cre-ated. In Vygotsky's (1987d, p. 244) terms:

> Word meaning, then, is a phenomenon of both speech and intellect. This does not, however, represent a simultaneous and external mem-bership in two different domains of mental life. Word meaning is a phenomenon of thinking only to the extent that thought is connected with the word and embodied in it. It is a phenomenon of speech only to the extent that speech is connected with thought and illuminated by it. It is a unity of word and thought.

Thought touches language at first through word meanings be-cause the assigning of a word to a group of sensory or perceptual events involves thought processes that partake in categorization and generalization. With this advance, the child becomes capable of combining thoughts rather than being bombarded by sensory and perceptual events which cannot be sequentially ordered. Thought can now encompass multiple domains, including thoughts about other thoughts. Vygotsky was unequivocal in his belief in the centrality of word meanings for the acquisition of mind. He noted that "… it may be appropriate to view word meaning not only as a unity of thinking and of speech, but as a unity of generalization and social interaction, a unity of thinking and communication" (1987dp. 49). In this way, the word becomes capable of the reflection of all mental life—the word is "a microcosm of human consciousness."

Over the course of development, word meanings take on new and specifiable relations to other psychological processes. Initially, there is a disjunction between thought and word. Vygotsky thus describes how language and thought are initially separate, yet as soon as they establish concurrence, each radically alters the other. During the prelinguistic period, "thought" manifests itself as action patterns and affectomotor discharges that make up the infant's earliest form of engagement with the object world. At this time, the infant's babbling is a forerunner of speech. Because it does not reflect thought, it is still mere sound. Only when united with thought, forming what analysts would view as a complex of earliest wishes, do these sounds begin to accrue meaning. Vygotsky defines stages in the evolution of word meanings, proceeding from "unorganized heaps" to "complexes" to "concepts." The reader is referred to Vygotsky (1987d) for an elaboration of these stages. In a later evolution, the word is seen by the child as an inherent part of the object it connotes, and is treated as inseparable from that object. At yet a further point in the development of word meanings, the child comes to grasp the social and pragmatic connotations of language that may run counter to its fixed grammatical meaning or structure. At this time, the ability to use language for communication implies the necessity for an understanding of context, prosody, and tropes. Prosody is defined by Thoman (1981) as the melodic line produced by the variations of pitch, rhythm, and stress of pronunciation, that bestow both semantic and emotional meaning to speech (see Halliday, 1967); (Chafe, 1974), (1980); (Prince, 1981); (Brown, 1983). Tropes are defined as any literary or rhetorical device that consists of the use of words in other than their literal sense. This includes metaphor, simile, metonymy, synecdoche, irony, and many others. The acquisition of the ability to grasp prosody and tropes can only transpire within the intimacies of primary relationships.

This last point deserves emphasis. The addition of meaning to sound (the introduction of word meaning) begins in a social context, within the dyadic interplay of infant and caregiver. These meanings are forged in what has come to be called "referential intersubjectivity." In line with our discussion, we find it most useful for psychoanalysis to define intersubjectivity according to linguistic communications theory (e.g., Rommetveit and Blakar, 1979), as when two or more interlocutors share some aspect of their situation definitions in the negotiation of sense. With this definition in hand, intersubjectivity can become an important concept, one not heretofore present in the psychoanalytic literature. At this stage the caregiver-child milieu is essential for language processes during their inception. The significance of the context of primary relationships remains constant,despite qualitative shifts in the relation of language to thought. Although some aspects of language development proceed via biological maturation, the use of language for the creation and articulation of meaning can only take place in the shared context of an intimate object relationship. The dyad provides the motivational force—that is, to have a wish or a need met by the object—for the form, structure, acquisition, and usage of words. These interactive processes provide one significant link between linguistics and psychoanalysis.

In his discussion of the acquisition of language, Vygotsky makes a further crucial distinction—between word sense and word meaning. He defines sense as the significance of the word in all of its changing contexts over time. Sense fluctuates widely with context and emotional state. Word sense will continue to change and develop and is sensitive to new interpersonal contexts of situation and word use. Meaning is the fixed definition of the word abstracted from the totality of its contexts. Put another way, the meaning of a word is akin to its unyielding private definitional status to a person, or what we might find in one's idiosyncratic unconscious dictionary, if such a thing could be imagined. Meaning is much more stable and unchanging than is sense. It is the more abstracted version of word sense, and underlies all of the more particular contexts in which word sense has evolved. Word sense can never be permanently defined, but instead has permeable and fluctuating boundaries. In Vygotsky's terms (cited by Wertsch, 1985, p. 124):

> The sense of a word ... is the aggregate of all the psychological facts emerging in our consciousness because of this word. Therefore, the sense of a word always turns out to be a dynamic, flowing, complex formation which has several zones of differential stability. Meaning is only one of the zones of the sense that a word acquires in the context of speaking. Furthermore, it is the most stable, unified, and precise zone ... meaning is nothing more than a potential that is realized in living speech. In living speech this meaning is only a stone in the edifice of sense.

Word sense always includes the social and affective aspects of word meaning, the potential from which a word derives its semantic force. When a word is spoken, it inevitably enters the plane of word sense, but reflects the underlying word meaning which can never be fully articulated. The archeologist of personal history can discover keys to the developmental history of the individual lying in the multiple word senses and the more stable word meanings that exist behind the manifest presentation of a word. Sense has a Januslike referential and creative nature. Sense is created anew in each novel affective and social context in which a word is used. The focus of sense is not just the discovery of preexistent meanings. The psychoanalytic situation, with its amplification of affective context, is one prime setting where crucial word senses can be created. In this way, the interpretive work of the analyst can be directed toward the creation of new structure through the expansion of word senses.

We belabor the distinction between word sense and word meaning because of two additional apparent implications for psychoanalysis. First, analytic investigation of word meanings offers a window into hidden emotional climates by unearthing clues to the context and affective conditions under which word meanings were originally forged. The explication of word meaning then can further foster the activation or gathering of the transference by making consensual these phenomena, which are initially masked by language. Conversely, the state of the transference allows an analyst to infer or clinically confirm the hidden word meaning. Second, this distinction allows us to recognize how rare true communicative success actually can be in most dialogue (see also Grice, 1975). What seems to be an implicitly acknowledged definition of a word often does not take into account the idiosyncratic skews of word meaning which every individual possesses and which colors the overt semantic presentation. How often then do people talk past others while believing they are understood? In psychoanalysis we are offered the unique opportunity to understand and track these communicative disjunctions, and thus to overcome some inherent limitations built into our status as language users. In part, the potential for tracking these word meanings exists because in analysis we encourage the arrival of inner rather than social speech, with its closer proximity to core processes that constitute the self.

Psychoanalysis and Vygotsky: Steps toward an Integration

In stipulating the points of reference between Vygotskian psychology and psychoanalysis, we can see that the acquisition of word meanings must be linked to the vicissitudes of early object relations. Although the potential for word meaning exists prior to language acquisition, word meaning is made manifest and communicable through the linkage of a word and its unique referents. The referents that are included within the generalizations of a particular word meaning are idiosyncratic, unique to each individual. During the child's early years, word meanings are initially acquired within the processes of identification that give life to the social context. Once formulated, word meanings are woven into and elaborate these identifications by giving them a unique stamp. In addition, other aspects of the child's motivations will contribute to the personalization of word meanings. In the context of the fantasies and developmental anxieties that characterize the inner lives of children, one can surmise that many of these referents are more unusual than the given dictionary definition that speakers can mistakenly assume words are intended to convey. The more bizarre or unacceptable referents are perhaps quickly repressed by the child, and the acceptable ones more readily consciously retained. The motive for the repression can originate from demands of inner and/or outer realities. We should emphasize that we develop this line of reasoning when studying Vygotsky; he himself only tangentially alludes to such a conflicted/motivational aspect to his theory. Vygotsky tended to focus on the normative side of the study of language processes; he did not concentrate on the context of volatile or psychopathological conditions in which the pairing and unpairing of language and thought was caused by conflicted inner disturbances or stressful external conditions.

Once language acquisition and the relation of language to thought is understood in the above manner, it becomes immediately relevant to clinical psychoanalysis. The dynamic context of language acquisition then comes under the umbrella of actions that are repeatable, within a broadly conceived notion of transference. The history of both psychic conflict and the emotional climate within which language is acquired are preserved in word meanings, among other places. Questions emerge that can best be answered in the psychoanalytic situation. Why does the child wish to internalize the speech of the parent? Does speech itself represent a subprocess of identification? How is language acquisition and use altered by the key conflicts of childhood? Why and in what manner does the child strive to internalize the speech of the parent or defend against the anxieties of aspects of this relationship through distortions of speech? How does the child unconsciously experience his newly found power of speech? How does the acquisition of speech map onto other developmental tasks and fantasies, e.g., separation or infantile omnipotence? However, such questions have not heretofore been systematically explored. With the exception of Brett (1981), we could find virtually no literature that directly addresses such questions, and even this paper takes as the basis of its inquiry a literary figure rather than an analytic patient. Even Bruner (1983) does not examine, beyond how it finds expression, what the unconscious motivation is for the child's adaptation to and solicitation of the LASS. Psychoanalytic scrutiny of these motivations will shed light on at least some subset of the motivations for and component processes of language acquisition and language usage. Perhaps the clinical psychoanalytic situation is the optimal setting in which the "why" can be tested; it is hard to think of another where it is so frankly highlighted. We suspect the reason there has not been a more systematic exploration of this issue is because of the lack of a relevant theoretical conceptualization, although to be sure the significance of word meanings has long been a focus of scrutiny in papers concerned with the theory of technique.

There are indications in Vygotsky's later writings that he recognized the insufficiency of any view that ignores the central role of emotional development. On the basis of remarks scattered through his writings, it appears that Vygotsky was aware of how emotion served as an integrating and motivational force within the mind. His concern for the volatile and abnormal is clear in his recently published lecture titled "Emotions and Their Development in Childhood" (1987a, p. 335), where he notes that:

> ... it is difficult to understand why the emotions cause such profound and extended behavioral disorders, to understand why we cannot think consistently when we are ill, cannot act with consistency or according to plan when our feelings are disordered, cannot be responsible for our own behavior and control our actions in an intense affective state.

There is no reason his description of the relation between language and thought cannot be used to understand phenomena embedded within a context of emotional turbulence, infantile sexuality, and wildly skewed wishes and childhood fantasies. These factors interact with language acquisition in influencing how an object's functions, regulations, and characteristics are interiorized as word meanings and inner speech by the child. What Vygotsky's theory lacks is an understanding of archaic motivations, defensive protection, the vicissitudes of psychosexual development, affective turbulence, and the multiple anxieties accompanying early internalized object relations, which can disrupt the smooth and adaptive pairing and unpairings of language and thought. This limitation of his theory seems not to have escaped Vygotsky. In a surprising and provocative passage, at the very end of *Thinking and Speaking,* Vygotsky (1987d pp. 282–283) notes:

> Thought has its origins in the motivating sphere of consciousness, a sphere that includes our inclinations and needs, our interests and impulses, and our affect and emotion. The affective and volitional tendency stands behind thought. Only here do we find the answer to the final "why" in the analysis of thinking . . . A true and complex understanding of another's thought becomes possible only when we discover its real, affective-volitional basis . . . Understanding the words of others also requires understanding their thoughts. And even this is incomplete without understanding their motives or why they expressed their thoughts. In precisely this sense we complete the psychological analysis of any expression only when we reveal the most secret internal plane of verbal thinking—its motivation. With this, our analysis is finished.

It is certainly a curiosity that while Vygotsky ends his masterwork on this provocative claim, his call for the affective/ motivational as the final plane of the analysis of thought does not really inform the model he creates in this or any other text. This is another example of how Vygotsky never possessed an experimental methodology that could keep pace with his penetrating grasp of the processes of growth and change (cf. Wertsch, 1985). We can look to psychoanalysis to provide the most profound answer to this final phase of the analysis of thought and speech. We underscore that psychoanalysis is explicitly about this *secret internal plane* of motivation.

From a psychoanalytic perspective, the child's internalization of language must help to solve developmental conflicts (including such well-known calamities as fear of loss of the object, loss of the object's love, or superego and castration anxiety). The psychoanalytic theory of language acquisition can encompass the

Vygotskian notion of the significance of word meaning, and complement such a view by stipulating that word meaning must be embedded within a context of what we know about the vicissitudes of identification, in addition to the organization of thought. Otherwise, Vygotskian psychology remains estranged from the crucial motivational implications basic to the psychoanalytic understanding of all thought processes.

Psychoanalysts after Freud were left with uncoordinated sets of postulates concerning the relation of language to thought. We believe that analysts knew more about language clinically than was contained in their unfolding theoretical formulations, which generally tended to cluster around studying the relation of language to dreams, metaphor, technical aspects of interpretation, and the acquisition of psychic structure. The literature on the relations among language, thought, and dreams is vast and in large part irrelevant to Vygotskian psychology. The role of metaphor requires us more directly to struggle with the relation of thought to language, whereas in technical aspects of interpretation and the acquisition of psychic structure we see this relation highlighted more vividly. It is in the effort to understand the relation between language and interpretation and structure formation that we see the need for a unified model of language and thought more starkly displayed. The clinical efficacy of psychoanalysis is predicated on the assumption that we can modify psychic structure through verbal communications. Yet as Edelson (1988 p. 78) succinctly states: ". . . we have no adequate theory either of the psychoanalyst's act of understanding or the psychoanalyst's act of making an interpretation." Perhaps Vygotskian theory can provide, not a replacement for existing psychoanalytic thought in this regard, but an additional aspect to the systematization of the efficacy of analytic interventions. We plan on returning to some of these issues in a future communication (Wilson and Weinstein, 1992). For now, we conclude this paper by saying that Vygotsky's work can help psychoanalysis to understand the dynamic transformations of early thought, how language comes to express the history of the individual, and how language comes to play a role in the structuring of his primitive fantasies, early objectrelations, and psychophysiological experiences.

References

Atkin, S. (1969). Psychoanalytic considerations of language and thought. *Psychoanalytic Quarterly* 38:549–582.

Balkanyi, C. (1964). On verbalization. *International Journal of Psychoanalysis* 45:64–74.

Basch, M. 1981). Psychoanalytic interpretation and cognitive transformation. *International Journal of Psychoanalysis* 62:151–175.

Brett, J. (1981). Self and other in the child's experience of language: Hofmannsthal's "Letter of Lord Chandos." *International Journal of Psychoanalysis* 8:191–201.

Brown, G. (1983). Prosodic structure and the given/new distinction. In *Prosody: Models and Measurement,* ed. A. Cutler & J.R. Ladd. Berlin: Springer Verlag, pp. 67–77

Bruner, J. (1983). *Child's Talk.* New York: W.W. Norton & Company.

Call, J.D. (1980). Some prelinguistic aspects of language development. *Journal of the American Psychoanalytic. Association* 28:259–289.

Caray, S. (1985). *Conceptual Change in Childhood* Cambridge, MA.: MIT Press.

Cavell, M. 1989a). Interpretation, psychoanalysis, and the philosophy of mind. *Journal of the American Psychoanalytic. Association* 37:859–879.

———(1989b). Solipsism and community: two concepts of mind in philosophy and psychoanalysis. *Psychoanalysis &.Contemporary.Thought* 12:587–613.

Chafe, W. (1974). Language and consciousness. *Language* 50:11–133.

————(1980). The deployment of consciousness in the production of a narrative. In *The Pear Stories: Cognitive, Cultural, and Linguistic Aspects of Narrative Production*, ed. W. Chafe, pp. 9-50. Norwood, NJ: Ablex.

Dore, J. (1989). Monologues as re-envoicement of dialogue. In *Narratives from the Crib*, Ed. K. Nelson, pp. 231-260. Cambridge, MA.: Harvard University Press.

Edelheit, H. (1969). Speech and psychic structures, *Journal of the American Psychoanalytic Association* 17:381–412.

Edelson, M. (1972). Language and dreams: the interpretation of dreams revisited *Psychoanalytic Study of the Child* 27:203–282.

————(1975). Language and Interpretation. In *Psychoanalysis*. New Haven, CT: Yale University Press.

————(1988). *Psychoanalysis: A Theory in Crisis*. Chicago: University of Chicago Press.

Emde, R. (1988). Development terminable and interminable *International Journal of Psychoanalysis*. 69:23–42; 283–296.

Freud, A. (1965). *Normality and Pathology in Childhood. Writings 6*. New York: International Universities Press.

Freud, S. (1887–1902). *The Origins of Psychoanalysis*. New York: Basic Books, 1954.

————(1895). Project for a scientific psychology. *Standard Edition 1*.

————(1888). *On Aphasia*. New York: International Universities Press, 1953.

————(1910). Leonardo Da Vinci and a memory of his childhood. *Standard Edition 11*.

————(1911). Psychoanalytic notes on an autobiographical account of a case of paranoia (dementia paranoides). *Standard Edition 12*.

————(1915a). Instincts and their vicissitudes. *Standard Edition 14*.

————(1915b). Repression. *Standard Edition 14*.

————(1915c). The unconscious. *Standard Edition 14*.

Grice, H.P. (1975). *Logic and conversation In Syntax and Semantics 3: Speech Acts*, ed., P. Cole & J.L. Morgan. New York: Academic Press.

Halliday, M. (1967). Notes on transitivity and theme in English part 2. *Journal of Linguistics* 3:177–274.

Horton, P. & Sharp, S. (1984). Language, solace, and transitional relatedness *Psychoanalytic Study of the Child* 39:167–194.

Kris, E. (1947). The nature of psychoanalytic propositions and their validation. In *Selected Papers* New Haven: Yale University Press, 1975 pp. 3–23

Lennenberg, E. (1967), *Biological Foundation of Language*. New York: Wiley.

Litowitz, B. & Litowitz, N. (1983). Development of verbal self-expression. In *The Future of Psychoanalysis*. Ed., A. Goldberg, pp. 397-427. New York: International Universities Press.

Loewald, H. (1960). The therapeutic action of psychoanalysis. *International Journal of Psychoanalysis*. 41:16–33.

———(1973). On internalization. *International Journal of Psychoanalysis* 54:9–17.

Meltzoff, A. 1985 The roots of social and cognitive development: models of man's original nature. In *Social Perception in Infants,* Eds., T. Field & N. Fox, pp. 1-30. Norwood, NJ: Ablex.

Olson, D., Ed. (1980). *The Social Foundations of Language and Thought: Essays in Honor of Jerome Bruner.* New York: W.W. Norton & Company.

Panel (1968). Language and the development of the ego, H. Edelstein, reporter. *Journal of the American Psychoanalytic Association* 16:113–122.

Panel (1969). Language and psychoanalysis, V. Rosen, reporter. *International Journal of Psychoanalysis* 50:113–116.

Panel (1977). Language and psychoanalysis, S. Leavy, reporter. *Journal of the American Psychoanalytic Association* 25:633–639.

Peller, L. (1966). Freud's contribution to language theory *Psychoanalytic Study of the Child* 21:448–467.

Prince, E. (1981). Toward a taxonomy of given-new information. In *Radical Pragmatics* Ed. P. Cole, pp. 223-255. New York: Academic Press.

Rommetveit, R. & Blakar, R. (979). On the architecture of intersubjectivity. In *Studies of Language, Thought, and Verbal Communication*, pp, 93-107. New York: Academic Press.

Rosen, V. (1977). *Style, Character, and Language.* Eds., M. Jucovy & S. Atkin.

New York: Jason Aronson.

Shapiro, T. (1979). *Clinical Psycholinguistics* New York: Plenum Publishing Corp.

———(1986). *Sign, Symbol, and Structural Theory in Psychoanalysis: the Science of Mental Conflict,* ed., M. Willick & A.D. Richards, pp. 107-125 Hillsdale, NJ: Analytic Press.

Thoman, E. (1981). Affective communication as the prelude and context for language learning. In *Early Language,* ed., R. Schiefelbusch & D. Bricker, pp 183-200. Baltimore: University Park Press.

Vygotsky, L.V. (1962). *Language and Thought.* Cambridge, MA.: MIT Press.

———(1978). *Mind in Society: The Development of Higher Psychological Processes* Cambridge, MA.: Harvard University Press.

———(1981). The genesis of higher mental functions. In *The Concept of Activity in Soviet Psychology.* ed., J. Wertsch, pp. 144-188. Armonk, NY: M. E. Sharpe Publishers, Inc.

———(1987a). Emotions and their development in childhood. In *The Collected Papers of L.S. Vygotsky,* Vol. 1, ed. R.W. Rieber & S.A. Carton, pp. 325-338. New York: Plenum.

———(1987b). Imagination and its development in childhood. In *The Collected Papers of L.S. Vygotsky,* Vol. 1, ed. R.W. Rieber & S.A. Carton, pp. 339-350. New York: Plenum.

———(1987c). The problem of will and its development in childhood. In *The Collected Papers of L.S. Vygotsky,* Vol. 1, ed., R.W. Rieber & S.A. Carton, pp. 351-358. New York: Plenum.

———(1987d). Thinking and speaking. In *The Collected Papers of L.S. Vygotsky,* Vol. 1, ed., R.W. Rieber & A.S. Carton, pp. 39-228. New York: Plenum Publishing Corp.

Waelder, R. (1930). The principle of multiple function In *Psychoanalysis: Observation, Theory, Application,* ed., S.A. Guttman, pp. 68-83. New York: International Universities Press, 1976.

Wallerstein, R.S. (1988). One psychoanalysis or many. *International Journal of Psychoanalysis* 69:5–22.

Wertsch, J. (1985). *Vygotsky and the Social Formation of Mind.* Cambridge, MA.: Harvard University Press.

Wertsch, J. (1991). *Voices of the Mind.* Cambridge, MA: Harvard University Press.

Wilson, A. & Malatesta, C. (1989). Affect and the compulsion to repeat: Freud's repetition compulsion revisited. *Psychoanalysis & Contemporary Thought* 12:243–290.

———Passik, S. & Faude, J. (1990). *Self-Regulation and Its Failures In Empirical Studies in Psychoanalytic Theory,* Volume III, Ed., J. Masling, pp. 149–213. Hillsdale, NJ: Erlbaum.

———& Weinstein, L. (1992). Language and the clinical process: psychoanalysis and Vygotskian psychology Part II. *Journal of the American Psychoanalytic Association* 40:3.

CHAPTER 12

LANGUAGE AND THE PSYCHOANALYTIC PROCESS: PSYCHOANALYSIS AND VYGOTSKIAN PSYCHOLOGY, PART II

In the first part of this investigation (Wilson and Weinstein, 1992), published here as Chapter 11, Vygotsky's analysis of the relation between language, thought, and internalization and its potential value for psychoanalysts was described. Points of convergence and divergence between a Vygotskian perspective and psychoanalytic theory were examined. Some ways were proposed in which psychoanalysis can encompass consideration of two approaches to language acquisition and use, specifically the nativist universals of brain function (e.g., Chomsky, 1957), (1966) and those aspects of sociolinguistics that study interactive phenomena through which the particulars of language development are forged (e.g., Bruner, 1983). These dual domains are united in nature and only separable in our theories of nature. The developmental progression of forms of language, from external (social) speech to egocentric speech to inner (private) speech, and their coexistence in the lexical repertoire of the adult was explicated. A psychoanalytic construal of the basic premises of Vygotsky's work suggests that over its developmental course the word becomes inherently polysemic (i.e., has a diversity of "meanings") and carries the successive historical layers of infantile and subsequent experiences, which may be observed clinically through the vehicles Vygotsky describes of word meaning and word sense.

In this paper, our previous theoretical discussions are further expanded in the direction of some clinical implications of Vygotskian premises. We focus on how his emphasis on language processes enables psychoanalysts better to attend to subtle and easily overlooked early experiences and their manifestations in the clinical situation. We do not aim to replace any aspect of psychoanalytic theory and technique with linguistically based formulations. Rather, the intention is to articulate and develop those bridging constructs necessary for clinical psychoanalysis to gain access to a substantial extant body of scholarship—one heretofore not conceptually available to psychoanalysis—through examination of the roles of language and thought in primal repression, metaphor, and inner, egocentric, and social speech in free association. (For further background on language, Vygotskian psychology, and psychoanalysis, see Peller, 1966; Edelson, 1975; Rosen, 1977; Shapiro, 1979; Forrester, 1980; Basch, 1981; Wertsch, 1985).

Primal Repression

Theoretical Background

Contemporary psychoanalysis which traces its lineage to Freud is predicated on the root assumptions of the primacy of intrapsychic conflict and the existence of unconscious processes. Integrating Vygotsky's views on early language-thought relations with psychoanalytic notions of early ego and structural development helps to specify the role of conflict in the various stages of repression and to clarify the structure of the unconscious. His thinking provides one way of conceptualizing the prototypic defensive activity of primal repression. It is important to remember that between 1910 and 1915, Freud used the concept of repression as a prototype for all defensive activity. So, too, might Freud have intended primal repression as an umbrella term that includes those early defensive operations used to ward off overstimulation, what we are familiar with today as splitting and primitive projection and denial. Likewise, when we speak of primal repression, we think of a prototype of defensive activity rather than a particular defense as mechanism.

In his body of writings, Freud depicted primal repression in only four of his theoretical works (1915a), (1915b), (1926), (1937), and it figured in one of his case studies (Freud, 1911). Freud developed his idea of primal repression when attempting to understand the earliest origins of mental life and levels of censorship. He afforded the concept varying degrees of importance to the extent that he was sympathetic to preoedipal determinants at any particular stage of his career. Each of his descriptions of primal repression is strikingly brief and underdeveloped. In "Repression," Freud (1915a) defined primal repression as occurring when the ideational representation of an instinct is denied access to the system preconscious. Thus, there is no "afterpressure," such as that which characterizes the second stage of repression proper. In primal repression, the instinctual vicissitude has never become accessible to the system pcs., whereas in repression proper, the barring of the idea from preconsciousness leads to the ever-present possibility of the return of the repressed. Once established, the unconscious nuclei constituted in primal repression then can participate in repression proper. A web of unconscious fantasies is then spun that "proliferate in the dark" (Freud, 1915a) and derivatives of which the system pcs. must countercathect in order to keep from awareness. In "The Unconscious," Freud (1915b) describes how primal repression is characterized economically by "anticathexes," by means of which the pcs. protects itself from an unconscious idea by cathecting another element that prevents the repressed idea from emerging. An example of anticathexis (a synonym for countercathexis) might be the cathexis of the idea of an animal in a phobic state in order to prevent, through displacement, the repressed idea of the father as castrator as well as the child's own projected murderous wishes toward the object from emerging into awareness. The anticathexis then accounts in part for the stability of the phobic symptom. Anticathexis is, to Freud, the sole mechanism of primal repression, as contrasted with the anticathexis and the withdrawal of the pcs. cathexis (also called decathexis) of a particularly unpleasant idea in repression proper. Withdrawal of pcs. cathexis and anticathexis thus imply each other in repression proper, as noted by Laplanche and Pontalis (1973). In *Analysis Terminable and Interminable* (1937), Freud returned only briefly to primal repression, but now to downplay its importance. This was his response to the technical experimentation of Otto Rank, who rendered the trauma of birth the apotheosis of neurosis and hence elevated in significance the ensuing primal repressions for all psychopathology and, indeed, all mental life. One problem with Freud's formulation is how to differentiate between situations in which there is an exclusive use of anticathexis and when there is an additional withdrawal of the preconscious cathexes—the specific clinical referents are unclear.

Freud also specified something of a timetable for the progression along a continuum from primal repression to repression proper. In *Inhibitions, Symptoms, and Anxiety,* Freud (1926) noted, "Far too little is known as yet about the background and preliminary stages of repression" (p. 94). Initially, primal repression would suffice to ward off trauma or environmentally generated stressors, because overstimulation from outside is the primary danger prior to the development of a differentiated psychic structure and the concomitant appearance of intrapsychic conflict as a source of pathogenesis. Freud then cautiously suggested that repression proper probably succeeds primal repression after the formation of the superego. Repression proper becomes necessary because during the oedipal period, for the first time the dangerous impulses of the id must be permanently excluded from aware-ness at the behest of the superego. The implied distinction is that following the internalization of conflict accompanying superego development, a constant expenditure of energy (the decathexis of the idea) becomes necessary.

Theorists as diverse as Hartmann (1964) and Kernberg (1975) date the acquisition of repression to approximately the oedipal period. Neither found much use for the concept of primal repres-sion as a necessary first stage for repression. Primal repression received some attention in psychoanalytic writings after Freud (e.g., Rapaport, 1951); (Brenner, 1957); (Frank, 1969); (Gedo and Goldberg, 1973); (Gedo, 1979), because of an increasing interest in studying early nuances of thought. Gedo and Goldberg (1973) in their hierarchical conceptualization of models of the mind recommend that the concept of primal repression be retained as the predominant mode of defensive activity during the earliest mode of functioning (mode 1); subsequent modes lead to its be-ing superseded by projection, introjection, and splitting as defensive activities. At present, the idea of the gradual evolution of primal repression into repression proper and the assumption of continuity between them is no longer generally held in psy-choanalysis. The concept of primal repression as the primary defensive activity of the preoedipal period has been supplanted by an understanding of a host of other defensive processes and mechanisms.

To Freud, primal repression was not so much a defense qua mechanism as it was a result of the infant's inability to establish an active line of defensive processes because of the immaturity of the psychic apparatus. Freud drew his distinctions between primal re-pression and repression proper in psychoeconomic terms (anticathexes and the withdrawal of preconscious cathexes, as dis-cussed above). Stepping outside of Freud's energic assumptions and his reliance on the topographic point of view, how can the difference between primal repression and repression proper be articulated? In our definition it is proposed that although primal repression does serve a defensive function, it is a normative aspect of the development of mind, subject to alterations similar to those that affect the development of early ideational, motoric, and perceptual functions. Its mode of deployment—the way it works—can be linked to processes of early language and thought. One might be able to articulate similar lines of ontogenesis for motoric and perceptual functions, but these have been less comprehensively studied than language and are more difficult to observe, especially in the clinical situation. Vygotsky's explication of the intertwining of speaking and thinking throughout development provides one such possibility for how primal repression can be reconceptualized.

Briefly, Vygotsky described three overarching disjunctive stages in the evolution of word meanings, which define patterns of translation between language and thought. These inevitable disjunctures of the relation between language and thought provide one key to understanding primal repression and distinguishing it from repression proper. First, language cannot reflect thought, but is mere sound. Until language is united with thought, these rudimentary forms cannot provide sufficient leverage to adequately meet adaptational needs. Second, a word and its meaning are treated as if they were truly one. For example, a six-year-old boy, asked what he would name his identical "twin" stuffed toy lobsters, immediately replied "Sam and Sam," because it was so obvious to him that their identity as twins necessitated identical names. Third, the child must come to know both semantics and phonetics and distinguish between the two, and to understand the social and pragmatic connotations of language which can run counter to its grammatical structure.

As noted in our earlier paper, Vygotsky did not have any theory resembling a dynamic unconscious, in part because he did not attempt to study conflicts or the motivational underpinnings which led to the barring of ideational content from immediate awareness. However, Vygotskian theory can help elucidate one aspect of the descriptive unconscious—word meanings that exist at the interface of language and thought and are therefore inaccessible to consciousness. This view can provide psychoanalysis with a theoretical explanation of how some early experiences can be represented unconsciously, not because of defensive afterpressure, but because they are embedded at one of the junctures of language and thought, a fate that is inevitable during the course of language acquisition. Freud (1915b) described how psychoanalysis possessed three perspectives for the examination of the unconscious—the descriptive, systemic, and dynamic. Since the systemic unconscious is not germane to our argument, we shall address only the dynamic and descriptive perspectives. The descriptive unconscious defines unconscious content that is capable of becoming conscious with the provision of attention cathexes, i.e., it emphasizes potential recallability. The descriptive unconscious provides a conceptual basis for understanding unconscious mental life that is not dynamically repressed (due to countercathexes). All that is dynamically unconscious is also descriptively unconscious, but not vice versa. The dynamic view of the unconscious is the familiar one of conflict over forcefully repressed mental content. Clinically, dynamically repressed mental content is made conscious through fantasies, memories, parapraxes, dreams, jokes, and puns. Psychoanalysts have always made reconstructions of dynamically repressed experiences which were excluded from consciousness despite the fact that they had reached linguistic representation, such as a reconstruction that deals with a childhood fantasy that may never have been conscious but explains a variety of symptoms and behaviors (Greenacre, 1981). It has been much more difficult to apprehend material that has never reached linguistic representation.

We shall now expand our definition of primal repression. In primal repression, the points of connection between language and thought are primitive but intact. The development of the earliest referential categories inherent in word meanings protect the child by acting as a bulwark against stimulus bombardment, which would necessarily follow from the need to mnemonically store each perceptual image of an object. However, early word meanings can be vague and oceanic, encompassing even the psychophysio-logical senses that accompany a word. These latter word meanings become inaccessible to consciousness, because they cannot be grasped or integrated by that aspect of the ego that promotes ad-aptation, tests reality, and is secondary-process oriented. Our view is thus akin to Noy's (1969), (1979), Holt's (1967), and Loewald's (1978) views on some distinction between primary- and second-ary-process thinking. Noy describes how it is the organizational mode of each system, the functions assigned to each, that makes them distinctive. Primary process organizes and can "make sense of" thought that is self-centered and "alogical"; secondary process organizes and makes sense of thought that is reality-oriented and logical. Both modes are intrinsic to and necessary for all complex thought; neither is inferior or superior to the other. In our recon-ceptualization of primal repression, the linkage between a language and thought element may be unable to reach precon-scious representation because the word meaning that is created is either alogical, bizarre, too global, or otherwise inassimilable. But it is *not* necessarily dynamically repressed. What then is the fate of these representations that are inaccessible to secondary-process organization? Since no other representation exists apart from the unconscious one, there is no need to destroy the linkage. Instead, the child's mind must simply continue to function in such a way that the linkage does not emerge into awareness (i.e., exactly like Freud's concept of anticathexis in primal repression).

Extending the above definition to the second stage of repression (repression proper), the word meaning that results from the pairing of language and thought can be apprehended and assimilated by the more mature psychic apparatus. As such, it constitutes a potential threat that must be barred from consciousness through the mobilization of an active defense. The relation between the word and the thought must be subject to revision by repression proper (i.e., exactly like Freud's withdrawal of preconscious cathexes). However, the linkage can only be weakened but not permanently demolished; once a connection is made between language and thought, the potential for its reconnection must be continually defended against. Just as Freud insisted that any repressed idea retains its cathexis in the unconscious, so too will the pairing once made remain immortal (see also Schafer's (1968) related idea of the immortality in psychic reality of the object—and its various fates). The possibility of the return of the repressed through the repairing of the thought with the language element will continue to exist. This reuniting leads to the potential amplification of a latent meaning, thereby necessitating the constant vigilance of repression proper. To the extent that repression is defined in terms of the fate of language and thought elements, primal repression can be seen as a forerunner to repression proper.

We contrast our definition of primal repression with that of Cohen and Kinston (1983) and Kinston and Cohen (1986). They offer a trauma-centered definition, the handling of which they believe is the central task and focus of psychoanalytic treatment. They describe how early traumatic events lead to "holes" in the representational system, which are deficit states characterized by a lack of psychic structure. They further hypothesize that the effects or derivatives of primal repression are made manifest through need states which are not connected with ideational derivatives or "wishes." These effects or derivatives of primal repression can be witnessed in such forms as volatile affects, accident-proneness, and primitive panic, all of which are preverbal and cannot be reached directly through interpretation. The task of the analyst in their view is not to "seal these holes over" through interpretation (which only gets at repression proper), but to allow the expression of the resulting states in the transference and then to mediate the needs, thereby creating structure where no structure had existed.

Although the importance of the primacy of emotional states and the difficulties of tapping these states only through the interpretation of ideational conflict is undeniable, our understanding differs considerably from that of Cohen and Kinston. Rather than a deficit state characterized by a lack of representational capacity which is brought into existence following trauma, primal repression can be thought of as normative. As such, it neither engenders further deficits nor requires actual need-gratifying mediation by the analyst. Primal repression thus is one ubiquitous aspect of early structure formation that results in skews and distortions that can but do not necessarily have pathognomic implication. Cohen and Kinston frame infantile helplessness and view the child as *ipso facto* victimized by the environment, inevitably traumatized by the natural course of actual life events. In contrast, the definition we offer emphasizes not actual traumata as the basis of primal repression, but instead the unavoidable futility of the child's attempt to translate between language and thought. Until language can meet thought on near equal footing, some precision must be lost in translation. That which is primally repressed is epigenetically linked with repression proper and all subsequent developmental occurrences. Conflict will then infiltrate the disjunctures, which will come to act as the *anlagen* for later defensive operations. However, later phenomena are not seen as epiphenomenal. Our definition more closely approximates Freud's effort to understand levels of censorship (primal repression—> repression proper—> second censorship) and does not posit the primacy of one particular developmental level over another. While primal repression is one core aspect of a personality organization, the supraordinate task of analysis is not, as Cohen and Kinston suggest, to strip away all later conflict in order to arrive at this fundamental basic core. By conceptualizing primal repression in terms of language and thought rather than trauma, we see the roots of primal repression later than do Cohen and Kinston, as at Gedo and Goldberg's mode 2 (the period of initial language acquisition) rather than mode 1, and with connecting branches extending throughout the life span.

Clinical and Technical Implications

An example of how analysts can glimpse crucial material behind the manifest facade of the word follows: A young woman was chastising her analyst after his last interpretation struck a chord she did not like. The analyst then noticed that while she was angry, her speech changed, and she began dropping her r's at the end of some words. He commented on how her dropping her r's must reflect something important, perhaps worth examining. She was surprised, but associated to this observation. Her associations led them to understand more clearly how she regressed to primary identification with her Southern mother with such an accent, who also dropped her r's. The patient returned to her syntactic past in order to sustain the rage she felt. When this was interpreted, important analytic material followed, as she fantasized that without the presence of the internal mother of a primary identification to steer her, she would be incapable of rage or any strong emotion, a tightly controlled and inhibited "leaf blowing in a storm," at the mercy of all to be taken advantage of.

The Vygotskian view suggests that the earliest communicational climates between infant and caregiver become ground into the composition of the word itself. These seminal interactions fall within the domain of primal repression. These words recombine under the natural rules of grammar to form new combinations, but retain an original essence. By deconstructing language into its constituent meanings, aspects of the original caregiver-child climate in which words obtained derivation may be brought into the analysis. The succession of senses through which a word acquires connotations over time carries the imprint of one's affective history. Arlow's (1969) proposition, based on data inferred from within the clinical situation, that unconscious fantasies must contain a linguistic as well as imagistic or pictorial component, is consistent with our perspective. Beyond semantics and syntax is pragmatics, how language gets things done—and all are clinically important. Whereas syntax links words with other words, and semantics links words with things, pragmatics links words to the context in which they are articulated, what a person accomplishes through language usage. It is through engagement with the latent intentionality conveyed through the forms of the word and its purpose in being articulated (e.g., "markers," tropes, prosody, polysemy), the archaeologic excavation of word meaning, and the concurrent expansion of word sense, that previously primally repressed inchoate experience can be elevated into the flow of the analytic process. How the word is uttered, i.e., the *prosodic* aspects of language which include pitch, rhythm, and tonality, can be a manifest form through which crucial material excluded from consciousness by primal repression can be glimpsed, a part of the totality of a word meaning or sense. Loewenstein's (1957) point that the words of an analysand are compromise formations that bear traces of the interplay of forces that led to the compromise is an example of a technical understanding that is compatible with the proposals in this paper. Loewenstein notes that an analyst should formulate interpretations using an analysand's "key words" because such words promote a regrouping of the patient's salient thoughts and emotions, which can lead to further recall and insight. Another way of formulating Loewenstein's point is that the analyst adds to the sense of the word by connecting it through interpretation with associated experiences.

All of the implications for psychoanalysis of the questions that have been raised cannot possibly be addressed in this paper. We would, however, like to make note of the implications for what is known about transference. Vygotsky was always concerned with the perseverance of the past within human relationships and the limitations it placed on the mutability of lived experience. He had a preferred data base for demonstrating these points. He illustrated the interdependence of past and present through an understanding of the relation of word meaning to word sense, with multiple examples from poems, novels, and plays (e.g., 1988,pp. 243–285). Hypotheses and evidence of mutability in speech can as well be marshaled from the analytic transference, and tested in the clinical situation (Edelson, 1984). As Greenacre (1968) implies, attention to the Vygotskian emphasis on the word can reintroduce the history of the earliest meaning-producing social nexus and its subsequent patinas into the transference:

> The misuse of speech . . . may be reflected not only in the basic transference, but in that very part which is the gateway to and blends with the transference neurosis. Such deformations represent a fixation in

early ego development, at which incipient defense reactions have begun to form at the very threshold of the oedipal period. This is after
the acquisition of speech, when it is in the process of adaptive refinement to the new relation to reality, consistent with logical and abstract
thinking. Such disturbances in the development of speech may contribute to an insecure transference as well as to a tendency to act out
in the course of treatment (p. 770).

Methodologically, we believe that it is through analysis of the
transference that one can resurrect the original meaning situation which has become "fossilized" (Valsiner, 1988) and also
through which subsequent transformations can be observed. Hierarchical transference repetition can issue from any level of
early development, including the earliest period when the infant's mind can be thought of as consisting of interpsychological
dyadic processes rather than as a "privatized" entity. Thus, an
early word meaning can become one carrier of the "primal"
transference (Stone, 1961) or "basic" transference (Greenacre,
1954). In the terminology of Vygotsky, one can see the varied
contributions to the sense of a word throughout development. A
number of analysts, including Jacobs (1986), Arlow (1987), and
Sandler (1988), have recently described how the analysis of
transference provides the most trustworthy route to the past, one
which enhances a patient's experienced veracity of any reconstructive work. Through the evocation and interpretation of the
transference, the analysis can further add to the sense of a word
at the same time as the more stable underlying meaning of a word
points to the earliest internal climate that can be unearthed. The
early word meaning is like an underpainting, each successive word
sense another coating, and the concurrent sense is the word's final
canvas. In a successfully proceeding analysis, there is a dynamically experienced reciprocity between past and present, where

both enrich and enliven each other as the analysis deepens. Much of the literature that advocates reconstruction (e.g., Blum, 1980); (Greenacre, 1981) makes essentially the same point, of the mutually enriching reciprocity and mutual dependency between past and present, as does Schafer (1983) in his conceptualization of some clinical implications of narration.

Continuing the investigation of language processes and the ineffable, we shall now examine the metaphoric and free association. In doing so, we shall proceed to additional aspects of the psychoanalytic and Vygotskian views on speaking and thinking.

The Metaphoric

Vygotsky's contributions to the relation between language and thought, specifically his explication of word sense, can help explain several clinical and technical observations on the importance of metaphor. Spence (1987) carefully addresses metaphor in psychoanalysis and follows the philosopher Hesse (1980) in defining metaphor as the transfer of the associated ideas and dynamic implications of a primary figurative system, usually unconscious, to a secondary system that is within the domain of analytic observation. The primary system then emphasizes or suppresses elements which are seen through the frame of the secondary system. Several excellent examples can be found in Arlow's (1979) classic paper on metaphor and unconscious fantasy.

In the view of classical rhetoric, metaphor is a trope that has historically borne a somewhat controversial relation to other tropes, one of which is termed metonymy (the use of the name for an object or concept for another object or concept to which it is related, e.g., "scepter" for "sovereignty"). Psychoanalysts at times refer to metaphor as if it existed only as a specific linguistic construction (a trope) separate and distinct from the metaphoric aspects contained in all language. The linguist Roman Jakobson (1956), (1960) presaged the perspective on the metaphoric as a property of all language when he highlighted the universality of the "pole" between the metaphoric and the metonymic. The tension between the metaphoric and the metonymic (i.e. between the symbolic and the contiguous) was emphasized. The metaphoric became an organizational principle that defined the symbolic interrelation of multiple entities of all sorts, from aphasias to poetics to all of culture. Jakobson examined the relation between the principles of primary-process ideation and these ways of organizing entities, and described how symbolism can be considered metaphoric and condensation and displacement metonymic. He thus laid out a blueprint of sorts for how the metaphoric and the metonymic can be linked to the psychoanalytic unconscious, each configuring a particular type of thought organization. According to Jacobson, all discourse tips eventually toward one or another end of this pole. Symbolic transformations and the history of the word naturally belong to the metaphoric end, since the metonymic tends toward the ahistorical. The significance of the tension between the metaphoric and the metonymic can also be seen in the processes of clinical psychoanalysis. There is alternating movement between the use of dreams and other symbolic events where multiple layers of experience are superimposed on one another (the metaphoric end of the pole) to the use of actual process analysis, for example, where a patient's contiguous thoughts are related to one another and offer a hidden subtext of salient issues (the metonymic end of the pole). Ricoeur (1978) has also contributed to a Vygotskianlike view of the metaphoric. He describes how the metaphoric is not confined to its classical grammatical structure (e.g., "she is a rose"), but is embedded within the larger units of natural substrates of conversational grammar. Lakoff and Johnson (1980) have gone even further and described how our very engagement of the world is inherently metaphoric, how levels of ubiquitous metaphoric constructions gird our ability to order, grasp, and make sense of reality.

In this spirit, that the metaphoric is ingrained in any use of language, Vygotsky's perspective on language and thought provides for an expanded definition of the metaphoric that can be brought to the clinical situation. More specifically, Vygotsky's explication of word sense as opposed to the decontextualized meaning of a word highlights the affective elements inherent in its metaphoric extension. The disjunctures between modes of translation and different symbol systems that arise during development are bridged through metaphoric extensions that find expression in language use. It is through the metaphoric that the earliest affective turbulence and noteworthy sensations can find subsequent expression. The metaphoric is created by the infusion of early affectivity. It represents the attempt of language to transcend itself—to express experiences that as yet have no words. The history of the metaphoric is the history of its constituent word senses.

Some attention psychoanalysis has given to metaphor within the clinical situation concerns the ability of language to give expression to earlier bodily experiences. Sharpe (1940) noted that metaphor fuses infantile sense experience (especially of a psychophysiological nature) and thought in language, thus providing a window into the time when the word was the representation of the unitary experience. She examines one function of the word, which is to provide a channel for discharge of infantile affects. This function is largely carried through prosody but also through the choice of word. By insisting that affectomotor discharge also informs the metaphor, she secures the role of affect in metaphor. Thus, the final choice of word or phrase (including how it is said) is a compromise between repetition of infantile experience and the semantics of the word. To Sharpe, a metaphor is a final common pathway, one that condenses multiple senses that can then be explicated in order to arrive at insight. To both Sharpe and Vygotsky, the history of the word (its meaning as it has passed through multiple senses) carries into the present prior affective meaning and experience. This thinking is not compatible, however, with the thinking of most nativist linguists.

Yet, the importance of the metaphor extends beyond psychophysiological states to the word meanings inherent in all language. Most clinicians agree that a patient's metaphoric expressions are a rich source of potential insight when translated. However, if we follow Vygotsky's logic concerning the development of word meaning and its evolution through multiple word senses, then we see that the metaphoric is already a particular kind of self-insight (cf. Shengold, 1981). Through the metaphoric, links to early ideational and sensory organizations that have been superseded by later structures are established. A patient's metaphoric use of language brings into the hour the rudiments of a self-interpretation which the analyst can best observe and encourage, but not provide. The self-interpretation is at first a personal and private one, which gradually expands as the metaphoric expands and preconscious derivatives and recognizable affective themes can be interpreted by the analyst. There is a simultaneous expansion of what is available for interpretation along with an increasing precision of designation (Shapiro, 1970) as the interpretive process proceeds.

While the more apparent symbolic translation of any specific metaphoric use of language may be easy for the analyst to apprehend, the affective context that also contributes to its meaning is rarely as readily known, and awaits its manifestation in the transference before a mutative interpretation will be most effective.

Further, as Goodman (1976,1984) noted in relation to metaphor, the attribution of similarity is ever ready to solve difficult problems too easily, because similarity is an "imposter." The metaphor can also provide "spurious certainty" because it possesses much surplus value. To interpret or translate the metaphoric into other words prematurely contains the danger of reducing early experience that cannot be conveyed in any other way into words without original feeling states attached to them, and replacing a felt connection with an intellectual understanding. Thus, a true understanding of the metaphoric must be as much within the domain of the experiencing ego as the observing ego, because the metaphoric is the funnel through which a history of overwhelming sensation, affectivity, and states of confusion can be poured, shaped, and articulated, and hence must be safeguarded. The affective context of the transference provides a guide as to whether the translation offers only spurious certainty.

Given the history of word sense, it becomes clear why premature translations miss the point. A word goes through numerous transformations, as affective and relational connections which infuse sense into a word accumulate. It is the affective connotation that drives the metaphoric because the multiple word senses are created in the context of emotional volatility. Thus, one component of the metaphoric is a hidden affective memory, contained within language in a manner similar to the way manifest images of a dream point to affects despite the apparent blandness or the lack of experienced emotion accompanying a dream (see Freud, 1900, pp. 460–487). Failure to make use of the transferential context in timing the interpretation parallels interpreting the manifest content of a dream without taking into account a patient's associations. Like the transference, the metaphoric allows the introduction of warded-off experience into the psychoanalytic situation because both permit a wider accrual of linkages between the past and the present than those available to secondary-process thought. Both the metaphoric and transference function initially in the clinical situation as action outside of awareness—they begin in various types of experiencing and only later become available to the observing ego. It is after the necessary insight previously described has occurred that the translation into secondary process and the connection with key developmental experiences and affects can most meaningfully take place.

Free Association and Who the Analysand Talks to

At first glance, the rejoinder appears obvious—the analysand talks to either the analyst or the self. However, Vygotskian psychology leads to the suggestion that the person to whom the analysand apparently speaks, either the self or the analyst, is never the exclusive target of utterances. An analysand is invariably talking to both the self and the analyst at the same time. This will vary depending on any particular set of conditions, for there is a coterminous existence of inner and social speech during the act of articulation. Wertsch et al. (1980) and Vygotsky (1981) demonstrated experimentally that this is particularly salient during times of joint problem-solving, an endeavor that characterizes much of the psychoanalytic enterprise. Yet, there are profound differences between speech directed to the self and to the other. Because of these differences, inner and social speech also mediate thought differently. Vygotsky (1988) was explicit that inner speech is an entirely unique, independent, and distinctive speech function, that it is completely different from external speech. This justifies the view that inner speech is an internal plane of verbal thinking which mediates the dynamic relationship between thought and word (p. 279).

Teasing apart some of these differences may provide some insights into the psychological processes at play during free association. Vygotsky stressed three defining *semantic* features of inner speech—the phenomenon of agglutination, the predominance of sense over meaning, and the infusion of sense into a word. In agglutination, separate words undergo abbreviation so that only part of each appears in a greater overall word, and the resulting complex word emerges as a structurally and functionally unified word, although not a bizarre combination as might be seen in condensation. This is one way simple words come to convey complex concepts. Agglutination is somewhat similar to condensation, except in agglutination the result of the combination is always a unified word that is recognizable. The regression inherent in analysis is broad and multidimensional, and includes cognitive fluctuations based on the powerful wishes evoked. One result is the fluidity and plasticity of language. When an analysand agglutinates, it is a sign that there is a predominance of inner speech at that moment. For example, an analysand was struggling with vivid homosexual wishes toward his analyst, and had recently engaged in some acting-out sexual activity that had been interpreted. He was then speaking of his desire to have "fresh friendships" with other men. Intending to say "where fresh friendships take me with other men," he said instead, "where freshmen take me." When drawn to his attention, his associations to this slip converged around his being a fresh man and a freshman. His associations revealed the multiple senses of both fresh and men. He was a fresh man because of his wish to engage in sexual activity, a freshman because of his fervid preoccupation with youthful potency and his passive longing to accept sexual gratification from behind in the analysis, like a young man. His associations provided evidence that his agglutinized (inner) speech contained a key aspect of the state of the transference at that moment.

The predominance of sense over meaning suggests that the concurrent intralinguistic context predominates over the stable denotation of the word, and thus word meanings tend to be hidden by the sharp fluctuations of context which are transformed by and which transform the word. The predominance of sense over meaning may also contribute to the analyst's words to the analysand at times being heard in a seemingly "distorted" way. However, the notion of distortion fails to take into account the inherent polysemy of language and its role in constituting perceptions of reality. The point is that the words are heard and construed in a particular "sense" that predominates at that moment. What can be thought of as a distortion can be better defined as momentary nonoverlapping or incompatible senses, better analyzed than corrected. The infusion of sense into a word was addressed earlier, referring to how a word's sense is influenced and changes swiftly as a function of its intralinguistic context, whereas a word's meaning does not. These latter two semantic principles are crucial because they help explain how we capture the essential skews of inner reality through inner speech, rather than through the more conventionally garbed trappings of social speech which is less rich and more stereotypic because it is devoid of the infusion and predominance of sense.

The predominant *syntactic* feature that characterizes inner speech is predicativity. Predicativity means that there is a dropping of reference to the subject of a sentence, with a subsequent emphasis on the predicate, the assumption being that the self already knows the subject. In fact, this often corresponds to the rules of the *new and given* information in conversational discourse (see Chafe, 1974; Clark and Haviland, 1977). Because an internal dialogue is one in which the listener and speaker are the same, much more information can be taken as given, and the only words that need to be spoken are the new words, which carry the force of the intention. The extent to which speech is truncated depends on the amount of information known to both discussants. Shared context, shared history, and shared prenegotiated assumptions and word definitions all contribute to the minimization of articulated language. Language use exists along a continuum, with written language at one end being the most decontextualized, fully explicated form (Bellin, 1983) and inner speech as a subset of dialogue at the other end. Language can be truncated to the degree that speakers share a common context, including intentional subtext and nonverbal information, as well as shared history and prenegotiated vocabulary. Thus inner speech functions as a dialogue that can be maximally truncated, since the greatest possible amount of information is held in common with the self.

Speech directed to the self has different syntactic and semantic properties than speech directed to the other. Its abbreviated, telegraphic, predicative (subjectless) properties will be emphasized in our discussion of free association. As crucial as they are to keep apart, these aspects of speech also merge in conversational language usage; listening to a speaker, one often cannot readily tell the difference. Understanding the distinction is pragmatically useful in psychoanalysis. At many points in an analysis, inner speech is the native tongue of an analysis that is alive and moving. Gedo (1986) suggests that when an analysis is proceeding well there is no true distinction between the analyst's and analysand's voice; their speech is interchangeable. The origin of speech, the subject and object of discourse, becomes an irrelevance when the analysis is going well. Put another way, the interventions of the analyst optimally blend into the inner, private speech of the analysand, without forcing the inner speech to prematurely become social, which would result in a change of form, content, and intention. Putting words in the form of social speech can pull an analysand away from the flow of inner thought and into a convention-draped conversational style divorced from personal and dynamic significance. In other words, the analyst comes to mediate between inner and social speech, just as he does between free association and self-observation, and between waking and sleeping states of consciousness (Lewin, 1955).

The facilitative analytic situation creates the necessary conditions for the analysand to communicate inner speech. The effective analyst knows imperceptibly not to discourage these inevitable speech acts. The therapeutic alliance can be understood in part as the history of the analyst-analysand's intimacy, safety, and familiarity that builds toward a tolerance welcoming the arrival of inner speech and makes its continued use feasible. The manner in which we listen to an analysand allows for the development of shared assumptions, so that the essential syntactic feature of inner speech—predicativity—might emerge and bind the two. Another way of understanding this situation is to note that the effective analysis can promote a flexible partial regression to the period when the distinction between social and egocentric speech was blurred—when they coexisted, before they bifurcated. One analysand, when the derivatives of a particular sexual conflict appeared in the transference, would insist that he could not understand what the analyst was saying, no matter how simply put. Every detail, including instances from a previous hour, had to be painstakingly spelled out before he would allow himself to understand the analyst's message and intent. His insistence on explication, as if talking with a stranger, expressed his attempts to defend against the erotism of the transference. He dealt with a conflicted sexual wish by attempting to assert distancing erotic control through altering the form of their usual linguistic intimacy, and to express their closeness by making sure they together recounted everything of the previous hour.

He accomplished these aims by switching to the assumptions and features of social speech at these moments, which were in sharp contradistinction to his more usual creatively expansive approach to analysis. By doing this, he both destroyed the syntactic features and shared assumptions that characterize the arrival of inner speech, and simultaneously warded off the intimacy of the erotically tinged transference.

It is important to understand in further detail how Vygotsky views egocentric speech and its relation to social and inner speech. To Vygotsky, egocentric speech does not reflect egocentric thinking; rather, it is a transitional form of external speech. Its origins lie in social, realistically oriented speech, and it is on the way to inner speech. Vygotsky describes how, for the child, there are three conditions under which egocentric speech first becomes differentiated from social speech—when there is the illusion of understanding by others, the necessity or opportunity to vocalize, and the presence of potential listeners. He demonstrates experimentally that when any of these are removed from the child, there is a tendency for egocentric speech to decrease. When we look at each of these—the presence of a listener, opportunity to vocalize, and assumption of being understood—they can be seen as necessary conditions for an analysis to proceed. If the analysand should come to believe that the analyst is absent, or believes that there is no possibility of being understood, or something compromises their capacity to vocalize, then egocentric speech is going to decrease, and there will be a greater reliance on social speech. Problems in any of these three areas can come from factors emanating in the intrapsychic activity of the analysand (e.g., resistance, superego pressures), or the actions of the analyst (e.g., subtly communicating to the analysand that a topic is not to be talked about). When such analytic pitfalls are initiated by the analysand, any of these can also be thought of as a manifestation of resistance. It is useful to note that these are all paraverbal or structural phenomena built into the communicative nature of the analytic process, each outside of what is delivered by the semantic content of the spoken word. Our formulations are a way of conceptualizing some of the silent dangers not frequently spoken of in theory, but which many analysts intuitively recognize in the "feel" of an hour.

On the way from egocentric speech to inner speech, the subject and object of discourse changes from inner-outer to inner-inner. Presumably, some inner "presence" must have been set up in order to mediate this development. We propose that the dialogic nature of Vygotskian psychology presupposes a concept of inner objects, a point similar to one elaborated in depth by Bakhtin (1981). The dialogic nature of inner speech assumes two intrapsychic representations in an intimate involvement, which may eventually come to be so habitual that it is only experienced as syntonic self-direction, not as recognizable inner conversation. This is our psychoanalytic construal of something inherent in Vygotsky's discussion of the status of inner speech, but not one that he elaborates on. However, there are suggestive similarities to Loewenstein's (1956) description of what takes place during self-analysis. Loewenstein describes how something akin to inner speech plays a central role in the therapeutic action of psychoanalysis outside of the clinical situation. He notes:

> . . . its effectiveness [is] in the form of a continuation of a previous analysis with an actual analyst . . . it is then usually a solitary continuation of dialogue with the latter or with an imaginary analyst. In this respect it might be viewed as an imaginary dialogue in which the subject is able to play both parts, that of a patient and that of an analyst, and thus to some extent involving inner speech (p. 467).

The importance of internal dialogue is further highlighted by pointing to a body of experimental evidence (Ziven, 1979) suggesting that it is through the inner dialogue of the self with the internal object, spoken in the phonetically silent tongue of inner speech, that a child is able to gain access to other crucial component processes of self-regulation. Egocentric speech appears at about the age of three, disappears at about seven, and peaks in the middle. *Parallels to the oedipal stage are no coincidence.* The process of egocentric speech being transmuted into inner speech accompanies the internalization of the self-regulating functions characteristic of the development of the superego. A similar point was recognized by Isakower (1939), when he noted the exceptional position of the auditory sphere in the formation of the superego. Hence, it is not surprising that the re-externalization of conflict which accompanies a superego regression in the transference can be paralleled in the analysis by the temporary articulation of egocentric speech "out loud." As the analysand again takes over the self-regulating functions which were abrogated during the course of the analysis, the egocentric speech can be reinternalized as inner speech, following structural change.

The key aspect of analysis is the gathering of the transference and the amplification of its intensity. The gathering and amplification of transference are fostered by the setting of conditions which allow inner speech to become a more readily available form of discourse. This is accomplished through a combination of the analysand's reclining, a delimiting of the perceptual field, and the analyst's maintenance of relative neutrality, abstinence, anonymity, and silence. Further, the analyst can be sensitive to the differential trappings of inner, egocentric, and social speech, and attempt to make it possible for inner speech to emerge at the right time and under manageable conditions of ease. By discouraging an analytic regression, an analyst may also be issuing a subtle yet profound dictate that the analysis proceed in the language of social rather than egocentric speech, thus impeding the unveiling of inner speech with its greater proximity to core thought processes and power to convey and alter transference repetition.

In order to further clarify the relation between free association and the relation between social and inner speech, two conceptual nodes will be distinguished, which Freud and others after him tended to blend in their thinking about free association. First, the concept of free association contains an implicit assumption of how memories are encoded. Through free association, an analyst can perform his version of an archaeological dig to uncover memories that are encoded in their original and unchanged form, along with other memories of like symbolic or emotional content—a view of the mind that Rorty (1979) deems a mistaken "mirror of nature." Freud's implicit assumption was that, through free association, analysis can bring a person back to a lost reality or a forgotten fantasy that accompanied an external event. This model was first and most clearly articulated in the *Project for a Scientific Psychology* where Freud (1895) described how experiences are deposited in neuronally encoded memory systems in a manner influenced by each experience's relation to other deposited material. Stripped of its neurological coating, this view continues to inform contemporary thinking about free association. Rapaport's work on memory (1942), (1950), where he discusses how drives affect memory functioning, make this point vividly clear. Recent investigators who have examined this aspect of free association have suggested that it is *far from free* (Schafer, 1978;Spence, 1982; Brenner, 1983; Kris, 1983), but that it is inevitably tendentious in ways that can be specified.

The second conceptual node is that free association has an indispensable role in the analysis of transference. As Freud (1912)

440

put it:

> For our experience has shown us—and the fact can be confirmed as
> often as we please—that if a patient's free associations fail the stoppage
> can invariably be removed by an assurance that he is being dominated
> at the moment by an association which is connected with the doctor
> himself or with something connected with him (p. 101).

This aspect of free association relates to its capacity to promote deeper transference states. It is to this second node of free
association that Vygotsky's perspective is most germane. Free association, along with perceptual isolation and the use of a couch,
provides an analysand with an invitation to strategically ignore
the presence and responses of the listener, to ignore the "actual"
dialogue in favor of inner and past dialogic experiences. Free association thus becomes an invitation to articulate the skews and
distortions that characterize inner reality and are most clearly expressed through inner speech, and to simultaneously maintain
yet subtly overlook the actual presence and impact of the analyst
in the treatment situation. What seems like a contradiction
(maintaining yet overlooking) is resolved when we see that it is
primarily an invitation to utilize the features of inner speech
while settling for its emergence through the necessary articula-
tions of more social speech—no analysis can be conducted solely
according to the features of inner speech, which is actually phonetically unarticulated.

It is a constructive tension in the analytic situation, similar to
Vygotsky's distinction between inner and social speech, wherein
Gray (1986) identifies a key potential for the analysis of the conflict-
motivated activity of the ego. He describes how an analysand free-
associates and then is interrupted by the sound of the analyst's voice,
and thereby is forced to attend to the analyst's voice. The analysand

then rationally attends to what the analyst is saying, strives to grasp the conflict identified by the interpretation, analyzes the inhibition or risk associated with the emergence of the conflict, and strives to gradually reduce the danger. Then, the analysand can return to the essential task of free-associating, having obtained a more spontaneous access to conflictual material with greater freedom, increased conscious control, and less risk in letting the conflict emerge.

We thereby suggest that one additional element of analytic utility to the basic rule is that it promotes a necessary transition to inner speech. The analyst and the analysand form a speech community of two, which generates a linguistic code that to an outsider may be coherent but whose full and resonant meaning can only be guessed at. The value of free association can be communicated by the analyst to an analysand as an opportunity to share the thoughts accompanying inner speech. The analysand in turn free-associates, yet relies on the analyst's skill to decode inner speech and reconstruct and transform it into the language and thinking that accompanies more social speech. Not to let the communicative features of inner speech emerge for both the analyst and analysand constitutes, in our opinion, a profound yet often invisible form of resistance, a kind of compulsory superficiality, a resistance to being moved by the importance of the analysis.

Of course, much of what takes place and has been gained in the analysis will ultimately reenter repression after termination. In the termination phase of an analysis, what has been brought into the shared discourse also becomes consolidated as inner speech. It can also then be repressed and/or made available silently as psychic structure. It is hoped that the areas of the personal and emotional life that have been analyzed have been greatly widened, and there is no longer a need to make them the focus of conscious communication as is the case during termination. During a successful termination, free association as a means of access to and a way of dealing with inner speech also becomes interiorized as a new capacity of thought. This self-analytic function remains as the permanent capacity to have access to and greater facility with the widened scope of inner speech, especially helpful under conditions of emotional turbulence.

Conclusion

We have developed a perspective on the relation between language and thought which, while departing from the traditional psychoanalytic viewpoint, does serve to bridge certain clinical considerations with other currently prevailing views on language and thought. Although Freud moved away from classifying psychic events according to their degree of access to consciousness when he relinquished the topographic point of view, he never fully developed ideas about language which fit his new structural perspective. One legacy of Freud's topography is that psychoanalysis has focused primarily on the "referential" aspect of language, with its assumption of factual historicity. One example of an overemphasis on the referential in psychoanalysis can be seen in Glover's (1931) influential argument on inexact interpretations. He described how therapeutic progress can be made through inexact interpretations that reinstate old repressions, although such progress is inimical to the true task of psychoanalysis. An interpretation thus had to be exact in order to liberate deep layers of unconscious fantasy from old repressions; inexactness or incompleteness of interpretation, though, could lead to therapeutic progress *only* because of the reinstitution of old repressions which lessened anxieties, or because of the setting up of displacement symptoms through suggestion.

We are now entering the seventh decade since Glover wrote his paper, and the mutative factor of psychoanalysis is still widely held to be interpretation. In this paper, we have conceptualized how to bring aspects of the ineffable into the purview of interpretation, through the examination of primal repression, the metaphoric, and free association, and we now propose some linguistic factors not available to Glover which promote the effectiveness of interpretation. We have argued that the referential must coexist with the "constitutive" in our understanding of the role language plays in the clinical situation. We claim that how an individual comes to "define" a word is a final pathway, the outcome of multiply determined forces, not the objective process it is often purported to be. Then, how a word is defined determines in part how one will act in the world. Although the essential ideas of the constitutive can be found in earlier writings, some current philosophical perspectives on language, which found their most original spokesmen in the paradigmatic contributions of Wittgenstein (1953), Searle (1962), Austin (1962), and Goodman (1984), stress how language use is inextricably tied to the creation of both inner and outer realities, ranging from the theories of "language games" (Wittgenstein) to "speech acts" (Austin, Searle) to "world-making" (Goodman). In the analytic situation, language use brings the dyad into symbolically constructed realities; attending only to the referential can mislead analysts into thinking that these constructions function as absolute, objective, and unambiguous data. A thoughtful solution to this thorny epistemic problem in psychology is provided by Bruner (1986), in his proposal for a robust pluralism as an alternative to deconstruction and reductive hermeneutics on the one hand and dogmatic scientism on the other.

An appreciation of the constitutive, dialogic nature of language can help explain why interpretation can have such a profound impact on intrapsychic structure. The efficacy of interpretation also rests on the fact that it is the nature of words to accrue perseverative "senses." The coordination of senses leads to reorganizations that are one aspect of structural change, which in turn allows for the further uncovering of "meanings" that are grounded in factual history.

In clinical work, the referential and constitutive faces of language are not opposed to one another. Interpretation in psychoanalysis is poised at the indivisible juncture of uncovering while begetting, the blend of discovering and revising the old while forging the new. Bird (1972) has made the related point that in the transference we see an intersection of spontaneous experiences with the reworking of old ones. Similarly, Loewald (1975) proposes that the term transference neurosis be reserved for the new creations that arise out of the analytic work, rather than the repetition of the infantile neurosis. We propose a perspective on language and thought that is logically consistent with these and other appealing notions of transference. Tests in the clinical situation now should guide the next step of evaluation of these ideas, for the success of our clinical work remains as always the best guide for how, what, and why we do what we do in psychoanalysis.

References

Arlow, J.A. (1969). Unconscious fantasy and disturbances of conscious experience. *Psychoanalytic Quarterly* 38:1–27.

———(1979). Metaphor and the psychoanalytic situation. *Psychoanalytic Quarterly* 48:363–385.

———(1987). The dynamics of interpretation. *Psychoanalytic Quarterly* 61:68–87.

Austin, J.L. (1962 *How to Do Things with Words*. Oxford: Oxford University Press.

Bakhtin, M. (1981). *The Dialogic Imagination*, Ed. M. Holmquist. Austin, TX: University of Texas Press.

Basch, M.F. (1981). Psychoanalytic interpretation and cognitive transformation. *International Journal of Psychoanalysis* 62:151–175.

Bellin, E. (1983). The psychoanalytic narrative: on the transferential axis between writing and speech. *Psychoanalysis and Contemporary Thought* 7:3–42.

Bird, B. (1972). Notes on transference: universal phenomenon and hardest part of analysis. *Journal of the American Psychoanalytic Association* 20:267–301.

Blum, H.P. (1980). The value of reconstruction in adult psychoanalysis. *International Journal of Psychoanalysis* 61:39–52.

Brenner, C. (1957). The nature and development of the concept of repression in Freud's writings. *Psychoanalytic Study of the Child* 12:19–46.

———(1983). *The Mind in Conflict*. New York: International Universities Press.

Bruner, J. (1983). *Child's Talk*. New York: W.W. Norton & Company.

———(1986). *Actual Minds, Possible Worlds*. Cambridge, MA: Harvard University Press.

Chafe, W. (1974). Language and consciousness. *Language* 50:111–133.

Chomsky, N. (1957). *Syntactic Structures*. The Hague, Switzerland: Mouton.

———(1966). *Cartesian Linguistics*. New York: Harper & Row.

Clark, H. & Haviland, S. (1977). *Comprehension and the Given—New Contrast in Discourse Production and Comprehension*, ed. R. Freedle, pp. 1–40. Norwood, NJ: Ablon.

Cohen, J. & Kinston, W. (1983). Repression theory: a new look at the cornerstone. *International Journal of Psychoanalysis* 61:421–423.

Edelson, M. (1975). *Language and Interpretation in Psychoanalysis*. Chicago: University of Chicago Press.

———(1984). *Hypothesis and Evidence in Psychoanalysis*. Chicago: University of. Chicago Press.

Forrester, J. (1980). *Language and the Origins of Psychoanalysis*. New York:

Columbia University Press.

Frank, A. (1969). The unrememberable and the unforgettable: passive primal repression. *Psychoanalytic Study of the Child* 24:59–66.

Freud, S. 1895 Project for a scientific psychology. *Standard Edition* 1.

———(1900). The interpretation of dreams *Standard Edition* 4 & 5.

———(1911). Psychoanalytic notes on an autobiographical account of a case of paranoia. (dementia paranoides) *Standard Edition* 12.

———(1912). The dynamics of transference. *Standard Edition* 12.

———(1915a). Repression *Standard Edition* 14.

———(1915b). The unconscious. *Standard Edition* 14.

———(1926). Inhibitions, symptoms, and anxiety. *Standard Edition* 20.

———(1937). Analysis terminable and interminable. *Standard Edition* 23.

Gedo, J.E. (1979). *Beyond Interpretation: Toward a Revised Theory for Psychoanalysis*. New York: International Universities Press.

———(1986). *Psychoanalysis and Its Discontents*. New York: Guilford Press.

———& Goldberg, A. (1973). *Models of the Mind*. Chicago: University of Chicago Press.

Glover, E. (1931). The therapeutic effect of inexact interpretation. *International Journal of Psychoanalysis* 12:397–411.

Goodman, N. (1976). *Languages of Art: An Approach to a Theory of Symbols* Indianapolis, IN: Hackett Publishing.

———(1984). *Of Mind and Other Matters*. Cambridge, MA: Harvard University Press.

Gray, P. (1986 On helping analysands observe intrapsychic activity In *Psychoanalysis: The Science of Mental Conflict*. ed. A. Richards & M. Willik, pp. 245–262. Hillsdale, NJ: Analytic Press.

Greenacre, P. (1954). The role of transference: practical considerations in relation to psychoanalytic therapy In *The Capacity for Emotional Growth*. Vol. 2, pp. 627–640. New York: International Universities Press, (1971).

———(1968). The psychoanalytic process, transference, and acting out In *The Capacity for Emotional Growth* Vol. 2, pp. 762-775. New York: International Universities Press, 1971.

———(1981). On reconstruction. *Journal of the. American Psychoanalytic Association* 23:693–712.

Hartmann, H. (1964 *Essays on Ego Psychology.* New York: International Universities Press.

Hesse, M. (1980). *Revolutions and Reconstructions in the Philosophy of Science.* Bloomington, Ind.: University of Indiana Press.

Holt, R.R. (1967). The development of the primary process: a structural view. In *Motives and Thought: Psychoanalytic Essays in Memory of David Rapaport* eds. R.R. Holt. Psychol. Issues Monograph 18/19, pp. 345-383. New York: International Universities Press.

Isakower, O. (1939). On the exceptional position of the auditory sphere. *International Journal of Psychoanalysis* 20:340–348.

Jacobs, T. (1986). Transference relationships, the relationships between transferences, and reconstruction. In *Psychoanalysis: The Science of Mental Conflict,* eds. M. A. Richards & M. Willik. Hillsdale, NJ: Analytic Press, pp. 301–320.

Jakobson, R. (1956). Two aspects of language and two types of aphasic disturbances. In *Fundamentals of Language,* ed. R. Jakobson & M. Halle, pp. 55–82. The Hague, Switzerland: Mouton.

Jakobson, R. (1960 Linguistics and poetics In *Style in Language* ed. T. Sebeok, pp. 350-377. Cambridge, MA.: Harvard University Press.

Kernberg, O.F. (1975). *Borderline Conditions and Pathological Narcissism.* New York: Jason Aronson.

Kinston, W. & Cohen, J. (1986). Primal and repression: clinical and theoretical aspects. *International Journal of Psychoanalysis* 67:337–356.

Kris, A. (1983 *Free Association: Method and Process.* New Haven, CT: Yale University Press.

Lakoff, G. & Johnson, M. (1980). *Metaphors We Live By.* Chicago, Ill.: University of. Chicago Press.

Laplanche, J. & Pontalis, J.B. (1973). *The Language of Psychoanalysis.* New York: W.W. Norton & Co.

Lewin, B.D. (1955 Dream psychology and the analytic situation. *Psychoanalytic Quarterly* 24:169–199.

Loewald, H.W. (1975 Psychoanalysis as an art and the fantasy character of the psychoanalytic situation In *Papers on Psychoanalysis, pp. 352-371.* New Haven, CT: Yale University Press, 1980.

———(1978). Primary process, secondary process, and language. In *Papers on Psychoanalysis, pp. 178-206.* New Haven, CT: Yale University Press, 1980.

Loewenstein, R.M. (1956). Some remarks on the role of speech in psychoanalytic technique. *International Journal of Psychoanalysis* 37:460–468.

———(1957). Some thoughts on interpretation in the theory and practice of psychoanalysis. *Psychoanalytic Study of the Child* 12:127–150.

Noy, P. (1969). A revision of the psychoanalytic theory of the primary process. *International Journal of Psychoanalysis* 50:147–154.

———(1979). The psychoanalytic theory of cognitive development. *Psychoanalytic Study of the Child* 34:169–216.

Peller, L. (1966). Freud's contribution to language theory. *Psychoanalytic Study of the Child* 21:448–467. New Haven: Yale University Press.

Rapaport, D. (1942). *Emotions and Memory* New York: International Universities Press,

———(1950). On the psychoanalytic theory of thinking. In *The Collected Papers of David Rapaport* ed. M. M. Gill, pp. 313-328. New York: Basic Books, 1967.

———(1951). *Organization and Pathology of Thought.* New York: Columbia University Press.

Ricoeur, P. (1978). The metaphoric process as cognition, imagination, and feeling *Critical Inquiry* 5:143–159.

Rorty, R. (1979). *Philosophy and the Mirror of Nature.* Princeton, NJ: Princeton Univ. Press.

Rosen, V.H. (1977). *Style, Character, and Language.* New York: Jason Aronson.

Sandler, A.M. (1988). Aspects of the analysis of a neurotic patient. *International Journal of Psychoanalysis* 69:317–326.

Schafer, R. (1968). *Aspects of Internalization.* New York: International Universities Press.

———(1978). *Language and Insight.* New Haven, CT: Yale University Press.

———(1983). *The Analytic Attitude* New York: Basic Books.

Searle, J.R. (1962). *Speech Acts.* Cambridge & New York: Cambridge University Press.

Shapiro, T. (1970). Interpretation and naming. *Journal of the American Psychoanalytic Association* 18:399–421.

———(1979). *Clinical Psycholinguistics.* New York: Plenum.

Sharpe, E.F. (1940). Psychophysical problems revealed in language: an examination of metaphor In *Collected Papers on Psychoanalysis, pp. 155=169.* London: Hogarth Press, 1950.

Shengold, L. (1981 Insight as metaphor. *Psychoanalytic Study of the Child* 36:289–306 New Haven, CT: Yale University Press.

Spence, D.P. (1982). *Narrative Truth and Historical Truth: Meaning and Interpretation in Psychoanalysis.* New York: W.W. Norton & Company.

———(1987). *The Freudian Metaphor.* New York: W.W. Norton & Company.

Stone, L. (1961 *The Psychoanalytic Situation.* New York: International Universities Press.

Valsiner, J. (1988). *Developmental Psychology in the Soviet Union* Bloomington, IN: Indiana University Press.

Vygotsky, L. (1981). The genesis of higher mental functions In *The Concept of Activity in Soviet Psychology,* ed. J. Wertsch, pp. 144–188. Armonk, NY: M.E. Sharpe Publishers, Inc.

———(1988). *Thinking and Speaking in the Collected Papers of L.S. Vygotsky* Vol. 1, ed. R.W. Rieber & A. S. Carton, pp. 39–288. New York: Plenum.

Wertsch, J. (1985). *Vygotsky and the Social Formation of Mind* Cambridge, MA.: Harvard University Press.

————McNamee, G., McLane, J. & Budwig, N. (1980). The adult–child dyad as a problem–solving system, *Child Development* 51:1215–1221.

Wilson, A. & Weinstein, L. (1992). An investigation into some implications of a Vygotskian perspective on the origins of the mind: psychoanalysis and Vygotskian psychology, Part I. *Journal of the. American Psychoanalytic Association* 40:357–387.

Wittgenstein, L. (1953). *Philosophical Investigations*. London: Blackwell.

Ziven, G., Ed. (1979). *The Development of Self-Regulation Through Private Speech*. New York: Wiley.

CHAPTER 13

THE TRANSFERENCE AND THE ZONE
OF PROXIMAL DEVELOPMENT

Introduction

The Zone of Proximal Development (ZPD) is discussed, a construct
that, when introduced into psychoanalysis, advances understanding of the key clinical relationship between the intrapsychic and the
interpersonal. Strands from several psychoanalytic formulations
are brought together and forged into a coherent construct, which is
then contrasted with the transference. It is shown how the ZPD provides the transference with its mutative potential. Just as the
transference provides the motivation for the recruitment of objects
to accomplish its purposes (repetition), the ZPD leads to the recruitment of objects in order to accomplish its purposes (to learn
by ushering individuals into a speech and internalization community). Under the sway of the transference, objects are sought so that
early dysregulating experiences can be repeated and an opportunity
provided for a better resolution. The ZPD works in tandem with the
transference, capitalizing on the impetus provided, allowing for the
possibility of internalization, a beneficial outcome to transference
repetition which otherwise would have no agent of conflict resolution. In analysis, when the transference and the ZPD enjoin
smoothly, the potential outcome is "insight" in a broad sense.
The processes of the ZPD define the optimal interpersonal context of psychoanalysis, one that allows the intrapsychic to be best
reached by analytic interventions. Given the inevitability of

mutual influences between analyst and analysand, the analyst strives simultaneously to be in the ZPD yet outside the transference with the analysand, a crucial tension that is a constant, precarious technical factor. This useful tension casts light on such procedural guides as optimal frustration and abstinence.

Psychoanalysis and the ZPD

When analysts are troubled by treatment impasses, puzzling failures to progress, or some negative therapeutic reactions, there is a tendency to look to early developmental processes for an explanation of these clinical crises. Often, actual interactive processes referred to in overly general terms, such as profound early maternal deprivation or failure of basic trust, are implicated, or residua of trauma are blamed. The search for pathogenic intrapsychic processes is often circumvented. The apparent reasoning is that if the pathology is profound, it must be early and its causes must be "real." It is often overlooked that the assumption that the earlier, the worse, is in current psychological thinking only one of several plausible approaches to understanding and modeling human development (Wertsch, 1992). By contrast, Freud (1905) proposed a developmental vulnerability model of psychosexual development, with the oedipal crisis situated at the nadir of a U-shaped curve, abrogating both assumptions of earliness and realness.

This paper is likewise an effort to conceptualize an alternative position to the view that worse necessarily implies earlier. Another possibility, one that implicates a family of processes, especially those having to do with the ways in which object use influences speech acquisition, will be proposed. These processes are set into motion early on and then amplified and made visible through later developments. In investigating these issues, several questions that ultimately bear on the essence of analyzability will be taken up. In order to do so, the paper will wind its way through a host of topics related to analyzability, especially the psychoanalytic theory of internalization (learning), the role and function of speech, and the nature of transference. Although topics with branches outside of clinical psychoanalysis are discussed, the proposals put forth will be rooted in the special demands the clinical situation makes upon theoretical constructs.

Recent contributions will be built upon that have emphasized new developments in linguistics and the role of speech, the complex relationship between "one-" and "two-person" psychologies, as well as the affective climate which is central to the bidirectional communicative flow between the analyst-analysand. It comes as no surprise that people interested in these psychoanalytic questions are beginning to pay attention to the writings of the Russian psychologist Lev Vygotsky, whose work decades ago foreshadowed such theoretical developments, although certainly not from a psychoanalytic orientation.

In previous papers on the subject (Wilson and Weinstein, 1992a, b), it was suggested that Vygotskian psychology is particularly useful for psychoanalysis in integrating some complexities of early object relations, and in understanding fantasies and psychophysiological experiences, which are most directly observable within the pragmatics of language use in the clinical situation. Vygotskian psychology was described as providing additions to, and not a replacement for, existing psychoanalytic hypotheses and theory. The present paper focuses on the clinical implications of another aspect of Vygotsky's oeuvre, a concept he termed the *Zone of Proximal Development* (ZPD; *zona blizaishego razvitia*[1] in

---

[1] Valsiner (1988) indicates that translation decisions might have led to the phrase zone of potential rather than proximal development, thereby minimizing the impression of a concept characterized by the reified notion of distance rather than by a psychological meaning.

Russian). This concept was adduced in order to make sense of how and why two people, in conjunction, can mobilize the intrapsychic and interpsychological resources that make cognitive and emotional growth possible for the less developed member of the dyad. One person, who possesses more sophisticated psychological skills (an example of which is knowing how the mind works), comes to function in a prostheticlike manner, creating the scaffold necessary for the evolution of capacities in the one with less developed or sophisticated psychological skills. As in the analytic situation, a pair creates capabilities beyond the limits of one alone (also in this regard see Wood, Bruner, and Ross, 1976). The concept of the ZPD provides certain advantages over other related explanatory concepts, such as the therapeutic alliance, because the dialogic interchanges that comprise the surface of the ZPD can themselves be further analyzed, allowing one to anatomize how actualities can follow from what initially seems to be invisible potential. These processes have previously been examined largely in the context of cognitive learning, as we will discuss later in this paper. The concept of the ZPD was originally formulated with respect to the dynamics of linguistic mediation as a way station toward understanding how and when internalization occurs. However, more globally, these processes have to do with any and all aspects of learning that partake of an interactive context.

Vygotsky invariably was more interested in the function than the content of psychological processes. The ZPD is an attempt to formulate how learning is made possible, but not what is known. The term refers to a set of interactive processes, themselves in constant evolution, rather than the actual knowledge a person might possess. The ZPD refers to a vital state; thus being in the ZPD "calls to life in the child, awakens and puts in motion an entire series of internal processes of development. These processes are at the time possible only in the sphere of interaction with those surrounding the child and in collaboration with companions, but in the internal course of development they eventually become the internal property' of the child" (Vygotsky, 1956, p. 450, cited by Wertsch, 1985, p. 71). Rather than referring to cognitive or conscious mental content, the ZPD exists proximally to "those functions that have not yet matured but are in the process of maturation, functions that will mature tomorrow but are currently in an embryonic state . . . the 'buds' or 'flowers' of development rather than the 'fruits' of development" (Vygotsky, 1978, p. 86). For this reason, Vygotsky depicted how instruction should proceed ahead of development, arousing abilities that might otherwise lie dormant. Later, we will propose that optimal and tactful interventions in psychoanalysis must likewise target such embryonic potentials that exist only within the currently ongoing viable interactive context.

The Americans who first grappled with the concept of the ZPD usually cite Vygotsky's definition, wedded to pedagogy, from *Mind in Society*, which is "the distance between the actual developmental level as determined by independent problem solving and the level of potential development as determined through problem solving under adult guidance or in collaboration with more capable peers" (1978, p. 78). Brown and Ferrara (1985) have developed an empirical research program measuring the ZPD in children. It is clear from the recently retranslated and expanded *Thinking and Speaking* (1987, chapter 6) that Vygotsky had more in mind than problem solving. He was attempting to formulate a principle that captured the dynamics underlying the inherent interdependence of self and object in human development. Vygotsky's emphasis on the initially interactive origins of psychological phenomena found concrete expression in his nodal hypothesis of the "general genetic law of cultural development" (Vygotsky, 1981), which stipulates

that everything internal began at one time as an external phenomenon. Everything internal must appear twice, first externally and
then again internally, although now transformed by the processes
of interiorization. These at-first external phenomena are initially
concentrated in and communicated through the primary caregivers, the original objects with the child in the ZPD. The ZPD acts as
a scaffold, adding an additional purpose to the object relationship,
namely, the entrance into what we are terming an internalization
community and, indeed, culture at large. Thus, the rather dry and
enigmatic definition of 1978 does not do justice to its potential richness. A modified definition of the ZPD is proposed, specifically
tailored to the clinical situation, which is consistent with the spirit
of Vygotsky's formulation in *Mind in Society*: the processes that
beget the differences between an analysand's ability to advantageously make use of the dyadic nature of the clinical situation as
contrasted with *solitary* introspection or self-analysis, in order to
acquire insight and capacities that promote self-knowledge and
ultimately self-regulation. In order for the insights of analysis to
take place, there has to be a transference object; ultimately, there
is really no such a thing as self-analysis, except in a colloquial
sense. Even Freud's self-analysis partook of Fliess as his transference object; *The Interpretation of Dreams* (1900) can be read as a
record of the resolution of that transference.

From the day Freud documented Breuer's revolutionary technical experiments with hysterical and neurasthenic patients,
psychoanalysis has in fits and starts defined itself with respect to
other fields of inquiry. It is remarkable that psychoanalysis has
not put forward a clinical concept like the ZPD over the last century, for how one learns is so crucial for so many lines of
investigation into human dynamics and processes. (The flawed
notion of the therapeutic alliance, which will be examined later
in thischapter, comes closest.) Perhaps this state of affairs has to

do with the sociology of knowledge, how and under what conditions psychoanalysis finds merit in other fields and areas.

There are concepts from outside psychoanalysis that fit seamlessly and those that do not. The history of psychoanalysis is filled with examples of concepts borrowed from outside which then became successfully normalized: on a grand scale in France, Lacan's appropriation of de Saussurian structural linguistics, or, in America. Hartmann and his colleagues' forays into development psychology that were eventually to inform the adaptive point of view of metapsychology. In both cases, a bold proposal was subject to intensive testing through which its seamlessness was assessed. A seamless fit, as we try to develop for the ZPD concept, lends itself to a deeper and different understanding of clinical processes, has a wide explanatory range, opens up new ways of looking at a wide range of phenomena, and sharpens the existing concepts it comes into contact with. It does not interfere with psychoanalysis as it is known and practiced, although it provides new angles on clinical matters. A non-seamless fit, like most current neurophysiological concepts as well as those outside of depth psychology, resists such translation. Perhaps it is useful to tease apart how the proposals in this paper can be scrutinized and critiqued in a narrow as opposed to a wide sense. The narrow sense is concerned with the place of the ZPD concept for clinical work in and of itself. The wider sense asks: how, when, and under what conditions does it make sense for psychoanalysis to look outside of itself as it is now constituted, for its continuing evolution, toward a concept such as the ZPD?

Precursors of the ZPD Concept Within Psychoanalysis

Some of the processes which we suggest comprise the ZPD have been previously seen as nested within the transference, and viewed as part of transference repetition, while others are variously described as extra-analytic and part of the real relationship. An example of the former is Stein's (1981) expansion of Freud's (1912) concept of the unobjectionable positive transference, which Gill (1982) correctly notes was, in Freud's hands, a distinction between transference that facilitates the analytic process and transference that resists the process—the critical juncture that the ZPD explicates, as will be shown.

The latter is typified by such constructs as the therapeutic alliance or the holding environment. It is suggested that the ZPD, as a hypothetical construct, can lead to a more precise understanding because it supersedes the false dichotimization of real relationship and transference, and does not overtax the concept of the transference, so that it is not synonymous with virtually everything that is conveyed by the analysand to the analyst. This section addresses previous psychoanalytic scholarship that alludes to aspects of the transference similar to the ZPD, but which tended to mistakenly focus on the content (what transference displacements and distortions tell about a particular analysand) rather than the function of earliest transference repetition (what furnishes the transference with its motive force).

The subtext of any psychoanalytic paper can usefully be read and interpreted as in some way speaking to the controversies that are in the air at the time in which it is written. Some of the most trenchant theorizing about these issues took place in the 1950s and extended for over a decade, as ego psychology was stretching itself in order to accommodate new findings, particularly with respect to early object relations. One could classify the historical controversies during this tumultuous era, which found expression in papers that were wrestling with the issues of how the transference comes to be internalized, in the following ways: First is the issue of hierarchical levels of transference. Second is the role of speech in the earlier or lower levels of transference, and how this guides an analytic view of the interactive analytic context. Third is the role of scaffolding and maturation in the clinical situation.

Greenacre and Stone both aimed at articulating and explaining levels of transference through analogy with human development. Greenacre (1954) referred to a basic transference which grows out of the original mother—infant quasi-union during the first months of life, and lends itself as a foundation to the later oedipal transference configuration. While Greenacre notes that the basic transference includes the rapport between analysand and analyst which merges into but is not identical with the transference neurosis, whose nucleus is the Oedipus complex, she never satisfactorily explicates how the basic transference is functionally related to other levels of the transference. Stone (1971) likewise notes the maternal interactive quality of the earliest transference, which he terms the primordial transference, and which serves as a backdrop for the later transference neurosis. Because he sees the primordial transference as being within the domain of ideational conflict, Stone's focus is on interpretation. He does not highlight or partial out the internalization-promoting aspect of this early transference that sets it apart from the later oedipal transference, and which he sees as contributing a central aspect of the transference's mutative potential. However, he notes that, "Insofar as an individual has achieved more than a physical—perceptual—linguistic separation from the primal object . . . the actual manifestations of primal transference . . . may play little or no role in the empirical realities of a given analysis" (1971, p. 77), thereby distancing the importance of his findings from clinical technique. Parenthetically, it should be remembered that in arriving at their views both Greenacre and Stone are generalizing from single cases. In any individual analytic case, processes of the ZPD and the transference are so inextricably intertwined that technically they must be simultaneously addressed. It is only from the remove of clinical theory construction that the distinction can be neatly sorted. Thus, although Greenacre and Stone report the germane processes, they do not put forward the theoretical distinctions suggested here. Although Greenacre and Stone further depicted the developmental processes informing the transference, in their hands this recognition did not, in the course of a usual analysis, alter the analyst's basic technical stance.

The recognition of hierarchical levels by Kohut led him, on the other hand, to radically alter analytic technique. Described in daunting terms, Kohut's (1971) valuable technical contribution to the treatment of severe narcissistic states is at bottom one of preemptively tuning in to the ZPD. However, with narcissistic patients, Kohut's attention to such processes often, perhaps at times necessarily, preempted the analysis of conflicts repeated in the transference. Apart from its clinical utility, Kohut's theory conflates staying in a viable interactive context with a patient with a genetic—developmental hypothesis about a patient's tendency toward certain types of regression. In some cases, the goal of staying empathically attuned can only be achieved by allowing a regression to primary identification. Modell (1988) similarly blends the distinction between technical recommendation and genetic explanation in his discussion of the "holding/ containing transference," so influenced by Winnicottian ideas. Thus, although the processes of the ZPD are encompassed in these contributions, the tendency to find isomorphisms between the observed transference and a reconstructed version of childhood, attenuates the clarity of the investigation into what the processes actually might be about.

Another angle on the multileveled view of transference and the interactive role of the analyst, one which also does not posit the necessity of providing support through a concept such as holding, is provided by Bird (1972). While sensitive to the developmental precursors of the processes taking place in the consulting room, he does not seek actual correspondence between them. He depicts how later transference is built upon powerful dyadic interactions, similar but not necessarily identical to earliest object relations. To Bird, transference is a "universal mental function which may well be the basis of all human relationships. In these several respects, transference would seem to me to assume characteristics of a major ego function" (1972, p. 267). Bird goes on to distinguish between overall reactions in the analytic situation, symbolic repetitions of past events (which he calls the "broader" transference), and the transference neurosis proper. As with Greenacre and Stone, the broader transference serves as a scaffold on which the transference neurosis rests. In an effort to delineate the transference neurosis, he describes how it evokes an earlier dual inside-the-body and outside-the-body quality, involving a transient and partial loss of identity difference between analysand and analyst. A transference neurosis is seen as fleeting, occurring at moments, and then receding temporarily while the broader transference takes precedence. Thus, the transference neurosis involves in part an enactment and exteriorization of previously internalized phenomena, with the analyst at such a time playing the part of an internalized function (but not necessarily a past object relationship), before any influential change can occur and be reinteriorized as altered psychic structure. Yet, only at moments when the transference neurosis comes to the fore can the most potent change occur, bringing the neurosis, a "walled off and independent institution," back to the mainstream of the analysand's emotional life and accessible to analytic influence once again. Bird is describing (in our words) how the ZPD and the transference flow into each other on a moment-by-moment basis, as seen in the progressive and regressive fluidity of analytic process.

The second historical controversy of this era, the role of speech in the earlier or lower levels of transference, is also a topic spotted by previous theorists. Both Greenacre and Stone were also exquisitely sensitive to the relationship between these transferences and the particulars of speech acquisition. Both boldly time the divergences of the primordial and the basic transferences from the transference neurosis, and yoke it to the acquisition of the pragmatics of language, as opposed to the hard-wired acquisitions of syntax. Stone further notes that it is through the pragmatics of language (how and in what way a word is used) that one is enabled to reach back into the subtleties of the primordial transference and witness its pull.

The importance of speech in the clinical situation (as opposed to development) was contemporaneously noted by Loewenstein. In discussing the role of speech in analytic technique, Loewenstein (1956) observed the following: "When the analyst believes, on the basis of preparatory work, that the time has come, that the patient is ready for it, he lends him the words, so to speak, which will meet the patient's thoughts and emotions half way." He also observed that, "interpretations given by the analyst ... might to some extent be compared to a kind of scaffolding which the patient's thought can gradually fill" (p. 465). Loewenstein's prophetic ideas represented a departure from the then prevailing psychoanalytic understanding of the role of speech in the analytic situation. Loewenstein's (1956, 1957) writings on this topic implied that what had previously been subsumed under tact and timing within the interpretive act could be further studied in terms of component psychological processes, particularly those having to do with the pragmatics of language use. To wit, an interpretation can accomplish more than an uncovering and codification of consensually agreed upon phenomena, an aspect of language use elsewhere termed referential (Wilson and Weinstein, 1992b). In the act of articulation, the analyst's words that serve as the vehicle for an interpretation also create a dialogic condition whereby canonical meaning negotiations will occur, further personalizing the interpretation, fleshing it out with the analysand's own thoughts and associations.

Loewenstein's observations also imply an expansion of the interactive role of the analyst. No longer exclusively the focus of transference distortions to be deciphered, interpretable as an externalization of interiorized conflict, the analyst now lends the analysand subtle mental attributes indispensable to analyzability. Previous literature has described such examples as some ego functions, such as the initial capacity for self-observation; another example is expanding the affective repertoire, such as the ability to enter into analysis of transference through freeing, remembering, and reliving by recognizing conditions of danger and safety (Sandler, 1960). These attributes follow from the point that the analytic dyad, when in an analytic process, creates capabilities in each other that either participant alone does not possess. Loewenstein's point is strikingly reminiscent of Bakhtin's (1986)[2] provocative claim and demonstration, from a perspective he terms translinguistics, that in any dialogic situation the meaning of a word belongs to a minimum of two people, and his investigation into how and under what conditions any speaker owns the meaning of a word.[3] Even more to the point,

---

[2] Although this particular work of Bakhtin's was not translated and published in the United States until 1981, most of the essays in this volume were conceived in the 1930s.

[3] That is to say, the "word" has a particular functional role common to both clinical psychoanalysis and Bakhtin's translinguistics. In both usages, the word is not a referential vehicle, best studied by, for example, linguistics implications in semantics and/or syntax. Rather, the word is the "dynamic milieu" (Kristeva, 1986) within which

dialogicity is at play at all times, even when only one person is speaking, as in free association. It fell to Bakhtin to depict how there is really no such thing as a monologic text; a sophisticated analysis of any text, written or spoken, unveils the multitude of contributing voices in conversation with one another, each inexorably altering the other as the text builds toward any variety of communicative meaningfulness. The concept of a monologic text—a voice with no influences—is an absurdity, yet much scholarship presumes exactly such an isolated and fractured entity. Bakhtin's ideas introduce a vast new terrain for psychoanalytic exploration. All of these authors have sought to address key questions; how do analysands come to imbue an ostensibly neutral relationship with intense meaning, and make use of this relationship to recapture and articulate memories of long-forgotten patterns and experiences?

What silent characteristics of human life fuel this profound authority, so that analysts can utilize engendered repetitions in order to remake the very fabric of an analysand's life? All imply that there must be an anlage in human development for the function of transference, otherwise where would its motive force arise? All are concerned with how and why a patient is able to make use of the analyst as an object of transference and as a tool in the process of recovery. In doing so, they inevitably touch upon larger questions, such as the function of repetition, and the developmental origins underlying how repetition provides for healing.

In more recent times, others have sought to explain such phenomena, some in ways quite different from the clinically focused

---

exchanges take place. Words are fluid constructs with tendrils in many places, at the intersections and junctures of all forms of communication, and which inevitably bear the imprint of a speaker's personal and subcultural history. Similarly, Bakhtin (1981) suggests that the meaning of a word when spoken is always half someone else's; no one person is ever solely in possession of the meaning of any utterance.

methods just examined. In evaluating such contributions, it is useful to tease apart reasons from causes. Reasons tend to be overly general; if they were more specific, they might be candidates to function as causes. Some contemporary explanations offered as answers to the above questions, such as a "lack of basic trust" when unstable transferences appear or "insecure attachment" when studying infant and mother interactions, actually paint a picture of reasons and not causes. They do not pinpoint the motivations, defenses, and conflicts specific to a causal psychoanalytic hypothesis, and hence require further specification. These important findings do suggest, however, that there must be some capacities, forged in the earliest dyadic interactions, that are necessary to support the function of transference, capacities which themselves are subject to further permutations and repetitions during development. It is in this inherently developmental arena, in conjunction with a sophisticated epigenetic theory of repetition and learning, that the relevance of the ZPD for a clinical theory can be found. Linking these findings with the psychoanalytic hypotheses put forward during this earlier period, in a way that does justice to both theoretical systems, becomes an important task, one expanding the data base of psychoanalytic theory and inquiry.

A wholly different attempt to introduce answers to such questions is offered by Loewald, perhaps the theorist most influential in investigating the third historical controversy of the time, scaffolding and maturation. Loewald strove to grasp the subtleties of why, in the midst of instinctual frustration and renunciation, an analysand might be motivated to tolerate the pain accompanying transference repetition. In a paper that served as a template for much of his later work, Loewald (1960) saw the analytic process as a period of ego disorganization and reorganization promoted through the medium of transference. The transference neurosis is set in motion by both the skill of the analyst (to whom objectivity and neutrality remain central tools) as well as the analyst's availability as a constantly recreated transference object. The analyst not only interprets transference distortions but also subtly yet tellingly conveys a new and less deceiving reality which the analysand comes to internalize. Loewald describes how the analyst must possess a dual image of the analysand, one as he or she now is, the second of the analysand as someone who can be freed of the strictures of the neurosis. The latter image, conveyed to the analysand in unapparent ways, provides an impetus for continuation in the face of the necessary optimal frustration as the manifestations of the neurosis are continually elicited and brought into the purview of the analysis. The analyst stays slightly ahead by having in rudimentary, not fully articulated form, an image of "what needs to be brought into its own." It is in the disparity between this reachable next step and the analysand's actual presentation that many mutative interpretations can usefully be formulated. Unfortunately, Loewald does not sufficiently specify how this enigmatic image of work in progress is conveyed. In contrast, the concept of the ZPD, because it is grounded in a substantial research literature, touching on aspects of learning, pedagogy, and socialization, that explicates just how this body of processes might actually take place, provides us with the additional technical leverage that follows from when a somewhat mystical concept is replaced by one capable of careful psychological specification.

The following discussion further explicates how the processes contained in the concept of the ZPD are applicable to psychoanalysis. Yet the areas where Vygotskian psychology and psychoanalysis find common ground and where they do not must be carefully delineated. With this obvious caveat in mind, we will proceed to investigate a question at the heart of both development and the clinical process—how and why is it that conflict resolution and mutative insight require another person? Note that all of the analysts discussed in this section have sought to assess the relative weights of the intrapsychic and interactive factors native to the clinical situation. With regard to these factors, this then leads us to ask: how and why does a two-person situation unleash a distinctive set of processes that are impossible in a one-person situation?

The Intrapsychic-Interactive Structure of the ZPD

Contemporary structural analysts have attempted to fathom the preeminent role of the intrapsychic, at the same time as they address the interactive context central to analysis. Contemporary structural analysis is not a well-conceived theory of exclusively intrapsychic treatment factors, for the intrapsychic and the interactive are not opposed to each other. It is only in the interactive context that the unconscious can be made manifest, subject to examination, and ultimately reorganization. While the endogenous content is present, the interactive context makes personal the intrapsychic. If one keeps in mind that the interactive is the context rather than the dynamic field itself, what then becomes the role of interaction? Pursuit of exactly this line of inquiry leads to the ZPD. The ZPD defines the native interactive context that opens or shuts a moving window of access to the intrapsychic. How an analyst opens up and takes clinical advantage of this window of access, then, emerges as a critical question, both for theory construction and technique.

The processes of the ZPD only make sense when speaking of two persons in some form of interactive engagement—learning. The problem of gaining access to the ZPD has been systematically explored to date in America with respect to the dynamics of tutoring, one of Vygotsky's original bases of description for the

ZPD concept. Perhaps a turn to these studies may provide psychoanalysis with a helpful vantage point. Accordingly, we would like now to explore this area that may be informative concerning the origins of the ZPD, but is rarely, if ever, mentioned in the psychoanalytic literature—what makes someone an effective tutor with very young children.

Distilling from Bruner (1986) and Lepper, Aspinwall, Mumme, and Chabey (1990), seven points summarize what makes a good tutor of young children:

1. A good tutor invariably mediates the child's experience of challenge. Children are not allowed to become overwhelmed by the anticipated challenge of a task, because the tutor is tuned in to how cognitive decisions are overridden by affective and motivational considerations. A realistic bridge is built between a child's present abilities and the challenge of what is to be embarked upon. One particularly superb tutor kept saying to children: "Ah, yes, perfect, but you missed this part" as a way of helping them to realize that they are already able to master what they have yet to undertake.

2. A good tutor distinguishes between the objective difficulty and the perceived difficulty of a challenging task. He then "masks" the perceived difficulty in order to prepare the child for the challenge of the task. This is preliminary to aiding the child to figure out how to answer the problem in the right way without providing the answer themselves.

3. A good tutor rarely if ever gives a child the answer to a problem, nor does he exhort. He rarely labels incorrect answers as incorrect; rather, he enables children to self-correct mistakes, without making direct suggestions as to how this should be

done. The tutor steers the child toward self-propelled attempts at solving enigmatic problems in order to provide him or her with an opportunity to think through a process leading to an incorrect answer.

4. A good tutor forestalls only some errors. The value of a productive error is recognized. He shifts children toward productive errors, realizing that by going back to them, a child stands to benefit. Good tutors only interdict "disruptive" errors that serve to derail the processes of learning.

5. Tutors are effective when they motivate a child to accept responsibility for their success or failure, particularly when the actual success or failure is not yet known to the child.

6. A good tutor gives a child information that would ordinarily be threatening, in the least threatening way.

7. A good tutor prompts problematic or learning phobic children to ask for increasingly difficult problems to solve. The nature of their relationship empowers an inhibited child to want to take in what the tutor has to offer, in an incremental series of gradations of difficulty.

Indeed, it is astounding to come face to face with how dynamically saturated the interactive processes of learning are for young children.[4] A successful tutor does not so much teach as he creates and exemplifies the conditions whereby learning is made possible. Note how it is the imperceptible background factors

---

[4] Chomsky (1976) makes a similar point about the subtle yet insidious appearance of incapacity, which adults are vulnerable to who are in subcultures nested within an unfamiliar culture that overrides their own.

embedded within object relations in tutoring that makes pedagogy plausible to a child. Might the processes through which an analysand comes to internalize the insights arrived at during the analysis of the transference be similar to that of the tutored child? After all, many of the observations of what makes a tutor a good tutor can be viewed as being within the jurisdiction of the analyst's tact (Sledge, 1989).

One might critique this analogy between tutoring and analysis by noting that the best approach to intrapsychic life is through its endogenous roots rather than interactive experiences. This argument perpetuates the false dichotomy, because it overlooks that the interactive context supports the intrapsychic and gives it definition and form. Although the intrapsychic and interpersonal can be pitted against one another in a semantically constructed version of opposition, they are distinguishable only in theory, not in nature. In actuality they are mutually potentiating, necessary for each other's continued evolution, and rely upon the other for their shape and function. Both feed into the analytic task of prioritizing psychic reality, which is thus not rooted exclusively in intrapsychic processes. In analysis, "real" external objects are rarely the focus of concerted attention; external knowledge is at best approximated, usually changing with the tides of the analysis and becoming a backdrop for the emotional climate of the day-to-day "facts" spoken to one another. From a developmental point of view, Sandler and Sandler (1978) likewise collapse the distinction between intrapsychic and interpersonal by demonstrating that even the earliest object relations involve wishes that emanate from the endogenous life of the child, both of which are subject to repetition and will later be an influence on the unfolding mind.

Everything known about the intrapsychic by the contemporary structural analyst, painstakingly won over a century of clinical observation and testing, is maintained when grafting the concept of the ZPD onto the intrapsychic focus of psychoanalysis. The ZPD thus provides psychoanalysis with a clinically grounded model of an interactive context, and one not mired in a focus on the real relationship. To be sure, Vygotsky's concept of the ZPD can be, and has mistakenly been, thought of as necessarily related to real objects. Valsiner (1988) points out how if a child is left on his own, he constructs a ZPD out of whatever resources are available. To quote Valsiner (1988, p. 149), "the developing child is constantly in the process of constructing his own future development, sometimes by his own means (in play) and at other times with explicit assistance from others (under instruction). For the analysand, it is both internal and external objects that constitute such available resources, although these resources required at one time some interactive presence, which was internalized and then further embellished. When in analysis the transference becomes re-externalized and the analysand seeks an object in order to repeat a transference configuration, conterminously the analyst offers himself as a partner in the ZPD, thereby allowing for entrance into an internalization community. Working together, they allow for the success of clinical psychoanalysis, and prevent the endless and ubiquitous transference repetition that goes on outside of the clinical situation. The tutor and the analyst, working with completely disparate content, both can ask the same questions: How do I get this person to learn what I am trying to impart to them? And, then again, both are geared toward their initial importance and their eventual dispensability, so that they can also ask: How can I get him to learn so that when the time is right, he will no longer need me?

The ZPD and the Analytic Alliance

Vygotsky's definition of the ZPD assumes a benign transference relationship that is relatively free of affective turbulence. The assumption of nonvolatility is inevitably altered in the clinical situation, where the presence of aggressive and sexual passions, of impulses and the defenses mobilized to contain them, find expression in the transference. In a successfully proceeding analysis, there is rarely a smooth partnership over a prolonged course of time. Vygotsky does not satisfactorily address the variegated drive and object relational issues associated with aggression or psychosexual development (although he hints at understanding the problem, see 1987, pp. 282–283). In the psychoanalytic situation, the ZPD involves far more than mere instruction. Modell (1990), the only American analyst to date who has discussed the role of the ZPD in clinical work, briefly alludes to this direction as well. So, prior psychoanalytic explanation of how the analytic process evolved, despite inevitable ferment, were forced to move outside of the analytic process itself and call on the real relationship. The resulting constructs (e.g., holding, repairing, alliance) often refer to the nonconflictual positive relationship, or simply the rational intention merely to get better. They tend, then, to contraindicate the welcome presence of intense aggression, because it comes to be seen only as a destructive force in the treatment. An example of the ZPD, in contrast, might be when an analyst can make an interpretation that leads to a patient feeling hurt or embarrassed, and the patient can angrily return the next day with a dream that inadvertently expresses the unconscious meaning of the interpretation to the patient. Even a patient's spiteful and hateful execration toward his analyst might reflect engagement in the ZPD, because the repeated action and its associated affects in the present can lead to the recovery of long-forgotten memories or fantasies which spawned the aggression that is being expressed.

That intense aggression and its derivatives could potentially further the work is a point made by Kris (1956), when he distinguishes the "good hour" from the "deceptively good hour" by the presence in the latter of compliance, so that ego integration does not occur because ego functioning is not truly autonomous. Rather, compliance serves the covert aim of winning the analyst's love or of gaining union with him or her. Kris (1956) described how a significant amount of analytic work was accomplished for some patients only under the aegis of the aggression characteristic of the negative phase of transference. For all patients, the analysis of aggression, particularly the aggression released with the successful analysis of defense, and its clinical counterpart, resistance, offers unique opportunities for structural reintegration, that do not exist in any other aspect of analysis. One advantage that the ZPD construct offers, over other explanations of an analysand's fortitude, is that it does not rule out aggression, and hence does not oppose well-tested clinical wisdom.

The ZPD should not be confused with the benign intentions of the clinician and patient. The ZPD does not refer to the idea of a therapeutic alliance, conscious cooperation, the willingness to work hard, or compliance that can be readily enlisted upon suggestion. There are also significant differences between the ZPD and many current empirical uses of the concept of the therapeutic alliance (Allen, Newsom, Gabbard, and Coyne, 1984). The therapeutic alliance is often understood and measured as a conscious and collaborative intent to get therapeutic work accomplished (Marziali, Marmar, and Krupnick, 1981; Hartley and Strupp, 1983; Frieswyk, Allen, Colson, Coyne, Gabbard, Horwitz, and Newsom, 1984). Clinical psychoanalytic descriptions of the therapeutic alliance, although more cognizant of the usefulness of potential oppositionality and resistance (Greenson, 1965; Dickes, 1967; Kanzer, 1981), still stress the collaborative element. We suggest that the processes that comprise a therapeutic alliance as defined by many of these theorists are first the byproduct and then the outcome of a well-conducted treatment, not a precondition for one.

However, if we think of support as emanating from the phe-nomenological world of the analysand, as opposed to the analyst's technique (Schlesinger, 1973), the ZPD can be seen as providing the basis for the experience of support in psychoanal-ysis. It is the experience of the analysand who can access a ZPD that provides a context for support, not the technique of exhort-ing, praising, affirming, bolstering, or mirroring a patient. Being in the ZPD is experienced as supportive, no matter what the technical intervention, whereas when the analyst acts support-ively, various forms of trouble can result. This helps explain why often the most painful and seemingly troublesome moments of an analysis are so often experienced the next day, or later re-called, as feeling supportive.

Optimal frustration can be gauged at any one moment in the analysis by paying attention to the conjunction of the ZPD with what material is active and heated up in the transference. Ana-lysts often talk knowingly about optimal frustration, but this has been quite difficult to define. The aim of frustration in analysis is to create the optimal conditions for the re-evocation of past patterns of behavior in the transference, as opposed to the im-mediate gratification of wishes—to activate memories and to gather the transference. At times, the bounds of optimal frustra-tion are difficult to clearly discern, and vary precariously with the ebbs and flows of the analysis.

Optimal frustration is only optimal if it fosters internalization and structural change, as it exists within the transactions charac-teristic of the dynamic meaning of the prevailing material. For example, early in his analysis, one analysand began his hours by making various bids to have an impact, any impact, on his ana-lyst. He did not so much want any response, whether talking, greeting, or praise, as he wished to feel that his spoken words led to a reaction from the analyst. The analyst's reaction indicating that an impact had been made could be communicated in a virtually endless variety of ways. Unless this bid was handled by letting the impact be known, his associations were sparse, were felt as futile, and seemed to point to little of unconscious significance. Once he felt that he had made an impact on the analyst, he usually would come alive and shift into an extraordinarily useful mode of deeply felt analytic involvement. Thus, early in his analysis, the optimal frustration that opened the window of access to the ZPD was minimal and pegged to this particular dynamic factor. Later in the analysis, when it was both useful and possible, the analyst was more overtly frustrating, thereby allowing the analysis of this pattern of behavior.

Abstinence is usually thought of as forestalling the gratification of a wish, in order that the wish might be put into words and analyzed rather than put into action. It is noteworthy that this definition is divorced from a theory of ongoing process. An analyst can, hence, easily not gratify a wish and, although technically correct, can set up the conditions for an analysis to be untenable. There is no single construct in an analyst's technical repertoire that points to the dangers of such clinical events, warned against by Lipton (1977), as undue abstinence that could produce iatrogenic, narcissistic-like phenomena in the analysand, who is self-referential and grandiose because he feels futile and rebuffed. With the ZPD in place, it is possible and useful to be abstinent vis-á-vis those wishes active and pressing in the transference. When the analyst is not usefully engaged in the processes of the ZPD with the patient, the frustration arising from abstinence tends to serve to anger and disappoint the patient. An analyst abstains from gratifying those transference wishes that the processes of the ZPD can reach and, once evoked, pull toward

integration. This sense of optimal abstinence is one of the processes that moves an analysis forward, and now others as well
will be investigated.

ZPD Transference and Repetition:
What Moves an Analysis Forward

Before attempting to differentiate the ZPD and the transference
with regard to the function of repetition, it is important to note
that the separation is largely heuristic. In the analytic situation,
it is virtually impossible to isolate a single bit of data and assign
it to either the transference or the ZPD. Inevitably, all psychic
conflicts are anchored in both. Likewise, in the course of development the processes that promote access to the ZPD cannot be
singled out from processes subject to transference repetition. In
fact, the processes that allow for entrance into the ZPD are themselves susceptible to conflict. However, the distinction is made
here because it leads to useful technical recommendations.

What ultimately distinguishes the ZPD from the transference is
the different functions of repetition and how each makes use of objects in the evoked interactive context. In the transference, objects
are recruited for purposes of repetition, whereas in the ZPD, objects
are recruited for purposes of learning and entry into an internalization community. As Freud (1914) noted, transference and
repetition bear an intimate and causal relationship, and, now we
add, so does repetition and the ZPD. Let us turn for a moment to
look at the different functions of repetition as they apply to the ZPD
and the transference. Each person when young constructs a unique
internalization community, as objects come to take on differential
importance. At all hierarchical levels, repetition provides for familiarity. The child tends to prefer to transform passive repetition to
active repetition, because the active mode implies mastery over

potentially traumatic events (Loewald, 1971; Klein, 1976; Wilson and Malatesta, 1989). By insuring that not everything will seem new, repetition organizes the chaos of infinite arrays of experience into recognizable and habitual forms. Internalization, with its provision of new structure and increased opportunities for self-regulation, provides the antidote to repetition, obviating the compulsion to recreate the old. But transference repetition does not necessarily lead to internalization. By itself, repetition accomplishes nothing with respect to internalization.

While one function of repetition is to recruit objects for the task of conflict resolution (the unconscious wisdom of object choice), internalization is necessary to successfully reach such a goal. Around any one repeated conflict, the content of the conflict will best explain why object recruitment has not been successful in the past. How an analyst handles that conflict will either allow for a widened access to an internalization community, or will position the analyst inside the conflict, unable to alter it. This is the conjunction of the ZPD with the transference. The end goal is not for the analyst to serve as a new object to undo pathological repetition, although he may temporarily and usefully do so, nor to repair conflicts. Rather, he creates the conditions for evoking the conflicts in a way that does not interfere with their ultimately being analyzed and worked through. One result of mutative interpretation is to widen the patient's ability to recruit objects for purposes of useful growth rather than futile repetition. Everybody has access to objects for repetition, but not everybody has access to objects for internalization. In introducing and regarding one's own personage as important to analyze, the analyst becomes a transference object as a step on the way to a widened and richer ZPD.

With respect to interpretation, the ZPD can then be operationally defined as the analytic space within which the analyst is able to formulate mutative interpretations that can be assimilated by the patient. The point has repeatedly been made that a good interpretation is slightly ahead of the patient's unfolding thought sequence, tapping preconscious material that just requires a nudge to reach conscious awareness, yet not so far ahead that the interpretation is unintelligible or easily intellectualized. Greenacre (1968) suggests a similar link between a patient's ability to take in an analyst's words and his relationship to objects, when she succinctly makes the following point:

> For the extent to which the interpretation can be made assimilable to the analysand depends not only on the analyst's sensitivity to the content of the patient's transference productions and his adequate knowledge of technique and principles but further on the construction—the stuff of which the patient's early attachments and identifications have been made in the period up to and including the acquisition of speech and the time immediately afterward [1968, p. 214].

As Greenacre notes, the capacity for assimilating interpretations depends in part on the nature of the patient's earliest attachments and identifications, particularly around the time of language acquisition. She notes that seemingly intact patients who are ultimately not analyzable are not precisely because of the nature of these conflicts. In the terms we set here, with such patients the problem is of the ZPD, not the transference.

The optimal range of the ZPD can be lost for a variety of reasons, cutting across diagnostic categories and levels of disturbance, ranging from a regression to primary identification, through a wish to win the love of the analyst through pseudocompliance. When this happens, there is a loss of the ability to learn through the analysis, and a consequent difficulty in maintaining a

ZPD that can sustain the buffeting of transference. Such a loss of the ability to learn from and through the analyst involves a return to earlier forms of internalization, such as only allowing the registration of affective, interactive ways of knowing the object, a reliance on imitation and action, and a loss of libidinal object constancy (Gedo, 1993). The concept of the ZPD prompts analysts to think carefully about the antecedents to transference interpretation, what must be first accomplished in order that the interpretation of the transference becomes and remains a useful undertaking to the analysand. Transference material is too often prematurely or precipitously wrenched into the analytic dialogue in a way that does not lend itself to being gainfully analyzed and internalized. "Prestages" of all procedural guides, such as abstinence, anonymity, and neutrality, are often of make-or-break importance early in an analysis, before an analysand settles into the smooth course characteristic of their understanding of what analysis is and what it is not. Stone's (1971) point that abstinence is part and parcel of the contrapuntal essence of the analytic setting, which is best characterized by both people working toward the eventual shared recognition that not gratifying wishes is the most useful way for the analysand to be helped, implicitly assumes a much earlier stage in which this must be negotiated and tested out in order for it to become agreed upon.

In an optimal analysis, the analyst and analysand co-construct the ZPD setting about analyzing the needs and wishes emanating as much as possible from the analysand that comprise the transference. The ZPD is a true co-construction, one which then allows the transference not to be co-constructed. This leads to the following technical conclusion.

An analyst strives to be inside the ZPD but outside of the transference. This distinction is key; the fictitious and oft-caricatured blank screen analyst stands outside of the transference and the ZPD, which few competent analysts actually do. On the other hand, those analysts who speak of the co-construction of the transference cannot be really analyzing the transference because they are not striving as best as possible to position themselves outside of it (in an absolute sense obviously an impossibility, in a relative sense, a clinical necessity). By co-constructing the transference, the entire meaning of the concept of the transference is altered (Wilson, 1995), because, among other changes, free association tends to be superseded by the concept of dialogue. Dialogue has dramatically different manifest features than free association, although both are intrinsically dialogic (but in different ways). Thus, rather than one person free associating and two people examining the thematic yield, two people are speaking according to conventional pragmatic rules of discourse. It is then unclear why an analyst would seek to intensify a patient's awareness of transference, since intensity of transference would then become more of a danger to the continuity of the relationship than an opportunity to analyze. In other words, given the inevitability of mutual influences, an analyst can be actively engaged with the patient around many facets of the analysis, yet can strive as best as possible to avoid determining the nature of the transference. The co-construction of the ZPD is an essential prelude to the analysis of the transference and constitutes a major challenge often more prominent during the opening phase of analysis, but a continual challenge throughout the analysis as new conflicts emerge. This co-construction is usually sotto voce in a smoothly proceeding analysis.

Although at first glance a contradiction, actually being "inside the ZPD" and "outside the transference" is an apt description of a tension which characterizes sound analytic process. Technically, it guides interventions aimed at both providing the opportunity to learn (or structuralize) from the back-and-forth flow of processes inherent in the analytic situation, while pre-serving the centrality of the externalization of unconsciously represented configurations that will be visible as the transfer-ence. The tension can be somewhat eased by seeing that the analytic path for the unfolding of the transference in most cases does not have to be protected as assiduously as historically has been thought and recommended, especially when its protection pushes the ZPD into the background. When neutrality, anonym-ity, and abstinence are recognized as relative rather than absolute aims of the analyst by which to steer an analysis, the inevitable trade-offs between being inside the ZPD and outside the trans-ference, that occur in the tempestuous currents of an hour, become part of the necessary and usual aspects of guarding the analytic process. This is why good analytic process can usefully be conceptualized as a concatenated series of trade-offs between being outside the transference and inside the ZPD, as well as fol-lowing from the time-honored gold standards of relative neutrality, anonymity, and abstinence.

Perhaps no one has investigated the relationship between the conceptually partitioned elements of the transference as deeply and thoroughly as Gill (1982), although his conclusions do not overlap with ours. Responding to Freud's (1912, 1913) dictums that the unobjectionable positive transference provides the nec-essary context for the continuation of the analysis when under the gun of negative transference, and that transference should not be interpreted until it has gelled into a resistance, Gill (1982) concludes that: "The unobjectionable positive transference which Freud argued was the necessary context for cooperation in the analytic work—the therapeutic alliance—is not something that has to be fostered by other means. It is promoted by the very process of the elucidation of the transference" (p. 178). Gill thus recommends early attention to resistance to the awareness of transference, which then evolves into interpretations of resistance to the resolution of transference, thereby fostering the "necessary context for cooperation" that an analysis with its necessary staying power and mutative potential.

While the conceptual distinctions Gill makes are similar to the ones made here, his way of technically solving the problem, of transference volatility and its relationship to the continuity of analysis, is to thoroughly alter the stance of the analyst. The analyst becomes a participant-observer who does not stand outside of the transference, which now largely results from the back-and-forth actual interaction between the analyst and analysand. Willfully participating in the here-and-now transference does not privilege the analysand's ability to externalize and then reinternalize by way of interpretation the unconscious fantasies underlying transference repetition. Gill dilutes the usefulness of the analyst remaining as best as possible outside of the transference, whereas striving to remain outside the transference but within the ZPD provides a technical guide that gives the analysand the opportunity to externalize unconscious fantasies with minimal clouding by the back-and-forth of the "real" interaction.

Language and the ZPD

To come full circle to the role of speech for clinical psychoanalysis, with the analysis and resolution of the transference, the person of the analyst as a member of the immediate internalization community recedes as his interpretive words are taken in. Around the scaffolding they provide the analysand can further articulate and restructure his own past and present experience. The capacity to restructure evolves into an ongoing self-analytic capacity.

Inherent in the concept of the ZPD is the idea that the analyst navigates being ahead of, with, and behind the analysand, while necessarily promoting the analysand's forward-moving activity. The notion of a reachable next step, particularly as described by Loewald (1960) who advocates this feature in analysis, of staying slightly ahead, has an important correlate in the contemporary field of sociolinguistics, where similar processes have been demonstrated during language acquisition. It has been shown that the competent caregiver tends to use semantics and syntax that are consistently months ahead of the given chronological age of the child. Some developmental psycholinguists (e.g., Lucariello and Nelson, 1987) have found that the caregiver must remain developmentally ahead of the child in her presentation of how event knowledge maps onto language ontogenesis, if the child is to pass through normative and optimal stages of language acquisition. For example, the infant says "ba' '—the mother replies and says, "Oh, you want milk!" and feeds the infant. Several months later, when the child's capacity to articulate has matured somewhat, the child no longer is rewarded for saying "ba," but must point or make a closer linguistic representation, such as "bada" or "bati" for bottle (depending upon how their consonants arrive). The child grows within and only within the mother's ever-increasing expectations. Similarly, the child might say "da," and the mother will again foster both conflict and development, as well as entry into the overall speech community, by remaining ahead of the child and saying "Daddy is at work," thus communicating several complicated ideas in rudimentary form to the child; namely, you miss daddy, daddy is away but will come back, and so on. In these examples, the expansion of the child's mind depends on the mother's intuitive understanding that the infant requires the stresses and strains that accompany being introduced to what lies ahead, in order to form categories, ask questions, acquire new syntactical rules, and to obtain new and necessary ways of apprehending the world. Through the properties of language, the mother approximates a developmental zone within which growth is awarded its potential. Note how the spoken word serves a function far removed from referentiality. The upward organizing momentum is provided by the words of the caregiver who provides the child with the wondrous sense that his or her inner states can be transmuted into forms of advanced representational knowledge. What Loewald is suggesting is that a similar forward push is provided by the analyst through the experienced magic of interpretation.

Loewald's and related views have been criticized for implying that the analyst knows more than the analysand and inevitably directs the course of the analysis. In fact, "staying ahead" is not an attempt to impart a body of already existing knowledge, but rather to communicate through interpretation the decontextualized structure already present in an analysand's activity. By focusing on the analysand's underlying action structure and separating it out from the context within which it is embedded, the analyst attempts to bring previously inchoate experience under the ever-expanding hegemony of speech. The analyst is not ahead of the analysand, except insofar as he or she is capable of a less conflicted awareness of the operative dynamics and therefore of how the mind works (Gray, 1973).

The history of the "ownership" of the meaning of a word is the invisible internalization community of one's past, for as Bakhtin (1981, 1986) asserts, it is only through two voices (or intentionalities) coming into contact (or conflict) that meaning is produced. A word, then, becomes one's own only when it is arrayed with one's entire self, appropriated for use with one's own semantic and expressive intentions. Once so internalized, the words of the analyst transform into the analysand's own words, and certain meanings belong to both of them and no one else. Loewenstein (1957) also warns against the use of words without a shared affective history in the act of interpretation. In analysis, private language is not transformed into socially comprehensible meanings by expansion; rather, the speech community of two forges words that constitute a unique set of experiences and insights, private to only the analyst and the analysand. The co-owned words are embellished intrapsychically, made into psychic structure, and serve subsequently as a constant safeguard against any renewed threat of the repetition of neurosis. The analysis of the transference opens up the expansion of the ZPD. Through the analysis of the transference comes a ZPD that is flexible and increasingly under the conscious sway of the analysand, and hence a ZPD that does not require but rather can embrace an external object when wished for or necessary.

Conclusion: Why Does a Person Have a Transference, Anyway?

Many have bemoaned the lack in psychoanalysis of a tenable theory of how learning takes place. Rapaport (1960) concluded that in part the difficulty followed from inherent problems in Freud's views on transformation from primary to secondary process, and pointed toward Piaget's genetic epistemology as one way out of this cul de sac. Although others have persisted in the effort to develop a broadly based and integrative psychoanalytic theory of learning (e.g., Greenspan, 1979; Schwartz, 1987), Schafer (1968) makes the telling point that clinical analysis can best lead us to understand the "deep involvements" that set learning into motion, as contrasted with, one might add, the universals of genetic epistemology. Any clinically based psychoanalytic theory of internalization must follow from a concept like the ZPD, which provides a dynamic theory of internalization, one compatible with a theory of intrapsychic conflict and psychic structure. The concept of the ZPD emphasizes how variable learning in fact is, as well as how situationally distributed is the sphere within which internalization takes place. The ZPD cannot be thought of as the long-sought Rosetta Stone of psychoanalysis—a general theory of internalization, but on the other hand such a general theory is not as germane to clinical psychoanalysis as one that centers on the dynamics of how learning is situationally distributed. Furthermore, it is the only theory of learning that emphasizes the inherent object relations underlying the growth of cognition and the self. Freud (1917, p. 445) hinted that the overcoming of obstacles in the way of learning optimally takes place in the context of the positive transference. The ZPD could better be substituted for the term positive transference in this sentence. Likewise, the distinction between positive and negative transference is not as remarkable as had been depicted; this distinction initially drawn by Freud (1912) emphasizes the affective coloring to the transference at the expense of an appreciation that both accomplish the same function. When the smoke clears, there is only transference and the phases through which it accomplishes its purposes.

Then, too, the issue of deficit can be seen in a new light. The focus on and examination of the vicissitudes of the ZPD with many analysands is initially more important than is the analysis of the transference. During early volatile stretches, developing a ZPD that can sustain the therapeutic action emerges as an immediate and neces sary first step. The hypothesis that volatile transference is unstable because there is no operant ZPD to sustain its intensity recasts the notions of "the sensorimotor use of the object" or "psychological deficit" into the context of the situationally specific nature of the object relations involved in learning. The question of "having" or not having a psychological deficit becomes moot. In support of our view, a host of studies have shown that individuals who appear not to have a particular ability in one context, that is, are diagnosed as deficit-laden, can in fact demonstrate that same ability provided they are in a different context (Lave, 1988; Rogoff, 1990).

A related question involves the assessment of analyzability. Clinicians who base their assessment of a prospective analysand's treatability on responses to trial interpretations during consultation have intuitively endorsed the concept of the ZPD. Green (1986) has described how the assessment of analyzability must be located at the intersection of the clinician—analysand interaction over time rather than in the analysand or the analyst at any one time. A capacity to conduct therapeutic work in an area of which they are not yet conscious, rather than the insight already possessed, is evaluated. Analyzability should be defined as an abstraction created and recreated on a moment-by-moment basis, which must continuously be enforced and renewed. Analyzability denotes a process, not a characteristic, and like all processes is defined by flux over time. The best way to predict analyzability is to make an in-domain prediction based on a representative microanalytic sample of analytic process, involving an assessment of both transference and the ZPD. Thus, analyzability cannot be causally linked to static factors such as adequate ego functioning (Bellak and Meyers, 1975) or any systematic metapsychological assessment of the personality (Greenspan and Cullander, 1973) in a meaningful way. It is not surprising that the history of research using a roster of isolated predictor variables in the analysand has yielded precious little (Bachrach, 1980). Even such uniquely psychoanalytic skills as the ability to free associate is suspect as a predictor of analyzability. A. Kris (1982) has similarly suggested that the capacity to free associate is, for some, a readily available style of thinking, which in itself predicts nothing about the ultimate course of an analysis. Rather, the focus of the evaluation for analyzability, can be on the analysand's ability to make use of the analyst—and the analyst's skill in offering himself to the analysand—in those ways defined as within the analytic process, which Shapiro (1984) also advocates and terms transference readiness, but is actually much more.

I have asked earlier why people have transference at all. What furnishes transferences with their motivational impetus? We are led to the following conclusions. The transference seeks an object in order to pull the object into multiple cyclical repetitions of the neurosis. The transference will misfire if what the object evokes can be too overwhelming to be integrated. The ZPD provides the context so that the evoked repetition need not be overwhelming. The transference is not a tool for change without the ZPD. Unless the internalizing function of the ZPD is harnessed, the transference will endlessly repeat what will continue to be unresolvable conflict. Brenner (1982) declared that the transference is ubiquitous, and the primary distinguishing factor of the clinical situation is that the transference is gathered rather than dispersed. Yes, of course, this is so, but something additional must now be appended: gathering it is not enough without its conjunction with the ZPD. The ZPD precedes and undergirds the transference and provides the transference with its mutative potential. The interactive context brings to life the latent potential of the intrapsychic.

The sheer existence of the transference is a consequence of and compensation for having had, at one time, an immature psychic apparatus. Transference has a biological function; if it were possible to be born with a mature psychic apparatus, there would be no need to have a transference, because self-reflection would be sufficient to enable one to acquire the requisite knowledge to self-regulate and smoothly link the past, present, and future in a continuum of dynamic stability. The transference recruits and then uses objects for its purposes, one of which is to overcome the multiple effects of early dysregulating experience, such as helplessness, the inevitable calamities of childhood, and trauma. In analysis, the transference and the ZPD create a partnership greater than either component alone, that takes the form of a self-healing capacity, which works toward the evoked repetition not being fruitless. This is why, in a beneficial analytic process, the transference must make things go wrong, in order that the ZPD can then make them right. The transference, in all its volatility, is inevitably an ally of the analyst, because in the analytic office it furnishes the raw materials for the psychological changes required so that, when paired with the ZPD, mastery might at long last occur.

References

Allen, J.; Newsom, G.; Gabbard, G.; & Coyne, L. (1984). Scales to assess the therapeutic alliance from a psychoanalytic perspective. *Bulletin of the Menninger Clinic* 48:383–394.

Bachrach, H. (1980). Analyzability: A clinical-research perspective. *Psychoanalysis & Contemporary Thought* 3:85–116.

Bakhtin, M. (1981). *The Dialogic Imagination: Four Essays by M.M. Bakhtin,* Eds. M. Holquist, tr. C. Emerson & M. Holquist. Austin: University of Texas Press.

———(1986). *Speech Genres and Other Late Essays,* ed. C. Emerson & M. Holquist, transl. V.W. McGee. Austin: University of Texas Press.

Bellak, L & Meyers, B. (1975). Ego function assessment and analyzability. *International. Review of Psychoanalysis* 2:413–427.

Bird, B. (1972). Notes on transference: Universal phenomena and the hardest part of analysis. *Journal of the American Psychoanalytic Association* 20:267–301.

Brenner, C. (1982). *The Mind in Conflict.* New York: International Universities Press.

Brown, A. & Ferrara, R. (1985). Diagnosing zones of proximal development. In *Culture, Cognition, Communication: Vygotskian Perspectives,* Ed. J. Wertsch, pp.273–305. Cambridge & New York: Cambridge University Press.

Bruner, J. (1986). *Actual Minds, Possible Worlds.* Cambridge, MA: Harvard University Press.

Chomsky, N. (1976). Equality: Language development, human intelligence, and social organization. In *The Chomsky Reader,* ed., pp. 183=202. J. Peck. New York: Pantheon Press, 1987.

Dickes, R. (1967). Severe regressive disruptions of the therapeutic alliance. *Journal of the American Psychoanalytic Association* 15:508–533.

Freud, S. (1900). The interpretation of dreams. *Standard Edition* 4 & 5.

———(1905). Three essays on the theory of sexuality. *Standard Edition* 7:123–243.

———(1912). The dynamics of transference. *Standard Edition* 12:97–108.

———(1913). On beginning the treatment (Further recommendations on the technique of psycho-analysis, I). *Standard Edition,* 12:121–144.

———(1914). Remembering, repeating, and working-through (Further recom- mendations on the technique of psycho-analysis, II). *Standard Edition* 12:147–156.

———(1917). Introductory lectures on psychoanalysis. *Standard Edition* 15 & 16.

Frieswyk, S.; Allen, J.; Colson, D.; Coyne, L; Gabbard, G.; Horwitz, L; & New-som, G. (1984). Therapeutic alliance: Its place as a process and outcome variable in dynamic psychotherapy research. *Consulting and Clinical Psychology* 54:32–58.

Gedo, J. (1993). The hierarchical model of mental functioning: Sources and applications. In *Hierarchical Concepts in Psychoanalysis: Theory, Research, and Clinical Practice,* ed. A Wilson &J. Gedo, pp. 129-152. New York: Guilford Press. Gn.t. M. (1982)

Gill, M. (1982) *Analysis of Transference,* Vol. 1. New York: International Universities Press.

Gray, P. (1973). Psychoanalytic technique and the ego's capacity for viewing intrapsychic activity. *Journal of the American Psychoanalytic Association* 21:474–494.

Green, A. (1986). The analyst, symbolization, and absence in the analytic setting. In *On Private Madness, pp. 30-59.* Madison, CT: International Universities Press.

Greenacre, P. (1954). The role of transference. *Journal of the American Psychoanalytic Association* 2:671–684.

———(1968). The psychoanalytic process, transference, and acting out. *International .Journal of Psychoanalysis* 49:211–223.

Greenson, R. (1965). The working alliance and the transference. In *Explorations in Psychoanalysis,* pp. 199-224. New York: International Universities Press, 1978.

Greenspan, S.l. (1979). *Intelligence and Adaptation: An Integration of Psychoanalytic and Piagetian Developmental Psychology. Psychological Issues Monograph.* 47I48. New York: International Universities Press.

———Cullander, C. (1973). A systematic metapsychological assessment of the personality: Its application to the problem of analyzability. *Journal of the American Psychoanalytic Association* 21:303–327.

Hartley, D. & Strupp, H. (1983). The therapeutic alliance: Its relationship to outcome in brief psychotherapy. In *Empirical Studies of Psychoanalytic Theories,* Vol. 1, Ed., J. Masling. pp. 1-27. Hillsdale, NJ: Analytic Press.

Kanzer, M. (1981). Freud's "analytic pact": The standard therapeutic alliance. *Journal of the American Psychoanalytic Association* 29:69–87.

Klein, G. (1976). *Psychoanalysis: A Study of Essentials.* New York: International Universities Press.

Kohut, H. (1971). *The Analysis of the Self.* New York: International Universities Press.

Kris, A. (1982). *Free Association.* New Haven, CT: Yale University Press.

Kris. E. (1956). On some vicissitudes of insight in psychoanalysis. *International Journal of Psychoanalysis* 37:445–455.

Kristeva, J. (1986). *The Kristeva Reader,* Ed. T. Moi. Oxford: Basil Blackwell.

Lave, J. (1988). *Cognition in Practice: Mind, Mathematics, and Culture in Everyday Life.* Cambridge & New York:: Cambridge University Press.

Lepper, M.; Aspinwall, L; Mumme, L; & Chabay, R. (1990). Self-perception and social- perception processes in tutoring: Subtle social control strategies of expert tutors. In *Self-Inference Processes: The Ontario Symposium,* Vol. 6, pp. 217-237, Eds.,J. Olson & M. Zanna. Hillsdale, NJ: Erlbaum.

Lipton, S. (1977). The advantages of Freud's technique as shown in his analysis of the Rat Man. *International Journal of Psychoanalysis* 58:255–273.

Loewald, H. (1960). The therapeutic action of psychoanalysis. *International Journal of Psychoanalysis* 41:16–33.

———(1971). Some considerations on repetition and repetition compulsion. *International Journal of Psychoanalysis* 52:59–66.

Loewenstein, R. (1956). Some remarks on the role of speech in psychoanalytic technique. *International Journal of Psychoanalysis* 37:460–468.

———(1957). Some thoughts on interpretation in the theory and practice of psychoanalysis. *Psychoanalytic Study of the Child* 12:127–150. New York: International Universities Press.

Lucarrielo, J. & Nelson, K. (1987). Remembering and planning talk between mothers and children. *Discourse Processes* 10:219–235.

Marzjali, E.; Marmar, C.; & Krupnick, M. (1981). Therapeutic alliance scales: Devel- opment and relationship to psychotherapy outcome. *American Journalof Psychiatry* 138:361–346.

Modell. A (1988). The centrality of the psychoanalytic setting and the changing aims of treatment. A perspective from a theory of object relations. *Psychoanalytic Quarterly* 57:577–596.

———(1990). *Other Times, Other Realities.* Cambridge, MA: Harvard University Press.

Rapaport, D. (1960). Psychoanalysis as a developmental psychology. In *The Collected Papers of David Rapaport,* ed. M.M. Gill, pp. 820-852. New York: Basic Books, 1967.

Rogoff, B. (1990). *Apprenticeship in Thinking: Cognitive Development in Social Context.* New York: Oxford University Press.

Sandler, J. (1960). The background of safety. *International Journal of Psychoanalysis* 41:352–356.

———Sandler, AM. (1978). On the development of object relationships and affects. *International Journal of Psychoanalysis* 59:285–296.

Schafer, R. (1968). *Aspects of Internalization.* New York: International Universities Press.

Schlesinger, H. (1973). Diagnosis and prescription for psychotherapy. *Bulletin of the Menninger Clinic* 33:269–278.

Schwartz, A 1987). Drives, affects, behavior and learning: approaches to a psychobiology of emotion and to an integration of psychoanalytic and neurobiology thought. *Journal of the American Psychoanalytic. Association* 35:467–506.

Shapiro, S. (1984). The initial assessment of the patient: A psychoanalytic approach. *International Journal of Psychoanalysis* 11:11–25.

Sledge, W. (1989). The psychoanalyst's use of tact. *Psychoanalytic Study of the Child*, 44:137–149.

Stein, M. (1981). The unobjectionable part of the transference. *Journal of the American Psychoanalytic Association* 29:869–892.

Stern, D. (1985). *The Interpersonal World of the Infant.* New York: Basic Books.

Stone, L (1971). *The Psychoanalytic Situation.* New York: International Universities Press.

Valsiner, J. (1988). *Developmental Psychology in the Soviet Union.* Bloomington, IN: Indiana University Press.

Vygotsky, L (1934). *Thought and Language.* Moscow–Leningrad: Sozekgiz.

———(1956). *Selected Psychological Investigations.* Moscow: Izdatel'stvo Akademii Pedagogicheskikh Nauk.

———(1978). *Mind in Society: The Development of Higher Psychological Processes.* Cambridge, MA: Harvard University Press.

———(1981). The genesis of higher mental functions. In *The Concept of Activity in Soviet Psychology,* ed. J. Wertsch, pp. 144-188. Armonk, NY: M. E. Sharpe Publishing, Inc.

———(1987). Thinking and speaking. In *The Collected Papers of L.S. Vygotsky,* Vol. 1, ed, RW. Reiber & AS. Carton.,pp. 39-288. New York: Plenum Publishing Corp.

Wertsch, J. (1985). *Vygotsky and the Social Formation of Mind*. Cambridge,MA: Harvard University Press.

———(1992). *Voices of the Mind*. Cambridge, MA: Harvard University Press.

Wilson, A. (1995). Mapping the minds of relational psychoanalysis: Some critiques, questions, and conjectures. *Psychoanalytic Psychology* 12:9–29.

———Malatesta, C. (1989).Affect and the compulsion to repeat: Freud's repetition compulsion revisited. *Psychoanalysis. & Contemporary Thought* 12:243–290.

———Weinstein, L (1992a). An investigation into some implications for psychoanalysis of Vygotsky's views on the origins of mind: Psychoanalysis and Vygotskian Psychology, Part I. *Journal of the American Psychoanalytic Association* 40:357–387.

———(1992b). Language and the clinical process: Psychoanalysis and Vygotskian Psychology, Part II. *Journal of the American Psychoanalytic Association* 40:725–759.

Wood, D., Bruner,J. & Ross, G. (1976). The role of tutoring in problem-solving. *Journal of Child Psychology and Psychiatry* 17:89–100.

IV. The Epigenetic Assessment Rating System (EARS)

CHAPTER 14

EARS ADMINISTRATION AND
SCORING MANUAL

I. Introduction

The Epigenetic Assessment Rating System (EARS) is an instrument designed for psychoanalytically informed personality research. As its name indicates, the EARS is based on a hierarchical, epigenetic approach to the organization of personality. Described simply, hierarchy in this context refers to the fact that multiple levels of a system coexist, while epigenesis refers to the correlation among those levels. These concepts will be further described below. Unlike many common assessment techniques, the EARS relies on the clinical inference capabilities of the researcher, rather than the measure itself. In this way, the EARS serves to bridge a gap between the needs of the researcher and those of the clinical analyst.

One way to bridge psychoanalytic practice and psychoanalytic research might be found in the development of an empirical technology that allows researchers to measure their variables of interest in a manner similar to how psychoanalysts listen and respond to their patients. That is to say, the clinical inference process of the rater doing research and the analyst can be identical, thereby not seeking to squeeze the in vivo ambiguities of the clinical focus out of the basis of the research enterprise. Far too much research seeks to limit or minimize the role of the rater, making the measure rather than the person and his/her clinical skill the object of reliability and validity claims, thereby inevitably distancing it from most pragmatic concerns of the clinical analyst. We have sought to reach for what to me is this necessary, if not sufficient, goal of studying the clinical inferences of the rater, rather than a measure in the Epigenetic Assessment Rating System (EARS), an empirical approach to the identification of levels of dimensions of psychic structure. The EARS is actually a way of explicating a usually implicit clinical inference making procedure. It formalizes and truncates the analyst's task of inference making in the clinical situation.

The developmental continuum upon which the EARS is based was first formulated by Gedo and Goldberg (1973) and later by Gedo alone (1979, 1981, 1984). In these publications, Gedo showed the value of organizing data from various clinical settings into modes of organization, each of which correspond to key developmental acquisitions. The system itself focuses on 10 specific dimensions of psychological functioning which are organized at 5 developmental modal levels of personality structure. Utilizing such a model for the EARS makes it possible to integrate data from therapy sessions with data from other situations.

Epigenesis serves as an overarching theoretical principle connecting many different areas of research. Epigenetic principles account for developmental change with four underlying assumptions: 1) the predominant level of personality organization depends upon the psychic structure formed out of the successive transactions between the individual and the environment; 2) the outcome of each level of organization depends upon the prior outcome of each previous level; 3) each higher level of organization integrates the lower levels under a new principle of regulation; 4) each level is defined by its own emergent properties. These 4 principles will be more fully discussed in Section II. Implicit in this definition of epigenesis is the view that once a given level of organization has been integrated into a higher level, the lower level remains available as an adaptive or maladaptive strategy for functioning. In this way, lower levels remain contained within, and can therefore influence, higher level psychological processes.

The EARS accounts for five broadly conceived epigenetic levels of personality organization, which are called "modes." The ten personality dimensions measured by the EARS are the following: affect tolerance, affect expression, personal agency, centration-decentration, threats to the self, defenses and defensive operations, empathic knowledge of others, use of an object, adaptive needs, and temporality. General features of these modes that are common to all ten dimensions as well as specific features of the modes will be discussed in detail in Section III of this manual.

The EARS is designed to be applied to narratives. What constitutes a narrative can be broadly defined, as a unitized speech sample. There are many kinds of narratives. Initially, the EARS was developed to be utilized in conjunction with a subject's response to the cards of the Thematic Apperception Test (TAT). The design of the EARS makes it possible to use other types of narratives as well. For example, five-minute monologues, Luborsky's Relationship Anecdote Paradigm Test, early memories, and therapy transcripts have been subsequently used.

The EARS is designed to be sensitive to both the thematic and structural aspects of a narrative and allows the various dimensions of psychological functioning to be assessed according to their developmental level. Important properties of a narrative are present in both the content of the story and the form in which it is presented. These are referred to as the thematic and structural features, respectively. The manner in which narratives are constructed reflects crucial aspects of personality organization (Mandler and Johnson, 19XX), which correspond with particular levels along the developmental continuum of the EARS (Wilson and Passik, 1993).

Any subject's personality functioning will be organized at multiple modal levels, although one mode often predominates. It should be noted that personality as reflected in modal level is quite situationally determined. In particular, the degree of arousal present will determine whether the organization tends to be progressive or regressive. In instances where environmental and internal demands are minimal, a subject should have access to his or her most efficient developmental strategies. In contrast, under conditions of high arousal, it is likely that regressive strategies will be employed. The EARS, used concurrently with the clinical acumen of the researcher, is constructed to detect these shifts in organization. Thus, the EARS makes it possible to study the overall developmental patterns of personality functioning for various populations. These and other aspects of administering the EARS will be discussed in Section IV of the manual. In addition, the central issues of reliability and validity will also be reported in Section V.

The EARS can also be utilized to evaluate progressive and regressive shifts along ***particular*** personality dimensions on a moment-to-moment basis as different intrapsychic and/or environmental demands are placed on the subject. In effect, the EARS can assist a clinician in determining which specific components of the personality are most stable or unstable under different conditions.

Inherent in the construction of the EARS is a sensitivity to early developmental modes of organization, which is another feature distinguishing it from traditional assessment tools. Through metaphor, polysemy, prosody, and other rhetorical tropes, the EARS can assess the psychological period predating language—the preverbal period. Examples of how the presubjective realm is scored, and complete scoring instructions, including a tutorial, are presented in later Sections of this manual.

II. The Modes

This section will describe the principles that correspond to each of the modal levels, the rationale behind a hierarchical, modal system, a brief description of the five modes of the EARS instrument, and the rationale for a developmental continuum.

The EARS is based on the assumption that an individual will constantly fluctuate in the developmental level of their personality functioning, with an increasing ability to functionally differentiate between self and other as a standard of this development. This model is organized in a hierarchical arrangement of development. Development is organized at five levels or "modes" which correspond to basic principles in development. Each mode is further characterized by a typical problem and an all-inclusive goal. The distinguishing feature of each modal level can be seen to roughly correspond to the following levels of personality organization: the primary problem of a Mode II might be the disruption of self-cohesion, while at Mode III the primary problem might be the persistence of illusions. The object relation of Mode III might be idealization/devaluation, while at Mode V it might be appreciation of the actual relationship. These descriptions illustrate the developmental pattern that emerges one of increasing differentiation, increasing independence and increasing reality testing.

This model also assumes an inherent interdependence between modes. The principle of epigenesis is proposed as a framework. Epigenesis is a metatheory of development specifying the way in which transformations occur between levels of organization. Epigenesis has been used by theorists interested in models of development in the psychological sciences as a way of conceptualizing a superordinate principle that explains movement from psychobiological to more explicitly psychological functioning (Wilson & Passik,1993). To briefly summarize the biological view of epigenesis, it has these distinct tenets: 1) a casual sequence of interactions exists between organism and environment; 2) earlier and more undifferentiated structures in the organism interactions exists between organism and environment and cause more differentiated structures to unfold in the organism; 3) these structures unfold in a series of levels, stages, or modes; 4) these structures come to possess increased levels structures come to possess increased levels of complexity and differentiation, and organization; 5) particular "emergent" qualities characterize each new level. Thus a particular level of mode: 1) is characterized by a specifiable degree of complexity and differentiation of structure; 2) possesses certain emergent qualities; 3) denotes particular interplay between the organism and the environment; and 4) casually relates to all past and future modes through the nature of successive transactions that reorganize structure and experience. This leads to a primary focus on the transformational properties and principles of structure and a secondary focus on content, or the phenomena that is undergoing transformation. One advantage of this approach is that we can understand the changes in mental life that have both qualitatively continuous and discontinuous qualities.

One must extrapolate from biology to psychoanalysis in order to find concrete application of this metatheory of development. We adduce several additional derivative postulates that characterize the importance of epigenesis for psychanalytic theory, in particular; 1) the formation of psychic structure is a result of successive reorganizing transactions between the child and the caregiving environment, each of which can be termed as a "mode"; 2) the form of structuralization of each mode of organization depends on the outcome of each previous mode and subsequent effects of the experience: 3) each mode integrates previous modes and results in new and more differentiated and articulated levels of organization and regulation; 4) each mode is defined by its own emergent properties. Furthermore, there are two important corollaries to these postulates: 1) once a given mode has been integrated by a higher mode, the more archaic form nonetheless remains as a potential end point of regression, at which time it can become the overriding organizer of experience: 2) lower modes are contained within and can continue to exert influence over higher-order advanced psychological processes despite their having yielded to developmental transformation.

These transformational principles add a breathtaking complexity to how analysts can model the process of internalization, taking us far beyond psychosexual and cognitive metaphors. Epigenesis provides a potential blueprint for the ontogenesis of the mind in relation to both endogenous and exogenous forces. Dimensions of psychic structure can be seen as subject to more or less constant regressive and progressive influences. Regression and progression are constant aspects of clinical reality, as a person can assess structures at virtually any levels, and at any moment. Any pattern of habitual action becomes accessible under the tax of regressive influence. The nature of the mind is now of a different sort that analysts customarily depict—it is far more fluid and momentarily reactive. This psychic structure view departs from Rapaport and Gill (1967) and Kernberg's (1975) definition of structure as stable and slowly changing, and it supports Loewald's (1960) view the analysand through volatile cycles of regression and progression, always turning into their present state, always offering analysands the sense that regression can be met and that higher states are available and even realized. In this way, new and less deceiving reality beckons. Through psychoanalysis one spirals forward and upward as one works through conflicts and internalizes insights. This movement forward is thwarted if the ability to internalize is compromised. The analysand, limited in his ability to internalize, is unable to reach higher developmental levels. Thus, it is imperative that the analyst consistently and carefully examine an analysand's capacity to internalize throughout the analytic hour so that decisions can be made about the transference positioning.

This model also assumes that personality organization is fluid and subject to regressive and progressive shifts in response to biological, psychological, and environmental factors. Thus, an individual may function at any modal level depending on internally or externally generated conditions of stress or arousal. Relative to a given situation, an individual's personality functioning will be organized at a mean modal level. Presumably, instances where adaptational demands are minimal, an individual will be able to function at the most efficient developmental level they have acquired. Conversely, when the integrity of the personality organization is threatened, it is likely that some regressive strategies will be employed. The EARS method detects such shifts and postulates that regression will be the automatic result of high arousal.

Thus, these qualities are encompassed as the basic structure for the five modes which are described below:

Mode 1 refers to a biologically driven "action self" in which there is little distinction between self and other and the primary feelings states are pleasure and unpleasure. Overstimulation is a primary threat.

Mode II may be understood as a transitional period between sensorimotor and imagistic representations in which others are "separate but attached" and are experienced solely in terms of their ability to provide basic needs. Affect states are highly polarized as good-bad. The primary threats are situations of separation, issues of autonomy, and intrusiveness.

Mode III may be understood as a period in which proper positioning of the self with the object world as the superordinate task. Self-enhancement and the maintaining of self-esteem are the main concerns. The disruption of wishful illusions is the primary threat.

Mode IV is a period characterized by oedipal conflicts in which moral anxieties around issues of competition and self-assertion dominate. Primary threat is the anxiety resulting from intrapsychic conflict.

Mode V is a period characterized by healthy, reality-based resolution of conflict. Creativity and generativity are the basic needs. Real dangers are perceived as the primary threats.

The EARS divides the continuum of development into two basic areas: the "presubjective" which is the earlier phase prior to the development of symbolic representation, and the "subjective," which suggests a sense of self based on developmental acquisitions such as language, separation responses, and relational phenomena. In keeping with the epigenetic construct, early preverbal life will have a profound impact upon the content and development of later psychic structures. Thus, the five modes can be separated into a presubjective and subjective areas. Modes I and II are considered presubjective, while Modes III, IV, and V are viewed as the subjective modes. This places great emphasis on the developmental differences (a developmental break, if you will) between the Modes II and III, suggesting critical lack of development in areas of self-other differentiation as a separation to these modes. The five modes of the EARS system can now be incorporated along ten personality variables or "Dimensions", discussed in the next section.

III. The Dimensions
Psychological Dimensions Assessed by the Narrative

Dimension 1: Affect Tolerance

Tolerance is a formal dimension of affective life. The way in which a person manages their affective arousal can take many forms. Through development and early socialization, a person comes to possess characteristic ways of tolerating emotions. These range on a continuum from highly unsocialized and immature forms to sophisticated and mature forms. Characteristic of immature forms is the avoidance of unpleasure and dedifferentiation and somatization of affects. Highly polarized affective states would characterize a midrange form. States that include either a strong or muted tone, and the integration, modulation, and acceptance of the nuances of one's emotional life may characterize mature forms of affect tolerance. In the creation of a narrative a person must confront the affects that the stimulus evokes. The response will depend upon an individual's ability to tolerate emotions. A subject's ability to modulate affective arousal will shift depending on the meaning each story has for the individual. These shifts provide useful diagnostic information, as they suggest how the subject reacts to and tolerates different kinds of affective arousal across degrees of stress.

Mode I: The subject's response indicates an extreme intolerance for affect. This may be displayed in either the subject's reactions to the story or in the story's content. Persons may be prone to explosive outbursts or impulsivity. Affects may be discharged through direct action designed to avoid unpleasure. Affective states are characterized by rapidly fluctuating and fragmented affect states.

Mode II: Due to fragmented responses, the cohesiveness of the narrative may suffer from the subject's attempt to keep contradictory affects apart. The subject's response indicates polarized affect states which may be highly charged with minimal affect tolerance. The responses may reflect an oscillation between extreme positive and negative affective experiences. In the story, the resulting manifestations of affect may be confused, bland, glib, logically fluid, or idealized/grandiose.

Mode III: Affects may be either euphoric or dysphoric without any underlying rage or destructiveness. The subject's response indicates a basic integration of opposing affects. Either positive or negative affects predominate. Though the non-dominant affects are minimized, they are still present. It may be that the tolerance for another's affect is through projection linked to one's own affect.

Mode IV: The subject's response indicates a simultaneous conscious representation of multiple affective experiences. This simultaneous representation produces conflict and anxiety but is tolerated. These affect states do not impede problem solving and working towards a resolution of the conflict.

Mode V: The subject's response indicates an acceptance of conflictual affect states. Acceptance of such conflictual states leads to the creative management of these affects, and the person is comfortable and at peace with what he or she is feeling.

Dimension 2: Affect Expression

Affect expression is a dimension that identifies how an individual's emotions come to play a role in a communicational matrix with others. Thus, affects as understood in a bidirectional communicational matrix requires two vectors: from self to other and from other to self. Whereas affect tolerance reflects how an individual handles emotion that are incoming – directed towards the self, affect expression reflects how an individual handles emotion that are outgoing – directed towards others or objects. The narrative a person creates will exemplify one's affective experiences. Their intensity and differentiation are clues to the typical ways in which a person expresses emotional states.

Mode I: The subject's narrative indicates global and undifferentiated affects organized around unpleasure or overstimulation. Discrete affect states are not yet differentiable from the experience of global unpleasure. Affects are undifferentiated and fragmented and can serve to obliterate the experience of the self. Sleeping or expressions of rage may be examples of actions expressing unpleasure or its relief.

Mode II: The subject's narrative indicates discrete affects in highly polarized and charged form. These affects stem from a disruption of self-cohesion. The typical affects expressed in this mode may be helplessness, primitive guilt which is manifest in a sense of badness of the self, rage which is destructive to self and other, free-floating anxiety, and positive feeling that has as a basis a fundamental need-gratifying dependence on others.

Mode III: The subject's narrative indicates affects stemming from illusory beliefs about the self or other. The typical affects expressed in this mode may include: the emptiness coming from failed grandiose aims, anger over others' noncompliance, idealized love and affection, pleasure in self-importance, and hypersensitive reactions to criticism such as vindictiveness and envy.

Mode IV: The subject's narrative indicates any full range of affects and diverse affect states may contradict one another. The typical affective experiences of this mode may be loss of self- esteem, guilt over failure to live up to expectations, joy taken in achievement and competition, conflictual love or eroticism, jealousy, or feelings about ego-ideal ambitions and conflicts. The respondent may express anxiety-provoking but modulated forms of anger, sadness, or other ambitions.

Mode V: The subject's narrative indicates affects stemming from the tolerable frustrations and conflicts of consciously lived experiences. The typical affective experiences of this mode tend to be acceptable and ego-syntonic. Mature forms of grief, anger, sadness, happiness, joy, and love, are all handled with an acceptance and wisdom appropriate to the situation at hand.

Dimension 3: Personal Agency

In classical psychoanalysis, the concept of "drive" was used to describe a motivational impetus. In the dimension of personal agency, we likewise strive to depict human motivation. In the EARS, motivation can be understood in the light of the developments informing a sense of self that emerges in a narrative production. Personal agency is one's cognitive architecture. Domains of selfhood are laid down in infancy and childhood and once in place exert influence upon self experience throughout one's development. Thus, levels of motivational constructs can be conceptualized. Earliest forms of self experience are based on sensorimotor action patterns, i.e., "I cry therefore I am." Over the course of development, action patterns are replaced by later constructs based upon attachment or of "being-with-others", and the motivation underlying the self is relationally defined. Still later, the self becomes capable of the revolutionary step of language usage. More refined and complex verbal representations lead to a quality of autonomy and self initiation. The highest forms of motivation are based on a person's abillity to integrate the three levels (action, iconic or image, lexicality).

Mode I: The self is an "action self." Others tend not to be implicated in the narrative. It is behavior rather than any sense of another's' inner life that defines the narrative description. The person is defined primarily by the physical activity or behavior in which he or she is engaged.

Mode II: The self is conceived as a "self-with-other." The sense of agency derives from one figure's intense connection to others. Many variations define an "intense connection" – for example, the self may be defined in opposition to an undesirable other or through an identification with an idealized other. However, both the self and other appear to have no lasting and sophisticated psychological qualities. One person helps organize the inner experience of another, and in the absence of the regulating person, action and behavior are chaotic. The interaction between self and other overrides an enduring sense of the psychological qualities of the self.

Mode III: The self may be conceived of as an "imagistic self." The sense of agency is mainly contingent upon fantasized images rather than a realistic appraisal of limitations and abilities. Stereotypic, exaggerated, or skewed images provide for a sense of agency. The response may be bound to the images perceived or the fantasies engendered, so that there is a certain inflexibility to perception and thought. What often underlies these images is the idealized other or the grandiose self, although many other possibilities exist.

Mode IV: The self may be conceived of as a "lexical self." Words paint a picture and the conflict is between the ideas expressed. Distance is the primary conveyer of a narrative of life and self. Words are not preempted by actions or images. There is a rich freedom from the image or fantasy. Conflict is rich and can be multi-thematic. In situations of stress or conflict, the lexical capacity can serve the function of compromise formation. A rich sense of personal agency emerges from the communicative flexibility afforded by the reliance on words as an advanced representational system. Interpersonal communication is usually between the self and complex, differentiated others.

Mode V: Responses are marked by flexibility and creativity. There is an acceptance of the self's strengths and limitations and an integration of actions and images with lexical representations. Under stress, this flexibility is not lost or compromised.

Dimension 4: Centration-Decentration

Centration-decentration is a dimension involving a person's ability to distinguish between the psychological life of self and other. A person's ability to see the world through another's point of view will depend, on a large part, on how decentrated they are and the extent to which others count in their way of viewing the world. Some processes of human development are the steady movement from extreme egocentrism to a more mature sense of one's place in the world. At mature levels, one can gauge one's place in the world realistically and have an appreciation and understanding of the subtlety of others. A healthy acceptance marks this mature understanding of one's own strengths, weaknesses, uniqueness, and ordinariness. Thus, at the highest level, centration and decentration are well balanced. At the lowest levels, the self is so expansive and egocentric that there is no delineation between self and other; the expansive self becomes all one can see. The way in which characters respond to each other and the subject's ability to distance oneself from the narrative are indications of the level of decentration. The level of decentration will shift according to how much defensiveness and arousal exist.

Mode I: The subject's narrative indicates there is no differentiation between the psychological life of self and other. The boundaries between self and other are weak and permeable. Others cannot exist as separate psychological entities because the self expands to allow no room for others to coexist. Responses may be marked by a confusion between one's sensations and perceptions and another's sensations and perceptions.

Mode II: The subject's narrative indicates his or her "place in the world" is characterized by a struggle over either enmeshment or flight from external control. Forging a basic identity among powerful others is a fundamental concern. Self-regulation is also an overarching concern, such that regulation of one's sensations, tensions, and actions are seen as the responsibility of others.

Mode III: Narratives are characterized by an overemphasis on the self. One's own world is understood in some detail and nuance while other's worlds are understood in less detail. The interpersonal world may be experienced as threatening or innocuous. Other's possessions may be regarded with envy, or one might see Pollyannish representations of cooperation and bliss without any sense of interpersonal discordance.

Mode IV: The subject's narrative is indicative of conflict and struggle surrounding one's proper and realistic place in the world. This conflict may take the form of tensions involving aggressive strivings alter achievement, competitiveness, jealousy, or feeling guilt over these strivings. One is not seen as the center of other's worlds but rather existing among well-differentiated others.

Mode V: The subject's narrative indicates an integrated and mature acceptance of one's place and status in the world. The characters have the capacity to attain their goals and values while realizing the proper import of these goals. Others goals and values are accepted regardless of the person's value system. There is a comfortable acceptance of self and other.

Dimension 5: Threats to the Self

Threats to the self is the dimension that examines which internal and external dangers are perceived as threats by the subject. There is important diagnostic information in assessing these threats, especially when measured against a subject's typical coping mechanisms. Besides the objective threat presented by a given situation, there are subjective perceptions of threats that a person's choice of neurosis has generated. They will perceive an internal or external reality situation as essentially threatening depending on the person's sense of vulnerability and ability to cope adaptively. They reflect this in the reading each subject makes of the dangers depicted in the story. We can define the nature of threats to the self along a continuum. Whereas, in early stages of development, loss of self poses as a pervasive threat, in later stages of development objective loss and failure to live up to one's goals or expectations emerge as the primary threats.

Mode I: The primary threats to the self are failure to regulate tensions. Responses are marked by a preoccupation with overstimulation, physical discomfort, annihilation, and loss of the self.

Mode II: The primary threats to the self are the loss of a self-regulatory other or of being overwhelmed by an intrusive other. Physical discomfort and overstimulation are construed in terms of this loss.

Mode III: The primary threat to the self is feeling small in relationship to dominant others, deflation, or disillusionment. This is defended against through contempt of others or holding an inappropriately overvalued sense of self. Threats may ensue from strict and unyielding adherence to rigid value systems and may be expressed through fears of others' aggressivity, badness, disapproval, criticism, etc.

Mode IV: The primary threat at this level if loss of love as opposed to loss of an object. The failure to love up to one's goals and expectations are characteristic of this mode. Complex social relations such as competition, jealousy, envy, guilt, or frustration may provide threats in this response. The fear of regression may also be represented as a particular threat in this response.

Mode V: Threats may take may forms in the response but they are manageable and realistically perceived. Threats relate to one's ability to creatively and adeptly manage stressful situations as they arise.

Dimension 6: Defenses and Defensive Operations

Defensive operations can be imagined along a continuum of increasing sophistication and adaptive value. Defensive operations are designed to modify or ward off unpleasure, anxiety, and information that threaten the stability of the self. Defenses are assigned a mode based on the predominant operations that minimize threatening states in a narrative. Early defensive operations are characteristically action oriented, i.e., crying or screaming as opposed to mature defenses that are more sophisticated verbal/symbolic ones, i.e., humor. The particular occasion for the emergence of defensive operations is important information for understanding how a person will defend himself.

Mode I: The primary defensive operations is discharge through action with the goal of returning to a preferred state of tension. Crying, screaming, and violent activity all serve to restore equilibrium. An example may be represented in such statements as, "he cried until he fell asleep." This discharge is accomplished without recourse to others.

Mode II: The primary defensive operation involves a splitting off of unpleasurable states into all good and all bad domains which remain unintegrated. The results are primitive forms of idealization/devaluation, deanimation/reanimation, delusional projection, lack of constancy, grandiosity, and denial. The pleasure/unpleasure dichotomy is difficult to integrate.

Mode III: The primary defensive operations serve to protect self-enhancing illusions against threatening aspects of reality. This may occur through disavowal, avoidance, minimization or diffusion which serve to distort or nullify aspects of reality which the individual finds threatening to his or her self-concept.

Mode IV: The primary defensive operations serve to create compromises between emotions, attitudes, and behaviors with an explicit or implicit concern for propriety. One may confront disagreeable situations and feelings with repression, rationalization, intellectualization, successful reaction-formations, moralization or mild self-punitive gestures. Dilemmas are resolved through minor inhibitions of thought and action.

Mode V: The primary defenses are flexible and not disruptive to selfhood or inhibiting of social expression. Interests and humor may be examples of Mode V defensive operations that result in adaptive conflict resolution.

Dimension 7: Empathic Knowledge of Others

Empathic knowledge is the dimension interested in the way a person understands another. Throughout development the ability to know other people and to empathize with them evolves. Early in life, contagion of affect is the basic element of empathy. Thus, when one baby cries in a nursery, neighboring babies will cry also. The child has no understanding of the basis of the affect. Later, one learns to understand others based on stereotypic functions and roles, and later still as individuals with separate psychologies and perspectives. The narrative a subject creates will reveal his level of empathic knowledge of others through the way characters' understanding of one another and the way he understands the structural qualities of the story's hero.

Mode I: There is no description of internal mental states depicted in the response. People are only understood in terms of their external physical characteristics and empathy is expressed only as a contagion of affect or action without further elaboration of internal states.

Mode II: People are recognized as somewhat separate, and internal states are understood solely on the basis of external characteristics. The internal states of others may be perceived in global terms, i.e. pleasure versus unpleasure or good versus bad. Since the internal world of the other is not differentiated, there may be a tendency to characterize the other through one's projections.

Mode III: People and their internal states are stereotyped according to function or role. There is some recognition of the inner life of others but it is not recognized as rich or complex. Self-gratification may provide the basis for selective empathy, which is the knowing of selective parts of the other. This selective empathy can at times result in a stark contrast between the psychological understanding of the need gratifiers who in the narrative are well understood and the peripheral characters who are less understood. Characters in the story are known largely for their capacity to gratify basic needs and those who cannot gratify these needs are not worthy of the empathic effort.

Mode IV: Others are understood as having a relatively independent and rich psychological existence. External characteristics, function, and internal states can be combined in the understanding of people but there is a failure to fully integrate contradictory elements.

Mode V: Others are understood and accepted as having an independent and integrated psychological existence. Both enduring and changing qualities of the individual are woven into the response.

Dimension 8: Use of an Object

There is a developmental range of object relationships beginning with the use of an object for the sole purpose of stabilization through self-enhancement, through mutual enhancement of both parties and leading to collaborative relations. Interpersonal relationships evolve during development from basic dependency through mature intimacy. In truly mutual and mature relationships, they subsume lower level functions and go on in silent fashion. Under conditions of disturbance or stress, they may concentrate interpersonal relations on lower level uses of objects in a person's life. The interpersonal relationships in a person's narratives reflect his typical use of objects and patterns of interpersonal contact. This will be seen also in the subject's use of the examiner and relationship to the hero of his story. Interesting comparisons can be made between the way a subject uses objects and the way he understands them.

Mode I: The response indicates a solely physical use or representation of the object to enhance the self. There is no enduring use of people beyond continuous physical processes. The onset of traumatic overstimulation or displeasure preempts any further use of objects.

Mode II: The object is used for or the self is enhanced by a life-sustaining parasitic, need-gratifying relationship, or objects are avoided because they threaten a fragmentation of self-experience.

Mode III: The object is used for or the self is enhanced by realistic or unrealistic feedback in the service of self-esteem maintenance or regulation. Thus, the object may be minimized or avoided in the pursuit of the maintenance of primary illusions.

Mode IV: Objects are used for or the self is enhanced by healthy competition, nondestructive rivalry, allegiances, ambitiousness, mature intimacy, or pedagogy. Some interpersonal relationships may be restricted to protect against anxiety-provoking conflict.

Mode V: The object is used unselfishly for the enhancement of others as well as the self. This is attained through sustained, co-operative relationships leading to a mutual gain and satisfactions. Interactions with objects may be restricted to avoid impinging upon others autonomy.

Dimension 9: Adaptive Needs

Understanding a person's most pressing needs is important diagnostic information. It can indicate the form of therapeutic intervention most consequential at a given moment. There are various levels of need which individuals' evidence in their attempts to adapt to the demands of their environment. A person's narrative will help the interpreter to formulate what the subject's most pressing needs are, both in the subject's overt reactions to the card and within the narrative itself. Life-sustaining and life-enhancing needs are characteristic of a mature level and the need for regulation of inner tensions are characteristically lower levels needs.

Mode I: Subjects narratives are characterized by the need for regulation of inner tension. Such needs might concern temperature, feeding, soothing, respiration, etc. The intensity of these needs tends to make one oblivious to possible internal or external sources of relief or comfort.

Mode II: The primary need indicated in the narrative is for a self-regulating other. There may be a clinging or life-sustaining dependence upon parents, friends, lovers, or treasured objects for enlivenment and/or the soothing of inner tensions.

Mode III: The subject's narrative indicates a need for a realistic self-enhancement and adaptive feedback form the world, especially concerning illusions, grandiosity, and the regulation of self-esteem. This enables one to position the self vis-a vis others.

Mode IV: There is a need for the synthesis of conflicting aims and values through insight, explanation and perspective taking. This allows for the entertainment of conflicting motives which opens up the possibility of adaptive gratification.

Mode V: The subject's narrative indicates a need for mature intimacy and creative expression. Opportunities to realize these needs are actively sought. The needs focus more on life-enhancing than on life-sustaining issues.

Dimension 10: Temporality

A person's ability to form a continuum of time is an important aspect of his or her cognitive ability to make sense out of the events in his or her world. With a clear and separate sense of past, present, and future, a person can order ambitions, aims, and events easily and most importantly be able to infer causality in an accurate manner. However, when logic no longer dominates, distinctions between past, present, and future are compromised and temporality is lost. Confusion and panic can follow. At high levels of arousal, defensiveness, and wishful thinking are some of the factors which can cause an ordered time to be compromised. This process can be reflected in the subject's narratives. The degree to which the narrative is structured by a clear sense of time with the inclusion and integration of past, present, and future will indicate his ability to construct a time-ordered world.

Mode I: No time continuity is present in the subject's response, either due to the absence of a concept or past, present, or future or because they are confused. The primary time organizer is the termination of a state of discomfort.

Mode II: Time is distorted in relation to activities or affective states. Thus, time may be rapidly fluctuating or standing still. The temporal organization of the response may be vague, nonsequential, or discontinuous. When a respondent is prompted to incorporate past, present, or future, he or she is unable to adequately meet the demands in terms of a substantive response or a more integrated temporal continuum.

Mode III: Past, present, and future are accessible but the accuracy of time is compromised. This may be because of the interference of pressing needs. Answers may reflect disproportionate emphasis on past, present, and future or the response may demonstrate the capacity for daydreaming or reminiscence. Past, present, and future may be filled when the subject is prompted. Answers may also be marked by the present as the most important and the past and future not given much importance. In this case, past and future are tacked on, usually when the subject is prompted to do so.

Mode IV: Past, present, and future are included in the answer, usually without prompting, and time is realistically represented in the answer. The response may indicate a general facility with time, although minimal distortions are easily corrected. Such minimal distortions are clearly motivated by conflictual or disturbing dynamic concerns rather than structural impairments.

Mode V: Past, present, and future are accurately and realistically included in the response. The response shows a rich evolution of time within the story, subjective and objective temporality can be compared, and there is a rich fluidity of time in the story. Time can be used in such a way that a narrative can fold back upon itself in the service of reflectivity.

IV. Administration

The EARS scoring system is applied to narratives. In the initial reliability and validity studies, a narrative was defined as an individual's verbal and nonverbal responses to the Thematic Apperception Test (TAT) stimuli. Multiple studies were done using the TAT as the primary stimuli (Keller and Wilson, 1993; Houston, 1993; Miele, 1994; Feldman and Wilson, 1998; Menos and Wilson, 1998; Scarpellino, 1999; Robinson, 1999; Camlibel, 1999). Other studies revealed the strength of the instrument's use in other narrative construction forms such as Luborsky's Relationship Anecdote Paradigm Interview (Faude, 1991), five minute spontaneously generated monologues (Passik, 1990), early memories and holocaust memories (Adelman, 1993), somatic memories (Blaustein, 1995), and psychotherapy transcripts (Kling, 1998; Schack, 2000). Thus, a variety of narrative forms can be scored with the EARS, provided both verbal and nonverbal components of the response process are assessed.

Narratives were chosen as the medium for the EARS because narratives reveal important personality aspects in both story content and its form of presentation. How an individual constructs a narrative can reflect crucial aspects of his/her personality organization. The act of constructing a narrative can be viewed as an analog of a specific style of mental functioning. It reveals distinctive features of an individual's psychological life. The EARS provides an empirical system for developmentally identifying these psychological features.

Obtaining narratives does not require an understanding of the EARS. Once the narrative is constructed, however, rating the narratives along the ten EARS psychological dimensions requires a particular expertise. To rate psychological processes using the EARS, the ten EARS psychological dimensions and its five modal levels must be understood. Once the fundamental nature of these dimensions and their developmental progression are understood, a rater can then assign scores to each of these psychological dimensions based on the narrative produced. This can be done only if the narrative is complete and it contains each of the dimensions in some form. Since these dimensions are central to human experiencing, they are generally found in narrative construction and have been consistently found in certain psychological techniques designed to tap narrative construction (Wilson and Passik, 1993). For example, during the administration of a TAT, an individual is asked to conceive and articulate a story about a presented picture. A trained administrator asks questions that tap the thoughts and feeling of the characters as well as temporal aspects of mental functioning. Once the narrative is constructed, expert raters evaluate it. These raters assign a modal score (I-V) to each of the ten psychological dimensions. Consensus scores are given for each dimension. The consensus scores are a subject's EARS scores for that particular narrative. Please see the scoring section for scoring examples and dilemmas.

V. Reliability and Validity

For the purpose of investigating EARS validity and reliability, we initially sought a situation affecting the environmental and intrapsychic conditions that a subject faces when creating a narrative.

We, therefore, required our subjects to respond to TAT cards that were judged by consensus to possess high and low arousal stimulus properties. Three practicing clinicians selected the high and low arousal TAT cards. The three clinicians ranked Card13-MF - a man standing with a downcast head buried in his arm, while behind him is the figure of a woman, naked to the waist, lying in bed- as the most arousing card. They ranked card 1- a young boy pondering a violin on a table in front of him- as the least arousing card. We then chose to present these cards to subjects with the task of constructing a narrative under two different arousal conditions. (see Ehrenreich {1991} for empirical support of the gradients from most to least arousing TAT cards).

Presenting subjects with high and low arousal stimuli allowed the examiners to observe a subject's regressive and progressive shifts in their narrative construction strategies along the epigenetic continuum for each dimension included in the EARS. Wilson, Passik, and Kuras (1989) further discuss the selection and preliminary research supporting the high and low arousal continuum.

Inter-rater reliability

The reliability of the EARS scoring system is presented in inter-rater reliability form because it does not lead to automatic underestimation and, thus, validity, encountered with other reliability forms (Wilson, et al., 1989). Split half or alternate form reliabilities are not appropriate because one cannot predict equivalent halves or forms of TAT stimuli that will hold up across subjects. Internal consistency is not applicable because TAT stimuli present highly heterogeneous content. Test-retest reliability is no applicable because the constellation of themes competing for expression on the TAT changes from time 1 to time 2, while nevertheless condensing the same underlying motives.

The first reliability trials begun with four graduate students in clinical psychology following a series of readings, discussions, and practice protocols supervised by the senior author. Of the four students, one was considered "advanced" (internship level) and two were "beginners" (pre-clinical master's level). In addition to the training mentioned above, all had been involved in the preparation of a training manual for the scoring of EARS dimensions. Each student was given a 3 card TAT protocol (Cards 5, 10, 15) to score and were blind to the fact that it had been obtained from a hospitalized schizophrenic man. Thus, each student provided 30 judgments (10 per card). We set the criteria for qualification as an expert rater at the following level: 90% of the judgments had to be between +1 and -1 scale point with a minimum of 50% exact matches, all compared with those of an already qualified expert rater. The results of this first trial fell slightly short of our criteria for satisfactory inter-rater reliability. Overall, 82 % of the judgments fell between +1 and -1 scale points with 45% exact matches. However, only the two beginning level students had failed to qualify as expert raters. Following the discussion of the protocols, and further training and rewriting of the EARS items with the lowest degree of agreement, all the raters were given the same TAT protocols (5, 10, 15) of another patient. All were again blind to the diagnostic status of the respondent, in this case a hospitalized borderline patient. The results of this second trial met our criteria for expert rater status for each of the four raters. Pearson Product-Moment correlations of the scores provided by each rater ranged from .85 (the beginning student) to .92 (the advanced students). Final Spearman-Brown Coefficient of Reliability scores, which provides an average of pairwise correlations, were calculated for the entire set of raters. This coefficient was .88, supporting the high inter-rater reliability capable of being obtained on the EARS after training.

The current expert rater qualification criterion is as follows: 90% of scores within 1 scale point of an existing expert rater's scores with a minimum of 50 % exact matches. Established inter-rater reliability levels are presented for 5 different uses of the EARS scoring system:

1.) The EARS adaptations for TAT narratives (EPI-TAT)
Wilson, Passik, and Kuras (1989) report Pearson Product-Moment Correlations of scores provided by raters ranging from .85 for beginning level graduate students to .92 for advanced level graduate students. A final Spearman Brown Coefficient of Reliability scores of .88 was calculated for the total set of raters.

2.) The EARS adaptations for the Relationship Anecdote Paradigm Interview (EPI-RAP)
Faude (1991) reported exact agreement ratings of 64% and ratings deviating by one modal level at 96%. Furthermore, 62% of the scoring disagreements fell between modes 1-2, 3-4, or 4-5, and not between modes 2-3, the pivotal point between presubjective and subjective levels of functioning.

3.) The EARS adaptations for Five-Minute Monologues (EPI-LOG)-Validity
Wilson, et al. (1989) demonstrated factorial validity for the psychological dimensions measured for the EPI-TAT. Each of the ten EARS psychological dimensions were shown to be independent, measuring different components of personality functioning. A principal components analysis, using twenty variables representing the ten psychological dimensions crossed with two levels of arousal, from an aggregated 80 subject data set, was performed using varimax rotation. Each dimension appeared with a high loading on one component (between .533 and .866) and less salient loadings on

other components (.366 or less). The principal components analysis yielded evidence that the twenty dimensions were largely orthogonal to each other, consistent with the hypothesis that there are twenty constructs being measured (ten psychological dimensions by two levels of arousal).

A principal components analysis was also performed for correlations within and across arousal conditions to detect any meaningful differences in data distribution across arousal levels. Median correlations for homogeneous and heterogeneous arousal dimensions calculated for the three studies are presented in order of low-low, high-high, and low-high respectively: Study 1, .447, .654, .348; Study 2, .730, .718, .586; Study 3, .694, .802, .574. While the median correlations vary across studies, the pattern remains the same and the heterogeneous correlations are considerably lower than the homogeneous correlations. This analysis supported the notion of ten independent dimensions of personality organization that can change relative to level of arousal.

VI. Rules for Scoring the EARS

The EARS is scored by analyzing a narrative along ten psychological dimensions. Narratives, for the purposes of this instrument, may consist of transcribed therapy sessions, TAT responses, descriptions of memories, or any other form of thematic verbalization. All ten dimensions are represented in a completed narrative. Each dimension is broken down into five developmental levels, or "modes."

Though the EARS can be a relatively simple instrument to use, there are certain situations that require some guidelines. Situations which may be more problematic in terms of scoring include scoring both the verbal and nonverbal features of a response, being aware of narratives that may contain features of two different modes, and keeping the various dimensions independent of one another during the scoring. The following are guidelines, which should help clear up some of the potential areas of confusion:

Though the "rules" for scoring the EARS will be presented with the TAT narrative in mind, the same rules apply to other types of narratives. For example, in rule #1, there need not be presentation of a TAT card to assess actions as being part of the response: actions during interviews which are gathering narrative data are also considered part of the response. If specified portions of psychotherapy sessions are being used as the narratives under assessment, then both verbal and nonverbal material are considered part of the response.

RULE 1: Just as a clinician sees any action or reaction as a "response," one must also take a broad view of what constitutes a response within a narrative. Any action, verbal or nonverbal, on the behalf of the respondent, following the presentation of the TAT card, then, constitutes a response. A response might be the telling of a story or the refusal/inability to tell a story. We move beyond the words spoken. For example, some patients may become excited or angry upon viewing a card. This becomes part of the scoring. This scoring principle will often be seen on the ADAPTIVE NEEDS dimension, where it will often be necessary to move beyond the manifest content of the story itself to clinical inferences based on the prevailing need states communicated in the entire context of the response.

Thus, if a patient needs to be calmed down in order to begin his or her narrative, this must be figured into the scoring. As can be seen, the dimensions on the EARS must be scored according to the inference skills of the clinician. The person administering the EARS must be conscientious about noting nuances in the response process, especially those not put into words.

RULE 2: For each dimension, the response is scored at a mode based upon attributes projected onto the figure(s) on the card by the subject and by the subject's emotional and verbal/behavioral reactions in responding to the card. Our use of the terms person or people refers either to the respondent or to the figures in the narratives. In this manual, we will use the term "subject" to refer only to the respondent. Also, our use of the concept of "self and other" refers to two types of self/other differentiation:

a) first, differentiation between respondent and the character(s) in the narrative;
b) second, differentiation between characters within the story;
c) third, differentiation between the respondent and the tester.

RULE 3: For an "other" to be seen as influential to a response, he or she does not have to be pictorialized in the narrative. The "other" can be explicit as well as implicit.

RULE 4: Each dimension is conceptualized as being independent of the others and should be scored independently of the others. In order to create a rich, heterogeneous profile of each respondent, one which captures the momentary flux of regressive and progressive aspects of personality functioning, no dimension should be seen as contingent upon any other. It is crucial that the scorer allow for a range of modal levels between dimensions, and not be guided by a pull towards a "regression to the mean" effect (e.g., scoring every dimension within a response as a "3").

V. SCORING OF SAMPLE RESPONSES

Rater training proceeds best when the novice rater is trained by scoring the narratives of normal subjects as well as those of pathological populations.

Raters-in-training seem to become more comfortable and feel that they have a "grasp" on scoring as they produce more heterogeneous scores, and less "collapsing" towards the middle (e.g., beginning to see a variety of scores, and not just all "3's") Most responses, when properly scored, span different modes. Novice raters tend to rate all the scores along one modal level, with insufficient regard for conceptual differences between dimensions.

Examples of narratives and discussion of their scoring

In order to illustrate how different types of narratives can be utilized in the EARS scoring process, three variations of anecdotal material will be presented:

1. A TAT response
2. Excerpt(s) from interviews describing Holocaust memories
3. Depressed subjects' narratives about interactions with others
4. Excerpt from 5-minute monologue describing subjects' parents

Example 1

The following response was given to Card #15 by a 17-year-old male psychiatric inpatient diagnosed with Borderline Personality Disorder and having a history of multiple brief psychiatric hospitalizations. Card #15 of the TAT is described by Henry Murray, who introduced the TAT, as follows: "A gaunt man with clenched hands is standing among gravestones."

"This looks like the cover of a Frank Zappa album. The picture is not even reality wise. This guy is someone who committed a murder and has six months later come to visit the body. He will leave and live happily ever after...He killed his mother, nah, you're not going to say that I want to kill my mother. I'd say this guy has no feelings whatsoever. He is not happy or sad, feels no guilt, maybe feels a slight sense of accomplishment...killing, doing what he wanted to do."

This response received the following EARS scores from an expert rater:

DIMENSION SCORE

Affect Tolerance	II
Affect Expression	II
Personal Agency	I
Centration/Decentration	I
Threat to Self	I
Defensive Operations	III
Empathic Knowledge	II
Use of an Object	III
Adaptive Needs	I
Temporality	III

<u>Discussion of Scoring</u>: The trained rater submitted the following explanation for his scoring: The respondent's narrative has at least three outstanding features.

First, the respondent distances himself from the card through the use of glib, rather facile humor. Given the content of the response, these can be viewed as defensive maneuvers which serve to maintain certain dimensions of his personality organization on a relatively higher level of organization. It appears that by remaining somewhat removed from the stimuli, the respondent is able to maintain some organizational capacities. For example, he is able to frame the response within a time continuum and he is able to extract some self-esteem, albeit even within the context of the figures' rather primitive actions (dimensions scored modal level III).

Second, there are portions of the narrative where the respondent is unable to remain at a distance from his narrative. This inability impacts upon certain dimensions. For example, he clearly identifies with the figure in his response. There is an understanding of the figure he created only through the projection of his own characteristics. Despite sensing that he may be compromising his position by referring to matricide, he states clearly that he assumes a concordance between himself and this figure. Having stated this, it is quickly disavowed as are the negative affect states that conceivably would accompany an act of this sort. His personality organization is alternately maintained through intense attachments to figures in the response and/or avoidance of potentially disrupting experiences (dimensions scored modal level II).

Third, this response indicates that there is another level of organization in the present narrative. On certain dimensions, distancing maneuvers are not functional and his tendency to identify and then avoid are not able to manage some of the adaptational demands. Thus, certain dimensions are organized at a lower level organization, best exemplified by his loss of differentiation between self and other and his tendency to discharge unpleasurable tension through action (dimensions scored modal level 1).

It is important to note that the modal levels of each dimension, though scored at the same level, remain independent. In this example, Personal Agency, Centration/Decentration, Threats to the Self, and Adaptive Needs are all scored at modal level I. This implies that, for this respondent, these dimensions are most vulnerable to regressive shifts. Similarly, the respondent's Defenses and Use of Objects appear to remain at a higher modal level. Therefore, this narrative creates a relatively egocentric psychological world characterized by primitive needs and threats that are managed by comparatively more advanced defensive structure. This, incidentally, corresponds to the clinical picture of this patient as reported by his therapist.

Example 2

The following is an excerpt from a mother-daughter interview, inspecting ways in which the Holocaust experience bears upon the mother-daughter relationship. It involves a mother who grew up in Warsaw and who was 15 years old when the war broke out:

> "At that time - I was alone - I wrote poetry. It just came and I wrote everything down, what came to me. It was a sort of salvation for me. I had, when the war ended, I had a rather large book filled with that, and somehow - I met a friend and she said, "Let me have it, I'll publish it." So I gave it to her and that was the last I saw of it. She lost it somewhere along the way... This was - not possible to reconstruct. I had no more of those feelings I had then and I just didn't remember, it's impossible. No, I lost my language. When I came here I couldn't write, I had no... At that time it was just flowing, I guess, suffering... I don't know, I'm not going to go into it ... You could not duplicate this" (Adelman, p.135).

When these links were severed, her narrative itself was disrupted: her speech became more halting and the flow of the story more disjointed." The author describes Ruth as intense and riveting: "There was poetry to her narrative that went beyond her words, interlaced throughout her speech and the piercing images of her narrative." She was poised, articulate, and graceful. At times she asked that the tape recorder be turned off, and she would gather her thoughts, offer tea, then resume. "The poignancy of her narrative was also interwoven with a hard, remote quality. She displayed little emotion. Her reserve was occasionally disrupted by an unexpected show of feeling - a brittle laugh or sudden, tearless crying. She was cynical and disdainful, expressing low expectations of what the world will bring her or of the inadequate response she anticipates from others."

As Ruth spoke, the author heard tension between her wish to remain matter-of-fact and the sharp undercurrents of intense emotions which she did not articulate. Though she seemed not to want to feel the emotions herself, they were powerfully evoked in the listener. Ruth provided rich detail, sometimes getting lost in the telling of the story, forgetting anyone was listening, "searching inwardly for the links which would reconnect her to the thoughts, feelings, and experiences she had during her experiences in Warsaw. Sometimes in her search, she would come up against the blankness and loss of feeling that she had experienced during the war: 'I had no feelings or no thoughts.' At other times, what she discovered in her looking back were her truncated connections to her past experiences. She found she was unable to rediscover and re-experience what she had felt.

(OR)

"It was an adventure. I was going places. I was afraid I'll miss something at that time...Jewish schools were closed and the air raids were on Warsaw. We left. I was very happy going. After the first day of walking I was less happy. I was tired. My feet hurt. I was thirsty. I saw dead horses laying on the road. And I ran away into a ditch hiding from the planes that were shooting at us. But I never thought I was in any danger. There was adventure. And we slept outdoors. It was terrific. I never slept outdoors before, under the trees...This was a real adventure" (Adelman, p. 136).

The author states: Her memory of the beginning of the war is of an exciting, almost exhilarating sense of escapade. Yet, as she describes her "adventures," what comes through as subtext are the terrifying and harsh conditions that confronted her as a 15-year-old school girl. Although she denies being afraid, her narrative reveals the terror and uncertainty that lay just beneath the surface. It is striking that even in retrospect, she is unable to acknowledge the horrifying reality that confronted her. In actuality, it may have actually felt like an adventure at the time, with the terror becoming real only afterwards. There is thus a broad gap between what she conveys nonverbally and what she is willing to put into words.

(OR)

"I was working at the time... making fabric from threads. First the threads were put on the row, and then this was put on the bar and this was feeding the machine, and machine was making the fabric and the fabric was coming out. Was very interesting. First, I was working when it was going out from spools, and I was watching spools. And there was a man there, making a big roll from the threads. And then one day there was a, they were taking people away, so they took that man. And he said to me, 'You know how to work it, so now you go work this part.' He was standing in the door, and he waved to me, said 'Bye! I'll meet you on the shelf with the soap!' There were rumors that they were making soap out of Jews. But that was rumors. Who believes that? So he made the joke. 'I'll meet you on the shelf with soap.' I don't know whether he survived or didn't. I have no idea. One thing is for sure, I was not on the shelf with soap" (Adelman, p. 139).

The author discusses the dynamics: Ruth's sense of time and tempo of her story fluctuates from lingering over minute details to skipping to the next event. Her emotions are frozen - she becomes grim and impassive, like "an anthropologist commenting microscopically on customs and beliefs that are alien and unfathomable..." Ruth views this period as suspended in time and meaning. Her account of this period is detailed, but lacks a center.

SCORING:

Example 3

The following are taken from a study (Faude, 1991) which utilized the Relationship Anecdotes Paradigm Interview (RAP) in examining depressed individuals on different variables. These are similar to TAT stories, except that the anecdotes that are told by the subjects are not fictional narratives, but are accounts of actual experiences. In order to illustrate scoring examples of the five modes, CCRT wishes that correspond to that modal level are provided:

"Examples of Different Modal Level Wishes Drawn from Subjects' RAP Narratives":

Mode I: "I feel I have to do something. It's like I got to exercise or whatever is going on inside me is just, um, it has just spoiled my whole day. I had to find some way to, um, reach some peace inside myself. So that night—that was the night when I didn't get to sleep for 3 or 4 hours."
(Wish: TO SOOTHE SELF/AVOID PAIN)

Mode II: "If I could—if the others I could leave a cake or cookies or something on the doorstep and leave, okay, and run. I, I feel I can't do that with new people."
(Wish: TO BE CLOSE, YET PHYSICALLY DISTANT FROM OTHERS)

Mode III: "You see, my relationship with V. is such that, um, in the past respect he feels I've tried to control his life. In a sense I was but I was trying to do it in the background."
(Wish: TO HAVE CONTROL OVER OTHER)

Mode IV: "As I reviewed the situation, I was thinking that somebody from downtown should have come out and talked to the parishioners. They owed us that much. I wanted to do something about it but I didn't want to be known as a troublemaker."
(Wish: TO DO THE RIGHT THING)

Mode V: "I wished I would have taken her to lunch and I wished I would've, um, just not pressured her about her son at this point even though he's kind of in a crisis. But she's in a crisis too. I feel kinda sad because I didn't pay more attention to the situation and couldn't respond to her in a more tactful way."
(Wish: TO BE INVOLVED WITH OTHERS/ TO BE CREATIVE AND ATTENTIVE)

Example 4

The following excerpt(s) are borrowed from a study involving subjects who experience chronic physical symptoms (Blaustein, 1995). Cindy is a married female in her mid-20s, whose somatic distress has had a major impact on her sense of herself. Cindy made the following comments about a weekend she had just had:

"'Well, I hope you feel better,' (mother said dropping her off), and then they left. So I kind of felt abandoned, but really they couldn't have really done anything if they would have stayed. But then when (husband) came home, you know, that makes me feel good and so I felt better so, I don't know, it was just kind of strange...I don't know, just, that it, there are so many strange things going on. You know, (husband)'s parents and then my parents and then I've got three brothers and I try to, you know, I'm only there for a couple of days so I kind of like catch up with them so I had, and then the (visiting) student, so it's almost like I have four siblings and then we had this wedding and you know, just feel like I'm being spread out trying to do all that and when I come here and it's just the opposite, you know, I'm by myself and I have nothing to do and I kind of like, I mean I like it today, I feel so much better and I have energy to get things done, but I wish I had a happy medium" (Blaustein, 1995, pp.157-8).

Scoring:

(OR)

Cindy fantasized about the possibility of finding emotional connection through becoming a mother and relating to a baby. At one point, she thought she might actually be pregnant, since her period was late:

"I thought, oh, god, how am I going to tell my mom and ... I mean, I was kind of ... I mean, I don't know ... I didn't ... I was kind of hoping, not hoping but ... I don't know. I've been thinking lately that that would be ... that I want to have a baby and so when that came up, it was ... I didn't know how to feel I guess. Because even if I was happy, (husband) wouldn't be happy and his parents wouldn't be happy and I don't know how my mom would feel (chuckle) you know, so I guess for some reason it didn't really matter if I was going to be happy. It wasn't really the right thing, you know... Just ... I don't know ... just the ... (husband) doesn't really want to you know, he doesn't ... he does ... well he's very uptight anyway, so, if that would be it would just mess up his whole ... you know, plan, and I don't want to cause ... I mean, I don't want to do it on purpose or anything else like that, you know. That would be...." (p. 159).

The author of this study writes: It seems that Cindy had yearnings about becoming a a mother that she couldn't fully share with her husband. Her longing to be closely connected to someone, in the painful absence of that kind of intimacy with her mother or her husband were only hinted at but not openly expressed. Cindy's anger and disappointment expression were rarely full-blown. Her anger came in the form of violent dreams and fragmented presentation of her experiences. She repeatedly broke off her sentences with, "I don't know." She would get very close to expressing herself, then would pull back in silent rage and painful longings for empathic merger.

EARS SCORE SHEET

Subject # _____   Group # _____   Rater _____

Card # _____   Card # _____

DIMENSION	HIGH AROUSAL	LOW AROUSAL
Affect Tolerance		
Affect Expression		
Personal Agency		
Centration/Decentration		
Threats to Self		
Defensive Operations		
Empathic Knowledge		
Use of an Object : :		
Adaptive Needs : :		
Temporality : :		

CHAPTER 15

AFFECTIVITY IN COCAINE AND OPIATE ABUSERS

Psychoanalytic theorists concerned with substance abuse suggest that the affect tolerance and affect expression of addicts are impaired due to preverbal influences. However, psychoanalytic contributions have largely been limited to clinical speculations and case study reports. The present study investigated the hypotheses that opiate abusers will demonstrate more impaired affect tolerance and affect expression than cocaine abusers, and that both groups would appear more impaired than a sample of normals. To investigate these hypotheses, a recently developed instrument, the Epigenetic Assessment Rating System (EARS), was employed. The EARS empirically measures verbal and preverbal phenomena theoretically linked with stages of development. The subjects were 25 opiate, 25 cocaine abusers, and 25 normals, matched according to age, gender, and SES criteria. Results supported the hypotheses that opiate and cocaine abusers' affect tolerance and affect expression were significantly impaired as compared to normals. Although affect tolerance did not distinguish between opiate and cocaine abusers, affect expression did. Cocaine abusers were less impaired than opiate abusers by preverbal modes of affect expression, although under stress cocaine abusers regressed to similar states.

This study empirically investigates affectivity in substance abusers from a psychoanalytic perspective. Psychoanalytic theorists have suggested that the affectivity in substance abusers is profoundly impaired, resulting in a need for self-medication

(Greenspan 1977; Khantzian 1985; Krystal and Raskin 1970; Treece 1984; Wurmser 1974). Based on this point of view, psychoanalytic theorists have proposed that substance abusers use drugs to offset difficulties in tolerating and giving verbal expression to painful affects (Krystal 1975). According to these theorists, substance abusers' affects are experienced as dedifferentiated, overwhelming, and preemptory. As such, affects are difficult to tolerate and, owing to their dedifferentiation, difficult to verbalize. Wurmser (1978) has referred to problems in the verbal expression of affects as "hyposymbolization," whereas Krystal (1987) attributes to this phenomenon a form of alexithymia.

Related to the self-medication theory is the hypothesis that the particular drug selected to modulate affects is not random (Milkman and Frosch 1973). Rather, a "drug of choice" helps the abusers substitute a preferable for an undesirable affect state, based upon an interaction between the pharmacologic effect of the drug and the psychodynamics of the individual. Wieder and Kaplan (1969) have called this the "Pharmacogenic effect." They and others (e.g., Greenspan, 1979; Krystal, 1975) have postulated that such pharmacologically induced affect states serve as correctives for disturbances in affectivity deriving from different preverbal periods of human development.

There is a mounting body of empirical support for the hypothesis of impaired affectivity in drug addicts. Descriptive psychiatric studies have consistently observed the presence of psychopathology in different types of addicts. Among opiate abusers there are high rates of depression (e.g., Berzins et al. 1974; Gossop 1976; Kandel et al. 1978; Rounsaville et al. 1982; Woody et al, 1983) as well as some forms of personality disorder, typically antisocial or borderline types (e.g., Gerard and Kornetsky 1955; Kleber and Gold 1978; Koston et al. 1982; Vaillant 1966). Similarly, numerous MMPI studies (reviewed by Craig,

1979a, 1979b) consistently reveal elevated Depression (D) and Psychopathic Deviate (PD) scales.

The literature on cocaine abusers, though less extensive, reveals trends similar to the findings of opiate addiction. Weiss et al. (1986), Gawin and Kleber (1986), and Runsaville et al. (1991) reported that 50-60% of abusers met criteria for some form of affective disorder. Weiss et al. (1986) also studied personality disorders in their sample and reported that 90% met criteria for some personality disorder, with borderline and narcissistic types predominating. MMPI data obtained on cocaine abusers also tend to reveal the elevated D-PD profile observed in opiate abusers (Helfrich et al. 1983).

The ego psychology approach that employs the Bellak et al. (1973) scales consistently shows that the ego functions most impaired are affect control and object relations (Blatt et al. 1984; Milkman and Frosch, 1973; Treece, 1984). Milkman and Frosch (1973) found opiate abusers' affect control somewhat more impaired than amphetamine abusers. Treece (1984) compared the Milkman and Frosch (1973) data on opiate abusers with norms provided by Bellak et al. (1973) for schizophrenics and neurotics. She found that although heroin abusers' ego functions paralleled neurotic functioning on a number of scales, the drug group's affect control scales duplicated those of schizophrenics. The data from these studies clearly point toward problems in affectivity and object relations in various groups of substance abusers.

Psychoanalytic object relations studies, which emphasize human development with a focus on the preverbal period, also reveal impaired affectivity in addicts. Within this genre, Wilson et al. (1989a) developed a methodology in which projective techniques can be used to investigate affect with respect to substance abuse. They underscore the role of affect regulation and they refer to disturbances in the preverbal realm as "failures of self-regulation." Wilson et al. (1989a, 1990) found that opiate abusers were significantly impaired on a "structural/nonverbal" factor, which has its roots primarily in the preverbal period, where self-regulation is largely influenced by affect tolerance and expression. They also demonstrate that projective techniques are more useful than standard self-report methods for gaining access to preverbal phenomena.

Although impressive, with the exception of Wilson et al., the above-cited studies do not attempt to establish relationships between disturbances in addicts' affectivity and the developmental precursors posited by psychoanalytic theorists (e.g., Khantzian 1985; Krystal and Rasbin 1970). Recent progress in psychoanalytic theory construction has converged on a hierarchical and epigenetic conception for human personality development, which now makes this possible. In a series of papers, Wilson and his colleagues (1989a, 1989b, 1990, 1992) have traced the implications of this epigenetic and hierarchical conception for the understanding of personality and clinical processes. They have adapted a hierarchical conception initially proposed by Gedo and Goldberg (1973) and elaborated by Gedo (1979). The hierarchical model integrates developmental principles and highlights the preverbal period. Gedo (1979) outlines a hierarchical arrangement consisting of five developmental stages, which he calls "modes." Each mode is characterized by a typical problem, an overarching aim/goal, and reflects the successively greater differentiation of the self-organization and the environment. The epigenetic hierarchy assumes that once specific achievements occur within a mode, they are then assimilated into the next mode of development. These achievements are therefore never lost or outgrown but may continue to exert influence throughout the life course. Thus, any individual, regardless of his or her overall level of psychological development, is capable of functioning in any of the five modes.

Wilson's adaptation of the five-mode hierarchy is presented below. Table 1 presents the relevant psychodynamic factors in this theoretical model.

As can be gleaned from Table 1, insights from different psychoanalytic schools of thought pertain more to certain modes than others. Thus, the data of interest to object relations theorists and self psychologists tend to cluster in Modes 1-3, whereas the conflict neuroses with which ego psychology has typically been preoccupied cluster in Modes 4-5. The present model views every individual as capable of functioning at moments in all modes, in that the model assumes an individual's functioning to be a complex shifting balance of various aspects of personality rather than a static entity. For a further elaboration of the theory and details of the modal characteristics, see Wilson et al. (1989b) and Wilson and Passik (1993).

The boundary between Mode 2 and Mode 3, which corresponds to the boundary between presubjectivity and subjectivity, is of special importance. This boundary defines the difference between a self capable of autonomous psychological life and one dependent upon the ministrations of another. In Mode 2, the child depends on another to perform functions that later he or she will be able to perform on his or her own. In Mode 2, the child "thinks" motorically instead of symbolically. Language is not yet available as a source of representational complexity (Wilson and Weinstein 1992). The first two modes are more submerged in a psychobiological, presymbolic, dyadically-based framework. In Mode 3 the child becomes more autonomous and is capable of language and more advanced forms of symbolic mediation. The enhanced representational skills of Mode 3 permit freedom from the constraints and limitations of the preverbal period.

Application of this model to psychoanalytic theories of substance abuse helps integrate various psychoanalytic observations on substance abuse phenomena into a single coherent model.

References to poor affect tolerance and expression (e.g., Wurmser 1974; Krystal 1975; Khantzian 1985) refer to Modes 1-3, wherein affects are regulated and expressed through either nonverbal, self-with-other affective attunements described by Stern (1985), Izard (1977), Greenspan (1979), and Wilson and Malatesta (1989); or in the earliest forms of the representational self and imaginal thinking. Other affective impairments such as the pharmacogenic effect (Wieder and Kaplan 1969), hyposymbolization (Wurmser 1974), and alexithymia (Krystal 1987) also correspond with Modes 1-3. The findings of Milkman and Frosch (1973) fit into this model quite nicely: heroin abusers would be located at Mode 2; amphetamine abusers at Mode 3; neurotics/normals at Modes 4 and 5. Again, the data of Wilson et al. (1989b) on self-regulation in opiate abusers conform with the above scheme since the nonverbal difficulties observed are consistent with Mode 2 phenomena. Even the data of studies from a descriptive psychiatric orientation fit neatly into the framework. Opiate abusers typically manifest borderline or antisocial personality disorders that correspond to Mode 2; cocaine abusers have largely been diagnosed as narcissistic and borderline, which correspond to Modes 2 and 3.

This hierarchical model is adaptable for the purpose of empirical research. Wilson and his colleagues (1989b,1993), in researching their model, have developed an assessment system called the EARS—the Epigenetic Assessment Rating System. One form of the EARS system is called the EPI-TAT, in which TAT narratives are the data base. The EPI-TAT is suited for the investigation of psychodynamic hypotheses regarding substance abuse since two of the variables it assesses are affect tolerance (AT) and affect expression (AE). The EPI-TAT measures three variables in both high and low levels of arousal. This permits an assessment of the degree to which subjects may regress on these psychological dimensions under stressful conditions.

Table 1

MODAL CHARACTERISTICS AND THE DYNAMICS OF ADDICTION[a]

	Presubjective			Subjective	
	Mode 1	Mode 2	Mode 3	Mode 4	Mode 5
Characteristic psychological problem	Overstimulation or traumatization	Disruption of self-cohesion	Persistence of illusions	Intrapsychic conflict	Frustration
Typical danger	Overstimulation	Separation from caregiver	Parental disapproval or sanctions	Moral anxiety	Dangers from reality
Defensive operations	Primal repression	Projection and related mechnisms	Disavowal	Repression (proper)	Renunciation
Affect tolerance	Extreme intolerance	Minimal tolerance	Moderate tolerance	Enhanced tolerance for affects in conflict	Full tolerance
Affect expression	Global and undifferentiated	All-good or all-bad affects	Beginning of integration of complex affects	Broad expression of conflicting affects	Full range of affect expression
Specific depressive experience	Empty bewilderment	Abandonment depression	Self-esteem depression	Guilt-ridden depression	Appropriate grief
Typical function of drug	Drug as mediator of global unpleasure	Drug as mediator of internalization of bad self-with-other representations	Drug as mediator of need for omnipotent control over self and objects	Drug as mediator of oedipal anxieties and object relations	Drug as mediator of actual frustrations and real dangers

[a] Adapted from Wilson et al. (1989b).

The study tested the hypothesis that opiate and cocaine abusers would score significantly lower than normals on the AT dimension of the EPI-TAT. In like manner, it was hypothesized that opiate and cocaine abusers would score significantly lower than normals on the AE dimension. It was also predicted that opiate abusers would score significantly lower than cocaine abusers on these scales.

Because where one scores on the EPI-TAT dimension is of central theoretical importance, it was hypothesized that for both AE and AT, under the low-arousal condition, opiate abusers would score at about Mode 3, cocaine abusers between 3 and 4, and normals at about Mode 4. Under the high-arousal condition, for both AE and AT, opiate abusers were expected to score at about Mode 2, cocaine abusers between 2 and 3, and normals at about Mode 3.

METHOD

Subjects

Subjects were 25 cocaine abusers, 25 opiate abusers, and 25 non-drug-or-alcohol-abusing volunteers who served as normal controls. Subjects were matched for age, sex, and Hollingshead criteria for social class (Hollingshead and Redlich 1958). Substance abusers were patients admitted for cocaine or opiate abuse/dependence at an outpatient substance abuse treatment unit. Normal subjects were recruited as volunteers through ads placed at several northeastern universities, but not all normals were college students. In order to be included in the study, all substance abusers had to: meet DSM-III-R (American Psychiatric Association 1987) criteria for either cocaine abuse or dependence based on psychiatric interviews conducted by the clinical staff; score in the pathological range of the drug abuse scale on the

Millon Clinical Multiaxial Inventory (MCMI-Millon 1983); state that the drug for which they sought treatment was their drug of choice. Subjects were excluded from any of the groups if: an opiate abuser has used cocaine or a cocaine abuser had used opiates within a year previous to treatment; any drug-abusing subject could not achieve at least 1 week of abstinence (to control for effects of withdrawal) or had been in treatment for longer than 1 month (to control for possible confounding effects of treatment); a volunteer in the control group scored in the pathological ranges on any of the MCMI scales (to control for comorbid psychopathology as well as undetected substance abuse). Use of the MCMI drug and alcohol abuse scales was chosen in lieu of a toxological assessment for the normals. Table 2 lists subjects' demographic characteristics and substance use history.

Comorbidity studies with substance abusers suggest that alcohol use may be quite high in cocaine and opiate-abusing populations (Carroll and Rounsaville 1993; Weiss et al. 1988). To control for this possibility, the study utilized the MCMI alcohol abuse scale to classify alcohol-abusing and non-alcohol-abusing subgroups within each of the drug-abusing samples. Fifteen cocaine abusers and 13 opiate abusers scored in the pathological range of the MCMI alcohol abuse disorder scale.

The decision to use normals as controls was based upon the following considerations: Other psychiatric populations are hypothesized to share difficulties similar to those of substance abusers in AT but for different reasons. Although using another psychiatric group might have added more specificity and allowed for finer-grained differences, we do not expect decrements in AT and AE to be unique to substance abusers. Had we hypothesized this, then a psychiatric control group would be vital and necessary. Although we recognize that this is a potential limitation to this study, we note that this problem is one of the thorniest in the

Table 2

SUBJECT CHARACTERISTICS

	Cocaine (n = 25)	Opiate (n = 25)	Normal (n = 25)
Age			
$\bar{x}$	29.3	28.9	28.3
range	19–44	23–45	19–41
Sex			
% male	64	64	64
Positive Substance Abuse Diagnosis			
DSM-III-R	25	25	NA
MCMI	25	25	0
Years of Use			
$\bar{x}$	3.68	3.44	NA
range	1–10	1–8	NA
Route of Administration			
Intranasal	10	1	NA
Intravenous	6	19	NA
Freebase	9	0	NA
Oral	0	5	NA
Positive MCMI Alcohol Abuse	13	12	0

entire substance abuse literature; it is what Khantzian and Treece (1979) called "the diagnostic dilemma for psychiatry."

Instruments

The EPI-TAT version of the EARS (Wilson et al. 1989b), a rating system for TAT narratives, was the primary projective measure of AT and AE. The instrument contains 10 dimensions, along which scores regress and progress within the five modes depending upon personality organization, adaptive capacities, and environmental demands. Thus, anyone is capable of operating in any mode along any dimension as biological, psychological, and environmental circumstances dictate. Since the EPI-TAT is concerned not only with a person's typical enduring modes of functioning—that is, level of personality organization (Kernberg 1976, 1984)—but also regressive and progressive shifts in functioning, the instrument introduces the notion of low-and high-arousal conditions. The instrument assumes that low and high arousal will be correlated with regression and progression, respectively. Low-and high-arousal conditions represent end points between which a subject will regress and progress. In the past, researchers have operationalized arousal level either by a video presentation of scenes of graphic violence, or by presenting electric shocks. We, in contrast, rely upon the perceptual activation of intrapsychic processes, elicited by TAT stimuli. Thus, arousal was operationalized by first polling three senior clinicians, each of whom rated Card 1 the least arousing and Card 13MF the most arousing of the set of TAT cards. Then, this classification was empirically tested for variables theoretically linked to arousal states associated with levels of regression. Ehrenreich (1989) rated TAT cards for directness/intensity of drive experiences and level of defenses. He found that Card 13MF consistently elicited the most drive expressions and was also most consistently "direct/unsocialized," whereas Card 1 had the least drive expressions and also elicited responses that were primarily "direct/socialized" and secondarily "weak/disguised." A statistically significant similar pattern with respect to these two cards held for defenses. For a fuller discussion of the relevant evidence for this construct, see Wilson et al. (1989) and Wilson and Passik (1993).

Interrater reliability for the EPI-TAT has been obtained on several occasions, with raters at multiple levels of professional development. Treating the scale as continuous yields interclass correlations averaging 0.75, with Finn's statistic averaging 0.92. When treating the scale as categorical, Scott's pi coefficients averaged .70. Wilson et al. (1989b) demonstrated factorial validity for the psychological dimensions in a principal component analysis from data pooled from several studies. A second form of validity demonstrated by Wilson and his colleagues involves how arousal level can lead to meaningful differences in how data are distributed. When interdimensional correlations are broken down by arousal conditions, a consistent pattern of results holds up in studies reported by Wilson et al. (1989b). Thus, correlations of low-arousal dimensions with themselves and correlations of high-arousal dimensions with themselves are higher than the correlations obtained when low-arousal dimensions are correlated with high-arousal dimensions.

Because the reliability and validity of the EPI-TAT has not been fully established, we decided to include a reliable and valid self-report measure derived from similar psychoanalytic views. The Toronto Alexithymia Scale (TAS) developed by Taylor, Ryan, and Bagby (1985) was used for this purpose. The TAS is a 26-item self-report inventory. Reliability was assessed with spilt-half and test-retest procedures. The split-half reliability coefficient was 0.672, accounting for 45.2% of the variance. Test-retest reliability for the TAS was r = 0.82, p <0.0001. The TAS has four factors: (1) ability to differentiate affects from one another and from bodily sensations; (2) ability to verbalize affects; (3) ability to fantasize and daydream; and (4) concrete, externally oriented thinking. Each factor is relatively independent of the total alexithymia score. For this study, only the first two factors were used, as they are most applicable to the concepts of AT and AE of the EPI-TAT.

The Millon Clinical Multiaxial Inventory (MCMI) is a 175-item inventory designed to parallel and complement the DSM-III diagnostic system (Millon 1983). It was employed in the present study as a control to ensure that normals did not exhibit psychiatric symptoms, personality disorders, or drug and alcohol abuse.

Procedure

Informed consent was obtained prior to the administration of the battery of instruments. Each subject in the substance-abusing groups was then required to produce a urine sample. Order of administration of the TAT cards and the self-report inventories was counterbalanced across subjects. The self-report inventories were presented in randomized order for all subjects. The TAT cards (1 and 13MF) were counterbalanced to control for order effects. Subjects' responses were recorded by either an advanced clinical psychology graduate student or a doctorate-level clinical psychologist. Examiners also recorded significant nonverbal behaviors, such as changes in tone of voice, affect, posture, movement, and silences that occurred during the test administration.

Before being tested in the study, both cocaine and opiate abusers had to demonstrate they were not currently using drugs or alcohol by producing a negative urinalysis for the presence of all substances. For subjects in the cocaine group, administration of the testing did not occur until at least 1 week after their last use of cocaine so that post-abstinence symptomatology (Gawin and Kleber 1986) had sufficient time to remit. Subjects in the opiate group were not tested until at least 1 week of naltrexone maintenance was achieved.

After testing, subjects were debriefed and provided with an explanation of the study. The principal investigator scored all self-report inventories. TAT narratives were then scored by raters trained on the EPI-TAT scoring system. The study employed two raters, both of whom had achieved expert rater status according to the criteria described by Wilson et al. (1989b). To minimize potential perseverative tendencies to score modes consistently within subjects, different raters scored different dimensions for each subject. The first rater scored Subjects 1-37 for AT and 38-75 for AE. The second rater scored Subjects 1-37 for AE and 38-75 for AT. Thus, the raters scored the data in a counterbalanced manner. Raters were blind to subjects' performance on self-report inventories, group membership, and the hypotheses of the study.

RESULTS

Prior to testing the major study hypotheses, the matching variables (age, sex, SES) were tested to determine if any statistically significant between-group differences existed. One-way analysis of variance (ANOVA) revealed that the groups did not statistically differ in age or social class. A chi-square revealed that the groups did not significantly differ on gender. Tests were used to compare alcoholic with nonalcoholic opiate abusers as well as alcoholic versus nonalcoholic cocaine abusers on all dependent variables. No significant differences were found. Thus, it was decided not to use alcoholism or any demographic variables as covariates.

To analyze the EPI-TAT data, the study utilized a 3 x 2 factorial design (Groups x Level of Arousal). The two EPITAT dimensions were analyzed for statistical significance using a repeated measures ANOVA. Arousal was the repeated measure. Means and standard deviations for the EPI-TAT and the TAS are presented in Table 3. Significance values are presented in Table 4. As predicted, the groups were significantly different in AT. The effect of arousal was also significant. The Group x Arousal interaction was nonsignificant.

Post-hoc Fisher's LSD tests were performed to determine if the overall between-groups main effect derived from differences between normals and substance abusers or if a significant difference between cocaine and opiate abusers existed as well. As predicted, both cocaine and opiate abusers scored significantly lower than normals on AT. However, opiate abusers did not score significantly lower than cocaine abusers as the study had predicted. Means for these groups, however, were in the predicted direction, as seen in **Table 3.**

Table 3

MEANS AND STANDARD DEVIATIONS
FOR NORMALS, COCAINE ABUSERS,
AND OPIATE ABUSERS ON THE
EPI-TAT AT, AE; AND THE TAS

	$\bar{x}$	SD
EPI-TAT		
AT-Lo		
Normal	4.04	0.61
Cocaine	3.64	0.75
Opiate	3.12	0.83
AT-Hi		
Normal	3.40	0.91
Cocaine	2.64	1.07
Opiate	2.48	0.77
AE-Lo		
Normal	3.96	0.73
Cocaine	3.52	0.91
Opiate	2.96	0.68
AE-Hi		
Normal	3.32	0.85
Cocaine	2.72	0.74
Opiate	2.20	0.76
TAS		
Total		
Normal	50.84	10.72
Cocaine	64.20	11.64
Opiate	69.08	12.22
Factor 1		
Normal	19.16	6.86
Cocaine	24.44	6.88
Opiate	27.24	6.73
Factor 2		
Normal	15.16	5.13
Cocaine	17.36	5.38
Opiate	19.84	4.49

Further inspection of Table 3 reveals that mean AT scores for the three groups under low arousal were just below 4 for normals, slightly above 3.5 for cocaine abusers, and slightly above 3 for opiate abusers. These values conform to the predictions of the study. Although the groups dropped in the predicted direction under high arousal, an examination of Table 3 also indicates that only cocaine abusers dropped one whole modal level. Nevertheless, it should be pointed out that whereas cocaine abusers score in the midrange of Mode 3 under low arousal, opiate abusers are located at the lower limit of that mode and are, therefore, closer to the point at which preverbal, psychobiological forms of AT begin to manifest themselves.

AFFECTIVITY AND DRUG ABUSE

Table 4

F TESTS FOR EPI-TAT AT,
EPI-TAT AE, AND TAS

Instrument	F	p
1. *EPI-TAT AT (ANOVA)*		
Groups	10.30	0.0001
Arousal	60.54	0.0001
G × A		NS
Post hoc (Fisher LSD)		
Cocaine vs. Normal		0.05
Opiate vs. Normal		0.002
Cocaine vs. Opiate		NS
2. *EPI-TAT AE (ANOVA)*		
Groups	17.00	0.0001
Arousal	49.79	0.0001
G × A		NS
Post hoc (Fisher LSD)		
Cocaine vs. Normal		0.05
Opiate vs. Normal		0.001
Cocaine vs. Opiate		0.05
3. *TAS Total (ANOVA)*		
Groups	16.72	0.0001
Post hoc (Fisher LSD)		
Cocaine vs. Normal		0.05
Opiate vs. Normal		0.01
Cocaine vs. Opiate		NS
4. *TAS Factor 1 (MANOVA)*		
Groups	9.03	0.0003
Post hoc (Fisher LSD)		
Cocaine vs. Normal		0.05
Opiate vs. Normal		0.05
Cocaine vs. Opiate		NS
5. *TAS Factor 2 (MANOVA)*		
Groups	4.38	0.02
Post hoc (Fisher LSD)		
Cocaine vs. Normal		NS
Opiate vs. Normal		0.05
Cocaine vs. Opiate		NS

Cocaine abusers' performance on AT in the low-arousal condition is about midway between normals and opiate abusers. However, under the high-arousal condition, performance for cocaine abusers declined nearly to the level of impairment demonstrated by opiate abusers. Thus, cocaine abusers' affect tolerance is more sensitive to high arousal than either of the other groups.

The second hypothesis of the study was concerned with the expression of affects in cocaine and opiate abusers compared to normals. As predicted, the groups were significantly different in affect expression as measured by the EPI-TAT. The effect of arousal was also significant. The Group x Arousal interaction was nonsignificant.

Post-hoc Fisher's LSD tests revealed that both cocaine and opiate abusers scored significantly lower than normals on the EPI-TAT affect expression scale. This time, however, as predicted, opiate abusers also scored significantly lower than cocaine abusers.

The three groups' modal levels drop approximately equal amounts under the high-arousal condition. Inspection of Table 3 suggests that modal shifts approximate the predictions of the study: Normals begin at just below Mode 4 (3.96) under low arousal and drop to the lower range of Mode 3 under high arousal (3.33); cocaine abusers begin in the midrange of Mode 3 under low arousal(3.52) and drop to the midrange of Mode 2 under high arousal (2.72); and opiate abusers begin just below Mode 3 under low arousal(2.96) and drop to the low range of Mode 2 under high arousal (2.20). What is impressive about these findings is that opiate abusers' affect expression is strictly confined to Mode 2. In contrast, cocaine abusers only enter Mode 2 in response to arousing, conflictual stimuli. This tendency was apparent but not significant on AT; it comes into sharp relief in terms of AE.

For the TAS, the study employed a one-way ANOVA to test for between-group differences on the TAS total alexithymia score and multivariate analysis of variance (MANOVA) on the two TAS factors. On the TAS total, the groups were significantly different. Post-hoc Fisher's LSD test revealed that both cocaine and opiate abusers were significantly more alexithymic than normals. However, the substance-abusing groups did not significantly differ from one another, though the group means differed in the predicted direction.

On Factor 1 of the TAS—the inability to differentiate emotions from one another as well as from bodily sensations - a MANOVA for the two factors revealed that the groups were significantly different. On post hoc tests both substance-abusing groups scored significantly higher than normals on Factor 1. However, though the means for the cocaine and opiate abusers differed in the predicted direction, they were not significantly different.

TAS Factor 2 estimates the subjects' capacity to verbalize feelings. The MANOVA revealed that the groups significantly differed on Factor 2. In contrast to Factor 1, the post-hoc tests revealed that only opiate abusers scored significantly higher than normals on Factor 2. Although cocaine abusers were not significantly different from either opiate abusers or normals, inspection of Table 3 indicates that the mean for cocaine abusers is about midway between normals and opiate abusers. In fact, the TAS Factor 2 score for cocaine abusers is actually closer to that of normals than opiate abusers.

The overall TAS score significantly correlates with both AT and AE at high and low arousal. Under high arousal, the TAS significantly correlates with AT ($r = 0.338$, $p < 0.005$) and AE ($r = 0.373$, $p < 0.001$). Under low arousal, the TAS significantly correlates with AT ($r = 0.313$, $p < 0.01$) and AE ($r = 0.296$, $p < 0.01$).

These findings lend preliminary support to the construct validity of the AT and AE measures, as a projective measure is cross validated with an objective instrument.

DISCUSSION

The results of the present study suggest affective impairments in both opiate and cocaine abusers as compared to normals, along a number of dimensions. On each of the EPI-TAT affective dimensions—affect tolerance (AT) and affect expression (AE)—both opiate and cocaine abusers were significantly more impaired than normals. Compared to normals, subjects in both groups tolerate and express emotions poorly. In addition, both groups are more alexithymic than normals. These findings lend support to the almost ubiquitous assertion in the psychoanalytic literature that substance abusers suffer profound difficulties in the affective sphere of experience (Khantzian and Treece 1979; Krystal 1975; Krystal and Raskin 1970; Treece 1984; Wieder and Kaplan 1969; Wurmser 1974).

On the EPI-TAT, under low arousal, mean scores for normals' AT were at Mode 4, defined as a level in which multiple affect states may be experienced simultaneously and where conflicting affects may be tolerated consciously. Under high arousal, normals regressed only to the midrange of Mode 3, where some tolerance and integration of opposing affects is still possible, though to a lesser extent. In contrast, both opiate and cocaine abusers' mean AT scores under low arousal were located within Mode 3 and under high arousal regressed to Mode2, where AT is severely compromised. Yet the regression to Mode 2 for drug abusers poses much graver difficulties than the regression to Mode 3 for normals. Mode 2 is defined as a presubjective organization in which affects are highly polarized—that is, organized as either all good or all bad. Affects at this level tend to be experienced as overwhelming tension states, because they are difficult to differentiate from somatic components. As noted, previous research (Wilson et al. 1989b) suggests regression to this level is an indicator of potential severe psychopathology and maladaptation, in part because the person requires the constant presence of a regulating other to maintain equilibrium. Thus, affect regulation in Mode 2 typically requires an other, because self-regulation is not possible. In the absence of self-regulatory capacities or some regulating other, a drug might become necessary as a surrogate.

The above finding is not startling with respect to opiate abusers. Previous studies have repeatedly demonstrated the presence of poor AT in this population (Milkman and Frosch 1973; Treece 1984). Moreover, Wilson et al. (1989a) have demonstrated failures in ability to self-regulate in opiate abusers. However, based on Milkman and Frosch's finding that amphetamine abusers were less impaired than heroin abusers in their control of affects as measured on the Bellak scales (Bellak et al. 1973), the present study had anticipated that cocaine abusers would display similarly better AT than opiate abusers on the EPI-TAT. Although the two groups tended to diverge in the predicted direction, the means were not statistically different.

One possible explanation of the difference between Milkman and Frosch's results and those of the present study is that it arises as a function of the different methodologies employed. Both studies attempt to assess typical levels of adaptiveness, the Bellak via structured interview, the EPI-TAT via low-arousal performance. However, in contrast to the Bellak, the EPI-TAT introduces the dimension of high arousal. In so doing, it attempts to induce a stressful, conflicted emotional state in the subject and observes deviations from typical capacities on each of the dimensions. Thus, the present study assesses AT over a range of conditions. Since the Milkman and Frosch (1973) study did not introduce arousal or something similar in its evaluation of affect control, it becomes problematic to compare their results with ours. If we think of the EPI-TAT low-arousal condition as akin to the conditions in which

Milkman and Frosch (1973) conducted the Bellak interviews, then the means for AT under low arousal in the present study ought to parallel group differences in the Milkman and Frosch study. In fact, group means in AT under low arousal indicate that cocaine abusers were located about midway between opiate abusers and normals, with cocaine abusers slightly closer to normals. These low-arousal results strikingly resemble those of Milkman and Frosch, whose amphetamine sample was located about midway between normals and heroin abusers on the Bellak affect control scale. Although it is problematic to compare group means from different studies using different measures, it seems highly likely that the disparity in the overall findings on AT, as compared to the earlier study, may be accounted for by the use of a high-arousal condition.

Our argument also helps to clarify other findings in the literature on opiate abusers using the Bellak. Treece (1984) found that Milkman and Frosch's (1973) affect control scores for opiate abusers were strikingly similar to those Bellak et al. (1973) found in schizophrenics. Notwithstanding opiate abusers' poor affect control, Treece's data appear surprising because one would expect schizophrenics to be most impaired on this personality dimension. However, if we compare AT in opiate abusers measured by the EPI-TAT with the data of Wilson et al. (1989b) on AT in an inpatient psychotic sample, we find that both groups under low arousal begin at just above Mode 3. Under high arousal, however, opiate abusers regress only to the midrange of Mode 2, whereas psychotics regress to the upper range of Mode 1 (Wilson et al.

1989b, p. 45). Thus, the EPI-TAT clarifies an important relationship because it includes arousal levels. On this basis, we would say that opiate abusers' affect control mirrors that of psychotic subjects under ordinary conditions; however, under the impact of stress, psychotic subjects regress to a far greater degree than opiate abusers.

Both opiate and cocaine abusers were significantly more impaired than normals in AE as measured by the EPI-TAT and the TAS. As with AT, this finding supports numerous anecdotal references in the psychoanalytic literature that substance abusers have difficulty in differentiating affects from one another and especially in verbalizing affect states. More importantly, the present study is the first empirical demonstration of impaired affect expression in drug abusers.

Cocaine abusers were significantly less impaired than opiate abusers on AE as measured by the EPI-TAT. In contrast to AT, all three groups are significantly different on AE. Inspection of Table 3 indicates that under low arousal, cocaine abusers' mean AE scores are located in the midrange of Mode 3, in which rudimentary affect differentiation as well as nascent forms of symbolizing (e.g., the capacity to verbalize) are present. In contrast, opiate abusers, even under low arousal, are already located in Mode 2, in which affects are less differentiated and far less capable of verbalization due to the predominantly psychobiological character of Mode 2 forms of representation. Under high arousal, AE declines for both groups, into the upper-middle range of Mode 2 for cocaine abusers and to the lower range of Mode 2 for opiate abusers. Thus, whereas opiate abusers' difficulties with affect verbalization are already in evidence under low arousal and are exacerbated by high arousal, cocaine abusers maintain their capacity to verbalize affects when adaptational demands are minimal, with impairments only coming into focus in the face of stress.

This finding is paralleled and in part clarified when the alexithymia results are considered. Cocaine and opiate abusers did not significantly differ on TAS Factor 1, which measures the capacity to differentiate emotions from one another as well as from bodily sensations. Both groups were more impaired than normals, though cocaine abusers differed in the predicted direction. However, on TAS Factor 2, which measures the ability to verbalize affects, cocaine abusers were not significantly different from either opiate abusers or normals. Thus, the greater capacity of cocaine abusers to express affects, as seen on the EPI-TAT, is suggested on the TAS, and this hint implies that it is within the verbal sphere.

If the findings on AE are now considered together with those obtained for AT, we see what distinguishes the two groups. Cocaine abusers' greater capacity for verbalization of affects suggests that they are less enslaved to strictly psychobiological forms of affectivity, in which preverbal modes for handling and expressing affects predominate. Though it is true that cocaine abusers, like their opiate counterparts, may regress to Mode 2 forms of AT and AE, it appears that the latter group is more fully submerged within the preverbal, psychobiological domain. In contrast, cocaine abusers have, as it were, one foot in and one foot out of the "psychobiological door."

How are these findings related to the self-medication hypothesis found in the psychoanalytic literature? The findings of the study are highly suggestive that what is being self-medicated by the use of drugs is not limited to the presence of negative affects, though this may often be the case. Rather, the findings suggest that the drug user also self-medicates his/her inability to tolerate and/or express such affects. As these latter capacities become compromised, affects are experienced as diffuse and preemptory. It thus appears likely that the drug abusers' reaction to the presence and intensity of such affects also undergoes self-medication.

There is a plausible rival hypothesis to the above view of self-medication. One might argue that drug abuse is the cause rather than the consequence of personality and psychological variables such as poor AT or underlying psychiatric disorder. This is an extremely thorny issue and very difficult to disentangle. Although a number of theorists and researchers have conceptualized drug abuse as a symptom of underlying psychiatric disorder or developmental deficit (e.g., Klober and Gold 1978; Krystal and Raskin 1970; Wurmser 1974), others have produced evidence to support the idea that drugs themselves give rise to psychiatric disorder (Khantzian and Treece 1979). Until now, this issue has been controversial because of the glaring lack of prospective research that examines this question over time. Recently, however, Block et al. (1988) have reported a longitudinal study in which ego under control of impulses at age 3 was found to be the best predictor of adolescent marijuana and hard drug abuse. This finding complements the findings of the present study. Although it is likely that the use of such drugs as cocaine and heroin diminishes one's ability to tolerate affects, poor affect tolerance appears to be in evidence prior to the onset of addiction. Thus, the issue of causation seems to require an integrated model.

Several avenues of further research are suggested by the positive findings of our study. Because the ability to verbalize affects is a critical aspect of psychotherapy and differentiates substance-abusing groups, it would be worthwhile to study ability to verbalize feelings within the context of psychotherapy of substance abusers and observe the degree to which it influences both the process and outcome of therapy.

Another avenue of research suggested by the study involves the measurement of drug craving. At present, other than simple self-report, no reliable and valid measures of craving exist. The present findings suggest that a craving inventory should include items relating to AT. In addition, our findings suggest that drug craving may be a broader construct than has heretofore been conceptualized in the empirical literature. We suggest that chronically impaired AT interacts with environmental cues in eliciting craving responses (Gawin and Kleber 1986)—the Mode 2 dilemma. Our results also help explicate the concept "apparently irrelevant decisions" (Marlatt and Gordon 1985), which implies that the drug user begins craving the drug without being aware of it. The results of the present study suggest that failure to detect affect states may well play a part in such unawareness.

References

American Psychiatric Association. (1987). *Diagnostic and Statistical Manual of Mental Disorders,* 3rd ed., rev. Washington, D.C.: American Psychiatric Association.

Bellak, L., Hurvich, M., & Gediman, H.K. (1973). *Ego Functions in Schizophrenics, Neurotics, and Normals.* New York: Wiley.

Berzins, J.J., Ross, W.F., English, G.E. & Haley, J. (1974). Subgroups among opiate addicts: A typological investigation. *Journal of Abnormal Psychology* 83:65–73.

Blatt, S.J., Rounsaville, B.J., Eyre, S., & Wilber, C. (1984). The psychodynamics of opiate addiction. *Journal of Nervous and Mental Disease* 172 (6):342–52.

Block, J., Block, J.H., & Keyes, S. (1988). Longitudinally foretelling drug usage in adolescence: Early childhood personality and environmental precursors. *Child Development* 59:336–55.

Carroll, K.M. & Rounsaville, B. (1993). Alcoholism in treatment seeking cocaine abusers: Clinical and prognostic significance. *American Journal of Drug and Alcohol Abuse* 54(2):199–208.

Craig, R.J. (1979a). Personality characteristics of heroin addicts: A review of the empirical literature–part I. *International Journal of the Addictions* 14(4):513–32.

————(1979b). Personality characteristics of heroin addicts: A review of the empirical literature–part II. *International Journal of the Addictions* 14(5):607–27.

Ehrenreich, J. (1989). Psychodynamic aspects of personality and sociocultural identity. Unpublished dissertation, New School for Social Research, New York City.

Gawin, F. & Kleber, H. (1986). Abstinence symptomatology and psychiatric diagnosis in cocaine abusers: Clinical observations. *Archives of General Psychiatry* 43:107.

Gedo, J. *Beyond Interpretation: Toward a Unified Theory of Psychoanalysis.* New York: International Universities Press, 1979.

————& Goldberg, A. (1973). *Models of the Mind.* Chicago: University of Chicago Press.

Gerard, D., & Kornetsky, C. (1955). Adolescent opiate addiction: A study of control and adult subjects. *Psychiatric Quarterly* 29:457–86.

Gossop, M. (1976). Drug dependence and self-esteem. *International Journal of the Addictions* 11(5):741–53.

Greenspan, S. (1977). Substance abuse: An understanding from psychoanalytic developmental and learning perspectives. In J.D. Blain & D.A. Julius, eds., *Psychodynamics of Drug Dependence. NIDA Research Monograph No. 12,* pp. 73–87.

Greenspan, S. (1979). Intelligence and adaptation: an integration of psychoanalytic and Piagetian developmental psychology. *Psychological Issues* 47/48. New York: International Universities Press.

Helfrich, A., Crowley, T.S., Atkinson, C.A., & Post, R.D. (1983). A clinical profile of 136 cocaine abusers. In L.S. Harris, ed., *Problems of Drug Dependence. NIDA Monographs Series No. 41* pp. 343–50.

Hollingshead, A.B., & Redlich, F.C. (1958). *Social Class and Mental Illness.* New York: Wiley.

Izard, C. (1977). *Human Emotions.* New York: Plenum Publishing Corp.

Kandel, D., Kessler, R., & Margulies, R. (1978). Antecedents of adolescent initiation into stages of drug use: A developmental analysis. In D. Kandel, ed., pp.73-99. *Longitudinal Research on Drug Use.* New York: Hemisphere.

Kernberg, O.F. (1976). *Object Relations Theory and Clinical Psychoanalysis.* New York: Jason Aronson.

———(1984). *Severe Personality Disorders.* New Haven, CT: Yale University Press.

Khantzian, E. (1974). Opiate addiction: A critique of theory and some implications for treatment. *American Journal of Psychotherapy* 28:59–70.

———(1976). The ego, the self, and opiate addiction: Theoretical and treatment considerations. *International Review of Psychoanalysis* 5:189–98.

———(1985). The self-medication hypothesis of addictive disorders: Focus on heroin and cocaine dependence. *American Journal of Psychiatry* 142(11):1259–64.

———& Treece, C. (1979). Heroin addiction: The diagnostic dilemma for psychiatry. In R. Pickens & L. Heston, eds., *Psychiatric Factors in Drug Abuse, pp. 21-43.* New York: Grune & Stratton.

Kleber, H.D., & Gold, M.S. (1978). Use of psychotropic drugs in treatment of methadone maintained narcotic addicts. *Annals of the New York Academy of Sciences* 311:81–98.

Koston, T., Rounsaville, B.J., & Kleber, H. (1982). DSM–III personality disorders in opiate addicts. *Comprehensive Psychiatry* 23 (6):572–81.

Krystal, H. Affect tolerance. (1975). *Annual of Psychoanalysis, Vol. 3, pp. 179-219.* New York: International Universities Press.

———Alexithymia and the effectiveness of psychoanalytic treatment. *International Journal of Psychoanalytic Psychotherapy* (1982/83) 9:353–78.

———*Integration and Self-Healing: Affect, Trauma, and Alexithymia.* Hillsdale, NJ: Analytic Press, 1987.

———& Raskin, H.A. (1970). *Drug Dependence: Aspects of Ego Function.* Detroit, MI: Wayne State University Press.

Lichtenberg, J. *Psychoanalysis and Infant Research.* Hillsdale, NJ: Analytic Press, 1983.

Marlatt, A., & Gordon, J.R. (1985). *Relapse Prevention: Maintenance Strate-gies in Addictive Behavior Change.* New York: Guilford Press.

Milkman, H.A., & Frosch, W. (1973). On the preferential abuse of heroin and amphetamines. *Journal of Nervous and Mental Disease* 156(4):242–48.

Millon, T. (1983). *Millon Clinical Multiaxial Inventory Manual,* 3rd ed. National Computer Systems.

Rounsaville, B., et al. (1991). Psychiatric diagnosis of treatment seeking co-caine abusers. *Archives of General Psychiatry* 48:43–51.

———, Weissman, M.M., Kleber, H.D., & Wilber, C.H. Heterogeneity of psychiatric disorders in treated opiate addicts. *Archives of General Psychiatry* (1982) 39:161–66.

Stern, D. (1985). *The Interpersonal World of the Infant.* New York: Basic Books.

Taylor, G., Ryan, D., & Bagby, R.M.(1985). Toward the development of a new self-report alexithymia scale. *Psychotherapy and Psychosomatics* 44:191–99.

Treece, C. (1984). Assessment of ego functioning in studies of narcotic addiction. In L. Bellak & L.A. Goldsmith, eds., *The Broad Scope of Ego Function Assessment,* pp. 47-69. New York: Wiley.

Vaillant, G.E. (1966). A 12-year follow-up of New York narcotic addicts. III. Some social and psychiatric characteristics. *Archives of General Psychiatry* 15:599–609.

Weiss, R.D., Mirin, S.M., Michael, J.L., & Sollogub, A.C. (1986). Psycho-pathology in chronic cocaine abusers. *American Journal of Drug and Alcohol Abuse* 12:17–29.

——————Griffen, M.L., & Michael, J.L. A (1988). Comparison of alco-holic and nonalcoholic drug abusers. *Journal of Studies on Alcohol* 49:510-15.

Wieder, H., and Kaplan, E.H. Drug use in adolescents: Psychodynamic meaning and pharmacogenic effect. *Psychoanalytic Study of the Child* (1969) 24:399–431.

Wilson, A., & Malatesta, C. (1989). Affect and the compulsion to repeat:

Freud's repetition compulsion revisited. *Psychoanalysis and Contemporary Thought* 12:243–90.

———& Passik, S. Explorations in presubjectivity. In A. Wilson and J. Gedo, eds., *Hierarchical Connections in Psychoanalysis, pp. 76-128. New York:* Guilford Press, 1993, pp. 76–128.

——————& Faude, J. Failures of self-regulation. In J. Masling, Ed., *Empirical Studies in Psychoanalytic Theory*, Vol. 3, pp. 149-211. Hillsdale, NJ: Erlbaum, 1990.

——————Abrams, J., & Gordon, e (1989a) A hierarchical model of opiate addiction: Failures of self-regulation as a central aspect of substance abuse. *Journal of Nervous and Mental Disease* 177:390–99.

——————, & Kuras, M. An epigenetic approach to the assessment of personality: The study of instability in stable personality organizations. In C.D. Spielberger and J. Butcher, Eds., *Advances in Personality Assessment,* Vol. 8, 1989b, pp. 63-95. Hillsdale, NJ: Erlbaum,

Wilson, A. & Weinstein, l. (1992). An investigation into some implications for psychoanalysis of the Vygotskian view on the origins of mind. *Journal of the American Psychoanalytic Association* 40:357–87.

Woody, G.E., Luborsky, L., McLellan, A.T., O'Brien, C.P., Beck, A.T., Blaine, J., Herman, I., & Hale, A. (1989). Psychotherapy for opiate addicts. *Archives of General Psychiatry* 40:639–45.

Wurmser, L. (1974). Psychoanalytic considerations of the etiology of compulsive drug use. *Journal of the American Psychoanalytic Association* 22:820–43.

———(1978). *The Hidden Dimension.* New York: Jason Aronson.

———(1987). Flight from conscience: Experiences with the psychoanalytic treatment of compulsive drug abusers. *Journal of Substance Abuse Treatment* 4:169—179.

CHAPTER 16

AFFECTIVE EXPERIENCES AND LEVELS OF
SELF-ORGANIZATION IN MATERNAL
POSTPARTUM DEPRESSION

This study explores the following underlying psychological processes and shifts in personality organization occurring in
postpartum depressed women: (a) the extent to which postpartum
women experience challenges in tolerating, differentiating, and
expressing affective experiences, as well as alterations in their experiences of self and other; (b) the relationship between depressive
severity and the extent to which depressed participants' narratives
are fueled by "presubjective" concerns; and (c) the extent to which,
in postpartum depression (PPD), severity of depressive experiences is associated with affective experiences that are highly
polarized, less finely differentiated, modulated, and integrated.

It has been observed that 30% of depressions in women are
associated with reproduction-related life events (Weissman,
Leaf, & Tischler, 1988). The risk of a psychiatric disorder increases during the postpartum period (Hopkins, Marcus, &
Campbell, 1984). Women are more likely to experience depression following childbirth than at any other time in their life (Cox,
Murray, & Chapman, 1993; Hopkins et al., 1984). Community
surveys have suggested that 80% of depressive reactions following childbirth are undetected and untreated (Gise, 1992; Howell
& Bayes, 1981), which raises concern because it has been found
that, untreated, it tends to recur with subsequent pregnancies
(Melges, 1968) and that it can exert a profound impact on the

child, spouse, and other important relationships (Anthony, 1983; Cogill & Kaplan, 1986; Kumar & Robson, 1984; Robson & Kumar, 1980).

At the beginning of this decade, research on this difficult experience remained minimal (Gruen, 1990). Although there has been some controversy as to whether or not it can be considered a distinct diagnostic entity (Gotlib, Whiffen, Wallace, & Mount, 1991; Hamilton, 1992; Philipps & O'Hara, 1991; Purdy & Frank, 1993; Whiffen, 1992; Whiffen & Gotlib, 1993), recent research has led to its inclusion in the fourth edition of the *Diagnostic and Statistical Manual of Mental Disorders* (DSM—IV; American Psychiatric Association, 1994) as a diagnostic specifier under depression, in contrast to its glaring omission in the revised third edition of the *Diagnostic and Statistical Manual of Mental Disorders* (DSM-III-R; American Psychiatric Association, 1987) (Gorodetsky, Trapnell, & Hamilton, 1992). Studies using stringent diagnostic criteria have revealed a relatively high incidence (20%) of PPD reactions in the mild to moderate range with about half of these cases reaching moderate to severe levels of severity (O'Hara, Rehm, & Campbell, 1982; Paykel, Emms, Fletcher, & Rassaby, 1980).

Research into predictive factors for PPD has not yielded any consensus identifying the germane variables (Hopkins et al., 1984; Kumar & Robson, 1984). Much of the nonepidemiological research on PPD has been correlational in method, focusing on socio-psychological risk factors. Although a plethora of variables have been linked to PPD, several authors have noted the absence of theoretically grounded, empirical research in this area (Brown & Shereshefsy, 1972; Sherman, 1971; Hopkins et al., 1984). Cutrona (1983) pointed out that previous studies examining the role of psychological factors in PPD have assessed a large number of theoretically unrelated variables, leading to potentially spurious correlations. With respect to depression in general, studies examining the relationship between demographic variables and PPD have not yielded consistent associations (Hopkins et al., 1984; Nolen-Hoeksema, 1987). Empirical data focusing on psychodynamic concerns in this area have been sparse (Cutrona, 1983; Greene, 1995; Manly, McMahon, Bradley, & Davidson, 1982; O'Hara, Rehm & Campbell, 1982; O'Hara, 1986). Most dynamically oriented articles have relied on clinical observation and anecdotal reporting, which may be related to difficulties operationalizing psychoanalytic concepts (Abraham, 1955; Benedek, 1959, 1970; Bibring, 1961; Deutsch, 1947; Klein, 1932; Lester & Notman, 1986, 1988; Winnicott, 1958).

Given the tendency to approach PPD from the lens of descriptive psychiatry, from a psychoanalytic perspective, an investigation of empirical gaps in this area suggests the following as worthy of exploration. First, psychoanalysis can usefully study psychological phenomena such as affective concomitants, including affect tolerance, differentiation, and expression. Second, following Benedek (1952), psychoanalysis can approach PPD from a psychobiological perspective (i.e., the extent to which severity of puerperal depressive experience is associated with a developmental level in which psychological and biological concerns are enmeshed). Psychobiological is defined as mental life that is characterized by endowed mental attributes that operate automatically, and although potentiated, are not created de novo, by interactive experiences. Third, self—other differentiation, defined as the evolutionary process through which the dyad develops from a global amorphous unit to a more differentiated and individualized one, has often been described (Bibring, 1961; Mahler, Pine, & Bergman, 1975), but the impact of this process on maternal psychological functioning has not been empirically addressed. Fourth, most psychodynamic perspectives on PPD stress that regression occurs in all pregnant women, which may be experienced as pleasurable or frightening (Domash, 1988; Pines, 1972) and may reactivate early unresolved issues. Several analysts have noted that, with its multiple arousal of old and new thoughts, feelings, impulses, fears, wishes and relational experiences, the puerperium also possesses the potential for tremendous growth and change (Deutsch, 1947; Klein, 1932; Winnicott, 1958).

The variables of (a) affectivity, (b) psychobiological factors, (c) self—other differentiation, and (d) regression are all operationalized in the Epigenetic Assessment Rating Scale (EARS). The EARS uses as a touchstone Gedo and Goldberg's (Gedo and Goldberg 1973; Gedo, 1993) epigenetic model of personality organization, an approach to regressive and progressive movements emphasizing their daily existence in the moment-by-moment flux of mental life (Loewald, 1981; Wilson & Passik, 1993; Wilson, Passik, & Kuras, 1989). In this view, psychological functioning is understood as a fluid, complex, constantly shifting balance of various aspects of personality rather than a static entity. Developmentally earlier modes of functioning continue to exist and are potentially activated under the influence of increased arousal or stress. Psychological shifts can occur in limited areas, with other dimensions maintaining their intactness. Such partial regressions are a normal feature of mental life. Thus, any individual, regardless of his or her overall level of psychological development, is capable of regressive or progressive functioning in any of the modes (or levels of organization) at any one time. The concept of regression, as measured by the EARS, is an important one in this research. The present study was based on the notion that puerperal women are presented with an increased potential for such regressive shifts.

In a series of papers, Wilson and his colleagues (Wilson, Kuras, et al., 1989; Wilson & Passik, 1993; Wilson, Passik, & Faude, 1990;

Wilson, Passik, Faude, et al., 1989; Wilson, Passik, & Kuras, 1989; Wilson & Weinstein, 1992, 1996; Keller & Wilson, 1994; Feldman & Wilson, 1997) have explored the empirical implications of an epigenetic, hierarchical model, consisting of five developmental levels or "modes." Each mode is characterized by a typical problem, an overarching aim or goal, and reflects the successively greater differentiation of self-organization and interactions with the environment. Wilson & Passik (1993) outlined these modes for operationalization through the EARS as follows:

Mode 1 is understood as a presubjective period of development. There is a limited distinction between self and other. Information is encoded in sensorimotor or action-oriented forms. The primary feeling states are pleasure and unpleasure. Avoidance of global unpleasure is the predominant defensive activity. Overstimulation or understimulation are the primary dangers.

Mode 2 is a transitional period between sensorimotor representations and representations encoded in imagistic forms. Significant others are represented as "separate but attached" because they provide for basic needs, such as soothing. This leads to the other being represented in a polarized fashion—good— bad. Intense attachment to or extreme avoidance of others is prominent. The independent volition of others tends to be not understood, and projection is the predominant defensive activity. Separation and issues of autonomy and intrusiveness are the primary danger situations.

Mode 3 is a period in which the proper positioning of the self in relationship to the object is the superordinate task. Self-enhancement and the maintaining of self-esteem are key concerns. A powerful need is the protection of those wishful illusions about both one's and important others' capabilities and capacities, those that support and bolster one's self-esteem. Denial and disavowal are the predominant defensive activities, and the primary danger situation is prohibition from external authority figures. Lexical representational capacities develop and with them a mature communicational ability.

Mode 4 is a period of Oedipal level conflicts. Moral anxieties and derivatives of castration fears are the main sources of threat. Subjectively accessible intrapsychic ideational conflict, especially around competition and self-assertion, is the principal danger. There is guilt over sexuality, but genital sexuality is also desired. The predominant defense activity is repression.

Mode 5 is a period characterized by the benevolent resolution of conflict. Creativity and generativity are the basic needs. Aggression is well contained; competition is not a major threat. There is a sense of containment deriving from one's realistic appraisal of a realistic place and role in the object world. The primary dangers involve undistorted reality factors, and the predominant defensive activity is renunciation. Table 1 presents the relevant psychodynamic factors in this theoretical model for PPD.

For the present study, the boundary between Mode 2 and Mode 3, which corresponds to the boundary between presubjectivity and subjectivity, is of importance. Passing through this boundary defines the difference between a self capable of autonomous psychological life and one being, in a myriad of ways, dependent on the ministrations of another. This boundary marks the transitional point between predominantly psychobiological and psychological aspects of mentation (see Wilson & Passik, 1993).

Table 1

Epigenetic Assessment Rating Scale Organization and Dynamics of Postpartum Depression

Variable	Mode 1	Mode 2	Mode 3	Mode 4	Mode 5
Postpartum dyadic feature	Psychobiologic undifferentiation	Overidentification or disengagement	Individuation yoked to maternal self-esteem	Greater differentiation accompanied by conflict and anxiety	Awareness of complex other: conflict handled as further growth
Typical danger	Over- or understimulation	Separation from caregiver	Parental disapproval or reprimand	Moral anxiety	Dangers from reality
Depressive experience	Empty bewilderment	Abandonment	Self-esteem fluctuation	Guilty self-condemnation	Appropriate grief
Personal agency	Action self	Self determined by interaction	Imagistic self	Lexical self with compromise formations	Flexible agency with acceptance of strengths and limitations
Affect tolerance	Extreme intolerance	Minimal tolerance	Moderate tolerance	Enhanced tolerance for affects and conflict	Full tolerance
Affect expression	Global and undifferentiated	All good or all bad affects	Beginning of integration of complex affects	Broad expression of conflicting affects	Full range of affective expression
Optimal intervention	Pacification	Unite disparate self-experience	Optimal disillusionment	Interpretation of ideational conflict	Empathic witness to introspection

In this study, dimensions of personal agency, affect tolerance, and affect expression are scored using the EARS system. Each of these dimensions is scaled at 5 modal levels, as can be seen in **Table 1.** The three dimensions are now explicated: Personal agency refers to the underlying motivation that characterizes an individual's actions, the architecture of a sense of self, ranging from actions and enactments at a low level, through imagistic representational skills at an intermediate level, and finally reaching higher levels of lexicality. Affect tolerance refers to an individual's ability to manage an ever-widening array of deeply felt emotions. The way in which a person manages affective arousal, ranging from highly unsocialized and immature forms (e.g., simple avoidance of unpleasure and dedifferentiation and somatization of affects) to a mid-range (where one-sided and highly polarized emotional experiences predominate) to more mature modes (in which the nuances of one's emotional life are largely integrated, modulated, and accepted). *Affect expression* refers to an individual's ability to communicate emotionally encoded information to another, that is, how an individual's emotions play a role in a communicational matrix with important others. The affects expressed, including their intensity and their differentiation (global or specific), are indications of a person's level of affective ties to others.

To help explicate the EARS, what follows is a sample of a narrative of the Thematic Apperception Test (TAT; Murray, 1943) Card 1 provided by a 19-year-old woman diagnosed with anorexia nervosa, along with an explanation of the scoring of this narrative along the three dimensions scored in this study.

> The . . . before the picture . . . the kid . . . someone told him to do his homework. At the time of the picture, he is studying his homework and feeling that it is not what he wants to be doing, and, after the

picture, he leaves and feels that he has not studied enough and should have done more (Should have done more?) I don't know why, he doesn't know why, but he knows that wasn't enough. (Enough?) It wasn't enough unpleasurable activity doing his homework. (Feeling?) Guilty after the picture because he hasn't done enough."

Affect tolerance is scored here at Mode 2. The response does not show the extreme intolerance for affect that characterizes Mode 1, but it should not be considered a Mode 3 response, because positive and negative affects are not both present, even in rudimentary form. Instead, there is only a bland and illogical feeling of guilt and displeasure, which indicates that there is only the minimal affect tolerance, characteristic of Mode 2.

Affect expression is also scored at Mode 2. The expression of affect shows some minimal differentiation, but the full range that is expected in the higher modes is not present. The affects expressed are helplessness and primitive guilt, which is distinguished from the guilt characteristic of Mode IV by the lack of strong or conflicting emotions. Instead, the guilt is vague and has no apparent connection to the situation depicted.

Personal agency is also scored at Mode 2 because in this response the self is not an "action self" of Mode 1 but shows some ability to define itself in terms of its thoughts and feelings. However, the self and other depicted are vague and determined solely in relation to each other.

In this study, differences between postpartum depressed women, postpartum nondepressed women, and controls along the dimensions of personal agency, affect tolerance, and affect expression, as operationalized by the EARS, will be explored. It was hypothesized that regression would occur in all women under conditions of stress, more severely with the clinically depressed postpartum women, and least severely with the control participants. Operationally this suggests that postpartum depressed women's narratives would be characterized by the lowest scores on these dimensions and the controls by the highest.

METHOD

Participants

The sample consisted of three groups: two postpartum groups (within 1 year after delivery) and one control group. Participants in a first group ($n = 29$) were postpartum women with elevated scores on the Beck Depression Inventory (BDI; Beck, Ward, Mendelson, Mock, & Erbaugh, 1961; above a score of 9). Postpartum women in the second group[1] ($n = 27$) scored between 0 and 9 on the BDI. These participants were recruited from Depression After Delivery (a national self-help organization) support groups and mailing lists, postpartum support groups (in hospitals and birthing centers), breast-feeding support groups, obstetricians and gynecologist (OB/GYN) private offices and baby exercise classes (only 4 participants were recruited from the latter). To control for the potentially confounding factors of teenage or single motherhood, postpartum women were eligible if they were married and older than 20. The third group ($n = 28$) consisted of women with scores below 9 on the BDI who had never given birth and were not currently pregnant. They were recruited from OB/GYN private offices and small businesses. An independent group t test showed no significant differences between the postpartum groups with respect to number of children.

---

[1] Usually the cutoff score on the BDI that suggests clinical depression is held to be 10. However, we eliminated one item from the inventory, which taps recent weight loss. Therefore, we changed the clinical cutoff score to 9.

The subjects' demographic characteristics by group are presented in Table 2. The groups are largely homogenous on all variables except for marital status, where both postpartum groups of women were required to be married, although this was not the case for the control group. Because epidemiological characteristics do appear to be relatively well balanced across the three groups, heterogeneity was not considered a threat to external validity. In previous studies of age (Blair et al., 1970; Pitt, 1968), social class (Hayworth et al., 1980; Kendell, Chalmers, & Platz, 1987), and educational level (Hopkins et al., 1984), there has not been any significant relationship between these variables and PPD.

Participants were recruited to obtain an overall sample of 90 participants to ensure sufficient power ($p = .80$; $\alpha = .05$) so as to detect medium level effect sizes (Cohen, 1977). The research began with 99 women. Ninety-two participants returned their questionnaires, 7 did not. There was no difference between the groups in return rate—2 participants in each group did not return their questionnaires; 1 control returned her questionnaire too late to be included in the analysis. Eight of the women recruited as controls were eliminated from the study due to their elevated (>9) BDI scores, leaving a final total of 84 women.

Instruments

Epigenetic Assessment Rating Scale (EARS). The EARS rates 10 psychological dimensions along five epigenetically defined modes of personality organization. It can be applied to any narrativized speech sample. When used with TAT narratives, the two TAT cards suggested for use that capture the extremes of levels of stimulus arousal are Card 1, depicting a young boy contemplating a violin that rests on a table in front of him, and Card 13 MF, depicting a

Table 2
Personal and Demographic Characteristics by Group

	Postpartum depressed participants (n = 29)				Postpartum nondepressed participants (n = 27)				Controls (n = 28)			
Characteristic	M	SD	N	%	M	SD	N	%	M	SD	N	%
Participant age	30.8	5.0			33.2	4.2			31.6	5.7 (F = 1.70)		
Infant age	7.5	3.6			6.9	3.5						
Income (thousands)	78.3	61.9			66.4	29.0			68.5	52.0 (F = 0.43)		
Ethnicity												
White			26	89.7			23	85.2			22	78.6
African American			2	6.9			2	7.4			2	7.4
Hispanic			1	3.4			1	3.7			2	7.4
Asian			1	3.4			2	7.4			2	7.4
Marital status												
Married			29	100.0			27	100.0			15	53.6
Single			0	0			0	0			13	46.4
Educational level												
High school graduate			4	14.3			2	7.4			0	0.0
Some college			2	7.1			4	14.8			2	7.1
College graduate			13	46.4			10	37.0			10	35.7
Some graduate school			2	7.1			0	0.0			7	25.0
Graduate degree			7	25.0			11	40.7			9	32.7
Husband's educational level												
High school graduate			5	17.2			2	7.4			0	0.0
Some college			9	31.0			3	11.1			1	6.7
College graduate			5	17.2			7	25.9			8	53.3
Some graduate school			1	3.4			2	7.4			0	0.0
Graduate degree			9	31.0			13	48.1			6	40.0

Note. For the participants, χ^2 (8, N = 84) = 15.1, p = .058; Kruskal-Wallis test, χ^2 = 2.93, p = .23. For their husbands, χ^2 (8, N = 71) = 14.7, p = .065; Kruskal-Wallis test, χ^2 = 5.21, p = .074.

man standing with a downcast head buried in his arm, while behind him is the figure of a semi-clothed woman in bed. Cards 1 and 13 MF were consensually judged by three practicing clinicians ranking a full set of TAT cards to depict the least and most arousing situations, respectively (Wilson & Passik, 1993). The sensitivity of the EARS to shifts in the predominant mode of responding from low- to high-arousal conditions, as exemplified in Cards 1 and 13 MF, has been repeatedly demonstrated (Wilson & Passik, 1993). Increased arousal is produced by heightened degrees of perceptual ambiguity and sexual or aggressive stimuli, and generally results in regressive response modes. High arousal stimuli have been empirically demon-strated to present greater adaptive and integrative challenges to the individual's personality and to cause a regressive shift in adaptive strategy (Feldman & Wilson, 1997; Keller & Wilson, 1994; Wilson et al., 1989). In terms of empirical support for the concept of levels of arousal for the particular TAT cards, Ehrenreich (1989) examined and rated multiple TAT cards and rated them according to intensity of drive experiences and levels of defense exhibited, both of which are theoretically associated with degree of regression. Card 13 MF con-sistently elicited the most drive expressions, and Card 1 had the least drive expressions. A similar pattern held for defenses exhibited.

Wilson and Passik (1993) have presented factorial validity de-fining independence of the dimensions for the EARS in the following manner. The results of three earlier studies were aggre-gated to form one larger data set. A total of 20 variables (10 psychological dimensions crossed with the two arousal levels) were used in a principal components analysis and rotated to vari-max criterion. Each dimension appeared with a high loading on one component (between .533 and .866), whereas the remaining dimensions on a given component appeared with loadings of .366 or less. Although each dimension in and of itself could not define a factor, a principal components analysis revealed that the 20 dimensions were relatively independent of each other.

High interrater reliability on the EARS has been demonstrated after intense training in the underlying theory of the scale, along with practice sessions. To qualify as an expert rater, we required that 90% of judgments be within 1 scale point, 50% of judgments be exact matches, and an overall intraclass correlation of at least .80 when used with continuous variables, compared with judg-ments produced by an already qualified expert rater.

Affects Balance Scale (ABS; Derogatis, 1980). The ABS is a multidimensional self-report adjective mood scale that assesses positive affect, negative affect, and the difference or "balance" between the two. It is a 40-item adjective checklist that has participants indicate the degree to which they experienced the 40 emotions (half positive and half negative) under consideration during a designated time frame (in this case, 1 week). This study will use the Positive Score Total and the Negative Score Total.

BDI. The BDI was used as the primary measure of depressive severity. Studies of PPD suggest that it is sufficiently similar to other forms of depression to be assessed with the same measures (Paykel et al., 1980; Pitt, 1968; Saks, 1985).

Procedure

Prior to the administration of any assessment procedures, each participant was given a consent form explaining that the study involves an exploration of how women, at different stages of life, think and feel about themselves and others. The consent form described the study and the procedures involved. Women were told that their data would be coded with numbers rather than names to protect their confidentiality. One individual assessment session was held for each participant. At this time, two TAT cards (1, 13 MF) were administered by an advanced-level graduate student. The TAT cards were presented in counterbalanced order to control for sequencing effects. Responses were recorded verbatim. In addition, any significant nonverbal responses, including change in affectivity, tone of voice, posture, physical movements or silences were recorded. Participants were then provided with a packet containing the ABS and BDI and instructions to fill them out within the next 2 weeks, without consulting anyone about their responses, and return them in the stamped, self-addressed envelope. A telephone number was then provided in case of any post-testing distress.

The women's narratives were scored according to the EARS by three advanced graduate students and one licensed clinical psychologist, trained in the use of this system, having already achieved expert status in reliability trials according to the criteria described by Wilson and Passik (1993). To further test for rater drift during scoring, the four experts rated a common pool of 10 stories, included within the set of narratives scored in the study. The Pearson product-moment correlations for this common pool ranged from .91 to .93, and the Spearman-Brown coefficient of correlation score for the total set of raters was .92. To minimize rater perseveration effects between scores between dimensions, the scorers rated each assigned story on 5 of the 10 dimensions. Half of the subjects' narratives were rated by two of the raters and the other half by three of the raters. Raters were blind to the participants' performances on self-report inventories and group membership.

Results

To examine group differences on demographic variables, a one-way analysis of variance (ANOVA) was used to compare depressed postpartum, nondepressed postpartum, and control women on the interval scale variables of age and annual income. No significant differences were observed among the groups with respect to these variables.

The participant's highest level of education and the highest level of education of her spouse were measured as ordinal categories, ranging from "elementary school" to "graduate degree." *Table 2* presented the cross tabulations of these variables by participant group. The significance of group differences on these variables was assessed by means of both chi-square and Kruskal-Wallis nonparametric procedures. The results indicate no significant differences among the groups with respect to education.

On the basis of the view that regression to preverbal modes of experience is especially problematic for PPD women, it was hypothesized that participants in the PPD group would be characterized by significantly larger numbers of scores at Modes 1 and 2 of the EARS than either of the other two groups. To test the notion that regression occurs universally postpartum, it was further hypothesized that the postpartum nondepressed group would have significantly higher numbers of scores at Modes 1 and 2 than control group participants.

To test this hypothesis, the number of Mode 1 and 2 scores for each participant across the 10 EARS dimensions for each stimulus card was tabulated. Next, a two-way mixed-model ANOVA was run on these scores. The independent variables in this analysis were group, a between-subjects factor, and card, a within-subjects factor. The ANOVA yielded significant main effects due to both group, $F(2, 81) = 7.85$, $p < .001$, and stimulus card, $F(2, 162) = 82.36$, $p < .001$). Post hoc Scheffe contrasts were carried out to determine the significance of pairwise differences among the marginal means of the three groups. These contrasts indicated that the mean score of the PPD group (5.4) was significantly higher than the mean score of the other two groups. However, the mean of the postpartum nondepressed group (3.7) was not significantly higher than the mean of the control group (3.2). In the absence of a significant interaction, it is assumed that these differences apply across stimulus cards. PPD women had significantly more Mode 1 and 2 scores than postpartum nondepressed or control women. However, postpartum nondepressed women did not differ significantly from controls. It was further hypothesized that PPD women would score significantly lower than nondepressed postpartum women and controls on the EARS scores representing affect tolerance, affect expression, and personal agency. It was expected that this would occur across stimulus conditions. To test this hypothesis, a preliminary multivariate analysis of variance (MANOVA) was run to guard against the accumulating probability of Type 1 error, and this MANOVA was followed by univariate analyses for each of the EARS scores.

Table 3
EARS Scores by Group and Stimulus Card and EARS Affect Tolerance Scores by Group and Stimulus Card

Stimulus card	Postpartum depressed participants ($n = 29$)		Postpartum nondepressed participants ($n = 27$)		Controls ($n = 28$)		SS	df	MS	F
	M	SD	M	SD	M	SD				
Card 1	2.8$_a$	0.8	3.4$_b$	0.8	3.3$_b$	0.8				
Card 13 MF	2.0$_a$	0.7	2.1$_a$	0.7	2.5$_b$	1.0				
Marginal	2.4		2.7		2.9					
ANOVA summary table										
Group							10.45	2	5.22	4.98**
Error (between)							85.02	81	1.05	
Card							39.72	2	19.86	54.19***
Group × Card							2.00	4	0.50	1.37
Error (within)							59.37	162	0.37	
EARS affect expression scores by group and stimulus card										
Card 1	2.6$_a$	0.9	3.5$_b$	0.8	3.5$_b$	0.8				
Card 13 MF	2.1$_a$	1.0	2.0$_a$	0.9	2.4$_b$	0.9				
Marginal	2.4		2.7		2.9					
ANOVA summary table										
Group							15.03	2	7.52	7.16**
Error (between)							85.10	81	1.05	
Card							43.04	2	21.52	41.42***
Group × Card							7.02	4	1.75	3.38**
Error (within)							84.19	162	0.52	
EARS personal agency scores by group and stimulus card										
Card 1	2.6$_a$	0.9	3.4$_b$	0.8	3.2$_b$	0.8				
Card 13 MF	1.9$_a$	0.9	2.3$_b$	0.9	2.5$_b$	1.0				
Marginal	2.3		2.8		2.8					
ANOVA summary table										
Group							15.32	2	7.66	4.98**
Error (between)							84.33	81	1.04	
Card							30.93	2	15.46	27.33***
Group × Card							2.43	4	0.61	1.08
Error (within)							91.65	122	0.57	

Note. Groups with different subscripts are significantly different from one another. EARS = Epigenetic Assessment Rating Scale; ANOVA = analysis of variance.
**$p < .01$. ***$p < .001$.

The MANOVA, in which all 10 EARS dimensions were included as dependent variables, yielded a significant main effect due to group, $F(20, 146) = 1.92, p = .015$; a significant main effect due to stimulus card, $F(20, 62) = 8.38, p = .001$; and a nonsignificant interaction, $F(40, 126) = 1.22, p = .207$. These findings provided justification for performing univariate analyses on the EARS variables of interest for the hypothesis, which is reported in Table 3.

All three ANOVAS yielded significant ($p < .01$) main effects due to group and significant ($p < .001$) main effects due to stimulus card. The ANOVA for affect expression also yielded a significant Group X Card interaction, $F(4, 162) = 3.38, p < .01$. In view of the nonsignificant multivariate interaction, however, this univariate interaction was discounted as a possible Type I error.

Post hoc Scheffe contrasts were calculated to determine the significance of the differences between the means of the three groups. With respect to both affect tolerance and affect expression, these contrasts indicated that, in the low arousal condition, the mean scores of both the controls (3.3 on affect tolerance, 3.5 on affect expression) and the nondepressed postpartum women (3.4 on affect tolerance, 3.5 on affect expression) were significantly higher than the mean score of PPD women (2.8 on affect tolerance, 2.6 on affect expression). These contrasts also indicated that, in the high arousal condition, mean affect tolerance and expression scores for the PPD women (2.0 on affect tolerance and 2.1 on affect expression) and postpartum nondepressed women (2.1 on affect tolerance affective dimensions (2.5 on affect tolerance and 2.4 on affect expression). The depressed and nondepressed women mean scores did not, however, differ significantly from each other in this high arousal condition.

With respect to personal agency, in the low arousal condition, the mean score of the depressed group (2.6) on personal agency was significantly lower than the mean scores of the nondepressed and control groups (3.4 and 3.2, respectively), which did not differ significantly from each other. In the high arousal condition, however, the mean score of the depressed group (1.9) was significantly lower than mean scores for both nondepressed (2.3) and control (2.5) postpartum women, which did not differ significantly.

Exploring the overall means scores on the EARS dimensions, it was hypothesized that under the standard high arousal condition, PPD women would score at Mode 2 and that nondepressed and control women would score at Mode 3. The mean for PPD women did fall near Mode 2 in the high arousal condition (with mean scores 2.0 on affect tolerance, 2.1 on affect expression and 1.9 on personal agency). On affect tolerance and affect expression, however, the mean scores for the nondepressed postpartum women was lower than anticipated, with their mean scores closer to Mode 2 than Mode 3 (2.1 on affect tolerance and 2.0 on affect expression). With respect to personal agency, however, the mean score of the nondepressed group (2.3) was significantly closer to the mean score of the control group (2.5) than the mean score of the depressed group (1.9). Although closer to Mode 3, the control participants scored slightly lower than anticipated on these dimensions in the high arousal condition (with mean scores of 2.5 on affect tolerance, 2.4 on affect expression, and 2.5 on personal agency).Exploring the relationship between depression and modal level, it was hypothesized that there would be a significant negative relationship between BDI scores and EARS scores on affect tolerance, affect expression, and personal agency. Correlations were calculated between the BDI and these EARS scores, and are reported in Table 4. Significant negative relationships with the BDI were observed for all three EARS dimensions for Stimulus Card 1 (low arousal condition) and for two of the three EARS dimensions for Stimulus Card 13 MF (high arousal condition). Significant negative relationships with the BDI were observed for affect tolerance, affect expression, and personal agency in the low arousal condition, and for affect tolerance and personal agency in the high arousal condition.

Table 4

Pearson Correlations Between Beck Depression Inventory and Epigenetic Assessment Rating Scale Scores on Affect Tolerance, Affect Expression, and Personal Agency (N = 84)

	Stimulus card	
Variable	Card 1	Card 13 MF
Affect tolerance	−.28**	−.26*
Affect expression	−.31**	−.19
Personal agency	−.28**	−.35***

*p < .05. **p < .01. ***p < .001.

Further exploring the role of affectivity, it was hypothesized that EARS scores on affect tolerance at Mode 3 would be associated with a pattern of scores on the ABS in which the distance between positive and negative affective poles is greater than that found with scores of 4 or 5 on affect tolerance, and smaller than that found with scores of 1 or 2. To test this hypothesis, a different score was calculated by taking the absolute value of the difference between the ABS T score for positive affect and the ABS T score for negative affect. A one-way ANOVA was run on these different scores. The ANOVA was significant, $F(2, 80) = 4.37, p = .016$). Post hoc Sheffe contrasts indicated significant differences between the means of those people who scored 2 or less (22.1), those who scored 3 (14.2), and those who scored 4 or 5 (11.6).

The proportion of participants in each group with positive affect T scores 1, 1.5, 2, and 3 standard deviations from negative affect T scores was tabulated. On the basis of these tabulations,

Table 5 further illustrates the difference between the groups with respect to the extent to which positive and negative affects are polarized.

Discussion

The regressive hypothesis in the postpartum psychoanalytic literature suggests that postpartum women return to earlier modes of functioning in affective, relational, perceptual, and memorial realms, including alterations in their sense of self, a regressive shift that is particularly problematic for women who are depressed postpartum. In support of this view, PPD women had significantly more total Mode 1 and 2 scores across all 10 dimensions measured by the EARS than postpartum nondepressed or control women. At these earlier modes of functioning in which primarily preverbal modes for handling and expressing affects are relied on, affects are communicated somatically and nonverbally, dedifferentiated or avoided when they are unpleasurable. Within this context, the finding of postpartum onset of panic disorder does not appear to be a coincidental event (Metz, Sichel, & Goff, 1988; Spivak, Spivak, & Wistrand, 1993). This finding also lends support for Blum's (1978) observation that the reconstruction of preoedipal precursors is an important component of treating PPD.

Contradicting the traditional psychoanalytic view of the postpartum, the other two groups (the controls and postpartum nondepressed women) did not differ in their total Mode 1 and 2 scores across all dimensions of psychological functioning. Thus, the results of this study suggest that a regression to presubjective realms of psychological functioning does not appear to be a universal feature postpartum, but that it occurs in women who are experiencing problematic adjustments at this time.

Table 5

ANOVA Comparing Modal Groups (EARS Affect Tolerance [AT] Dimension [Low Arousal Condition]) on Distance Between ABS T Score for Positive Affect and ABS T Score for Negative Affect

	Mean difference between positive and negative affect	SD	Distance between positive and negative affect scores			
			1 SD (%)	2 SD (%)	3 SD (%)	4 SD (%)
Participants scoring 1 or 2 on AT ($n = 29$)	22.1$_a$	10.4				
Participants scoring 3 on AT ($n = 33$)	14.2$_b$	11.6				
Participants scoring 4 or 5 on AT ($n = 21$)	11.5$_c$	10.4				
Participants scoring 2 on AT ($n = 21$)			72	52	48	29
Participants scoring 3 on AT ($n = 34$)			53	41	29	0
Participants scoring 4 or 5 on AT ($n = 27$)			44	33	24	0

Note. Groups with different subscripts are significantly different from one another. Analysis of variance (ANOVA) summary for between source: $SS = 1,418.28$, $df = 2$, $MS = 709.14$, $F = 4.38$, $p < .016$; for within source: $SS = 12,957.89$, $df = 80$, $MS = 161.97$. EARS = Epigenetic Assessment Rating Scale.

It was further hypothesized that affect tolerance, affect expression, and personal agency would be vulnerable dimensions postpartum, with a regressive pull for all women during this time. Although this was true for the depressed women, it was not universally true under the low stress condition in which the postpartum nondepressed group looked much more like the controls. Under high stress, however, in the affective dimensions, affect tolerance and affect expression, the postpartum nondepressed group did not differ significantly from the postpartum depressed group in the extent of regression displayed. This suggests that affective tolerance and affective expression are areas of particular vulnerability for all women postpartum in high arousal, or stressful, conditions. Under low levels of stress, a well-adjusted mother appears able to escape the clutches of presubjectivity. Under high stress, she may be vulnerable, particularly in her ability to tolerate, differentiate, and express her emotions.

It is important to stress that in the postpartum, a nonpatho-logical group functions like a pathological group along affective dimensions when under the regressive tax of stress. The control group did not display such shifts, suggesting that the effect is directly related to the childbirth experience. In terms of the regression hypothesis, it can be hypothesized that PPD mothers display a global regression to presubjectivity, whereas postpartum nondepressed mothers display a vulnerability to regress to presubjective modes of affective functioning, which only becomes activated in the context of high stress.

Women's decreased ability to tolerate and express their emotional experiences under conditions of stress may be related to the general "intensification of affectivity" noted by Benedek (1970) in postpartum women. Affectivity is the communicational system in early development that may lead to a generally heightened level of emotional arousal postpartum. Several factors may therefore contribute to the flooding of affective experiences postpartum: (a) the effects of dyadic sharing that includes raw, primitive, potentially uncomfortable psychobiological states; (b) the experienced loss of an often cherished state of pregnancy and expectation, which may trigger a heightening of emotions related to loss and separation; and (c) the biological processes occurring postpartum.

It is a woman's ability to be open to or to be identified with her own regressive level of experience that facilitates her attunement to her infant. Mothers can only help their infants tolerate, differentiate, and express affect states when they themselves are capable of it. The results of this study suggest that adaptation to the demands of this stressful time depends on the flexibility of self-organization. The ability to shift from adult modes to presubjective realms and then back again appears to be key in differentiating pathological responses from well-adjusted ones. A maladaptive response to motherhood seems to consist of insufficient reversibility of the necessary adaptive access to psychobiological states.

Only the depressed postpartum women in this study were vulnerable to irreversible shifts along the dimension of self—other differentiation, as witnessed in the Mode 2 level of functioning in personal agency under the high arousal condition. Recognizing personal agency as a central dimension in the postpartum period illuminates the finding that women who return to work following childbirth are less vulnerable to depressive experiences at this time (Paykel et al., 1980). Maintaining other interests, activities, and relationships may facilitate flexible shifting between various levels of self-experience. These findings are consistent with the view (Linville, 1985) that complex and differentiated self-representations can provide an organizing buffer against the overwhelming effects of stressful life events. In addition, it would be important to explore the extent to which forming a symbiotic bond with another may be used to ward off depressive responses (Gedo, 1991). Melges (1968) observed the difficulties postpartum depressed women have in tolerating their infant's needs, which he related to their own unfulfilled dependency needs. This issue may also help understand the low levels of marital satisfaction often found in PPD women (Gotlib, Whiffen, Wallace, & Mount, 1991; O'Hara et al., 1982) and the extent to which the poor quality of an important relationship may be associated with nonremission of depression (Krantz & Moos, 1988).

In this study, a direct link was established between increased levels of psychological stress and depressive severity. Significant negative relationships with the BDI were observed for all three EARS dimensions in the low arousal condition. Significant negative relationships with the BDI were also found with affect tolerance and personal agency in the high arousal condition.

These findings are in line with a general framework of the psychodynamics of depression during the postpartum (Arieti, 1978) viewing depressive withdrawal in its defensive function, protecting against potential intensification of overwhelming affectivity. The increased levels of withdrawal observed in PPD women (Harberger, Berchtold, & Honikman, 1992; Herz, 1992) may be understood in this light.

The relationship between level of psychological organization on affect tolerance and the extent to which positive and negative affects are experienced in a polarized way, defined by how many standard deviations apart these poles were on the ABS, was explored. Clear differences emerged between the groups, with lower scores on the EARS corresponding to more polarized experiences of positive and negative affect. The more developmentally advanced an individual's scores on affect tolerance, the less polarized their positive and negative affect scores. These findings support an understanding of affective development as a growing tolerance for tension and a growing variety of means for appropriate discharge (Jacobson, 1964). With maturity, finer and more modulated emotional shadings emerge, more differentiated and consciously experienced. These results also provide convergent validity for both the EARS and the ABS.

The following potential limitations of this research exist. The generalizability of the findings may be limited in that many postpartum women were recruited from support groups. A differential selection bias may exist in that none of the controls were recruited from support groups. The homogeneous quality of the sample, with respect to ethnicity and marital status, raises a question concerning external validity. As presented, however, the findings strongly support the view that the postpartum is a developmental time of potential psychological crisis (Benedek, 1959, 1970; Bibring, 1961; Deutsch, 1947; Lester & Notman,

1986; Winnicott, 1958), and shed some light on the nature of this crisis. Finally, this study does lend powerful support to the operational usefulness of the EARS and, therefore, of the epigenetic—hierarchical schema.

The evolutionary process through which the postpartum dyad develops—from a global amorphous unit to a more differentiated one—appears to provide opportunities for women to learn to tolerate, differentiate, and express a multiplicity of affective and self-other experiences. PPD may reflect a sense of hopelessness in the face of these difficult tasks. If provided the benefit of therapeutic opportunities and worked through, however, this research demonstrates that the developmental tasks of the postpartum period may well result in progressive shifts in psychological functioning. Such shifts will inevitably affect all of a woman's significant relationships, particularly with her children.

Summary

Three groups totaling 84 women were compared: postpartum depressed (PPD) women, postpartum nondepressed women, and a control group of matched normals. Participants filled out the Affects Balance Scale (ABS) and the Beck Depression Inventory. Raters scored participants' narratives, elicited at different levels of arousal, with the Epigenetic Assessment Rating Scale (EARS), along dimensions of affect tolerance (AT), affect expression (AE), and personal agency. PPD responses were characterized by a global regression to earlier levels of personality organization. AT and AE were areas of vulnerability for all postpartum women under conditions of stress or high arousal. There was a strong relationship between level of organization on AT and the extent to which positive and negative affects were polarized on the ABS, supporting both the hierarchical structure of the EARS and an understanding of affective development as a growing ability to tolerate, differentiate, and express emotions, with increased modulation at higher levels.

References

Abraham, K. (1955). Psychoanalysis and gynecology. In H. Abraham (Ed.), *Selected Papers* (pp. 91–97). London: Hogarth.

American Psychiatric Association. (1987). *Diagnostic and statistical manual of mental disorders* (3rd ed., rev.). Washington, D.C.: American Psychiatric Association

———(1994). *Diagnostic and statistical manual of mental disorders* (4th ed.). Washington, D.C.: American Psychiatric Association.

Anthony, E.J. (1983). An overview of the effects of maternal depression on the infant and child. In H.L. Morrison (Ed.), *Children of Depressed Parents* (pp. 1–17). New York: Grune & Stratton.

Arieti, S. (1978). Postpartum depression. In S. Arieti & J. Bemporad (Eds.), *Severe and Mild Depression* (pp. 254–268). New York: Basic Books.

Beck, A. T., Ward, C. H., Mendelson, M., Mock, J., & Erbaugh, J. (1961). Inventory for measuring depression. *Archives of General Psychiatry* 4:561–571.

Benedek, T. (1952). *Psychosexual Functions in Women*. New York: Ronald Press.

———(1959). Parenthood as a Developmental Phase—A Contribution to the Libido Theory. *Journal of the American Psychoanalytic Association* 7:389–417.

———(1970). The psychobiology of pregnancy. In J.H. Williams (Ed.), *Psychology of Women: Behavior in a Biosocial Context* (pp. 246–251). New York: W.W. Norton & Company.

Bibring, G.L., Dwyer, T.F., Huntington, D.S. & Valenstein, A.F. (1961). A Study of the Psychological Processes in Pregnancy and of the Earliest Mother-Child Relationship—I. Some Propositions and Comments. *Psychoanalytic Study of the Child* 16:9–24.

Blair, R.A., Gilmore, J.S., Playfair, H.R., Tindall, M.W., & O'Shea, M.W. (1970). Puerperal depression: A study of predictive factors. *Journal of the Royal College of General Practitioners* 19:22–25.

Blum, H.P. (1978). Reconstruction in a Case of Postpartum Depression. *Psychoanalytic Study of the Child* 33:335–362.

Brown, W.A., & Shereshefsy, P. (1972). Seven women: A prospective study of postpartum psychiatric disorders. *Psychiatry* 35:139–159.

Cogill, S.R., & Caplan, H.L. (1986). Impact of maternal postnatal depression on cognitive development of young children. *British Medical Journal* 292:1165–1167.

Cohen, J. (1977). *Statistical Power Analysis for the Behavioral Sciences.* New York: Academic Press.

Cox, J.L., Murray, D., & Chapman, G. (1993). A controlled study of the onset, duration, and prevalence of postnatal depression. *British Journal of Psychiatry* 163:27–31.

Cutrona, C.E. (1983). Causal attributions and perinatal depression. *Journal of Abnormal Psychology* 92:161–172.

Derogatis, L.R. (1980). *The Affects Balance Scale.* Towson, MD: Clinical Psychometric Research.

Deutsch, H. (1947). *The Psychology of Women* (Vol. 2). New York: International Universities Press.

Domash, L. (1988). The postpartum period: Analytic reflections on the potential for agony and ecstacy. In J. Offerman-Zuckerberg (Ed.), *Critical Psychophysical Passages in the Life of a Woman* (pp. 133–145). New York: Plenum.

Ehrenreich, J. (1989). *Psychodynamic Aspects of Personality and Sociocultural Identity.* Unpublished doctoral dissertation, New School for Social Research, New York.

Feldman, M., & Wilson, A. (1997). Adolescent suicidality in urban minorities and its relationship to conduct disorders, depression, and separation anxiety. *Journal of the American Academy of Child and Adolescent Psychiatry* 36:75–84.

Gedo, J. (1991). *The Biology of Clinical Encounters.* Hillsdale, NJ: Analytic Press.

———(1993). *Beyond Interpretation* (rev. ed.). Hillsdale, NJ: Analytic Press.

———& Goldberg, A. (1973). *Models of the Mind.* Chicago: University of Chicago Press.

Gise, L. H. (1992). Psychiatric implications of pregnancy. In S.H. Cherry & I.R. Merkatz, Eds., *Complications of Pregnancy: Medical, Surgical, Gynecologic, Psychosocial and Perinatal* (4th ed.; pp. 194–250). Baltimore, MD: Williams & Wilkins.

Gorodetsky, G. M., Trapnell, R.H., & Hamilton, J. A. (1992). In J.A. Hamilton & P.N. Harberger (Eds.), *Postpartum Psychiatric Illness.* Philadelphia: University of Pennsylvania Press.

Gotlib, I.H., Whiffen, V.E., Wallace, P.M., & Mount, J.H. (1991). Prospective investigation of postpartum depression: Factors involved in onset and recovery. *Journal of Abnormal Psychology* 100, 122–132.

Greene, K.J.T. (1995). Postpartum emotional disorders. In B.K. Rothman (Ed.), *Encyclopedia of Childbirth* (pp. 311–313). Phoenix, AZ: Oryx Press.

Gruen, D. S. (1990). Postpartum depression: A debilitating yet often unassessed problem. *Health and Social Work* 15(4):261–266.

Hamilton, J.A. (1992). The issue of unique qualities. In J.A. Hamilton & P. N. Harberger (Eds.), *Postpartum Psychiatric Illness* (pp. 15–33). Philadelphia: University of Pennsylvania Press.

Harberger, P.N., Berchtold, N G., & Honikman, J.I. (1992). Cries for help. In J. A. Hamilton & P.N. Harberger (Eds.), *Postpartum Psychiatric Illness,* pp.41–61. Philadelphia: University of Pennsylvania Press.

Hayworth, J., Little, B.C., Bonham Carter, S., Raptopolous, P., & Priest, R.G. (1980). A predictive study of postpartum depression: Some predisposing characteristics. *British Journal of Medical Psychology* 53:161–167.

Herz, E.K. (1992). Prediction, recognition and prevention. In J. A. Hamilton & P.N. Harberger (Eds.) *Postpartum Psychiatric Illness* (pp. 65–78). Philadelphia: University of Pennsylvania Press.

Hopkins, J., Marcus, M., & Campbell, S.B. (1984). Postpartum depression: A critical review. *Psychological Review* 5:498–515.

Howell, E., & Bayes, M. (Eds.). (1981). *Women and Mental Health*. New York: Basic Books.

Jacobson, E. (1964). *The Self and the Object World*. New York: International Universities Press.

Keller, D., & Wilson, A. (1994). Affectivity in opiate and cocaine abusers. *Psychiatry* 57:333–347.

Kendell, R.E., Chalmers, J.C., & Platz, C. (1987). Epidemiology of puerperal psychoses. *British Journal of Psychiatry* 150:662–673.

Klein, M. (1932). *The Psychoanalysis of Children*. London: Hogarth.

Krantz, S.E., & Moos, R.H. (1988). Risk factors at intake predict nonremission among depressed patients. *Journal of Consulting and Clinical Psychology* 58:863–869.

Kumar, R., & Robson, K.M. (1984). A prospective study of emotional disorders in childbearing women. *British Journal of Psychiatry* 144:35–47.

Lester, E.P. & Notman, M.T. (1986). Pregnancy, Developmental Crisis and Object Relations: Psychoanalytic Considerations. *International Journal of Psychoanalysis* 67:357–365.

———Notman, M. T. (1988). Pregnancy and Object Relations: Clinical Considerations *Psychoanalytic Inquiry* 8:196–221.

Linville, P. (1985). Self-complexity and affective extremity: Don't put all of your eggs in one cognitive basket. *Social Cognition* 3:94–120.

Loewald, H.W. (1981). Regression: Some General Considerations. *Psychoanalytic Quarterly* 50:22–43.

Mahler, M.S., Pine, F., & Bergman, A. (1975). *The Psychological Birth of the Human Infant: Symbiosis and Individuation*. New York: Basic Books.

Manly, P.C., McMahon, R.J., Bradley, C.F., & Davidson, P.O. (1982). Depressive attributional style and depression following childbirth. *Journal of Abnormal Psychology* 91:245–254.

Melges, F.T. (1968). Postpartum psychiatric syndromes. *Psychosomatic Medicine* 30:95–108.

Metz, A., Sichel, D.A., & Goff, D.C. (1988). Postpartum panic disorder. *Journal of Clinical Psychiatry* 48(7):278–279.

Murray, H.A. (1943). *Thematic Apperception Test.* Cambridge, MA: Harvard University Press.

Nolen-Hoeksema, S. (1987). Sex differences in unipolar depression: Evidence and theory. *Psychological Bulletin* 101:259–282.

O'Hara, M.W. (1986). Social support, life events and depression during pregnancy and the puerperium. *Archives of General Psychiatry* 43:569–573.

O'Hara, M.W., Rehm, L.P., & Campbell, S.B. (1982). Predicting depressive symptomatology: Cognitive behavioral models and postpartum depression. *Journal of Abnormal Psychology* 91:457–461.

Paykel, E.S., Emms, E.M., Fletcher, J., & Rassaby, E.S. (1980). Life events and social support in puerperal depression. *British Journal of Psychiatry* 136:339–346.

Philipps, L.H.C., & O'Hara, M. W. (1991). Prospective study of postpartum depression: 4 1/2 year follow-up of women and children. *Journal of Abnormal Psychology* 100:151–155.

Pines, D. (1972). Pregnancy and motherhood: Interaction between fantasy and reality. *British Journal of Medical Psychology* 45:333–343.

Pitt, B. (1968). Atypical depression following childbirth. *British Journal of Psychiatry* 114:1325–1335.

Purdy, D., & Frank, E. (1993). Should postpartum mood disorders be given a more prominent or distinct place in the DSM–IV? *Depression:* 1(2):59–70.

Robson, K.M., & Kumar, R. (1980). Delayed onset of maternal affection after childbirth. *British Journal of Psychiatry* 136:347–353.

Saks, B. (1985). Depressed mood during pregnancy and the puerperium: Clinical recognition and implications for clinical practice. *American Journal of Psychiatry* 142:728–731.

Sherman, J.A. (1971). *On the Psychology of Women: A Study of Empirical Studies.* Springfield, IL: Charles C Thomas.

Spivak, L., Spivak, D., & Wistrand, K. (1993). New psychic phenomena related to normal childbirth. *European Journal of Psychiatry* 7:239–243.

Weissman, M., Leaf, P., & Tischler, G. (1988). Affective disorders in five United States communities. *Psychological Medicine* 18:141–153.

Whiffen, V.E. (1992). Vulnerability to postpartum depression: A prospective multivariate study. *Journal of Abnormal Psychology* 97:467–474.

———Gotlib, I.H. (1993). Comparison of postpartum & nonpostpartum depression: Clinical presentation, psychiatric history and psychosocial functioning. *Journal of Consulting and Clinical Psychology* 61:485–494.

Wilson, A. (1986). Archaic transference and anaclitic depression: Psychoanalytic perspectives on the treatment of severely depressed patients *Psychoanalytic Psychology* 3:237–256.

———(1988). Levels of depression and clinical assessment. In H. Lerner & P. Lerner (Eds.), *Primitive Mental States and the Rorschach Test* (pp. 441–462). New York: International Universities Press.

———Kuras, M., Passik, S., Morral, A., & Turner, A. (1989). *The EPI-TAT Administration & Scoring Manual.* An unpublished manuscript, New School for Social Research, New York.

———Passik, S. (1993). Explorations in presubjectivity. In A. Wilson & J. Gedo (Eds.), *Hierarchical Concepts in Psychoanalysis: Research, Theory, and Clinical Practice* (pp. 311–324). New York: Guilford.

———————& Faude, J. (1990). Self-regulation and its failures. In J. Masling (Ed.), *Empirical studies of psychoanalytic theories* (Vol. 3; pp. 149–213). Hillsdale, NJ: Erlbaum.

———————Abrams, J., & Gordon, E. (1989). A hierarchical model of opiate addiction: Failures of self-regulation as a central aspect of substance abuse. *Journal of Nervous Mental Disease* 177:390–399.

———& Kuras, M. (1989). An epigenetic approach to the assessment of personality: The study of the instability of the stable personality organization. In C. Spielberger and J. Butcher (Eds.), *Advances in Personality Assessment* (pp. 63–95). Hillsdale, NJ: Erlbaum.

———& Weinstein, L. (1992). An investigation into some implications of a Vygotskian perspective on the origins of mind *Journal of the American Psychoanalytic Association* 40:357–387.

———(1996). The Transference and The Zone of Proximal Development. *Journal of the American Psychoanalytic Association* 44:167–200.

Winnicott, D.W. (1958). Primary maternal preoccupation. In D.W. Winnicott (Ed.), *Collected Papers* (pp. 300–305). London: Tavistock.

CHAPTER 17

ADOLESCENT SUICIDALITY IN URBAN MINORITIES AND ITS RELATIONSHIP TO CONDUCT DISORDERS, DEPRESSION, AND SEPARATION ANXIETY

This study investigates the underlying personality/structural dimensions mediating suicidal behavior in psychiatrically hospitalized, largely minority adolescents. Although socioeconomic status has not been demonstrated to differentially affect suicide rates (Berman and Jobes, 1991), the study population represents a particular subculture, a predominantly poor, urban minority, with familial, sociocultural, and economic deprivation factors that may contribute to vulnerabilities that need to be better understood. Jessor (1993) points to "troubling lacunae" as studies of adolescence have largely ignored impoverished youth.

Studying depression cannot substitute for directly studying suicidality (Hendin, 1963). Kazdin et al. (1983), using a modified Beck Hopelessness Scale, have failed to explain suicidal behavior in other psychiatric groups (Allen, 1987; Carlson and Cantwell, 1982; Kuperman and Stewart, 1979; Mattsson et al., 1969).

An alternative to depression research examines the role of aggression, especially as diagnostically formulated in conduct disorder. Studies find high coexistence of suicidality and aggression/conduct disorders in suicidal adolescents (Apter et al., 1988; Shaffer, 1974). Adolescents with conduct disorder who attempt suicide often deny depression and demonstrate nonsuicidal, self-mutilatory behavior. Many suicidal adolescents have had legal troubles, and incarcerated adolescents are at extreme risk for suicide

607

(Shafii et al., 1985). Given the high prevalence of conduct disorders in adolescence, and that such states have a poor prognosis (Loeber et al., 1985), suicidality and conduct disorders must be research priorities.

Difficulty in correctly identifying adolescents at risk for suicide may be due to a lack of attention to differences among developmental levels in suicidality theories (Erlich, 1978). Constructs heretofore used to explain suicide in adults do not adequately explain suicide in children and adolescents in the throes of developmental progression. Miller (1981) describes suicidal adolescents as "prisoners of the present" lacking a finite sense of time, having little sense of future or irreversibility, and thinking concretely. The level of cognitive/affective development requisite for such developments as guilt and self-blame in suicide has not been carefully empirically studied, since appropriate measures did not exist.

In addition to depression, aggression, and developmental level, separation plays a role in childhood and adolescent suicidality. Studies of suicidal adults have found early separations from parents and vulnerability to separations and losses later in life (e.g., separation from partners, loss of the ability to work, loss of possessions) (Wasserman, 1988; Hendin 1963, 1986) suggests that psychodynamic constellations seen in suicide can be conceptualized as responses to loss, separation, or abandonment—separation equates with death. One major psychological task of adolescence is separation from parents and infantile dependencies and wishes, and the finding of new people to love (Blos, 1962; Freud, 1958, 1969). Suicide has been termed a "failed attachment" (Adam, 1986).

Hansburg (1980a) developed the Adolescent Separation Anxiety Test (SAT), a semiprojective measure of reactions to separation experiences. The SAT's theoretical underpinnings lie in Bowlby's

(1969, 1973, 1977) attachment theory. Hansburg (1980b) sees separation problems as involving a balance between separation-individuation and attachment-interdependence. Wade (1987) used Hansburg's SAT to study suicidal teenage girls. She found the suicidal adolescent girls to be less individuated, with more regressive/symbiotic attachments, than nonsuicidal teenage girls. The adolescent girl seeks relief from abandonment depression and separation anxiety by recapturing in suicide a symbiotic state.

Thus far, the roles of depression, aggression, developmental level, and separation in suicidality have been considered. A hierarchical approach to personality organization will now be put forward that integrates these seemingly disparate phenomena. A hierarchical approach emphasizes levels of personality organization and specifies the epigenesis (or rules of transformation) of later levels with respect to earlier ones. Integrative J potential exists through assigning the disparate phenomena to different hierarchical levels. This approach emphasizes phases prior to the development of symbolic representation, which are termed preverbal. This period is presubjective and psychobiological because its representational imprint is not consciously accessible to an adult's later recall (Emde, 1988; Wilson and Passik, 1993).

Wilson and his colleagues (e.g., Keller and Wilson, 1994; Wilson et al., 1989a,b, 1990a,b; Wilson and Passik, 1993), in explicating the Epigenetic Assessment Rating System (EARS) approach, describe personality organization as flexible, fluid, and subject to rapid fluctuations. The succession of modes represents a transition, albeit with key continuities and discontinuities, from a primarily psychobiologically based period of presubjectivity (Modes I and II) to a more psychologically based period of subjectivity (Modes III and V).

Wilson's group describe how each EARS mode is cast along 10 personality dimensions. A person can function in any one of the five modes, for each of the personality dimensions. The five modal levels are now explicated:

Mode I. Presubjective, preverbal period; limited distinction between self and other; sensorimotor encoding of information; primary feelings states are pleasure/ unpleasure; defensive activity is primarily avoidance of global unpleasure; primary threat is overstimulation.

Mode II. Transitional period between sensorimotor and imagistic representation; others are "separate but attached," providing for basic needs; defensive activity primarily projection; primary threats involve separation, intrusiveness.

Mode III. Period in which subjectivity arrives; primary concerns are self-enhancement and self-esteem maintenance, including protection of wishful illusions; lexical capacities develop and with them a mature communicational ability; predominant defensive activities are denial and disavowal; primary threat is prohibitions from authorities.

Mode IV. Period of oedipal-level conflicts; primary threats from moral anxieties and derivatives of castration fears; guilt over sexuality, but genital sexuality is also desired; primary defense is repression; primary threat involves conflicts around competition and self-assertion; are "separate but attached," providing for basic needs; defensive activity primarily projection; primary threats involve separation, intrusiveness.

Mode V. Period characterized by benevolent resolution of conflict; conflict and generativity are basic needs; aggression is well-contained and competition is not a major threat; sense of acceptance deriving from realistic appraisal of place and role in world; predominant defense is renunciation; primary dangers stem from undistorted reality factors.

In this research, the EARS dimensions used to study suicidality include Affect Tolerance (AT), Affect Expression (AE), and Use of an Object (UO). They are explicated as follows:

Affect Tolerance. The way in which a person manages affective arousal, ranging from highly unsocialized and immature forms (e.g., simple avoidance of unpleasure and dedifferentiation and somatization of affects) to a mid-range (where one-sided and highly polarized emotional experiences predominate) to more mature modes (in which the nuances of one's emotional life are largely integrated, modulated, and accepted).

Affect Expression. How an individual's emotions play a role in a communicational matrix with important others. The affects expressed, including their intensity and their differentiation (global or specific), are indications of a person's level of affective ties to others.

Use of an Object. Object relationships at low modes involve the use of another for the purpose of stabilization through self-enhancement, develop to mutual enhancement of both parties, and then to intimate relations.

These and other key dimensions germane to suicidality, scaled along the five modal levels, are heuristically depicted in Table 1.

SUICIDALITY

To assess the fluidity of personality organization, the EARS evaluates regressive and progressive shifts in functioning. Wilson et al. (1989a) thus introduce the notion of low and high arousal levels. Arousal level is a function of the particular stimulus to which

TABLE 1
Epigenetic Assessment Rating System
Characteristics and Personality Organization

	Mode I	Mode II	Mode III	Mode IV	Mode V
Characteristic pathogenic feature	Over- or understimulation or trauma	Disruption of self-cohesion	Persistence of illusions	Intrapsychic conflict	Frustration
Typical danger	Overstimulation	Separation from caregiver	Parental disapproval or reprimand	Moral anxiety	Dangers from reality
Depressive experience	Empty bewilderment	Abandonment	Self-esteem fluctuation	Guilty self-condemnation	Appropriate grief
Quality of object relation	Search for optimal level of excitation	Gratify concrete needs	Manage idealization and devaluation	Promote identification and complex self	Appreciate actual relationship
Optimal intervention	Pacification	Unite disparate self-experience	Optimal disillusionment	Interpretation of ideational conflict	Empathic witness to introspection

the individual responds. It has been empirically demonstrated that narratives given in response to low arousal stimuli reflect the most efficient developmental strategies an individual has acquired, and those most typically relied upon (Keller and Wilson, 1994). High arousal stimuli are defined as presenting much greater adaptive and integrative challenges to the individual's personality and cause a regressive shift in adaptive strategy.

It was hypothesized that the suicidal groups would score lower on the AT, AE, and UO dimensions than nonpsychiatric patients and that subjects with conduct disorder would score the lowest of the groups. It was also hypothesized that suicidal subjects would show regression into the presubjective realm of functioning when affective tensions (Wilson and Malatesta, 1989) become overwhelming. The lower modes on the AT dimension describe a period of extreme intolerance for affective experience, with impulsivity and the discharge of affects through direct action and explosive outbursts—hallmarks and defining characteristics of conduct disorders. Without secure object relations, the individual is vulnerable to feelings of annihilation and fragmentation, loss of sense of self, and overwhelming dependency, as is ascribed in the lower modes on the AE dimension.

The UO dimension is an object relational dimension measuring the aims and ends that relationships serve to the individual. In the lowest modes, objects are used to enhance the self with no enduring use of people beyond physical processes, or relationships are life-sustaining, parasitic, and need-gratifying, and objects may be avoided because they threaten a fragmentation of self-experience. In later modes, the self is enhanced by mature intimacy and allegiances, and objects can be used for more mutual gains and satisfactions. Patients with conduct disorder are characterized by the callous use of people for their own gain and to satisfy their own immediate needs, and they have difficulty delaying gratification. Thus, their scores are predicted to be the lowest of the groups.

It was hypothesized that a mean EARS scores of 2.5 and below would prove to be a better predictor of suicidality than a measure of depression. The 2.5 score marks the boundary between subjectivity and presubjectivity. Adolescent suicidality corresponds to a level of psychic organization in which there is poor differentiation of self and other. Impaired object representations leave the adolescent vulnerable to separation and overwhelming feelings of dependency and fragmentation (Jacobson, 1973). This level corresponds to Mode Il on the EARS. This hypothesis assumes that the role of acting on impulses is a significant component in suicidal behavior, not accounted for by a focus on depression, and would appear in low scores on the EARS.

It was hypothesized that suicidal groups would have a higher percentage of attachment factor responses on the SAT than non-suicidal subjects.

The implications of scoring below 2.5 (i.e., crossing into the presubjective realm) on the EARS was explored for all subjects.

METHOD

Subjects

Subjects in the experimental groups were recruited from a child and adolescent inpatient psychiatry service at a large municipal hospital.

An overall sample of N = 104 was predetermined to ensure sufficient power (power = .80) to detect medium-level effect sizes (Cohen, 1977). Subjects were recruited from all consecutive new admissions, until 26 subjects (13 males and 13 females) in each of four groups were obtained. Each potential subject and his or her parent/legal guardian was approached within 10 days of the adolescent's hospital admission and asked to participate in the study. Only two subjects refused to participate in the study when approached (one boy with conduct disorder and one suicidal girl with conduct disorder).

Suicidal behavior was assessed by noting all references to self-harmful behaviors with suicidal intent in each patient's chart for 10days, including emergency room notes and treatment team notes. Self-mutilating teenagers without suicide intent were excluded. Each patient was then rated according to the Pfeffer Child Suicide Potential Scale (Pfeffer, 1986). The validity of this scale for research on suicidal adolescents is established and presented by Pfeffer et al. (1993). This scale is along a 1 to 5 spectrum, rating the severity of a child's suicidal behavior during the past 6 months:

1. Nonsuicidal behavior—No evidence of any self-destructive thoughts or actions
2. Suicidal ideation—Thoughts or verbalizations of causing injury or death to oneself
3. Suicidal threat—Verbalization of impending self-destructive suicidal action and/or a precursor action, which, if fully carried out, could lead to harm
4. Mild attempt—Actual self-destructive action that realistically would not have endangered life
5. Serious attempt—Actions that realistically could lead to death and may necessitate intensive care
   A score of 3 and above was used to identify suicidal subjects.

The suicidal subjects were divided into two groups: those with a conduct disorder diagnosis and those with other diagnoses. A third group consisted of subjects who had a diagnosis of conduct disorder but no evidence of suicidality. Diagnosis was taken from the 10-day working diagnosis on the treatment plan in the patient's chart. Diagnoses met DSM-III-R (American Psychiatric Association, 1987) criteria and were made by the attending physician on each patient's unit. Final diagnosis upon discharge was subsequently recorded and changes noted. If diagnoses no longer met criteria of the study, the subject was dropped. Patients with a diagnosis of mental retardation, organic brain syndrome, or schizophrenia were not included.

A control group of 26 nonpsychiatric subjects were recruited from local community groups. This group consisted of adolescents, matched with experimental subjects for age, sex, race, and socioeconomic status, and who, with the consent of their guardians, agreed to participate in the study. Using analysis of variance (ANOVA) and nonparametric analyses, we found that the control group did not differ significantly on any demographic (age, socioeconomic status, race) variables.

Subjects' ages ranged from 12.0 to 16.0 years, with an overall mean age of 13.10 years. The mean ages of subjects in each group varied by only 4 1/2 months (Table 2).

Socioeconomic status was calculated with the Hollingshead and Redlich (1958) Two Factor Index of Social Position, which yields a classification ranging from the highest class of 1 to the lowest class of 5. There were no subjects in class 1, and only 5.8% of the sample were in class 2 (see Table 2). A majority consisting of 42.3% of the sample were in class 5, and the remainder of subjects were equally divided, with 26.0% in each of classes 3 and 4.

Instruments

Epigenetic Assessment Rating System. The EARS can be applied to any narrativized speech sample; in the present study, it is applied to responses to two Thematic Apperception Test cards, one

TABLE 2
Demographic Data

Group	Mean Age
Suic Cond Dis	13 years, 9.2 months
Cond Dis	13 years, 8.7 months
Suic Noncond Dis	13 years, 9.5 months
Control	14 years, 1.5 months

Race

Group	Black		Hispanic		White		Other	
	No.	%	No.	%	No.	%	No.	%
Suic Cond Dis	13	50.0	8	30.0	4	15.4	1[a]	3.8
Cond Dis	20	76.9	5	19.2	0	0	1[b]	3.8
Suic Noncond Dis	13	50.0	9	34.6	0	0	4[c]	15.2
Control	15	57.7	9	34.6	1	3.8	1[a]	3.8
Total sample	61	58.7	31	29.8	5	4.8	7	6.8

Social Class

Group	1		2		3		4		5	
	No.	%	No.	%	No.	%	No.	%	No.	%
Suic Cond Dis	0	0	1	3.8	5	19.2	7	26.9	13	50.0
Cond Dis	0	0	2	7.7	3	11.5	7	26.9	14	53.8
Suic Noncond Dis	0	0	2	7.7	11	42.3	5	19.2	8	30.8
Control	0	0	1	3.8	8	30.8	8	30.8	9	34.6
Total sample	0	0	6	5.8	27	26.0	27	26.0	44	42.3

Note: Social class was rated according to Hollingshead and Redlich (1958). Suic Cond Dis = suicidal conduct disorder; Cond Dis = conduct disorder; Suic Noncond Dis = suicidal non-conduct disorder.
[a] Black/Hispanic.
[b] Black/white.
[c] Black/white; black/Hispanic; black/Indian; Arab.

low arousal (Card 1) and the other high arousal (Card 13 MF) (Wilson et al., 1989b). Wilson et al. (1989b) demonstrated the validity of the EARS by testing the factorial independence of the psychological dimensions as well as demonstrating that arousal was a meaningful entity in that various levels of personality dimensions appeared in response to changing task conditions in both normal and psychiatric subjects. High interrater reliability on the EARS has been repeatedly demonstrated after rater training. To qualify as an expert rater, it is required that 90% of judgments are within 1 scale point, 50% of judgments are exact matches, and there is an overall Pearson *r* of at least .80, compared with judgments produced by an already qualified expert rater.

Children's Depression Inventory. The Children's Depression Inventory (CDI) (Kovacs, 1982; Kovacs and Beck, 1977) is a self-report questionnaire consisting of 27 items, designed for children aged 8 to 17 years. Reliability testing has demonstrated satisfactory internal consistency, inter-item and item-total correlations, and temporal stability (Strober and Werry, 1986). Self-report measures are widely used in the study of depression because affective states are likely to be manifested in subjective evaluations of one's own experiences (Kazdin, 1981). In this study, the CDI was administered aloud to each subject and verbal responses were recorded verbatim to minimize the possible contaminants of poor attention, immature cognitive abilities, or disturbing responses to inner affective states (Pfeffer, 1986).

Separation Anxiety Test. The SAT (Hansburg, 1980a,b) is a semiprojective instrument that consists of 12 black-and-white drawings, each depicting a child and an attachment figure, in various situations of separation or loss. Kroger (1986) conducted a factor analysis of the scales of the SAT to provide a matrix of empirically derived factors. The scale scores for a total sample of 80 female and 55 male subjects were intercorrelated, and the matrix was subjected to a principal-components factor analysis. Factors with eigen values greater than 1 were extracted and rotated to a varimax solution. Seven factors were derived. Kroger found an attachment factor which partially replicated the attachment factor defined by Hansburg. This empirically derived factor, defined by positive loadings on rejection, anxiety, and loneliness scales, was utilized in the current study. Internal consistency of the items on the SAT, split-half correlations, and test-retest reliability were found to be satisfactory (Black, 1986; Kroger and Green, 1990).

Procedures

All measures were administered to each subject in the experimental groups within 10 days of admission to the inpatient service. To ensure confidentiality, all data were coded numerically and no names were used. The Thematic Apperception Test narratives from which the EARS is scored (Cards I and 13 MF) were administered first, followed by the CDI and the SAT. The EARS narratives were rated by two independent expert raters. The raters were blind to group membership as well as to the subject's performance on the CDI and SAT. Each rater scored 5 of the 10 dimensions on each card, alternating halves to be scored (Keller and Wilson, 1994). On the preliminary trial, which involved 100 ratings, there was exact agreement between the raters on 70% of the scores, and 95% agreement within 1 score point. To provide a further check of interrater reliability between the raters, and to assess drift and guarantee that the raters were using the same internal scale consistently throughout the entire rating procedure, each rater also scored expertly prescored dummy protocols which were interspersed in each group of 10 study protocols to be rated. On the dummy protocols, which involved 100 ratings, there was exact agreement on 63% of the scores and 96% agreement within 1 score point. The Spearman-Brown coefficient of reliability for the dummy protocols was .94. No significant differences between the raters or the raters and an expert were later found on the dummy protocols, indicating that the raters maintained the same internal scale reference points during as before the ratings began.

RESULTS

A one-way ANOVA with group membership as the independent variable and mean EARS score on the AT, AE, and UO dimensions as the dependent variable revealed significant differences on the EARS scores among the groups (Table 3). Mean scores for each group were lower in the high arousal than in the low arousal condition on the EARS. Mean scores for the control group were highest in both arousal conditions. Mean scores in each arousal condition for the suicidal non—conduct disorder group were higher than for the conduct disorder groups. To attenuate for type 1 error, a Scheffé correction (Fcrit **(3.101)** = 2.68 X 2) was used and pairwise comparisons were conducted between the means. Significant differences were found between the means of the suicidal conduct disorder and both the suicidal non—conduct disorder and control groups in each arousal condition. Significant differences were also found between means of the conduct disorder and both the suicidal non—conduct disorder and control groups in each arousal condition. As expected, the means of the suicidal conduct disorder and conduct disorder groups did not significantly differ from each other in either of the arousal conditions. Although the mean of the suicidal non—conduct disorder group did differ significantly from the control group in the high arousal condition, the suicidal non—conduct disorder group did not differ significantly from the control group in the low arousal condition. This was due to the mean score of the control group being lower than anticipated in the high arousal condition.

The distribution of mean scores across the AT, AE, and UO dimensions in each arousal condition was calculated to determine what percentage of subjects in each group had modal scores falling into the presubjective (2.5 and below) versus subjective (above 2.5) ranges in each arousal condition. In the low arousal condition, 12% of the suicidal conduct disorder and 35% of the conduct disorder subjects scored in the subjective range, whereas 77% of the suicidal non—conduct disorder and 96% of the control subjects fell in the subjective range. In the high arousal condition, 100% of the conduct disorder subjects fell in the presubjective range; 19% of the suicidal non—conduct disorder and 46% of the control subjects remained in the subjective range.

We calculated the number and percentage of subjects in each group scoring 13 and below (the cutoff score for depressive symptoms) versus above 13 on the CDI, and the number and percentage of subjects in each group scoring 2.5 and below versus above 2.5 on the EARS. Forty-six percent of the suicidal subjects ($n = 52$) scored above the cutoff for depression on the CDI. (Forty-two percent of subjects with conduct disorder [$n = 52$] and 15% of the control subjects [$n = 26$] scored above the cutoff.) Sixty-seven percent of suicidal subjects scored below the cutoff of 2.5. (Eighty-five percent of subjects with conduct disorder and 23% of control subjects scored below this cutoff.) A χ2 analysis was performed to test the frequency distribution of suicidal and control subjects on each instrument (CDI and EARS). When we explored differences between the suicidal subjects with conduct disorder, suicidal subjects without conduct disorder, and control subjects, both the CDI and the EARS were able to identify a significant proportion of suicidal subjects. For the CDI, $df = 1,76$, $\chi2(1) = 7.13$ ($p = .008$). For the EARS, $df = 1,76$, $\chi2(1) = 13.60$ ($p = .002$). To determine the amount of shared variance between each instrument and group, a ϕ coefficient (a measure of association between the variables) was calculated. The CDI accounted for 9.14% of the variance whereas the EARS accounted for 17.44% of the variance. The results of the overall χ2 analyses were followed by pairwise comparisons using a series of two (2 analyses for each instrument, corrected for type 1 error using the Dunn-Bonferroni correction ($p < .05/2 = p < .025$). When we analyzed the frequency distribution of suicidal conduct disorder subjects and control subjects, the $\chi 2$ for the CDI was not significant, whereas the $\chi 2$ for the EARS was significant ($p < .001$). Based on the ϕ coefficient, the CDI accounted for 8.83% of the variance whereas the EARS accounted for 55.45% of the variance. When we analyzed the frequency distribution of suicidal non–conduct disorder subjects and control subjects, the $\chi 2$ for the CDI was significant ($p = .008$), but the $\chi 2$ for the EARS was not significant. Based on the ϕ coefficient, the CDI accounted for 13.61% of the variance but the EARS accounted for only 2.78% of the variance. Thus, while the EARS identified more of the suicidal subjects than the CDI, based on the cutoff scores, further analysis of the suicidal groups found that the EARS was better than the CDI at identifying suicidal conduct disorder subjects, but the CDI was better at identifying suicidal non–conduct disorder subjects.

A stepwise multiple discriminant analysis was performed to identify which of the independent variables best predicted group membership. The three EARS dimensions at each of the two arousal conditions, the CDI, and the SAT served as the discriminating variables. The first step, AE-low arousal, best predicts group membership (multiple $r = 596$, R2 = .355, F = 56.18, $df = 1,102$, $p < .0001$). On the second step, AE-high arousal is added to the equation (multiple $r = .627$, R2 = .393, 2,101, F = 32.82, $p < .01$). After this second step, no other discriminating variables obtain statistical significance on the stepwise procedure.

An ANOVA was performed to test whether subjects in the suicidal groups would have a significantly higher percentage of Attachment factor responses on the SAT than subjects in the nonsuicidal groups. Group membership was the independent

TABLE 3

Comparison of Group Means for Combined Epigenetic Assessment Rating System Dimensions Affect Tolerance, Affect Expression, Use of an Object

Group	Card 1: Low Arousal		Card 13 ME: High Arousal	
	Mean	SD	Mean	SD
Suic Cond Dis	2.189	.343	1.458	.327
Cond Dis	2.291	.483	1.562	.386
Suic Noncond Dis	3.138	.611	2.151	.647
Control	3.342	.538	2.497	.591

Group Means and Standard Deviations

Group Comparison	Arousal	F	p	df
All groups	Low	35.09	<.001	3,100
	High	24.61	<.001	3,100
		$F_{enhanced}$		
Suic Cond Dis vs. Cond Dis	Low	0.54	.465	1,100
	High	0.54	.463	1,100
Suic Cond Dis vs. Suic Noncond Dis	Low	46.18*	<.001	1,100
	High	24.36*	<.001	1,100
Suic Cond Dis vs. Control	Low	56.68*	<.001	1,100
	High	44.35*	<.001	1,100
Cond Dis vs. Suic Noncond Dis	Low	36.76*	<.001	1,100
	High	17.63*	<.001	1,100
Cond Dis vs. Control	Low	68.25*	<.001	1,100
	High	54.71*	<.001	1,100
Suic Noncond Dis vs. Control	Low	2.15	.146	1,100
	High	6.06*	.016	1,100

Difference Between Group Means

Note: Suic Cond Dis = suicidal conduct disorder; Cond Dis = conduct disorder; Suic Noncond Dis = suicidal non-conduct disorder.
* Significant using Scheffé correction; Scheffé $F_{critical}$ = 5.1.

variable and percentage of Attachment factor responses on the SAT was the dependent variable. An ANOVA for all groups yielded a significant difference on percentage of SAT responses among the groups ($p = .012$). To attenuate for type 1 error, the Scheffé correction (Fcrit (**3.101**) = 2.68 X 2) was used and pairwise comparisons were conducted between the means. The suicidal groups had a significantly higher mean percentage of Attachment factor responses than the conduct disorder group but did not differ significantly from the control group. The suicidal non–conduct disorder group had a significantly higher mean percentage of Attachment factor responses than the conduct disorder group but did not differ significantly from the control group. The conduct disorder groups did have a significantly lower mean percentage of Attachment factor responses than both the suicidal non–conduct disorder and the control group. The conduct disorder group differed significantly from the control group, but the suicidal conduct disorder group did not differ significantly from any of the other groups (Table 4).

TABLE 4

Comparison of Group Means of Attachment Factor Responses on the Separation Anxiety Test

Group	Group Means and Standard Deviations	
	Mean	SD
Suic Cond Dis	19.19	5.45
Cond Dis	16.85	4.87
Suic Noncond Dis	21.42	6.22
Control	22.00	7.50

Group Comparison	Difference Between Group Means
	F
All groups	3.87[a]
	$F_{(obtained)}$
All Suicidal vs. Cond Dis	5.60*
All Suicidal vs. Control	1.34
Suic Noncond Dis vs. Cond Dis	7.34*
Suic Noncond Dis vs. Control	0.12
All Cond Dis vs. Suic Noncond Dis	5.42*
All Cond Dis vs. Control	7.41*
All Cond Dis vs. All Noncond Dis	9.56*
Cond Dis vs. Control	9.31*
Suic Cond Dis vs. Cond Dis	1.93
Suic Cond Dis vs. Suic Noncond Dis	1.74
Suic Cond Dis vs. Control	2.76

Note: Suic Cond Dis = suicidal conduct disorder; Cond Dis = conduct disorder; Suic Noncond Dis = suicidal non–conduct disorder.

[a] $p = .012$

* Significant at $p < .05$ using Scheffé correction; Scheffé $F_{(crit)} = 5.1$.

A *t* test was performed to determine whether subjects with an overall EARS mean of 2.5 and below would have a significantly greater total number of responses on the SAT than subjects with an overall EARS mean above 2.5. A significant difference was found, whereby subjects with an overall EARS mean of 2.5 and below had a mean of 91 responses on the SAT, whereas subjects with an overall EARS mean above 2.5 had a mean of 68 responses on the SAT ($p < .001$).

DISCUSSION

Studying an urban minority population, one should be careful about generalizing any results to adolescents from other socio-demographic strata. As the three groups were each so disturbed to require hospitalization, it may be initially assumed that significant similarities exist among groups. Differences among the groups must therefore be given special credence as elucidating critical characteristics of adolescent suicidality and conduct disorders.

Modal level of functioning on a particular cluster of EARS dimensions linked to affectivity and object relations was found to be associated with group membership. This suggests that impairment in the toleration and expression of affects, including a tendency to discharge intolerable affects through aggressive/impulsive behavior, is related to both suicidal and conduct disordered behavior. Lower psychological functioning in these areas was greater when a conduct disorder presented concurrently with suicidality.

Mean EARS scores in each group regressed with greater stress. Conduct disorder groups had lower mean scores than non—conduct disorder groups. Of particular interest is the finding concerning the distribution of scores "across the boundary" from subjective, language mediated psychological functioning to presubjective, preverbal, action-dominated functioning. Even under low stress, where the highest modal functioning generally available to the individual is assumed to be reflected, the large majority of all subjects with conduct disorder had modal scores below this boundary point. This suggests these individuals characteristically suffer major impairments in negotiating interpersonal relationships and in modulating affective arousal. Under high arousal, conduct disorder subjects' modal functioning fell in the presubjective range. Under low stress, most of the suicidal non—conduct disorder subjects remained in the subjective range. It was under high stress that they regressed into the presubjective range. Thus, under high arousal the overt aggression of conduct disorders and the self-destructive acts of suicidal adolescents are means of discharging intolerable affects through impulsive action. Under low stress, virtually all of the control subjects scored in the subjective range, and, under high stress, half remained in the subjective range. As differences were found between suicidal adolescent groups with and without conduct disorders, important dynamic distinctions between suicidal adolescents can be made, and subsets of suicidal adolescents can be identified. These results are consistent with the suggestion of Pfeffer et al. (1983) that there are two types of suicidal children: those who have relatively stable ego functioning and reality testing, who do not become aggressive, but who decompensate with environmental stress; and those suicidal children with distinct ego deficits with more chronic rage and extreme temper outbursts. The findings also support the argument of Erlich (1978) that there are progressive and regressive fluctuations between concrete and abstract thought, and action and symbolic modalities, in suicide-prone adolescents.

With respect to the depression/suicidality relationship, despite long-standing assumptions that depressive symptoms are a key warning signal of possible suicidal behavior, fewer than half of the study's suicidal adolescents were identified as depressed on a depression scale, and there were a substantial number of depressed, but not suicidal, adolescents with conduct disorder. This parallels previous findings of studies (Carlson and Cantwell, 1982; Kuperman and Stewart, 1979; Mattsson et al., 1969; Pfeffer et al., 1983; Shaffer, 1974) that fewer than half of suicidal children and adolescents are depressed and that many depressed individuals are not suicidal. There was a significant association between scores above the cutoff point for depression on the CDI and being in the suicidal groups. However, the depression cutoff score, while significant in identifying suicidal non—conduct disorder subjects, did not identify suicidal conduct disorder subjects. That depressive symptoms were found in more of the suicidal subjects who did not have conduct disorder than in suicidal subjects with conduct disorder suggests a subset of suicidal adolescents exhibiting significant signs of depression. Clinicians should be aware that relying on the assumed link between suicide and depressive symptoms and ignoring a more complex variable, level of organization, may result in overlooking the majority of adolescents at risk for suicide.

The remarkable finding that AE at both levels of arousal is the best predictor of group membership underscores the crucial significance of an affectivity aspect in distinguishing the groups. It is not depression, nor separation, nor how affects are tolerated, but how affects are expressed that sets the groups apart. This finding holds up over levels of arousal, further highlighting the strength of this feature of affectivity.

It was demonstrated that there is a relationship between low EARS scores (in the presubjective range) and extreme anxiety or emotional reactivity in the face of separation experiences as measured by greater reactivity to separation stimuli on the SAT. Subjects whose overall psychological functioning is in the subjective range maintained their equilibrium when faced with anxiety-provoking separation stimuli. Those whose overall psychological functioning is in the presubjective range are vulnerable to psychological disorganization and regression to reliance on prepsychological action patterns.

Clinical Implications

The hierarchical model offers a framework for understanding the psychodynamics of adolescents at serious risk for aggressive/self-destructive behavior. Under high stress the modal functioning of suicidal subjects, particularly in the areas of affectivity and object relations, is in modes highlighting issues of separation. Intense or persistent anger weakens attachment bonds, and aggression becomes revengeful and malicious. While the suicidal non–conduct disorder patient maintains some hope of reunion with, rather than destruction of, attachment figures, the suicidal conduct disorder patient "crosses the border" into chronic anger and destructive aggression.

Following from the optimal interventions implied by the hierarchical model, adolescents organized at a preverbal level will not verbalize affects, and thus clinicians must look for expressions of affects in sensorimotor forms, i.e., a proclivity to action orientations. Interventions in the form of support, pacification, or unification, as opposed to interpretive interpretations, are indicated. As functioning of suicidal adolescents regresses into modes highlighting issues of failures in self-regulation, impulsivity, and poor self-other differentiation, then traditionally focused-upon issues may also examine how the level of disturbance in the areas of affectivity and object relations are exhibited in different types of suicidal behavior. The nature, frequency, severity, and aim of suicidal behavior may differ as a function of structural/dynamic variables associated with different diagnostic categories. Future research can fine-tune diagnostic precision by using a structured diagnostic interview in the selection of subjects.

Summary

This research investigates personality variables—aggression and disorders of conduct, depression, and separation anxiety—mediating suicidal behavior in psychiatrically hospitalized urban minority adolescents. Method: Four matched groups of 26 subjects (N = 104) participated: suicidal adolescents with, and suicidal adolescents without, a conduct disorder diagnosis, nonsuicidal adolescents with a conduct disorder diagnosis, and a nonpsychiatric control group. Subjects were assessed with three dimensions from the Epigenetic Assessment Rating System (EARS), the Children's Depression Inventory (CD'), and the Separation Anxiety Test (SAT). Results: A conduct disorder diagnosis was related to lower modal EARS scores. The EARS and the CDI each identified a different subset of suicidal adolescents. Adolescents with lower modal EARS scores exhibited greater reactivity to separation experiences on the SAT. Conclusion: Relying on depressive symptomatology to identify suicidality overlooks a majority of at-risk adolescents. Structural personality variables as measured by the EARS identify and distinguish subsets of suicidal adolescents.

References

Adam, K.S. (1986). Early family influences on suicidal behavior. *Annals of the New York Academy of Science* 487:63–76.

Allen , B.P. (1987). Youth suicide. *Adolescence* 22:271–289.

American Psychiatric Association (1987). *Diagnostic and Statistical Manual of Mental Disorders*, 3rd edition-revised (DSM-III-R). Washington, DC: American Psychiatric Association.

Apter, A., Bleich, A., Plutchik, R., Mendelsohn, S., Tyano S. (1988). Suicidal behavior, depression, and conduct disorder in hospitalized adolescents. *Journal of the American Academy of Child and Adolescent Psychiatry* 27:696–699.

Berman, A.L., Jobes, D.A. (1991). *Adolescent Suicide: Assessment and Intervention.* Washington, DC: American Psychological Association.

Black, H.M. (1986). The reliability of the Separation Anxiety Test. In: *Researches in Separation Anxiety: A Third Volume on the Separation Anxiety Test,* Hansburg, H.G., Ed. Melbourne, FL: Krieger Publishing.

Blos, P, (1962). *On Adolescence.* New York: Free Press.

Bowlby J (1969). *Attachment and Loss.* New York: Basic Books.

———(1973). *Attachment and Loss, Vol 2: Separation Anxiety and Anger.* New York: Basic Books.

———(1977). The making and breaking of affectional bonds. Aetiology and psychopathology in light of attachment theory. *British Journal of Psychiatry* 130:201–210.

Carlson, G.A., Cantwell, D.P. (1982). Suicidal behavior and depression in children and adolescents. *Journal of the. American Academy of Child Psychiatry* 21:361–368.

Cohen, J. (1 977). *Statistical Power Analysis for the Behavioral Sciences.* New York: Academic Press.

Emde R (1988). Development terminable and interminable I and Il. *International Journal of Psychoanalysis* 69:23–42, 283–296.

Erlich, H.S. (1978). Adolescent suicide: maternal longing and cognitive development. *Psychoanalytic.Study of the Child* 33:261–262.

Freud, A. (1958). Adolescence. *Psychoanalytic Study of the Child* 32:255–278.

———(1969). Adolescence as a developmental disturbance. In: *Adolescence: Psychosocial Perspectives* S. Lebbovici & G. Caplan, Eds. New York: Basic Books .

Hansburg, H.G. (1980a). *Adolescent Separation Anxiety Test.* Melbourne, FL: Krieger Publishing.

———(1980b). *Adolescent Separation Anxiety: A Method for the Study of Adolescent Separation Problems,* Vols 1–2. Melbourne, FL: Krieger Publishing.

Hendin H. (1963). The psychodynamics of suicide. *Journal of Nervous and Mental Disease.* 136:236–244 .

———(1986). Suicide: a review of new directions in research. *Hospital Community Psychiatry* 37:148–154.

Hollingshead, A.B., Redlich, F.C. (1958). *Social Class and Mental Illness.* New York: Wiley.

Jacobson, E. (1973). *Depression: Comparative Studies of Normal, Neurotic, and Psychotic Conditions.* New York: International Universities Press.

Jessor, R. (1993). Successful adolescent development among youth in high risk settings. *American.Psychologist.* 48:117–126.

Kazdin, A.E. (1981). Assessment techniques for childhood depression: a critical appraisal. *Journal of the American Academy of Child Psychiatry* 20:358–375.

———French, N.H., Unis, A.S., Esveldt-Dawson, K., Sherick, R.B. (1983). Hopelessness, depression, and suicidal intent among psychiatrically disturbed inpatient children. *Journal of Consulting and Clinical Psychology.* 51:504–505.

Keller, D., Wilson, A. (1994). Affectivity in opiate and cocaine abusers. *Psychiatry* 57:333–347.

Kovacs, M. (1982). Children's Depression Inventor. Pittsburgh: Western Psychiatric Institute and Clinic .

———Beck, A.T. (1977). An empirical clinical approach cowards a definition of childhood depression. In: *Depression in Children,* Schulterbrandt JG, Raskin A, Eds. New York: Raven Press.

Kroger, J. (1986). Factor structure of the Hansburg Separation Anxiety Test. *Journal of Clinical Psychology.* 42:605–611.

Kroger, J., Green, K. (1990). Subscale structure and stability of the Hansburg Adolescent Separation Anxiety Test. *Journal of Clinical Psychology* 46:850–856.

Kuperman, S., Stewart, M.A. (1979). The diagnosis of depression in children. *Journal of Affective Disor*ders 1:213–217.

Laeber S., Rolf W., Schmaling. K.B. (1985). Empirical evidence for overt and covert patterns of antisocial conduct problems: a meta-analysis. *Journal of Abnormal Child Psychology.* 13:337–352.

Mattsson, A., Sees, L.R., Hawkins, J.W. (1969). Suicidal behavior as child psychiatric emergency: clinical characteristics and follow-up results. *Archives of General Psychiatry* 20:100–109.

Miller, D, (1981). Adolescent suicide: etiology and treatment. *Adolescent Psychiatry* 9:327–342.

Pfeffer, C., Klerman, G., Hurt, S., Kakuma, T., Peskin, J., Sieker, M. (1993). Suicidal children grow up: rates and psychosocial risk factors for suicide attempts during follow-up. *Journal of the American Academy of Child and Adolescent Psychiatry* 32:106–1 13.

———(1986). *The Suicidal Child.* New York/London: Guilford Press.

———Plutchik, R., Mizruchi, S. (1983). Suicidal and assaultive behavior in children: Classification, measurement, and interrelation. *American Journal of Psychiatry* 140:154–157.

Shaffer, D. (1974). Suicide in childhood and early adolescence. *Journal of Child Psychology and Psychiatry* 15:275–291.

Shafii, M., Carrigan, S., Whittinghill, J.R., Derrick, A. (1985). Psychological autopsy of completed suicide in children and adolescents. *American Journal of Psychiatry* 142:1061–1064.

Strober, M., Werry, J.S. (1986). The assessment of depression in children and adolescents. In: *Assessment of Depression,* N. Sartorius & T.A. Ban, eds. Berlin: Springer-Verlag.

Wade, N.L. (1987). Suicide as a resolution of separation-individuation among adolescent girls. *Adolescence* 22: 169–177.

Wasserman, D. (1988). Separation: An important factor in suicidal actions. *Crisis* 9:49–63.

Wilson, A., Maltesta, C. (1989). Affects and the compulsion to repeat: Freud's repetition compulsion revisited. *Psychoanalytic Contemporary Thought* 12:243–289.

———Passik, S. (1993). Explorations in presubjectivity. In: *Hierarchical Concepts in Psychoanalysis: Research, Theory and Practice, A.* Wilson & J. Gedo, Eds. New York: Guilford Press.

—————Faude. J. (1990a). Self-regulation and its failures. In: *Empirical Studies of Psychoanalytic Theories,* Vol 3, Masling J, ed. Hillsdale, NJ: Analytic Press.

—————————Gordon, E., Abrams, J.A. (1989a). Hierarchical model of opiate addiction: failures of self-regulation as a central aspect of substance abuse. *Journal of Nervous and Mental Disease* 177(7):390–399.

—————Kuras, M. (1989b). An epigenetic approach to the assessment of personality: the study of instability in stable personality organizations. In: *Advances in Personality Assessment,* C. Spielberger & J. Butcher, Eds. Hillsdale, NJ: Erlbaum.

———Weinstein, L. (1990b). Language, Thought, and Interiorization: A Psychoanalytic and Vygotskian perspective. *Contemporary Psychoanalysis* 26:24–40.

V. Surviving the Holocaust

CHAPTER 18

AFTERMATH OF THE CONCENTRATION CAMP:
THE SECOND GENERATION

A composite reading of varying reports circulating through the mental health community of the United States suggests that a new and unique group is emerging into a historical niche at this time—the children of those individuals who survived imprisonment in Nazi concentration camps or Soviet labor camps during the Second World War. Although these children may range on a mental health continuum from extremely healthy to extremely maladjusted, they all, nevertheless, seem deeply affected by the experience of their parents. The particular trauma at issue, the Holocaust, seems to exert an influence on either health or illness in the children, depending upon how the parents adapted to postwar life and to their parenting functions.

Let us specify what is meant by "children of survivors." Kestenberg (1972) suggests that the term may apply to any individual who was himself not subject to persecution, but is the child of at least one parent who was. This definition encompasses surviving in many ways, e.g., hiding in woods, moving from town to town, etc. In contrast, we do not include in our study a sample of the wide group of refugees and their children, but limit our discussion to children who have at least one parent who survived either a concentration or labor camp. This narrowed definition follows because the concentration camp experience was unique in its horror, and is the differentiating factor which renders the plight of these survivors unique. For organizational

637

purposes, Kestenberg's definition is satisfactory. For psychological purposes, it is not.

Investigators (Kestenberg, 1972; Klein, 1974) report great difficulty concerning research and treatment around the issue of the Holocaust. Hochman (1978) reports the following vignette from a psychoanalytic clinic in a major city:

> Two cases came up for discussion, where social and ethnic factors were important. One was an Irish Catholic and one was the daughter of Polish Jews. While there was an extensive discussion about the importance of the cultural factors in the first case, there was little such discussion in the second case, with no recognition of the importance of the Holocaust. . . . Many analysts have been affected directly and indirectly by the Holocaust. In spite of extensive analytic discussions of the death instinct and murderous and sadistic fantasies, discussions of murderous and sadistic reality take on an unsettling presence in the analyst's consulting room.

We contend that the vicissitudes of development in the children of survivors are best understood, not in the light of mental illness, but within their historical niche as children of survivors. Their dynamics emerge from intergenerational, cultural, and psychological factors, and all have to be considered if these individuals are to be properly understood. We further contend that the psychodynamics which have given rise to the emotional characteristics of these individuals are historically unique, and efforts to study them with reference to any other population can only serve to blur distinctions unique to each group.

These individuals are different, and working with them can cause unique transference and countertransference problems. For perhaps the best description of the possible difficulties in the countertransferential realm when working with a victim of the

Holocaust, we turn to Des Pres (1976), an English professor, not a psychologist. Here, one does not have to entirely agree with Des Pres to know that he is feeling a collective pulse of our times:

> Merely because they are survivors, the men and women who passed through the camps are suspect in our eyes. But when we consider the specific nature of their identity—not only as survivors, but survivors of those places—suspicion deepens to shock and rejection. The concentration camp experience represents an evil so appalling that we, too, when we turn to face it, suffer psychic unbalance. We too flounder in nightmare, in a torment having nothing to do with us yet felt in some strange way to be very much a part of our deepest, most secret being. The terror of the camps is with us. Some hideous impression of Auschwitz is in every mind, far removed from conscious thought but there; and not only as a repressed perception of historical events but as an image that stirs up the demonic content of our worst fears and wishes and anything connected with it, anything which starts it into consciousness, brings with it a horror too large and intensely personal to confront safely.

Kestenberg (1972) recognizes this danger, and notes that the personal difficulties a clinician may have in facing this horror may lead to a reluctance to probe for the relationship between the difficulties of a child of a survivor parent and the parent's experiences in the camps. This "pact of silence" appears to be an all-too-frequent occurrence, a covert contractual arrangement, if the clinician is not consciously aware of the significance of the Holocaust as an organizing principle of psychological development.

The Sample

A brief discussion of our sample and issues of generalization is called for. The first author interviewed extensively 18 children of survivors, all of whom were between the ages of 22 and 34. We aimed at obtaining information about the interviewees, but also obtained anecdotal information about other children of survivors and family members. The interviewees were reached by advertisement and word of mouth. None of those contacted refused to be interviewed. Those interviewed differed markedly from each other in socioeconomic status and extent of educational attainment, ranging from high school dropouts to Ph.D. students. All were Jewish; ten were female, and eight were male.

The bulk of our information was obtained from a background questionnaire, a structured clinical interview, other literature already reported, and clinical impressions. The background questionnaire provided us with the hard data we needed about the children's and parent's past. Information gathered in the background questionnaire included known personal history of the children, the parents, and their prewar family life, postwar adjustment, themes of accommodation to American culture, familial attitudes towards therapy and other forms of help, and other related effects of the Holocaust. The structured clinical interview was taped and transcribed. We looked particularly for nuances and reflections about interpersonal relations, emotional climate at home, the parent's marriage, themes of personality, emotional difficulties, self-other-world attitudes, life satisfaction, achievement motivation, issues of separation-individuation (including life-span involvement with the parents), Jewish identity, and avenues of communication available between parent and child vis-à-vis concentration camp themes. Tangential speculations and associations were usually encouraged.

The Parents view, which focuses on the life span unfolding as well as the interaction along the life span with the parents, In our opinion, in trying to understand the individuals in our study, as the survivors themselves, who carry with them the dynamics at

issue, constitutes a satisfactory "genetic" (Cohler, 1979) explanation.

Bettelheim (1943) saw the camps as a monstrous assault upon
the human will, in which the survivors were those who possessed
the quality of "autonomy," who never gave up, who persevered
defiantly despite the obstacles. To Bettelheim, when the state of
rebelliousness, of heroism, was overcome by the experience of
life in the camps, then all was lost, and the prisoners became like
children—culpable victims. Rather than celebrate suicidal opposition as an avenue to "autonomy," Des Pres (1976) uncovers the
multitude of ways, many of them far more heroic than Bettelheim is prepared to see, in which the camp inmates were able to
support themselves, resist, and at times create the conditions
whereby they could save themselves. Des Pres claims that Bettelheim is mistakenly addressing a psychological level he terms
"primary adjustment," which is the level of overt subordination
to the camps, a level of existence which to the camp inmates had
no meaning other than survival on a moment-to-moment basis.
For all intents, Des Pres believes, this level of existence was without symbolic or interpretive value, unmediated by multidetermined symbol systems.

Bettelheim goes on to assert a regression hypothesis, which
postulates that inmates regress to forms of behavior and defenses
which are characteristic of infancy or childhood. He points out
that the prisoners were helpless like children, and were tortured
in ways in which a cruel and domineering father might physically torture or emotionally debase a child. They were forced to
soil themselves as they had done in early childhood. Like children, they lived only in the immediate present, because it was
impossible to plan for the future or to give up whatever immediate pleasure was possible in order to obtain greater satisfaction
in the future. With people being killed all the time around them,

concentration camp inmates were unable to establish durable object relations. Daydreaming and identification with the aggressor were among the very few defenses left to them by means of which to protect themselves from total emotional annihilation. Des Pres, whose sympathetic voice is a welcome antidote to the transparent condescension Bettelheim holds for inmates, nevertheless employs a mistaken ad hominem argument in disputing this interpretation. His argument, directed at Bettelheim, erroneously generalizes in his charge of an inability of psychoanalytic theory to account for the camp experience, and the apparent derogation of the inmates. While we agree with Des Pres that Bettelheim is wrong, we hope to demonstrate that psychoanalytic insights may deepen our understanding of life during and after extremity.

The distinction Des Pres (after Goffman, 1961) draws between primary and secondary levels of adjustment will be stressed in this paper. In extremity, he argues, life is split into these two coexistent levels, and Bettelheim is depicting the primary level (symbolless cognition and outwardly-seeming capitulation), whereas the inmates actually survived through access to the secondary level of adjustment (multisymbolic cognition and surreptitious organizational resistance). As Des Pres describes it, the primary level refers to the facts of required life, of coopted activity to the camp situation, while the secondary level is defined as the unauthorized ways, means, and ends which allow an inmate to stand apart from his role as inmate, apart from the self controlled by the captors. Thus, Des Pres concludes, Bettelheim's picture of inmate pathology is in error precisely because of his failure to see the extent of the inmate's powers of adaptation and self-help behaviors, and his confusion of primary level behaviors for the inmate's total characterological personality formation.

If we grant Des Pres this primary/secondary bifurcation (not to be confused with primary and secondary process), then one still must question exactly what were the consequences of the abuse on the primary level which the inmates received. Des Pres seems to prefer to overlook this aspect of the psychological life of the inmates, whereas Bettelheim seems not to see past it to survival adaptations. To us, these levels must both be recognized as simultaneous and real. The crafts and tools necessary for survival are to be found on the secondary level, yet one is also subject to the psychological consequences of abuse on the primary level.

On the primary level, there is enough evidence to conclude that certain behaviors and defenses which resemble developmentally early defenses were employed by the inmates in the service of survival. However, this does not necessarily imply a pathological type of regression. These defenses, some of which have been cited by Bettelheim, include identification with the aggressor, feelings of omnipotence, hallucinatory wish-fulfillment (Freud, 1916), and the attribution of animism to environmental objects. However, these defenses and behaviors should not be considered pathological in that they served the purpose of survival, of adaptation to an impossible situation. They are primary-level-of-adjustment phenomena. On this primary level, any show of resistance usually meant certain death. Degradation was so rampant that any civilized behavior would have been unrealistic. One may either resist and by doing so commit suicide (which seems to be Bettelheim's preference), give up and, by doing so, commit suicide, or allow oneself to be driven, adapting in order to survive, into a regressive/passive state characterized by a dulling of cognitive and affective abilities (Bychowski, 1968) as well as the development of the above-mentioned defenses and behaviors. Victor Frankl (1955) referred to emotional death as a "necessary mechanism of self-defense." In the case of the survivor, it may be more accurate to speak of regression in the service of survival rather than classic pathological regression. Although regression in the service of survival occurs under different social conditions and operates in a different (although not as yet fully understood) fashion, we are not suggesting that it is less devastating than pathological regression to the organismic world of the inmate (cf. Lifton, 1976).

On the secondary level of adjustment, the inmates erected what amounts to nothing less than a survival culture, amazing in its capacity to sustain life in the face of such overwhelming obstacles. Rules were made and enforced, groups were organized, resistance acts were undertaken, help was given—all surreptitiously. It was at these times that the inmates were able to recharge themselves. During these hours, they could cognize and emote without retaliation. Life for a few hours existed on a multisymbolic level of free and individual meaning.

A final note on the distinction of primary vs secondary levels of adjustment. To survive, the inmate had to create psychic space for the formation of an impoverished psychological level characterized by symbols which could be translated as either life-sustaining or death-producing. We, who take our civilized life and culture for granted, must make a superb effort to grasp the fact that what are symbols of defilement to us might have been symbols of life to the inmates. Even Paul Ricoeur, the theologian/phenomenologist, assumes a priori the existence of a civilized status in his book, *The Symbolism of Evil* (1967), where he discusses how symbols of corruption, decay, and excrement embody our symbolic perceptions of evil. But what if these symbols, from which we flinch as if by reflex, come to represent the continuation of life? Does not being bombarded by excrement represent a far more desirable alternative than being burned in an oven? We ask the reader to consider how alien such forms of symbolic mediation are to him, and to appreciate how inadequately the classical concept of pathological regression accounts for such phenomena. It becomes an ethnocentric superimposition of man-in-civilization upon man-in-extremity.

Hence, the concentration camps may be seen as an alien culture, one which radically departed from any other culture yet known to civilized man. The problem of comprehending the concentration camps is thus related to the problem of gaining access to a foreign culture's meanings (Geertz, 1973). Further, Geertz, after Weber (1947), views culture semiotically, where understanding begins through the interpretation of social symbols, in pursuit of the culture's unique web of meanings. Herein lies a difficulty of interpretation: in the concentration camps, there was not a unique panorama of multidetermined symbols and meanings; rather, there was a winnowing down of symbols in which they actualized themselves at the lowest possible level of meaning (life and death).

After liberation, the survivors of the camps were faced with severe problems. They were physically deteriorated. According to Niederland (1961), the survivor may be chronically anxious, depressed, beset by physical symptoms, reliving past terrors through repetitive nightmares, obsessed with "survivor guilt" (self-directed aggression due to the reality of one's survival while others perished), and extreme social isolation. Krystal (1968) further asserts that the old concept of traumatic neurosis may be an appropriate diagnosis, but has to be extended to account for the survivor's long-term, stable, crystallized traits and symptoms. Traumatic neurosis is defined by its immediate onset after a trauma, with an amelioration of symptoms likely. The concentration camp survivor, according to Krystal, is experiencing a state similar to a traumatic neurosis, but which may also be characterized by unremitting symptoms, a "symptom-free interval" before onset, as well as unique psychoneurotic adaptations. These investigators recognize that traditional concepts of mental illness are not suited for this particular population, and that they cannot be grouped with the mentally ill. We actually go further and suggest that Holocaust survivors cannot be grouped with any other populations, neither with survivors of other disasters nor with modern extirpated technological man and his existential plight.

Matussak (1971) has empirically demonstrated that the neurological-psychiatric illnesses which beset the survivor not only unfold individualistically, depending upon the survivor's past history of problem-solving and his ongoing sociofamilial situation, but also are not comparable to previously described syndromes in the psychiatric literature.

At liberation, the life of the survivor was extremely difficult. He had been failed by the important institutions in life, viz., religion, family, country. Alone, abandoned, and distrustful, many of the survivors, despite harsh treatment by authorities and low immigration quotas, succeeded in relocating either in America or in what was soon to become Israel. As both Koenig (1964) and Hillel Klein (1971) note, many of these survivors, finding that they had lost most of their families, entered hasty and ill-planned marriages in order to alleviate the intense mourning and separation anxiety they were undergoing. These marriages were frequently arranged by distant relatives or friends, and often the spouses barely knew each other before betrothal. In other cases, marriages were arrived at in DP camps, again with spouses one barely knew, except insofar as the feat of survival was common to both partners. There were limited courtship rituals, and these marriages tended to be centered around themes of procreation. What seems to have taken place was a pattern characterized by euphoria after liberation, and then profound mourning, depression, and resignation as the realization crept in that the loved ones were gone forever. Many of the female survivors, then,

married and bore their children while in a state of profound bereavement for losses which could never be replaced. In this way,
the generation of the children of survivors began, in about 1946-
48. For future research, a comprehensive ethnography of the life
of the survivor during these turbulent years is needed.

For the survivor, the role of memory functioning is important. As Krystal and Niederland (1968) noted, the survivor
may have difficulty owning up to memories and related mental
material, at times confusing past for present. In order to start life
anew, the memories of the camps had to be banished from consciousness, so that they would not hinder the survivor in his new
life. This is the route of adaptation. Recent psychoanalytic investigation has focused on memory as an adaptive function rather
than as forgetting explained from the vantage point of repression. Schlesinger (1969) has pointed out that forgetting is not
necessarily negative and nonadaptive, and is an important factor
in the continuing efficiency of memory. Schachtel (1959), as part
of his critique of repression, asserts that memory as a function of
the living personality can be understood only as a capacity for
the organization and reconstruction of past experiences and impressions in the service of present needs, fears, and interests.

Memories, to be acted upon, do not have to exist in consciousness. In the case of the survivors, it seems probable that memories
are more dissociated than repressed, and that they are capable of
sharply influencing behavior if precipitated or aroused, to the det-
riment of the integrity of the psyche. The survivor cannot help but
preconsciously live with his memories, and he has to struggle to
cope successfully with them. A "selective memory" is needed, one
which allows access to memories but prevents an overflow of painful affect. It may be an inability in some survivors to constitute this
selective memory which has led the majority of clinicians to refuse
to recommend psychodynamic therapy for survivors (Kestenberg,

1972). If this selective memory is understood as an adaptive mechanism, then it follows that an event, person, or thing which provokes a failure in the selective memory's defensive function may cause deep conflict. We think that many survivors tailor their lives in such a way that it remains intact at almost any cost. We would further speculate that if this selective memory mechanism is in some way overwhelmed or fails, some manifestation of aggression or shame will be the outcome: aggression against the other for precipitating the reaction, shame in regard to the self both because of the precipitated memories and because the observing ego recognizes the inappropriateness of such a reaction. These phenomena have often been observed, but have been attributed to the rather loose concept of "survivor guilt." Barocas and Barocas (1973) noted that survivors may have great difficulty neutralizing their aggressive discharges. Our data confirm this.

The Children

The survivors were usually living in an unfamiliar foreign place when their children were born. Often they faced a new and unfamiliar culture. As we discussed, in a state of mourning, giving birth to a child can acquire a special significance. Children may mean many things to the survivor. They may serve to restitute lost objects, goals, and ideals (Trossman, 1968). If the child is begotten to restitute lost family members, the newborn infant becomes a symbiotic restitution object (Klein, 1971). In this case, there may arise an excessive involvement with the children, who become a repository for a complex web of wishes and fears. Like others, the child is capable, no matter how inadvertently, of causing the failure of the selective memory, even before he is old enough to do so intentionally. Perhaps the essential safeguard in the early life of the child of the survivor may be an ability not to reawaken the searing dissociated or sequestered memories of life in the camps for the parents. The deeper the child is tied into the parents' network of fantasies, feelings, and Holocaust-related memories, the more the child will be influenced by the consequences of their rekindling. What is important is that the early life span of the child of the survivor is characterized by the very same behaviors and defenses the survivor employed in the camps, e.g., attributions of animism, satisfaction in daydreaming rather than action (symbolic play), and extreme passivity, helplessness, and dependency. The child's early behaviors and defenses parallel the behaviors and defenses which the parents employed on the primary level of adjustment in the concentration camp, and evoke dissociated and sequestered memories which have been eliminated from consciousness in ethe service of adaptation to living in the normal world again. In the child of the survivor, then, normal development may be threatening to the parents. The child at birth exists in a state which is not dissimilar to that which was termed the parents' primary level of adjustment earlier in this paper. He has limited symbols, he can be shaped, he is stark naked, and his mortality is evident and clearly an issue. He is helpless and dependent upon others for his survival. The infant thus simultaneously becomes both a recapitulator of the dissociated or the sequestered memories as well as the symbolization of a chance for the parents to undo the trauma associated with these memories. Here, we see the forerunner of the later conflict between the survivors carrying on a desperate and forced attempt to obtain their own identifications through their children (Barocas and Barocas, 1973), and a fearful, often suffocating overprotectiveness (Lipkowitz, 1973). Tragically, the children, born out of the parents' hope of banishing the Holocaust from their lives, become agents whereby the Holocaust is relived. Perhaps this cannot be avoided. Possibly the children may learn to defend against it when they attain a sufficient level of cognitive maturity to comprehend the problem. They then can learn to take evasive steps to avoid those behaviors which would lead to breakdowns in the parents' empathy.

Hence, we believe that the major difficulties in these parent-child relationships are Holocaust-derived, and in large part related to ego, superego, and projective identifications. For example, over and over again, the parents deal with the children's aggression and disobedience by calling them the likes of "little Hitler" or explosively responding to them with counteraggression.

Let us now hear from two children whom the first author interviewed, discussing their fathers, in both cases survivors:

> I did not know him very well. . . . He would not speak to me. He was withdrawn. He would have temper tantrums occasionally, keeping things in all the time, and then there would be occasional explosions, which were inevitably directed towards myself in the way of physical beatings, severe physical beatings.

And:

> I would get hit, but he just had to look at me in the wrong way and I would start crying. They [her brothers] were beaten severely. He [her father] would go crazy, he would just lose control practically. The more my brothers would answer back the more he would go wild. Usually with his hand or with a stick and sometimes he would even throw things. I remember I could not take that.

In both cases, one must wonder for whom these beatings were really intended.

In survivors, we believe there are four separate clusters of available identifications (Schafer, 1968) which may appear after the birth of their children. First, the child evokes identifications which assisst the mother in her maternal duties. Benedek (1959) has described how a woman's "motherliness" is derived from the developmental vicissitudes of primary identifications with her own mother. The developmental phase of initial parenthood reactivates self and object representations which were integrated during her own oral phase, bringing about a repetition of the intrapsychic processes which occurred many years earlier, except that she is now the mother, and the infant is who she once was. Benedek further points out how these identifications help the mother develop confidence in her "good-mother-self." Thus, it is not the fact of evoking identifications in the mother which may result in empathic and caretaking difficulties, but the kind and quality of the identifications which the child evokes. We are postulating three additional clusters of identifications, maladaptive ones, which issue specifically from the camp experience. The child, at times when his existence leads to a failure of the selective memory, may be identified by the parent as (a) someone in the camps, either the parents themselves or comrades, or (b) the captors, or (c) loved ones lost during the Holocaust, particularly the survivor's first set of children if a family had been reared before the war. H. Klein (1971) found that before the birth of their children, survivors were able to articulate their belief that their soon-to-be-born children were a source of security and gratification, an undoing of destruction, and a restoration of lost family. He also found a paralyzing fear of damage, in which survivor mothers had vivid fantasies concerning damage to themselves and their children during pregnancy. The fluctuating nature of these fantasies may be responsible for Krystal's (1971) report of a puzzlingly high abortion rate among female survivors.

It may be helpful to discuss some dynamics which seem to permeate the entire life span via the ever-evolving but continual parent-child bond. Trossman (1968) notes that survivors may treat their children as symbols of their own inner emptiness, of all they have been denied by fate, and not as individuals. Needy parents may use the child as restitutive self-objects, rather than allow the child to use them as structuring, optimally frustrating, self-objects. As Lipkowitz (1973) reports, these parents' meanings are more important to the parents than the needs of their children. This leads to a phenomenon of "parenting the parents," and is consistently present in the older children's reports of being held accountable for the happiness and welfare of their parents. This responsibility seems to take two forms. First, the child may be overloaded by messages that living fully and apart from the parents is a sign of betrayal, an act of disloyalty. If the child enters into a pact whereby the experience of extrafamilial gratification represents a denial of the bonding with the parents, what is reported is a depressed, troubled early life span. Usually in these instances, the children report growing up in a household pervaded by an ambience of gloom, an underlying sense of imminent catastrophe, as if the Holocaust were on a cycle of eternal return. Second, the happiness of the parents may be associated with extrafamilial achievement and growth. This alternative allows the child to leave the physical propinquity of the parents, and to establish durable object relations and later a career away from home. He or she is more likely to succeed, whereas the other children tend to fail, often seemingly intentionally. Failure for this first group, in our sample, took such forms as drug addiction, psychopathology, social isolation, a lapse into ego-dystonic homosexuality, and academic failure. These seem to be purposive, in that failure reinforced the parent-child bond, and frequently brought the children back under control of the parents. One of the children we interviewed had gotten married, and after seven months, during which time the marriage was never consummated, moved back in with his parents, where he resumed a deadly avocation of mediating their fights in the hope of keeping them together and available to him. The differences between the two above-mentioned groups may be qualitative rather than quantitative, i.e., some degree of both forms may be present in many families.

What criteria may we use to distinguish a priori between groups of favorable and less favorable outcome? We propose that two variables enter into this picture, which may enable us to identify those children at risk for later difficulty and those headed for a less conflicted life course. The two variables may be seen as "orienter variables" towards outcome, but clearly they are not themselves dynamic. They point to the pivotal dynamic, the parenting pattern, and should not be confused with it.

First, we suspect that a prognostic indicator is the parents' willingness or capability to empathically discuss their experiences in the camps with their children (cf. Epstein, 1979). If this pathway of conscious and preconscious communication is open, there seem to be a number of beneficial consequences. The identifications which lead to self-boundary dissolution are minimized, and so the parent can view the child, not as a representation of an idealized, distorted, or emotionally laden memory, but as a child. It also suggests that the selective memory is intact and well fortified, can tolerate the admission of painful or conflictual input without having to defend against it. This implies that the child can recapitulate the parent's experience, i.e., attain age-appropriate defenses and behaviors, without being driven into an emotional cul-de-sac. Further, these parents may be more at peace with their past, and experience less need to protect their children from real or imagined dangers. In our sample, we found that a number of these children had entered professions which stressed helping others and human authenticity. Some of them struck us as among the most genuine, caring people we had ever met; yet, the effects of the Holocaust were still present. They had succeeded in employ-ing their parents' pain in the service of their own growth. One child, a clinical psychology student, put it this way:

> I have a great need to help others. I do not see it as a strength in myself, I see it as a weakness, something which is changing. I am aware that it is a major contradiction in my life. But I have also felt that the product of my social, my cultural experience, has given me an ability, has de-veloped a capacity within myself to do things on my own, to rely on myself in ways that many other people cannot, and the use of that abil-ity is one of the reasons that led to my choice of clinical psychology as a profession.

"Parenting the parents," the necessity of developing empathic and introspective sensitivities in order to protect the parent from his memories, may be in some individuals excellent early prepa-ration for the helping professions.

On the other hand, the survivors who do not grant their chil-dren an intellectual or affectively appropriate understanding of their predicament, despite the fact that the consequences of the camps are transmitted to and lived out by the parents and children on a moment-to-moment basis, seem to have far more difficulties with their parenting duties. These seem to be the parents who ex-pect their children to participate in their world view of hostile suspiciousness (Trossman, 1968), in which most of the children's autonomous activities elicit overprotection (Barocas and Barocas, 1973). If it is true that the refusal to speak of the camp experience in many of these parents is due to a depletion of the personality of the survivor (Sigal, Silver, Rakoff, and Ellin, 1973), then perhaps these parents could not provide appropriate feedback and empa-thy to their children when they were growing up in part because their personality resources were so highly overtaxed. As Kohut

(1977) stresses, the parental satisfaction of needs may be less influential in early childhood than the child's optimal experience of
a merger with the empathic parental self-object. Exquisite attunement to the child's nascent self may be more important than good
caretaking abilities. Winnicott (1962) also notes that "it is indeed
possible to gratify an oral drive and in so doing violate the infant's
ego function, or that which would later on be jealously guarded as
the self, the core of the personality."

Although not phrased in these terms, this appears to be the
early situation which Sigal et al. encountered. Despite the best-in-
tentioned and diligent caretaking, the children seem to have been
used for or influenced by the parents' Holocaust-derived identifications (hence the term restitutive self-object), which in turn
affected the children's ability to use the parents as average, expectable, structuring objects. In this respect, Crapanzano, a cultural
anthropologist, has suggested to us that "the unsayable" accurately
conveys the fear associated with the camp recollections which the
survivors withhold from their children (personal communication). It should be noted that it is the intrapsychic dynamics
associated with the ability to speak about the camp experience
with the children which are at issue here, not the actual behavior.
We might say that it is the ability to empathically create the channel in the service of the child's needs which marks it as
constructive. Thus, there will be parents who do not speak to their
children of the camp experiences who nevertheless are capable of
soothing their children's tensions and of being attuned to their
children's subtle needs. So, too, will there be parents who speak
inappropriately of the camps. For instance, one of our subjects informed us that she grew up in a house where the concentration
camps were dwelled upon at every possible moment by the parents, both survivors. This led to a family setting in which the
children grew up "overwhelmed by each other's innermost

secrets," and ultimately the concentration camps became an excuse for the parents to exercise a smothering overprotectiveness against fantasized dangers, and, later, a rationale for any triggering of irrational parenting. Nevertheless, this woman, although afflicted with an anxiety neurosis, was able to separate from her parents, move 1000 miles away, become successful in her chosen career, and advantageously utilize psychoanalytic assistance.

The second variable which may suggest outcome is the status as first family or as a second family reconstituted from one lost during the war. If the children are a second family, then we might expect that the parents' losses resulting from the Holocaust were that much more devastating. Winnik (1967) notes that inmates in the camps who had lost children tended to be more passive in the camps and to shun resistance activities, more than inmates who had not lost children. Klein (1974) has found that active inmates adjusted to postwar life far better than passive inmates. Thus, activity on the level of resistance, which has been termed the secondary level of adjustment, may be seen as a secondary prognostic indicator of the survivor's ability to parent. In the passive survivor who has lost children, the dynamic of the child's evocation of the parent's camp memories may trigger exceptionally deep feelings of loss; he may resonate more profoundly to shame, helplessness, and capitulation than active inmates do. Further, if the second family becomes identified with the lost children, a complex matrix of difficulties may arise. Binding his children into the nuclear family may become more imperative. If the survivor idealized the lost children, and if he himself as an immigrant could not attain his potential, the successful academic, social, or professional accomplishments of the second group of children may stir up feelings of loss and envy, in which the second children may be seen as simultaneously living out the aspirations of the parents as well as those they had for the first set of family. Here, the conflict between the parents' smothering overprotectiveness, their view of the world as malevolent and catastrophic, and their need to realize their own ego ideals through the activity and accomplishments of their children may be at its most acute. Kestenberg (1972) asserts that survivors who find a new love object after the camps, be it husband, wife, or child, will experience severe guilt about their perceived betrayal of the original love objects. This, too, may promote maladaptive identifications with the lost loved ones of the parents. What is so striking about these particular identifications is that the survivors' emotions are not confined to feelings about the loss, but extend to feelings which in fantasy belong to the lost loved ones. Projection has led to personification, which in turn is followed by identification. This particular mental sequence has the implications of a projective identification, as coined by M. Klein (1946).

However, not all children of survivors show the above difficulties. After interviewing a number of the exceptions to predicted outcome, i.e., children with robust selves who can play, work and love, but are the reconstituted second family of parents who did not speak to them of their camp experiences, we feel that despite emotional hardships, some of the children nevertheless were able to seek out and find "good-enough" (Winnicott, 1962) parenting. In this instance, Kohut's (1971) observations on the father's role in the bipolar self of ambitions and ideals are germane. In Kohut's (1977) terms, even if the child is denied an empathic merger with the mirroring grandiose self-object, he may yet obtain sufficient esteem from an empathic union with the paternal idealized self-object, and thus emerge from early childhood with a cohesive self. The child may be able to actively seek a salubrious alternative to the unempathic self-object. From an object relations approach, Abelin (1971) discusses the importance of the father in development, particularly during the practicing subphase (when the child "hatches" from the symbiosis) and the rapprochement subphase (when the "ambitendencies" occur which enable the child to integrate good/bad internalizations). The father, in Kohut's self psychology, represents the "second chance" to sustain a cohesive self. In our group, we found that greater difficulties accrue to those who were denied a deep relationship with the father, who were not pulled out of the symbiosis by the "uncontaminated" (Mahler and Gosliner, 1955) father. In more than one of our sample, this effect could be traced directly to the Holocaust's impact upon the mother, who viewed the father as a danger to the child, not dissimilar to individuals outside the family. The hostile suspiciousness of the world often seen in survivors' families thus can intrude into the family, affecting the parents' relationships with each other, and profoundly affecting the child. Conversely, the exceptions to the orienter variables may be those in which the father has a good deal of involvement with the child and in which the mother is able to "let go" of the child in favor of the father.

Our research suggests that some survivor fathers may have unusual difficulty with their children's aggression. As previously noted, such aggression may precipitate projective identifications (e.g. "little Hitler") which threaten the integrity of the parents' selective memory. Barocas and Barocas (1973) assert that since survivors had such difficulty dealing with their own aggressive impulses, they may unconsciously facilitate the expression of aggression in their children. Although the paternal response of counteraggression to the child's constituents of aggression is important, we believe that it is part of a more global picture of father-child asynchrony, especially concerning the father's reluctance to allow himself to be idealized. As previously noted, many survivor fathers tend to be withdrawn, passive, and ashamed, and have occasional explosive outbursts of aggression which have a retaliatory sense. Such fathers rebuffed their children's attempts to initiate idealized self-object relationships. In our sample, several of these children reported feeling empty and un-fulfilled by the successes of their lives and careers, even when a parental injunction around ambivalent achievement did not ex-ist. Thus, we are speaking of a genetically based internalized structural issue, not a sense of failing to please a demanding par-ent. In our sample, these fathers became and remained urgently important to the children, who strained, even in adulthood, to elicit reactions which would appear to be capable of filling in the emptiness and unfulfillment which life and career could not do. In this sense, our observations support Kohut's views on the re-lationship, in the narcissistic sector, between the growth and management of ideals and the empathic paternal response as a way station towards self-cohesion and vigor.

A striking example of the ambivalence associated with aggres-sion and counteraggression is a survivor son, aged 24, whose father was distant, passive, and explosive, but idealized, largely due to his son's excellent capacity for compassion and empathy. During his teen years, after the child had been harshly punished for a seemingly trivial act of disobedience, he retaliated against his father in a fit of rage, punching him and in so doing cutting his own hand. For a year, he kept this cut open and bleeding, re-fusing to allow a scab to form and the healing process to begin, until the parents, against his wishes, had a cast put on to prevent him from inflicting any more damage to himself.

The two variables discussed may also point to households in which there is ubiquitous suspicion of a world which allowed the Holocaust to occur, the sense that all life outside the family is dangerous, and overprotectiveness from real and imagined threats. All of these work against a loose, relaxed, playful home atmosphere with such restraints at a minimum, and work against the likelihood that there will be significant others to act as surrogates to fill the breach and perhaps serve as alternative identification figures. In support of this notion, we refer to H. Klein (1974), who has noted a dread of separation in disturbed children of survivors, a dread which is shared by both the child and the parents. Frequently, there are marriages between a survivor and a nonsurvivor, through which the above-mentioned characteristics will certainly be modulated or altered. In fact, the effects upon the children may be significantly different with the presence of a nonsurvivor and the culturally adaptive patterns he or she may bring into the family fold.

An uncanny testimonial to the constrictive mutuality of the parent-child bond is the so-called "anniversary reaction" (Hilgard, 1953). In children of survivors (Axelrod et al., 1980), this tragic event can occur when they are at the same age as their parent(s) were upon incarceration. The child's unconscious sabotage of his life may take many forms, e.g., a collapse of interpersonal relations or a clinical depression. In our sample, we were informed of several anniversary reactions in which an abrupt transition in parental relations led to the child seemingly seeking symptoms as a way of reestablishing or maintaining a longed-for parent-child bonding. The most striking symptom in this context was anorexia nervosa with amenorrhea, in a woman who engaged in particularly vivid fantasies of what her mother had undergone in the camps. Allowing her mother to be the precipitant of and later to become privy to the resolution of her emaciation represented, we suspect, this child's effort to heal herself and her mother at the same time. Pollock (1970), speaking of anniversary reactions in other traumatized populations, finds that they may be delayed mourning reactions triggered by a psychologically contiguous stimulus. He further remarks that the precipitating trauma need not be recalled in order to be reexperienced. What is striking about the anniversary reaction in the children of survivors is that quite a few of the apparently self-sabotaging children do not know at what age their parents entered the camps, because of the parents' refusal to speak of the camp experiences. They suffer their parents' anniversary reaction. It may be that, at this particular time, the parents will panic and strive to pull the child back into the family process, thus causing the child to collapse and, as a result, return to the hegemony of the parents. Compassionately sacrificing his own mental health or autonomy may be experienced by the child as a way of protecting his parents, as well as of assuring them of his availability and of the meaning he provides to them. This kind of communications network may be a lifelong or periodic phenomenon, and does not find expression only in the anniversary reaction. This phenomenon has been informally termed "the compassionate sacrifice" (Danieli, 1979). The anniversary reaction of the child of survivors, then, is in part the mourning which causes the child to be drawn back into the symbiotic orbit, and the compassionate sacrifice represents the child's willingness to do so.

In our interviewing, we found that some children of survivors tended to recall early and unremitting images and fantasies of death, violence, and persecution. Although we recognize that fantasies of death and violence are characteristic of the generation of mass media-influenced children, we feel that in the children of survivors such fantasies represent the lingering effects the Holocaust has had upon their parents. This may be seen in the persecutory quality of many of these fantasies. It also seems that the children of survivors who do not speak of their camp experiences participated equally in this tendency with those whose parents did speak of their camp experiences. Perhaps all the survivors did "speak" about their camp experiences in some manner, through channels not necessarily verbal in nature. One woman whose grandparents were both survivors was haunted by a recurring memory from early childhood. Her grandfather would unexpectedly creep up on his wife and, apparently for no reason, try to scare her. The woman recalls believing that her grandfather was trying to scare her grandmother to death. She described her grandmother as never having recovered from the Holocaust, and her grandfather's behavior as "what Nazi prison guards must have been like." In the other interviews we conducted, we were continually noting the many references made to death-related themes, frequently humorously, sometimes with no concomitant affect, often with a flood of painful affect. Some of the children reported an early, virulent obsession with death and its implications. One child lived with a phobia which extended back as far as he could remember, in which he feared death in the form of a huge rock which would fall off a building on top of his head when he was not looking. Another interviewee, whose parents never spoke of the camps, recalls an overpoweringly experienced childhood fantasy of wishing to lock up all the children her age into cages. She eventually grew up to become an ardent advocate of adolescent incarceration reform.

Conclusion

Analysts, therapists, and researchers working around the issue of the Holocaust have to come to expect, at times, to be overwhelmed by the gruesomeness of this barometer of man's horror to his fellow man, and to be repelled into yearning for work on a clearer topic which might make the investigator feel better about himself and those who share this world with him. This has certainly been the case with ourselves. Indeed, we suspect that no other response would be an appropriate one. We hope that this paper will serve to stimulate others in picking up these threads, working with and thinking about this crucial problem of contemporary life.

The reader will notice that we have avoided endorsing any of the current paradigms prominent in psychoanalysis. While we admire such paradigms as separation-individuation, ego psychology, or the psychology of the self, their application to the phenomenology of the child of survivors presents some difficulties. It is essential for a clinician to directly address the psychic imagery such individuals have of their and their parents' lives.

For example, a common fantasy in our sample was that mother survived through prostitution, father by collaboration in the camps. The task of the clinician is to confront this imagery, to decode the concentration camp-related symbols and fantasies. To relegate these themes to a theoretical paradigm is to reduce their subjective impact, to make the concentration camp-related material secondary to the chosen paradigm. Doubtless, adherents of paradigms will publish articles that demonstrate how the experience can be seen through their theoretical lens; we believe that in the case of survivors and their children, such undertakings may be misdirected. We doubt that psychotherapeutic attempts which subordinate the second-generation experience to a paradigm will be sufficient. It is the hermeneutical effort, the creation of narrative sense, the interpretation of meaningfulness out of the inchoate past that are called for therapeutically.

The child of survivors is, in many ways, out of place in modern culture. In a narcissistic society which advertises pleasure as an easily obtainable end, he is rooted in his and his parents' pain. Where autonomy is seen as desirable, he has intense parental bindings. In a society where obsession with the past is considered by definition neurotic, he either renounces his identity or suffers conflicts around self-disclosure. Like his parents, the child may be ostracized if he persists in speaking of the camps, in bringing the demonic into the world of prosaic life. One of the psych-social tasks many children may face in therapy is clarifying the tension between the ideals of modern society and the heritage they are born into.

In our group of second-generation survivors there was a prevalent sense that a person offering professional help was not to be trusted, that psychoanalysts and psychologists were not able to be of any assistance when one was suffering. Yet, many of these individuals would probably have flourished in therapy. Perhaps their reluctance is linked to an observation H. Klein (1971) made, in Israel, of a need to feel protective towards one's survivor parents, with an accompanying need to emphasize the heroic aspects of the parents' past while negating or denying the suffering. Perhaps helpers also bring along with them a threat, a threat which the helpers may easily overlook in their eagerness to help. Attachment to another person, good or bad, is preferable to no attachment at all. Freedom from constrictive bonds may be experienced as no freedom at all. With this in mind, reconstructive and recollective work may be pursued, slowly and with care. Hopefully, each therapeutic involvement will also serve to minimize any deleterious effects of the Holocaust on the third generation of survivors, a generation whose time is now upon us.

References

Abelin, E. (1971), The role of the father in the separation-individuation process, in J. McDevitt and C. Settlage (Eds.), *Separation-Individuation: Essays in Honor of Margaret Mahler*, pp. 229-252. International Universities Press, New York.

Axelrod, S.,O.H. Schnipper and J. H. Rau (1980), Hospitalized offspring of holocaust survivors: Problems and dynamics, *Bulletin of the Menninger Clinic* 44.

Barocas, H. and C. Barocas (1973), Manifestations of concentration camp effects on the second generation, *American Journal of Psychiatry* 130, 821.

Benedek, T. (1959), Parenthood as a developmental phase: A contribution to the libido theory, *Journal of the American Psychoanalytic Association* 7:389–417.

Bettelheim, B. (1943), Individual and mass behavior in extreme situations, *Journal of Abnormal Social Psychology* 38:417–452.

Bychowski, G. (1968), Permanent character changes as an aftereffect of persecution, in H. Krystal (Ed.), *Massive Psychic Trauma.*, pp. 75–86. New York: International Universities Press.

Cohler, B.J. (1979), Adult developmental psychology and reconstruction in psychoanalysis, in S. I. Greenspan and G. H. Pollock (Eds.), *Human Life Cycle Developmental Psychology*. Government Printing Office, Washington, D.C. (N.I.M.H.).

Crapanzano, V. (1979), Personal communication.

Danieli, Y. (1979), Personal communication.

Des Pres, T. (1976), *The Survivor: An Anatomy of Life in the Death Camps.* Pocket Books, New York.

Epstein, H. (1979), *Children of the Holocaust: Conversations with Sons and Daughters of Survivors*, Putnam, New York.

Frankl, V. (1955), *The Doctor and the Soul: An Introduction to Logotherapy.* New York: Alfred A. Knopf.

Freud, S. (1916), A Metapsychological Supplement to the Theory of Dreams. *Standard Edition* 14:222–235.

Geertz, C. (1973), *The Interpretation of Cultures*, New York: Basic Books.

Goffman, E. (1961), *Asylums.* New York: Anchor Books.

Hilgard, J.R. (1953), Anniversary reaction in parents precipitated by children, *Psychiatry* 16:73–80.

Hochman, J. (1978), Unpublished manuscript.

Kestenberg, J. (1972), Psychoanalytic contributions to the problem of children of survivors from Nazi persecution. *Israel Journal of Psychiatry and Related Sciences* 10:311–325.

Klein, H. (1971), Families of survivors in the Kibbutz: Psychological studies, in H. Krystal and W. Niederland (Eds.), *Psychic Traumatization* (Vol. 8 of *International Psychiatry Clinics*), pp. 11-28. Boston: Little, Brown, and Co. Boston

Klein, H. (1974), Children of the Holocaust: Mourning and bereavement, in E.J. Anthony (Ed.), *Children of the Holocaust, International Yearbook of Child Psychiatry*, Vol. 12, pp. 393–409.

Klein, M. (1946), Notes on some schizoid mechanisms, in *Envy and Gratitude and Other Works, 1946–1963*, New York: Delacorte Press / Seymour Laurence, 1975.

Koenig, W. (1964), Chronic or persisting identity diffusion, *American Journal of Psychiatry* 120:1081–1084.

Kohut, H. (1971), *The Analysis of the Self*. New York: International Universities Press. (*Monograph Series of the Psychoanalytic Study of the Child*, Number 4).

Kohut, H. (1977), *The Restoration of the Self*. New York: International Universities Press.

Krystal, H. (1968), Studies of concentration camp survivors, in H. Krystal, Ed., *Massive Psychic Trauma*, pp. 23-30. New York: International Universities Press, New York.

———W. Niederland (1968), Clinical observations on the survivor syndrome, in H. Krystal (Ed.), *Massive Psychic Trauma*, pp. 327-348, New York: International Universities Press.

———(1971), Trauma: Considerations of its intensity and chronicity, in H. Krystal and W. Niederland (Eds.), *Psychic Traumatization* (Vol. 8 of *International Psychiatry Clinics*), pp. 11–28. Boston: Little, Brown, and Co.

Lipkowitz, M. (1973), The child of survivors: A report of an unsuccessful therapy, *Israel Annals of Psychiatry and Related Disc*iplines, 2:141–155.

Mahler, M. and B. Gosliner (1955), On symbiotic child psychosis: Genetic, dynamic, and restitutive aspects, in *Psychoanalytic Study of the Child*, Vol. 10, International Universities Press, New York, pp. 195–212.

Matussak, P. (1971), Late symptomatology among concentration camp inmates, in S. Arieti (Ed.), *The World Biennial of Psychiatry and Psychotherapy*: Vol. 1, pp. 353-374. New York: Basic Books.

Niederland, W. (1961), The problem of the survivor, *Journal of Hillside Hospital* 10:232–247.

Pollock, G. (1970), Anniversary reactions, trauma, and mourning, *Psychoanalytic Quarterly*39:347–371.

Ricoeur, P. (1967), *The Symbolism of Evil* (tr. Emerson Buchanan), New York: Harper & Row.

Schachtel, E.G. (1959), *Metamorphosis: On the Development of Affect, Perception, Attention and Memory*. New York: Basic Books.

Schafer, R. (1968), *Aspects of Internalization*. International Universities Press, New York.

Schlesinger, H. (1969), The place of forgetting in memory functioning, *Journal of the American Psychoanalytic Association.*, 17:358–371.

Sigal, J., Silver, D., Rakoff, V. & Ellin, B. (1973), Some second-generation effects of survival of the Nazi persecution. *American Journal of Orthopsychiatry* 43:320–327.

Trossman, B. (1968), Adolescent children of concentration camp survivors. *Journal of the Canadian Psychiatric Association J.* 13:121–123.

Weber, M. (1947), *The Theory of Social and Economic Organization*. Glencoe: IL: Free Press.

Winnicott, D.W. (1962), Ego integration in child development, in *The Maturational Processes and the Facilitating Environment*, pp. 56–63. London: Hogarth Press.

Winnick, H.Z. (1967), Further comments concerning problems of late psychopathological effects of Nazi persecution and their therapy. *Israel Annals of Psychiatry and Related Disciplines* 5:1–16.

CHAPTER 19

ON SILENCE AND THE HOLOCAUST:
A CONTRIBUTION TO CLINICAL THEORY

I am concerned in this paper with the capacity of children of Holocaust survivors to tolerate affects and the construction, in collaboration with a therapist, of a narrative account of data from the remembered, fantasized, and hitherto unexplored past. I suggest that tolerance for certain affects which are Holocaust sequelae is enhanced by the commitment to historical explanation and that such a narrative commitment, when supported by a therapeutic holding environment, constitutes a facilitative element of the treatment process.

I also examine a particular aspect of how trauma is perpetuated from one generation to the next. Several clinicians have examined this issue. Auerhahn and Prelinger (1983) cite the principle of repetition, in which the parent induces a re-creation of Holocaust images, fantasies, and experiences in his child in order to work through conflicts relating to meaninglessness and self-fragmentation originating in the death camps. The child, in turn, promotes the re-created images, fantasies, and experiences in order to make sense out of a turbulent parental biography shrouded in pain and ambiguity. Wilson and Fromm (1982) describe the way the survivor parent may use his child as a "restitutive self-object," in which the child may simultaneously represent both a recapitulation of searing dissociated memories as well as the symbol for the parent to undo the trauma associated with those memories. In this way, sequestered Holocaust themes in the parent emerge and become enacted within the context of the parent-child relationship. The child, the object of identification with prior figures, may be overprotected or expelled, may be delegated to succeed or fail, or may fulfill the thwarted ego-ideal ambitions of the parent or be the object of their thwarted ego-ideal conflicts. Others have spoken of the parents' inability to absorb their children's aggression (Barocas & Barocas, 1973), the transmission of global mistrustfulness and fear which is part of a "survival complex" (Kestenberg, 1980), the necessity of a "parentogenic alliance" in which parents must forge a safe place between them, which contains their own developmental failures, fixations, and fantasies lest these forces overflow and envelop the vulnerable child (Herzog, 1982), and the intrafamilial vectors arising from the parental attempt to reverse their encounter with death and destruction (Trossman, 1968; H. Klein, 1974; Lipkowitz, 1973; Sigal et al., 1973).

There are many children of survivors whose parents have empathically and with appropriate concern prompted them to know the past and creatively integrate it. I am concerned here primarily with individuals who either do not know, avoid knowing, or defend against knowing. The concepts contained here, though, have implications for those survivor families in which the parents could not help but dwell and obsess on the Holocaust and thus violated generational boundaries, which led to the children's needs to seek refuge in isolation, away from the overwhelming intrusiveness of the parents' innermost secrets.

Affects and Affect Tolerance

Affect was originally viewed largely within the economic point of view, as a means of drive representation that corresponded with discharge process (Rapaport, 1953). Both affect and ideation were associated with memory traces—affects were the unstructuralized response of the ego to a cathexis of a memory trace, while ideation was the structuralized response. Both Schur (1953) and Rapaport (1953) argued that affects themselves constitute structures and thus undergo a structuralization process. Their contributions set the stage for development theorists to study early mental life and the genesis of affective life. Issues such as the role of early object relations, the intertwining of cognition with specified affects, and the relationship of affects to psychobiological life became the focus of scrutiny. As a result, affects began to be viewed as ego states independent of complex metapsychological considerations. The work of Bibring (1953), Sandler and Joffe (1965), and Bemporad and Wilson (1978) in conceptualizing depression as a basic psychobiological affect are examples. While affects have thus been scrutinized, the notion of affect tolerance has received relatively scant attention in the clinical psychoanalytic literature. Joffe (1969), Zetzel (1970), and Kernberg (1975) have addressed the notion of affect tolerance in some way, but Krystal's (1975) paper remains the most comprehensive evaluation of this concept.

Affect tolerance is the comfort, established incrementally through gradual familiarity and recognition, of a particular feeling state within the context of the self. This construct implies that we pay attention not to the absence or presence of an affect, but rather to the manner by which we experience, handle, or defend against an affective state. What clinically often looks like the absence of an affect may be a condition wherein a patient cannot control, master, or bear the affect; the intolerable affect therefore becomes repressed or dissociated and fails to be integrated into an expanding affect array. At other times, an affect may be accessible to conscious self-observation but minimized because it signals overwhelming tensions over which the patient possesses inadequate controls. Self-regulation of one's own affective experiences occurs through a gradual characteristic patterning of modes of action and defense, which usually are internalized functions of the self inherited from an early parent-child attunement.

In early development the good-enough mother allows her child a tolerable affective experience, intuitively knowing her child's capacities and how a child's affect array expands. She empathically organizes and filters through doses of increasingly strong and varied affective states until the experience approaches a traumatic level of overload, at which time she intervenes and frees the child from the unpleasure that has developed. This is part of the theory of the mother as an external or auxiliary stimulus barrier. The mother's specific influences on her child's developmental acquisition of affective states are complex and varied, as discussed in detail by Benedek (1956), Winnicott (1960), and Mahler (1966). Jacobson (1964), too, has described affects not as unpleasurable tensions but as the discharge of psychic energies along preferred pathways that develop through the experiences of early object relationships. These object-relations views of affect-formation are complemented by the work of theorists such as Tompkins (1962), Schmale (1964), Basch (1976), and Pine (1980), who note the interaction of innate constitutional, biological, and instinctual factors with the role the mother plays.

What is generally agreed is that it is the caretaking experience that is essential to the form of affect development, the parent's ability to sense and organize the child's affective experience. When the child reaches higher levels of developmental maturity, the patterning of affective experiences becomes further fixed by age-specific internalization and self-regulatory processes. The dreading of emotions and characteristic ways of warding off emotions are further elaborated through the lifespan. As Zetzel (1970) emphasizes, ways of dealing with affect are an ever-evolving lifelong developmental phenomena.

Of particular importance to my thesis is the intertwining of affects with unconscious and conscious ideation. Brenner (1974), among others, emphasizes that affects occur in the presence of associated ideas, which are internalized reflections of early social experiences. In particular, he believes, anxiety and depression function in this way. In Brenner's view, anxiety is associated with the idea that something bad is about to happen, whereas depression is associated with the idea that something bad has already happened. Depression and anxiety perform a signaling function and act as a motive for defense or action. Jacobson (1964) has asserted that, depending upon individual social experiences, many affects can perform a similar signaling function.

Tolerance for an affect is established developmentally through increasingly intensive and varied exposure to an affective state under conditions of security. The mother intuitively understands her infant's and toddler's threshold, above which the affective experience becomes unmanageable and potentially traumatic. The mother's regulatory function is eventually internalized by the child. The signal of traumatic overload represents a failure of the self-regulatory function during conditions of affect intolerance.

For children of Holocaust survivors, the affects cited by Brenner (depression and anxiety), as well as rage, often serve this signaling function and are particular adult manifestations of ideation resulting from early experiences with their parents. The survivor parent who communicates to his or her child the idea that bad things will happen may thus promote a lack of anxiety tolerance. If the parent conveys to the child the idea that he or she has done bad things, a lack of depression tolerance may be the result. The survivor parent who communicates the idea that the child's aggression is overwhelming or destructive may promote a lack of rage tolerance. When children of survivors enter treatment as adults, affect tolerance can be enhanced through the therapeutic investigation of these ideas, with the result that the affects no longer serve as signals for action or defense; they can then be integrated into the group of affective experiences that are safe and tolerable.

Clinically, it is relatively easy to overlook affect tolerance as a goal of treatment. It is difficult to empathically perceive another person's regressed affective states because these are frequently lacking in obvious behavioral manifestations. Additionally, state-dependent primitive mental conditions are difficult to discern in patients because of the clinician's repression of the memories of his own infantile affects. This limitation is especially germane when the clinician is faced with the recognition of another's severe emotional pain. In the absence of his ability to recognize another's affect, a clinician may tend to assume that it is one in his own repertoire (Krystal, 1974). Thus, to the extent that affects are subject to regression, i.e., when state-conditions lead to regressions that result in primitive mental affective conditions, a clinician is vulnerable to projecting his own feeling state or mistakenly identifying a feeling state with which he can experience comfort or familiarity.

Holocaust-Affect Tolerance

The clinical observations in this paper derive from psychoanalytic psychotherapy with children of survivors. One patient, Mr. A, was a 31-year-old man whose rage and lust for revenge against persecutors and victimizers often spilled over into many sectors of his life. He was unusually intelligent and articulate but could not stabilize himself in a career and eventually allied himself with an escapist cult group. His treatment was unusually difficult and was intermittently punctuated by fierce diatribes against mental health professionals, whom he perceived as representing a parasitical element that survived by passive reflection rather than active op-position to various social injustices. His parents, both survivors, had met in a deportation camp shortly before coming to the United States in 1946. Mr. A noted that the only time his father willingly talked about the camps was in recollecting the time he secretly pasted a picture of Hitler on the wall of a latrine, thereby risking death. Mr. A's mother was hypochondriacal and overpro-tective. Mr. A suffered from severe depression, which at times was defended against by over-ideational impulsivity. It was not until the first half of the second year of treatment that he was able to begin to examine the effects upon him of his parents' concentra-tion camp experiences without retreating into rage and invective. The therapist attempted to remain interpretive and analytically neutral through the storms; gradually, as the patient's rage abated, he began to speak more and more of the hardships his parents had undergone. He initiated a deeper relation with his parents and coaxed them into telling him more about their camp experiences. At around the same time, he became capable of reflecting upon his turbulent moods and depressive states with an increased capacity for self-observation, and joined the therapist in constructing a plausible history to explain their origins. As the Holocaust mate-rial unfolded, Mr. A was able to stabilize himself in treatment with a newly emerging positive transference and was able to reevaluate his relation with his parents. As he developed insight, his ongoing relation with them changed. His rage toward his father for the lat-ter's emotional unavailability and refusal to be pleased by any of Mr. A's accomplishments abated. His rage against helpers was un-derstood to derive, in part, from his mother's attempt in times of panic attacks to identify him with her own father (killed during the war), who had protected and soothed her and whom she ide-alized. After these panic episodes, she belittled Mr. A's attempt to perform this same soothing function and made him feel "toxic" to others and ashamed of himself. His parents also seemed to have a great deal of difficulty handling and absorbing his aggression, and often responded either counter-aggressively or by withdrawing when he asserted himself against their wishes. The gradual intro-duction of Holocaust-related data brought about a new level of insight into his parents' lives, as well as a sense of how the Holo-caust had entered into his life through his parents. When termination prematurely occurred (the therapist was moving to a different city), he was still symptomatic, but began work with a new therapist and continued to improve. His affective life was far more buoyant, and he no longer experienced his rage or depres-sion with such overwhelming intensity. During the termination phase, he asserted that, in part, it had been the therapist's willing-ness to withstand his affective states without recoiling that had contributed to his ability to integrate them and not to feel as if he were "out of control" all the time. Depression, rage, and severe anxiety no longer signaled the onset of an ego-alien mental state that made him feel strange and isolated, compounding his lack of affect tolerance.

Mr. A's development of self-regulation through the expression and exploration of aggressive wishes in the transference is remi-niscent of Winnicott's (1971) discussion of the value of the therapist who survives while he simultaneously allows himself to be destroyed as the patient wishes, so that the patient can be re-assured that the therapist has the capacity to survive his unbridled psychic destructiveness. To Winnicott, such aggres-sive wishes represent an unresolved residue of the infant's normal unintentional destructive urges, arising from the natural vigor of his primary needs. What I wish to draw attention to is how the analyst's holding function exemplifies the therapeutic provision of affect tolerance, of holding and containing the vicissitudes of aggression (however it manifests itself in feeling states) so that aggression is no longer dreaded and the patient no longer experiences himself as out of control.

After liberation from the death camps, many survivors presented an ominous clinical picture (although, to be sure, many did not). Manifold sequelae were directly traceable to the appalling camp experience. I Various clinicians described states of chronic reactive aggression, distorted identification with the dead, severe "survivor's guilt," and massive dependency conflicts with unresolved mourning. The turning of aggression against the self was seen to potentiate depression that was triggered by guilt. Chronic anxiety and tension states were seen to lead to disturbed family ties.

In survivor families, certain of the children's feeling states are frequently proscribed because they evoke Holocaust-related memories, identifications, and fantasies in the parents. Krystal (1978, p. 92) remarks that in severely traumatized adults, "... the fear of affects frequently represents the dread of the return of ... trauma." As with Mr. A, parental explosiveness often becomes associated with the evocation of certain feeling states; at other times, parental withdrawal results when dreaded or overwhelming affect states emerge into felt experience. What occurs may be understood as an intergenerational transmission of trauma: One generation's trauma leads to the next generation's lack of affect tolerance. Certain affects in the children become intolerable, split off, and their emergence into awareness is difficult and painful. The affects are feared and avoided by parents because the reawakening, remembering, and reliving in themselves is too immense and painful an ordeal.

Anthologies edited by Krystal (1968) and Dimsdale (1980) provide detailed descriptions of psychiatric symptomology and treatment of survivors. In much the same protective way, and for a variety of reasons (e.g., avoiding parental withdrawal or sensing severely conflictual and painful affective states), the children may collaborate with their parents' aim of forgetting by splitting off or dissociating affects that trigger horrible memories in their parents. The threshold of tolerance for these particular affects consequently becomes lowered and the affect is not integrated within the normal developing affect array. Discomfort with these affects may lead the child to avoid situations outside of the family in which they might be experienced, resulting in poor peer relations (Sigal et al., 1973), a sense of the world as hostile and malevolent (Barocas & Barocas, 1981), and the sense of the family as the sole source of pleasure, gratification, and protection (H. Klein, 1974).

When the child experiences difficulties in mastering and expressing such affects as anxiety, rage, or depression,[1] it may be due not so much to overt traumatization as to the child's failure to be helped to experience necessary increments of these affects when the affect in normal development had to be mastered, made familiar and comfortable, and then modulated. It is not gross trauma that lead to most difficulties with such individuals, it is the subphase inadequacies that began with uneven and ineffective modulation and then extended into other sectors of the personality.

Case reports of offspring of Holocaust survivors are sometimes described in which these affective states are not linked to sequelae of their parents' experience in the death camps. Quite often the survivor's child himself does not know this is the case and misidentifies the roots of his affectivity as ahistorical, his and his alone.

---

[1] Anxiety, rage, and depression intolerance does not characterize every child of survivors, just as not every parent presented a characteristic survivor syndrome. These descriptions originate from a "normative" rather than "privileged" competence (Spence, 1982), implying a description based upon the tendencies depicted in broad psychoanalytic research descriptions rather than the web of specific meanings unique to a particular case.

The survivor child, preferring to view the parent as a hero rather than a victim, is bereft of a historical perspective while experiencing the repetition of psychodynamics issuing from the amorphous past. The pathway to insight, through comprehending that his affective difficulties represent the perpetuation of an ongoing intergenerational tragedy, is often not open to him.

Children of survivors, seen in psychoanalysis or psychotherapy, may characterologically have grown to dread and avoid Holocaust generated emotions. They may settle into a style of object relations in which a multitude of events that might trigger them, such as nu ances of intimacy or interpersonal conflict, are avoided. One rather schizoid and anhedonic patient, who strove to avoid expressions of affects that might make him feel "attached" to another person, had never had a relationship outside his family in which he felt a reasonable amount of comfort and intimacy. He fantasized that this could only be possible were he to move to Israel. He described Israel as both a Jewish as well as a highly aggressive country. The relocation fantasy was understood to symbolize an unconscious idea that attachment to another person was possible only if he could truly understand himself as a Jew, but this required a surrounding milieu in which aggressivity could be tolerated, unlike the situation in his family. Like their parents, children of survivors tend to live with the dread that split-off, painful, maladaptive affective states will reach consciousness and overwhelm them. Thus the therapeutic context may provide a basis for a creative reintegration, a concept similar to but more than what Zetzel (1970) called "bearing it. " At issue here is the acquisition of Holocaust-affect tolerance— establishing comfort and constraints in the therapeutic relationship around anxiety, rage, and depression.

During the treatment of individuals with lowered Holocaust affect tolerance, the clinician must be wary of the facile appeal of the hydraulic metaphor, which equates expression with riddance. Should the clinician find himself thinking in such abreactive terms, he might identify this thought as a specific countertransference response—his wish that the patient rid himself of an aversive mental state so that he too may be rid of the problem of treating it. In such cases, the hydraulic concept is an antiquated anal metaphor that can only confuse one's therapeutic vision. This countertransference reaction may lead to severe acting out or the often-seen clinical phenomenon of the affect storm. One also runs the risk of losing patients who are naturally suspicious of psychotherapeutic help by encouraging cathartic release when the tolerance that would enable a patient to withstand such a release is absent.[2] One of the outcomes of countertransference-generated acting out might be the heightening of paranoid ideation and suspiciousness regarding the therapist's motives, perhaps resulting in the abrupt termination of the treatment. Because affect tolerance is the problem, the articulation and experience of these affects is frightening, and character structure is likely to be organized around their minimization. It should also be stressed that the other extreme—when the therapist is frightened of the patient's mental states and blocks the expression of affects—results in an upsurge in the patient's dread of his feelings. This error also fails to address the therapeutic goal of tolerating previously intolerable affective states.

The effect on the child of experiencing the repercussions of the Holocaust while not knowing about the event may be paralyzing. What is in the air must be put into words, if not at home, then in the therapist's office. It is in the therapist's office that the silent parent can safely be heard, albeit through the imaginative

---

[2] A Second Generation patient who leaves treatment in this way may experience a need to emphasize his parents' heroism while denying their suffering; or he may develop a mistrust of the clinician with the underlying belief that he is a persecutor; or he may deny conflict with an accompanying sense that he does not require assistance.

discourse of the child and the interpretative reconstructive commitment of the therapist. It is precisely at this point in the treatment that it becomes important for the therapist to be acutely sensitive to what, in the patient's recounting, is constituted of fantasy and what of factually derived evidence. This is because fantasy has deeper meaning, but discourse of what was true of the Holocaust is at times beyond conflict and thus beyond formations arising from motives versus countermotives. Images of what occurred are not necessarily compromise formations. There might be no more rational way of viewing them. Psychoanalytic theory and practice, dating back to Freud's 1897 famous and fateful 69th letter to Fliess (Freud, 1887-1902), with its emphasis upon dreamwork, early memories, screen memories, and the necessity for free association, has never sharply defined a consistent distinction between what actually transpired in the object field of the patient and what meanings the patient has superimposed onto his experiences.

It has been argued that many factors prevent the accurate retelling of early experiences, although analogic correspondences are most frequently discerned through the transference. Such issues as the defensive function of memories (G. Klein, 1966; Loewald, 1976), one's position on the lifespan (Schafer, 1978), the context of time (Loewald, 1973), and the inherent subjectivity of the analytic process itself (Schimek, 1975) cast doubt upon the objectivity of the process of recollection. And what of the survivor? Do his recollections become subject to these principles of regulation? Wiesel (1969, p. 42) described how in his camp ". . . flames were leaping up from a ditch, gigantic flames. They were burning something... little children. Babies? Yes, I saw it—saw it with my own eyes . . . was I awake? I could not believe it . . . no, none of this could be true. It was a nightmare." If only we could treat this as dreamlife, the product of primary-process condensation and displacement, the royal road that points us to unconscious infantile wishes, a symbolization of current conflicts. But this incredible madness was real, it occurred in this world and must be dealt with as such.

When a child of survivors discusses the Holocaust, dreams about it, fantasizes about it, we may be faced with the psychological representation of a rendition of the past upon which the bizarre logic of the nightmare reflects real events rather than the intrusion of unconscious processes. Comfort in this case is established through trust in the containing therapeutic holding action, not through the discovery of deeper meaning. Through this reliance on the therapeutic holding action, these data can be apprehended with clarity, and the child of survivors can appreciate the implications for his and his parents' lives, weaving past, present, and future into a meaningful continuum. Schafer (1979) makes the point that in the course of a useful analysis a sense of multiple histories is usually created. As one looks backward from the present and forward from the past, past and present interact in a circular development of interpretations. As the life history continuum becomes established through the explication of memory, fact, and fantasy, the past, too, will evolve and assume an increasingly intelligible coherence. Loftus and Loftus (1980). from the perspective of experimental psychology, have shown that the manner in which we talk about a memory and the questions we ask of it tend to become part of the original memory. Thus, for the survivor's child, speaking of the past to a therapist serves the purposes of rewriting what is already known, as well as discovering what is new. The past that is constructed through such a recounting fills in the gaps and clarifies the distortions induced by the vicissitudes of silence.

Holocaust-affect tolerance is most likely to be developed gradually and indirectly, through two concurrent processes. The first is through the establishment of a narrative competence—a construction of the past, composed of fantasies, memories, and information that is organized textually, possesses verisimilitude (the appearance of truthfulness), and offers a historical framework for containing, explaining, and understanding. At the same time, in the therapeutic relationship, the comfort and modulation around affects that the good-enough mother intuitively provides becomes reenacted in the holding environment. Thus, what is unknown, unspoken, but pervasive enters into verbal discourse and becomes consciously negotiable therapeutic data. Here, the applicable formula is not only the topographic model of making conscious what was unconscious—and the structural model of creating ego where id had been—it is also the narrative model of rendering sayable what was unsayable.

To Know or Not to Know:
Narrative Commitment and Affect Tolerance

A notion of narrative commitment as an aspect of psychoanalytic explanation was initially formulated by Sherwood (1969, p. 281), who stated that "Psychoanalytic explanation begins with an individual case history, and the real job of explanation occurs through ordering the mass of biographical material and attempting to organize it into a coherent whole. This is accomplished by constructing some sort of narrative account containing as much of the material as possible."

Sherwood discusses narrative commitment within the context of psychoanalytic epistemology, asserting that much of what is considered to be explanation and generalization is really a commitment to present case-history data in a coherent and consistent form.

By contrast, narrative commitment in this paper may be understood as the willingness, despite discomfort, to create in the therapeutic context a coherent and meaningful verbal account of the personal past out of whatever shreds of information (whether in fantasy or reality) are available. Its truth claim (Ricoeur, 1977) is to be evaluated, not in terms of reliance on the actual occurrences of events, but in terms of consistency, narrative intelligibility, and success in integrating meaningful information. The question of the explanatory potential of the narration is at first detectable by the therapist rather than the patient, because of the inherent nature of the listening process (G. Klein, 1965). The patient "feels" a particular affective configuration, which is the outcome of the situation whereby vital information has failed to be consciously represented in a way that spurs insight, self-regulation, and fosters the therapeutic alliance.

Des Pres (1976, p. 170) warns: "The concentration-camp experience represents an evil so appalling that we too, when we turn to face it, suffer psychic unbalance.... Some hideous impression of Auschwitz is in every mind, far removed from conscious thought but there ... and anything connected with it, anything which starts it into consciousness, brings with it a horror too large and intensely personal to confront safely." This, then, is a dilemma of the child of survivors—how to confront the appalling realities safely, how to transcend self and parental injunctions against knowing, how to counterbalance the psychic imbalance, how to tolerate the affective experiences whose origins and genesis are shrouded in mystery and cloaked with fantasy. In the treatment office, this dilemma becomes the therapist's as well. Because of the danger of both knowing as well as not knowing, the relationship between interpretation and the construction of the narrative subtly changes. Usually, in therapy, the construction of a narrative occurs through the interpretive work of the analytic process (Schafer, 1980; Spence, 1982). In the case of patients of the Second Generation, narrative commitment is constructed parallel to the narrative itself.[3] The patient provides bits of information which, in essence, are symbols that serve as preliminary interpretations of the past. The therapist then reinterprets the patient's symbolic or incomplete interpretation in the service of narrativity, conflict and defense, and verisimilitude. Narrative commitment is forged between therapist and patient; together they construct meanings and intentions that are an integral aspect of the therapeutic transaction. Thus, narrative commitment is a dialectical process; it is present in the therapist, in the patient, and is synthesized between patient and therapist.

I have already stressed the value of the holding environment that the therapist provides for the child of survivors. The issue of what "holds" a patient in treatment and motivates a patient to keep coming back and to strive for health is controversial and dates back to Freud's papers on transference (1910, 1912, 1915). In these papers, he puzzled on a major paradox of psychoanalytic technique: The transference is simultaneously the major form of both attachment and resistance. How can the therapist rely upon something in the patient that must be resolved? How is a therapist to evoke in the patient the interest and energy necessary for treatment while curbing the impulses from which this interest and energy are powered? Loewald (1960) has suggested that a particular childhood need sought in therapy is the need to identify with one's potential for growth as seen in the eyes of a parent. This type of therapeutic response provides hope and also structures one's vision of reality in a promising, optimistic way. The therapist thus holds the patient by being experienced as a guide

---

[3] The construction of a narrative and the collaboration around narrative commitment has been written about and recommended by clinicians who treat children of survivors as a technique that appears to have the status of a parameter (Eissler, 1953). Gampel (1982) offers a poignant example of this process in a case she calls "A Daughter of Silence."

to the riches the world offers. In essential agreement with this position, Friedman (1969, p. 150), discussing the therapeutic alliance, asserts that the therapist "... must convey to the patient not only the direction he wants the patient to move in, but also the confidence that the movement is inherent in the patient, which means that what the uncured patient wants is indeed a representation, however distorted, of what the cured patient will get. To the extent that the analyst fails to do the latter he will naturally lose significance to the patient."

For children or survivors, this direction of movement that the therapist conveys "holds" the patient when it takes the form of encouraging the encounter with Holocaust-derived memories and fantasies, narrativizing them, and promotes tolerance of their affective repercussions. Thus, beyond the patient's recognition that an alternative and better life is possible, an identification with the therapist's resoluteness in facing Holocaust themes constitutes an essential element of the holding environment. While empathically acknowledging a despairing world view, which follows from confrontations with the past, the therapist must also represent to the patient a direction out of the despair. The therapist's communication of confidence that the patient can withstand the confrontation with the past and that such a confrontation will lead to increased mental health provides a security as well as a motive for the patient to persevere. The patient may then identify with the therapist's conviction that affects associated with Holocaust material need not be dreaded or avoided but can be mastered.

The enhancement of affect tolerance is thus facilitated by construction of a historical narrative, which includes the Holocaust legacy, by support of such a remembered and discovered past in the holding context of the therapy and through the typical concerns of the transference. These processes are not mutually exclusive; clinically, they comprise complementary aspects of the therapeutic interaction. Certain affects express basic parental identifications, and these identifications need to be experienced affectively in the course of a successful treatment (Schafer; 1964). Information that is organized in the therapy according to narrative principles will simultaneously be played out in the dynamics of the transference as well as experienced according to one's tolerance for affective expression.

The defenses and resistances mobilized when the Holocaust survivor's child commits himself to the explication of Holocaust material are different from those a therapist finds when analyzing the analytic transference. The former arise from diverse sources: the patient's reluctance to assess his parents' victimization; the wish to cleanse himself of the repugnance of the death traces of the past; the dissonance with positive idealized transference elements; fear of destabilizing the balance of the present relation with the parents; or hesitance to abandon a seething hatefulness of certain aspects of the past in favor of an understanding tempered by forgiving and understanding. An important difference is that the therapist does not always attempt to dissolve them or bring them into awareness through interpretations from a position of technical neutrality. This is because they may serve a restraining function due to a lack of affect tolerance. The technique of interpreting defenses before impulses holds when the patient can tolerate the analysis of the defenses. It is for this reason that the therapist who treats these patients may, when the patient begins to assess the Holocaust-related material, have to assert an inordinate amount of control over the treatment and allow himself to be a receptacle for hostile or paranoid projections; he may have to actively struggle with the patient through confrontation and clarification. Then, too, he may have to abandon the technique of following the patient's associations and instead be prepared to lead the patient into the aversive material. Through evoking this material and then tolerating it without relegating it to the realm of a disguising fantasy to be interpreted, the therapist may serve a stimulus-regulating function parallel to the one the survivor's parent may have failed to serve many years earlier.

An example of this type of therapeutic action is the case of Mr. B. Mr. B was an energetic, at times hypomanic, man, who lived a fairly frantic life, which left him little time for relaxation or recreation. He had a long series of unsuccessful heterosexual relationships, which tended to end because he became bored and irritated with his partners. Action-oriented, he felt restless and anxious when his girlfriends demanded intimacy and closeness. Mr. B spoke of his past as if it were unreal or an illusion that could be brushed aside and had no impact upon his present life. His parents were both survivors. His father, a prominent European intellectual before the war, received compensation payments from the government of West Germany. The father maintained a tie with the past in part through an abstract philosophical preoccupation with the freedom of the human individual, a message with which he constantly harangued his son. Much of this preoccupation concerned his own experience of survival and the freedom of choices open to him after the utter tyranny of incarceration. Mr. B's mother, on the other hand, refused to speak about her life before coming to America and giving birth to Mr. B. It was understood in his family that she was not to be upset, and father and son protected her through a conspiracy of silence. In the therapy, it gradually became clear that, like his mother, Mr. B was striving to not have a past. Like his father, he sought freedom by pitting himself against oppression, which in his case he contrived. Comments linking this dynamic with his parents' lives were well received, but made Mr. B quite anxious. Part of the therapeutic task at this juncture became to provide him with a history that could be experienced as alive. I led him into this material, despite the increasing level of his discomfort. As Mr. B spoke of his past, we both also came to understand that love and nurturance were not provided in his family when a member dwelled on the past. He was, though, loved at other times, and both parents took pride in his intellectual and athletic prowess. However, the dread of the past had passed into his life and profoundly influenced his intimate relationships. He unconsciously expected that a sharing of personal history jeopardized relationships, introducing stresses that would overwhelm the love and care in the relationship.

Children of survivors can construct a multitude of bridges to the past. Perhaps the most taxing and fantasy-laden is through initiating a new level of dialogue with their parents. Mr. A, described earlier, insisted for over a year that he could not speak with his parents about the Holocaust experience, because such communication would provoke his father to murderous rage. When he did initiate this dialogue, he found that he did indeed rekindle rage in his father, but it was not directed at him. Although the exchanges were filled with stress, he also discovered pleasure in experiencing his father as an assertive and powerful figure, and proudly produced a series of fantasies and dreams concerning what his father had been like before imprisonment.

Conclusion

I have examined the importance of narrative commitment and the therapeutic holding environment in the treatment of children of survivors in mastering Holocaust imagery, unconscious fantasies, and defective affect tolerance that have been generated by intergenerational transmission of death-camp trauma. I am suggesting that affect tolerance is enhanced by the commitment to historical explanation, and that such a narrative commitment constitutes a facilitative element of the therapeutic holding environment and the treatment process. Insofar as the survivor's child experiences are unknown incomprehensible repetitions of the parental past, the establishment in therapy of a narrative that spans the boundary of the generations permits the child to overcome destructive forces, to make integrative use of the parent's induction of Holocaust repetitions and of the child's reception of such repetitions. The resolution of concentration camp sequelae may be viewed as necessitating symbolic restoration of obliterated or disguised meanings, as the individual organizes and assimilates overwhelming messages and disguised images whose origins lie in the distant past. Therapist and patient collaborate on the interpretation of hidden or obscure themes and allusions, translating into words various forms of meaningful silence that conceal important personal history.

The affects cited (anxiety, rage, depression) may remain split-off and intolerable until the Second Generation individual can juxtapose them against the backdrop of the Holocaust as an organizing experience for his parents and for himself. Each new bit of historical information will change the narrative, which continually evolves in order to accommodate new findings and make sense out of the inchoate amorphous past. As these affects become less fearful, less aversive, fact and fiction become increasingly extricated from each other, and the process of affect tolerance gets under way. The patient increasingly becomes immersed in the psychoanalytic and psychotherapeutic process. The clinician provides the holding environment that promotes comfort with these affects and wherein they can be safely experienced, tolerated, explored, and explained. It is a fundamental psychoanalytic tenet that human memory retrieves information selectively in the service of current fears and conflicts. As a result, the exploration and differentiation of affects hitherto dreaded or inaccessible will also lead to the reevaluation of memories and ongoing experiences.

The word silence has emerged into prominence largely in the context of ethics and morals in Holocaust-informed studies. It has been argued that much of what reaches public discourse either fails to capture the essence of the event or cheapens it through misrepresentation. Some prefer the alternative to such public discourse—silence rather than an image tarnished and trivialized. For those concerned with the ethical aftermath, with the preservation of the values and the moral indignation the Holocaust demands, such a position is fully understandable and perhaps laudable. But for clinicians charged with the health of the patients they talk to, discourse is different; it is not trivial; the event is not lost or explained away. Therefore, I am led to the conclusion that individuals touched by the horror of the Holocaust must define their personal involvement with its reverberations through the generations, rather than submit to the invisible forces of a pathogenic silence that perpetuates the destructiveness.

References

Auerhahn, N. & Prelinger, E. (1983). Repetition in the concentration camp survivor and her child. *International Review of Psychoanalysis* 10:31–46.

Barocas, H. & Barocas, C. (1973). Manifestations of concentration camp effects on the second generation. *American Journal of. Psychiatry* 130:820–828.

———(1981). Wounds of the fathers: The next generation of holocaust victims. *International Review of Psychoanalysis* 6:331–341.

Basch, M.F. (1976). The concept of affect: A re-examination. *Journal of the American Psychoanalytic Association* 24:759–777.

Bemporad, J.R. & Wilson, A. (1978). A developmental approach to depression in childhood and adolescence. *Journal of the American Academy of Psychoanalysis.* 6:325–352.

Benedek, T. (1956). Psychobiological aspects of mothering. *American Journal of Orthopsychiatry* 26:272–278.

Bibring, E. (1953). The mechanism of depression. *In Affective Disorders,* ed. P. Greenacre, pp. 13-48. New York: International Universities Press.

Brenner, C. (1974). On the nature and development of affects: A unified theory. *Psychoanalytic Quarterly* 43:532–556.

Des Pres, T. (1976). *The Survivor: An Anatomy of Life in the Death Camps.* New York: Oxford University Press.

Dimsdale, J., ed. (1980). *Survivors, Victims, and Perpetrators: Essays on the Nazi Holocaust.* New York: Hemisphere.

Eissler, K. (1953). The effect of the structure of the ego on psychoanalytic technique. *Journal of the American Psychoanalytic Association* 1:104–143.

Freud, S. (1887–1902). *Origins of Psychoanalysis.* New York: Basic Books, 1954.

——(1910). The future prospects of psychoanalytic therapy. *Standard Edition* 11.

——(1912). The dynamics of transference. *Standard Edition* 12.

——(1915). Observations on transference. *Standard Edition* 12.

Friedman, L. (1969). The therapeutic alliance. *International Journal of Psychoanalysis* 50:139–136.

Gampel, Y. (1982). A daughter of silence. In *Generations of the Holocaust,* ed. M. Bergmann & M. Jucovy, pp. 120-136. New York: Basic Books.

Herzog, J. (1982). World Beyond Metaphor: Thoughts on the Transmission of Trauma. In *Generations of the Holocaust,* ed. M. Bergmann & M. Jucovy, pp. 102-119. New York: Basic Books.

Jacobson, E. (1964). *The Self and the Object World.* New York: International Universities Press.

Joffe, W.G. (1969). A critical review of the status of the ego concept. *International Journal of Psychoanalysis* 50:533–547.

Kernberg, O. (1975). *Borderline Conditions and Pathological Narcissism.* New York: Jason Aronson.

Kestenberg, J. (1980). Psychoanalyses of children of survivors from the holocaust: Case presentations and assessment. *Journal of the American Psychoanalytic Association.* 28:775–804.

Klein, H. (1974). Children of the holocaust: mourning and bereavement. In Children of the Holocaust, ed. E. J. Anthony. *International Yearbook of Child Psychiatry* 12:393-409.

Klein, G. (1965). On hearing one's own voice: An aspect of cognitive control in spoken thought. In *Psychoanalysis and Current Biological Thought,* ed. N.S. Greenfield & W.C. Lewis, pp.245-273. Madison: University of Wisconsin Press.

———— (1966). The several grades of memory. In *Psychoanalysis—A General Psychology: Essays in Honor of Heinz Hartmann,* Eds. R.M. Lowenstein, L.M. Newman, M. Schur, & A.. Solnit, pp.377-389, New York: International Universities Press.

Krystal, H., ed. (1968). *Massive Psychic Trauma.* New York: International Universities Press.

———(1974). The genetic development of affects and affect regression. *Annual of Psychoanalysis* 2:98–126.

———(1975). Affect tolerance. *Annual of Psychoanalysis* 3:179–219.

———(1978). Trauma and affects. *Psychoanalytic Study of the Child* 33:81–116.

Lipkowitz, M.H. (1973). The child of two survivors. A report of an unsuccessful therapy. *Israel Annals of Psychiatry & Related Disciplines* 2:363-374.

Loewald, H. (1960). On the therapeutic action of psychoanalysis. *International Journal of Psychoanalysis* 41:16-33.

———(1973). On internalization. *International Journal of Psychoanalysis* 54:9-17.

———(1976). Perspectives on memory. In *Psychology Versus Metapsychology: Psychoanalytic Essays in Honor of George Klein,* ed. M. Gill & P. Holzman. *Psychological Issues, Monograph 36,* pp. 299-325.

Loftus, E.F. & Loftus, G.R. (1980). On the permanence of stored information in the brain. *American Psychologist* 35:409–420.

Mahler, M. (1966). Notes on the development of basic moods: The depressive affect. In *Psychoanalysis—A General Psychology,* Eds. R.M. Loewenstein, L.M. Newman, M. Schur, & A.J. Solnit, pp. 152-168. New York: International Universities Press.

Pine, F. (1980). On the expansion of the affect array: A developmental description. In *Rapprochement: The Critical Subphase of Separation-Individuation,* Eds. R.L. Lax, S. Bach, & J.A. Burland, pp. 217-233. New York: Jason Aronson.

Rapaport, D. (1953). On the psychoanalytic theory of affects. In *Collected Papers,* Ed. M.M. Gill moo, 476-512, New York: Basic Books.

Ricoeur, P. (1977). The question of proof in Freud's psychoanalytic writing. *Journal of the American Psychoanalytic Association* 25:835–871.

Sandler, J. & Joffe, W.G. (1965). Notes on childhood depression. *International Journal of Psychoanalysis* 46:88–96.

Schafer, R. (1964). The clinical analysis of affects. *Journal of the American Psychoanalytic Association* 12:275–300.

(1978). *Language and Insight: The Sigmund Freud Memorial Lectures 1975–76,* University College London. New Haven& London: Yale University Press.

———(1979). The appreciative analytic attitude and the construction of multiple histories. *Psychoanalysis and Contemporary Thought* 2:3–24.

———(1980). Narration in the psychoanalytic dialogue. *Critical Inquiry* 7:29–53.

Schimek, J. (1975). The interpretation of the past: Childhood trauma, psychical reality, and historical truth. *Journal of the American Psychoanalytic Association* 23:845–865.

Schmale A. (1964). A genetic view of affects. *Psychoanalytic Study of the Child* 19:287–310. New Haven: Yale University Press.

Schur, M. (1953). The ego in anxiety. In *Drives, Affects, Behavior,* Ed. R. Loewenstein, pp. 67-104. New York: International Universities Press.

Sherwood, M. (1969). *The Logic of Explanation in Psychoanalysis.* New York: Academic Press.

Sigal, J., Silver, D., Rakoff, V., & Ellin, B. (1973). Some second-generation effects of survival of the Nazi persecution. *American Journal of Orthopsychiatry* 43:320–332.

Spence, D. (1982). *Narrative Truth and Historical Truth: Meaning and Interpretation in Psychoanalysis.* New York: W.W. Norton & Company.

Tompkins, S. (1962). *Affect, Imagery, Consciousness,* vol. 1. New York: Springer.

Trossman, B. (1968). Adolescent children of concentration camp survivors. *Journal of the Canadian Psychiatric. Association* 13:121–123.

Wiesel, E. (1969). *Night.* New York: Avon.

Wilson, A., & Fromm, E. (1982). Aftermath of the concentration camp: The second generation. *Journal of the. American Academy of Psychoanalysis* 10:289–313.

Winnicott, D.W. (1960). The theory of the parent-infant relationship. In *The Maturational Processes and the Facilitating Environment, pp 37-55.* New York: International Universities Press, 1965.

———(1971). The use of an object and relating through identifications. In *Playing and Reality, pp. 86-94.* New York: Basic Books.

Zetzel, E. (1970). *The Capacity for Emotional Growth.* New York: International Universities Press.

(Circa 2020)

Most of these papers have been written over the last few decades. In this book, I have approached psychoanalysis from many perspectives—analytic practice, analytic theory, empirical observation, experimental and quasi-experimental science. I aim to coordinate multiple perspectives. I will suggest that in a broad sense mastering multiple perspectives is one of the central tasks of the contemporary analyst. When the coordination of multiple perspectives is competently handled, it can result in a meeting of minds in a distinctively psychoanalytic manner. Schweder (2003) is a visible spokesperson of this trend, and uses the terms "postmodern humanism" and "the view from manywheres" interchangeably. Schweder notes that postmodern humanism is suspicious of any total or unitary world view, and seeks and celebrates difference rather than sameness. It is a way of thinking based on a single maxim: "The knowable world is incomplete if seen from any one point-of-view, incoherent if seen from all points of view at once, and empty if seen from nowhere in particular." (2003, p. 2) Therefore, the contemporary theorist should always be on the move, embracing alternative points of view to one's own favorite, which is a kind of default position lurking with danger. Seeing matters from multiple viewpoints without prioritizing one and using it to denigrate others is the only way to restore integrity to alien voices on other sides of fault lines embedded within culture. Therefore, one special role psychoanalysis plays in the community of ideas is to test the limits of pluralism. Ethnocentrism, the hatred of other points of view when patients' lives are at stake, is the opposite of the view from manywheres; it is the single-mindedness of the view from only here. Schweder usefully contrasts both the view from manywheres and the view from only here with the view from nowhere; he claims that incoherence and chaos arise when a theorist holds firmly to no view, no perspective at all, the view from nowhere in particular.

The conceptual problems introduced by the coordination of multiple perspectives, as I will soon define it, are not at all native to psychoanalysis—they are endemic to modern Western life. Such attendant problems already live everywhere around us, and have infiltrated the very fiber of the vast world of contemporary ideas. However, I do not think that they have yet been adequately explored by psychoanalysis, in order to locate itself in the modern world. Doing so provides a portal within which to exchange ideas without the inevitability of committing category errors in translation. I hope to have shown that the coordination of multiple perspectives is native to psychoanalysis, but is not firmly entrenched within its tradition, for a variety of reasons.

All traditions to some degree or another must change. Outside of psychoanalysis, the pace of change in this modern world of ideas is accelerating, and the reverberations are mind boggling. Struggling to adjust to this tempo is a challenge for everyone trafficking in the business of ideas—in university departments, in the many segments of health care delivery, in Western culture writ large. Amidst a barrage of information, at times swarming in its impact and too overwhelming to properly digest, those interested in the evolution of these ideas face the responsibility of sober appraisal, of distinguishing the ever-diminishing figure from the ever-expansive ground. Separating the wheat from the chaff is an unending obligation, since change is constant. The stakes are high, and it is wiser to play out this struggle along multiple fronts than to forfeit the outcome.

In trying to be true to this responsibility, in this book I am concerned with how one comes to function within the role they assign to themselves when they determine who they are. It is not so easy in these rapid currents. There are telltale rites of passage that boundary off any person's entry into those professions that minister to culture. They confer the privilege of taking part in the evolutionary processes—becoming a guardian of ideas—and these rites of passage themselves must likewise evolve as our cultural institutions do what they must, which is to perpetuate themselves. It is in these rites of passage that bound tensions mount, like a coiled spring about to snap. These pressure points often act so as to safeguard the past against those changes that might be imagined as destructive. Yet, it is only those changes that can safeguard the future. Consider that in a science, the rites of passage flexibly adapt; in a religion the rites of passage are more likely to strive to remain immutable and timeless. A curriculum— the core of what is taught to fledglings so as to prepare them to properly function—is a dynamic object, and is as well remarkably historically sensitive, a mirror of cultural shifts. Thus, turn of the century British children were taught courses in the art of conversation and proper manners, seen fully as essential as history and mathematics. (Clearly, they knew something back then that we now do not.) Thirty years ago, American junior high school boys all dutifully took shop, while the girls banded together and headed straight toward home education with nary a peep, both gender-laden assumptions of what is important to convey—indeed, a strong statement about how lives were to be lived, which would be unthinkable now. For better or worse, curricula away from churches, mosques, and synagogues have always been calibrated with the evolution of culture, and people are educated to be players of that historical moment, akin to the educational lag that leads so many professional practitioners to remain frozen in loyalty to the methods they were once taught during their formative years of training. Venture into the nimbler American universities circa 2020 and witness the possible majors of today's college students—technology and culture, gender and queer studies, robotics. Then imagine how obsolete these majors may well be in thirty years.

For besieged psychoanalysts who seek to balance loyalties to the past and future, it becomes ever more important for the sake of the field to stay abreast of current matters amidst this dizzying rate of change. Balancing past and future is a never-ending proposition, and it is rare to get it just right. Perhaps it is impossible to do so in a way that satisfies everyone, and is best conceived as a necessary and ultimately benevolent tension that simply cannot be resolved, nor should it disappear. This work represents my effort to pay homage to this tension with respect to some of the crucial principles that comprise a contemporary Freudian understanding of psychoanalysis. It also represents my effort to understand the necessity for doing so.

To describe oneself as a contemporary Freudian implies exactly what these words impute—it is to embed Freudian ideas in a contemporary intellectual and clinical climate. It is not to rigidly hold onto ideas that stubbornly resist coming into dynamic conflict with other ideas for the benefit of both. It most certainly includes the understanding what takes place when a patient is seen four or five times a week over a course of many years, under the prevailing condition of relative neutrality, with interpretation the predominant verbal intervention, and with transference and resistance key points of contact. To locate oneself as a contemporary Freudian, though, is not to be an unabashed defender or an apologist for Freud. Rather, it brings along an obligation to point out where and when Freud was inconsistent or mistaken, and to then place these problems in the context of the evolution of

Freud's thinking and the importance of our understanding that evolution as we continue to assess, revise, and build new psychoanalytic theories. In order to maintain some continuity with the past, it is very important that psychoanalysts agree upon a way of reading Freud somewhat akin to this, much as Mahoney (2002) described a "processive" reading.

Freud's cultural surround was quite rich, and he never suffered from a poverty of influence and stimulation. It is clear, though, that the cultural surround contemporary Freudian psychoanalysis is embedded within is remarkably different from that of Freud. The vein running through most of the contemporary intellectual world is concerned with the wide-ranging varieties of human subjectivity, and the relationship of human subjectivity to interaction, language, culture, and society, and the many sides of development, i.e., the assets and liabilities of understanding derived from studying ontogenetic change over time of multiple entities. These concerns saturate the understanding of contemporary scientific life and have already infiltrated the contemporary Freudian literature to some extent, but have not yet taken on a characteristic and widely recognized psychoanalytic form. Therefore, the ideas presented here concerning the coordination of multiple perspectives do not arise de novo. The distinctions I make and the clinical issues discussed are latent in a rapidly unfolding literature and shared sensibility. I am not after novelty so much as I am trying to develop a conceptual structure that enters these debates and is intended to best allow such contemporary linkages and ideas to flower and evolve in classical psychoanalysis.

Inevitably, the Eitingon educational system forged in Berlin when psychoanalysis was launched, which has since determined how young analysts are educated, is implicated in this tension. Having fretted about the problem for years, I think I finally have a better grasp of something the formal education of psychoanalysts today has difficulty imparting to candidates. A formal psychoanalytic education is an oxymoron. Too many things intervene in the course of training that are not in the better interests of the candidate, and this does not escape them. A formal analytic education becomes too intertwined with systemic conflicts that benefit the entrenched institute rather than the candidate. It is not so much that the current models of education are obsolete, although I would not quarrel with those who hold this view; rather, it has to do with a failure to grapple with why aspiring analysts would wish to learn about psychoanalysis. Practical patches grafted onto existing structures will not make this dilemma disappear. The dilemma is close to the bone, embedded within but hidden by the self-evident. It is this. If one needs to rely upon instrumentalities, the problem goes underground, shielded from sight. Goals, benefits, ends—all instrumentalities— have come to dominate lives; everything has a pragmatic purpose and value. But what must now be admitted is that there is little instrumental payoff in really learning about psychoanalysis. A love for the field, for its way of inquiring, for making sense of oneself, for touching other peoples' lives, must trump the practicalities and offer a basis for self-sacrifice of a sort. A good analyst has to be an analyst because it is as if, to each one, there is no other viable choice for a career. So, many aspiring analysts often do not, confusing metrics like graduation and certification and the size of their practice with educational accomplishments, replacing acquiring an education with a search for what the practice of psychoanalysis can do for them. Again, we are led back to Freud. The moment concrete incentives are built in is the same moment that those limits are imposed that changes it into something else, what Freud was afraid would happen in America (privately, he was known to contemptuously refer to America as "Dollarland").

Many "reasons" to learn about psychoanalysis tend to undermine, if not bankrupt, the essence of this enterprise. Psychoanalysis is today a poor feeder of creature comforts. Perhaps we would be in a different and better place if it had always been so. Psychoanalytic education is an end in itself; it can find few reasons to justify itself. For those who perceive this, the exploration of psychoanalysis can become an unending joy. Their vision is restored, and it is clear what can be found where. A psychoanalytic education has a momentum of its own. It seeks out those who merely seek to expand an inner space, not bearing upon what they have, but nesting within the eternal question of who they are. This book is also about my encounter with my version of this joy, and it is my hope that the reader can share in it. I fear that for the reader who is looking for the typical instrumentalities, such as what to say to a particular patient at a particular time in a particular way, I will not have very much to say, or far worse to my mind, that they will be bored by what I have to offer.

To learn about psychoanalysis from the inside is to progressively gain access into a different world than the one that we all adapt to from birth onward. It can make a person lonelier than before they learned about it. Once committed, you can go around saying odd things that make others nervous. You often have to hold your tongue. Many heretofore profound things come to seem banal. You learn to split off what you understand from what you are socially allowed to say. To all but those who have likewise made this commitment, psychoanalysis is *prima facie* implausible, and no matter how much we yearn for it, in a general sense plausibility and psychoanalysis make for a bad marriage.

I think that one of the most important conflictual issues faced by a psychoanalytic writer has to do with how isolation is handled. Talking around to other analysts who do not feel quite right unless they are writing about what they see and do, it seems to me that the influence of isolation is pervasive, but that isolation can be something that defeats you or strengthens you, as the case may be. I have come to see that some analysts write in order to become isolated, from those fantasy figures that in their internal world persist in making demands, all the while consciously believing that they write in order to connect and not to feel isolated. Writing for a psychoanalyst can then be an act of defiance, a self-regulatory necessity, a concealed rebellion against a revered teacher, the outcome of genuine curiosity and intellectual passion, a bid for acclaim and tribute, identification with an admired forbear, or any combination thereof. Depending upon one's motives, writing can then come easier or become more difficult.

David Rapaport used to comment that it is a bit of a minor miracle that clinical analysts ever write at all. By this, he meant that clinical work and writing constitute two such different modes of thought that one person could not be expected to master both, and that it may be that in order to turn one on the other has to be turned off. This is truly a shame, since it is exactly this balance that must be obtained if going forward we are enabled to continue to have a viable psychoanalytic literature. In this regard, I consider myself fortunate, having had the benefit of relationships in which isolation felt like a blessing rather than a deprivation, because of the value accorded my own autonomy. Then, too, such relationships have always emphasized these strange schisms, and pushed me to never tilt too far to either side. This book as well emerges from my effort to balance upon this most fragile tightrope, to have both sides of me—the writer and the clinical analyst—enter into the discussion and be true to their origins and roots.

I would like to offer apologies to certain respected colleagues in advance. Many discerning scholars—analysts and non-analysts alike—have worked in the areas I will be investigating. I have read some of them and cited them. I have read others and not cited them, and yet there are many others whom I have not read but whose work is certainly applicable. Everybody who belongs just cannot be invited to this particular party. It is our lot to be located within a vast and fragmented landscape, and it is virtually impossible to include everybody who justly deserves recognition.

I am a sworn mortal enemy of jargon. My attempted demonstration of the coordination of multiple perspectives in this book will hopefully be neither mystical nor obscure, but grounded in straightforward psychological processes that can readily be understood and seen once conceptualized. These processes, however, can be fleeting to the eye and readily overlooked if one assumes that their vision of things at any one moment can encompass the entire prevailing analytic observational field, or that one's favored theories are all inclusive and sufficiently explanatory, and do not require growth and expansion. We are all greater-wider-deeper, more complex—than anything that can be seen, heard, or said about one another or to oneself. No one can be captured in their entirety.

I would like to make one more parenthetic note in this concluding chapter. Much of the writing in this book assumes a familiarity and a background in psychoanalysis. This background has to be taken at face value. In approaching a body as vast as psychoanalysis, not everything can be described; certain things simply exist as assumed constructs because they constitute the bricks and mortar of a tradition. For example, if I do not directly address key clinical concepts, it is not because I do not consider them important. It is because my focus is on certain matters, and my aim is to drive those matters in particular into a place of conceptual coherence, which is where they promote the most useful examination of other matters not directly picked up. I believe that I am clear in the body of this work what the tradition I envelop myself within is. I embrace my loyalties, and yet I am trapped by and cannot escape them, and that is finally my, and perhaps every analyst's, inevitable plight.

References

Mahoney, P. (2002). Freud's Writing. His (W)rite of Passage and its Reverberations. *Journal of the American Psychoanalytic Association* 50: 885–907.

Schweder, R. (2003). *Why Do Men Barbecue? Recipes for a Cultural Psychology*. Cambridge, MA: Harvard University Press.

www.ingramcontent.com/pod-product-compliance
Lightning Source LLC
Chambersburg PA
CBHW062107020426
42335CB00013B/882